To Tracey
Merry Christmas 2004
love from Mike
Mum x x x

Margot Fonteyn

Margot Fonteyn

MEREDITH DANEMAN

VIKING
an imprint of
PENGUIN BOOKS

VIKING

Published by the Penguin Group
Penguin Books Ltd, 80 Strand, London WC2R 0RL, England
Penguin Group (USA) Inc., 375 Hudson Street, New York, New York 10014, USA
Penguin Books Australia Ltd, 250 Camberwell Road,
Camberwell, Victoria 3124, Australia
Penguin Books Canada Ltd, 10 Alcorn Avenue, Toronto, Ontario, Canada M4V 3B2
Penguin Books India (P) Ltd, 11 Community Centre,
Panchsheel Park, New Delhi – 110 017, India
Penguin Group (NZ), cnr Airborne and Rosedale Roads, Albany,
Auckland 1310, New Zealand
Penguin Books (South Africa) (Pty) Ltd, 24 Sturdee Avenue,
Rosebank 2196, South Africa

Penguin Books Ltd, Registered Offices: 80 Strand, London WC2R 0RL, England

www.penguin.com

First published 2004
5

Set in Bembo
Typeset by Palimpsest Book Production Limited,
Polmont, Stirlingshire
Printed in Great Britain by Clays Ltd, St Ives plc

A CIP catalogue record for this book is available from the British Library

ISBN 0-670-91337-5

To Paul Daneman and Paul Golding

Contents

List of Illustrations

Every effort has been made to trace the copyright holders and we apologize in advance for any unintentional omission. We would be pleased to insert the appropriate acknowledgement in any subsequent editions.

Endpapers: Scene from *Swan Lake*, Margot Fonteyn and Michael Somes, presented by Sadlers Wells at the 1956 Edinburgh Festival, The Scottish Tourist Board.

Acknowledgements

Given a subject as adored as Fonteyn, I have been witness to inordinate acts of kindness and special protection, made for Margot's sake, not mine. Complete strangers have faithfully met me at remote airports at two in the morning (Jan Power in Auckland) and I have been conveyed around Panama like a princess by Margot's former manservant, Buenaventura Medina, who, when I decided I wanted to walk barefoot in the Pacific at La Quinta Pata, took a revolver from the glove compartment of his jeep to ensure my safety. But, most of all, because of the compelling nature of my subject to her friends and colleagues in the ballet world, I have been given interviews of extraordinary liveliness and meditative grace which have fallen to me like blessings, as though Margot – just as Ninette de Valois intimated – were still controlling her destiny from beyond the grave. Some of the people who contributed to this book have died during the long years of its writing and I regret not having met *their* deadlines with my thanks. They were: Lord Annan, Harmodio Arias, Trumbull Barton, Svetlana Beriosova, June Brae, Peter Brinson, Richard Buckle, William Chappell, Sir Ashley Clarke, Dame Ninette de Valois, Fiore de Henriquez, Lila de Nobili, Jane Edgeworth, Leslie Edwards, Annabel Farjeon, Christopher Gable, Patricia Garnett, Jean Gilbert, Charles Hassé, Margaret Hodson, Idell Hookham, John Lanchbery, Louis Martinz, Anthony Powell, Alfred Rodrigues, Herbert Ross, George Rylands, Bud Smith, Michael Somes, Joseph Stull, Alard Tobin, Ann Todd, Irene Worth and perhaps others, news of whom may not have reached me.

For their wonderful spoken testaments, my thanks are due to: Dalal Achcar, William Akers, Heather Albery, Querube Arias, Rosario Arias de Galindo, Ana Cristina Alvarado, Basil Appleby, Clive Barnes, Michael Bentley, Christina Berlin, Graham Bowles, Joy (Williams) Brown, Isabel Browne, Susan Carlton Jones, Theodora Christon, John Craxton, Zoë Dominic, Nitzia Embiricos, Michael Fontes, Patricia Foy, Celia Franca, Moira Fraser, Pauline (Clayden) Gamble, Maude

(Lloyd) Gosling, Robert Gottlieb, Alexander Grant, Jill Gregory, Dame Beryl Grey, Gabriel Galindo, Judy (Tatham) Hassé, Anne Heaton, Hans Werner Henze, Jane Herrmann, Margaret Hewitt, Ronald Hynd, Lady Jellicoe, Leo Kersley, Al Khoner, Otilia Koster, Annie Lambert, Christopher Lawrence-Price, Eva Loeffler, Alastair Macaulay, Donald MacLeary, Lady MacMillan, Dame Alicia Markova, Monica Mason, Pamela May, Buenaventura Medina, Gail (Thomas) Monahan, Ivan Nagy, Nadia Nerina, April Olrich, Annette Page, Georgina Parkinson, Roland Petit, Marguerite Porter, Lady Violet Powell, Anthony Russell-Roberts, Galina Samsova, Lynn Seymour, Moira Shearer, Dame Antoinette Sibley, Alan Sievewright, Wayne Sleep, Wendy Ellis Somes, Maria Tallchief, Joan Thring, Sir John Tooley, Violette Verdy, David Wall, Garth Welch and Sir Peter Wright.

For their support, time and generosity in either professional or private spheres, I would further like to thank: Neil Ambrose, Terence Bainton, Margaret Barbieri, Irina Baronova, Dick Beard, Michael Beare, Alida Belair, Zamira Benthall, Barbara Booroff, Michael Boulton, David Brown, Michael Brown, Peter Brownlee, Tanya Bruce Lockhart, Jane Buchanan-Michaelson, Marilyn Burr, Lady Clarke, Fiona Colbert, Frederika Davis, Myra Demetriou, Violetta Elvin, Richard Farley, Peter Fontes, Adrian Fontes, Joy Fontes, Anna Furse, Katya Furse, David Gayle, Tony Giacomin, Charles Gordon, Joan and Monica Halliday, Baroness Hoyningen-Huene, Lady Hunt, Luke Jennings, Jennifer Kinmont, Barry Kitcher, Paul Kramer, Gerasimos Kanelopulos, Richard Koster, Attilio Labis, Michael Lehmann, Janine Limberg, Jill Montgomerie, Carol Macready, Laurel Martyn, Rebecca Miller, Geraldine Morris, Brian Masters, Andrew Motion, Alex Martin, Suzanne Musitz, Sally (Ashby) Neale, Jean Newton, George Nicholson, Jaime Ortiz Patino, Elizabeth Panourgias, Jean Percival, Nicholas and Flora Phillips, Wallace Potts, Jan Power, David Rees, Simon and Sophie Robson, Roy Round, Marian St Claire, Lady Sainsbury (Anya Linden), Mischa Scorer, Lady Southward, Pippa Southward, Felicity Thompson, Lady Walton, David Walker, Doreen Wells (Marchioness of Londonderry), Sarah Woodcock, Belinda Wright and Jelko Yuresha.

At the Royal Opera House Archive, Francesca Franchi and her staff were always generously accommodating to me, as was Anne Meadmore at the Royal Ballet School Archive. And in New York, I am especially grateful to Joy Brown, who, with Robert Gottlieb, recently staged an acclaimed Fonteyn exhibit; over the years, she sent me reams of valuable notes and cuttings, and allowed me to use the gorgeous photos of her and Margot on holiday in 1948. David Scrase was also enormously helpful, making sure that no snippet of information about Fonteyn ever escaped my attention and opening up his correspondence with Margot to me. Jennie Walton was a source of endless assistance, searching out wills and family trees, and giving me access to her wide-ranging collection of press-cuttings, letters and photographs, particularly the scrapbooks of Neil Ambrose. And Johanna Adams was kind enough to let me walk away with a treasure trove of cuttings on which I have absolutely depended for piecing together the colourful press version of Margot's story.

In the practical field, I must first acknowledge Maggie Pringle who, unbeknown to me, originally broached the mad idea in some boardroom that I should take on Fonteyn's biography. Three times I declined the daunting task, but Sally Ashby, whom I had known since our Royal Ballet School days, would not take my 'no' for an answer. She arranged for Margot's close friends Al Khoner and Bud Smith to convey a letter to Margot in her Houston hospital. I agreed, certain that Fonteyn, with her well-known insistence upon privacy, would deny me permission to embark. But she was too ill to read the letter, and died without granting me the refusal which would have resolved my moral dilemma. And, beyond her death, there arose for me the issue of courage – that trait which Margot herself had so exemplified – and thus the infection began. What ultimately drew me in was the chance to reconnect with my childhood longing – that overwhelming aspiration which afflicted so many girls of my generation: to *be* Margot Fonteyn. (Take care, they always say, what you wish for.) I was shored up, from the start, by Gill Coleridge, who has proved to be so much more that a mere agent. She has fought my corner for thirteen years, not once losing faith, despite my slowness. The book has seen three editors: Louise Haines, who was so encouraging at the beginning, Tom Weldon, who sent me flowers when the manuscript was only *half-finished*, and finally and fittingly, Juliet Annan, the daughter of Noël Annan who happened to be at Cambridge with Tito Arias. My thanks to them all, and to Kathryn Court, my kind and exceedingly patient editor in New York. On the London Viking team I am grateful for the visual discrimination of Kate Brunt, and for the meticulous attention to detail of Annie Lee.

Also at Cambridge with Tito Arias was Paul Kramer, whose knowledge of Panamanian politics was a mainstay. And I am grateful to Judy Hassé for her lively written account of the 'revolution,' and to the late Annabel Farjeon for her fascinating 'Dutch Journal'.

But chief among those whom I must single out for special thanks is Margot's step-daughter, Querube Arias de Clark, who, in deciding as she did to trust me, offered me a direct experience of the warmth and wit and irresistible charm with which the Arias family must have held Margot entranced. My heartfelt thanks, also, to Fonteyn's English family, Lavinia Exham and Phoebe Hookham, who, late into the writing of the book, gave me permission to quote from Fonteyn's letters and papers, and granted me access to the kind of document that biographers dream of discovering: BQ's candid and animated memoir.

Keith Money paved the way for that breakthrough – my thanks to him for his kindness, and for the enlightening hours I spent with him in New Zealand. His wonderful pictorial books on Margot were forever open on my desk, as were Julie Kavanagh's thrillingly outspoken biography of Ashton, Mary Clarke's classic history of the Sadler's Wells Ballet, and James Monahan's unsurpassed critical assessment of Fonteyn. When the writing was done, James's widow, the former dancer Gail Thomas – having already proved what a staunch friend she was to me by effortlessly opening doors to the elite of the ballet world – now came into her own. With her laser copy-editor's eye, organizational gifts and vast ballet knowledge, she tirelessly helped me to pull the reference pages into shape. My other saviour was Alastair Macaulay, who having already proved his generosity by placing the heavily researched 60,000-word version of his recently published short biography of Fonteyn at my disposal, now brought the full force of his specialist brilliance and strict insistence upon dates and chronology to bear upon my manuscript, proof-reading it not once, but twice, and faxing me over 100 pages of salutary and indispensable notes. Such is the devotion that Fonteyn's cause can still inspire.

Inspiration – that most precious and elusive of commodities – was selflessly sustained in me by two people: my late husband and editor-to-the-last, Paul Daneman, and Paul Golding, who has watched over every sentence of this book as though it were his own.

Prologue

Margot dancing: I must start with that. But how to put something so visual, so potent with theatrical moment that even film cannot capture it, into plain words? How to explain why it is that when, to a particular strain of music, an ordinary mortal steps forward on to one leg, raises the other behind her and lifts her arms above her head, the angels hold their breath? It fell to Margot Fonteyn to become what little girls dream of being: the most famous ballerina in the world. And the legend that grew up around this neat-limbed, olive-skinned, dark-haired, grave-eyed girl was inherent from the beginning. 'She had,' said her first partner, Robert Helpmann, 'the curious quality of making you want to cry.'[1] Her soft, unshowy lyricism and limpid purity of line have entered the poetic imagery of our age. 'It's hard on the dancers who have followed her,' said Maude Lloyd,[2] wife and writing partner of the critic Alexander Bland. 'When I watch them dancing, all I can see is Margot.'

And Margot is what I must call her, despite the beauty and resonance of her half-invented surname, which tells a cooler and more formal truth about her. I must forgo 'Fonteyn' reluctantly, along with my own sense of propriety at doing so, and adopt the intimacy of her Christian name, which was also not hers to begin with, but into which she grew with her simple and instinctive grace. Margot it must be because of the insistent way that people who have told me about her have used it – possessively, proprietorially, in clipped English, in drawn-out American, in the sweet rolling tones of Panamanian Spanish: 'Margot was like that,' or 'That was Margot'; dwelling on their pleasure in repeating it, conjuring her in two syllables, revelling in their right to drop the 'Dame'. It would be dishonest for me to call her anything else, accustomed as I have become to bandying

I

her name about – that arrangement of six letters which has been such a potent trigger to her friends; repeating it back to them incessantly and shamelessly in my effort to touch the nerve of their experience of her, this one and only woman who was also a great dancer.

The fans, of course, even in the early days, when she was still plain Miss Fonteyn, would never have dared call her Margot to her face. And she herself was quite strict about these niceties; she had a way of walking straight past admirers whom she considered to be impertinent. But 'Margot' was what they whispered, what they waited for, as they clustered outside the stage door. They felt that they knew her. And you could hardly blame them, because when she came on to the stage there was, beyond the mystery and glamour that ballet famously engenders, an ordinary familiarity about her. Even if you had never seen her dance before, at some deep level you recognized her; she was like something you'd already imagined, coming true. Great performers tend to possess this quality, this ability to take you with them, to get you automatically on their side. Certainly, for a fellow dancer, watching her from the stage or the wings, every step she took, every gesture she made, however impossibly beyond you technically, terrified and rewarded you in some personal way, as though you were doing it yourself.

She didn't take the stage by storm. She took it reticently, modestly, in deference to the great difficulty of what she was attempting. Perhaps because, in her teens, she had been promoted so fast, always a little ahead of her proficiency – which caught up, let's face it, quickly enough – there always seemed a sense of awe about her finding herself centre-stage, a naïve excitement tempered by an overwhelming gravity of spirit. Physically she was beautiful enough, although not in the plasticine way of modern ballerinas, whose backs bend in half and whose legs fly over their heads and back again; the angles which Margot's limbs formed with her torso were geometrically limited, but the artistry lay in that very limitation, as artistry so often does. Her drop-shouldered, low-armed, relatively low-legged *arabesque*, with the unforced line of her jaw following in perfect accord above it, and her eyes, with their quiet, dark-pupilled gaze projecting the line forward and upward, beyond the physical confines of her body, was a thing of incomparable integrity which, desperately as every dancer in the land tried to reproduce it, remains completely distinctive to her. The word most often used about her is 'proportion'. She was perfectly proportioned. Her measurements from shoulder to elbow to wrist, from neck to waist to hip to knee to ankle, had been worked out by the gods at their most mathematically meticulous, with the setting of her head upon her neck being the most immaculate touch of all. I have deliberately left out her feet, as they were the most criticized part of her, being less expressively arched than the divine Pavlova's, and not particularly strong in recompense. 'I think we may be just in time to save the child's feet,'[3] pronounced Ninette de Valois when the fourteen-year-old arrived at the Sadler's Wells School, and Frederick Ashton always referred to them as 'Margot's pats of butter'. But, in fact, visually they were all of a piece with the rest of her in their soft, unexaggerated elegance; and steely enough, in the end, to support the cruel contortions through which she was to put her body for so long.

But even in an art as visual as ballet, appearances can only go so far. The outer reflects the inner, and Margot's unity of physique was served by a deeply unifying mental approach to her work, an obedience and submission to the letter of each step which somehow imbued the smallest movement with an orderliness and unclutteredness that made it speak. And what it spoke, of course, was the music.

It is impossible to think of Margot dancing without whole passages of Tchaikovsky or Stravinsky or César Franck breaking into one's mind. And this is strange, since in her private life – once her long (eight-year) liaison with the composer and conductor Constant Lambert was over – she abjured music anywhere but on the stage, and later, in her married life with Roberto Arias, listened to it not at all. Her great Russian partner,

Rudolf Nureyev, when he first stayed with her in London at the Panamanian Embassy, was appalled to find that she made no background use of it in her daily life. 'I am like dying,' he said, when she asked him what was the matter; 'four days, I hear no music.'[4] But Margot's relationship with it was too professionally intense for off-duty pleasure. She described her musicality as an inner tape-recording that she was always trying to match to the outer orchestral sound: when the two ran concurrently, she was on form.

In which role would one most wish to invoke her? As Odette in *Swan Lake*, her womanly eyes lidded with the self-sacrifice she played out so controversially in real life? Or as the Firebird, most inhuman of feathered heroines, so dashing and sparkling and rare? Or would one have her discovered in repose, curved sideways in abstract profile, as in *Symphonic Variations*? Or as the water nymph, Ondine, where Ashton found for her a character as vulnerable and implacable as her own? No; one would have to settle for the obvious: Princess Aurora in *The Sleeping Beauty* – the Rose Adagio. It was with this ballet that Margot conquered America. She did it, she thought, 'by smiling'.[5] Her smile was what got stuck in all our hearts. It was the smile of a true princess, who was lucky and had everything, yet could still be capable of an unspoilt, trembling happiness.

Everyone knows the fairy story. There is nothing to tell. There is just this girl who pricks her finger, falls asleep and is awoken with a kiss. It was by no means Margot's favourite role. She preferred being forlorn, or mad; and, despite seeming lady-like enough to the naked eye, enjoyed 'flinging [herself] about the stage happily tearing a passion to tatters'.[6] Here, in *The Sleeping Beauty*, there was 'nothing to act except a young girl celebrating her birthday'. And yet, as in all these apparently simple and light-hearted tales, there is a profound psychological truth at the core, to which something innate in Margot's nature must have responded. The archetype portrayed by the Sleeping Beauty is that of a spirit locked in eternal girlhood, unpenetrated by life, a spirit whose passive existence must remain frozen in time until it is roused into womanhood by passion. It can't have been for nothing that, at least until the time of her marriage, Margot was actually referred to as 'the Sleeping Beauty' by members of the company, with all the irony as well as the affection that the nickname implies.

The ballet starts with a Prologue, in which the heroine is no more than a doll in a cot, being visited by wand-waving fairies. It is not until the second scene that she comes running on to the stage, in a pale pink tutu, legs in silk tights, arms, as befits a princess of modesty and decorum, discreetly clothed in gauze sleeves. The memory of Fonteyn at that moment is like a burst of inner sunlight in one's brain, so that in describing the first entrance of Aurora, one is automatically describing the woman herself.

People who can move us with movement are marked by some elemental affiliation. Markova was identified with a cool, airy lightness. Pavlova could quicken the heart with her dramatic fire. Spessivtseva's weeping spirit opened the floodgates to the emotions. But Fonteyn drew her magic from the humble element of earth. There was something tangible and terrestrial about her, a sensuous embracing of the here and now. The short solo that precedes the Rose Adagio is fast and full of jumps, and although elevation was hardly Margot's strong point, she danced it incomparably, *terre à terre*. Emotionally, too, it was perfectly pitched: we had waited for her, through the parading of courtiers and the waltzing of garlanded maidens, and this, her first dance, expressed the heart-racing happiness we felt, now that at last she was here. But then the music slowed and swelled to the elegiac strains that suited her most, and, though her smile did not falter, her spirit grew dignified and serene. She kissed her mother. Her father kissed her. The Rose Adagio began.

The choreography to this fabled set-piece of Tchaikovsky, by the French-born Russian master Marius Petipa, is, in a way, an oddity, since it is in essence a solo with four partners. We hardly spare a glance for the princes from India, England, Italy and Spain who have come to pay court to the sixteen-year-old

Aurora on her birthday. Since none of them means anything to her romantically, they are unlikely to be distinguishable to us in their wigs and finery, but are simply there to support, pivot, lift, catch, hand her roses, and, above all, prepare her for the virtuoso balances *en attitude* which are to amaze us. And at the music's climax she abandons them all anyway, to perform, centre-stage, a simple, turning *bourrée* on the spot, with sweeping *port de bras*, bending back to watch us over her shoulder, twisting her head to keep us in her sights as though we were a mirror, and she, a teenager cavorting, with private exultation rather than vanity, in front of herself.

And yet, throughout, although the lushness of the music exhorts the dancer to vulgarity, what predominates in Margot's performance is her reticence: her clean, classical, unadorned English restraint. After the last collection of roses is flung to the winds (with such sensitivity for their vulnerable petals that we would hardly believe that fresh flowers, for reasons of super-stition, are never used on the stage), she embarks on her final, testing balances. And these she holds, not with flashy aplomb, but with a tentative, internalized excitement so charged that we feel pride in her on the absurd scale that a parent does watching its child stand unaided for the first time. But, of course, when the long sustained *attitude* opens into a full-blown *arabesque*, and, after a supported triple *pirouette* which she has the knack to make seem six, she steps back into the *révérence* which concludes the grand Adagio, it becomes all too clear once more that this is no novice, but a woman of rare and schooled grace.

If you were lucky enough to have seen Margot dance this ballet at her zenith, in the 1950s, then you do not need me to tell you how great was your privilege. But even if you saw her in the early 40s or the late 60s, you will still have witnessed much the same performance. In her youth, she was capable of a precocious maturity; and, late in her career, of an unsullied, perpetuated girlishness. Duration and reliability were everything with her; she would never have let you down.

'Margot had no high-lights to her dancing,' Dame Ninette

de Valois was fond of remarking.[7] Just so. Nor had she any low-lights. One does not remember her for a particular capacity to jump or spin or float. She did what consummate artists in all fields do: transcend technique. The steps which she danced – for all that they mattered – might hardly have had names, or cost her years of work in the studio, since she laid her mastery of them unequivocally at the altar of expression. And what she expressed, and why this purely classical ballet suited her so perfectly, despite the fact that she was a more than passingly good actress, was *herself*. The simplicity and tenderness and vivacity of her own nature. Of course she had extraordinary gifts of body and mind. And she was lucky, too. England needed her: its turn had come to produce a great ballerina, and her rise was in fact the rise of the Royal Ballet: she rode the passionate wave of wartime patriotism that produced it. But the question persists: why her? She was, of course, the choice of de Valois, unquestionably one of the most visionary and forceful women of the last century, who lighted on her, loved her and lived through her. And, moreover, Margot had Frederick Ashton, who chose to invest her with his choreographic genius. The era into which she was born spawned other legends: Alonso and Tallchief in America, Chauviré in France, Ulanova in Soviet Russia; yet, rightly or wrongly, Fonteyn's stature came to overshadow them all. Indeed, her reputation has remained unchallenged by the generations of superb dancers who have followed. And yet, strangely, she did not provoke envy: there was something about her to which even the most arch of her rivals conceded. Professionally, she seems to have engendered almost tiresomely universal love and respect.

Ballet is an iron discipline: it takes more than a milk-sop sweetness of nature to succeed in it, let alone to become the most famous ballerina in the world. True art, in the end, is to do with character. Beyond the beauty or cleverness or power of what we see or read or hear, what reaches us is the essence of a person. And we could not take our eyes off Margot Fonteyn.

So the mystery to be unravelled is a moral one: it is the qualities of heart that made her so exceptional a being that must be the subject of this book.

In the earliest photographs, she is neither sleeping nor a beauty. Her hair, so sleekly coiffed in later life, stands scraggily on end. Her eyes, wide open, are of a dark un-Englishness that is not so much 'Chinese' (the word famously ascribed to her faintly exotic look in adolescence) as Semitic. She looks old, as the newborn sometimes do: she might grow up to be anything. There is certainly nothing about her pudgy cheeks that could be said to portend the fragile facial contours of a ballerina. The most promising features are her ears, which are neat and set close to the head. And, perhaps, her high eyebrows, although one suspects the photographer of having retouched them in the high style of the day; for it was at the dawn of the 1920s that Margot Fonteyn was born – between 4 and 5 a.m., on 18 May 1919.

She was christened Margaret Evelyn Hookham – Margaret after her father's (unmarried) sister, and Evelyn after her mother's (unmarried) mother – but the Margaret was soon down-graded to Peggy, which, combined with her unprepossessing surname, would, in its jokey unsuitability, come to delight the press in years to come. *Peggy Hookham*. Not an article could ever appear without some sniggering allusion to it. For it was, in its way, the perfect birth-name for the first truly British ballerina-to-be. It spoke of modesty, of the profound British distaste for overt aspiration. Fame was only acceptable if it took you by surprise. And how could anyone with a name like Peggy Hookham have presumed to greatness?

In reality, she was only British on her father's side. Her mother's parents were Irish and Brazilian – her maternal grandfather, Antonio Gonçalvez Fontes, known to Hilda Hookham as A.G., having been, according to a great-grandson, Michael Fontes, 'about the richest man in South America. I think the old man had quite a lot of illegitimate children – he had a simply huge family. He bought and sold things on a grand scale. The big thing to come out of England at the time was cotton cloth from Lancaster, so he must have fathered Margot's mother on a visit. He wasn't the sort of man who slept alone at night.' The girl who shared his bed, Evelyn Maud Acheson, whom A.G. had met at an ice-rink, was to die of cirrhosis at the age of twenty-nine, before the child conceived on that visit, and born in the Derbyshire town of Matlock on 19 December 1894, was nine years old. Hilda, fostered at first by a sweet-faced countrywoman, Mrs Moorley, and later brought up by her black-bonneted Acheson grandmother, was effectively parentless, glimpsing the dashing foreign gentleman who was her father but twice in the first twenty-one years of her life, and only remembering the young woman, who no one saw fit to inform her was her mother, as a tragic figure in a Victorian deathbed tableau, 'her long auburn hair flowing over the pillow'. Mrs Hookham's recall of her father is more detailed. In a memoir written when she was eighty, she tells of a surprise visit which he paid to the house of her foster-mother in Salford: 'I was frightened and hid behind an armchair till brought out and shown a beautiful doll he had brought for me. He was very well dressed and smelt nice, so after a while he took me on his knee and was talking nicely to me when he turned up my frock and looked at my underclothes to see if they (and I presumably) were being kept clean. I was most indignant and jumped off his knee, but have never really forgotten the incident – and that was the last time I saw my father for fourteen years.'

His disappearance from her life was due to a row which blew up when Hilda's Irish-Protestant grandmother refused to comply with A.G.'s wish to have the child brought up by nuns in a convent. Instead, Grannie Acheson took the six-year-old to live with her in Manchester, at 7 Cecil Street, Chorlton-cum-Hardy. There, although Hilda's companions were her cousin Stanley and her Aunt Cissy (later known as 'Purdie'), and despite the fact that the child shared a bed with her grandmother, physical affection was scarce: Hilda would only remember having been kissed by those women once, when she went on holiday to Blackpool. Nor did she ever kiss Stanley, until, at the age of eighteen, he left for the Great War, never to return. During her teens, Hilda changed her name to Nita, short for Juanita; but a new, Hispanicized flourish to her first name could do nothing to assuage the blushes which her sham surnames, Moorley Acheson, caused her: 'Only older people now will be able to imagine the disgrace of having an illegitimate child or, for that matter, being one. The Victorian attitude was merciless. You were an outcast, soiled goods which no man would want except as a mistress and finally, when he tired of you, you would have to keep on that path until you became a prostitute. Believe me that was drummed into me when I reached puberty, although at that time I did not know what sex relations were. Only that I must never let anyone touch me, or my clothes, or go into any house or place alone with a man, but no explanation as to what or why. I had no warning of menstruation either, and thought I was dying when my clothes were suddenly stained with blood and screamed for Grannie. When she told me that it was going to happen every month for nearly all my life I just couldn't believe it. It was horrible! I was shocked and ashamed later to find that men knew about it but it didn't happen to them.'

Nita, however, looked older than her years, and would later remember: 'While I was only twelve or thirteen, men used to look at me with apparent interest.' The men who interested *her* had tended to be foreign, until, at the age of twenty, an engineering student at Manchester University caught her eye. 'In the window at the side of No. 2 Cecil Street, a corner house opposite us, a young man was sitting holding his head and looking very sorry for himself. I looked up and laughed at him and made some silly remark at which he groaned. I went on home, but a day or two later we met again as he was coming in from college and I was coming in with some shopping. We got talking and he asked me to go for a walk that evening to which I agreed. He was very good-looking and seemed very nice, though I still didn't care very much for English students. However, after that we saw each other more and more and gradually over several months decided that we loved each other. His name was Felix, which I must admit I didn't believe at first, and have never really liked!'

On 2 June 1915, Hilda Acheson married Felix Hookham at St Bartholomew's Church in Sydenham, London. But the discovery, the minimum number of weeks thereafter, that she was pregnant caused Nita to feel not just 'scared and upset', but 'shattered'. The doctor who attended the birth of her son, Felix, did not help matters by asking: 'Would you like it slow and bad or quick and worse?' And although the baby, once delivered, amused her with its 'snorts and grunts, just like a piglet', mother-hood struck so alien a note with Nita that she spent the first four months of her second pregnancy doing all that she could to abort England's future Prima Ballerina Assoluta – 'by means of . . . a strong peppermint essence called Penny Royal, which left one breathless for seconds; jumping down the stairs four at a time; doing violent exercises, and drinking some horrible herbal brew that someone recommended. All in vain, of course, so in the fifth month I gave up and resigned myself to the inevitable.'

As it transpired, the second half of Nita's term was even more precarious than the first, since she, her husband and her small son all developed scabies, caused by a mite which burrows under the skin to lay its eggs. So, when 'the inevitable' finally took place, Nita was understandably apprehensive. 'I had my previous nice old nurse with me, and the very first thing I said was "Is it all right?", fearing that all those weeks of irritation and my early efforts to terminate the pregnancy might have had some horrible effect.' But the object of Nita's dread turned out to be the source of her deepest gratification. 'Oh precious day that was in Reigate those many moons ago,' she would write in old age to her ageing daughter, 'how happy I was that you had arrived safely and were all complete. It is a pity I could not see all those good fairies that must have been around, the one that gave you a kind and loving disposition, another who gave you a beautiful body and face, another great intelligence, another grace of movement to give pleasure to millions of people. It certainly was the luckiest day of my life.' And, of course, those fairies *did* all roll up to the house called North Redlands, by the railway station, where Peggy lay in her crib. The Fairy of the Crystal Fountain. The Enchanted Garden Fairy. The Fairy of the Woodland Glade. The Songbird Fairy. The Fairy of the Golden Vine. And, to complete the cast, that most magical and protective of well-wishers, the Lilac Fairy. But I said all: the wicked Carabosse came too, old and ugly, the harbinger of bad fate. Fairy stories are all the same. You cannot have the light without the dark.

Like the Princess Aurora's, however, the child's early years remained unclouded. But that is as far as the royal comparison can be taken. For the Hookham side of the family prided itself – despite various bookish uncles and a composer grandfather – on its lower-middle-class orthodoxy and utter lack of exception. 'We settled down to ordinary family life,' writes Mrs Hookham, almost with relief, 'and I don't think anything remarkable happened. There were family things, children and things and household things, which made the years slip by.' Yet a mother who has no personal experience of being mothered is bound to be more singular than she realizes.

Wartime privation had dictated that the Hookhams share their Reigate house with another family, the Cullys, who also had a baby son. But although Nita was able to compare practical notes with the wife, Mabel, essentially she operated from an intuition which, though often sound, could be strangely inconsistent. Physically undemonstrative and emotionally contained, on the one hand, in her dealings with her children – to the extent that she would claim, later in life, hardly to know them – she possessed, on the other hand, a maternal instinct primal enough in its untutored power to be heedless of the normal barriers between parent and child. Her sense of identification with her daughter was, from the start, so acute that her own role and Peggy's could seem interchangeable. 'For instance,' she writes, 'when she fell and bumped herself and I picked her up crying, I had only to pretend I had hurt myself or that something was wrong with me, and she would stop crying at once. I would kiss her better and then she would kiss me better, and that would be the end of the tears.'

She'd had no such luck, however, in hushing the protestations of the boy, Felix, who lacked the placidity and responsiveness of his baby sister. 'He would wake at about 5 a.m., and of course so did everyone else, which was particularly hard on his father, who had to travel long hours and work at the Arsenal.' But, even if Peggy possessed the sunnier nature, she could yell much louder than her brother. Indeed, such was the capacity of her infant lungs that family lore would later have it that, had she not danced at Covent Garden, she would surely have sung there. She was not especially impatient to walk, having developed a speedy and efficient way of hauling herself about by 'putting out one hand and swinging her body out after it'. Her prime motivation for movement seemed to be the fanatical pursuit of her elusive brother, to whom, by the time she was three, she had become a devoted slave. 'If he was playing with building toys or anything,' their mother was to write, 'and something was missing that he wanted, it was she who went up to the nursery, kneeling on every step as she went up, and coming down, bumpity-bump on her bottom.'

A more imposing Tudor-style staircase was a feature of the newly built three-bedroomed house in Waldeck Road, West London, to which the Hookham family soon moved. The genteel suburb of Ealing suited them well, since Mr Hookham had, now that the war was over, been dropped from his engineering job at the Arsenal and was able to find work a mere bus-ride away – with the American Oil Company, in Westminster. Like many a wife of the time, Mrs Hookham seems, in her memoir, unsure of the precise nature of her husband's work; 'but I do remember a time when he brought home lots of oil-burning signal lamps and dotted them about the house to test how long the oil took to burn out under different conditions.'

It was on the polished oak staircase of the house in Waldeck Road that Margot claims to have had an experience of flying. Most of us would have called it falling, since Peggy was propelled into mid-air, and landed, unhurt, rather lower down the stairs than she had started. But the child was so excited at finding herself airborne that she made every effort to launch herself into free-fall once again. Luckily the footwork for the take-off proved, technically, just that little bit too demanding.

A year later, Peggy took her first dancing class. Yet, young as she was, she can hardly have connected holding on to a wooden rail, and being told to turn her feet out, with the transcendental urge to defy gravity. It was enough that a girl of her staid background should learn to stand up straight. Apparently she had a way of hunching her shoulders, and of screwing up her eyes when reading or concentrating, that was less than ladylike. It is her father, we are told, whom history has to thank for having casually remarked that dancing might be of benefit to his daughter's deportment. That, at least, is what the press, over the years, was either fed, or would cook up. Margot herself was more ambivalent. In a 1973 radio interview with Esther Rantzen she would argue: 'That's the story but I think it's just a legend. I have no idea whether it's accurate or not because my parents, who are the people concerned, can't remember.'[1] Mrs Hookham, in her version of events, seems to remember all too vividly. And the discrepancy is worth noting since it illustrates Margot's curious and often perverse relationship with the truth. We are back to the thorny subject of ambition, from which perceived vulgarity Margot was keen, all her life, to distance herself. Yet the impetus behind that very first lesson is crucial. Esther Rantzen, in the interview, presses Margot to acknowledge some early sign of an obsession with ballet: 'Can you remember yourself the moment when it first caught your imagination?' But Margot will not play. 'I don't think it caught my imagination.'

Poor Rantzen struggles on. 'I think for so many little girls across the country there will be a moment when perhaps they've seen you . . . perhaps in a film, and think, "That is the most romantic thing I've ever seen, I wish I could do that," but you, yourself, never saw ballet in that light?' 'No,' persists Margot flatly. 'I think I was . . . er . . . I just danced. I don't think I ever thought about it very much.'

But *someone* must have done so at the beginning. The implication that this was the father sounds about as likely as the suggestion that poor posture can seriously take root in a four-year-old. We know perfectly well whose idea those ballet lessons must have been. Nita Hookham considered the bodies of both her children to be 'straight as young saplings and beautifully proportioned'. So, if the issue of deportment really did arise, we can picture the gleam in her black-browed Latin eyes as she persuaded her husband to agree, on remedial grounds, to something at which he might easily have baulked on artistic ones. For it goes almost without saying that behind the carefree, modest, unassuming figure that Peggy Hookham cut all the way to becoming Margot Fonteyn, there must have stood, as behind so many great performers, the powerful, compelling force of an ambitious mother.

It is not an archetype which commands much respect. As Noël Coward wagged in his song about Mrs Worthington, the theatre is rife with pushy women determined to put their daughters on the stage. And the dancing profession has coined its own damning term for that despised and formidable breed: Ballet-Mother. Yet Mrs Hookham, despite her constant heavy backstage presence and passionate identification with her daughter's career, was never to be branded thus. Instead, she would earn from Margot's colleagues a nickname more grand than derisory: Black Queen. In *Checkmate*, the ballet from which the nickname was lifted, the Black Queen is the leading female part, and there was something about Mrs Hookham – the sheer, sweeping common-sense of the woman – that could command nothing less than star billing. And if she was widely respected it was because people took their cue from Margot, who accepted her mother's perpetual presence with affectionate and un-embarrassed naturalness. In these solipsistic days we take a dim psychological view of so unbroken an umbilical connection. Yet to yearn for the success of someone other than oneself is often the purest and most potent form of wishing. The key to the child's radiant achievement is the shadowy, unlived aspiration of a mother who would never herself have dreamed of taking ballet lessons, mindful as she was of her grandmother's acerbic remark: 'Ach, poor child, you've beef to the heels like a Mulinger heifer' – in other words, you've got thick ankles.

Bad legs, perhaps, but a good clear head. When Nita was still a girl in Manchester, a friend who worked as a typist for a firm of importers remarked, in casual conversation, that her boss 'had just come back from Brazil again and sparks were flying round and he was finding fault with everything in the office'. Nita asked what the firm was called, and was never to forget how her friend's reply – A.G.Fontes & Co. – 'really shook me. By this time I think I was about sixteen and a half, and after Grannie's death Purdie had told me the story of the family tragedy . . . Without telling Purdie or Stanley I sat down and wrote a letter to A.G. saying I was now old enough to think for myself and thought it was silly to carry on all this refusal to have anything to do with him and that I would like to meet him if I could.' That same afternoon, Nita received a telegram – the first of her life: 'Come to office at 12.30 tomorrow.' A.G. received her, intro-duced her to his partner, her uncle Manoel, took her to the best restaurant in St Anne's Square and bought her a necklace. 'Apparently,' she writes, 'he was very pleased with me and complimented me on my quick tongue.' A.G. disappeared again, but not without instructing Manoel to welcome Nita into his family in Altrincham, and providing her with an allowance of £3 per week. And when, in 1917, A.G. died in Paris, he bequeathed Mrs Hookham a private income of £600 a year. 'That, of course, was wealth to us, and one of the first things I did was to go to a big new shop called Selfridges and buy myself

17

a black seal musquash coat.' With the passage of the years that annual bequest, needless to say, hardly amounted to a fortune; but it did allow Mrs Hookham a certain freedom to follow her heart. And her heart, from the day of Peggy's birth, ran with her own second chance: her dark-eyed daughter.

One sunny day in 1923, Nita and Peggy set off for dancing school. They did not have far to go. They were heading – only round the corner, conveniently enough – for an establishment run by a Cornishwoman, Miss Grace Bosustow. Not that Mrs Hookham, who, even in those early days, was a great one for research, would ever have based her choice on mere geographical convenience. She had found out that Miss Bosustow's pupils were in demand at local charity shows, and that the letters A.O.D. on the name-plate stood for Association of Operatic Dancing (now the Royal Academy of Dancing, of which her daughter would eventually become President). But really Mrs Hookham, whose personal experience of dancing was limited to the Veleta, the Boston and the Military Twostep, knew nothing about ballet. So it is a tribute to the way in which fate looks after its chosen that Miss Bosustow just happened to be an excellent teacher.

The school was on the ground floor of a three-storey Ealing house, not unlike the Hookhams' own. While mother and teacher sat in the garden, discussing terms and times, Peggy picked daisies, a flower to which she would be compared by Cecil Beaton fourteen years later, on the first night of Ashton's *Apparitions*. 'She possessed a wistful, childlike quality which made her appear as fresh and guileless as a white marguerite.' That the comparison was evident when she was four is doubtful, for, although Miss Bosustow did recall later, 'To me she had the most perfect grace I have ever seen in an untrained child,'[2] the pronouncement sounds like hindsight. The few photographs of Peggy at that time portray her as round-faced and sturdy-limbed, with her dark, Dutch-bobbed hair cut in a heavy fringe unsuited to what was actually an exceptionally low hairline. A description from Miss Bosustow's niece, a contemporary at the school, sounds more objective (or perhaps less so, since Peggy won the prize – a pink sash – for dancing the best polka): 'A grim little thing – a black-eyed Susan and not a child you'd look at twice except for the neatness of her.'[3]

It was agreed that Peggy should attend junior classes every Friday. Soon she was also having a private lesson on Mondays. Most of Miss Bosustow's pupils stuck to one course, but Peggy tried everything: ballroom, ballet, Greek and tap, with equally solemn enthusiasm. 'From the first,' said Miss Bosustow, 'I thought her a very sweet little girl and very original. Though I don't think she was shy, in the usual sense of the word, she seldom spoke unless spoken to and would never say "yes" if a nod would do as well. Her manner was very grave and somehow remote. She was not at all vivacious and everything she did was placid and determined.'[4] She was accompanied at all times by her mother, who watched and learned. 'In fact,' Mrs Hookham has written, 'we both learned together, so that I also knew what each movement should be.'[5] And, not altogether accurately, she reels off a few: 'First you point your toe in front of you with the little toe on the ground, then you learn the five positions. 1st, heel to middle of instep; 2nd, point to front; 3rd, point to side; 4th, point to back; 5th, feet together, toe to heel of opposite foot.'

Teachers, these days, go to great lengths to keep such intense maternal involvement at bay, forbidding anyone to sit in on classes – even with the youngest students. But, from the beginning, Margot's mother seems to have had a shrewd understanding of the pitfalls of her rather ignominious role. 'Of course many parents can be perfect nuisances. They become jealous, ambitious and over-protective. The trouble is that a group of mothers with children all think that their child is best, and I did too, but I kept my mouth shut about it. Every teacher will tell you of the typical ballet mother who babbles on about her child's talent, who criticizes the teacher and other children's ability, who literally thinks and talks as though the parent and child were one and the same person . . . Children, especially young children, are very sensitive to their parents' feelings and the last thing a fledgling dancer needs is this kind of pressure. One of the most important things I have learned in my life is to say very little. Think plenty, but say nothing.'[6]

Her style must have been acceptably low-key, for Margot records unblushingly that during school displays at Miss Bosustow's, 'It was usual for my mother to stand in the wings and whisper "Put your tongue in. Smile."'[7] And, years later, Mrs Hookham, now dubbed Black Queen by Frederick Ashton, still had *carte blanche* to sit in Margot's dressing-room and pass critical comments on her daughter's speed and attack in, say, Act III of *Swan Lake*. If, in the end, selfless help became stifling interference, the dutiful daughter never allowed it to show.

But one thing did betray the deep and exaggerated sense of responsibility which Peggy felt, and which she was to feel all her life, towards the elevated expectations of others. Always in those early years she would run a high temperature for three days before a dancing examination. She would recover just in time and go on and fulfil their best hopes for her. But something in her was being pressed beyond her healthy ability to resist. Young as she was, it was not failure that she feared, but letting people down – 'people' being, first, her mother, later, Ninette de Valois, and finally, the indulgent yet ever-exacting eye of the general public.

Yet there was one capacity in which Peggy was entirely her own mistress, and that was in the classic area of food. She would not eat what she was given. It seems extraordinary to think of that streamlined, thoroughbred body being built up cell by cell on an unrelieved diet of carbohydrates, but that was indeed the case. She loathed everything her mother considered good for her, particularly eggs, which she would not touch unless, said Mrs Hookham, 'scrambled with Bovril or in a custard pudding. She did not like meat or fish in any form but lived on bread and butter with jam. She liked potatoes, but her favourite of all was Heinz baked beans on toast. The fruits she preferred were bananas, apples and the summer fruits, with Bird's custard but not cream. Sweet cakes, particularly doughnuts and sweet scones, went down well; but any new suggestions were flatly refused. Once I even took her to the doctor to ask if all this starchy food without vegetables or meat was all right for her. On looking at her he said it must be, or she would not look so well or have so much energy.'

In the early days, Mrs Hookham would try to tempt or trick her daughter into sampling meat and vegetables by means of clever recipes, and, once, in desperation, resorted to a blindfold. But the child was implacable, and, if crossed, capable of becoming ill for three foodless days. So there was nothing for it but to toast more bread and open another tin of baked beans. Peggy, after all, seemed to thrive on it – independence, perhaps, being as strong a requirement as protein.

Thus began Margot's lifelong reputation for 'stubbornness', although you could say that it looks more like protest, since there is no more symbolic characteristic in a mother than her capacity for nourishing and providing. 'Stubborn' was to stick, and is used again and again by colleagues and friends as they grope to find some fault with the bland-sounding virtue of Margot's nature. But the more they use the word, the more it seems, in one so obedient and dutiful, like a saving grace.

Luckily, Mrs Hookham was equally graceful in defeat. 'Like any mother, I dare say, my daughter seemed to me an ordinary but good child. Certainly she was extraordinarily self-controlled and well behaved, but from the age of three one knew exactly what she would and would not do; I learnt never to force an issue but to skirt round it. Her will was stronger than mine if it came to a showdown, so I had to avoid such situations wherever possible . . . As a sample of her strength of will, or should I say obstinacy: one day after lunch . . . I gave her permission to leave the table, and she left the room but left the door wide open. I called after her, "Close the door, darling"; she came back, looked at me, then went off leaving the door. Somewhat shocked, I called again, and she returned but just said, "I don't want to." I told her that I thought she was a very rude and unkind little girl and that she had better go and stand in the corner in the hall and think about it, which without a word she did. She stayed there until I had finished my lunch. I asked her later why she didn't want to close the door; she just said, "I didn't want to." So I left it at that.'

These female confrontations do not seem to have been matched by similar battles of will between Peggy and her tolerant, even-tempered father, who would lie under his second-hand 'touring' Stoneleigh, tinkering for hours with the engine, while his wife chafed, picnic packed, to be off on some promised jaunt into the countryside. The blue sky could cloud over all it liked; Mr Hookham would only emerge, wiping the oil from his hands, when his intricate technical adjustments were good and done.

Patience was not the only lesson he had to teach. He was also a great tease. Yet Margot, who would in adult life turn out to be such an inveterate giggler, was, by her own admission, a remarkably solemn child. She could not see the funny side of herself. What she learned from her father's leg-pulling was that it was wise to laugh, even when the joke was against you. And from this conscious effort to conquer her innate *amour propre* was to emerge her much-quoted and admirable maxim: 'The one important thing I have learnt over the years is the difference between taking one's work seriously and taking oneself seriously. The first is imperative and the second disastrous.'[8]

But an earnest nature can have its impressive side in a four-year-old. Here is Mrs Hookham, on the soundtrack of Keith Money's 1969 film, made to mark Fonteyn's fiftieth birthday, which I quote in full, as much to illustrate the passionately involved and entertaining maternal tone as to relay the relative ordinariness of the incident itself. 'As a small child of about four [Margot] had one of those kiddy-car things, and it ran away down a hill. And she fell off at the bottom and she *bellowed*. Windows flew open: the voice would fill the Albert Hall in *those* days. Someone said, you have to bring the little girl in, because her knees were bleeding, and we took her to the cloakroom and mopped her up and then we sat in the drawing-room and she started controlling herself. Great big sobs . . .' (Mrs Hookham demonstrates graphically) '. . . but she controlled herself. Even at that age, without any saying from me. So she's got an inborn natural control. It's evident in everything she does.'[9]

It was not a quality immediately exploitable by Miss Bosustow. She was more inclined to pounce on the talents of Mrs Hookham herself, whom she roped in to run up costumes for concerts and competitions. Peggy liked nothing better than to pore over the designs in *Weldon's Book of Fancy Dress Costumes for Parties*, imagining herself as the Penguin, the Gipsy, or the pointed-toed, forked-tailed Mephistopheles. But the resources of that versatile publication must have been tested by the demands of Peggy's first appearance at four years of age; heaven knows what she can have worn as 'A Wind'. Mrs Hookham must have found more gratification in dressing her son Felix, then aged seven, who seems to have appeared in the same programme in a leading role – boys at dancing schools having been, during those pre-Nureyevian days, in such woefully short supply. But although Felix was later to become a photographer, of ballet among other things, family memory seems to have blotted out this early foray into the world of pink tulle and rosebuds: no doubt he was just dragged along for the ride.

Though Mr Hookham's prized Stoneleigh had a folding hood and side-screens for bad weather, it tended to 'conk out' if subjected to too much rain, so the family moved to a bigger house – 3 Elm Grove Road, close to Ealing Common – in order to gain an extra ground-floor room which could be converted into a garage. In the general spirit of joy-riding, Mrs Hookham learned to drive and was rewarded with an Austin Seven, which she duly banged into the garage wall. But never mind any damage to the car: pains in her knees sent her hobbling to a specialist who diagnosed the beginnings of osteoarthritis, a condition that would dog her all her life.

She did, however, become an extremely capable driver, and the car came in handy for ferrying Peggy and her friends to the various parish halls where Miss Bosustow held her dancing recitals. Peggy was not a good passenger: journeys, whatever the form of transport, made her turn green and suffer the pervasive misery that is travel-sickness. And yet ignoring physical discomfort was already an ethic of her upbringing, so that when the car deposited her, she would rush into the hall with the others, her cheerful, healthy self again. After all, Miss Bosustow relied on her. Because of her unwavering sense of rhythm, rather than any particular technical prowess, Peggy, right from the start, had been called upon to lead a group of eight children on to the stage in a scene called 'The Little Co-Optimists' (the real, full-sized Co-Optimists being England's most famous concert troupe in the 20s). Miss Bosustow's infant octet sat on milking-stools in a semi-circle, waiting, with coloured cloaks over their national costumes, to reward their mothers' long hours of sewing with their allocated solos. When Peggy's turn came, she was revealed to be wearing a green satin skirt and white apron, her thick fringe poking out from under a red headscarf, and Mrs Hookham's Celtic blood warmed to the sight of her daughter performing an Irish washerwoman's jig. Peggy loved character dancing much more at this stage than she loved the perverse and inhibiting discipline of ballet, and, while mastering the loose-ankled footwork, would flash her missing milk-teeth quite unprompted by her mother.

The child's scholastic endeavours had by now begun – with rather more aplomb than they would end – under the tutelage of a governess whom she shared with four other children, including Roy and Roger Cane, the sons of a well-heeled neighbour on the other side of the Common. Despite Peggy's unease in larger gatherings (she hated parties for their milky blancmanges and bursting balloons, and would make straight for a chair, on to which she would climb and sit solemnly), she showed, in the familiar company of the Cane boys, a carefree taste for animated, mind-expanding argument, not to say a marked aptitude for competition. The photographer Keith Money, Margot's friend and biographer, writes: 'The dichotomy that existed between Peggy's view of dance exams and her view of school exams was extreme. Her father once told me that the school variety held no terrors for his daughter. With a chuckle, he suddenly recalled walking her across Ealing Common for some important day at an early school, and Peggy bursting out with: "Oh Daddy, I do like exams. You never know whether you are going to come out the top or the bottom!" '[10] Peggy, according to her mother, 'could never stand to be number two in anything'. Money continues: 'Of course, in the company of her brother or other boys, she was *hors concours*, which suited her admirably.'

The coquette in her was already taking precedence over the tomboy. Reprimanded by her maiden aunt Margaret, who had caught her in the ungainly act of clutching her ankles and looking out at the upside-down world with her head between her legs, Peggy wandered forlornly to the end of the back garden, where her injured, tearful femininity was not lost on a neighbour who, on the other side of the fence, happened to be trimming his herbaceous border. And it was from him that she received the first floral tribute of her life: a bunch of snapdragons, with puppet jaws which he showed her how to open and shut. Next day, she returned to the back fence and duly received a second presentation. 'It's not polite to ask for presents,' said her mother in horror;[11] but Peggy hadn't. She had simply tried smiling instead of crying.

The maternal aspect of the girl's nature was rather less to the fore. She did not like dolls any more than, later on, she would much care for the idea of babies. But she did possess a toy animal to which she displayed, according to her mother, 'the virtuous side of [her] determination . . . It came out as complete loyalty to things and people, once adopted.' When Margot was four, Louise, Manoel's wife, sent her a life-size furry rabbit. 'She loved it and took it everywhere with her and called it Week because it was the sound I made for it when we played together. Every night it had to sleep with her. She used to suck her thumb and pluck at the fur till he was nearly bald.' Week had to wait in the dressing-room with Mrs Hookham whenever Peggy took her ballet examinations. For Grade I she was awarded 95 out of 100; for Grade II, the next year, 85, and for Grade III, 70. But it was for a classical dance in a short silver tunic that she earned her first newspaper review. The occasion was a concert at the Rudolph Steiner Hall in aid of the League of Pity; the date, 4 July 1924. 'In *The Silver Ballet* there was a remarkably fine solo danced by Peggy Hookham, which was vigorously encored,' noted the *Middlesex County Times*. It was enough to make Peggy and her mother keep tabs on other dancers who could command publicity. The sight of a playbill displaying a photograph of Anna Pavlova incited Peggy to ask her mother, 'Who is that lady?' Her mother replied that it was the greatest ballerina in the world. 'Then I'll be the second greatest,' said Peggy. Nor was she properly overcome when her mother managed to get seats for them in the upper circle of the Palace Theatre to see Pavlova dance *The Fairy Doll*.

Frederick Ashton, living as a child in Lima, Peru, had been present at a Pavlova performance in 1917, and had responded dramatically. 'Seeing her at that stage was the end of me. She injected me with her poison, and from the end of that evening I wanted to dance.'[12] His future muse, however, remained un-impressed. What was it that the rather aged ballerina could do that she, Peggy, could not? Well, better *retirés* for one thing, pointed out Mrs Hookham, sensibly picking on one of the few steps humble enough to come within the basic sphere of Peggy's weekly classwork. Peggy was mortified by this want of maternal solidarity. But even if she could not spot the genius of Pavlova, she could, and did, work harder at her next lesson. In the exer-cise of *retiré*, one pointed foot is drawn up the supporting leg to lodge at the side of the knee, so that the two turned-out legs, one straight, one bent, make the shape of a printed figure four. Often it is just an interim, unsustained position, prepara-tory to some unfolding of the working leg *à la seconde*, or into *arabesque*, or so forth. As a step on its own, it usually has a sharp, staccato, snatched-up feel to it. But as Margot explains in her illuminative appendix to *A Dancer's World* (a handbook which she wrote in 1978 for students and parents), these 300-year-old steps have evolved away from their original representation, as has indeed the usage of the French language. The literal translation of *retiré* is 'withdrawn', 'contracted', 'secluded'. That such a pedantic emphasis should be laid, even in an unreliable family anecdote, on so introverted and modest a movement is somehow typical of the care and subtlety of Fonteyn's very earliest training. Pavlova, after all, was forever dancing something incandescent, or unearthly, that went far beyond the bounds of ordinary technique; and a less responsible mother would have encouraged her daughter to fling herself about the drawing-room as a Dragonfly or a Dying Swan. But Mrs Hookham, guided by Miss Bosustow, seems to have understood that her daughter's immature limbs could only be prompted, not pushed. The safe haven of Ealing was about to give way to a wider and less scrupulous world. And the best information that a prospective dancer's mother could possibly have gleaned was this: no ballet class at all is better than a bad one.

In 1900, when Margot's father was eleven years old, his own father, also an engineer, had taken over the management of a small railway line in Brazil, running from Santa Catarina to Imbitules. The family of four – mother Alice, father John, son Felix, and his eight-year-old sister Margaret – had set sail for South America, where, for two years, the boy had been allowed to run wild on the beach, quite unencumbered by the pressures of education. And now, in 1927, a second-generation Felix and Margaret, his own son and daughter, had reached the corresponding ages of eleven and eight when, uncannily, a similar adventure opened up to them. Mr Hookham was to be posted to China as 'Number 2' to the Chief Engineer of the British American Tobacco Company, who was nearing retirement.

Yet the pattern did not quite repeat itself. This time, one member of the family had to be left behind. Despite the tempting offer to her husband, Mrs Hookham had great qualms: 'such a strange country, so far away, home leave for Felix only every four years, and what about the children? Finally it was decided that we should go; so we called on the man who had bought our house in Waldeck Road, and who, extraordinarily, had been consul in Shanghai, to ask about conditions there. He painted quite a rosy picture of life there, but said that it would be better not to take our son, since although there was quite a good school there for boys almost everybody sent their children back to England for their education. He added that it was very hard for children to be sent back without their parents, and advised us to send him to a boarding-school before we left, so that he could get used to it.'

Up to this point, young Felix had gone by bicycle to a local day school, Durston House, the headmistress of which, Mrs Pierce, happened to run a small preparatory school in Ripley, Surrey, so his removal there was straightforward as far as his mother could ascertain. 'He never said much about his new life, and hardly spoke at all on our last visit before we left. I told him that we had arranged for him to spend the Christmas holiday with Manoel's family in Altrincham near Manchester. There were five somewhat older children who would look after him, a large house, and at least two cars. I was sure they would have a good Christmas, and be very nice to him, which indeed they were. I was told later, however, that they could not get "close" to him, and that he spent most of his time either in the garage with the chauffeur, reading, or wandering about the garden.'

But no sooner had the boy been settled, and their passports been prepared, than something happened which forced the Hookhams to postpone their journey to the Far East. With the blithe disregard for political danger that was to characterize her attitude all her life, Margot, in her autobiography, dismisses the hitch as a 'minor Sino-Japanese conflict'. But in fact the situation in China in 1927 was both grave and complex. The many warring factions, tired of their exploitation by foreign powers, had formed a national party to free themselves of foreign domination. Earlier in the same year, Nationalist troops, led by

Chiang Kai-shek, had pushed northwards, and only the deployment of foreign troops had kept them out of the foreign settlements in Shanghai, where, at the same time, Communist-led labour unions had risen in a general strike. When the Nationalists attacked Nanking, they were halted by the British and US gunboats in the Yangtse.

Until the trouble had, as Margot puts it, 'blown over', the Hookham family was diverted to America, where Mr Hookham could use the hiatus to study the tobacco business in the Southern States. Peggy and her parents were to set sail for New York on 5 November 1927. On the eve of the Atlantic crossing, they slept at the St Pancras Hotel in London before catching the boat train to Liverpool the next morning, so that Mr Hookham's parents could join them for a farewell dinner and reminisce about their own departure, long ago, to Brazil. But the St Pancras was 'a great gloomy barracks of a place', which served, to Peggy's disgust, oxtail soup. So sure was she now that her likes and dislikes held sway that she hardly even bothered to glance at her mother for permission to leave the horrid brown brew. But she was reckoning without her grandmother. Mr Hookham *père* had a sweet disposition and a great sense of humour; but his wife, Alice, who ruled him, had a biting tongue and 'boasted she could make anyone quail'. She chose this moment to insist upon her Victorian doctrine that children must eat what has been put in front of them. Yet it was the grandmother, not the child, who learned a lesson. At three in the morning in her hotel bedroom, Peggy was violently and repeatedly sick; and she boarded the ship the next day ghostly pale but essentially triumphant.

Her smile, however, was only to fade, and her pallor to increase, as the ten-day crossing got under way. The cause, oddly enough, was not sea-sickness – since from the age of nine she would never, to her mother's surprise, ever suffer from travel-sickness again. A nobler indisposition had assailed the child: the pain of separation from her brother. As she stood on the deck, staring back over the widening water, her outer listlessness and inner distress were symptoms not of nausea but of a bout of melancholy and longing such as she had never felt before. This was not the first sea trip she had undertaken: the family of four had, some years earlier, crossed the Channel to Ambleteuse, and gone by boat to the island of Lundy. But now their number had fallen to three. And this voyage was Peggy's initiation into the world of sweet, sorrowful partings that she was to inhabit for so much of her life. The troubled, churning sea (the same mesmeric grey-green, she noted, as the linoleum of Miss Bosustow's classroom floor) became a metaphor for heartache. In those days before international flying, time and distance gave tangible measure to the enormity of the power of love. And the girl on the deck was to become the kind of woman who loves most what she can least possess.

2

The train from New York to Virginia, clanging its bell, ran through the streets of Richmond and deposited the astonished Hookham family directly outside the William Byrd Hotel. Margot was later to become expert at the art of travelling light – a couple of Dior suits would, after all, take you anywhere – and at airports she would teach her colleagues how to organize their hand-luggage so that journeying could unfold like a seamless *enchaînement*. But, in her childhood, huge cabin trunks and twenty pieces of luggage were the order of the day; and, being the kind of child that she was – homesick, uncommunicative, fussy about food – she might well have proved a reluctant vagabond, were it not for the fact that her parents showed such good humour in the face of the unknown. Wherever they went, her toy rabbit went too, his head poking out of Mrs Hookham's golf bag 'so that he could see everything' – from the skyscrapers of New York in the morning mist, to the poverty-stricken South, with its children and chickens running wild in the cotton-fields.

From Richmond the family moved to Louisville, where the British American Tobacco Company had provided them with an apartment. Located on the ground floor, it was thickly carpeted and, by English standards, fabulously equipped with kitchen knick-knacks and a fashionable Sunmon Bed-in-a-cupboard. Mr Hookham splashed out on an Essex car and, since Christmas was coming, drove his family to Covington to visit a college friend – an Episcopalian minister with an American wife and a five-year-old daughter, Wendy. 'The Whittles were very hospitable and kind,' writes Mrs Hookham, 'and of course devout; we on the other hand were rather easygoing. We practically never went to Church, or said grace at meals, although

I must confess I was brought up to do so; we were hardly the ideal Christmas guests.'

Once his daughter was safely settled with friends, Mr Hookham whisked his wife off, between Boxing Day and New Year, for a motoring tour, but those seven motherless days turned out to be purgatory for the child. Peggy later admitted to a life-long loathing for Wendy Whittle, who, as well as having lighted on the English girl's phobias about American mod-cons (the unfamiliar ring of the telephone, the whirlpool flush of the lava-tory), further mocked her with un-Christian zeal for not knowing the words to hymns. In the misery of her abandon-ment, Peggy must have had a taste of how it felt to be Felix, holed up in an English boarding-school and prey to more accom-plished tormentors than Wendy.

But Peggy was a girl; and if the sexual politics of the day decreed that her formal education counted for less than her brother's, then, by extension, her emotional needs were given far more credence than his. Mrs Hookham, on her return to the Whittles, was horrified to find that her daughter had sunk into the solemn silence which, with Peggy, was the only sure sign of the child's unhappiness. And so, despite a shattered wind-screen, the Hookhams set off post-haste for their flat in Louisville, driving over rough mountain terrain, through snow and bitter winds, with Peggy wrapped in a blanket on the back seat, clutching a hot water bottle.

It was during their three-month stay in Louisville that Peggy enrolled at an ordinary school. Mrs Hookham was pleasantly surprised by what was locally on offer to her daughter, which included lessons in homemaking as well as public hygiene and city management. 'Everything except pens and pencils was free. In England, of course, she would have gone to a private school where nothing would be free, uniforms compulsory, and expen-sive. It was quite near, and a large State school with mixed classes, but no negroes as they were called, as the South was still segre-gated.' Peggy, however, was less impressed than her mother. Children *en masse* frightened her; she disliked games; she objected to pronouncing her 'zeds' as 'zees'. Once again she fell unnaturally silent. But her reticence did not deter one small boy from walking into Mrs Hookham's kitchen without knocking, to ask, 'Can your Peggy be my sweetheart?' Mrs Hookham looked at him somewhat startled, and, after suggesting that he might like to remove his hat, said, 'Thank you for asking me first. I will go and ask her.' Mrs Hookham continues: 'Needless to say the answer was in the negative. I gave him the bad news and enquired why he chose Peggy over one of the other girls that he must have known longer and he replied, "Well she is different," and went off. That was her first admirer, a rather plump, pale-faced little boy of nine with a strong American accent.'

Peggy's reluctance to make friends provided the cue for Mrs Hookham to start looking for a dancing school. There was only one in the telephone directory. She took the precaution of watching a class before letting Peggy join, and what she saw did not please her. Even the basic five positions of the arms and feet had not been properly taught, and students as young as Peggy were being encouraged to do high-kicks and splits. Miss Bosustow would have had a fit. So ballet, for the moment, remained off the agenda. The family was, in any case, soon on the move again. They took a train to Seattle, joined the SS *President Jackson*, and began the long voyage to China. 'Compared to our experience of a British ship,' writes Mrs Hookham, 'discipline seemed rather lax; officers mixed with passengers in a relaxed way, and apparently anyone could go up on the bridge when they wanted.'

The bridge was the best place to be when, six weeks later, the water through which the American vessel was passing grew murky and discoloured, heralding the estuary of the Yangtse Kiang. Into its tributary, the Whang Poo, the ship steamed, past huge junks with slatted sails and tiny sampans – stacked high with produce and housing entire families – manoeuvred at high speed, with one oar, by lone oarsmen. Days later, within sight of the Bund, the ship at last dropped anchor. The solid Victorian buildings which lined the shore were a curious source of comfort to Peggy: Shanghai seemed so much more like England than America had done.

And despite the sweltering streets teeming with rickshaws, and the cars hooting and the people shouting and the bicycle bells ringing, this comforting impression could be sustained so long as one restricted oneself to the privileged, European part of Shanghai, with its exclusive clubs, racecourse and manicured public gardens, and did not cross the bridge to the seamy, cabbage-smelling district where starving beggars munched on their own body lice. The Hookhams were staying in the British concession at the Astor House Hotel, and were much taken with the huge Victorian beds swathed in musty mosquito net and the antique commodes which were emptied daily by a coolie. But after a fortnight of this cosseting, the family was sent to the much smaller town of Tientsin, the port of Peking: Old China. Here, at last, the utter differentness of the Far East, which is what, after all, we mean by exoticism, was borne in with the yellow winds that blow sand from the great Gobi Desert, and the scent of purple lilac from the wilds of Mongolia. Peggy and her mother joined the thronging blue-clad Chinese in the native quarter, and braved the dim interiors of brightly bannered shops to finger bales of silken cloth: blossom-embroidered gauzes and lace-encrusted grass-linens for fancy-dress costumes undreamed of by the Weldons.

In Tientsin, Peggy once again embarked on dancing lessons, this time with an elderly Russian, Mme Tarakanova. The distraction was not so much for Peggy's benefit as to fill the idle hours of her mother, who – with a staff of chauffeur, 'boy', watchman, cook and amah to run the splendid house in the Russian concession that the family had been allocated – would have lost face if she'd lifted a finger. Mrs Hookham's working-class upbringing had not equipped her for the snobberies of expatriate socializing, and she baulked at the prospect of spending her afternoons in the company of other nostalgic housewives around a mah-jong table. Instead she took, symbolically enough, to buying caged birds from street markets and setting them loose in her spare room. But the creatures did not thrive. So she turned her attention to rabbits, which, though they slept outside in hutches, were allowed, during the day, the run of the living-room. The image of Margot, in her last years on the farm in Panama, with cows wandering unchecked about the ramshackle veranda and into the house, and hens laying eggs on the bedroom pillows, seems not so strange when one considers those early, complicitous days of solace found in the company of animals.

Peggy ate well in Tientsin, having discovered a German pâtisserie where her mother would treat her to cheese straws and ice-cream on the way home from her dancing lessons. The family owned a wind-up gramophone which, together with some records that they had searched out locally – *Ballet Egyptien* and *Humoresque* – encouraged Mrs Hookham and her daughter to dabble in a spot of choreography. Between them they devised a dance which, according to a local critic, 'was easily the hit of the performance . . . the little girl's footwork being especially striking in the dance of a Turkish slave girl where she jangled her tambourine and threw herself into the dance with a gay abandon rare in such a young dancer'.[1]

But Mrs Hookham was not one to be fooled by such small-pond flattery: she kept her eye on bigger fish back home. Regular deliveries of the *Dancing Times* from London, however out of date, nevertheless fed her with the requisite information as to which school, or which teacher, currently mattered. The names of Nicholas Legat, Serafina Astafieva, Marie Rambert and Ninette de Valois had already lodged themselves in her consciousness. She yearned to see her son, and England; but her husband was enjoying his new job, and her olive-skinned daughter seemed perfectly assimilated as she set off daily, in the oppressive heat, to Tientsin Grammar School. Sometimes, on Saturdays, Peggy's father would take her to work with him, and she proved as susceptible to the romance of the factory as he. Between the wars, cigarettes exuded a cinematic glamour: they were regarded not as coffin-nails but as lifelines – the final consolation to be placed between the lips of dying heroes; the first prop to adorn the bright mouths of new, fast-talking heroines. The aroma of tobacco was still considered vampy and haunting, and Peggy had every reason, then, to be proud of her father's profession. Most thrilling to her were the handfuls of cigarette-cards with which she was presented on these outings, cards depicting oriental glories that she was sure would gratify her brother, who had now moved on from Ripley to a boarding-school in Gloucestershire. She would post her favourites to him and hang on his reaction, but none came: perhaps lush blossom and Buddhist temples and the faces of Chinese actors cut no ice in the playgrounds and dormitories of Cheltenham College.

The chance to find out was suddenly upon her. By June 1929 her father's work in Tientsin was done, and he was to be sent by the BAT to set up a factory in a town thought too remote for womenfolk. So it was decided that Peggy and her mother should return to England to see young Felix. No snail's-pace ship this time; the Trans-Siberian Railway would shrink the journey home to a mere fourteen days. And thus, with fourteen pieces of luggage, Mrs Hookham and her daughter boarded the wood-burning Russian train at Chang Chun and crossed the frontier at Manchouli. Amid wagonloads of peasants and soldiers travelling 'hard class', Peggy and Mrs Hookham basked in the opulence of a red-plush compartment which converted into a double sleeping-berth at night. Just as well that they were comfortable, for they were virtual prisoners in transit, their passports stamped 'On no account is it permitted to leave the train or change money.' Not that the landscape struck them as conducive: passing through Siberia, Mrs Hookham noticed 'some black bundles on the ground beside the fence, and wondered what they were until one moved. A thin arm came out and rearranged the wrapping around its head and shoulder; it looked like the extremity of poverty and misery. At the other end of the scale, but equally chilling, was when we stopped at Ekaterinburg where someone took the trouble to point out the biggish house up on the hill, and told us that it was where the

Russian Royal Family was murdered, which was only about ten years back at the time.'

In Moscow, passengers *were* allowed off the train, and were taken to a hotel where they were nevertheless forbidden a much-needed bath. Instead their time was to be spent on a tour of imposing buildings, but Peggy was less impressed by Lenin's tomb than she was by the life-size stuffed black bear in her hotel lobby. Nothing, however, entranced her so much as the Lorelei Rock, which she and her mother visited by boat when they reached Germany. The dark Rhine, mythically draped in white mist and flanked by steep mountains with unlikely turreted castles reaching up into the clouds, fed Peggy with a taste for the kind of scenery which, one day, would forever be dropping in around her from the flies, and swirling about her feet from dry-ice machines, and adorning the painted backdrops of *Swan Lake*.

At Victoria Station, Felix still made no mention of cigarette-cards. Dumbstruck with apprehensive excitement at the sight of him, Peggy did not speak of them either, nor indeed of anything else. They stood, estranged, on the platform – cosseted, much-travelled daughter, and isolated, insular son: Cheltenham versus China. Meeting can sometimes be even sadder than parting.

Mrs Hookham had booked rooms at a residential hotel in Ealing, the better to renew Peggy's association with Miss Bosustow. But Peggy had become more catholic than ever in her dancing tastes. Never mind the discipline of being coached for ballet exams: on this ten-month stay in England she preferred to develop her 'Turkish' dance for All England Competitions, and to appear at the Albert Hall with turquoise bows on her tap-shoes in a children's number, 'Pickin' Cotton'. She and her mother were subject, in any case, to thirteen-year-old Felix's term timetable, which was strict and inflexible and made no conces-sion to visiting families – not even those who had travelled 4,500 miles. Mrs Hookham held no brief for Cheltenham College. 'I think [Felix] hated it,' she writes, 'but he didn't complain. I thought it was awful. On that cold winter's day the boys were all walking about without overcoats, apparently unaware of the season – it wasn't "done" to wrap up.'

As soon as Felix was let out of school, the family made straight for Littleham, a small village on the hills above Exmouth to which Peggy's paternal grandparents had retired. For all of Peggy's exotic travels, she and her mother found the countryside of Devon and Dorset, from Lyme Regis to Dartmoor, more beautiful than any landscape they had seen abroad. Mrs Hookham bought an Austin Ten and drove her children to the seaside at Polzeath, where they stayed in a farmhouse on the sand-dunes. When the school holidays were over, mother and daughter returned to Ealing, where Mrs Hookham enrolled Peggy at a local day-school for two terms. But on their return to China, in the spring of 1930, Peggy managed, for six care-free months, to abscond from academic life entirely. Felix senior had his first 'local' leave in Hong Kong and the family stayed 'in a lovely old hotel overlooking Repulse Bay . . . a beautiful setting with the mountains behind and the island's inlets all around'. Not only was Peggy let off school, but the telephone directory failed to yield a viable dancing academy. Who cared? The child was in her element: the sea. She swam all day. And, alone on the beach, she found the next best thing to a ballet teacher: the first of her handsome, gallant, lucky dancing part-ners. Mr Olsen, a big-boned Norwegian diplomat, twice her height and four times her age, took to meeting her daily to talk of Karsavina, whom he had seen perform Aurora in St Petersburg. And in the afternoons he would escort her to tea-dances at their shared hotel, where no one thought it the least bit rum that a man in his forties should sweep an eleven-year-old round the dance floor in a *paso doble*.

Towards the end of their stay in Hong Kong, Mrs Hookham suffered a bout of malaria. She had never really been ill before, so dreaded a further attack, which came, surely enough, just as the family was on the move again, back to Shanghai. She took quinine and crawled into bed rather than call for a doctor; but, in fact, she hardly needed one, for it was at this point that she was made aware of the eagerly compassionate nature of her daughter. 'Little Peggy was my devoted nurse. She watched the time, gave me pills, and got me drinks while [her father] was away at the factory. This time I turned quite yellow and had all the misery of it, but for a much shorter time, thank goodness. It was only when I was sitting up again that I discovered that I had been taking double doses from my little nurse; though I must say that apparently it did me no harm and in fact I have never suffered from malaria since.'

On this second posting to Shanghai, Mr Hookham was promoted to Director as well as Chief Engineer of the British American Tobacco Company. Patsy Jellicoe, a contemporary of Margot's who grew up in Shanghai, recalls the snobbish, stratified society in which the socially insecure Hookhams found themselves: 'You were spoilt rotten. Wonderful restaurants. Everyone went out dancing every night. Of course it was very colonial, and the English wouldn't mix with anyone else. They had their own country club and this famous long bar where no one else was allowed to go. There was a sort of polo-playing, banking crowd, and then there was a middle, working crowd, which the Hookhams would have been part of. There was a very good orchestra with Italians, Portuguese, French, and Dutch playing in it, but that was more for the middle people, which included a whole White Russian contingent who were brilliant and gifted – none of the polo players would have been seen dead with them.'

Although even this period, from early 1931 to late 1933, was interrupted by an eight-month visit to England, it was in Shanghai that Peggy received what semblance of a formal education was ever to be hers. Here she attended an august British institution called the Cathedral School for Girls (now, paradoxically, a school for the performing arts, with a ballet studio in what was then the Assembly Hall). Margot was later to describe herself as academically 'fair', but that seems *un*-fair, since, considering the ground which she had lost, she must have done unusually well to have kept up at all. Patsy Jellicoe says: 'She had an extremely good mind, an *extremely* good mind. Very, very bright. Her father was a very quick and intelligent businessman and she was very like him. Small-boned like him. Very neat. And a precise, good mind.'

The actual nature of Fonteyn's intelligence is not, as yet, the issue; but what *is* interesting is its lineage. Everyone who knew Margot has something to say about Mrs Hookham's powerful influence over her daughter's life. But although Margot's father lived on until 1975, he, like the unwanted surname he bequeathed her, will virtually have disappeared from her story by the end of this chapter. Yet, tempting as it is to dismiss him as the formidable Black Queen's counterpart in the ballet *Checkmate* – namely, the gentle and infinitely vanquishable Red King – a photograph of father and daughter on the balcony of their flat in Shanghai, taken in 1931, bears out Lady Jellicoe's insistence on their resemblance, at least on the all-important physical level. He stands behind her, and is, indeed, a slight man, since Peggy's twelve-year-old bobbed head already reaches half-way up his chest. His hands rest lightly, one on her shoulder, the other on her elbow; and she is leaning against him, but not heavily. It is not just that their profiles match so closely; there is a restfulness between them, a shared, placid repose which clearly marks the ancestry of her distinctive serenity. And despite the baggy trousers of the day, and the institutional cuff-linked white shirt and tie, it is clear that the compact physique and delicate, arresting bone structure already evident in the bare arms and elegantly held neck of his cotton-frocked daughter must be his – not his wife's – genetic gift.

There is, however, another photograph, this time of mother and daughter; same dress, same balcony, same day. Once again Peggy leans against her parent, but now she relinquishes her whole weight. Mrs Hookham's face is preoccupied: what we look at, what she means us to look at, is not her, but her child. Peggy's head is lowered bashfully, yet her eyes are raised: their dreaming, rapt expression has caught the light. Physical likeness is neither pointed nor material here. Where there was calm with her father, with her mother there is excitement: here are two spirits presenting themselves as one.

Mrs Hookham was united with Peggy in her hatred of sport: after all, prospective dancers cannot afford tennis muscles or hockey injuries, and besides, the girl was hardly going to want for exercise. There were plenty of dancing schools in Shanghai, and Peggy was, by this time, as keen as her mother to seek one out. 'Even when we were on holiday,' claimed Mrs Hookham, 'Margot had to find a teacher before the family was allowed to unpack or go swimming. Once that matter was settled, we were permitted to enjoy ourselves.'[2] According to Audrey King, who taught Peggy at that time: 'She was a very shy little girl ... She had lovely straight legs and a beautiful *arabesque* from the beginning, and she was different from the other little girls in the class who were obviously only learning dancing because Mother thought it would do them good, or just for fun. Margot was always serious about what she was doing – in fact I think perhaps that is a part of her character, always to try to do things to the best of her ability. In Shanghai, of course, it was possible to learn all types of dancing and I know that Margot's mother felt that Margot was going to be a very good character dancer.'[3]

This is borne out by photographs taken in 1931, in which Peggy – under the auspices of another of her mother's experiments, the Rhomer-Peeler School, which espoused Greek dancing and callisthenics – appeared in a variety of cat-suits (with tail and ears), spotted tunics and gauze drapes. One of these pictures, featuring Peggy and a matching girl with a matching bob doing pointy things with their fingers and toes, travelled as far as the pages of the *Dancing Times* in London, where it appeared under the caption: 'Dragon Sprites'.

Given all this barefoot abandon, classical ballet can hardly have been a priority for Peggy. For – with the exception of Pavlova, who had just died, aged forty-nine – the child had never even seen a ballerina. But on her next trip to London she went with her mother and brother to see the new English ballet company about which they had read, the Vic-Wells, in some short ballets which, like their creator, Ninette de Valois, did not sound English at all: *Fête Polonaise*, *Homage à Belles Viennoises* and *Création du Monde*. And on another, more prophetic, evening, they saw the first performance of *A Day in a Southern Port* (which was later to be called *Rio Grande*), choreographed by Frederick Ashton to music by Constant Lambert and featuring Alicia Markova. But what made the greatest impression on Peggy was a performance of *Les Sylphides*, also danced by Markova.

Les Sylphides is romantic ballet incarnate. All the gorgeous silliness is there: the poet in pale tights and black tunic over billowing white sleeves, surrounded by long-skirted women in white tulle who waft in dreamlike formations to the nocturnes and preludes of Chopin. There is no story: rapture of movement is all; this is Fokine anticipating the glorious abstractions of Balanchine. Here at last was something to which Peggy could aspire. And at the centre of the vision was the unbelievably airborne and ethereal figure of Markova, who, however 'Russian' both in manner and name, was – Peggy knew from her mother's researches – just plain old Lilian Marks from Muswell Hill.

The image of Markova would have predominated on the long sea voyage back to Shanghai had not mother and child shared a more immediate grail. In Parkway, near to London Zoo, Peggy had spotted a ring-tailed lemur, which she begged Mrs Hookham to buy. 'It was £16, so I had to say no and that we would have to wait and see if we could find something at one of the ports.' Finally, in Penang, they tracked down 'a dark dirty shop full of tiny cages . . . The Chinese owner took us out to the back where there was a covered box on the ground. As he bent down two little paws reached out from the bottom and grasped at his robe and pitiful little cries came out. It was too much for us, and without seeing more I said we would have it whatever it was . . . When we arrived in Shanghai about two weeks later Felix was at the dockside to meet us with a friend. He shouted up to us, "I've got a nice new flat." I replied, "Splendid, we've got an otter." "A what-er?" "An Otter!" So we went ashore with Peggy screaming with laughter and excitement.'

The new apartment came with a comprehensive staff elected from what Mrs Hookham describes as the 'freemasonry of Chinese servants who knew everything and everybody and "arranged" themselves into the jobs . . . The Boys took great pride in their houses and work, especially their cooking and tables. If there was a dinner party, for instance, and our table cloth was not as good as some other Boy's missy's, then he would borrow the best he could find so as not to "lose face" by working for someone who did not have sufficient standing. There were stories told of people who, dining out with friends, would find themselves eating off their own table cloth, or with their own silver: next morning everything would be clean and laundered and back in place.'

It was under the critical eye of this self-regulating workforce that Mrs Hookham's final food-battle with Peggy was to be waged. 'For lunch one day there was some very good roast pork. I asked her to taste it, just a little – "No, I don't like it," she said. I asked her how she knew, never having tasted it – "I *do* know." I was a bit cross and told her, "You've just made up your mind not to like it, so you can go up to your room and stay there till I finish my lunch." Which she did without further comment. We had a very tall Chinese butler who served the rest of the lunch, and went out. When I had finished, I went up to Peggy's room. She was lying on the bed sobbing; he was standing beside her with a toy in one hand and a towel in the other saying, "No cry little missy, please no cry." As he went out he gave me the blackest of looks: I am sure I lost a lot of "face" with him after that.'

Lessons in ballet were now all-important: the latest trip to London had convinced Mrs Hookham that her daughter needed a more professional training. At the theatre where Peggy's concerts were held, Mrs Hookham spied an older girl, more accomplished than Peggy's fellow pupils, someone whose lyrical flow of movement set her apart. The girl's name was June Bear (later to become June Brae). Next morning, Mrs Hookham was on the blower to Mrs Bear. Who was it who was teaching her talented daughter? It turned out to be three people: a woman and two men. The woman had a studio, but the men, White Russian émigrés on their uppers, did not. One of them, George Goncharov, had danced with the Bolshoi in Moscow. His lessons were apparently conducted in the Bears' dining-room, and were shared by a girl called Virginia Browning, with Mrs Bear accompanying, not tremendously well, on a tinny piano. 'Could Peggy join in?' wondered Mrs Hookham.

'I was horrified,' June Brae remembers, 'because I was very grown-up at nearly fourteen, and this little girl of twelve came in with a black fringe, black hair, very, very proper – with her mother, of course. Mothers were always around. I thought, "Who on earth's *this*?" She was like a little Japanese doll. But we became great friends. She always wanted me to go and stay with her. And it was all-night pillow fights. They were her one thing in life. Her mother was quite jolly, but she was still stern. Margot and I had to watch it. She never missed a class, Mrs Hookham. She was always sitting there, making sure we weren't fooling around. I think she really pushed Margot hard. She was strict with her technically. She wanted everything to be technically correct.'

And Goncharov was the man to see to it. He was a teacher steeped in the discipline and style of the great Russian tradition, and it was a stroke of extraordinary luck that Margot should have fallen into his hands when she did. (She was later to reciprocate the felicity by signing his British naturalization papers and introducing him as a teacher into Sadler's Wells.) The classes which he gave were quiet and explanatory, with much emphasis placed upon musical feeling and response. And, in his response to Peggy, one hears, for the first time, the authentic appreciation of one artist for another, which makes no false claims but notes only and distinctively what could have been evident then. 'Directly I saw her I knew she had a ballerina's head. Her face – she was very attractive, with big dark eyes – seemed to talk to me. She held herself beautifully. She was always somehow *intent*, as though she had some idea that she knew what she was about.'[4]

The other male teacher, Elirov, did not exactly meet Mrs Hookham's stringent standards. He had never been a dancer, but taught his own brand of *plastique* movement, sitting at the piano and waving the girls along with his plump arms. 'We used to prance around and just make up the dances ourselves,' says June Brae. Yet the sessions seemed harmless enough, and unlikely to strain any muscles. Mrs Hookham gave short shrift, however, to the third, female, teacher. 'After watching, I decided that, according to our standards, she was ruining the children by letting them do movements that their muscles were not then ready for or strong enough to take. I also noticed that she was letting June turn her legs out from the knee and not from the hip, which was a very serious fault. I told Mrs Bear all of this and said I would not allow Margot to take the class, and advised her to take June out of it as well.'[5]

Who would dare disobey? Over the next two years, a great deal of competition would arise between the two girls, and indeed between the two mothers; but as Patsy Jellicoe puts it: 'Black Queen could wipe the floor with Mrs Bear.' Mrs Hookham writes: 'June's intense keenness stirred Peggy's ambition to try to be the best, so it was all to the good. I think we must have seemed quite mad . . . and now I can see it must have been a bit hard on the poor husbands, especially Mr Bear who was a rather strict Scotsman and could not be expected to approve of so much that was going on especially in his own home. At this time Shanghai was the most cosmopolitan city in the world and there was always something to do, so Felix could keep his distance from his dance-crazed family, and take a fatherly interest in the proceedings. However one night when we were out enjoying ourselves at a cabaret, a trio of dancers came on and did an adagio number. I turned to Felix and said that I knew that they were ballet trained and professional dancers. One of them turned out to be "our" Goncharov, and his two partners were friends of his from the Bolshoi Ballet, and as you can imagine they put on a wonderful act. Of course we got to know the other two; the man was Topiroff and the girl as she was then was Vera Volkova.'

Peggy and her mother had caught a glimpse of this Vera Volkova before – in the Bears' dining-room, when the beguiling Russian émigrée had walked, in a black picture hat, into the middle of Goncharov's class. The discovery that a perfectly trained student of the great Agrippina Vaganova should have been reduced to earning her living by performing a cabaret act in one of Shanghai's steamier nightclubs galvanized the two ambitious mothers, as did news, gleaned from the *Dancing Times*, that three Russian-trained 'Baby Ballerinas' – Tamara Toumanova, Irina Baronova and Tatiana Riabouchinska (all of them younger than June and none much older than Margot) – were currently taking London and Europe by storm. Now it was Mrs Bear's turn to 'wipe the floor' with her rival. 'The lure of the bright lights,' writes Mrs Hookham, 'brought about one of Mrs Bear's impetuous decisions. The first we knew of it was when Peggy and I went as usual to her house which had become our dance studio for Goncharov's class. The class over, she suddenly announced that she was taking June off to London so that she could have lessons with Nicholas Legat, the famous Russian teacher. I was somewhat shattered by this, [since], while Mrs Bear's plans were simple, there would be no studio or pianist for poor Goncharov to continue his lessons . . . We certainly wanted Peggy to go on studying dancing as she had made a lot of progress and enjoyed "being good at it". We were now almost forced to consider whether it was to be her career. After all, at that time, a career for a son was important, but most daughters would be succeeding with a husband and family . . . There was also young Felix at boarding school and reports of his progress were not so promising. His Aunt "Purdie" had written to say that he seemed lonely on his holidays.'

Of course, there were other, more sombre, reasons why a sensible English family should have considered leaving Shanghai at that time. Since 1931, the Japanese army in China (called the Kwantang Army, and not under the control of Tokyo) had occupied Manchuria, which in 1932 was declared independent and renamed Manchukuo. In January of that year the Japanese had tried to gain control of the major ports, and sporadic fighting had broken out in Shangai. As June Brae says: 'Actually, touch wood, we were lucky, because after we came home everything blew up in China, and even when we were still there we had times when we were told to stay in the house, not to go out, and you could see the soldiers walking along the street, shooting, just like that.' But the first rumblings of the full-scale war that would break out between China and Japan in 1937 did not, at this stage, come into the Hookhams' calculations. Mrs Hookham was simply torn between loyalty to her marriage and loyalty to her maternal ambition. It was no contest really. Within two weeks of the Bears' departure, the plan had been forged: Peggy and her mother were to travel to London several months ahead of Mr Hookham's next leave so that the girl's potential could, once and for all, be properly assessed.

It was only a trip to England like any of the others. But the enormity of the decision was illustrated by two factors. The first was Peggy's interview with her redoubtable headmistress at the Cathedral School, Miss Fleet, to whom she admitted that she was abandoning academic education completely. Mounting the oak stairs to Miss Fleet's office, Peggy found herself, for the first time in that daunting building, not the least bit afraid. 'You will regret this all your life,' said Miss Fleet, 'because you will find yourself an ignoramus among other people.'[6] And though Peggy, even then, could quite see her point, she dismissed the prophecy with a shrug. How could a headmistress be expected to under-stand that when you want to be a dancer and are already four-teen years old, time is running out? And the second act of faith was this: although the otter was handed over to Shanghai Zoo, Peggy and her mother took two pets – a hawfinch and a dazal bird – with their luggage to England. To all intents and purposes, Nita Hookham was abandoning the nest. Any semblance of family life for Peggy was at an end: the career of Margot Fonteyn was about to begin.

The London to which Peggy and her mother returned in 1933 was still the capital of the British Empire in a world where huge areas of the map were coloured pink. It was a safe, solid, complacent city, not the least bit rowdy like New York, nor raffish like Paris. The plumbing worked, and the gleaming Underground trains ran on time. Women, on the whole, stayed at home, and the work that men went out to remained defined by cloth caps or bowler hats. Summers were just as hot as on the Continent, but no restaurant owner would have considered putting chairs and tables out on the pavement. Nor, in winter, was there much in the way of domestic central heating. This was as symptomatic of stoicism as it was of poverty: the grander the house, the colder.

Plays and musicals flourished. *Cavalcade*, by Noël Coward, could command a cast of 400; audiences wore evening dress, at least in the stalls, which were, in any case, the prerogative of the upper classes who monopolized the West End – dining in its restaurants, working at its ministries, and living in the elegant houses of Mayfair and Belgravia. But ballet, which had long been institutionalized in France, Russia and Denmark, lacked, as yet, a national status in England. The magnificent masques of the Tudor and Stuart courts had failed to engender any public theatrical tradition. And although, in the 1830s and 40s, there had been an English vogue for ballerinas, these had all been strictly foreign: Taglioni, Elssler, Grisi, Cerrito, Grahn. By the late nineteenth century, the whole concept of women wafting about on their toes supported by wigged men in jockstraps had been relegated to the music hall, to places like the Empire and the Alhambra, where ballet was produced to the kind of popular standard that might these days grace an ice-skating spectacular.

So that when Diaghilev burst upon Covent Garden with his Ballets Russes, the unprecedented collaboration which he effected between the high arts of music and painting and dancing took London's intelligentsia by storm. All the writers and musicians and artists and dancers who were to shape the future of British ballet fell hopelessly under the Russian's spell. Marie Rambert, Ninette de Valois, Constant Lambert, Anton Dolin and Alicia Markova each worked and studied with him in some capacity or another. And in 1930, less than a year after the death of their mentor, these five joined forces with other eminent teachers, critics, designers, conductors and composers to form the Camargo Society,[1] dedicated to the occasional production of original and classic ballets, using the best talent to be found.

The best talent to be unearthed in England turned out to be Irish. Ninette de Valois, born in 1898 in County Wicklow, was christened Edris Stannus. 'My mother gave me the name Ninette for the theatre when I was too young to say much about it, but I had a lot of French blood in me. I don't know anyone any more who calls me Edris. It's rather a serious little name, I suppose. You outlive it, rather, a name like that.'[2] After an early career dancing 'the Dying Swan on every pier in England', she had joined Diaghilev and risen to the rank of soloist. But her interest did not really lie with performing. It was to Diaghilev's own scholarly and creative vision that she aspired: 'In him I encountered a higher form of genius, a state of mind capable of concerning itself with the basic principle of perfect unity in a creative work . . . Such people . . . see artists wrapped in their isolated interests – and with invisible strings they draw them together and coordinate the whole.'[3]

Actually, it is doubtful whether de Valois really imagined that she could follow in Diaghilev's footsteps, even though in describing him as 'by nature autocratic, proud and conservative'[4] she might easily have been defining her essential self. Despite the huge force of her character and intellect and pioneering pre-feminist spirit, she always deferred to men; and, on the death of Constant Lambert in 1951, mourned him as 'our only hope of an English Diaghilev'.[5] It was in the narrower field of choreography that she had originally hoped to carry forward Diaghilev's ideals, and to this end she had opened a school called, rather earnestly, 'The Academy of Choreographic Art'. She gathered around her a nucleus of dancers whom, with an early taste for the institutional, she dressed in tunics of a plum-coloured fabric that could only be tracked down at John Barker's in Kensington High Street. But the studio space she had found in Roland Gardens proved inadequate: she needed a theatre in which to display her students' efforts. Wearing a floppy hat, she crossed Waterloo Bridge to the Old Vic Theatre, over which presided Lilian Baylis, a woman of high religious fervour as well as entrepreneurial zeal, who saw theatre for the masses mainly as a means of clearing the drunkards off the streets.

Miss Baylis announced that she liked Miss de Valois's face. Confusingly, she went on to say that she preferred beautiful hands to beautiful faces. And the hands of her dramatic students at the Old Vic were, she had to confess, quite dreadful. None of them knew what to do with them. (One member of her existing Opera Ballet did in fact turn out to have a wooden hand.) So although she had no second theatre or rehearsal rooms, nor, for that matter, money to help launch a British ballet company, she was prepared to pay this Miss de Valois a pound a week to teach her actors to move, and two pounds a time to choreograph productions of Shakespeare, rising to a dizzying three pounds should more than one dance be involved. Thus it was that these two almost farcically contrasting women came to join their formidable forces, and British national ballet was born, albeit into the helplessness of infancy.

Its other mother, Marie Rambert, must be credited with having fostered, at her ballet club in the tiny Mercury Theatre in Notting Hill, much of the choreographic and designing talent of the day – notably that of Frederick Ashton, Antony Tudor, Sophie Fedorovitch and William Chappell. But, since everyone was paid a pittance and no one was properly contracted, most people, without any sense of disloyalty, took work from whichever source happened to offer it. Not even de Valois herself felt tied to the Old Vic: she would take her best students to the Festival Theatre in Cambridge, where she arranged choruses in Greek plays, and to Dublin, where she collaborated with W.B.Yeats on his *Plays for Dancers*. But Lilian Baylis had promised de Valois a proper home for her projected ballet company; and, in 1931, with the re-opening of the Sadler's Wells Theatre in Rosebery Avenue, she proved true to her word. The new auditorium, 'refurbished' in the midst of the Depression, sported no more than a dull grey curtain, and lacked carpets; but there were 1,648 tip-up seats, and Lilian Baylis's ventures at the Old Vic had bred a band of followers faithful enough to troop across London and sit on them. Nevertheless, the first salaried members of the company – Ursula Moreton, Freda Bamford, Beatrice Appleyard, Sheila McCarthy, Nadia Newhouse and Joy Newton, with de Valois herself as 'prima ballerina, director and principal choreographer' – had to content themselves with appearing incidentally, and sometimes demeaningly, as pages or trainbearers or corpses in operas. However, there was enough dancing involved in *Carmen*, *Aida* and *Faust* for Ninette de Valois to engage Frederick Ashton to partner her in her capacity as prima ballerina. The dancers spent much of their time dressed in scanty practice-clothes beneath their coats, and leaping on and off the No. 67 bus, which ran between the Wells and the Vic. And it was at the older of these two haunts, the Old Vic, that the first full night of ballet which Lilian Baylis dared risk took place – on 5 May 1931.

It went uncommonly well. Markova's celebrated Irish partner, Anton Dolin (born Patrick Healey-Kay), lent his international reputation to the evening, and de Valois persuaded her adored Constant Lambert, the composer whom she had befriended while working with Diaghilev, to conduct. Lilian Baylis was encouraged to repeat the performances twice at Sadler's Wells, with Maynard Keynes's wife, Lydia Lopokova, as guest artist, and the annual directors' report proclaimed that it was 'astonishingly satisfactory to discover so large and enthusiastic a public waiting

for this difficult and eclectic form of art, which has not hitherto been treated seriously in London unless it hailed from a
foreign country'.[6]

For English ballet to venture abroad was more daring still. In
1932, de Valois shepherded an assorted troupe, under the auspices
of the Royal Academy of Dancing, to Denmark, where her
dancers shared a gala performance with the Royal Danish Ballet
on the occasion of the King of Denmark's birthday. A Copenhagen newspaper greeted the prospect with scepticism. 'Let's
hope there are plenty of Russians. British people dance well
enough, and their step dancers are marvellous, but British ballet
– I know of nothing more horrible.'[7] A touring British journalist, however, toed a more loyal line: 'It is remarkable that we
have to come all the way to Copenhagen to have brought home
to us that we have such good dancers in England.'

In the event, the visitors were respectfully received, with de
Valois's own ballet, *Job*, being deemed to be in the vanguard of
artistic fashion, even if the Danes were mystified as to why
English dancers should feel prompted to affect Russian names.
But changes were afoot. A new recruit to the company, a gifted
and headstrong fourteen-year-old called Doris May, was only
required to alter her unmodish first name. 'The Prelude in
Sylphides,' said Miss de Valois, who had a peremptory way of
re-dubbing her dancers in print without recourse to consultation, 'cannot be danced by Doris May.'[8] The dancer in question, who had privately rather fancied becoming an Angela or
a Penelope, recalls one night at Sadler's Wells when 'Ninette
came to me and she said: "Oh, by the way, you're Pamela May
on the programme, and I put an 'e' on May." "Oh," I said, "no!
I'll look like a hat shop!" Ninette roared with laughter, she *died*!
She said: "Darling, you're absolutely right. I'll take the 'e' off." '[9]

For all the blossoming home-grown talent, the undisputed
star of those early Vic-Wells days was Alicia Markova, who first
appeared with the company, by then more than doubled in
number, in January of 1932. It was she who, although billed
below Anton Dolin, and in smaller print, aroused enough public

interest to warrant a full ballet season being mounted around her. The whole company was offered a year's contract, and performances which had been given once a fortnight were now stepped up to two a week. The school at Sadler's Wells flourished, and its profits were ploughed back into the theatre. But ballet training is a protracted and arduous process, and the technical and artistic gap between Markova and the other, disparately schooled, members of the company remained glaringly wide. De Valois longed not just to narrow that gap, but to create an English style in its own right. Certainly she admired and valued 'Alice', (as she would, erroneously, insist on calling her), who, twelve years her junior, had, after all, been Diaghilev's prodigy. But Markova, although only twenty-two in 1933 (and a mere nine years older than Peggy), already belonged stylistically to the past – and the Russian past at that. De Valois was now in a position to move forward, gradually drawing under her wing the architects of her company's future: the brilliant composer and conductor Constant Lambert; the gifted choreographer Frederick Ashton; and, from Australia, a young male dancer of great theatrical flair, if not technical schooling: Robert Helpmann. But what she lacked, what she needed, was a ballerina, fashioned from her own fiercely disciplined teaching methods and poetic Celtic vision: dark-haired and doe-eyed like Markova of course, but gayer, graver, simpler, subtler, more sensual. And more biddable. She was forever casting her eye around the rehearsal room at the Wells. But although there were plenty of pretty and talented pupils among the eighteen hand-picked female members of her school, she could not see the one for whom she was waiting, the girl already formed in her mind's eye.

For Mrs Hookham had not taken her daughter directly to Sadler's Wells. Peggy and her mother had followed the Bear trail to Nicholas Legat, whose Barons Court studio, as coincidence would have it, was next door to 149 Talgarth Road – the Burne-Jones house in which Mrs Hookham would one day live, next door, in turn, to the future premises of the Sadler's Wells School in what was then Colet Gardens. 'Needless to say,' writes

Mrs Hookham, 'we had a lot of catching up to do as Mrs Bear was impulsive and a fast worker; she had tracked down Legat's studio and enrolled June, who was regularly going to class there.' Legat had been Pavlova's partner, and, for a time, had trained de Valois. He taught rather lethargically from a seated position at the piano, where he improvised accompaniments to his *enchaînements*. But although de Valois had found him 'an inspiring and lovable teacher', with 'deep knowledge behind the apparently free and easy approach',[10] Mrs Hookham was not satisfied. 'When we got home that evening, I told Mrs Bear that I wouldn't take Peggy there as I didn't think our girls were old enough or up to his standard yet, as in Russia Legat had been noted as a Teacher of Perfection for the professionals. Mrs Bear said that June loved the classes and wanted to stay, so I said no more. June was two years older than Peggy and had a long flowing and soft style of dancing, but was not very strong in technique as her early teacher in Shanghai had let her "turn out" slightly from the knee instead of the hip. Still her mother absolutely adored her, and could never see a fault.'

On arriving in London, Mrs Hookham had managed to get hold of a cheap room with two beds at the same place as June and her mother: the Women's Residence Club in Barkston Gardens, Earls Court. The room had a gas fire with an attached gas-ring on a coin meter, which meant that they could save on not eating out. 'It was ideal for the tomato soup and vital baked beans on toast which were Peggy's mainstay,' writes her mother.

Shared digs notwithstanding, it was now time for Mrs Hookham to go it alone. 'Looking back, I am surprised at my "nerve", as I was never cut out to be a "pushy" dancer's mother.' Yet push for Peggy she did, having set her sights on a particularly lofty mentor: the Princess Serafina Astafieva, teacher to none other than Markova. Astafieva lived – and taught – at the Pheasantry, once a shooting lodge for Charles II, a house still standing in the King's Road, Chelsea. The Hookhams found the Princess not in the light, bright, hugely mirrored, eighteenth-century studio, but huddled gloomily by a gas stove in her small bedroom, which was stuffed with Russian tapestries. Astafieva was not well. Nor was she in the least bit welcoming. Gaunt and turbanned, smoking a Balkan Sobranie, shabbily elegant in exotic, trailing skirts and a washed-out pastel cardigan, she categorically refused to consider a new pupil. She was too old, she said, too tired to take on anyone; pupils were ungrateful, didn't care, never came to see her. But Mrs Hookham was not to be fobbed off. 'You *must* accept my daughter,' she insisted. 'I have brought her six thousand miles from China to study with you.'[11]

Mortally ill as she was, the Princess was no match for the Black Queen-to-be. 'OK,' she shrugged. 'I look.' Next day, Astafieva's assistant, Vera (Verishka), showed Peggy, who reminded her of a well-trained pony, into the studio. Mrs Hookham watched nervously, 'having rather expected that we [!] would be almost lost among promising young dancers, but I think there were only three others attending the class, including a handsome young boy. The class had not been going long before I could see that this was the same training as the dancers in Shanghai, Volkova and Goncharov, had in their youth in Russia. After the *barre* work was finished, Astafieva picked up her skirt and tucked it into her black silk knickers to demonstrate the steps she was teaching, and became totally involved in the art and technique of ballet . . . As the class came to an end, I looked at Madame, and she gave me a little nod and smile which filled me with pride, and relief.' Before they left that day, the arrangements were made: Astafieva would take Peggy on, at a fee of three shillings and sixpence (£0.16) for class and a guinea (£1.05) for private lessons. Peggy was enrolled for two classes and three private lessons per week, and instructed to invest in some new shoes. Apparently the soft ballet slippers she was accustomed to wearing were for male dancers only. For advanced classwork, girls of Peggy's standard were expected to wear pink satin *pointe* shoes – old worn ones, mind you, with the stiff, shellacked insoles cracked and ripped out. Strangely, after a while, these noisy, narrow-heeled, bulbous-toed pumps become both malleable and comfortable: more natural to a dancer than bare feet.

Peggy's time with Astafieva, however brief, was to prove vital – vital because, in the eccentric, expansive atmosphere of the Pheasantry, she could relax and let herself go in a way that would soon be denied her. Astafieva encouraged lightness and ease of movement, and her method of teaching was all to do with facilitation, the shedding of strain – sometimes by the simple knack of proper breathing. When she taught, the fifty-eight-year-old Princess was transformed from a stooped near-cripple into a tall, elegant creature of contagious grace. But she taught less and less. On days when there was no scheduled class, Peggy's half-hour private lesson was almost always delegated to an assistant. Once or twice, the stand-in coach was no less a luminary than Markova, who remembers Peggy as a plump though beautifully proportioned child, who giggled a lot in the dressing-room. 'I think a couple of times I worked with her at the beginning. How can I say? It's very difficult to think about potential, but at that time she didn't seem too interested. It was Mrs Hookham, you see, who was really interested. Margot was very good, you know, she went along with it. But at the beginning the mother was, I felt, more smitten, more ambitious than Margot was.'

It was certainly Mrs Hookham who instigated the next and most momentous move. In her opinion Peggy was 'losing the look of a girl who was just good at dancing, as she was expressing more feeling with the movements'. The time had come, she decided, to tackle the Sadler's Wells school. 'I enjoyed the classes, as a spectator,' she writes, 'every bit as much as Margot, but I realized that since she was approaching fifteen, it had come to the point where I had to know if this training was going to lead somewhere; I just couldn't afford to spend the time, money and effort on my daughter's occupation if it wasn't. The only place I could find out if she had the talent for a theatrical future was a place where that talent might be used – a ballet company.'[12]

Astafieva was indignant. Had she not predicted ingratitude? And Peggy did not want to obey her mother. She was carefree and contented where she was. 'I'm not nearly ready,' she protested. 'However,' writes her mother, 'she took my word for it.'[13] Perhaps the most awkward person to square things with was Mrs Bear, on whom Mrs Hookham could not help but feel she was stealing a march. But Mrs Bear's ambitions for June had taken another course. June had successfully auditioned for a lavish new musical, *The Golden Toy*, and was now nightly hoofing it at the Coliseum.

On the appointed morning in March, with Peggy 'still mumbling about not being ready and not wanting to go', Mrs Hookham and her daughter caught the bus to Islington and presented themselves, on the dot of eleven, at the stage door. There was no Ninette de Valois on hand to greet them. 'Expecting literally an interview, and after explaining to the busy stage doorman and waiting, we were taken upstairs to a small room out of the bustle of singers and dancers who, singing snatches and shouting, seemed to fill the narrow passages and stairways. I think we both felt like fish out of water, but were soon put more at ease by Miss Ursula Moreton, who asked about Peggy's ballet training in China and ambitions. However, stupidly, I had not anticipated Peggy being asked to do some dance steps so we had not brought along any practice clothes or shoes.' Miss Moreton suggested that Peggy take off her street-shoes and her dress and stand in first position at the *barre*. Thus it was that the immaculate Fonteyn was accepted into the Sadler's Wells School – in her petticoat.

She was to start the following Monday. 'I was delighted and relieved of course,' writes Mrs Hookham, 'but before the eventful day I had to bustle about to find the material, and make it up into the regulation mauve tunics that the students had to have, which I soon did, and of course I sent off the letter bearing the good news, which about eight weeks later would arrive in Shanghai and make Felix a proud father.' Ursula Moreton was a kind woman, and for the first few sessions – since Peggy was the youngest student – allowed Mrs Hookham to keep an eye on her in class, 'seated on a form under the window, well away from the teacher'. But when Miss de Valois turned up to take class in person, Mrs Hookham had the good sense to make herself scarce. So she was not witness to the famous exchange between Ninette de Valois and Ursula Moreton on the occasion of the former's first sighting of the fledgling Margot Fonteyn:

DE VALOIS: Who's the little Chinese girl?
MORETON: She's not Chinese, her name is Hookham.
DE VALOIS: Where does she come from?
MORETON: Shanghai.
DE VALOIS: What did I tell you?

Like any anecdote that enters legend and is allowed by its participants to filter, through the live net of private discrimination, into the stagnant pond of received public knowledge, this one sounds both edited and romanticized. But de Valois kept the press happy with it for the length of her, and Margot's, professional lives, and, even in her late nineties, would still trot it out with a freshness of delivery that gave it the ring, if not of precisely recollected dialogue, at least of her own mystically infallible judgement: 'There was the morning when I went up to the Wells room to see the junior girls, including some new arrivals. My eye swept round and on to one. Lovely child, I mused, with her elegant limbs and well-poised head. There was something about her though; she did not look English with those almond-shaped eyes. I enquired in a whisper about the little girl who looked Chinese. I asked where she came from and was told Shanghai. I flashed a look of triumph at Miss Moreton and returned to my inspection. Chinese or not, it was obvious that something wonderful and beautiful had come into our midst: not even the proof of a Yorkshire-born father and a mother of Irish descent could shake off this mysterious glamour . . . In those days her dancing had a colt-like quality, the smile was embarrassingly wide and guileless . . . Children are either gauche or graceful. Miss Hookham was both – in spite perhaps

58

of a remarkable inner poise, a poise that could only, at this particular period, prove itself through the fact that gaucherie and gracefulness never fell out of step.'[14]

To have Miss de Valois's sharp and ambitious eye light upon her was not, for a shy adolescent, an unalloyed blessing. The nagging that Peggy was used to from her mother was as nothing compared to de Valois's maternal ferocity; and, in a class full of aspiring students, there was clearly no future in remaining ignored. But to be picked on and raged at incessantly: 'No, no, that's still wrong; don't be so obstinate, go back and do it again as I want . . .'[15] did not at first seem like the rare compliment that it was. In an interview with Keith Money, de Valois would later say: 'I was struck with her great talent and equally struck by her great faults . . . I think she arrived just in time for us to save her feet; she was not even standing on them properly, they were in a terrible state.'[16] Since her return to England Peggy had always chosen to wear shoes made by Porselli, which she found soft and comfortable. 'Suddenly,' writes her mother, 'the command came to go to another maker. It took us both by surprise, but unquestioningly we quickly did so, though not without the usual objections from Peggy, who had to wear them.'

With her mother now relegated to the dressing-room, it made things no easier for Peggy that she had to endure de Valois's humiliating personal attacks without being able to catch the loyal and conspiratorial eye of Mrs Hookham, who, for her own part, felt let down and rather frightened to be suddenly robbed of her close day-to-day connection with her daughter's progress. 'The biggest change for me,' she writes, 'was that it was no longer "done" for me to watch classes and rehearsals. In some ways this was hard to bear . . . Still, we both had a lot to learn; my new roles soon became clear; personal maid and dresser, chaperone, and chauffeur as soon as I could afford a new Austin Ten.' Sometimes, in direct contravention of all the rules, mother and daughter would jump into the car and abscond together to Astafieva's, where the sun streamed through the French windows, and the Princess said, 'Good, darlink,' and you were allowed to wear whatever practice-clothes you liked. The sickly mauve of the regulation tunic on which de Valois insisted did nothing for Peggy's sallow complexion. The members of the company were, by contrast, elegantly attired in black tunics and pink headbands, and, for some obscure reason, referred to the girls in the school as 'the Bombs', treating them with lofty disdain. 'The Company used the dressing-rooms,' 'Margot would tell *Woman* magazine in 1961; 'students had to change in the ladies' lavatory at the back of the dress circle. The Company worked on stage. Students were confined to the Wells room, the big room above the theatre foyer, or even to the very unsuitable board room.'[17] And God help you if you arrived late for class. Pointless trying to slink past the glass door once *pliés* had begun. 'Come in at once,' de Valois would command in her high, clipped, piercingly haughty tone. But no sooner were you in, than you were out again. 'If you can't get here on time, you can't do class; get out!'[18] she would screech, flinging her cardigan across the floor and banging the stick that she carried in the style of her own and Pavlova's great teacher, Enrico Cecchetti, a devil for footwork – footwork being de Valois's great strength and Peggy's greatest weakness. Peggy would watch with some envy as the latecomer sloped off in disgrace, marvelling at a punishment that forbade you to submit yourself to further tyranny. Surely there must be more joy to dancing than this?

That was what baffled de Valois about 'Little Hookham'. Alone among her classmates, the child did not seem to care if she were taken into the company proper or not. 'They came over not really knowing what direction she should go in. She was just as interested in musical comedy work. I found her going on the sly to some school, for the fun of it, and I put my foot down: I sent for the mother and I said, "Not with this girl, I'm not going to allow it. You've got to choose whether she goes seriously, or *that* way." It came to an end quickly: they were charming about it, but she was a gay little girl, you see, and she was just as much at home in musical comedy, which rather alarmed me, because I suddenly saw her at Drury Lane in the *corps de ballet* of something. You just had to steady the boats . . . they really didn't know . . . the mother was a simple woman. Very simple, but intelligent in an ordinary way: an excellent mother for her – we got on very well, thank goodness.'

In fact, the reason why Peggy desisted – for a while – from going to outside classes was not because de Valois had outlawed them, but because her darling Astafieva died. Verishka broke the news to her at the end of a private lesson; it seemed that her switch of allegiance to the Wells had been all too timely. But the interview with de Valois did serve a purpose: Mrs Hookham, 'simple woman' that she was, cleverly managed to use the confrontation to resolve the difficulties which were besetting her personally. 'I explained my circumstances, my husband keeping our China home, our son an engineering student, and the living expenses in London. I needed to know what to do; make more permanent arrangements in London and find a flat, or take Peggy and perhaps young Felix back to Shanghai. She understood immediately, and replied in her decisive way, "No money you can spend on the child will be wasted. Unless some disaster occurs, I know she has a great future ahead of her." I must admit that it was more than I ever expected, and I was filled with gratitude for the definite answer as much as for the good predictions it contained. Though I could not conceal my exhilaration, I am afraid I did not tell Peggy the whole truth about the interview, though I am sure I told her that Miss de Valois was pleased with her work and said that if she worked hard and got more strength in her feet she would become a very good dancer. So weeks later, when the replies to my letters to Felix finally arrived, the die was cast and we were to stay in London, and it would not be long before Felix himself would be joining us on "home" leave.'

The interview worked in Mrs Hookham's favour in more ways than one. Anxious not to lose a promising student, de Valois now wasted no time in promoting Peggy. These days, even the most talented graduate to the Royal Ballet has usually already spent two years at the upper school, somewhere between the ages of sixteen and nineteen. But it was a matter of weeks before Peggy, though still aged only fourteen, was offered paid work with the company. History has it that she made her début as one of twenty-eight Snow Flakes in *Casse-Noisette*. Markova, whose younger sister, Bunny (Berenice Marks), began dancing with the company at the same time, remembers it differently. 'No, no, at the beginning the whole thing was they were little boys in the party scene. And then, after the snowflake scene, during the interval when the curtain came down, they had, in their little suits and pants, with brooms, to go on in front of the audience in the intermission and sweep up all the snowflakes ready for the last act, the big dancing act, you see. And they adored that because they were paid a little extra.'

Every little extra helps when you are sharing a bed-sit in a women's hostel. But a mother's gratification cannot be measured in coins for the gas meter. The great news, when it came, did so in the cursory form of a postcard, summoning Peggy to understudy 'Snow Flakes' for two shillings and sixpence per performance. In a television interview towards the end of her daughter's more-than-usually exciting career, Mrs Hookham still rated the arrival of that postcard as the most exciting moment of her life. She and Peggy 'danced round the room together' – the one and only time, perhaps, that Black Queen was actively borne, as an equal partner, in the arms of the talent to which she had given birth. Peggy duly presented herself for the specified rehearsal. But no such thing took place. On 21 April, Leslie Edwards remembers 'coming in for the matinée, and someone saying, "Oh, Joy Robson's off, and the new girl's going on." She hadn't rehearsed at all.'

Hurriedly hooked-and-eyed into an ill-fitting Snow Flake costume, Peggy had not even been told where the audience would be sitting in relation to the steps she had been hastily shown. Members of the *corps de ballet* talked her through: ('turn; kneel; follow me'). But despite the terror, she was swept up by the music (Tchaikovsky at its most sumptuous, complete with female backing chorus), and the changing lights, and the paper snowflakes raining on her head. This, then, apparently, was where her life was to be lived – in this strange, exposed, blindingly bright place, which smelled of fish-glue and sweat – to the tune of an inexorable beat which had its own outcome, and logic. Choice did not really enter into the equation. There was Miss de Valois now, as well as her mother, to appease, to say nothing of that hushed, rowdy, many-headed animal out there in the darkness, hungry for the sight of you, like it or no. But scared as Peggy was, she had no idea, then, of the *really* frightening thing: that alone among these others in white tarlatan who would get older and give up and be replaced, it was in this light, and with these smells, and to this beat, that she would spend almost half a century.

4

'Peggy Hookham? *That* won't look very glamorous on the bill-boards,' said Robert Helpmann when Ninette de Valois told him of her latest discovery.[1] De Valois herself was hardly in need of prompting when it came to imposing fanciful stage-names upon her prospective stars; but Helpmann, always one to be in at the beginning, liked to claim that he had been the first to address the compliant child as 'Margot'. In fact, Mrs Hookham had herself long been a dab-hand at the business of rechristen-ing, having changed her aunt's name from Cissy to Purdie, not to mention her own, from Hilda to Juanita, so it would be naïve to imagine that she and her daughter had not been pondering monikers and doodling possible autographs for quite some time. 'Peggy and I reached the same conclusion,' she writes, 'that Peggy Hookham would not be a good stage name, especially for a ballet dancer among all the glamorous names and −ovas. We both thought that my father's name Fontes would be much better, so I wrote off to Manoel Fontes to see if he would mind if Peggy called herself Margaret Fontes. Whilst we were waiting for a reply Miss de Valois also suggested that we found a new name, and I told her that I had written to the head of the family to see if Peggy could use their name. It was just as well I asked, because although it appeared in the next programme, a very definite "No" came from Manchester.'

Whether Uncle Manoel's snobbish objection lay in the un-desirable theatrical connection or in the illegitimacy of his half-sister remains unclear. 'My grandfather was a pretty tricky old thing,' says Michael Fontes. 'He only had one eye − nobody knew how he lost it.'

Either way, Mrs Hookham and her daughter − whose fame would in due course prove one in the eye for Manoel − took the rebuff in their stride. Not wanting to confuse the public with too radical a programme change, they looked up Fontes in the telephone directory. Fontanes, Fontannaz, Fontene, Fontenelle. Fontene sounded the most English, a detail which, when the time came to decide, would appeal to de Valois: 'We have at last found and created a British ballerina. For heaven's sake, don't let her sound Spanish.'[2] But the spelling would be changed to Fonteyn – an unconscious felicity, for not even de Valois had noted that the first ballerina of all time, a Mlle de La Fontaine (1655–1738), had been hailed as 'the Queen of the Dance', whose 'voluminous velvet and damask robes must have lent a dignified rather than sprightly quality to her dancing'.[3] Mrs Hookham, though not overly taken with 'Margot', considered it 'more suitable than Margaret; so Margot Fonteyn evolved. We kept our fingers crossed and hoped that no one would write and ask if we were related. Nobody did, so we left it at that.'

Printing costs being what they were, the interim name, Margot Fontes, went on featuring in programmes for rather longer than it should have done. Yet Peggy would surely have been flattered professionally by the concerted haste to invest her with a new identity, had not the change symbolized, outwardly, a profound inner crisis for a girl in the throes of puberty. 'She must have been about fifteen at the time,' writes Mrs Hookham, 'and struggling to adjust to her age and the confusing new situation in which she found herself, and which made her very quiet and reticent, so that all I could do was to be there and feed and cherish her as best I could. It took me back to my teens and the memory of my shyness which had had much the same effect. In Peggy's case, however, it was her way of dealing with life's problems; to become silent and concentrate until she came to some understanding within herself. I was reminded of Miss Bosustow, her first teacher, being surprised by quiet little Peggy who never spoke, but just got on, got it right, and always tried to be the best in the class.'

But there is a world of difference between a ballet student and a professional dancer. And, in the company of The Company,

Margot, as its newest, youngest incumbent, felt intimidated and inadequate. All her life she had tried to be a nice child; but in this closeted, camp, sophisticated society into which she had so precipitously been thrust, neither niceness nor childishness held any sway. The thing to be here was – at all costs – amusing. And if you lacked the facility to be witty by intent, you could be certain that, no sooner was your back turned, you would become the object of wit in others.

Robert Helpmann was the court jester, the one who set the company style. (The Germanic second 'n' tacked on to his Scottish name was his own doing, not de Valois's – this apparently on the advice of a numerologist.) 'That devil', 'That monkey', Dame Ninette called him until her dying day, her frail voice suddenly robust with remembered indulgence.[4] Known as 'Miss de Valois's colonial protégé',[5] Helpmann had captivated other powerful women of the theatre before her, notably Pavlova, who had let him study with her touring company in Melbourne; but also Gladys Moncrief, who had starred him in her Sydney Operetta; and the actress Margaret Rawlings, who had brought him back with her on the ship from Adelaide, delivering him with a glowing note to the Wells. De Valois wrote: 'I look up and see a figure standing in the doorway. Portrait of a young man, very pale with large eyes; he is wearing a huge camel-hair coat. I am struck by a resemblance in some strange way to Massine. He comes forward and speaks to me very politely – it appears that he had been waiting downstairs for some time. Instinctively I know that this is Margaret Rawlings' Australian find. Everything about him proclaims the artist born. I get on the phone to Miss Baylis a little later and beg to be allowed to engage him at once.'[6]

The 'artist born' was also the self-made sybarite who had learned the courage of his exotic convictions in a rougher and more intolerant school than any available to his English contemporaries. Once, at the age of seventeen, parading past the swimmers on Bondi Beach – attired in Oxford bags, pink shirt, purple tie and red nail polish – he had found himself hefted high into the air by a squad of hearty life-savers, who, reversing their standard procedure, dumped him in the crashing surf of the Pacific.

When he first appeared with Sadler's Wells in *Coppélia* – to his disgust as a mere member of the *corps de ballet* – he smeared his head with paraffin to make it gleam.

'Who is *that*?' Lilian Baylis asked de Valois.

'Bobby, the new boy I keep telling you about.'

'Then tell him not to put so much grease on his hair. I can't take my eyes off him.'

'I suspect that was the idea,' said Miss de Valois.

'Oh well,' said Miss Baylis after a pause. 'He does have a nice little bottom.'[7]

By the time Peggy first appeared with the company, Bobby's extraordinarily arresting, if somewhat eccentric, physiognomy was already firmly in the limelight. He had caused a sensation as Satan in de Valois's ballet *Job*, and she had created the role of the Master of Treginnis for him in *The Haunted Ballroom*. Less acclaimed as a dancer than as a mime, he nevertheless, in the absence of Dolin, regularly partnered Markova in the classics. Loved as well as feared for his wicked, pop-eyed mimicry and his vitriolic tongue, he, alone of the company, could be guaranteed to make even de Valois at her most furious scream with laughter. Peggy would laugh too, all the louder and more nervously for not having understood – especially when Bobby was in cahoots with the company's musical director, Constant Lambert, who, in Helpmann's own words, was 'worldly wise and sure of himself, able to talk about any subject from Picasso to Stravinsky, from the new trend in music to Edith Sitwell. All in all, the sort of person I longed to be.'[8]

In pursuit of this longing, Helpmann had once followed the huge, shambling, shabbily overcoated and probably half-drunk object of his admiration out of rehearsal and into the corridor, where he had bluntly announced: 'I'm completely uneducated. If I'm to become anybody I need to know more. Will you help me?'[9] Constant had hooted with laughter and walked off, protesting over his shoulder that he was far too busy conducting at the Wells and writing music reviews for the *Morning Post* to be of any use as a mentor. But Helpmann's disarming gall had wrought its charm. A few days later, Lambert sought him out with an exhaustive list of concerts to attend, paintings to look at, books to read. And, from that time on, Bobby was regularly invited to the opera as a guest of Constant and his beautiful wife, Flo, and included at weekend gatherings in the country, among such literary luminaries as Anthony Powell, Dylan Thomas, Peter Quennell and the Sitwells. Now that they were friends, the audacious pupil would make a point of publicly outwitting his genial tutor, and when the two sparred together, as they often did in the lull between class and rehearsal, Peggy would veer between shock at their bawdy language and dazzlement at their epigrammatic flair. Such articulacy made her feel as though she dared not open her own mouth – no less from fear of the suburban platitudes which might spout from it than because her accent, still residually Mancunian, was an embarrassment in snobbish, 30s London, where Noël Coward's clipped diction was all the rage. If Peggy practised hard at that time, it was for solace rather than from ambition. Dancing, she discovered, could be a refuge from social strain, a retreat into the silent language of the body where her sensibility would not be misinterpreted. Except that her motives immediately were. 'That horrid child,' she overheard one of the principal dancers say of her, 'is always showing off, practising *arabesques* in a corner.'[10]

The child often took her horridness home, not bothering even to talk to her mother. 'I went through a worse than normal period of adolescent antagonism towards her,' Margot would later confess to *Woman* magazine. 'Because she wasn't a "sophisticated intellectual", like "them", I wouldn't ask her help, thinking half ruefully, half irritably, that she wouldn't know anything more about "their" world than I did.'[11] But in fact, dull and insignificant though Peggy might have felt, 'they' were covertly watching her. Her great friend Leslie Edwards claims: 'With someone like Margot you can't fudge how you first met her. And I did notice her because she *looked* right. Automatically, from the word go.

It wasn't as though Miss Moreton had to say, "No dear, put your shoulder here and your head over there." I remember thinking that, out of the whole line of Swans, that girl stood absolutely as you should stand.'

Robert Helpmann saw no such distinction in her. 'I was told to keep an eye on her,' he admitted later, 'because Ninette thought she was very promising. It was rather a jaundiced eye, I'm afraid. To me, little Margot seemed rather uppity, tiresomely remote for one so young, and, in appearance, rather scraggy.'[12]

'Scraggy' is an odd accusation, since most people at that time, and photographs bear them out, considered the new girl – whether in her mauve practice tunic, or in her white, ethereal Wili costume – to be rather inappropriately plump. But 'uppity' must stick: even William Chappell, a much calmer and kinder character than Helpmann, admits that his original impression was of 'a rather annoyingly self-possessed child'.[13] As for 'remote', Chappell concedes in retrospect that remoteness is often a portent of promise: 'Later I discovered she was not only shy, but reserved, and already half-enwrapped in the veil of unconscious and accepted isolation that is common to . . . those who are to excel in any form of creative art . . .'[14]

But no sooner had Peggy been transmogrified into Margot, and been awarded the welcome wage of thirty shillings a week, than the season ended and the company disbanded for the summer. De Valois, however, made sure that there was continuity of work for her favourites, and Margot was included in the group which was to appear with the International Opera at Covent Garden. Rehearsals were held at the Chenies Street Drill Hall. Margot was cast in *Schwanda the Bagpiper*, *Turandot* and *Die Meistersinger*. If there was one composer to whom Margot was to suffer a lifelong allergy, it was Wagner; so it is ironic that her début at the great Opera House, scene of triumphs to come, should have been as an elderly gnome, struggling beneath the weight of a gold nugget, and obscured by a long grey beard and moustaches, in *Das Rheingold*.

The jokey and inconsequential nature of these appearances

lightened the atmosphere among her colleagues, who started to encourage her to come to lunch with them at the nearest ABC or Joe Lyons. Being included was, at that time, more important to Margot than being singled out. She and her friend Bunny, Markova's sister, cast as children in the crowd scenes of *Turandot*, would sing along forbiddenly with the choruses, their reedy voices drowned out by Puccini's grandeur. But such reassuring anonymity was not to last, was not even to survive the summer. Margot, one of a dozen dancers picked to appear in a ballet scene of a film, *Escape Me Never*, found herself 'doubling' for the actress Rosalinde Fuller. Never mind that her face was hardly glimpsed, or that her body was only visible in long shot: it was the discrepancy in fee that the other girls found hard to stomach. Used to being paid five shillings per performance in the Opera Ballet, they were staggered to find themselves raking in a princely two guineas a day. But Margot's daily filming rate was five guineas.

It was not a sum that was immediately going to resolve Mrs Hookham's current financial straits. 'I remember the children laughing at me,' she writes, 'because I had a box divided into compartments to keep the housekeeping money in; food, the rent, electricity and so on, which I replenished every month.' But now that Margot's salary was augmenting Mrs Hookham's income from her father's estate and her allowance from her husband in China, she decided to search for separate lodgings from Mrs Bear, so that Felix could spend weekends with his mother and sister. Mrs Hookham found a flat nearby, at 19 Hesper Mews, and Mrs Bear eventually took a basement flat in Barkston Gardens.

Peggy was compensated for the loss of June by two things: the chance to see more of her brother, and her budding friendship with Pamela May, who remembers visiting Hesper Mews, 'a tiny little place off the back of Earls Court. Margot and her mother had all these animals. A great big black bird which used to flutter around the room. And something in the bath – was it an otter? – something was swimming. I must have become

Margot's friend very quickly – I think because her mother could see that I was also going up the ladder. She had a very quick eye, the mother, and she would bring the people to Margot more than Margot would go out to them. She was quite a shy girl in a way. And then I met her brother, Felix, who lived there too. He used to take me out to dinner occasionally – in the most brotherly way – he never tried to pull a fast one or anything. Mrs Hookham just didn't have much time for him, and, quite frankly, didn't make much effort either.' Mrs Hookham herself makes no bones about the fact that her relations with her son were irreparably damaged by the eight long years of separation, and her disappointment in the boy seems poignantly at odds with her pride in her daughter. 'He had done badly at school, and had only the minimum qualification, called Matriculation, which he got by going to a "crammer" after leaving Cheltenham.' Following a student apprenticeship with an engineering firm in Kent, he 'scraped into King's College, London, but was unable to keep up because of his weakness in mathematics. Luckily he had always been interested in photography and got to know Ninette de Valois's brother Gordon Anthony, who was becoming well-known for his ballet and theatre photographs, and who took him on as an assistant . . . To me he was like somebody else's son for whom I was responsible. It was sad for me, but there seemed to be no way in which I could be accepted in his immature yet self-sufficient life, and every attempt I made seemed to increase the gap between us . . . Neither of my children could be called chatty and never talked to me about their thoughts or problems, they only gave the briefest answers to questions, so I really came to know very little about their adolescence . . . Come to think of it, everyone seemed to keep themselves more to themselves in the pre-war days.'

And no one more so than Nita Hookham herself, who had marital troubles of her own which she would never have inflicted on her children. True, she had left Shanghai of her own volition, but she had believed her separation from her husband to have been purely circumstantial. Her suspicions, however, were roused during Mr Hookham's much-anticipated home leave, when she had travelled to Budapest to meet him. 'One of the first things I noticed . . . was that Felix was wearing a ring. It rather shook me as he had never worn a ring in his life to my certain knowledge, so I could only think that a woman had given it to him . . . I knew enough to be prepared for him to have had some affairs while we were apart, but . . . the wretched ring seemed constantly on my mind, and eventually I could not stand wondering who had given it to him and why, so I had to ask . . . He explained that he had become friendly with an Austrian woman who he had met several times at the round of parties that was the social life in Shanghai, and had had an affair with her. He spoke as if it had not been very serious and was over, and said that she had gone back to Austria to her family. Apparently she had been married and divorced and had been living alone in Shanghai. The ring disappeared and my anxiety faded away . . . It must have been at least six months after Felix had left to go back to China [that] I got a letter from him which gave me a terrible shock. Would I divorce him? He said circumstances had changed, and the woman he had told me about had . . . travelled to Shanghai with him. They were living in the same flat and she wanted to marry him. I was really shattered . . . I wrote back and . . . begged him to think things over for two years, and if he still insisted then I would agree . . . I did not tell either Margot or young Felix about my changed circumstances . . . but inside myself I keened like a dog.'

Meanwhile Mrs Hookham had to scrape together the money to provide some sort of holiday for her children. Huddled stoically under canvas in the middle of a rain-sodden field in Devon, she had cause to regret the loss of the domestic comforts to which she had become accustomed in her marriage. 'It was dawn,' she writes, 'by the time I more or less settled down only to become aware of heavy breathing and strange noises around the tent. With my two children peacefully sleeping I screwed up my courage and crawled over to look outside and came nose to nose with a cow. It was a shock for both of us I can assure you, and an end to economy as far as I was concerned.' But no existence could be too basic for her daughter, who, in her brother's company, reverted to her childhood nickname, happy just to be Felix's little sister Peggy for that one last summer, before the burden of becoming Margot Fonteyn finally claimed her.

For who knows to what extent children are unconsciously driven to redeem their parents' lives? With her mother's marriage now laid firmly at the altar of her career, it was Margot's un-witting task to make her father rue the day he had ever taken it into his head to forsake his family. The child was now respon-sible for the mother's happiness, and nothing cheered Mrs Hookham more than news of Margot's advancement.

Dancers discover their fates on cast-lists impersonally pinned to noticeboards in draughty corridors as they arrive for ten o'clock class in the morning. When Margot reported to Sadler's Wells for the new season in September 1934, one such list read as follows:

The Haunted Ballroom

The Master of Treginnis	Helpmann
Young Treginnis	Fontes
Alicia	Markova
Ursula	Moreton
Beatrice	Appleyard
The Strange Player	Chappell

And underneath were typed the names of lesser lights who were to play assorted footmen and ghosts.

The Haunted Ballroom was a ballet written and composed by Geoffrey Toye and choreographed by Ninette de Valois. It had been made as a showpiece for Helpmann, who, as the Master of Treginnis, was obliged to dance himself to a gothic death in the manner of his ancestors, who had all been similarly fore-doomed. The part of Young Treginnis was only small, consisting mainly of mime, but it was a telling one. Dressed in a Little Lord Fauntleroy suit, head enlarged by a close-cropped wig, Margot's allotted character bore the double onus of opening the ballet and being left alone on the stage at its close. A dancer called Freda Bamford had originally made quite a hit in the part, since when it had become a test-piece for the dramatic aptitude of newcomers. 'As the Young Treginnis,' writes William Chappell, 'Fonteyn struck me as good – no better, for they had all been good – as any of her forerunners.'[15]

But there had been another, less ostentatious piece of casting on that noticeboard which was to prove more important to Fonteyn's future than any appearance in a ballet by de Valois. Margot's name was down with three others – Molly Brown, Joy Robson and Jill Gregory – to dance, on that same opening night of the season (2 October 1934) in a newly created *pas de quatre*. The number was to be added to *Les Rendezvous*, first choreographed a year earlier, and seminal to the work of Frederick Ashton.

Ashton had been in New York, being fêted, if not paid, on Broadway for his dances for Gertrude Stein's opera, *Four Saints in Three Acts*. But a fit of homesickness had driven him back to England, where vivid tales of his exploits reached Margot's ears long before she had laid eyes on him. 'Freddie was quite mad at the party last night,' she would overhear Helpmann say to Chappell. 'He danced for four hours without stopping.'[16] Or Chappell would say to Helpmann: 'I've never seen Fred so exhilarated. He did a hilarious *pas de deux* with a chair . . .'[17]

In the light of all this, Ashton seemed unexpectedly constrained when he walked with his languid short-stepped gait into rehearsal, dressed unsuitably in a suit. He eyed the four girls nervously, and said in a weary voice: 'Now, what are we going to do?' – as though he really expected them to tell him. Then he listened to a few bars of the music – by Daniel François Auber. And it was as if, within the formal fabric of his stiff suit, his torso had been abruptly turned into rubber. All of a sudden, his unexceptional male frame was invested with an extraordinary female flexibility. His diffident manner gave way to a violent zest which propelled him about the room in swoops and twists as he marked out chains of steps only vaguely reminiscent of any that Margot had ever encountered in the classroom. And then he stopped and smiled at them. 'What did I do?' he asked innocently. 'Now you do it.'[18]

Margot tried, but could not. The dance was to a sprightly, polka-like rhythm, and involved distracting little flicks of the wrists and an unbalancing throwing gesture from the shoulders. Ashton seemed to be watching her more intently than he did the others, and finding incessant fault with her. 'No, no, bend more; bend right over this side and then right over that side. Move your body more,' he said. 'Don't be so stiff.' But it was hopeless. If she relinquished her rigidity, she fell over. Ashton's scowl was that of a man whose point has been proved.

'I remember,' writes Mrs Hookham, 'she was very upset after the first rehearsal for the *pas de quatre* in *Les Rendezvous*, and kept saying she couldn't do it because it was all "opposites".' And Ashton reported back to de Valois that there had been a complete clash of personalities between him and the fifteen-year-old girl. He found her obstinate and 'strangely lacking in warmth, charm, temperament and variety; indeed she seemed positively lethargic in her approach to her work. I soon became aware that she thought me completely mad, and to me she was nothing but a tiresome little madam.' Even at the end of his life he could not properly explain this initial blindness to what would become the main conduit of his own inner vision: 'I didn't get on with her. I found her inadequate in what she was doing and also she seemed to me to have a sort of superior attitude which didn't appeal to me. I sensed a streak of stubbornness.'

De Valois agreed about the stubbornness; but pupils, for her, fell into two categories: 'Nice children' or 'Absolute devils'.[19] Give her a little devil any day. Refusing to let Ashton's lack of enthusiasm undermine her, she built on Margot's appearance in *Les Rendezvous* by trying her out in a classical solo: the Mazurka from *Les Sylphides*. No one could appear in this of all ballets without incurring unfavourable comparison with Markova, and 'Fontes' was no exception. She was too earthy, lacked the thistle-down lightness and spiritual other-worldliness of the Vic-Wells' beloved star. But certain members of the company were beginning to admit that there was something about the girl that commanded special attention; a youthful softness, a romantic tenderness that could not be dismissed. When it came to the Mazurka, William Chappell confessed, 'she bounded. Her line was clean and thrusting.' On a personal level, too, she was beginning to disarm him, but not with niceness, nor, indeed, with the self-effacing modesty to which, in his book about her, even he subscribes. 'She and I were great chums,' he said. 'For some mysterious reason she took to me very quickly.' (No mystery: she had an adolescent crush on the immensely courteous and outstandingly handsome Chappell.) 'She used to sit by me during rehearsals when we weren't taking part and give me her views on the company – which were very, very sharp, I may tell you. She despised everybody except Alicia. "They can't do it really," she'd say. "That one's no good, she's too big, isn't she." She was always right. It was fascinating. She used to make for me and murmur into my ear, "*She's* not bad, but Markova's the one that can dance." And she was, of course, the most wonderful technician, Markova, in those days.'

Markova, for her part, thought of little Margot as 'family'. 'Margot was always rather like another sister for me because she was tagged on to my sister, Bunny; I was very busy with my life, my responsibilities, and my mother said, "If you've got to attend receptions what are you going to do with Bunny?" And of course it was Mrs Hookham who always used to say, "Don't worry, I'll be with them." She had this weeny little car which she used to put the two of them into and off they'd go.'

The car was a boon in more ways than one: it put Mrs Hookham in the regular position of being able to offer Ninette de Valois lifts home. Ensconced in the passenger seat after Margot's first performance in *Les Sylphides*, de Valois took the opportunity to make a rather startling announcement. 'By the way,' she confided to the small figure in the back seat, 'I forgot to tell you. You need not wear students' rehearsal dress any more – you can wear a black tunic; you are in the company.'[20] It was hard to imagine where else Miss de Valois supposed that Margot had been for the best part of the last year.

But a more sophisticated line in practice-tights did not necessarily make for an improved standard of footwork. De Valois tried to shake her protégée from the lethargy of which Ashton had complained – by casting her against type as Papillon in *Carnaval*. But although she rehearsed Margot privately and mercilessly, the speed and sparkle of Fokine's choreography left her pupil struggling, and she had to be dropped from the part after a couple of unsatisfactory performances. Undaunted, de Valois stepped up her campaign by making Margot one of the four cygnets in Act II of *Swan Lake*. This *pas de quatre*, as irksome to dancers as it is delightful to audiences, constricts the use of the arms entirely to make a stunt of the automated unison of the head, legs and feet. When it was seen that Margot could pass this test in attack, neatness and placing, de Valois began to exhort Ashton to give the girl another chance. He agreed, but declined to coach her himself, foisting her on to the unsuspecting Markova, who remembers: 'The very first – shall I say – serious thing that Margot danced was with me, and that was in *The Lord of Burleigh*. Sir Fred did it first at the Camargo Society for me. I played Katie Willows, and one of the characters had a lovely dance with me – the original was Andrée Howard. And then when the production was given over to us at the Vic-Wells, naturally Fred had casting. He said to me, "What about the little Chinese girl?" So I said, "Yes, well, if you think so . . . I'm willing." But he said: "You'll have to teach her, you know exactly what we did." I remember her first performance, and she'd never had anything individual, you see, on the big stage. After we did it I said, "We have to take a call," and she sort of stood and looked at me, and I said, "Come on, give me your hand."'

But it was she, Markova, who was being led by the lamb to the slaughter. Ashton had been badly upset by her refusal to agree to dance in *Valentine's Eve*, a new piece he was planning for the Ballet Rambert. 'She'd become frightfully grand and thought she couldn't stoop to do my little things. We were having dinner at the Café Royal and I don't know if under my breath I said, "Fuck you, that's the end," but that's what it was . . . I cut her out of my life. If that's the sort of person you are – *out!*'[21]

When it came to his revival in the spring of 1935 of *A Day in a Southern Port*, renamed *Rio Grande* after Lambert's original score, Markova was not disposed to dance the role of the Creole Girl which she had created; so Ashton's vindictive spirit overruled his artistic scruples about the Fontes child. Reluctantly he began to agree with de Valois – 'She was the only one there. The one that had extra substance'[22] – and cast Margot, not yet sixteen, as a mulatto prostitute. Once again it was Markova who was given the job of handing on the role: 'I always tried to inspire because that was the Russian training, that one should always pass on what one knows. It was a great tradition. You carried the torch for as long as you could, and then it had to be passed on to somebody else.'

But *Rio Grande* (a collaboration between Ashton and the designer Edward Burra, to Constant Lambert's 1927 score) was no *Les Sylphides*, no *Swan Lake*. It was a highly innovative and impassioned work, set in a jangling tropical port, a dream-world of heat and colour and sex, a million miles from the cold, ethereal mists that swathed Markova's innately spiritual image. 'I was faintly shocked,' writes Mrs Hookham, 'at the completely transparent skirt of Margot's costume, and Lilian Baylis had made the designer paint out part of the backdrop which showed a naked lady sitting very inelegantly, pouring water over her head and down between her knees.' There were those in the lower ranks of the company who, resentful of Margot's rapid advancement, believed, in keeping with the – as yet uncorrected – political times, that she could not become an English ballerina because she looked 'dark-skinned'. They were reckoning without *Rio Grande*. The miracle of this particular ballet for Margot was that the whirling gaiety and syncopated rhythms of the piece spoke directly to her hot Brazilian blood. The sight of her still child-like body, half-clothed in that gaudy see-through costume, her smooth black hair frizzed out around her flashing eyes, extended and excited the staid public concept of what might constitute an English dancer. William Chappell, who partnered her, and into whose longed-for arms Margot joyfully propelled herself under cover of her amorous part, has written: 'It is from this time that I really remember her vividly. She proved to be ideal casting. Markova had not been. She was too fragile, too deli-cately built. Fonteyn was warm and very young. Made up the colour of a dark golden peach grown on some Southern shore, she glowed like a Mediterranean day and her wide radiant smile would have warmed a continent.'[23]

Margot admitted to him years later, in her practical, self-deprecating way, that she had enjoyed the ballet 'because I didn't have to wear *pointe* shoes'.[24] But the real liberation had been an emotional one: the chance to forget her adolescent shyness and gaze brazenly into the blue eyes of a man to whom she felt erotically drawn. It was the first of many instances where life could be lived more intensely on stage than off. For innocence does not hold out long in a ballet company, and Margot must have been aware that, personally and aesthetically enchanted by her as Chappell clearly was, his sexual responses were reserved for men.

But her physical charms, so specifically bestowed, had ranged far beyond him, and hit a more fateful mark. In the pit, conducting his own brilliant score, stood the man for whose shadowy, obsessional proclivities Margot might, in the extremity of her youth and nescience, have been perfectly fashioned. Constant Lambert was married. He had met his wife, Florence Chuter, when she was only fourteen. Flo's mother, who had lived down by the London docks, had died when the girl was still small, and her father was thought to have been an unknown Javanese sailor. Brought up in an orphanage, the child turned out to be an astonishing half-caste beauty: 'the most beautiful creature you ever saw in the world', Constant told his friend Anthony Powell[25] – and with good reason. 'It is difficult,' writes Lambert's biographer, Andrew Motion, 'not to suspect that he was drawn to her because her looks, in an English context, suggested vulnerability as well as a mysterious otherness. They made him want to protect her – to start with, at least.'[26]

And now, here before him, was another such tender creature, but with the fabulous added ingredient of God-given grace. An English girl, but native to the foreign landscape of his music. How could he not want to take her and shape her as he had taken and tried to shape his eager, overawed and completely uneducated wife? His efforts thus far with Flo had simply proved procreative – in a few weeks' time, on 11 May 1935, she was to give birth to their only child, Kit. This was hardly the time for Constant to embark, even in his dreams, on a new love affair. Yet the wrong moment is often the most potent one, and this vision of Margot in *Rio Grande* was fatally bound up with his attachment to his own most triumphant musical creation. In its original concert form, *Rio Grande* was a setting for solo piano, orchestra and chorus of a poem by Sacheverell Sitwell, and makes musical reference to the 'Gretchen' movement in Liszt's Faust Symphony. Angus Morrison, to whom *Rio Grande* is dedicated, writes: 'Would it be too fanciful to suggest that some part of the intense inner compulsion Constant felt about this special passage derived from its original identification with the character of Gretchen? By incorporating it into his own music did it thereby become the symbol of a central female figure, as necessary to him as Gretchen was for Faust: some coloured Marguerite, glimpsed every now and again amidst the thronging crowds and revealing herself finally in the single alto voice that rises out of the chorus to sing so movingly the closing words of the poem? It is here, surely, that he gives expression more completely than anywhere else in his music to the passionate longing he always felt for exotic beauty, and his perpetual sense of the beckoning wonder of distant and unattainable horizons.'[27]

But if Flo, who was already showing signs of psychological

disturbance, had been the victim of a Faustian seduction, not so the little Chinese/Creole Girl up there on the extravagantly painted, shimmering, palm-treed set. Acquiescent and obedient and unformed though she might have seemed to be, Peggy-Margot-Hookham-Fontes-soon-to-be-Fonteyn was nobody's Gretchen. The day would, of course, come when, worn down by his insistent desire for her, she would fall under the composer's sexual power, and let him mould her mentally and musically – use her as he would. Yet use has a way of rounding on the user. She was not destined to be the reflection of a great man's glory. Before he died, tragically early, at the age of forty-eight, he would find his genius reduced to a mere reflection of hers.

5

The question for Margot in 1935 was not really whether she had it in her to become an English ballerina. The issue was the much more urgent and patriotic one of whether English ballet itself had any future in the twentieth century.

'You've got to remember,' insisted Michael Somes, whose great partnership with Fonteyn spanned the 50s, 'that ballet was only *this* big. The Theatre, Musical Comedy, even Variety ruled the roost. As a body of people, we were all pioneering, we were all very new to the game. The Russian ballet was in the ascendancy, and those standards were as much a dream to us at the Sadler's Wells as they had been to me when I was a boy in Taunton. I'm sure Margot was the same, although she was farther along the line, further up the tree, much more into it than I was; better trained. But why should Mrs Hookham, with this precious daughter, commit her to a narrow little enterprise that performed on Tuesdays and alternate Saturdays and Friday afternoons up there in Islington for tuppence-ha'penny a week? All the big shots – Dolin, Bobby Helpmann and a lot of the older boys, Claude Newman, Billy Chappell – even Fred – they all had jobs in Cochran shows. They used to do two shows a night and run between them both and fit the ballet in as some sort of hobby. Nobody had any money, nobody was properly trained: that was the whole background to our lives. We were miles off from a state theatre. Only de Valois, who was the driving force, the one with the vision of the future, might have believed that such a thing was possible. We were paid five shillings for opera, ten-and-six for ballet performances: you were lucky if you netted thirty bob a week. You would walk rather than take the tram in order to get a roll and butter. And the wigs they gave us – terrible – and the tights, and the ballet shoes. Everything patched and dyed. Baylis would beg the audience for clothes to cut up for costumes, threatening: "If you want us to open, dears . . ." And the audiences *were* benevolent. Loyal, impoverished gentlefolk supported us: Brigadier Walters, eccentric Miss Pilgrim, Lady Tenterton, all sat, night after night, in the front row. Audiences today would scarcely believe how awful we were. But we did *begin.'*

Michael Somes's own part in that beginning was almost scuppered by the clock in Rosebery Avenue which, on the day of his audition for the Sadler's Wells School, was running fifteen minutes fast: 'I was due there at twelve and it said quarter past, and I thought, Oh, God, I'm late. Being late was a serious offence in those days, but when I got there, de Valois herself was dancing on the stage. *They* were late. The rehearsal was *Coppélia*, and she wasn't ready for me – I was nothing. Ursula Moreton, who was her assistant at that time, eventually told me to go and change in the bathroom, which I did. The clock was wrong. I think it still is. I jumped about a bit, and they were glad to have anything in those days; they would have taken on a dog.'

Self-effacement, the shadow-side of his nobility of countenance and bearing, was an innate quality in Michael Somes, and one which he was to sustain, to Margot's huge professional advantage, throughout their long partnership. But when he turned up at the school, he must have been the farthest thing from a 'dog' that the Wells had yet laid eyes upon. 'An absolutely magical creature' was how Lincoln Kirstein, the American dance commentator, would later describe the seventeen-year-old from the West Country. And Somes was – no two ways about it – tall, dark and handsome: the epitome of our most obvious dreams. And not just the dreams of women: de Valois had no trouble selling him to Frederick Ashton. Despite the fact that the seventeen-year-old's feet were ungainly and unyielding, and that there was little to recommend him technically beside an intense musicality and an unusually buoyant jump, the choreographer was smitten at first sight. Lilian Baylis wasted no time in procuring for Michael a patron who was prepared to pay his fees and equip him with a 'box' – a trunk containing both street- and practice-clothes – so long as the young man could answer three questions. Was Somes reasonably talented? Was he healthy enough? And was he Roman Catholic? The answer to this last enquiry – though No – must have been the right one, since a cheque for a hundred pounds was duly forthcoming. But when the mysterious donor finally turned up to see his protégé dance ('Look for the ugliest man in the foyer'), it transpired that, behind his pebble lenses, he was virtually blind.

Being the only scholarship boy at the Wells was bound to set Somes apart, but he was not by nature very sociable. Notwithstanding his insistence on family poverty, there was an unusual refinement to his background, and he would hold his head back and literally 'look down his nose' at the rest of the company, a mannerism which inspired both resentment and respect. Although the hit song of the day was 'These Foolish Things', Somes had no fashionable aptitude for folly. His humour had a bitter, self-castigating edge, and the overt earnestness of his ambition could not have been less attuned to an era when performers, however secretly serious, affected nonchalance and endeared themselves to one another by becoming known as Great Gigglers. Margot's inherent high spirits – even if a clever cover for her timidity – had by this stage earned her that accolade, so it was a credit to her emerging social grace that she should have been among the first to break through the stiff, reserved carapace which Michael Somes had constructed around himself.

This is how he described his first brush with the woman who was to become not just his famous partner but his first lover: 'We used to have a *pas de deux* class on Saturday mornings. Idzikowsky was taking this one, and in those days I was terri-fied of him – a great dancer, Cecchetti's pupil, a tiny little man, very fierce. All the senior people were given partners. I was last on the list, and there was no one left for me, so I was told just to stay there and be quiet. And then Margot came in – a little late, as it turned out – and found that everyone had been paired off. And then, even though I was a new boy and most of them would have turned their backs, she, being Margot, and the sweet-natured person that she was right from the beginning, came to me and got on *pointe* in front of me so that I had to put my hands on her waist. And I thought, Oh my goodness, what luck. But Idzikowsky immediately swished her around and sent her off to be with Bobby or someone, and pushed me with some big fat girl or other – he soon took me out of *her* hands.'

Double-work, often such a burdensome and unrewarding responsibility for male dancers, can sometimes have the effect of setting a female dancer free. Taught first to hang on to a *barre*, and then made to let go and perform her classroom exercises unsupported in 'the centre', she will often respond with a sense of liberation to a pair of strong hands spanning her spinning waist, or to someone else's muscle propelling her into the air, or steadying her as her limbs unfold at angles to her body too precarious to be sustained by her own capacity for balance. Margot had originally experienced this heady exchange of trust with an excellent dancer called Keith Lester at Astafieva's studio. 'What an extraordinary sensation it was,' she wrote, 'the first time I found myself held high in the air; rather like being caught up in a tree by the shirt tails!'[1]

But although her sense of communion with male bodies and their responses developed rapidly and naturally in class and performance, she was, in real life, far from sure of herself. She who, on stage, could as easily be a whore as a sylph, had no idea what persona to adopt when she stepped out on to the street as Margot Fonteyn. There were plenty of young men presenting themselves at the stage door, eager to convey her to the Savoy Grill; but they found it bizarre to watch her scanning the menu for her staple Heinz baked beans on toast. The first of these escorts who attempted to kiss her on the lips had his face soundly slapped for his trouble. She protests that it was the shock: that her artistically fashionable disdain for the movies had left her ignorant of the mechanics of osculation (although the slap itself, with its clichéd histrionics, seems typical of any

Hollywood film of the time). The truth is that a compromise had already taken place, a split between body and soul, made necessary by the world in which she found herself. Ballet companies, even to this day, employ at least a third more girls than they do boys; and, of the thirty-six or so members then with the Sadler's Wells Ballet, only a handful of the twelve males were likely to have been attracted to women. And in some ways these unambivalent 'he-men' would have been the least romantically acceptable of all: cocks of the walk, cutting a swathe through the ranks of the more foolishly susceptible girls in the *corps de ballet*. On stage, the ballerina is queen, she commands centre-stage and the audience's best attention; she is deferred to and tenderly presented by her partner. But backstage, simple statistics are usually against her. She has little hope of sexual supremacy. Yet the obsessional nature of her job, its rituals, its hermeticism, the terrible physical daring which it demands, render her, like a soldier, unfit for civilian life, unequipped for the ways of ordinary society. The fact that Margot lost her virginity at the (for then) startlingly early age of sixteen (to a young man from the BBC World Service, Donald Hodson, later nicknamed the Chipmunk) has little bearing on her sentimental education. This was taking place where her true allegiance lay: among her professional colleagues, amid the heat and sweat of her working life. If she broke her adolescent heart, it was for courtly Chappell, or remote Helpmann, or, more and more these days, for critical, fanatical Frederick Ashton. When you are young, it is sometimes strangely difficult to distinguish between sexual yearning and plain ambition. Especially when, by nature and upbringing, you have no conscious recognition of the pangs of the latter.

For it seems to have been with complete ingenuousness that Margot, when the news broke that Markova was to absent herself from the company, wrote to a friend: 'Isn't it terrible about Markova leaving? I cannot think what will happen next season without her; we shall all have to work very hard, but even hard work cannot make a ballerina if there isn't one.'[2]

The relinquishment of Markova from the Vic-Wells was a subtler manoeuvre than it seemed — as chilling as it was emotionally heated. De Valois was more than Alicia's employer: she was her friend; she was the woman who had been charged with the fatherless girl when Diaghilev had first taken her into his company at the age of fourteen. The two female dancers had met in a fog at Victoria Station, whence the twenty-six-year-old de Valois, with her continental gloss and command of French, was supposed to shepherd the speechless child, along with Guggy, her nanny, to Monte Carlo. 'Is that the brat?' she is said to have enquired, jabbing her finger at Alicia's singularly under-developed chest.[3] 'But she turned out not to be a monster at all,' de Valois recalls. 'There never was a sweeter child. She was always good — almost too good. Everything you told her to do she immediately did.'[4]

And between 1931 and 1934, Markova had done all that de Valois had bidden her. 'What kept the company going,' says the ballet critic Clement Crisp, 'was Markova. No doubt about it. Without Alicia there to do those ballets, they never would have happened. Dame Ninette pinned everything on her.' Yet when, in 1935, the general manager of the famous Windmill Theatre, Vivian Van Damm (who happened to be having an affair with Alicia's sister Doris), offered Markova a company of her own to tour the country, de Valois, distraught as she was at the premature loss of her star, did not beg Markova to stay. It was not part of the director's ethic to attempt to hold on to people whose loyalty was even *capable* of straying. Markova's own overriding loyalty was to her partner Dolin, whose services Sadler's Wells could no longer afford to retain. And de Valois understood well enough the inevitable lure of money. Markova had, over the years, virtually given her services to the Wells, accepting a paltry five pounds per performance (later raised, with reluctance, to ten and then fifteen); and even though it was no secret that she could earn many times that amount elsewhere, she 'wanted to stand by Ninette, and what she was trying to achieve . . . Ninette gave me the classics. She knew I wanted to dance them. She also knew that if she wanted to establish a company she had to do it with the classics. They are the training ground for dancers, just as Shakespeare is for actors.'[5]

But in the Shakespearean terms that she invokes, Markova had become something of a Donald Wolfit (the overbearing thespian prototype of Ronald Harwood's play *The Dresser*), distracting attention from all other performers around her. On nights when she danced, 2,000 people would turn out and there would be queues round the block for standing room. On nights when she didn't, the theatre would often be half-empty. Even Colonel de Basil at Covent Garden, with his Baby Ballerinas, could not compete. On 27 March 1935 the *Evening News* wrote: 'There may be, and there may have been better dancers than Markova, but I for one don't believe it.'[6]

De Valois was grateful to Markova, but wanted, sooner or later, to be rid of her. She dreamed of a British ballet that would shine in its own light – not in the reflected radiance of a star created by Diaghilev. 'She and Dolin thought they were old enough to go out on their own,' said de Valois. 'And I had people like Helpmann and Fonteyn coming up, so it was a natural change-over. They were getting famous and they wanted to get on with their own lives. There was a perfectly good friendship between us, there always has been, and there was no trouble.'[7]

But there *was*, and plenty of it – 'harsh letters, tears and threats of litigation between nearly everyone involved' – this while de Valois lay in hospital recovering from a hysterectomy, performed by a Dr Connell, the man who, much to the company's mirth, would duly come to be known as 'Arthur-my-husband'. Lilian Baylis was left to negotiate the terms of Markova's release with another redoubtable lady: Mrs Laura Henderson, a wealthy jute merchant's widow who was backing Van Damm's tour. 'You will do much good for British ballet but you will lose a fortune,' predicted Miss Baylis,[8] who had a well-known hot-line to God; and, indeed, Mrs Henderson was eventually parted from £30,000. But not before the company coffers had profited from the first tour, which, to Markova's detriment, went out, not under her own name, but under the widely publicized banner of Sadler's Wells.

De Valois, meanwhile, sat in her hospital bed, surrounded by flowers, less concerned by the imminent departure of her leading ballerina than by Robert Helpmann's temporary defection to the cast of *Stop Press*, a musical at the Adelphi Theatre, which meant that he could not play the Rake at the première of her forthcoming ballet, *The Rake's Progress*. Still, at least Markova could not lure him away to partner her in her new venture. Let her take Dolin – a man whom de Valois could not abide. Helpmann's revue at the Adelphi was bound to fold ingloriously, and soon enough he would be knocking on Lilian Baylis's door, begging to take over in the ballet that had succeeded without him. Most pressing of all was de Valois's need to secure the loyalty of Frederick Ashton, whose running feud with Markova made desertion to her camp unlikely; but just to make sure, de Valois, who, in the past, had fought shy of offering him a proper contract, now formally engaged him as resident choreographer, electing him over Antony Tudor, who was on the brink of creating his superb *Lilac Garden* and was eventually to take his slighted talent to America. De Valois always felt the need to defend her choice – and always with the partiality and literary allusion that must have attended her original decision: 'Tudor had wit,' she said, 'but he didn't have humour.'[9]

Ashton, however, had a surfeit of both, but he wasn't joking when he said to her: 'How can we come back to London next season when we have no ballerina?' De Valois braved it out. 'We've got a perfectly good ballerina. We've got Margot.' Yet the look which Ashton gave her sufficed to make her engage, and swiftly, three new female dancers: the angelically beautiful Pearl Argyle, poached from Rambert; the technically brilliant Mary Honer, who had mostly worked in musical comedy; and none other than Margot's old friend June Bear, renamed June Brae, whom de Valois had talent-spotted at the Coliseum in *The Golden Toy*. Elizabeth Miller, who had been with the company since 1931, and the promising Pamela May, with her clean, classical elegance, were also in de Valois's mind for promotion. 'The thing is,' says Markova, 'the year I left, it took four or five dancers to cover my work, because I was so versatile, I suppose.' Her claim is no less than the truth. But, as much to punish her hubris as to serve the future, Ashton now took a closer look at de Valois's favourite, and sought the advice of friends. Lydia Lopokova and Maynard Keynes tended to endorse his prejudice: if he was not convinced that Margot had talent, then he was probably right. However, Tamara Karsavina, the legendary star of the Maryinsky, thought otherwise. She told Ashton that Margot was indeed gifted, and quite unusually musical, but that what the child lacked was a proper understanding of *épaulement*, the carriage of head and shoulders. 'From tomorrow,' said Ashton, 'I will ensure that she does.'[10] And by the time that Markova left the company, he was seeing to it so thoroughly that the parting shot he claims to have fired at the defector would prove fatal for her. 'I'm going to take Margot,' he told Alicia, 'and make her much greater than you *ever* were.'[11]

Margot, meanwhile, was an innocent enough player in the contest to have asked Markova – who gave her last performance at Sadler's Wells on 1 June 1935 – for permission to keep, as a memento, Alicia's first costume from *Giselle*. Margot was slipped so unobtrusively – and mostly at matinées – into her idol's more modern roles that she herself hardly noticed the changeover, so busy was she learning the new parts assigned to her: the leading girl in *Rendezvous*, the Polka in *Façade*, and 'Alicia', no less, in *The Haunted Ballroom*. 'Mostly I just danced and danced,' she writes, 'leaving no time to analyse thoughts or feelings. Optimism and self-criticism chased each other by day; I ate heartily, and slept like a log by night.'[12]

This pragmatic ability to just 'get on and do it' was Margot's great mainstay, according to Clement Crisp. 'She may have agonized over certain technical problems, but I think the rest of the time she simply trusted her luck, trusted the people who helped her. And *look* at the people she was given: Ashton,

Lambert, Helpmann! Margot was just a talented girl. No more. It must have been terrifying for her to feel that the finger had touched her, and she was to take over roles from Alicia, Alicia who had *every* gift. And now this poor little girl had to step into her shoes. I'm surprised she didn't go mad. But she didn't. She found the strength. Remade her identity. The effort must have set a pattern for her life – of discipline and acceptance of responsibility. I think she was self-created, but she was not a totally artificial thing. There was a real girl there. It was a case of "What will God give us to do something with?" And He gave us Fonteyn.'

One might as easily have hazarded, at the beginning, that He had planned to give us June Brae, for Margot's finalized name, when at last it made it into print, often appeared lower down the billing than that of June, whom in 1936 de Valois had chosen to play the Other Woman in her new ballet, *Prometheus*. But the two mothers were delighted to resume their erstwhile rivalry. 'It was nice,' writes Mrs Hookham, 'to have Mrs Bear back again with her endless chatter about the dancers. We both, of course, had our anxious moments as our daughters took on new roles. We were used to watching every class, but of course that wasn't allowed at the Wells; now, instead, we hardly ever missed a performance.'

Mrs Hookham and Mrs Bear wasted no time in hatching a new plot: why not take the girls to Paris so that they could study with the great exiled ballerinas from Czarist Russia, about whom, in Shanghai, they had read so much? Pamela May remembers: 'Margot's mother came up to me and she said, "When you get your holiday in the summer I'm going to take Margot to Paris – would you like to come with us?" So we went. June and her mother and the three of us all stayed at the YWCA for about a pound a week. Classes, living, all our food, cost me about twenty pounds. But it was wonderfully generous, wasn't it, that they asked me to go?'

Right from the very beginning, Paris, above all other cities, exerted a liberating influence on Margot's closely guarded spirit.

The best writing in her autobiography is devoted to an evocation of the three ageing teachers with whom she was to work there, summer after summer, free from de Valois's possessive scrutiny and Ashton's nerve-racking displeasure: the impoverished, lovable 'Preo' (Olga Preobrajenska); the coquettish, effervescent Mathilde Kschessinska, who had been the Czar's mistress; and Lubov Egorova, 'full of dignity and the soul of old Russia'. Up to six classes a day were held at any one of their three studios – at Place Clichy, at Place de la Trinité, and at Passy – and, so long as you kept producing a five-franc note, you could stay from 9 in the morning till 7.30 at night, rubbing shoulders with leading ballerinas. 'Kschessinska's class was elegant,' writes Mrs Hookham, 'though I never felt that she cared very much about her foreign students. June loved her classes and stayed with her more than Margot who seemed to get on better with Egorova's cool, detached style, and more difficult lessons. Preobrajenska was probably the most interesting of the teachers, because she was the most experienced and had understudied all the chief dancers and their roles. She was a little woman with hunched shoulders and a short neck. Looking at her I rather wondered how she had managed to be a successful understudy to many famous ballerinas, but her personality and dedication must have carried her through.'

There were no regulation practice-clothes, and Margot and Pamela, enthusiastic dressmakers, began feverishly to sew, knocking out pale, flattering tunics to wear over pink silk tights, which were forbidden at the Wells except for the stage. Mrs Hookham, allowed to sit in on class once more, was the gayest of duennas, and given to sensible subversions of her own: it was at her instigation that the girls pinched the china and cutlery from their breakfast trays so that economical picnics could be prepared and secretly eaten in the YWCA dormitory.

Pamela, June and Margot arrived back in London greater friends than they had ever been rivals. And they were to need one another's support and good humour, for, if living conditions had been basic in Paris, these would prove rougher still in the North of England, where late that summer they toured briefly with the Markova company before the new Vic-Wells season opened in the autumn. Needless to say, Mrs Hookham toured too: 'As was the custom then, we stayed in theatrical digs . . . On the whole, digs were very good value with generous breakfasts and a good supper late at night after the show. However there was never more than one bathroom, and the beds were generally lumpy or sagging in the middle . . . but young people don't worry about such things, especially tired dancers.' Exhaustion and youth, however, were no protection against the ravages of bed-bugs, which infested the room where Margot and Alicia's sister Bunny stayed in Leeds; and although the girls sloshed whole bottles of wet-white over their inflamed skin, their exposed arms and throats and backs looked hopelessly red and blotched in the cool misty glades of *Les Sylphides*.

'I think it was on this first tour,' writes Mrs Hookham, 'that Margot acquired her first serious admirer. He was a brilliant and charming man, but much older than she was . . . I was pretty worried, but said nothing about it.' She is, of course, referring to Constant Lambert, whose effect on her daughter was markedly subverting: in Blackpool, with its funfair and seaside thrills, Margot at last began to give vent to a few overdue flashes of delinquency, eluding her mother's proprietorial eye to ride the switchbacks and bumper cars, and, horror of horrors, to swim without a bathing cap. Prospective ballerinas, scolded Mrs Hookham, were not supposed to walk about with their shoulder-length hair sopping wet; but, for the first time since the early clashes with her daughter over food, the mother got the worst of the argument. For Margot had a valour and audacity in the water that she did not always possess on dry land, and was 'far more proud of her American crawl than she was of her pirouettes'.[13] There is a telling passage in an essay by de Valois where she analyses Margot-as-mermaid with what amounts to erotic fascination: 'People never quite grasped her beauty, simply because she did not grasp it herself. I can recall seeing her one summer swimming in the South of France, covered, completely unabashed, in hideous mosquito bites. Her black hair streamed out behind her as she cut through the water and created for me a picture of a beautiful, skilful young seal.'[14] Sixteen years later, in 1951, on holiday in Greece after the launching of *Daphnis and Chloë*, Margot's underwater prowess was to provoke virtually the same response in Frederick Ashton: 'She was wonderful in the sea because she was so svelte; she swam like an Ondine with her hair hanging down.'[15]

But back in September of 1935, as the first season without Markova got under way, Margot was less the shimmering water sprite of Ashton's imagination than an earthbound novice with 'buttery feet', who would not *bend*, and who could not for the life of her grasp the luxuriant 'whooshes' which he had picked up from his mentor Bronislava Nijinska – creator of the original version of *Le Baiser de la Fée*, on which Stravinsky score Ashton was now at work. De Valois had talked him into casting Margot in the part of the Bride, whose bridegroom is stolen from her on her wedding day by a predatory fairy. The coolly sophisticated Pearl Argyle, whom Ashton adored, was to play the Fairy, whose kiss at the bridegroom's birth cannot be forsworn. But when it came to the forsaken Bride, Ashton badly missed Markova and the artistic collaboration which he had enjoyed with her. 'I don't think you can have that step,' she had been able to warn him. 'Why not?' he would ask.[16] And she would tell him from her vast experience that Massine or Balanchine had used it before, had already made it their own. But Margot came to him uninitiated. He felt 'set back' by having to take his inspiration from a stubborn child who seemed to have pitted her exasperating will against his. Rehearsing with her, he admitted to 'a great frustration in being unable to mould her as precisely as I wanted . . . She had a very difficult variation to do which required a tremendous attack and sharpness in her dancing which at that time Margot didn't have . . . I got very cross with her and went on and on at her relentlessly.'[17]

And then, by instinct, by birthright, from honest necessity, Margot did the thing that was to set the seal on both their fates.

The 'uppity', 'remote', 'self-possessed' child, who apparently had no temperament to speak of, suddenly burst into tears and rushed over to Ashton and threw her arms around his neck. 'I'm sorry,' she sobbed. 'I'm trying my best; I can't do any more.'[18]

Men never know when they have been conquered. To the end of his life, Ashton believed that it was he who had won the battle. 'I realized then,' he later concluded, 'that she had conceded to me, and that I would be able to work with her . . . From that moment we were never at real loggerheads again.'[19] And so it proved. *Le Baiser de la Fée*, premièred on 26 November 1935, was not an entirely successful work – no visual interpretation of the derivative Stravinsky score ever really has been – but there was no question that the collaboration between Ashton and Fonteyn presaged greatness. In this ballet, he made a *pas de deux* for her and Harold Turner, which, in its affecting lyricism, was more heartfelt than any he had ever invented for Markova. The critics were enchanted; one wrote: 'Mr Ashton has had the wit to create an original romantic figure – and Miss Fonteyn the inspiration to body it forth, with poignant ecstasy and pathos through the medium of her attested virtuosity. This person really lives.'

At the time of *Baiser*, Ashton was beginning to fall obsessively for the fundamentally heterosexual Michael Somes. Margot, in her turn, was already adored from afar by the tormented, married composer Constant Lambert. And now, a tender, youthful attraction began between the two innocents, Margot and Michael. Yet, historically, sex is neither here nor there. Amid all the carnal complications, the bond which fate intended to promote and preserve for posterity was a chaste one: the marriage between the creative artist and his muse. The qualities that irritated Ashton about Margot were the very ones which would prove his salvation. Certainly she was unable to impersonate his rendering of Pavlova's genius – that divine propensity to run across the stage 'like a comet trailing everything behind her'.[20] But Margot's stubborn English failure to reproduce the fire of the Russian's turns, or 'the drama she could make of an *arabesque*', paid a different kind of dividend; for the girl's restraint – her natural emotional discretion – was the perfect filter for the theatrical extravagance of Ashton's vision. Until he saw the energy of his talent flowing through the quiet un-mannered candour of her body, he did not realize how pure his style was meant to be.

'Even as a young girl,' he would tell Keith Money, '. . . she always had that great gift which she displays to this day – a wonderful sense of measure. Never once did she make a gesture which was not completely true; one that did not come from the heart. Nothing was exaggerated. If her performances then were lacking in any respect, then it was because she felt unable to indulge in anything that she did not feel . . . In the early days she was like a delicate plant; one that needed continual feeding and watering . . . Had I not been able to work with Margot I might never have developed the lyrical side of my work. As it was, it evolved into a personal idiom.'[21]

6

It was one thing for a young dancer to succeed in a ballet that had been tailored especially for her. But now de Valois decreed that the time had come for Margot to tackle the classics. Less than a month after the opening of *Baiser*, she was to dance her first Odette in *Swan Lake*. Since Margot was thought to lack the technical skill to cope with the double role, Mary Honer was cast as Odile; but in the event the Black Swan would be danced by Ruth French.

Once again Margot and her mother entered into their natural state of conspiracy. They sought out a certain Mme Manya in Maida Vale, who had made Markova's costumes and Pavlova's before her. There is a secret cut to a tutu which can only be passed on first-hand: the basque must sit low on the hips in order to lend definition and length to the waist, yet be high-cut enough for the legs to be shown at their longest; and there must be stature and depth to the layers of gathered tarlatan, which may neither droop, nor spring up. Mme Manya, though somewhat affronted by the bold approach of one so young and uncelebrated, agreed to make the dress (to a design by Hugh Stevenson) for £16 – a fortune in terms of what Margot would earn wearing it. Heaven knows where Mrs Hookham found the money, but she shelled out without a murmur, for she could now purloin Mme Manya's prototype and replicate it to her maternal heart's content. A beautifully fitting costume is more than a practical necessity for a performer: it is a magic talisman. Yet, although the temptation in this double-cast production was to ensure that the white swan be seen to greater advantage than the black, both Margot and her mother knew that the role of Odette/Odile was, in essence, a test of versatility: ultimately, Margot would find that the competition was between her own strengths and weaknesses. As James Monahan was to write: 'It is the achievement of Tchaikovsky and Ivanov (supplemented by Petipa) in *Swan Lake* to have epitomized in a single role the primary two-sidedness of the classical ballerina. Of course *Swan Lake* is not the only classic to demand of its ballerina virtuosity as well as elegance, pathos as well as flamboyance; all the other surviving ballets of the Imperial Russian nineteenth century make something of the same two-fold demand. But none of the others does it quite so bluntly. Margot Fonteyn is an Odette. This means that, well though she may acquit herself in the other part of the double role, it is in the elegiac atmosphere, the wistfulness and the slower tempo of the great adagio of the bewitched Swan Princess with her princely lover that she is "at home". Talent and application have made her an Odile; but nature made her an Odette.'[1]

Nature may well have made Ruth French an Odile, for she was a fine and experienced technician. But on the evening of 16 December 1935, even if her dancing had not been marred by a foot injury, no one would have had eyes for *her*. All eyes were upon Margot, urging her towards success, unprepared even to contemplate failure. 'I well remember Margot's first performance as Odette,' writes Mrs Hookham. 'That night I sat with Miss de Valois in the front row of the circle and we were both so tense and nervous that we were literally trembling, or at least I was. People on either side of us were looking to see what was making their seats shake. She did well, thank heavens, and almost before the curtain came down we were rushing up the long stairway, and were first in the bar for a quick brandy.'

Next day the press raised its own toast. 'Margot Fonteyn in the famous role gave a truly great performance. No other word will do,' wrote Arnold Haskell. His review, headed 'Birth of a Great Ballerina', was over-excited and premature to say the least, if the photographs by de Valois's brother, Gordon Anthony, are anything to go by. In her heavily feathered costume, and with her jewelled headdress carving an exaggerated V in her forehead (to make seem heart-shaped a face that is still, frankly, quite pudgily round-cheeked), Margot, as that first Odette, makes a strangely blurred and indistinct impression which gives little clue as to the honed, linear clarity and haunted fragility that would render incomparable her later Swan Queen. Gordon Anthony himself, reined in by his sister's strict realism, probably gives a more reliable account of the evening: 'I was thinking of many Odettes I had seen – great, good, bad and indifferent. As usual, Fonteyn was herself, and good. She wisely chose to stress her own natural qualities of lyricism and romanticism, rather than attempt to emulate the technical brilliance of her famous predecessor, which was only to be gained by experience. It worked well, and I for one was carried away by her rendering of the role: it was far better than a pale copy.'[2]

Margot's promotion in status was reflected by a move to a more fashionable address. Mrs Hookham's lease at Hesper Mews was running out and, with her usual luck, she managed to rent a large four-bedroomed maisonette at the top of 69 Egerton Gardens. The sitting-room looked out over Brompton Oratory and what was then Brompton Road tube station. Margot's growing reputation made her more of a target than ever for 'stage-door Johnnies', much to her mother's alarm. 'I got a bit more worried when she started to get invitations from the young men who followed the ballet and frequently took the girls out to fashionable restaurants. In fact, eventually I became so concerned that I cornered Frederick Ashton in the interval one evening, and told him of my worries and asked him if he would keep an eye on Margot . . . He smiled and said in his quiet quick way, "Don't worry, I'm a much better chaperone than you'll ever be." It was a great relief to me, and I suddenly realized another advantage for Margot of having joined a young ballet company where she was treated as if she was one of a big family of brothers and sisters.'

The true danger, however, could not have been closer to home. Maynard Keynes, anxious to use up the final funds still at the disposal of the Camargo Society, charged Lambert to stir Ashton into another creative collaboration. Lambert set about the task with passion – all the undeclared passion which he felt for under-aged Margot. The ballet concocted for her (with the help of Berlioz's synopsis to his *Symphonie Fantastique*), was *Apparitions*, which centred on a poet's opium-induced vision of his alluring but elusive *idée fixe*.

'Dear Fred,' wrote Lambert, 'I was up in London last night and pursued you from theatre to theatre like a symbolist foot chasing a courtesan and equally in vain. My object was to bore you with my new idea . . . I think that a Liszt ballet by you would be the ideal thing . . . I want as far as possible to use only unknown pieces mostly from the latest period though I may allow you *Valse Oubliée* and *Consolation* as a sop to your feelings. The genre is 1830 romanticism of the fruitiest type plus a leavening of surrealism . . . For that reason I think Sophie might be the best person for the décor if she can be juicy enough . . . The man's part will suit Bobby very well and the woman's part will be ideal for either Spessiva or Fonteyn (whom to my great surprise you don't seem to appreciate at her true level. Though obviously immature at the moment she is to my mind the only post-Diaghileff dancer with of course the exception of Toumanova, to have that indefinable quality of poetry in her work).'[3]

Needless to say, Spessivtseva did not come into it. Fonteyn was cast as the Woman in a Ball Dress, the dress in question being designed in the end not by Sophie Fedorovitch, who, juicy or otherwise, turned out to be too expensive, but by Cecil Beaton. He grandly donated his entire fee – a full fifty pounds – to Karinska, Balanchine's brilliant costumier, who personally made all the ball gowns, although not, unfortunately, in time for the dress rehearsal, which was a fiasco. The theatre was plunged into a royal gloom, scarcely helped by the fact that King George V had died two weeks earlier. 'The atmosphere was dead,' Lambert wrote to Beaton. 'One felt the awful weight of middle-brow opinion against the whole thing.'[4] After the doomed dress-run, there was a photographic session to which Margot rode with Ashton in a taxi. She appears, at that time, to have been in a complicated kind of thrall to him, a state of desperation for approval which, in a girl parted prematurely from her father, might easily be taken for love. Sitting unduly close to her, Ashton took the opportunity to pull her performance to pieces. He had hoped for enigmatic elegance. But the person he had seen on stage had turned out to be 'a sincere, simple girl with no guile and no affectation'.[5] For the second time in his presence, guilelessly, Margot wept, aware that, since the steps which he had devised for her in *Apparitions* were well within her technical grasp, she must have failed him not as a dancer but as a woman. Her success to date was useless to her; it only served to exacerbate her fear that she would let them all down – Fred, Constant, her co-star Robert Helpmann, Miss de Valois, the company, everyone. 'But,' she wrote, 'it is strange how such moments help foment the artist lurking deep inside the adolescent. The next night, by some alchemy of despair, I had matured just enough to meet the demands of the ballet.'[6]

The pain of unrequited love does seem to have effected a transformation that no amount of lecturing could have brought about. Overnight, Margot appears to have shed her puppy fat. Gordon Anthony speaks of 'a subtle increase of beauty of form and face . . .' on that first night; of 'the dawn of maturity. She was startling in the sudden changes of mood demanded of her, and gave indications of a possible fund of emotion not yet drawn upon.'[7] Even her dreaded guilelessness was romanticized by the arch-sophisticate Cecil Beaton, who was reminded of a humble marguerite by the girl whom he would one day famously dress as the dissolute Marguérite Gautier. His endorsement was hard won, however, for she had not endeared herself to the designer socially, announcing, upon introduction to him: 'Oh, I have heard of you.'[8] Later, she suffered the humiliation of hearing this gaffe repeated by Robert Helpmann to a group of sniggering dancers: 'Did you *hear* what she said to Cecil?'[9] And Beaton got his own back, when, on first sighting her in her costume, he bitched:

'Oh, dear! Couldn't we have something a little more glamorous in the way of eye make-up?'

There was one person, however, for whom Margot's glamour remained as constant as his own unlikely name. Constant Lambert was hardly given to fidelity. But he was implacably devoted to the chase and enduringly fixed upon the object of his desire, especially when that object evinced the instinct, initially, to thwart him. And in the spring of 1936 his quarry was unquestionably Margot. 'He was absolutely pining for her and rattling on her door for a long, long time,' says Ashton's nephew, Anthony Russell-Roberts, 'and she was very, very strong in pushing him away.' Lambert was forever dragging his broken heart to his friends, and begging them to intercede on his behalf. 'Constant used to drive Fred mad, sighing endlessly after Margot, making Fred's life a misery − it became a real cross for Fred to bear.' Lambert's great chum Anthony Powell said, 'One of the stories that has rather grown up about Constant is that he was some sort of Svengali, but he was, early on, the shyest man with women that you can imagine. Really, he was within about two or three months of my age, and he was tremendously awkward, and not the least experienced.'[10]

Pleased to call himself 'a Francophile English composer-conductor born to an Australian painter from St Petersburg',[11] Lambert was hardly the dashing, dapper figure that a sensitive young dancer, steeped in the programme synopses of romantic ballets, might envisage as her Count Albrecht, her Prince Siegfried. The territory was more Beauty and the Beast. Although, in his Royal College of Music days, Constant had been considered, with his strong, sensual features and swept-back hair, to be 'radiantly good looking'[12] (witness Christopher Wood's 1926 portrait), childhood illness had already ravaged him: eighteen operations for osteomyelitis had left him limping, and deaf in one ear. 'Although,' according to Anthony Powell, 'his clothes were ordinary, he never looked ordinary . . . His habit of hatlessness (followed also by Walton), slightly unconventional at that period, persisted from Christ's Hospital schooldays.

Getting into a stiff shirt or "morning clothes" for conducting, one or other form of "tails" required most days, was always likely to cause apoplexy.'[13] By the time Margot first set eyes on Lambert in 1934 his body was, by a dancer's stringent standards, unprepossessingly bloated, and his florid, fleshy face had become heavily jowled; he was drinking himself steadily into Tom Driberg's description of him: 'Bulky, untidy, in exuberance and girth a young Chesterton; slight lameness obliges him to walk with a stick which he usually contrives to drop inconveniently or tangle in his friends' legs.'[14] Yet girls of sixteen are notoriously less susceptible to physical charm than they are to intellectual acumen; and Maynard Keynes pronounced Lambert potentially the most brilliant person he had ever met. To Anthony Powell's mind, Lambert possessed 'a touch of genius . . . He had a natural gift for writing, a style individual and fluid, that brisk phraseology so characteristic of those musicians able to express themselves on paper . . . Lambert inwardly inhabited, often outwardly expressed, a universe in which every individual, every action, was instantly appreciated in terms of art.'[15]

For the company, his presence among their number was an inspiration. 'He was a musical director such as one's rarely known,' says Leslie Edwards. 'A great man. Terribly knowledgeable. And Margot was a very young girl. We all shared in his marvellous geniality. You could go to him and ask him questions about music. I remember him recommending books to read. I'm sure Margot's great love of reading stemmed from that time.' Pamela May agrees: 'He was always interested in talking to all of us, but particularly Margot. In a funny sort of way, he educated her. She used to say to her own mother: "Why on earth wasn't I educated properly?" I could barely add up two and two myself, but in our day we had to learn things by heart, and I used to drive Margot mad by suddenly quoting from Shakespeare, or something out of the Bible, and she'd look at me and say: "How do you *know* that?" in a sort of fury. I was never a great reader, whereas you couldn't put a book down that Margot wouldn't pick up. And I think this was where she talked to Constant – about wanting to read. Ninette had a story: she sat down next to Margot on a bus going up to Sadler's Wells one day and Margot was reading a book that was *banned*. Ninette snapped the book shut and said, "Put that back in your bag: don't let people see you – that book's *banned* in England." *Lady Chatterley's Lover*, or something. Ninette was hysterically funny about it. And a bit cross. "I'll bet it was Constant who gave it to you," she said. "If you *must* read it, take it home and read it there." '

Lambert's growing obsession with Margot unnerved de Valois on more than just the literary front. She herself had hero-worshipped him since her days with the Ballets Russes, when the fresh-complexioned young man with the mind that even then 'could rear itself above us all'[16] had dared to stand up to the artistic autocracy of Diaghilev. Lambert had always seemed to her to be 'an Englishman of another and more full-blooded day, perhaps because he was an Edwardian in both life and thought'.[17] She was, in short, in love with him; and had, according to Sir Sacheverell Sitwell, conducted a protracted and emotionally unreciprocated romance with the composer, a romance which had only ended when Flo came on the scene. And although de Valois was married now, and had set aside such longings, there was a strange combination of pain and gratification in seeing the man whom she had so admired fall for the girl who embodied her own professional dreams. 'Frankly, I wish they had married,' she once let slip,[18] although events had long since proved that the granting of this wish, however magnanimously made, would have proved more of a malediction than a blessing. At any rate, in Margot's version of the banned-book story, *Lady Chatterley's Lover* is upgraded to James Joyce's *Ulysses*, just as she prefers to call the lover who gave it to her 'an admirer'. 'Admirers,' she blithely explains, 'were a source of literary or musical information to the point where I liked best the young man' (Constant was almost twice her age) 'who could lend me the best books and records.'[19] She had at her feet someone of awe-inspiring talent, scholarship and artistic generosity, yet in none of her writings does she admit his primary sway over her heart and mind, let alone body. It is hard, in the current outspoken climate, to be patient with her. And yet the times, to which she was perfectly attuned, dictated that outlook, which was not so much prissy as passionate about privacy. Also, there was her mother to contend with − both her mothers, actually, since de Valois, for all her retrospective matchmaking, would, in those days, have brooked no scandal. She saw it as part of her mission that ballet dancers, who in the nineteenth century had socially been seen as little more than glorified courtesans, should be perceived as respectable by the middle-class parents whose sons and daughters she hoped to entice. And because, even at this early age, the weight of Margot's destiny was upon her, the girl bore the imperative obediently, like the crown princess she was of the company which would eventually gain a Royal Charter. She stuffed the offending book into her bag and, for a little while at least, resisted Lambert's adulterous advances.

Her way of resisting was by succumbing elsewhere. It was, in a sense, an artistic decision, for she could see that the virginal blandness of Markova would never be a great choreographer's ideal. The emotional demands that Ashton had made on her in *Apparitions* had shaken her: never again would she allow him to accuse her of naïveté. Guile was something that could be acquired, and she set about acquiring some, choosing her seducer from the safety of the other side of the footlights: Donald Hodson, whom she had met at a concert, and who was to rise to be Controller of Overseas Services at the BBC. Hodson was ten years Margot's senior, and his exuberant affair with the sixteen-year-old was interrupted by his falling for a beautiful socialite, Margaret Beaston Beale, wife, at the time, to Sir William Deakin. Four years later, Hodson would marry Margaret Deakin, but their romance in 1936 came as an early blow to Margot's nascent self-esteem. According to Margaret Hodson, Donald had found Margot rather childish and over-attached to her mother, and, as dancers tend to be, forever hungry. This apparent lust for food was well matched by a growing appetite for sex in a girl whose paramount means of communication had become her body. Asked, very tentatively, whether Donald and Margot had been good friends, Hodson's eighty-seven-year-old widow gamely snapped: 'Friends? Not especially. They were bedfellows.' Needless to say, although Margot introduced Donald to her mother, she kept the nature of their exploits secret, sneaking off to their trysts in the same anarchic spirit as she had escaped to ride the bumper cars at Blackpool. But something new in her daughter's appearance must have alerted Mrs Hookham, who prided herself on being able to read people's auras. For, as the summer approached and she prepared to chaperone a second trip to Paris (this time with Laurel Martyn and Molly Brown as well as Pamela May), she sat Margot down and, rather late in the day, regaled her with the facts of life.

But when it came to the crunch, Mrs Hookham, given her own shady background, could not bring herself to censure Margot's behaviour. In Paris, mother and daughter, having managed to rent a studio-room and bedroom, took up with two young Englishmen, acquaintances of Constant Lambert. One was Theyre Lee-Elliot, a famous poster artist at that time, who had designed *The Speed Bird* for British Airways, and the other, the more gentle and gallant of the pair, who quickly became smitten with Margot, was his young artist friend Patrick Furse. The four went about exploring the city together, until, 'one most beautiful moonlit night,' writes Mrs Hookham, 'Patrick asked me if I would mind him going all round the romantic old part of Paris with Margot. This was quite late at night and it was really a shame to go indoors, so of course I agreed. I woke about 6 a.m. and went to see if she had returned. They were both there with the door wide open, she, covered up in the bed, and he, lying fully dressed on top, both looking so young and idyllic that I couldn't possibly waken them and went back to my room with tears starting.'

This touching interlude works against Margaret Hodson's description of Margot as 'broken-hearted' by Donald Hodson's abandonment of her. But if there *had* been an element of heart-break, it would, professionally, have proved all too useful. In October, Margot began rehearsals for Ashton's new ballet, *Nocturne*, a piece which provided her with the chance to enact her distress at the hands of a man caddish enough (Robert Helpmann) to forsake a poor innocent flower girl (Margot) for a rich, sophisticated lady (June Brae). The score, a tone-poem by Delius – *Paris, Song of a Great City*, which had been suggested by the librettist Edward Sackville-West – initially met with dis-approval from Constant Lambert, who felt that such symphonic impressionism should be confined to the concert hall. But when *Nocturne* opened on 10 November, Ashton was deemed to have found 'an ideal ballet score which he transformed into move-ment which seemed to grow naturally out of the music and become part of it. It is one of the very few ballets where ears and eyes are engaged in equal degrees.' Margot later told Keith Money: 'One simply did not think about the steps very much; one thought about the expression, the mood . . . He had the atmosphere of that Delius music to perfection.'[20] The designs were by Ashton's friend and mentor, Sophie Fedorovitch, who dressed Margot in a grey-and-white costume of striking simplicity, reminiscent of a Manet. Ashton, once again, had been kind to his new muse and not pressed her technically beyond her powers, and it was in this ballet that Margot came into possession of perhaps her greatest dramatic quality: pathos.

In real life, however, the figure that she was cutting was far from pathetic. If Donald Hodson had broken her heart, it had mended quickly: she had a new bedfellow. Having successfully been seduced, she now tried her hand at seduction, setting her sights on the most covetable boy in the company – Michael Somes. 'She made all the running,' says his third wife, Wendy Ellis. 'Men and women adored him. She was his first lover, although he was not hers. She was the experienced one.'

How much conscious image-making was involved on either side is hard to assess, for each contributed greatly to the other's romantic glamour. Can Margot have known the risk she took of inciting Ashton's jealousy by coming between him and his unresolved passion for Somes? It seems unlikely. Ashton, at the time, was in a *Nocturne*-like triangle of his own, his infatuation with penniless, unworldly Michael lending an undertone of melancholic yearning to his more opportunistic affair with one of the richest and most elegant women in the land: Alice von Hofmannsthal. If anything, the sudden air of sexual intrigue surrounding Margot seems to have elevated her in Ashton's eyes. His own appearance as the Spectator in *Nocturne*, an authorial figure in a black cloak who tries in vain to comfort the spurned Flower Girl, seemed somehow to endorse Margot's enhanced status with him – at least on a metaphorical level – as the recipient of his meticulous concern and deep, fond, fatherly attention. She could, in fact, have done with some guidance, for if Ashton was not jealous of Somes's intimacy with her, then Lambert most certainly was, and, in his 'unstoppable' pursuit of Margot, grew more careless than ever about the sensibilities of his wife. Violet Powell tells how, before the first night of *Nocturne*, Flo asked whether Margot should be sent flowers. 'Constant said he didn't think it was necessary. Flo went to the flower shop to get something to put in her hair, and saw in Constant's unmistakable writing (he wrote like no one else – like music) a card addressed to Margot from him. She began to feel there was something going on.' Lambert did nothing to allay his wife's suspicions. He dealt with her jealousy by disparaging her want of sophistication; it was perfectly possible, he pronounced, to be in love with two women at once, and he escaped Flo's scenes by throwing himself ever more obsessionally into his work: a score which he was planning for a new ballet. 'At the end of the week,' he wrote to Ashton, 'if I can hobble about enough, I plan to go down to Captain Bertie's where I shall be free to look at *Horoscope* which has naturally been at a standstill. I do hope it will turn out alright. I may not be back in London until 18th. If you see Margot before I do, give her all my love and more and try to persuade her I'm not such a beast as might appear.'[21]

Even if this message was conveyed to Margot, it would only have been one of many on the same theme – a theme which, by dint of its very persistence, was beginning to wear her down. Emotional pressure, given how hard she worked physically, was the last thing she needed. The morning after the first night of *Nocturne*, the company was up at dawn, to face the rigours of a new medium: television. 'We used to meet at Broadcasting House at nine o'clock,' wrote Molly Brown, 'and were taken by bus to Alexandra Palace; there we rehearsed in the morning and then gave two live performances – one in the afternoon and one in the mid-evening. We rather enjoyed these excursions, and we very much appreciated the money which I believe was £4.'[22] In December, Margot danced her first television solo, the Polka in *Façade*; but those early live small-screen appearances were not especially successful, for the studios were hot and airless, and the dancing looked ineffective in a flickering blue eight-inch image. When Lilian Baylis saw it, she was disgusted. '*That's no good*,' she said disdainfully. 'Much too small. Those girls will never get married like that.'[23]

In spite of television, someone whom many took to be Margot's new suitor presented himself without her having had to stir from her front door. Theyre Lee-Elliot came to stay at Egerton Gardens, as Mrs Hookham's paying guest. He aspired to painting dancers, and Margot was happy to pose for him and to spend time with his painter friends, especially Patrick Furse, who by now was deeply in love with her. Her dalliance with Michael Somes had been short-lived; for, despite their later great compatibility as dancing partners, sexually they were unsuited. 'Michael adored Margot as a person,' says Wendy Somes. 'But he never really liked her in that way.' His eye had already strayed to Pamela May, who, with her blonde elegance and sensuous Englishness, was 'much more his type'. The two girls, Margot and Pamela, do not seem to have allowed their fluctuating romantic attachments to the same man to ruffle the surface of their deepening friendship, for 'with Michael we were all just ships that passed in the night', mutters May enigmatically. At

May's flat, a painting by Theyre Lee-Elliot of Margot in *Nocturne* still shares wall-space with a gouache by the same artist of herself and Elizabeth Miller spinning through the air as Red Girls in *Les Patineurs*. Lee-Elliot and Lambert were also good friends, and played cards and invented crosswords on train journeys; and it may have suited Lambert's purpose – and put Mrs Hookham off the scent – that Margot should have so many apparent escorts. For it was at this time that his passion and intensity overcame the girl's scruples, and he lured her at last into his bed.

A joke of the day went: 'I'm not that sort of girl – besides, where could we go?' And finding somewhere to go did pose a bit of a problem, since Constant, despite his heroic work-load, was on his financial uppers. Besides, even if he could have afforded the outlay, hotels in London (with the odd seedy exception where secrecy was impossible to sustain) did not endorse adulterous assignations. Finding a suitable venue was, according to Anthony Powell, 'one of Constant's favourite subjects. He had a very good idea for a short story. Two people who are in love pretend that they are looking for a house. They go round with orders to view and try out all the bedrooms on the market in London.' It was Ashton's influence with Alice von Hofmannsthal that provided the perfect love-nest: she lent Constant the gate cottage at Hanover Lodge, her magnificent Regency villa, locked safely behind wrought-iron gates in the middle of Regent's Park. In exchange for this favour, Lambert gossiped about Margot's sexual prowess to Ashton. Apparently it was considerable. Once she vanquished her moral anxiety, she was without inhibition – as finely tuned and responsive sensually as he already knew her to be artistically. Or, to put it more bluntly, as he did: 'Her cunt muscles are so strong that she can activate me of her own accord.'[24]

When *Les Patineurs*, Ashton's next ballet, opened on 16 February 1937, it was hailed as 'an almost outrageous triumph'.[25] Audiences, critics and dancers doted on it, and it remains in the Royal Ballet's repertoire to this day. But it certainly did not depend on Margot for its success. She and Robert Helpmann, both in white, performed a cool, decorous double-*adagio*, yet their thunder was easily stolen by the virtuoso Blue *pas de trois*, danced in this first instance by Harold Turner, Mary Honer and Elizabeth Miller. However, even these three had to struggle for the limelight, *Patineurs* essentially being an ensemble work which drew attention to the rising number of good dancers in the *corps de ballet*. In the *pas de huit*, Ashton had given Somes, in brown, what he called 'a moment', a sudden series of *jetés* which sent Harold Turner storming out of rehearsal when he saw them.

Nor was Margot the particular success of Ashton's next work, a comic piece with a specially written score by Gerald Berners and choral interventions by Lambert. *A Wedding Bouquet* was based on a Gertrude Stein play, the very title of which typifies the arch and studied fashion of the day: *They Must. Be Wedded. To their Wife* – an imperative increasingly flouted by Constant Lambert, whose name, coupled with Margot's, was set to figure over the next eight years in the visitors' book at Faringdon, Lord Berners's Palladian-style country seat in Oxfordshire. Life at Faringdon was aristocratic and not a little decadent, with pink fan-tailed pigeons strutting the lawns, dinner-courses themed in pink to match, and pornographic texts (disguised as leather-bound literature) casually placed on bedside tables. Margot seems to have taken it all in her stride, her signature growing with each entry, from small schoolgirlish script to a more swooping hand, not unlike Constant's own stylish, 'musical' flourish, which it invariably accompanied.

When *A Wedding Bouquet* opened, on 27 April 1937, the honours went unequivocally to Robert Helpmann who, as the Bridegroom, took his brilliant personal gift for burlesque on to the stage for the first time. Huge laughs, too, greeted Mary Honer, who was wonderfully daft as the Bride. As for Ninette de Valois, in the last dancing appearance of her career, she delighted the knowing audience by satirizing herself as a bossy, starchy maid, Webster. Margot, alone, seems to have struck a wrong note. As Julia ('known as forlorn'), she came in for the first vaguely censorious reviews of her career. 'The sincerity, which gives depth to all her characterizations, introduced an incongruous tragic element which was out of place in this heartless frolic.'[26] It was as though her solemnity – the former butt of her father's leg-pulling – had returned to haunt her. In a programme note, Constant Lambert called Julia 'a modern Giselle'. And perhaps that was the trouble: Margot's concentration was elsewhere – grappling with the demands of the real thing.

Just before the tour at the end of 1936, de Valois had confided to Mrs Hookham that she planned to revive *Giselle* (which had been dropped from the repertoire as a result of Markova's departure), especially, and only, for Margot, who reacted with genuine horror. 'I could hardly speak, I was so upset.'[27] She insisted that she could not do it, was not ready. 'That's for me to decide,' said de Valois;[28] and that, needless to say, was that. The first performance took place on 19 January 1937.

It is not that *Giselle* is technically so very exposing: there are no tutus to be worn, no balances to be held, no *fouettés* to be executed in the grand manner of the great Petipa–Tchaikovsky roles. The heroine is not a princess but a peasant, and, even as a ghost, she is the humblest of tragic spirits. Adolphe Adam's score – whacked out in a week – though ambitious for its day, has subsequently been supplemented, cut, revised. And, although the 1841 choreography was attributed to Coralli, Giselle's dances were originally arranged by Perrot, while both they and the Act Two ensemble work, still as glorious as any in classical ballet, were overhauled by Marius Petipa between 1860 and 1903. Yet despite all the tinkering this romantic drama has been hailed the *Hamlet* of ballet: on her success or failure in it, a dancer's career may turn. It is not even a straightforward matter of acting ability: the greatest dramatic ballerina of our age, Lynn Seymour, struggled more than most with the implausibility of Gautier's libretto, searching for some logic in the character's sudden disintegration into madness and death, which could so easily – especially to a prosaic English audience – seem like 'silly nonsense'.[29] In this particular instance, there was nothing falsely modest about Margot's terror. And yet she came through, as she always did, not with flying colours, nor in the shadow of Markova, but by the unostentatious use of her own luminous potential and beautiful, natural, 'stage manners'.[30] In other words: she abdicated any egotistical or analytical attempt to characterize, and simply became entirely reactive, almost passively absorbed in the fictional circumstances built up around her. Giselle's painted cardboard village and pre-arranged steps came, paradoxically, to constitute safety, a haven away from the 'wilderness of unpredictables in an unchoreographed world'[31] which had so beset the girl throughout her adolescence. 'It was so easy for me to step out into the limelight through the plywood door of Giselle's cottage and suffer her shyness, ecstasy, deception and madness as if it was my own life catching me by surprise at each new turn. It was a fresh, living experience for me at every performance as the drama unfolded.'

There is black-and-white evidence of this statement in an archive film of Act I, shot in 1937. The sequences are too jumpy and incomplete to sustain the addition of a musical soundtrack; but, watched in silence, they are astonishing. For Margot, with the sheer joyousness of her youthful presence, literally conjures the tunes out of thin air. If you know them at all, you cannot fail to hear them; they sing irresistibly through her body; and perhaps the influence of Constant Lambert can best be glimpsed in this newly conscious celebration of Fonteyn's musicality. The early scenes (danced with sympathetic, though rather lax-kneed, support from Robert Helpmann) are extraordinary in the development of their detail, which was to change very little over the years: as an artist, Margot seems virtually to have arrived fully formed. The fragments from the mad scene are less convincing, for there is about them an air of silent movie melodrama and a conventionality of mime that seem, in a dated way, to patronize the heroine's mental affliction. Yet some gestures – the stiff hands, pressed to either side of the mouth, for instance – must have been truthful enough in their intuitive conception to be applicable, later on, to real-life tragedy. Margot's stepdaughter, Querube, was with her in 1988 when she was told of the death of Mrs Hookham. Apparently Margot said nothing, but raised her hands to her wild-eyed face in an agony of distraction: 'Just like Giselle.'

There is no record from that period of Act II, where the real test of dancing begins; but James Monahan is correct in his assertion that Margot never really possessed 'the air of gossamer asperity which is proper to a Wili, especially in her treatment of young Albrecht, responsible as he is for her lovelorn premature ghostliness'.[32] Margot was only an actress up to a point. Great performers are often like that: they do not turn themselves into the character; they turn the character they are playing into themselves. And yet, what audience would choose asperity in a heroine over gentleness and humanity?

Markova and Dolin, who were appearing in pantomime at the Hippodrome, rushed over to the Wells after their act was finished, to see what Margot would make of the ballet that Alicia had made so much her own. They arrived just in time for the mad scene. But, eager as Margot was to impress her idol, she was astute enough not to try to emulate her – not least since Ashton had made it clear that, in his opinion, over-identification with the role of Giselle had been Markova's undoing. So anxious was Margot to seem professionally unassuming that, in her inexperience, she arrived at the theatre with barely enough time to dress and make up before the curtain rose, let alone open her first-night messages. But when, back in the dressing-room, with everyone standing around congratulating her, she did rip open her telegrams, there was one from de Valois which read: 'And some have greatness thrust upon them.'

Shame burned Margot's cheeks more effectively than any compliment could have done. For she did not know the quotation, nor its source, and had to stand there, with her bouquets wilting around her, while Miss de Valois was forced to explain that the words were part of the famous lines from *Twelfth Night*. But the only line which Margot could remember at that moment was the one uttered by her Shanghai headmistress, Miss Fleet: 'You will find yourself an ignoramus among other people.' How quickly the prophecy had fulfilled itself. And no mere ovation would take away its curse.

The closest brush that the dancers had with intellectual life was their annual visit to Cambridge at the end of May. The engagement at the Arts Theatre was only for a week, followed in early June by what, in the idiosyncratic tradition of England's senior universities, is known as May Week – Cambridge's post-tripos Bacchanalian rite. Most of the boys in the company, who felt socially as well as academically o'erparted, would drift back to London for a well-earned rest; but the prettier girls (and June and Pamela and Margot – dubbed 'the Triptych' by the dons – were easily the prettiest) were naturally pressed to linger awhile. Admission to the famous May Balls was both restricted and expensive, so Margot and her partner would have one pair of tickets, which she would throw out of the window to Pamela, who would then come in with *her* partner, only to send the same tickets fluttering down to be used by June.

Cambridge in the flush of early summer is probably one of the most enchanting places in the world; and Pamela May and Michael Somes stirred the romantic atmosphere – and Ashton's jealousy – by punting past, wrapped in each other's arms. Soulful girlish yearning and burgeoning student libido lazed on the grass all day and danced the night away. Noël Annan, an undergraduate at the time, wrote years later to Ashton: 'Were not those Cambridge days perpetual sunshine of glorious youth? With endless laughter and fun and drink and delicate romances of no duration. I think of them as some of the happiest times, and of Lydia's champagne laughter.'

Laughing Lydia (Lopokova) had done her dash as a ballerina, but it was in her honour that her husband, Maynard Keynes, had built the Arts Theatre. The ballet season at the Arts was followed by the Footlights Revue, produced by George ('Dadie')

Rylands, King's College historian and doyen of the university's theatricals, who snatched up any talent that happened to be passing. 'Bobby and Freddy became rather interested in helping me with skit ballets,' he explained. 'I saw quite a lot of Constant at that time, too, because he was a very great friend of Patrick Hadley, who was professor of music – Constant used to stay with him in Caius. Paddy Hadley was deeply in love with Margot. So was Constant. Everyone was.' But Margot eschewed the dazzling intellects arrayed before her, and embarked in 1937 on an adventure not of the head but of the heart. And – in the face of condescending English chauvinism – with a foreigner.

Roberto Emilio Arias was an eighteen-year-old undergraduate who, arriving the previous year, 1936, had taken Part I of the Economics Tripos only to switch later to Law. He belonged to the dynasty, half-Spanish, half-Indian, which had dominated Panamanian politics since the country had gained its independence in 1903. Not only had his father been the ruling president until 1936, but his uncle Arnulfo, elected four times to the presidency, was the charismatic hero of Panamanian democracy, such as it was. Roberto ('Tito') and his brother Harmodio ('Modi') were appearing in Dadie Rylands's Footlights Revue, performing the first rumba ever to be danced in Britain, with Tito, the younger of the two, who happened to have extraordinarily delicately boned legs, dressed, or rather undressed (no doubt at Helpmann's behest) as a coffee-complexioned girl. Drag was not Tito's thing, but a photograph, captioned 'Full Swing', shows him wearing his minimal costume with skinny aplomb. The brothers' new dance was in great demand after the show at parties, one of which happened, on a particular June night in 1937, to drift spontaneously into the rooms where the Triptych was staying. Late at night, Margot, mounting the narrow stairs to her digs above the King's Parade restaurant, heard a strange exotic sound coming from what must have been someone's portable gramophone. It was the Lacuona Cuban Band, playing the rumba. To the loud hypnotic beat that was in her blood as well as in her ears, Margot met the man destined to become her husband. And it is strange that, at this critical first moment – the moment which tends to dictate how the power between two people is to be apportioned – it was he who happened to be dancing and not she.

'Mrs Bear and I went to pick up our daughters,' writes Mrs Hookham. 'As we got into the room I saw Margot sitting on a settee-bed in a corner and just caught a look between her and the dark-haired boy beside her which made me think "I wonder?" To my knowledge she had never been in love with any of her boy or men friends but that look was different. Anyway, neither she nor I spoke of it and it was only when I read her autobiography that I learnt the truth of it.'

Margot claims to have been, like Juliet, lovestruck at first sight – or, at least, by the morning after. For, in her 1975 account, elsewhere so level-headed and unwhimsical, there ensues a passage which strains our credulity: 'After I woke up I stepped out of bed to find the floor was not as usual. My feet did not touch it as I moved across the room, so I returned and sat on the edge of the bed to think the matter out. I could not understand what was happening to me. The phrase "walking on air" came to my mind, and suddenly I remembered the dark-haired boy dancing the rumba the night before. That was it! I must be in love! I did not even know his name, except that they called him Tito.'[1]

This scene is not so much written as choreographed. She is virtually miming bewitchment for us, lending to the memory of her feelings the greatest validity that she knows: physical action. She discovers her emotions as an audience would – through her movements. She shows, rather than tells, what she is thinking, brings the full weight of her artistry to bear on what is essentially artless. Little wonder that the reader feels vaguely hoodwinked. All her life, her friends and colleagues were to question her attachment to Arias – whether it was real or just a role. But such doubts would only compel her to protest her devotion the more strongly, until, in the end, she would tolerate no one who did not profess unconditional admiration for Tito.

Her version of their meeting in Cambridge is the first of those demands which were to test so many loyalties over the years, and to isolate her from so many of her friends.

Cambridge does seem to have cast a disproportionate match-making spell: both June and Pamela met their husbands there, and a side of Margot wanted desperately to be like her contemporaries – bound for marriage and motherhood and an ordinary existence. But her extraordinary destiny had already laid claim to her, not least in the powerful figure of Constant Lambert, who, watching wryly from the sidelines while the young had their day, probably saw Margot's flirtation with Arias for what at the beginning it may simply have been – a bid to escape not just from his clutches but also from the tyranny of a relentless vocation. 'I just wished he would take me away with him and look after me forever,' writes Margot of Tito,[2] and we have to concede that, for British ballet's sake, it is as well that he did not. But what *does* ring with emotional truth is her description of her pleasure at the glancing lightness of his touch, the absent-mindedness of his attention, the elusiveness of his presence. 'He sat,' she would tell *Woman* magazine in 1961, 'with his arm around me all evening. He was there when we went up river to swim and have tea at Granchester. Sometimes he came to the theatre green room to have coffee with us, sat on the floor of my dressing-room to wait for me, and once, he kissed me.'[3] He talked – if at all – softly and indistinctly, and about his own life, not her dancing. 'Do you *like* ballet?' she would ask. 'No,' he would reply, in part to tease her.[4] And yet his answer struck her as original and refreshing. It amazed her that she might be admired not for what she did but for who she was. But who *was* she? Tito seemed to need no explanation. 'Having so little to say myself,' she confesses, 'it was perfect happiness to be with someone equally uncommunicative and yet totally compatible.'[5]

For once, she made no secret of her feelings. Leslie Edwards 'knew she had a crush on him, *natch*. Besotted, from the word go.' Dadie Rylands thought Tito 'a dear boy, but frankly, we were all pretty amazed'. Noël Annan found her romance 'as astonishing as Jackie's with Onassis'. And Pamela May, Margot's closest confidante in those days, admits, 'She was mad about Tito then. We all said, "It's the South American influence."' By the end of the week, when the company had to move on, he still hadn't asked to see her again, or told her that he loved her. But he had given her his address, and a Panamanian coin – a half balboa, dated 1933: the year his father had become President. Margot treasured this, along with some photographs of Tito taken by the river at Granchester, and when he returned to Panama for the summer vacation she sent him a photograph of herself, inscribed with a message that seemed to lose courage half-way: 'For my dear Tito – from Margot.'[6] But he did not write back. 'It was part of my code,' she would later admit, 'that it was terrible for a woman to be more in love with a man than he was with her, and in the long months of Tito's silence, I'd destroyed all my dreams and broken my heart.'[7]

There was, however, another man in her life, one who, as yet, loved her more than she loved him. And it may have been her humiliation over Tito, and the resignation and passivity which suffering engenders, that confirmed her surrender to Constant Lambert. The word 'rebound' comes to mind; yet it seems an inadequate description of the enormity of the plunge which she now took and of the courage which it required. It is sometimes the discovery of what we cannot have that defines what is most urgently meant to be ours. Lambert, though increasingly estranged from his wife, was nevertheless a husband and a father, not to mention a heavy drinker; and although Margot's upbringing had not been religious, it had been highly principled. Mrs Hookham, while neither a prude nor a spoilsport, was implacably opposed to the idea of a sexual liaison between Margot and the composer, and would, according to Patricia Garnett, glare at Constant whenever she met Margot off the company train. In June 1937 Mrs Hookham travelled with the dancers on their first visit to Paris, where they had been invited by the British Council, and she watched over Margot like a hawk, little knowing how far from the nest the bird had already flown. Tellingly, it was on this tour that Mrs Hookham acquired the nickname by which she would come to be known for the rest of her life: Black Queen.

The highlight of the season at the Théâtre des Champs-Elysées was to be the first performance of Ninette de Valois's new ballet, *Echec et Mat*, later known as *Checkmate*, but Margot only appeared in the small part of a Black Pawn, looking, Molly Brown and Jill Gregory privately agreed, 'just like the Imperial Bee on the honey jars'.[8] The actual Black Queen was danced by June Brae, with Pamela May as the Red Queen – typical of de Valois's democratic attitude, as once remarked on by Alexandra Danilova: 'What I particularly like is that *la petite Margot* has not so far been given the best parts in all the ballets . . .'[9] And perhaps this attests to a shrewd understanding on de Valois's part that if Ashton was to be as great a choreographer as she hoped, then he must be allowed to command the fidelity of his muse. Besides, the director knew her own strengths well enough to realize that her ballets were better vehicles for men than for women. Once again, it was Robert Helpmann – this time as the poignant Red King – who best exemplified her ironic and flinty sensibility. But when it came to a game which the company played, sitting about in the canteen between rehearsals, of naming the dancers' mothers after the characters in the ballet, there was no question as to whom Mrs Hookham should be. 'It was either Fred or Bobby who cast her,' says Leslie Edwards, 'but we all suddenly, in our giggling way, agreed with the choice for Black Queen. *Ideal* – Mrs Hookham! There were only a few women's parts, and we didn't go in for sex changes then, although one particular mother *was* cast as a Bishop [Helpmann's own]. Margot loathed the nickname Black Queen, which she modified to BQ, but you would hardly cast her mother in a small role. The name stuck because Mrs Hookham was a very stylish lady. She was great fun, but she could be very much on her dignity.' Baffled though she was, and more vulnerable than she seemed, Mrs Hookham bore the backhanded compliment with forbearance.

'I have no idea why that name has stuck to me, but all my friends and a lot of older ballet people call me by it – even Ninette, to my embarrassment. Anyway, I feel honoured and flattered by it as a sign of affection.'

The Vic-Wells dancers were in Paris to represent Britain at the International Exhibition of Industry and Art: as well as *Checkmate*, they had taken with them *Pomona*, *Apparitions*, *Nocturne*, *Les Patineurs*, *Façade*, *The Rake's Progress*, the Aurora *pas de deux* and the *pas de trois* from *Le Lac des Cygnes*; but they may as well not have bothered: the British Pavilion was almost as hard to find as any evidence of publicity for *Les Ballets Anglais*. Still, what did the dancers care if the theatre was only half full? It was summer, and they were in Paris, and the real dancing began after curtain-down, when, unfettered by any formal offers of hospitality, they did the rounds of all the *boîtes* and bars, 'gaily hysterical'[10] as they swung along the lamp-lit boulevards in an intoxicated pack. Sophie Fedorovitch and Alice von Hofmannsthal were in town, and even Bobby Helpmann's mother, over from Adelaide, and the spitting image of her son, tagged along. But Black Queen did justice to her new name by escorting her recalcitrant daughter straight back to their room at the Byron Hotel after each night's performance. Mrs Hookham's concern was justifiable: the foreign nature of the Exhibition had prompted a series of clashes between the right-wing Cagoulards and the gendarmes; bullets ricocheted outside the crowded cafés of Place de la Concorde. However, she could hardly prevent Margot from attending a garden party in the beautiful formal grounds of the Villa Trianon which merged into the park of the Palais de Versailles. The hostess, Lady Mendl, had engaged the most fashionable band in Paris, the Hot Club of France, led by Stephane Grappelli and Django Reinhardt, to play their innovative jazz. Lame Constant sat spellbound beside them on the terrace as, to the syncopated improvisations of violin and guitar, Margot led the revelling dancers through the topiary.

While Margot spent the rest of her summer in Paris taking classes with the old Russian ballerinas, Constant accepted an invitation for himself, his wife and their son, who was now two years old, to stay at Kammer, the von Hofmannsthals' Austrian retreat. Ashton, his sister Edith, Bobby Helpmann and Billy Chappell had already gathered there, the latter two 'goggle-eyed'[11] at the passing parade of grandees – which included Wallis Simpson, Margot Oxford, Iris Tree and the Duke and Duchess of Kent. But Flo Lambert, having just discovered that Alice had lent Constant and Margot her cottage at Hanover Lodge, was too distraught to care about social details. Flo was by now a thoroughly tragic figure, screaming drunkenly in public at Constant and throwing such histrionic fits that she and Kit found themselves ejected from the house by their hosts, while Constant made no move to defend his wife or child. Flo, however, claimed to Anthony Powell that it had been she who had been determined to walk out. 'I must add,' confided Powell, 'she said she was jolly well going to leave Constant despite a particular physical advantage that he had.' Ashton draws attention to this attribute more plainly: 'What did Constant give to ballet that no one else could have done? Very good balance, very reliable tempi, very large cock . . .'[12] In any event, and size notwithstanding, those scenes at Kammer marked the end of Constant Lambert's first marriage. He settled down for the rest of the holiday to work with Ashton on *Horoscope*, his ballet score that was to bear the brazen dedication: 'To Margot Fonteyn'.

In August, on her return to England for the autumn provincial tour, Margot found her enhanced romantic stature counterbalanced by a drop in her professional fortunes. Pearl Argyle had rejoined the company, and reclaimed first casting in several of Margot's new roles. The names Pearl Argyle and Robert Helpmann now topped the bill, with Margot Fonteyn and Harold Turner in second place. If Margot minded, she did not let it show. Besides, there was much for her to learn from watching the ravishing Argyle, about whose doomed beauty de Valois once murmured: 'Imagine waking up every morning and seeing that face in the mirror.'[13] Although technically rocky, and limited in range, Argyle (who was to die tragically early of a brain haemorrhage) possessed, in the classics, what Billy Chappell was forced to concede Margot still lacked: splendour. 'Pearl,' he writes, 'had such real beauty of face and figure and such an air of serene grandeur that she used to hold me riveted to every movement.'[14] Margot, whose speciality at that time was 'artless simplicity', may well have been grateful for someone to admire. Certainly, given the turmoil of her private life, she must have welcomed this respite from professional pressure. When Constant returned from Kammer, he moved straight out of the marital home in Trevor Place, took a flat in Hanover ('Hangover') Lodge, and paid a woman to play cards with him all night in a hotel, so that Margot should not be cited in his divorce. But Flo was not so discreet.

'She couldn't cope with it,' says Annie Lambert, Flo's daughter by her second marriage. 'Kit was farmed out to various grand-mothers and aunts while she walked around London, this beauty, with unwashed hair and no make-up. She then thought in her head, if he wants a dancer, right, I'll be a dancer, and she went off and did five classes a day – at the age of twenty-three. Tremendous will-power. After about two years she got herself into the company.'

'She wasn't actually *in* the company,' points out Patricia Garnett. 'She was a student. An extra. A Page in *Sleeping Beauty*. She wanted to get back at them: she was quite vindictive at that time. She enjoyed implying: I'm still here, you can't get rid of me. Flo used to do the most cruel imitation of Margot talking.' Annie Lambert confesses: 'My mother was tortured and terribly jealous and never lost it. She was always ready to call Margot by her real name – *Peggy Hookham*. That would come out with venom.'

The roles for which Margot had so far become known were mostly those of innocents. The heroine was usually vulnerable – the forsaken bride, the betrayed peasant, the jilted flower girl, the anguished white swan rather than the treacherous black one. But now, finding herself, for the first time, capable of personal intrigue and duplicity and of the sexual glamour that attends them, she could properly assume the double onus of the full-length *Swan Lake*, and Odette's maleficent shadow, the Princess Odile.

In her list of professional terrors, Margot places *Swan Lake* at the top – a fear which was to remain with her throughout her performing life. As she wrote in 1989, in an epilogue to her children's story-book based on the legend: 'I think one should be aware not only of the duality of the Odette/Odile roles, of good and evil, but also the duality within each role. Both are enigmatic characters; neither is what she seems. Odette is bird as well as woman. Odile is reality as well as illusion . . . I always found *Swan Lake* the greatest challenge in my repertoire.'[15]

Central to her apprehension were the famous thirty-two *fouettés* in Act III, a speciality of the original Odette/Odile, Pierina Legnani, and the bane of ballerinas' lives ever since. *Fouettés* are virtuoso turns on one leg, propelled by a repeated whipping action of the other; and the fuss made over them by audiences and critics is disproportionate to their artistic merit, or even their technical difficulty – for, being a knack more than an accomplishment, they might as easily be torn off by a confident student as defy an experienced star. In Margot's case, they were a struggle from the start. But although it is perfectly permissible and, sometimes, artistically preferable for a ballerina to substitute a more congenial step, it went against Margot's nature to admit defeat. Perhaps she had an innate understanding that purity of intention is more endearing to an audience than perfection of execution. One practical source of support was Robert Helpmann, who, since her unarguable success in *Apparitions*, had set aside his caustic wit and now helped her to make light of her *fouetté* phobia. Although, in those early days, she remained a little wary of him off-stage (where he, for his own part, professed hardly to know her), she adored working with him. 'Helpmann had only to walk on stage to draw all eyes to him, for he had a magnetic stage presence . . . To be constantly sharing a stage with such a personality . . . is to learn in a hard school, which is the best school, for only by a superhuman effort can one hope to hold the public's attention oneself.'[16] Yet despite his breathtaking self-centredness, Helpmann could be considerate and patient. He hated to over-rehearse, and taught her to rely on trust and instinct rather than on needless drilling.

De Valois, not long before Margot died, asked her who, of all her partners, had been her favourite. 'She said, "Helpmann!" I said, "*What?*" "Oh, Madam," she said, "he was wonderful. None of the others was ever like him." I'd expected her to say Somes, or the Russian boy. But she said that Nureyev wasn't such a comfortable partner, although he knew how to bring her out. I thought, this is extraordinary, and I went on and asked Markova. I said, "Alice, of all the men you've danced with, who was the best?" And she said, "Helpmann!" And not only had she been with Diaghilev's people, but she'd had a famous partnership with Dolin! But that other monkey had something up here. So intelligent. And yet he was still only really learning the job himself. But he knew how to handle them. Oh my God, what a man of the theatre Helpmann was. They don't appreciate him now, they don't realize what he did for us at that time.'

Certainly at the time of Margot's first full-length *Swan Lake*, Helpmann was busy ensuring that he was a man of more than just the ballet. His relationship with Frederick Ashton had always been competitive (to Chappell and Ashton he was known unaffectionately as 'La'), and the emergence of Michael Somes with his manly beauty and power over Ashton's heart made Helpmann doubtful about the chances of maintaining his position as *danseur noble*. He'd never had any intention, should his fame begin to wane, of 'wiping the noses of snotty little *corps de ballet* girls'.[17] Even as the rehearsals for *Swan Lake* began, he went to see Lilian Baylis to ask if he might audition for a straight acting role: Oberon in Tyrone Guthrie's forthcoming production of *A Midsummer Night's Dream*; and Miss Baylis, relieved not to have been pressed for a rise, refrained, for once, from her usual refrain: 'Sorry, dear, God says "No".'[18] Helpmann got the part and whizzed back and forth from the Vic to the Wells, and between the two most ravishing leading ladies in London, Vivien Leigh (Titania) and Margot Fonteyn (Odette/Odile), the green sequins of Oberon's fantastical make-up still clinging to his hooded eyelids as Prince Siegfried. But Lilian Baylis (otherwise known as 'the Lady') did not live to see her leading dancer – Australian accent elocutively suppressed – hailed 'not merely as an actor of imagination and grace but as a speaker of poetic fire . . .'[19] She died suddenly on 25 November, before either the *Dream* or *Swan Lake* had opened. Comically eccentric though the company had always found her, everyone was horribly sobered by the loss of Baylis. De Valois has described her as 'not unlike a sincere, shrewd, devout peasant . . . She informed me once that she was very ignorant, but she always knew *who* knew. What she did not know in her great and fearless simplicity was that she possessed something greater than knowledge – a natural wisdom; this wisdom sprang from experience, piety and kindliness, the paths that lead to human understanding.'[20]

'Do you believe in God, dear?' had been Miss Baylis's first words to Margot when, on the stairs backstage at the Old Vic, the fourteen-year-old student had bumped into the dumpy, frumpish, bespectacled, wispy-haired old personage.[21] Just as well the child had answered yes. For had she replied in the negative, one is tempted to conjecture that she might never have danced the Swan Queen, since neither God nor Miss Baylis would have countenanced it. And the company would have been deprived of what its members regarded as a miracle. For, in under four years, Sadler's Wells had spawned, from its own ranks, a home-grown ballerina capable of dominating a full-scale classical production. 'Well, somehow or other I did it,' writes Margot,[22] although in truth the dreaded virtuoso turns did not stay on one spot, or rise to the requisite number of thirty-two. The critics forgave her: 'I have never seen her so regal in manner or half so brilliant, in spite of indifferent *fouettés* and an occasional jerkiness,' wrote Arnold Haskell. Tangye Lean was no less indulgent: 'The peculiar atmosphere of poetry which infuses the smallest of her movements merged perfectly with the sinister gloom of the second and fourth acts, but in the third, which demands sheer technique and a certain hardness of acting, she rose to it with a stability that one had not seen in her before.'[23]

In a discussion two days before the death of Baylis, de Valois had spoken of a long and cherished wish, made possible at last by plans to enlarge the dressing-rooms and scene dock at Sadler's Wells. What the two women had talked about at that last meeting was their ambition to mount a production of a ballet that even Diaghilev had failed to stage successfully. And now that an English ballerina had proved equal to one of the two great Russian masterpieces, the time had come to brave the other.

Overwhelmed as she must have been by the reception of her first full-length *Swan Lake*, Margot can hardly have imagined the rapturous response which, in this next ballet, would one day be hers. It was, of course, Tchaikovsky's *The Sleeping Beauty*.

Notwithstanding his intellectual credentials and debunking sense of humour, Constant Lambert had an unashamed fascination with the occult. He liked to claim that the Prelude to his new ballet, *Horoscope*, had been dictated to him from the other side of the grave by Bernard van Dieran (who had died in 1936), and certainly the eerie musical palindrome bears little stylistic resemblance to the rest of Lambert's work. His initials acknowledge authorship of the rather sketchy programme note for *Horoscope*, which runs: 'When people are born they have the sun in one sign of the Zodiac, the moon in another. This ballet takes for its theme a man who has the sun in Leo and the moon in Gemini, and a woman who also has the moon in Gemini but whose sun is in Virgo. The two opposed signs of Leo and Virgo, the one energetic and full-blooded, the other timid and sensitive, struggle to keep the man and woman apart. It is by their mutual sign, the Gemini, that they are brought together and by the moon that they are finally united.'

The autobiographical reference was there for mystics to ponder in Lambert's own astrological chart, which, sporting Sun in Leo and Moon in Gemini, flagrantly decorated the cover of the first-night programme. But, beyond that, fiction partly prevailed. Margot, who of course danced the Young Woman with the Sun in Virgo, was born under the sign of Taurus, with Moon in Sagittarius. The owner of the Virgo/Gemini signature was, as it happened, Frederick Ashton, but that was still not quite the true picture. Lambert believed that because the moment of his birth coincided with the exact hour in which the Sun quits the sign of Leo to enter Virgo, his nature was fated to be the battleground where romantic vision pitted itself against material reality. So, despite its dedication to Margot, *Horoscope* was a musical description of what he took to be his own elemental struggle between earth and fire, rather than a hymn to any creature of flesh and blood.

It is both flattering and discomfiting to be the muse of a great artist; and Margot was not the only one to suffer this peculiar form of persecution. Hard on the heels of her surrender to Constant Lambert had come Michael Somes's sexual capitulation to Frederick Ashton. And, as in Margot's case, it was difficult to disentangle erotic response from the drive for artistic development. 'I suppose Michael saw a Diaghilev quality in Ashton that was very glamorous,' says Alan Carter, who danced one of the Gemini Twins in *Horoscope*.[1] Taking advantage of Helpmann's temporary defection to the straight theatre, Ashton had plucked the twenty-year-old Somes from the *corps* to be Margot's new partner. But whereas, in succumbing to Lambert, Margot was following her true, physically adventurous, emotionally biddable nature, Michael Somes's stability was severely threatened by the pressure which Ashton brought to bear on his responses. It did not seem to worry the choreographer that, as he put it, 'Michael was never queer in any way,'[2] nor, indeed, that the object of his affection should have been on the rebound from a youthful romance with Pamela May, who, like Margot, had already met the man she was to marry, at Cambridge the previous summer. The obvious disturbance caused to Somes pervaded the atmosphere of rehearsals, which, according to Alan Carter, were 'het-up' to say the least. While Somes's brooding rages found their way into the aggressively springing steps and defensively clenched fists of the Young Man with the Sun in Leo, Pamela May was cool and inhumanly remote as the Moon, presiding over Sophie Fedorovitch's cloud-banked, monochrome sky. But, where Somes's partnering was concerned, Ashton felt utterly justified in the choice of his new lover as leading man. 'He looked wonderful behind Margot,' he protested. 'A hundred times better than Bobby Helpmann did. When Michael and Margot presented themselves on stage they looked a wonderful couple. I'm not saying that he was the greatest dancer in the world – he wasn't – but he was perfectly efficient at what he did. Michael did great turns in the air, he was very musical . . . and a beautiful creature – so why not? Who else was there?'[3]

In a note to Michael Somes on the first night, 27 January 1938, Ashton took a less pragmatic tone: 'Dance like a god,' he exhorted the boy[4] – and the audience was duly worshipful: there were twenty curtain calls. How much of the acclaim was meant for Lambert's music is hard to gauge, since the complete score of *Horoscope* was to suffer an unhappy wartime fate: only a concert suite survives. This, Lambert's biographer, Richard Shead, praises faintly as 'excellent light music – of which the twentieth century has produced little'.[5] But, at the time, comparisons were made with Stravinsky, to whose work, ironically, Lambert was antipathetic; yet if *Horoscope* is redolent of anything, it is of the Sixth Symphony by the composer who, in his book *Music Ho!*, he considers the most inimitable: 'Of all contemporary music that of Sibelius seems to point forward most surely to the future. Since the death of Debussy, Sibelius and Schönberg are the most significant figures in European music, and Sibelius is undoubtedly the more complete artist of the two . . . We are not likely to find any imitation of Sibelius No. 7, such as we find of Stravinsky's *Symphonie des Psaumes*, because the spiritual calm of this work is the climax of the spiritual experience of a lifetime and cannot be achieved by any aping of external mannerisms.'[6]

As specialist books go, *Music Ho!*, published in 1934, enjoyed quite a popular success; but it seems heavy going now, as it no doubt did at the time to Margot, for whom, as mistress of the author, it would have amounted to prescribed reading. But although, near the end of her life, the most she could be drawn to say of Constant was that 'he was on an intellectual level that was way over my head',[7] in these early, innocent days she sat at his feet, entirely in thrall, not just to the *enfant terrible* but also to what Andrew Motion calls the 'filthy-but-clever-schoolboy'[8] whose great relish for words could as easily find expression in the invention of a limerick as a piece of literature. Tom Driberg quoted an example in his book *Ruling Passions*.

The Bishop of Central Japan
Used to bugger himself with a fan,
When taxed with his acts
He explained: 'It contracts
And expands so much more than a man.'[9]

Lambert's uproarious flights of fancy, however, could be matched by a spiralling descent into a vortex of depression. Margot, not yet nineteen, now found herself exposed to the ravages of dipsomania. Constant and Flo, in the intense physicality of their exchange, had often come to blows: 'Lambert's married life was always rather extraordinary, to put it mildly,' says Anthony Powell. 'One night, he and Flo apparently had an awful row, and he socked her, and they made such a noise that the police came up and she had to say, "I had a terrible toothache, couldn't control myself and I was yelling." That sort of instance rather tended to take place.' Annie Lambert, too, attests to her mother's violence, which endured into her second marriage; and certainly Flo's volatility must have gone a long way towards provoking Constant's wrath. But whereas it is unlikely that Margot's natural acquiescence would have invited such scenes, she did, according to Herbert Ross, later confide to his wife, Nora Kaye, that she had come in for some rough treatment at the hands of Constant. How early she was aware of exactly what she had taken on, we cannot know; and probably any physical fear of him which she may have felt would have been outweighed, not just by the excitement of their mutual sexual voracity, but by her compassion for his turbulent and thwarted genius. And yet, one way or another, some instinct for self-preservation in her seems to have figured from the start. Despite her frequent visits to 'Hangover' Lodge (which Lambert also dubbed his 'shooting box'), where his many cats stalked about among the scattered music scores, there was no talk of cohabitation, let alone of marriage. Lambert's own domineering mother was as socially prejudiced against uneducated dancers as Mrs Hookham was against inebriated composers; and Margot remained, in public at least, primly under her mother's ample wing. 'Margot loses her head but not her heart,' Ashton would say of her[10] – until, of course, her marriage to Arias. But Margot counters: 'In truth I lost neither.'[11] And perhaps we should take her at her word. Again and again in her autobiography one is struck by the fact that, though she misleads us by omission, and often fools herself, she does not actually lie. In the summer of 1938, she saw Arias again at Cambridge. 'To my surprise he held me closely and asked, "Are you still mine?" Turmoil and confusion in my mind! I had prepared myself so completely for his lack of interest. In a tiny voice I said a reluctant "no". At any rate I would not lie to him.'[12] Too bad that she cannot bring herself to be more honest with *us*. But her small-voiced denial acts as a kind of code. It is as near as she can come to admitting that, however intact her head and heart might still have been, her body and soul were by then committed to Lambert.

Keeping company with Constant drew Margot into the magic inner circle from which all influence radiated at Sadler's Wells. Lunching with de Valois, Ashton and Chappell, she was privy to discussions of the production of *Sleeping Beauty* planned for the new season. The others had all seen Diaghilev's array of Russian ballerinas: Spessivtseva, Trefilova, Egorova and Lopokova. But to Margot the ballet was a blank – without even the ingrained image of Markova to haunt her. 'Who will dance Princess Aurora this time?' she was naïve enough to ask.[13]

(But how naïve was she? She had been dancing the *pas de deux* from *Aurora's Wedding* since 1936. The only other person to have done that had been Pearl Argyle, who wasn't used to dancing full-length ballets.) De Valois was not taken in. 'Why, *you*,' she snapped,[14] and resumed her quarrel with Constant as to who should be hired as designer. He favoured Edmund Dulac; she, Nadia Benois. In 1921 the choice had been Léon Bakst, and the sets and costumes had been lavish – too lavish, in fact: 'The dress rehearsal was a disaster,' wrote Diaghilev. 'The stage machinery did not work; the trees in the enchanted woods did not sprout; the tulle skirts got tangled in the flats. The première suffered accordingly, and the financial losses that ensued were incalculable. By staging this ballet I nearly killed off my theatrical venture abroad.'[15] (The Russian impresario did not mention, and presumably neither did de Valois, to Margot, that Spessivtseva, making her excitedly awaited début in London, had slipped as she began her first variation, and fallen flat on her back.)

Diaghilev blamed, as well as his own timing, the ignorance of the public. 'I am fifteen years too early with this ballet,' he calculated.[16] Now, seventeen years down the line, de Valois was about to put his prophecy to the test. She was adamant that her version should not be encumbered by opulent plumes or complicated effects, and her will triumphed over Constant's: Nadia Benois was engaged. But Diaghilev's 'magnificent disaster' was, if anything, over-corrected. When Margot first saw the sketches and fabrics for her costumes, she almost burst into tears. They were plain to the point of drabness, like 'little cotton house frocks'.[17] Not a sequin in sight. Sharing Lambert's hedonistic way of life had caused her to grow plumper than she had ever been in her life, and she desperately needed the boost of a glamorous wardrobe. How would she ever be able to pass herself off as the Beauty of the fairy story? Just as well that the ballet had been renamed, as in Diaghilev's time, *The Sleeping Princess*. But how could she be even *that*, with a crown made of cardboard? Well, at least she had her own hair (which, unlike ballerinas of today, who scrape theirs back in a tight bun, she was to wear in a 'classical': parted at the centre, wound and pinned in two coils over the ears, and supported by a hairnet). Most of the budget seems to have gone on the boys' 'truly hideous wigs';[18] and having his name changed from Désiré to Florimund did not save Robert Helpmann, as the Prince, from finding himself saddled with the worst wig of all – 'a blond page-boy affair that flapped as he danced'.[19]

When it came to reproducing, as closely as possible, the original Petipa choreography, de Valois enlisted the services of Nicholas Sergeyev, former ballet master and notator of the Maryinsky, whom she had brought over from Paris, where, but for his precious smuggled manuscripts, he would have starved. '[Sergeyev's] rehearsals were a nightmare,' wrote Elizabeth Miller, 'and never got any easier – all of us prostrate on the floor, poring over his little pin-men, and trying to decipher which way they went, and where we were supposed to go, ending up with frayed tempers and utter frustration as he could not make himself understood . . . Madam tried to interpret, boiling inwardly.'[20] To confuse matters further, de Valois kept calling secret rehearsals, which only incited Sergeyev, a taskmaster at the best of times, into whacking the dancers' calves harder than usual with his fine malacca cane.

Margot's self-doubt, meanwhile, did not abate. 'She was sure she couldn't do a big important ballet like that,' writes her mother. 'The weather that year was very cold and foggy and coming out of the theatre she was miserable, so she needed a lot of cosseting for a while. The next time I saw Ninette I told her about it and she said, "Don't worry, she will be all right and do it well, but she is one of those people who have to frighten themselves into doing things they imagine they can't do."'

The opening night, on 2 February 1939, took place during one of London's pea-soupers – the thick fog which, before the Clean Air Act, could bring the great capital to a standstill. Against the odds, *The Sleeping Princess* succeeded. But, like Margot's own career, which this fairy-tale would come to epitomize, it was not an overnight triumph. It grew slowly in the public's esteem. And although it was the ballet chosen for the Command Performance – in honour of the President of the French Republic at Covent Garden on 22 March – the Prologue and three acts were considered too testing for so illustrious an audience, which included George VI, Queen Elizabeth and the two princesses; so only Acts I and III were presented, with a rest in the middle, during which Sir Thomas Beecham conducted the London Philharmonic Orchestra in Debussy's *Ibéria*.

When the ballet was televised – twice – at Alexandra Palace, it was again in this truncated two-act version. It seems strange, now, to consider what artistic prejudice could trust an audience to tolerate such unmelodic, starkly modern works as Bliss's *Checkmate*, or Lambert's own *Horoscope*, just because they did not last a whole evening, while doubting the chances of so accessible a composer as Tchaikovsky. Oddly, the music for *Sleeping Beauty* was not well known at the time. Constant Lambert makes no mention of it in *Music Ho!*,[21] and had, on his lectern, the only extant score in London. Yet, as the music swelled under his baton, he must surely have wondered how Tchaikovsky's melodies, so peerlessly conducive to movement, could possibly have been dismissed by the London critics in 1921 as 'circus music'.[22] Ironically, what needed to be developed was not public confidence; it was confidence in the public. There is, however, no greater testament to success than subsequent satire; and a mad burlesque called *The Creaking Princess*, shown in Herbert Farjeon's *Little Revue*, where Hermione Baddeley and Cyril Ritchard appeared as Mme Allova and Harold Helpmeet, proved just how fashionable a note *The Sleeping Princess* had struck. Despite their political estrangement, England and Russia were not as far apart, culturally, as they pretended to be. 'Keep your spirits up,' Diaghilev had written to Bakst. 'Strange as it may seem, our best classical ballets were fairy plays.'[23] London had taken this fairy play to its heart. And the day would come when America would do the same. Meanwhile, a strange accolade came to Margot from across the Atlantic: Walt Disney sent her a drawing of Donald Duck dressed as a ballerina. Her pleasure and amusement were tempered by genuine astonishment: 'How does he know about me?'[24]

The hand of fate, which seems to have guarded Margot's reputation as zealously as it promoted it, ensured that she was not cast in Ashton's next ballet, which would turn out to be something of a fiasco. *Cupid and Psyche* was, observed Mary Clarke, 'an attempt to treat a rather sad little story in an ultra-smart and witty fashion'.[25] But the joke misfired, culminating as it did in a chorus-line of fascist goose-stepping which was bound to offend nervous pre-war sensibilities. The dancer to whom the ill-starred role of Psyche fell was the enchanting Julia Farron, who, aged only sixteen, already had other problems: no sooner had Ashton discovered her than she found herself the latest object of Michael Somes's doggedly heterosexual advances. Sparks flew, too, over the questionable adequacy of Lord Berners's music, and Constant 'took to the bottle',[26] repairing himself only just in time to conduct the first performance. Pamela May, who sensibly fell ill, made no such timely recovery, so Margot, stepping in for her at the last minute in the small part of Ceres, was subject to the ignominy of being booed for the first and only time in her life. But, essentially, the failure of *Cupid and Psyche* did not reflect on her, and she ended the season triumphantly with a performance of *The Sleeping Princess* on 18 May, her twentieth birthday.

The usual dates of Cambridge, Oxford and Bournemouth were played before the company disbanded for the holidays. But, this year, Tito Arias, having graduated BA with third class honours in Law, was no longer at Cambridge to hold Margot close and interrogate her about her fidelity. It was his own that was in question. For, despite the fact that the last time Margot had seen him had been in Paris, when he had twice taken her to lunch, back in London an inadvertent remark by a friend had thrown her into turmoil. The friend in question was Charles Gordon (who coincidentally – after Painton Cowan had been killed in action – became the second husband of Pamela May). 'Charles was in Paris with Tito just before the war in '39,' says Pamela, 'and Tito went off with this girl – he was a bit frivolous.' The girl was American, and married, and her name was Mrs Gordon, so it is no wonder that Charles Gordon let mention of her slip. In a letter to Pamela and Charles after Tito's death, Margot has not forgotten. She wonders if they remember the American Mrs Gordon whom Tito had run around with in Paris. Love is no respecter of irony, and the fact that Margot was 'running around' with a married man herself at the time did not lessen the blow that this piece of idle gossip caused her, the pain of which was to last all her life. 'Interesting that she remembers it so clearly,' says Pamela. 'It so broke her heart.

Charles dropped a brick and she was heartbroken. That she even mentions it, so many years later, says so much.'

Margot thought she heard a porter shout something which made her blood freeze as he ran along the platform at Liverpool station, banging shut the doors of the train. It was Sunday, 3 September 1939, and while the rest of the nation had its ear pressed to the wireless, waiting for Chamberlain's broadcast, the company had boarded a train bound for Leeds.

'I think he said, "War declared," ' Margot ventured, but none of the others in her compartment would have it. Nonsense, they said, he was just shouting 'All clear', and went back to doing what dancers do on tedious train journeys: play cards, snooze, moan about their aches and pains. Bobby Helpmann had a routine into which he launched whenever boredom set in – one featuring an outrageously grand prima donna who must suffer the theatrical digs of a northern landlady called Mrs Snodgrass – and Constant would obligingly play stooge to his camp ravings. But when, an hour or two later, the train stopped at Crewe, all laughter and moaning abruptly ceased. This time there could be no mistaking the message being bawled through the loudspeakers. For the second time in twenty-one years, Britain was at war with Germany.

The dancers did not know what to do. Should they return home to London? De Valois decided that they should go on to Leeds, where at least they had hotel bookings – by tomorrow the picture would be clearer. But by that same evening they knew the worst: the Home Office had closed every theatre and cinema in the land. The company was to consider itself disbanded.

Nevertheless the troupe clung together, afraid, as everyone was, of an immediate apocalypse; and, indeed, a siren did sound in the night, causing Margot and Pamela to leap from their hotel beds and rush, wrapped in blankets, to an air-raid shelter in the basement. On their way, they ran into de Valois, who told them not to be ridiculous. 'Go back and get into your dressing-gowns at once,' she commanded.[27] More unflappable still was Constant

Lambert, who shuffled into the dusty cellar long after all the rest were huddled there, brandishing the *Times* crossword and demanding everyone's full concentration on the clues.

There was no air raid. But this first night of what was to become known as the 'phoney war' taught the girls a lesson – in style if not sense. Pamela May, who often stayed with Margot in Egerton Gardens, does not remember them ever going into an air-raid shelter together again. 'Margot's flat was on two floors,' she explains, 'so when a siren sounded we just ran down to the floor below.'[28]

Alone in London, Mrs Hookham remembers 'staring out of the window in the sitting-room across the road at the Brompton Road tube station which had recently been closed (it was later said it was a very hush-hush Government Operations place) and wondering what would happen to us all, and thinking this would be the second time I had been living in a 3rd floor flat when war was declared. All young men were to be called up and I thought of Stanley and young Felix. Was this going to be another carnage of young lives? Well, what can't be cured must be endured, so we must all live as normally as possible.'

As if responding to her advice, the company soon found a way of regrouping. Within two weeks the theatres had re-opened and Ashton had taken matters into his own hands: he extracted backing from Alice von Hofmannsthal and the art historian Kenneth Clark to take the company on tour through the provinces on a cooperative basis – principals and *corps de ballet* alike to be paid £5 a week. No orchestra: Constant Lambert would play the piano, as would the company's adored rehearsal pianist, Hilda Gaunt. They would, in de Valois's words, be 'like a little concert party';[29] and, for once, she felt no inclination to shepherd them. Ashton saw her sudden immersion in her 'private life', which usually got such short shrift, as a betrayal. 'Ninette – wonderful Ninette, said that a woman's place is in the home, and she went away and disappeared. She absolutely abandoned us. But that's never written about. When Ninette saw it was going to work she came back and took the whole thing in her hands again.'[30] But who is to say what spiritual blow the outbreak of war might have dealt a woman of de Valois's visionary idealism? Having been born into a military family, she was, in many ways, less an artist than a general, and, as such, she worried about her men, who, with the exception of Helpmann (on account of his nationality) and Lambert (on account of his lameness), stood to be conscripted. Yet how could she, the most passionate of patriots, countenance their not fighting for their country? Arthur-My-Husband's partner in his medical practice was soon to be called up; and if, for a while, she saw her duty as a wifely one, helping to run the surgery, who could blame her? Well – Ashton, to name but one. But his harsh judgement can perhaps best be explained by his resentment that de Valois should have failed to engineer his own exemption from military service. Instead, her darling Helpmann remained free not only to dance throughout the years of the war, but to usurp Ashton's position, while the choreographer himself was 'clapped into light blue serge and relegated to what fliers consider the lowest form of service life – that of ground staff'.

The company reassembled in Cardiff on 18 September, where they suffered the stiff and aching limbs which are bound to beset dancers flung back on to the stage after a fortnight without class. On 2 October they set off on the tour, which was to include Leicester, Leeds, Southsea, Brighton, Cambridge and Nottingham. In each town they gave six evening performances and three matinées per week. They had never worked harder in their lives, but received scant appreciation from the newly recruited troops who comprised the grudging audiences at the military camps where the ballets were staged, and who would walk out before the end, cursing and banging their seats as they went, utterly unpersuaded by floating sylphs, chess-pieces in tights and tormented signs of the Zodiac. Nevertheless, the dancers were glad to be dancing: camaraderie would never again be so strong as in those days when, half-starved, they braved the freezing dressing-rooms, the damp digs with outdoor lavatories, the lukewarm bath water, the tiny stages, the concrete floors, and the interminable trains crawling spasmodically through the blacked-out countryside.

Hunger can cure the most entrenched food faddiness, and even Margot found it hard to sustain her antipathy to real eggs in the face of dried-egg omelettes served up in north-country digs. Over one such repast Ashton grabbed the Bible and said he was going to read it from the first page to the last, by which time the war would be over. (Alas, he miscalculated by four years.) He began aloud, in tones of plangent piety, calculated to elicit groans from the company; but, in fact, the religious language infected him with a new spiritual fervour which was to colour, in contrasting ways, his next two beautiful and serious ballets, *Dante Sonata* and *The Wise Virgins*.

Margot, since her callisthenics in Shanghai, had only once danced barefoot – as a Slave Girl in the opera *Aida*. Now, in *Dante Sonata*, she had the chance not only to shed her *pointe* shoes but to let down her black silky hair for the sheer sensuous release of it, rather than to denote a character's derangement. Sophie Fedorovitch based her designs on John Flaxman's illustrations for *The Divine Comedy* and, again, the idea was to leave the dancers' bodies unfettered for absolute physical abandon. Pamela May remembers Sophie joining them on tour in Hull, where, 'between the matinée and the evening show she would pin yards of white material to our shoulders, trying to decide what length to make these dresses. "Now Margot – *run!*" It was tight round the waist, then it was loose, with a long train behind. "Pamela – *run!*" And it was such *fun*. You felt you were part of it all.'

Constant Lambert played for all the rehearsals, so that when he came to orchestrate the music – Liszt's sonata, inspired by Victor Hugo's *D'Après une Lecture de Dante* – the work had the rare unity that is particular to intense collaboration. Certainly the dancers were caught up in the great tumult of Ashton's emotional response to the war: 'I felt I hadn't said nearly enough to be ready to die on it,' which seemed to speak for all of them.[31] Margot Fonteyn and Michael Somes led the Children of Light, oppressed by the Children of Darkness, led by Robert Helpmann and June Brae; but, for all the ballet's warring forces of good and evil, Ashton did not mean it to be a propagandist piece. 'People said I was affected by the violation of Poland and all that,' he protested. 'I don't think I was. It was more about the futility of war and how nobody wins in the end.'[32] In fact, the power of the piece was therapeutic. 'Most of us,' P.W. Manchester thought at the time, 'feel that the world is too much for us, and we would give anything to be able to roll on the floor and tear our hair and scream. *Dante Sonata* does it for us.'[33]

The company returned to Sadler's Wells on 26 December for a month's trial, to see, despite the fear, as yet unrealized, of enemy aircraft reaching the capital, whether audiences would be brave enough to fill the theatre. They were not. Even though the gallery was as packed as ever, the stalls and circle remained woefully under-populated. It was *Dante Sonata* that saved the day; for what in peacetime might have seemed a turgid emotional wallow proved, in those early days of the war, a profoundly affecting experience; to have seen it became a patriotic necessity, and there was a scramble for seats, resulting in an extension of the season. In 'this simple and tragic *pièce d'occasion*,' wrote Elizabeth Frank, Fonteyn was 'a new and heartbreaking revelation'.[34]

From the frenzied opulence of Liszt, Ashton turned to the celestial serenity of Bach, the composer least used in ballet – possibly because his structural perfection can so easily make visual embellishment seem like impertinence. *The Wise Virgins* was the choreographer's 'holy ballet', drawn from a parable (Matthew XXV). Barefoot again, Margot was this time chastely wrapped by Rex Whistler in flowing robes reminiscent of an Italian Renaissance painting. Whereas in *Dante Sonata* there had been passionate angst, here was a mood of patient, dignified acceptance. The legendary Indian dancer Ram Gopal had recently appeared in London, and Ashton was inspired by the oriental delicacy of his hand-movements to make a particularly beautiful solo for Margot, laying emphasis on her rapt and meditative aptitude for stillness, which would be described one day, in another, greater, ballet, as 'the still centre of the world'.[35] Meanwhile, of Margot as the Bride, Gordon Anthony wrote: 'She seemed to surround herself with a great tenderness and peace. Fonteyn was as worthy of this ballet as it was of her.'[36]

It was April 1940, and already the bond between the dancers and their public had deepened. The war years, instead of being the cultural desert of glum prediction, proved to be remarkably fertile. Solace is most quickly found through poetry and music, and the once narrowly élitist preserves of opera and ballet began to gain an almost plebeian popularity. War was terrifying, of course, but it could also, between air raids, be monumentally dull. All over the country people sat around, separated from their families and lovers, in a state of restlessness which the authorities determined to mobilize.

Although Winston Churchill was himself a thoroughgoing Conservative, he was presiding over a coalition government, many of whose members were to form the innovative Labour administration of 1945. It was a passionate belief of the left, and a fashionable philosophy among intellectuals, that hope for the future lay in the cultural education of the masses. Here were thousands of young men and women, most of whom had never read a book, never gone to a theatre, never seen an original painting – youths whose only stimulation had been the escapist romances, musicals and thrillers of Hollywood. The opportunity for experiment was unique. Every army camp, naval depot, aerodrome, factory and mine was infiltrated with pale, young, bespectacled officers only too ready to lecture the befuddled inmates on Proust or Post-Impressionism.

But it was not all political patronage. From the ugliness of war emerged an appetite for beauty that was as urgent as it was genuine. The painters Paul Nash, John Piper and Graham Sutherland were recruited as war artists. They produced, rather than the expected odalisques or views from windows in Arles, images of what they actually saw around them. An astonishing exhibition of infernos was mounted by recruits to the fire service;

and burgeoning art lovers, while visiting the National Gallery, could also drop in for a piano recital given by Myra Hess, classical music's answer to Vera Lynn. Even the cinema grew high-minded: Noël Coward broke the mould by appropriating Rachmaninov's Piano Concerto No. 2 as background music for *Brief Encounter* (1945), and an absurdly romantic film, *Dangerous Moonlight* (1941), featured handsome Anton Walbrook, who, pausing on his way to become a Spitfire pilot, tore off a rip-roaring rendition of Richard Addinsell's Warsaw Concerto, which sold in its thousands and was endlessly requested on the wireless as a Forces' Favourite. The very stasis of so much service-life left people with little alternative but to read: small, new, inexpensive Penguin paperbacks of the classics and the best contemporary writing, which could hastily be slipped into the pocket of a soldier's battledress.

As for the theatre, it was in its golden age, with John Gielgud at the helm, giving, in 1944 alone, five plays in repertory at the Haymarket – *Hamlet*, *Love for Love*, *The Circle*, *A Midsummer Night's Dream* and *The Duchess of Malfi* – with Peggy Ashcroft as leading lady. In the same year, the great Old Vic season at the New Theatre starred Laurence Olivier as Richard III and Ralph Richardson as Peer Gynt. The provinces were bustling with tours of shows, put on by countless education and entertainment bodies, each with its plethora of capital letters: ABCA, CEMA, and Sadler's Wells's very own sponsor, ENSA – Every Night Something Awful, as it was fondly known.[37]

'It was incredible what Margot did during the war,' says Ninette de Valois. 'We thought nothing of asking her to do three *Lacs des Cygnes* in one week. No ballerina would *look* at that number of performances today. Mind you, it toughened her up.' Clement Crisp agrees. 'She knew she had a duty to keep herself performing. She was rarely off. Same with Helpmann, who was a more important figure than she was, then, and worked bloody hard too. During the war she knocked herself out – I've seen her dance six ballets in a day. Whatever came to her afterwards, she'd earned it. When the moment came, she never got it wrong. But you don't get it right just by luck; you get it right by being extremely skilled and extremely hardworking. The war played into her hands in a way – it sharpened the public's appreciation. And there was no rivalry. All those terrible Russians – Riabouchinska, Toumanova, Danilova – were out of the picture. Margot had a completely free run. It gave her time, as an artist, to grow up.'

9

The person who had the bright idea of sending a band of un-protected dancers – some little more than children – into the jaws of the imminent German *Blitzkrieg* was Lord Lloyd, head of the British Council. Lloyd was a great devotee of ballet, and the notion that the neutral countries would benefit from a little cultural propaganda in the form of a visit from Sadler's Wells seemed as good a way as any of convincing the Foreign Office that the call-up of valuable male dancers, even if not averted indefinitely, should at least be postponed for a couple of months. In 1940, the kingdom of the Netherlands stood apart from the rest of Europe. The Dutch, encouraged by the neutrality sustained in the First World War, had gone to great lengths to avoid providing Hitler with any excuse to attack them. But he had already invaded Denmark and Norway – without warning. And so, as the ballet company sallied forth from King's Cross Station, on 6 May, to a Holland quite unprepared for war, Bobby announced: 'If the ship gets hit, I shall swim breast-stroke, with my head well back. I could never look the Dutch in the face if my perm got wet and went into a frizz like one of those ten-shilling do's.'[1]

Though Helpmann's waves remained dry, the voyage across the rough North Sea was not exactly a breeze. The seasick company was herded into male and female communal cabins, with bunks from floor to ceiling – a luxury, had they but known it, compared with what was to come. But Rotterdam, when they disembarked, sparkled with sunshine and cleanliness, and the bus to The Hague overtook hundreds of leisurely cyclists, necks and handlebars garlanded with tulips. By evening, the whole company had become besotted with things foreign: the pink joints of ham and shining yellow cheeses; plentiful sugar and butter – unrationed, if you please; and, above all, the bright lights of the city against the navy summer sky – English nights having been plunged into gloomy blackout.

What was more, the first-night audience, in full anachronistic evening regalia (tiaras and long white gloves), adored the modern English offerings (*Checkmate* and *Dante Sonata*). In a poetic gesture at the curtain calls, tulip petals rained from high in the flies down over the dancers' bowing heads. The affirmation of friendship and cultural regard was all that the British Council could have dreamed of. But next day, on the bus to Hengelo, close to the German border, the dream began to sour. Most members of the company, who, like Margot, were lucky to have had a single day's schooling since the age of fourteen, had no notion of geography, and still less of history; but they could still tell a dangerous and unprotected landscape when they saw one. Vast areas of country-side had been flooded; ten-foot-high cement barriers with iron spikes stuck out into the road, which was fenced with massive barbed-wire entanglements. Apart from groups of soldiers standing around with fixed bayonets, there was not a soul in sight. There had clearly been a mass evacuation.

At Hengelo, when the unsoldierly-looking ballet boys and the girls in their pretty English spring frocks stepped down from the bus, they were jeered at by children and spat at by adults: the place was plainly teeming with German sympathizers. De Valois would have sent the younger girls back to The Hague at once, but it was impossible: the roads were blocked and the government had commandeered the trains. Nothing to be done but dance – even if the local orchestra did not exactly help. In what felt like an anti-British gesture, the Dutch musicians squeaked and squawked their way through Walton's *Façade*. 'Violins raced to catch up,' wrote Annabel Farjeon in her journal, *Ballet Behind the Borders*, 'woodwind started and stopped in the middle of a phrase while some deep instrument boomed on steadily, regardless of everything . . . Finally to our horror Constant began to sing. Like many conductors his voice was not musical, hardly in tune.'[2] He was not the only one to resort to song. And, in *The Rake's Progress*, he did not sing alone. The *corps de ballet* had made up a ribald ditty to accompany the brothel scene; and now the lyrics rang out, loud enough for the audience to hear: Oh dearie me / I do want to pee / and I don't really care if the orchestra sees me. 'After being shut up all day in that bus,' explained Farjeon, 'the rough theatre, the uncertainty of our welcome and the sense of dislocation in the town contributed to the release of all constraint.'[3]

Next morning, on a blackboard in the middle of the market place, some news about the English government was being chalked up. A South African girl in the company could make out the Dutch well enough to tell that it was something to do with the Chamberlain administration having fallen. And it was true that matters had reached a crisis at home. Public disquiet at the Anglo-French failure in Norway could not be glossed over; and on 13 May Winston Churchill, with his offer to the nation of nothing but 'blood, toil, tears and sweat', took over as Prime Minister. But here in Hengelo, the dancers' concept of sweat and toil was narrowly bound up in the exhaustion from the previous night's performance, and the preparation for the one to come – at the Philips factory in Eindhoven, which mercifully was less close to the German border. Most of the troupe used the five-hour journeys to and from The Hague to catch up on lost sleep. But the following day, not even the most exhausted and self-centred among them could close their eyes as the bus trundled towards their next date, Arnhem. Hundreds of refugees, dragging their children and their hastily bundled belongings, were trudging along the roadside – but trudging in the opposite direction to the bus: clearly they were fleeing from the very place where Sadler's Wells was due to perform. However, at the theatre, tulip petals – not bombs – rained upon them; and the English-Netherlands Society provided the usual sumptuous feast. Yet, despite the gluttony which can take hold of performers at the end of a show, the dancers left half-finished their platefuls of ham and salad, and piled back into the bus, as anxious to return to The Hague as de Valois was to get them there. It was 3 a.m. by the time they fell into bed.

An hour later they fell out again – two of the party more rudely awoken than the rest. The menacing throb of aircraft, and a sharp fusillade of gunfire, sent the dancers racing through the corridors of the Hôtel du Passage, bursting into one another's rooms, to announce that German troops had surrounded the city and were parachuting down out of the sky. And now, a second newsflash rocked the hotel. Margot Fonteyn had been discovered in bed with Constant Lambert. Stumbling down, half asleep, to the hotel lobby where the company had gathered, Annabel Farjeon remembered: 'I could not be bothered by the fact that the long expected invasion had begun. I was struck by Margot's dressing-gown.'[4] It was apparently a full-sleeved and high-waisted garment of extraordinary romantic allure, in purple and pale blue taffeta. Nobody could take their eyes off Margot that night, in her newly uncovered identity of fallen woman. 'Her long black hair fell over her shoulders, her face and hands were pale . . . She looked breathtakingly beautiful.'[5] And beside her, equally mesmerizing in his own voluminous way, was Constant. 'Looking very dishevelled,' says Patricia Garnett. 'Shirt all undone. No tie. What little hair he had, all disarranged. You could almost see that they'd . . . They looked so . . .' She cannot find the words, but the inference is that, despite the serious danger, the suddenly exposed lovers had about them the careless exultation of two people living intensely and defiantly for the moment, as lovers in time of war are wont to do.

Margot's fabled negligée – along with the scenery, costumes and scores for *Checkmate*, *Façade*, *The Rake's Progress*, *Les Patineurs*, *Dante Sonata* and *Horoscope* – had to be left behind in The Hague. The dancers would be lucky to get away in the clothes that they were wearing, and were told to confine their belongings to one hold-all apiece. At first they waited excitedly to be rescued, dashing up on to the roof to watch the planes unleashing showers of leaflets which read: 'The German army protects the life and goods of every peace-loving citizen. However the German troops will punish every deed of violence committed by the population with a death sentence.' Like the stars that they were, Margot, Bobby, Constant and Michael climbed on to an even higher roof, only to crouch behind a chimney-pot as a black bomber seemed to dive directly at them. Shooed down to the cellars by de Valois, they were kept cheerful by Bobby, who assumed the persona of an incorrigible fan telephoning the worried mothers: 'Those *poor* girls. Simply surrounded by Germans . . . *Poor* Margot. And such a promising little dancer . . .'[6]

In fact, Mrs Hookham was in Gloucestershire when she first got wind of the danger. Theyre Lee-Elliot had invited her to spend several months at his cousin's fifteenth-century house. 'We heard on the radio that the Germans had invaded Holland. Needless to say I was worried to death . . . I walked up and down the garden path for ages, wondering what to do and when I could get information. Anyway I must get back to London immediately. I went indoors to pack. Petrol was rationed but I still had the car and could get back.'

There was, however, no sign of transport for the sleepless dancers waiting at their hotel in The Hague. As time wore on, even Helpmann's mood grew sombre. Next day someone trying to tune in to the news picked up an English wireless programme called 'Up in the Morning Early'. It was a keep-fit class for housewives – 'And push, and bend, and *lift* your leg,' instructed a condescending BBC voice.[7] To everyone's astonishment, but without a hint of mockery, Bobby now rose in silence and took hold of the back of a chair, to follow the banal instructions as though he were taking part in that ritual sacred to ballet dancers – morning class. One by one the other dancers solemnly got up and followed suit, impervious to the broadcaster's voice: 'Little bounce, little bounce and UP!'[8] Suddenly the hotel lounge was alive with effort and energy; and, for the length of the programme, all anxiety was banished, as it is banished daily in a dancer's life, during that hour of absolute identification with the body.

Not until 6 p.m. did two buses finally come to fetch them.

Everyone was eccentrically attired. Some of the girls wore dinner jackets. De Valois had donned Ashton's, which he couldn't bear to leave behind. Margot was sporting boy's socks with her high-heeled shoes. And thus they bade farewell to their brave Dutch agents, who had taken such risks to arrange their escape, while Bobby, posing as Miss Hook of Holland, performed a valedictory clog dance, the mad wit of which would one day find its way into an Ashton masterpiece.

Their overcrowded charabancs crept fitfully through the streets, past a building sliced in two by a German plane, its domestic innards laid bare like an opened doll's house. It was the sort of sight that would soon be commonplace in London, but this was the dancers' initiation into urban horror. The darkening countryside beyond The Hague was lit by distant flames; its flattened stillness broken by closer gunfire. Their Dutch guards did not seem to know where they were headed: when questioned, one of them simply said: '*Ik ben een Jood. I bewaar der laste kogel vor Hitler.*' (I am a Jew. I am saving the last bullet for Hitler.)[9] Every half-hour the buses stopped and changed direction as new groups of parachutists dropped into the woods ahead. At one of these stops, Leslie Edwards recalls how 'a group of Dutch soldiers appeared and snatched one of their supposed company off the bus and started shouting at him: our driver managed to close the door and we moved off. However, the people in the rear seats, looking back, were aghast to see the guard, whom we had watched being interrogated on our bus, shot dead.'[10] Soon after, the two buses became separated. It took nine hours to travel fifty miles.

Suddenly, in the ghostly blackness, the dancers were told to get out, but to stick together. Gravel crunched beneath their feet. They were at a small nineteenth-century country estate in some place called Velsen. The shuttered house was crammed with refugees, and although a mattress was eventually found upstairs for de Valois, who had been stricken for days with one of her violent migraines, everyone else had to find floor-space in the reception rooms. But there was no hope of sleep.

Margot and Constant went out into the grounds to watch the day break. Being so far from home held, for them, one advantage – the absence of Margot's mother. And despite the waiting and the worry, here, in this enormous garden and within the indulgent atmosphere of the company, they were released at last from lies, and could be openly together. Love, when it stirs the heart, lays bare the senses and makes us intricately, almost painfully susceptible to the beauty of nature. And Margot's enraptured memory of that morning, her vivid description of its charm, reads like an allegorical admission of the degree to which she had fallen under Constant's spell: 'The chilly air was sweet and fresh, and trees took shape as the light grew. Slowly there came the miraculous unfolding of a picture so serene and exquisite, touched with morning dew and the promise of a fine warm day . . . A mist-laden lake, rushes, flowering shrubs, pathways and broad lawns came into view as the first vigilant birds alerted others to the hour of wakening. These stirrings of dawn quickly provoked more movement by the water's edge, as a variety of ducks shook their feathers, while herons, treading with extreme care, delicately lowered their long legs and stirred life into some deer who softly stretched and wandered away into the park to start a day that, for them, would not be different from any other.'[11]

Members of the company remember her energy that day – so marked in the face of their own fatigue – and how it cheered them through the hours of waiting. 'She made quite a joke of it,' says Moyra Fraser. 'I can see her larking about. I can see her playing football. She was quite a tomboy. Loved an occasion, joining in, being one of us.'

More refugees arrived, and the food – small pieces of tough steak and fried potatoes – ran out. It was midnight before the company could move on – marched out into the darkness in a crocodile, hanging on to one another's shoulders. They spent much of the ensuing three-hour journey flat on the floor of the buses, to avoid stray bullets. At the port of Ymuiden a long line of refugees waited to board an old cargo boat called *The*

Dotterel. The dancers stood in the thick snaking queue, edging a step forward every ten minutes while searchlights swooped low over their heads and bombs fell close by. When at last they braved the frightening gap between boat and jetty where the gangway should have been, they heard English voices calling: 'Vic-Wells, this way.'[12] But the way was down, deep into the tramp-steamer's dirty hold, where, by the light of hurricane lamps, people huddled in the straw. The smell was foul: there were no sanitary arrangements other than a few communal buckets behind a canvas curtain. Once again, the North Sea was rough and almost everyone was sick. The ship was bombarded all the way, as the Germans suspected Queen Wilhelmina to have been on board; and by the time the fifteen-hour crossing was at an end, and they were at last allowed on to the deck, romance had faded even for Margot: not only had Constant secretly consumed a whole bottle of brandy, pinched from Ashton's luggage, but he was pacing up and down, sweating with pain – not from any glorious war-wound, but from a speck of cigar-ash in his eye. As the ship came within sight of Harwich, Margot tidied him up as best she could, standing on tiptoe to re-tie the silk handkerchief that bandaged his head. But the ordeal was not yet over. They had dropped anchor outside the harbour on what happened to be Whit Monday, so no one from the Admiralty had given permission for a ship to enter. The official who informed them that they would have to spend another night aboard hadn't reckoned with de Valois. 'You're an idiot,' she roared. 'My good man, where's your common sense? Pig-headed fool! . . . No one minded putting up with the crossing: we knew it couldn't be helped. But to come back to one's own country to panic and stupidity and down-right incompetence . . . that's too much . . . You can get every man, woman and child off this boat before nightfall, and that is what you are going to do.'[13]

Unsurprisingly, a motor launch was brought alongside so that the crazy Vic-Wells woman and her charges could be hustled away. Two of the younger girls fainted when their feet touched dry land, but there were still endless formalities to be endured. Not until 3 a.m. did the train finally deposit the filthy and bedraggled dancers at Liverpool Street. There to meet them were a few dauntless fans – plus, of course, Mrs Hookham. Game, sophisticated Margot was suddenly a child again at the sight of her mother. She asked if she could bring Joy Newton, whose relatives were in the north of England, back to Egerton Gardens for the night. Such was the girls' exhaustion that Mrs Hookham herself had to bathe them. She cooked them an omelette – eggs – which Margot wolfed down without a murmur. Mrs Hookham asked no questions: 'I waited till the next day to hear all about it.' In fact, the girls would have slept the clock round, but an important date loomed – not Margot's twenty-first birthday in four days' time, but their regular appointment at the *barre*, in leotard and tights, at ten o'clock on Wednesday morning.

Professionals, the saying goes, can do it even when they don't feel like it; amateurs can't, even when they do. And because Margot had always been such an arch-professional, there were many, many times when she did not feel like working at all. There are few vocations with a higher reputation for dedication than the ballet. But 'dedication' was not a word that Margot would have dreamed of ascribing to herself. It would have struck her as far too precious and assuming, and would not have made allowance for the flighty girl who liked to stay out late at parties, or sometimes danced more carelessly in a small role than a large one, or who would cushion her aching feet in old, soft *pointe* shoes at the expense of proper support.

Yet Pamela May insists that, after a night of too much champagne, it would always be Margot who would be standing over her the next morning, trying to haul her out of bed for class – an attempt on Margot's part, perhaps, to muster support in her struggle against what she considered her greatest fault: laziness. Of course, by ordinary standards, such self-censure seems absurd. But, by the brutally exacting ethic which classical dancers must follow, the accusation was not devoid of substance. Ninette de

Valois, for one, endorses it – and in print – probably because Margot so loathed the dry, repetitive Cecchetti method in which de Valois's own formative training had been steeped. But the most gifted artists are often the least naturally hard-working, because the battle, almost from the beginning, is not against rivals but against the much subtler foe of their own inherent limitations. It was one thing for Margot to rush headlong into the challenge of a new role on stage before an audience; whereas to toil quietly in front of a mirror in a classroom, trying to consolidate, over many hours, the progress that her body had made in a moment of excitement, was quite another. She was twenty-one and could no longer be considered a promising child; indeed, so brief can be a ballet career that some of her contemporaries, if they were not soon to be put out of action by injury (Pamela May), were already beginning to drift towards motherhood (June Brae), or even retirement (Mary Honer). To sustain a calling is as much a matter of maintenance as it is of development, and Margot must now, in the face of the talent that was flooding into Sadler's Wells, strive conscientiously to hold on to the position which she had gained as de Valois's favourite, as Ashton's muse, and as the darling of the public. Two new recruits in particular put her on her mettle: the red-haired, porcelain-skinned Scottish beauty Moira King (who was to become Moira Shearer) and the long-limbed technical prodigy Beryl Groom (soon to be Beryl Grey), who, at fourteen, could not only execute a faultless *entrechat six*, but could knock out those elusive thirty-two *fouettés* as easily to the left as she could to the right. Margot would never jump so high nor turn so fast. But these shortcomings, far from defeating her, sharpened her wit and deepened her humility, enhancing her facility for learning. Even if, by de Valois's own admission, 'Margot's talent was average', her judgement was acute, and her way of conducting herself beyond reproach: 'She knew how to listen. She knew the people she *shouldn't* listen to. Always very quiet in everything she said. A very balanced person. I don't count people's emotional lives. Balance is a thing of the intellect, and

I'm talking about her intellect. I never saw her get hysterical, however deeply she felt. Terribly popular in the company. She had a way of keeping herself outside it all – and inside at the same time. At parties she was always there. There was no question of the ballerina not being with them.'[14]

Margot's contemporaries were not always as appreciative of this blandness as de Valois might have imagined. According to Annabel Farjeon, 'Margot was the most passive person I have ever known.'[15] Her social manner could also grate: 'A small flourishing whine invaded her speech, and a superficial giggle, which revealed a degree of self-consciousness you would never have suspected from the generally calm, assured manner.' But when it came to her dancing, all reservations evaporated. 'It was her tranquillity, her balance of mind, spirit and body that combined to produce perfect lyricism ... Every pose and action seemed held by some accurate counter-weight. Her technique was never perfect; *pirouettes* often went astray, off-centre, like a top running down, yet the effort to set herself right would result in a movement that was true and beautiful in itself.'[16]

This enchanting fallibility between difficult steps could still be glimpsed late in her career, in moments of preparation as well as recovery. Gail Monahan says: 'I can clearly picture her getting ready for a double *pirouette en dehors*. She would go to fourth position, focus carefully on something out in the auditorium, tuck her chin in very slightly and then take off. Other ballerinas, more confident in their techniques, sometimes launched themselves from less than perfect preparations and delivered perfect turns. Fonteyn seemed to feel that if she didn't do it the way she was taught to do it, disaster would strike.'

Luckily, the person best qualified to keep disaster at bay was, like the calm and beneficent Lilac Fairy, soon to make a timely return to the scene. Vera Volkova, who, in Shanghai, had already revealed herself to twelve-year-old Peggy as a vision in a black straw hat, now opened a studio at Cambridge Circus, to which all the foreign dancers passing through London flocked. De Valois still forbade members of her company to attend 'outside' classes. Beryl Grey thinks that 'Ninette possibly took it as an indirect attack on her methods – that people felt she wasn't good enough and other teachers offered more than she could. She didn't like that, and wouldn't suffer it.' But suffer it she must where her leading ballerina was concerned, for the balance of power had shifted, and, as Julia Farron puts it: 'By that time I don't think she could have done much about stopping Margot. Vera did absolute marvels for her, and Margot couldn't move without Vera guiding and helping her. Vera was marvellously Russian – but without the carry-on: absolutely pure. The best teacher Margot ever had, without any doubt at all.'

De Valois sensibly countered the defection among her dancers by luring Volkova, as well as George Goncharov, Margot's teacher in Shanghai, who had also turned up in London, to give occasional classes both at the school and the theatre. Margot was enormously fond of Goncharov, but it was for the small, bird-like, chain-smoking Volkova, full of physical effervescence and imaginative verbal flights of broken English, that she now pushed herself beyond what she perceived to be her limits. She says: 'I worked so hard in Volkova's class that I used to wish I could faint, as the great Taglioni is reported to have done at the end of two hours' training with her father.'[17] But Margot's body remained stubbornly conscious as her limbs sought to obey the quaint poetry of Volkova's exhortations: 'Arms are holding delicate flowers you must not crush,' or 'Pull God's beard,' or 'Leg does not know is going to arabesque.'[18] Sick with exhaustion after a particularly difficult *enchaînement*, Margot would look to her for praise, only to be told: 'Well somehow it didn't quite come out, isn't it.'[19] The story of a dancer's life.

But a story of greater consequence than might meet the eye. The French ballerina Violette Verdy elucidates: 'It's almost a privilege of our profession that we have to go about it the hard way. Margot's slow development, as exemplified in the way she worked with Volkova, is absolute proof of a truth which wants to be ignored these days, but which still exists – that nobody from the outside can impose something and pretend it looks real if it's not grown from the inside. The gorgeous result that we got with Margot could only have been achieved the hard way. It was a pilgrimage. There's no need to do it on your knee and bleed: Margot didn't look for unnecessary suffering. But whatever difficulty she had, she confronted honestly, with humility, and when you work like that, without anger, without unnatural forcing, it gives you a sense of reality. The strengthening of the foot leads automatically to the growth of character. It's surprising how, if you stick to the one thing you should do, life is going to deliver what you need.'

Courtesy of Theyre Lee-Elliot, Margot celebrated her twenty-first birthday at his cousin's beautiful black-and-white medieval pile in Gloucestershire. Kenneth Clark, who lived nearby, had brought the painter Graham Sutherland to meet her. Margot was now an inspirational enough figure in artistic circles for the introduction to encourage Sutherland to undertake the designs of a new Ashton ballet for her: *The Wanderer*. But that would be in the future, and it was hard to plan even a few months ahead when the present was so fraught and the day-to-day news so grim. Norway had fallen; France had capitulated; and on 4 June, when the company began its new season at Sadler's Wells, the last ships bore the remains of the British army (de Valois's elder brother among them) away from Dunkirk.

In the early days of the Battle of Britain, the Home Office had ordered that when a siren sounded all entertainments should cease for ten minutes, while the expected exodus from theatre auditoria took place. But as soon as it became clear that it was a matter of honour among audiences – even if London shook to its foundations around them – not to budge from their seats, nor to curb either their laughter or their concentration, the order was withdrawn in favour of a notice which ran: 'You will be notified by an illuminated sign that an Air Raid Warning has been sounded during the performance – but that does not mean that an air raid will necessarily take place. If you wish to leave for home or an official Air Raid Shelter you are at liberty to do so. All we ask is that –

if you feel you must go – you will depart quietly and without excitement.'

But Mrs Hookham 'never saw anyone get up and leave'. And, through the dark and dreadful days, the music at the Wells played on – although not always from the orchestra pit. *Dante Sonata*, with its morale-boosting potential, was the first of the ballets lost in Holland to be resurrected; but, although its simple sets and costumes were easily re-modelled, it had to be danced to a recording until the orchestral parts could be re-scored. De Valois choreographed a new, bawdy romp, ironically titled *The Prospect Before Us*, and tailored to Helpmann's clowning skills, which were known to lift the public's spirits. As in so many of her ballets, there was no part for Margot, who, in any case, was danced off her feet, often having to contend with inexperienced partners aged no more than sixteen, straight from the school. The ranks of the company were fast being drained of male talent: William Chappell had gone into the army; Richard Ellis and Stanley Hall into the navy; the Royal Air Force had claimed Sadler's Wells's first casualty, a twenty-seven-year-old Australian called Leo Young. *Les Sylphides*, with its virtually all-girl cast, could still be convincingly staged. But the Czardas and the Spanish Dance had to be dropped from *Swan Lake*; and, in *The Sleeping Princess*, Margot found herself rejecting Bobby Helpmann as a suitor in the Rose Adagio, only to embrace him a few scenes later, quick-changed into the guise of Prince Florimund.

The season ended on 6 September 1940, and the next day Margot and Pamela, Fred Ashton and Beryl de Zoete escaped to Cornwall where they spent a week at Greylands Hotel, gorging themselves on fried breakfasts and clotted-cream teas. They were lucky to be out of London, for, on the 7th, the bombing intensified and the Sadler's Wells Theatre was commandeered as a refuge for victims of air raids. The ballet school, alone, continued to be housed on the top floor, in the mirror-lined rehearsal room, beyond whose huge glass windows floated shoals of silver barrage balloons, while the basement of the building operated as a soup kitchen. Miss Baylis's missionary dream of a theatre that would succour the homeless had, finally and tragically, come true. Meanwhile, the homeless ballet company – though promised by Sir Bronson Albery a season at the New Theatre in St Martin's Lane the following January – went off on an ENSA tour of the garrison theatres, where the uncompromising response of the troops soon encouraged the boys to abandon their wigs and the girls to don strings of pearls in order to pass sexual muster. A tour of the provinces followed, and then, at Christmas time, a short period of 'rest and rehearsal' (surely a contradiction in terms) at Dartington Hall in Devon. It was here, between nutritious meals (the food came straight from the land) and nightly games of strip poker, that *The Wanderer* at last took shape. The music was Schubert's Fantasie in C major, Opus 15. Although Robert Helpmann played the angst-ridden traveller-through-time, and was on the stage throughout in a compelling *tour de force*, it was into the *pas de deux* for the mature lovers, danced by Michael Somes and Pamela May, that Ashton poured his romantic and sexual longing, displacing reality as he always did: Somes was now enamoured of Julia Farron, and May had married Painton Cowan, her Cambridge sweetheart. Margot envied this beautiful and eroti-cally explicit duet – the kind of lyrical adagio, all poetic charm and draped pastel chiffon, that usually fell to her. Instead, she was allotted the role of Success, and, garbed in modernist tunic, tights of crimson and black, long studded gloves and a huge waving head-feather, she was expected to hurl herself like a circus acrobat from one youth to another in a series of death-defying lifts. 'Fred was getting a bit wild at the time,' remem-bers Pamela May, 'and Margot didn't like it much. She was always rather scared of doing it – it was not at all what she was used to.'[20] Margot also loathed her Sutherland costume, which the *Spectator* described as 'Something between the Worst Woman in London and an equestrienne.'[21] But Ashton had her best inter-ests at heart. When *The Wanderer* duly opened at the New Theatre on 27 January 1941, the *pas de deux* with Helpmann caused a sensation, its fast, jagged movements forcing Margot to flash and glitter as she never had before, challenging the public's perception of her technical and artistic range. In this, the last of his three early wartime ballets, so urgently following one upon the other before he was snatched away by the RAF, Ashton, having, with *Apparitions*, 'laid a new atmosphere on Fonteyn', now, according to William Chappell, 'lifted her suddenly away from the rest of the company'.[22] The 'golden child',[23] who, to his amusement, had thrown herself into his arms in *Rio Grande*, had begun to exert a serious and passionate hold on the romantic imagination of Chappell. He might well have been speaking for a whole generation of young men of sensibility caught up in the British War Machine when he wrote: 'The sorrowing figure from *Dante Sonata* with streaming hair, the stylized bride from *The Wise Virgins* with her submissive antique gestures, and the wicked woman from *The Wanderer* with her proud plumed head − each one seemed more real than the khaki-clad figures that swarmed around us.'[24]

Rather less reverently, Margot's photograph was pinned up in the officers' wardroom of HMS *Aurora*. She had become what only war could have made her: a national mascot.

And, for a little while, it went to her head.

IO

The wartime schedule of the Sadler's Wells Ballet was enough to make its least member, let alone its hardest-working ballerina, lose all sense of proportion. Every eight to ten weeks spent by the dancers performing at the New Theatre in London had to be matched by a corresponding number of weeks spent touring the provinces. On one ill-fated tour, there was an air-raid in every successive town they visited: the theatre in Bath was hit and partially burned out while four of the girls were sleeping in the dressing-room after the performance, their lodgings having already been destroyed during an earlier raid. Astonishingly, no one was hurt. But, where the dancers had been accustomed to giving two or three performances a week, they were now expected to give nine. 'I danced so often,' Margot told *Woman* magazine, 'that sometimes I stood trembling in the wings, unable to remember if I had finished my solo before I left the stage.'[1] There was slightly less pressure at the New, where at first they played only matinées, since the West End audiences did not know them and there was none of the automatic enthusiasm that could be counted on in Islington. By September, however, the wartime boom in theatre-going had set in, and the demand on the part of Londoners for tickets grew so great that the company was compelled to give three performances in a row on Saturdays, with only a half-hour break in between. A stop was put to this when *corps de ballet* members took to fainting, but Margot confesses that she was quite sorry. The first evidence of her legendary stamina comes with the casual admission: 'It had been quite fun, in a way, while it lasted.'[2]

Perhaps non-stop work *was* the best tonic — better, anyway, than the peculiar green drink on the market at the time, to which the dancers became addicted, a beverage which purported to 'give you tomorrow's strength today'. ('All that happened,' Margot tells us wryly, 'was that tomorrow one felt even more tired, and drank even more green drink.'[3]) But at least, as liquids went, it was innocuous, unlike the huge quantities of wine and spirits that Constant was prone to put away. The loss of the *Horoscope* score had been hard for him to bear, for no full-length recording of the work had ever been made. 'Once he returned from Holland,' writes the poet and biographer Andrew Motion, 'Constant seems to have been afflicted with the idea that he should address himself directly to contemporary events.'[4] In a self-sacrificial mood – induced by the fighting he was not fit enough to join – he had, since the start of the war, taken on patriotic commissions, such as a film score for a documentary about the Merchant Navy. But such overtly 'English' music was not his strong suit; it failed to inspire him. He had been working harder than ever for the ballet, accompanying performances on the piano in the absence of an orchestra, and had 'rewarded himself by relaxing unusually hard too'.[5] Margot, with her long working hours and daunting responsibilities, could hardly be a companion to him in the bars and restaurants where he hung out late into the night, nor on his morning pub-crawls which invariably wound up at the George, known as the Gluepot. She had no choice but to abandon him to his literary cronies, such as Alan Frank, Norman Douglas, Michael Ayrton, and his particular kindred spirit, Dylan Thomas, whose wild romantic melancholy only exacerbated his own. By having 'laid a new atmosphere on Fonteyn and lifted her suddenly away from the rest of the company', Ashton had effectively isolated Margot. Besides, she was no longer one of a triptych: June, like Pamela, had married her Cambridge sweetheart, and both girls were on leave, having babies. Margot, alone in the No. 1 dressing-room at the New, became susceptible to the blandishments of fans and hangers-on. The higher you rise, the less you can count on finding the companionship of equals; and the temptation to mistake adulation for friendship was something with which Margot would have to wrestle for the rest of her life. People, she discovered, wanted to give her things: not just flowers or chocolates – so desirable because they were in such short supply – but their clothing coupons, their services, their time. Again and again, throughout her career and even beyond it, Margot's immensely pragmatic nature made it difficult for her to resist the notion that even the most sycophantic of offers could somehow be put to practical use. On the one hand, her personal barriers were very strong – most of the humbler members of the company now found her remote and hard to know. She would regularly arrive fractionally late for class, in order to avoid fraternizing with colleagues, and would busy herself during breaks in rehearsal by forever darning her *pointe* shoes. But with her admirers on the other side of the footlights, she was already showing a less than discriminating tendency to let those barriers drop. When fans told her that she was special, she fed on it: God knows she had been starved of compliments by both Ashton and de Valois. Yet, redeemingly, it is a fault for which she is the first to castigate herself. 'I developed a star complex,' she admits, 'and for a time I was really impossible, imagining that I was different from, and superior to, those around me.'[6] This was the same demon that was to possess her at the end of the war, when she would instruct the stage-door keeper, Mr Jackson, to refer to her not as 'Margot', but as 'Miss Fonteyn'. But, in 1942, the censure of a true friend delivered her from the influence of false ones. Pamela May came backstage to see the company, and had the courage to tell Margot that she'd become a bore. It was not just her words, but Pamela's tragic plight that filled Margot with shame. In an astonishing short solo in *Dante Sonata*, May had given haunting expression to what one critic called 'some terrible, unexplained grief'.[7] Now, like a premonition realized, that grief explained itself. Three weeks after the birth of her son, Pamela's husband had been killed in action.

Margot saw no such tragedy strike the people closest to her. Neither her lover nor her dancing partner had been called up. Her brother, now styling himself Felix Fonteyn, volunteered for the Fire Service in Chelsea, where, according to his mother, he 'made several friends though of course he never mentioned them to me. But one day he did come in to tell me that he was going to marry the daughter of a Brigadier General Sim. To say I was astonished is to put it mildly! [That] he had no money and no profession or real job and was going to ask a Brigadier General to let him marry his daughter struck me as the most courageous thing I had ever heard of. Of course, as in the 1914 war, people married immediately who would normally have waited, but "asking father" has always been a bit of an ordeal for most young men. Anyway, he was accepted, and in 1941 was married in Chelsea Old Church to Miss Idell Sim.'

Felix's own father was unable to attend the wedding, having been interned in Shanghai when the Japanese invaded China. Margot and her mother received no news whatever of him for the duration of the war; but, when it was over, they would have cause to be grateful to Felix senior's new paramour. 'If I had been in China,' writes Mrs Hookham, 'I should have been interned in a woman's camp. Beatrice, being a foreigner, was not interned and was able to get parcels of food to Felix. She was very clever and played the money market and she managed to keep their flat and belongings in spite of the Japanese. I could not have done anything like that of course.'

What Black Queen did do, however, was join the Women's Voluntary Service, 'collecting and sorting and giving out clothes to people who through bombing had lost all they had'. Everyone was expected to do his or her bit, ballet dancers not excepted. A newspaper article of 1941 ran: 'Critical days lie ahead. Although London is having plenty of ballet just now, balletomanes fear that it may soon all end . . . Margot Fonteyn and several other women dancers have registered [for National Service]. Now an appeal is being made for male dancers, especially those of the Sadler's Wells Company, to be exempted from service with the forces. It is pointed out that there is no book for ballets; the dancing has to be learnt and passed on from one to another. It is argued that if the continuity is broken, the repertoire of classical and modern work may be lost to this country.'[8]

Public opinion took a dim view of such special pleading. There were, in fact, only two reasons for exemption: a 'reserved occupation', one vital to the war effort, or unfitness – neither of which, obviously, a dancer could claim. For women, the rules were a lot less stringent; and there was never any real danger of England's Prima Ballerina being expected to stomp up and down a dusty drill-square with hundreds of other servicewomen. But on 21 June 1941, after a performance of *Dante Sonata*, in which Frederick Ashton had to take the place of the already departed Leslie Edwards as one of the Children of Light, Ninette de Valois stepped forward to make the announcement that everyone had been dreading. Ashton had just danced for the last time, and, along with Alan Carter and Michael Somes, was to leave that very night to join up. Margot, like many others, both on stage and in the audience, was in tears.

Latterly, her own brother had been called up. But his wartime career proved to be perhaps the least chequered of his life: he became an officer cadet and was sent to Sandhurst for training, where he was given a commission to the 23rd Hussars. Posted to Staffordshire and then to Whitby, he designed a gun turret for tanks and stayed there as a trainer all through the war till demobilization in 1946, so Idell was able to be with him throughout. Idell was somewhat startled by her new theatrical in-laws. 'She tells me that the first time she came to see me in Egerton Gardens,' writes Mrs Hookham, 'our conversation was interrupted by screams from the bathroom. I rushed in to find that Margot, who had a bad cold, had not stirred up the mustard I had put in the bath and had just sat on it, with very warming results.'

By now the lease at Egerton Gardens was nearly up, so Mrs Hookham accepted the offer of a cheap house at the corner of Pelham Street and Pelham Place 'which had been shaken by a nearby bomb', before moving, a year later, to a slightly more substantial three-storey house in Pelham Crescent, which she was able to secure without any premium at all and at a reasonable rent. 'Looking back, in spite of everything, this was a happy period in my life. Felix and Idell had the top floor to themselves and Margot and I had the rest. Many of the ballet people came in and out and we had occasional good parties.'

'Mrs Hookham, more than any of the other mothers,' said Leslie Edwards, 'was lavish in her entertaining – I suppose because of her time in Shanghai. I don't mean that she was doing the Charleston on the table, but she liked gatherings. Pimm's came in, so she gave a Pimm's party. And suddenly this sweet girl who had never touched liquor in her life was taken out feet first, when only an hour before she had been saying, "Oh, this fruit cup is delicious." So Mrs Hookham's parties seemed very sophisticated to us, with her sitting in the middle like a queen. None of us had any money except Bobby, who could always send home to kill a sheep.'

Ashton's darkest hour had become Helpmann's brightest moment. De Valois now encouraged him to try his hand at choreography. Being the extrovert that he was, he naturally placed himself at the centre of his first creation, *Comus* (1942), to a score by Purcell, suggested and arranged by Constant Lambert. But Helpmann had another mentor now: his lover, the brilliant young theatre director Michael Benthall. Collaboration with Benthall ensured that, in *Comus*, Helpmann pitted his talent against a subject of intellectual weight. Knowing his shortcomings as a dancer, Helpmann created a masque – less of a ballet than a drama of movement – subordinating the dancing to the progress of the plot and relying for effect on his clever skill for characterization and the contents of his make-up box. He spoke Milton's lines from the Messel stage-set which graphically depicted the dark intensity of the language: 'perplexed paths, the nodding horror of whose shady brows threats the forlorn and wondering passenger'. The passenger was Margot, as the Lady, lost in the ominous wood, virtuous and unassailable.

In Helpmann's next ballet, *Hamlet* – premièred 19 May 1942 – she was assailed on all sides, for in his phantasmagorical version, set to Tchaikovsky's eighteen-minute overture, her character, Ophelia, merged or was interchangeable with that of both the Player Queen and Gertrude. This fashionable, Freudian treatment of the play – which took its theme from the line: 'For in that sleep of death/what dreams may come'[9] – was conceived by Dadie Rylands, who would go on to direct a revival, in 1944, of John Gielgud's acclaimed *Hamlet*, not seen in London since 1934. Rylands would later recall how shamelessly his brain was picked: 'Bobby talked to me a lot about it during the time the Sadler's Wells were here in Cambridge. He played me the music and asked me what ideas I had. I said I thought it was very important that the same dancer should do Gertrude and Ophelia. And we worked it out in some detail – Constant taking part and Bobby and myself. And it was put on for the first time here at the Arts. Bobby was full of gratitude and praise – couldn't have managed without me and all that. But when it came to the first performance in London, he neither put my name on the programme nor invited me to the dress rehearsal to see it. Couldn't bear to share. That was naughty.'

Naughtier still was the sole credit that Helpmann took for the wonderful stage effect by Michael Benthall, which opened and closed the ballet and which has been emulated by Hamlets ever since, from Olivier to Kenneth Branagh: the prince's upside-down face, spot-lit in death, falling backwards from his stiff, high-hoisted body, borne on the shoulders of the pall-bearers. It was an image potent enough to make a public idol of Helpmann, who, in de Valois's words, became, for a while, 'a victim of balletomane hysteria',[10] to the extent that one fan was moved to write: 'Dear Mr Helpmann, I want you to know how very much I enjoyed your new ballet. As I have said many times to my husband, "Hamlet has been ruined by the words . . ."'[11]

Margot, who had always been sane and sensible enough to find the enactment of dementia the least of her problems, now, with the part of Ophelia, entered into Helpmann's dramatic world of delirium, relieved to be spared, at least for the time being, the tyranny of Ashton's insistence on intricate footwork.

Helpmann's limited choreographic vocabulary was hardly likely to test her technical powers, but, as an actress, she flowered under his tutelage. Keen to distinguish Ophelia's madness from Giselle's, Helpmann poached the tragic gesture of a war widow whom he had observed, on a daily basis, taking coffee at the Pavilion in Bournemouth. Whenever the Palm Court orchestra played, the woman would clasp her gloved hands above her head and twist them ritualistically, as though trying to wrench apart the entwined fingers. None of the other customers seemed to pay her any attention, but Helpmann took Margot to observe the woman's blank, matter-of-fact expression as she raised her arms; and those locked, writhing hands became Ophelia's signature. 'Is it not possible that in finding a great dancer, we have lost a great actress?' wondered de Valois. 'Watch her tender, solicitous start when Hamlet turns to her with a violence that makes it impossible for her to hide her sudden anxiety; it is here that one senses the fear of misunderstanding rather than the fear of physical violence. The movement is so intelligent, with its subtle timing and its refined control.'[12]

It may have been that this new command of emotional nuance resulted more from her private development as a woman than from any untapped thespian talent, for Margot was no longer an innocent in matters of the heart. It was not just that Constant had begun to prove as faithless – not to mention violent – as he had done with Flo. What she had to suffer, as her own idealized image shrank in her lover's regard, was the loss of her youthful ideal of love. For, when the muse deserted Lambert, it was she, Margot, who became diminished in his eyes. During the whole war he composed only one short work of which he could be proud: *Aubade Héroique* (1942), a piece reminiscent of, and dedicated to, Vaughan Williams. But this composition was retrospective in conception, having been inspired, in Constant's words, 'by a daybreak during the invasion of Holland, the calm of the surrounding park contrasting with the distant mutterings of war'[13] – the same scene which, in her book, Margot invests with such delicate nostalgia. That intensely shared half-dream of beauty would not come again. Reality in wartime Britain was too bleak, and Constant short enough of money to be forced to move from 'Hangover' Lodge into the house of his seventy-year-old mother in Peel Street, thereby dashing any hope of a domestic future with Margot. By the time Margot, who could not be rushed, had become truly interested in Constant, and wanted to commit to him, it was, from Constant's point of view, 'just a little bit too late', says Anthony Russell-Roberts. 'Constant had invested so much passion early on when nothing had happened, that it broke something in him and when that cord is snapped there is nothing you can do.' Lambert seemed even to regret the lost stability of his marriage, and confided to Anthony Powell: 'Do you know, in spite of everything, I'm not sure I won't try to make it up with Flo.'[14] And now, to Michael Ayrton, he described Margot, whom he had pursued with such ardour, as the OG (Old Girl). 'Like the character in *Apparitions*,' explains Ashton, 'Constant was looking for the Ideal One. Whenever he thought he'd found her, he got tired of it.'[15]

Solace lay for Margot, as it does for all true artists, in her work. Or perhaps some innate ill-adjustment to private life deepens the need, in performers bound for greatness, for direct interaction with the collective. But now, that same element of compromise that was souring her love-affair also had to be confronted in her professional life. For she found that she had to take on everything – light-hearted roles which did not really suit her, such as Columbine in *Carnaval* or Swanilda in *Coppélia*. De Valois had a quaint and rather prejudiced theory that girls with curly or springy hair were bound to play soubrettes, whereas straight-haired dancers were the lyric poets of movement. And Margot's shining black tresses could be coaxed to hang as straight as a die. It really did seem to follow that de Valois was right, and that Swanilda was not within Margot's range. Those who had seen Danilova or Lopokova were never to be convinced by Fonteyn's powers as a comedienne, nor by her mime, which was considered stilted. Aware, perhaps, of the implication inherent in de Valois's dictum, she herself confessed to 'not feeling the part'[16] – even though Herbert Farjeon found her interpretation exquisite: the very 'acme of comedy'.[17] Whatever the case, the limelight was inevitably stolen by Robert Helpmann, who left the partnering of Swanilda to Alexis Rassine, a Lithuanian newcomer from South Africa, and threw himself into the doddering role of Dr Coppélius, in which de Valois shame-facedly admits to having encouraged him to clown 'up to the heights of its utmost humour'.[18] He could never go too far for Margot, who relied on his improprieties, off-stage as well as on, to raise Constant's ever-plummeting spirits. At parties, Helpmann was known for passing round a plate, held well below waist-level, so that an extra, anatomical 'sausage' might be arranged among the *hors d'oeuvres*. Or he would tuck away his much-exposed parts between his legs, and lie naked and fully made-up on some boarding-house bed in Manchester, calling out to Constant in a cockney falsetto: 'I'm ready for you, Master.'[19] Once, in that same city, Bobby and Margot were invited to the Belle Vue Zoo, in order to name two zebras. But Bobby caught sight of a llama whose comical, rolling eyes reminded him of his own, and insisted on naming the benighted animal after himself. As always, Constant was drawn into the subversive spirit of Bobby's camperie, and turned up at the zoo the next day to confer the consolation of his own name upon the zebra who had been so sadly overlooked.

Margot's whole life was peculiarly overrun by animals, from the common rabbits and exotic otters of her Shanghai girlhood, to the imposing cows and beloved dogs of her last days in Panama. But her years with the composer were marked by a passion for cats. Constant, as president of the Kensington Cats' Club, delivered a talk on the radio titled 'Cats in Music', in which he attested that 'with one or two noteworthy exceptions, I know of no composer or executant worth his salt, who has not been devoted to the feline world'. So Margot, with her artistic credentials on the line, but hardly being in a position to mother the animals themselves, began to assemble a collection of glass and porcelain cats which became – at least until the press caught on and turned her private craze into a public stunt – a source of inordinate attachment. It was the closest thing to a hobby that she had ever allowed herself, and it provided an outlet for her increasingly stifled emotions. 'One could never tell whether Margot was upset or not,' says Patricia Garnett. 'It was very difficult to have a conversation with her. The only people she ever seemed to talk to were people who were mad about cats. Cat lovers could have great exchanges with her.' Margot would indeed have a long exchange of letters with one dancer, Guinevere Parry, to whom she always wrote in the guise of a cat, signing herself 'Fur-Legs', or 'Fifi Fantail'.

There was, of course, a strong factor of identification, as if, in her great passivity and suggestibility, she were assuming the qualities of the type of creature Constant most admired. As William Chappell was to write: 'The feline in her appearance has become emphasized as she has grown up. Her eyes appear larger, slightly more slanted. Her limbs sleeker, more satiny in texture. Her cheeks, faintly, romantically hollowed in repose, lift themselves when she smiles into a small pussy roundness; and the tilt of her brows, the neat curve of the top of her head add to the illusion. She is not a Persian cat, nor a tiger tabby; not a tortoiseshell nor a sleek blonde marmalade cat. She is a long-limbed, sinuous, fastidious little puss, with tiny paws and a coat of silk velvet. An aristocrat of oriental lineage, a Siamese with a dark head, but a freak, a special Siamese who by some dealings in cat magic has exchanged its disturbing blue gaze for a pair of brilliant dark eyes.'[20]

Yet, during this era, Margot was often called upon to forget her sleek fastidiousness, and prowl the streets like any common alley-cat in search of her wayward lover. 'She used to have to go out looking for him,' says John Lanchbery. 'Constant would find somewhere to drink after the show. She'd pick him up from the gutter.' Washing vomit from a fallen man's clothes – however mighty the wearer – is not exactly a romantic pastime, and it is to Helpmann's credit that he often escorted Margot on these nocturnal forays. But his kind deeds did not go unpunished; for Lambert, despite his personal affection for Helpmann, had growing misgivings about the effect of Bobby's naked self-interest on the artistic standards of the company and at one point threatened to resign, in order to lend weight to an unofficial letter from Kenneth Clark, which pressed for the release of Ashton from his prosaic post in RAF Intelligence. 'Helpmann is an admirable dancer, but he is a virtuoso, and does not command the confidence of the company as a whole in the way Ashton would do,' wrote Clark (who happened to be involved at the time in an affair with Ashton's sister, Edith). 'If Constant Lambert leaves I am afraid that Margot Fonteyn would leave also, and the whole Ballet would break up.'[21] Needless to say, no exemption for Ashton was forthcoming. But, in 1943, at least he was granted leave – six weeks in all – to choreograph a ballet called *The Quest*.

Margot had longed for this moment, as one might long for the return of a lover. For, in spite of the frightening technical demands that Ashton had always made on her, he had the power to bring to life some valued part of her which depended upon his presence for its existence: her sense of being not just an interpretative artist, but a creative one. Ashton, for his part, had found it an agony to be parted from the daily inspiration which Margot brought him. His nephew, Anthony Russell-Roberts, says: 'I think she was a kind of prize. I think she was so much his muse that he didn't want anybody else to be on that territory. He wanted her to be *his* discovery – for *him* to be the one to release her genius. So he was very protective, perhaps obsessive, certainly proprietorial. He did feel that he was creating her, and that Margot was really helping him and was truly *with* him, unlocking something very important within him, whereas de Valois, he felt, was blocking him all the time. De Valois was the director and she had to be even-handed – she had probably to think beyond Fred. But he was quite reproachful about her – how many ballets, he used to say, were immediately put on the scrapheap?'

Not to mention how many remained unwritten throughout the war. The whole company was overjoyed to have Ashton back, however briefly. Michael Somes, who was unable to join the cast of *The Quest* until 1945, later spoke of the pride he took in his own contribution to rehearsals. 'Fred's talent was so great,' he reminisced, 'but you had to prod him to get that little bit more. Margot and I did that – the three of us stirred the pudding. Nothing would happen without him but he allowed us the privilege of really creating with him; he had the sense to realize that it was coming out of us, and that it was to his benefit and advantage to *get* it out.' And there was an undeniable sensuousness to the exchange. 'Fred was an *angel* to work with,' says Maude Lloyd, remembering Ashton's early days with Rambert. 'He would hold one's hand and walk round, chafing one's cuticle.'[22] Even the *corps de ballet* partook of the intimacy. Annabel Farjeon wrote: 'He loved the feel of dancers, both physically and mentally, and greeted them with warmth. His long face would light up with joy as readily as a child's when we danced well. But there were days when he would turn up to rehearsal seemingly without an idea in his head and in my experience he never wrote anything down. Sitting on the bench before the window, his cheeks and neck would turn peony pink with anxiety. There was stillness and silence in the room. At last he would go to the piano and, leaning over the music to hide his embarrassment, say, "Play this bit, Hilda." Hilda Gaunt would lay her cigarette on the fingerboard and play. After a moment he would pick on a favourite dancer: "Do something! Go on darling, do something!" Then he, too, would start swooping about the room, dragging a couple standing at the side by the hands. "Try it like this. Try lifting her – no, one leg like this! No – yes! Lovely! Now reverse the whole thing." It was as though we were shapes with whom he was playing or experimenting, as a little boy might.'[23]

But the little boy in the now thirty-eight-year-old choreographer was sulking. Ashton felt stultified by two years spent in northern Nissen huts, doing work for which he had absolutely no aptitude. He did not bring his usual innocent energy to *The Quest*, nor, indeed, a strong enough grasp of his subject: a libretto by Doris Langley Moore, based on Book One of Spenser's *The Faerie Queene*. Taking the chivalric story of St George, England's patron saint, at face value, Ashton had hoped, by commissioning a score from William Walton (who was composing the background music for what was to be Olivier's rabble-rousing film of *Henry V*), to make the kind of patriotic contribution that the War Office would applaud. But the mystical and pacifist elements of Spenser's allegory could not easily be suppressed, any more than knightly deeds could adequately be represented by a cast almost entirely denuded of men. Worst of all, there was no *time* to conjure his usual magic – the company was on the road, and William Walton, with only five weeks to produce forty-five minutes' worth of music, would 'bribe guards on trains to take a minute or so's music to wherever Freddy happened to be with the ballet – to Wolverhampton or Preston or somewhere'.[24] Nor was there any proper collaboration with the designer John Piper, who preferred to rely on what he called 'an "accidental" unity'.[25] One such accident was a wig for Helpmann which, according to Walton, made him look more like the Dragon than St George. This delighted Ashton, who seems to have been more interested in venting his spleen than in protecting his ballet. In the last tableau, he obscured Helpmann behind a gauze, reasoning that 'It is better than seeing that sinful face sanctified.'[26]

Margot was allotted the part of Una, beloved of St George and the personification of Truth; and, in truth, Ashton did make some beautiful moments for her, not least with his signature, skimming, 'walking-on-air' step – originally invented for Pamela May in *The Wanderer*, but now remodelled and perfected in Margot's image. And yet, when *The Quest* opened at the New Theatre on 6 April 1943, there were – despite a heart-lifting reception for Ashton – only two victors in what was otherwise generally admitted to be a disappointing venture: the young rising contenders for Margot's crown – seventeen-year-old Moira

Shearer, full of 'shining beauty' as Pride, and Beryl Grey, still only fifteen, sharply arresting and extraordinarily technically proficient as the Duenna. Shearer's film-star looks were certainly one kind of challenge for Margot. But 'Beryl was the one who got to her,' a friend admits. 'The only person I ever remember Margot being less than generous about.'[27]

Envy was a new and shocking emotion for someone whose position had long been so inviolable that she had not even thought of herself as ambitious. But envy, which is often professional, only needs two people. Now Margot had to suffer its much more passionate and overwhelming counterpart – jealousy – which is invariably sexual, and requires a third party. To Sadler's Wells came a dancer called Sheila Fleming, whose stage name was Anne Lascelles. 'Anne was not exotic,' says Celia Franca, who was her friend, 'but she had a physique very much like Margot's: nice legs and feet, a slim body and a pretty head. Dark brown hair. Constant had his eye on her. She would be sitting on the stage as a fairy in *Nutcracker*, and he would be conducting and looking at her the whole time. It was a little embarrassing, but it was not a long-lived affair. Margot called me into her bedroom one day to speak about it – we were on tour somewhere and she would rest in the afternoons, so I went to her hotel. We chatted about it briefly – she was very cool and dignified – it was all typically British. Anne was very unhappy about it. She had a genuine fondness for Constant Lambert, but was in a difficult position.'

So was Margot, who, however threatened she might have felt, could hardly claim the high moral ground. As one of her colleagues puts it: 'Constant Lambert wasn't her property when she lifted him. He was married to someone else.' Margot's way of bearing upsetting things had always been simply, strictly, not to think about them. She had learned to ignore Constant's bouts of whoring, and, in particular, his liaison with Laureen Sylvestre, a black cigarette-girl from a club in Soho called the Nest on whom he relied for 'information about night life' and 'uncomplicated affection'.[28] Anne Lascelles was by no means the only

1. BQ as a little girl.

2. Felix with the newborn Peggy: 'neither sleeping, nor a beauty' (Cully children on the left).

3. Peggy and the boys (the Fletcher brothers, Pat Tattersall and Roger Cane).

4. With her father in Shanghai, 1931.

5. The newly-named Margot Fonteyn.

6. Constant Lambert.

7. As the Creole Girl in *Rio Grande* with William Chappell.

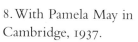
8. With Pamela May in Cambridge, 1937.

9. Tito as an undergraduate.

10. With Frederick Ashton.

11. With Constant Lambert, arriving back from Holland.

12. With Michael Somes in
    Horoscope, 1938.

13. *Dante Sonata* with
    Robert Helpmann, 1940.

14. *The Wanderer* with
    Robert Helpmann,
    1941.

15. On holiday in the South of France with 'Fitz', Pamela May, Charles Gordon and Charles Hassé.

16. In *Apparitions.*

17. In *Symphonic Variations* with Henry Danton and Moira Shearer,
Michael Somes, Brian Shaw and Pamela May.

18. In costume for Agathe, the catwoman,
in *Les Demoiselles de la Nuit,* Paris, 1948.

19. Cinderella.

20. On holiday in the South of France, 1948, with Joy Williams.

21. With Léonor Fini.

22. With Roland Petit.

23. The Messel production of *Sleeping Beauty*: with Henry Danton as the third prince in Act I.

24. New York, 1949: with Nora Kaye, Helpmann and Ashton.

member of the *corps de ballet* to whom Constant had made over-
tures, but she was the first to challenge company hierarchy by
responding publicly, thereby subjecting Margot to humiliating
gossip and the galling pity of her peers. Whether Lascelles and
Lambert slept together cannot be known: the proverbial fly on
the wall is beyond consultation. And human memory is longer-
lived but frustratingly subjective, with the result that accounts
of the sexual climate within the company are almost ludicrously
contradictory. 'Of *course* everybody was in and out of each other's
beds,' claims one surviving member. 'The war was on and we
stayed up all night because we might be dead tomorrow. We
were in the *theatre*, for God's sake – we'd all had contracts since
we were fourteen. If there was a man around you grabbed him.
There weren't many of them.' Others insist upon the innocence
and discipline of the time. 'We took things much more slowly
than the young do these days. It was all unconsummated love.
We were too exhausted anyway – even on Sundays, when we
weren't dancing, we'd be on our way somewhere by train.' But
on one theme, at least, all versions concur: the real deterrent to
emancipated sex was the fear of unwanted pregnancy. 'Before
the war, and for a while after, all the ballet companies had at
least one, if not two, people who knew a friend who knew a
friend who could arrange an abortion. And that person stood
in no fear of getting the sack because that knowledge was a
certain kind of gold dust, as you can imagine. It was quiet, but
on the other hand it was fixed. If anybody knew a secret like
that, it was better kept than the atom bomb. But it happened.'

It happened twice to Margot. According to the consultant
gynaecologist who diagnosed her cancer when she was sixty-
five, her medical history included two terminations of pregnancy. Friends tend to think that the first, 'or even possibly the
second', of these probably took place in the late summer of '43,
when she was absent from the company for two months of
unexplained sick leave. It was entirely unlike her to miss even
one performance. 'She was brave,' says Celia Franca. 'None of
us, I suppose, was in the best of health, but Margot never gave

in. Nothing was going to deter her from going on stage.'

And yet, in 1943, after the open-air season given for the second year running at Victoria Park in Bethnal Green, where Eastenders paid sixpence to 'watch the ladies dance' (in particular Margot as the Sugar Plum Fairy), something did indeed deter her from appearing at the New Theatre on the company's return there in August. The season opened quietly, without a leading ballerina. Pauline Clayden danced Margot's part in *The Quest*, and Beryl Grey stepped in as Ophelia. It was not until the new production of *Le Lac des Cygnes*, with designs by Leslie Hurry, had opened on 7 September that Margot reappeared to dance Odette/Odile. She was on fine form: ostensibly nothing had changed. But a new determination was in the air, which gripped, if not Margot herself, then the women who felt that the girl's welfare lay in their charge. Black Queen had chummed up with Doris Langley Moore, and, with de Valois's cooperation, they set about separating Margot from Constant by means of a little gentle match-making. They prevailed upon a film director called Charles Hassé to pay court to Margot, in the course of researching a documentary account of a dancer's life, commissioned by the Crown Film Unit for the Ministry of Information.

'The film never got made, in fact,' said Hassé. 'I was given a year to prepare it. The story of the life of a ballerina. How she began, and so on. That's how I met Margot. Ninette hated the idea of films of the ballet. But it happened that the script was going to be by Doris Langley Moore who persuaded Ninette that if Margot were to spend time with me, it might break up the relationship with Constant. There was even talk of their marrying at that time, and Ninette didn't want it. That was the real reason she agreed. So, for six months in '44 I went around with Margot, going to concerts and ballet classes and on tour with them. I took her out to lunch occasionally and of course always went round with flowers, but it was really rather boring. I didn't have much to talk about to her – it was just a job. Then, one evening, I joined Felix and Idell for tea at the Ritz and we went on to the ballet at the New Theatre. And afterwards, in

Margot's dressing-room, as she was taking her make-up off, I suddenly saw her looking at me very strangely in the mirror. And that clicked something with me. Most extraordinary. We all went on to the Milroy – Pamela, Freddy, everyone – and Margot played it very badly in a way because she danced with me practically the whole night. A number of them came back to my flat in Hammersmith Terrace, and we sat up all night, talking. Then we adjourned to Margot's mother's place, and then on to lunch. Margot had to go to Birmingham that night, so we saw her off, and that was that. Then, on Tuesday, I had a call at about two in the morning from Margot saying: "Get out of my mind!" '

The following Saturday, when Margot returned to London, the two sneaked away to a private supper at the Moulin d'Or. 'At her suggestion, strangely. It was where she always went with Constant. Afterwards, we got into a taxi and stopped outside her house, and then decided to come down to my flat, and that's where it began. We went to bed. She was marvellous, sexually. Completely natural. I don't think she'd had proper satisfaction with anybody. Constant was drunk, always. She told me that on tour she'd tried to go to bed with Michael Somes, but it hadn't worked out at all. Margot's mother was rather cross that she didn't go home that night. She was difficult about it at first. But I got to know her and became fond of her, and she was very fond of me.'

Like all the men who had once been in love with Margot and were still alive to tell the tale, Charles Hassé, at the age of ninety, was lit, when he spoke of her, with the bright flame of remembrance – and fired by something else, too: the pressing desire for the part he played in her life to be acknowledged. Constant Lambert may only have been awarded three passing mentions in Margot's autobiography; but Hassé was granted not one. He could not understand it. 'I had a very close relationship with her for four years. She spent three or four nights a week at my flat, or I'd go back with her to her mother's for the night. She rang me every night on tour, at two o'clock in the morning. For four years.'

With his suave good looks and part-Chinese ancestry, Hassé must, at the prime age of forty, have cut an elegant figure with twenty-four-year-old Margot. His steady and uncomplicated devotion to her, and his reassuring friendship with her mother, sustained Margot through the rigours and distractions of the war: the skies of London were now beset with 'doodlebugs', the terrifying, pilotless missiles whose sinister motorbike roar was preferable to their sudden silence. For silence, directly overhead, most likely spelt doom. Margot, in her dauntless way, so typical of the tenor of the time, makes a cheerful analogy with the gramophone needle being lifted abruptly from a record in a game of musical chairs: 'One dived behind the settee and hoped for the best.'[29] But on 5 June, at midnight, a buzz bomb came down on Pelham Crescent, killing nine people. Margot, who was out, 'missed all the fun', but BQ had quite a close shave: 'I had a very old friend, Vera Volkova, to supper and afterwards I had taken her up to Margot's room to show her Margot's latest hats. After a lot of talk and gossip she left to get the Tube at 11.30. Felix and Idell were in bed in their little top flat and Margot had gone out to supper after the performance. I was pottering around in the basement dining-room when I heard a bomb approaching, so I rushed up to open the front door and back doors to let any blast go through and as I just got to the front door the bomb dropped behind the houses on the other side of the road and after about two seconds the front door flew off its hinges and hit me on the behind, swung round, and laid itself neatly on the opposite wall.'

Perhaps it was the wartime vulnerability of buildings in general that made it acceptable for Hassé to sleep with Margot under Black Queen's roof. But for a lover to make an ally of the mother is always a two-edged sword, especially when, for the daughter, there remained unresolved issues of separation. Margot was by now twenty-five, yet still answerable as ever to her mother, who had turned the war years into an excuse to attach herself more closely to Margot's world in the unofficial capacity of Wardrobe Mistress. 'Oh yes,' says Beryl Grey, 'Mrs Hookham in the war – ra-*ther*. She looked after our costumes. I know Margot's tutus were *always* divine. When I fell through a chair and got stuck on a nail – I was fourteen, and had just joined the company – she was rushed in and was *wonderful*: sort of pulled me out of the chair and did a lot of bathing in antiseptic.' And, according to Constance Tomkinson, who toured as secretary with Sadler's Wells in 1946, Mrs Hookham was a far cry from 'the interfering mother of ballet legend, zealous only for the advancement of her daughter's career. She was devoted to the whole company. In order to see much of her daughter she had to be in the theatre and while she was there she busied herself doing something useful. If she wasn't pressing a tutu, running an errand or sewing a seam she would be comforting one of the company – listening to their troubles, fussing over their health, scolding them for their own good and in general taking the place of their own mothers.'[30]

Little wonder, then, that Margot should still sometimes have sought refuge from maternal solicitude in the disreputable company of Constant Lambert. She remained his Old Girl, even though, in February of 1944, he fled *his* mother's clutches and moved – lock, cat and piano – to All Saints' Place, into the house of his most roistering drinking companion, Michael Ayrton, with whom he shared an ability 'to look at any occurrence, any part of . . . life, any event in it, as at once a profundity, a mystery and a huge joke'. By this stage of his intensely lived, short life, Constant believed that his very presence on the street could produce a 'happening'. 'This morning's pub crawl produced two black ATS (and my God what beauties), a lesbian midget on crutches by Dadd, and (believe me or believe me not) outside the Bear and Rummer of all places, a woman in a tartan skirt with *two* bandaged legs both of which were bleeding.'[31] His power to hurt Margot was tempered, the older and more dissolute he became, by his inspired, unfailing power to make her laugh. 'Lambert was prodigal of his wit,' writes Anthony Powell. But: 'Even in his palmiest days there were good friends who could stand only limited stretches of the Lambert barrage of ideas, jokes, fantasy, quotations, apt instances, things that struck him as he walked through London, not because these lacked quality, on the contrary because the mixture was after a while too rich.' Margot became great friends with Joan Walsh, Michael Ayrton's mistress, and, despite Charles Hassé's belief that the ballerina was virtually living with him, she spent snatches of her time at Ayrton's glass-roofed studio flat in All Saints' Place, if no longer in physical love with Constant, then still in social and intellectual thrall to his bohemian existence. Lambert's own dependence on Margot remained as profound as it was grudging: 'Travelling to Hanley on Thursday,' he admitted in a note to Ayrton. 'We might go up with a bottle or two and blow raspberries at the OG in Giselle.'[32]

Whatever private disparagement Margot may have borne at that time, the public's romantic view of her could not have been more unsullied. On 1 February, the Old Girl danced the Young Girl in Fokine's *Spectre de la Rose*, in a revival produced by Tamara Karsavina who, with Nijinsky, had created the ballet for Diaghilev in 1911. A cameo specifically made to display Nijinsky's legendary leaping-power and Karsavina's touching command of pictorial stylization, *Spectre* was one of those ballets (*Marguerite and Armand* was to prove another) which does not successfully survive its original cast. If Alexis Rassine was no Vaslav Nijinsky, neither could Rex Whistler's over-elegant designs compete with the rapt, dreamy atmosphere so effortlessly invoked by Bakst. According to Mary Clarke: 'Fonteyn's costume was altogether too pretty and her curls and make-up were nearer Hollywood than ballet.'[33]

The role of the Young Girl, however, did yield one unprecedented bonus: the chance to be coached by the sixty-two-year-old Karsavina, who had not only been a major adornment of the Maryinsky and of the Saisons Russes in Paris, but was renowned for her huge cultural sophistication, rare among Russian dancers: the sharpness and breadth of a mind that could produce the unsurpassed ballet memoir *Theatre Street*. Margot would brook no criticism of her own performance in *Spectre* on the grounds that: 'Karsavina told me to do it like that and Karsavina's word is unalterable law.'[34] Herself once an acknowledged beauty of such velvet-eyed and classical fascination that she had been compared to the women of Greuze and Murillo and Caravaggio, Karsavina, in her turn, did not quarrel with her compatriot Mathilde Kschessinskaya's appraisal of Margot as: '*Pas belle, mais belle pour la scène.*'[35] Margot was flattered – why should she *not* have been? The split between reality and representation was now established, and the choice made: what matter if the woman in her suffer, so long as the artist thrive?

On 24 August 1944 there were still many months of bloody fighting ahead. But of all the great moments of relief and joy which marked, or foretold, the ending of the war, the date on which Paris was liberated from German occupation was perhaps the most thrilling and significant for cosmopolitan Londoners. The blacked-out streets of one great capital rang with songs and cheers for the restoration of the honour of another. 'In our favourite French restaurant, after the ballet,' says Margot, 'we drank more bottles of Algerian burgundy than ever before and cried tears of happiness with the proprietor's family.'[1]

Now, at last, without fearing to tempt fate, the dancers could plan for a civilized future. And the first plan was that in early 1945 the Vic-Wells should travel to Brussels, and thence to Paris, to entertain the British and American forces stationed there. After years of selfless rationing and making do, the ordinary human foibles of vanity and frivolity could reassert themselves: girls could once again be girls, and entertain that uppermost girlish thought: *What shall I wear?* They soon found out. 'We were issued,' Margot scoffs, 'with straight khaki skirts, military jackets, khaki stockings and flat-heeled shoes. Each of us got two shirts, a tie, a wool scarf and a very unbecoming soft military cap.'[2]

Pamela May had rejoined the company, and she and Margot took themselves off to the Queen's milliner, Aage Thaarup, to see what a bit of blocking could do for that shapeless headgear. But they also decided, on reflection, that they dared not abandon their regulation footwear in favour of the ankle-strapped platforms so dear to their hearts yet so ruinous to de Valois's nerves. Just as well; for, when they arrived in Brussels, the streets were ankle deep in snow. There was no electricity in the city during the daylight hours, and no heating or hot water at any time. Three weeks later, in Paris, they were even gladder of their greatcoats and sensible walking shoes, for the only food on offer in the middle of the night was miles from their hotel on the Champs-Elysées – at the Canadian Officers' Club near the Opéra, a theatre so cold that the French *corps de ballet* were given permission to wear white cardigans over their costumes during actual performances. The English girls refused to be fazed by the chronic lack of transport. 'Pamela and I rushed out of our hotel billet,' writes Margot, 'thumbed a lift in a jeep, and went to find Preobrajenska.'[3] And when the Vic-Wells arrived at the Théâtre des Champs-Elysées for the second half of their Paris season, their ENSA get-ups, far from seeming dowdy to the dashing Parisiens, proved a positive fashion hit.

'No!' insists Roland Petit. 'They were *very* chic in uniform, very, very chic. It was really very English and very nice. Here was this English ballet arriving in Paris, and they were the winner of the war. We had always listened to Radio London and it was for us very important. So I was touched.' He was touched in particular by de Valois's reaction to his ballet *Les Forains*, which the company had watched him rehearse. 'Afterwards,' says Petit, 'Ninette de Valois came up to me, and she said with her famous voice and the way she does her punctuations, and the scream she does in the middle of what she says: "You are *choreographer*, my dear!" So that, for me, really meant something because I had just left the Paris Opéra, and I was not twenty years old, and it was my first ballet, my first season. And then she presented me Margot, and I knew this girl from the pictures on the front of *Dancing Times* that came from Switzerland, and I had already fallen in love with her, so it was a great emotion to meet her.'

The feeling was mutual. Not only did Petit show brilliantly innovative flair as a choreographer and dancer, but he was handsome in a way that reflected his Italian mother as well as his French father, and thereby possessed of the feature that Margot felt most drawn to in a human face – perhaps because she saw in it reflections of her own Latin lineage: a pair of lustrous black eyes. She had not met so dark and ardent a gaze since her encounter with Tito Arias, in Cambridge. 'Margot had already,' says Petit, 'the aura of being the first English Great Girl. The one before [Markova] had taken a Russian name, and I had many Russians around me, so I was not always astonished by them. But Margot was just supreme – face, body, all. A young, beautiful, English, ballerina.'

Two nights later he saw her dance – in the Russian, hardly innovative, *Nutcracker pas de deux*. 'A little tense, the smile irreproachable and the little finger in the air, which made malicious Parisians say that she danced with a teacup in her hand, and her admirers, of whom I was unconditionally one, that she was carrying on the traditions of old England.'[4] At the call, Petit emitted a heartfelt cheer but his colleagues were not so susceptible. 'A very famous French dancer seated by me said, "Why do you scream like that? You think it's so good? I think it's nothing and they are no good at all." But I really fell in love with that company. And Margot most of all. She is one of the persons I love best in my life.'

Whatever was to evolve between Roland and Margot remained unspoken for the present, since Petit, at that time, had little English and Margot barely more than ballet terms in French – a situation soon to be remedied by Margot, who, as soon as chance allowed, would take herself post-haste to a London language school. Constant, of course, was Franco-fluent, and tried to instruct her in the way that was natural to him – through literature. Asked in later years how she had learned her good but thickly accented French, Margot replied: 'By reading Proust.'[5] It is true that she sent Baudelaire's poems back to England – as a present for Charles Hassé – but the latter reacted with scepticism: 'I don't think she really cared about Baudelaire. It was Constant Lambert who made her interested.' Meanwhile, Lambert's own personal interests were expanding. It was on this trip that he took up with Isabel Delmer, who, thirty-three, on the verge of divorce, bonily beautiful, and the consort of artists such as Derain, Miró, Epstein and Giacometti, was more

Lambert's intellectual equal than Margot could ever have hoped to be. Though Isabel's radical politics left Constant cold, her moral emancipation suggested a compatibility that he prized above all others: the capacity to match him drink for drink. She took him to the City Hotel, which, she says, enchanted him: 'especially the scaffolding, which filled him with interesting and fanciful thoughts. In the café overlooking the Seine it was clear that he was perfectly happy . . . One evening, without any warning, Margot Fonteyn and Ninette de Valois arrived outside the café. There we both were, sipping what was probably a Pernod, when Margot turned towards Ninette, smiling with glee, saying, "Enfin il a trouvé son ambiance." They had brought with them Roland Petit, who was astounded to find Constant frequenting such an unfashionable and broken-down habitation as the City Hotel.'[6]

When the company left Paris for the last Belgian lap of the ENSA tour, Constant lingered on for a few days with Isabel before going alone to conduct a series of concerts in Poland. He returned to London in a state of mental and physical collapse, which perturbed Ayrton: 'His emotional instability is becoming "chronic" as charwomen say. Of course we are all the same, but he takes it a step further than the rest of us.'[7]

Personal worries, however, were diminished by global relief. Two weeks into the spring season at the New, Hitler's charred remains were delivered into the hands of the Russians, and on 13 May 1945, five days before Margot's twenty-sixth birthday, the company celebrated Victory in Europe to Delibes's triumphal score, with Helpmann running riot as Dr Coppélius, decking Swanilda's balcony with Union Jacks. The men were coming home from the forces: Ashton, Somes, Harold Turner, Jack Hart, John Field. 'While awaiting demobilization,' rejoiced de Valois, 'they turned up at the theatre in uniform and army boots – getting down to a little practice and rehearsal, even before they had received their discharge papers.'[8] She went on to describe Constant Lambert as 'in his element' at being in command of a full-sized orchestra. But, in fact, his friends were trying desperately to make him scale down his responsibilities. They plotted to bring him the medical help that he needed – not an easy manoeuvre, since the torments of his childhood leg operations for osteomyelitis, which had left him lame, had taught him to scorn all doctors, a scorn further exacerbated by their inevitable dictum: stop drinking. The Sitwells came up with a Dr Child, a meeting between Constant and whom, wrote Ayrton: 'must be effected at the earliest opportunity. The middle of next week if possible. He can then be put out to grass for two full weeks. He *must be prevented* from working. Margot is frantic (and a party to our scheme). The old boy is spitting blood and in every way worse.'[9]

It was to be discovered posthumously that Lambert's alcoholism only represented half the picture: undiagnosed in his lifetime had been his diabetes mellitus, a condition aggravated by his propensity to forget about eating for long stretches of time when his work possessed him. What he had needed, but had never received, were injections of insulin. Saved from death in 1945, not by any medical intervention but by the iron constitution peculiar to fabled drinkers (and perhaps the zest that accompanies the prospect of a new love affair), he went on to conduct ten concerts at the Proms and to make a great success of them. It was Margot's own health that, with the ending of the war, suddenly and mysteriously broke down. The restricted diet, and the unremitting personal responsibility that she had shouldered for so long, told at last on her tender frame, infecting her skin and threatening to leave scarred – of all things – her face. Not that she attached much importance to her looks in close-up, when heavy make-up and footlights could disguise so much. What did she care if she were *pas belle* as long as she remained *belle pour la scène*?

'Oh,' she said to the specialist who treated her, 'my feet are much more important than my face.'[10] Scandalized by such a perverse want of vanity in a pretty young woman, Dr Isaac Muende injected the point of infection directly with the new wonder drug, penicillin. Luckily for posterity as well as for his patient, the unsightliness disappeared, leaving no trace. 'He treated me,' writes Margot, and her astonishment sounds genuine, 'as delicately as a film star.'[11]

Just in time. For *The Sleeping Princess* was about to assume its proper title: *The Sleeping Beauty*. What other ballet could so aptly celebrate the graduation of the Sadler's Wells Ballet to its new home at the Royal Opera House, Covent Garden, than this benevolent fairy tale of fate and transformation? Unlike Diaghilev, who had never considered his ballerinas' faces to be their fortune, de Valois believed that she had at least three potential Auroras who could legitimately be described as beautiful. Blonde, blue-eyed May and red-headed, cream-skinned Shearer were two of them. But only Fonteyn truly matched Tennyson's poetic vision: Love, if thy tresses be so dark / How dark those hidden eyes must be! / A touch, a kiss! The charm was snapt . . .'[12]

But the revivifying of the dormant Opera House was not so whimsically achieved, nor did it go uncontested. De Valois herself opposed it, or at least considered it premature. The newly formed Arts Council, headed by Lord Keynes, felt strongly that Covent Garden, which before the war had mounted glittering seasons of imported Grand Opera or Russian Ballet (only to stand empty for the intervening months), should be made the home of a resident opera company and a resident ballet company consisting mainly of British artists. Admittedly, a world-class national opera company would take years to build up, but a genuinely national ballet was already in existence. De Valois was invited not only to expand her ranks and make the Opera House her company's home, but to enlarge the school and form a second company to fill the vacant place at Sadler's Wells.

It was a bold idea which threatened to stretch the company's resources to the limit. For once, de Valois's vision failed her. She did not believe that the sets for the company's existing works, particularly her own, could successfully be up-scaled. More seriously, she feared that her dancers would be dwarfed by the huge proscenium, and that their technical shortcomings – resulting from years of reining in and toning down to accommodate raked and crowded stages and slippery and uneven surfaces – would be fatally exposed by so limitless a canvas. Moreover, backstage, the Opera House was a shambles. Dusty old wardrobes revealed racks of costumes from long-forgotten opera productions, and rats were to be found lording it in the dressing-rooms. 'It was a great theatre,' writes de Valois, 'haunted by shades of exotic Russian ballet . . . We were . . . challenging it, at the beginning with nothing less than a bedraggled war-weary company.'[13]

Ashton would stand for none of her faint-heartedness. 'If you don't, I will,' he warned,[14] and when de Valois, overruled by her board of directors, agreed to the move for a trial period of four months, he made it his business to teach the dancers, and Margot in particular, how to make their presence felt in the vast auditorium. 'I went all over the house and said [to Fonteyn], "You're still not registering. I don't know what's the matter. I've been upstairs, I've been downstairs," and then one day she held one pose a fraction longer and I went back and I said, "I've got it. You've got to *hold* everything much more so as to register." And that's how she started to do it. She said, "Where?" I took her through rehearsals and I said, "Here." And we got it.'[15]

Throughout the war, a different kind of dancing had made its mark within the hallowed walls. Mecca Enterprises had leased the building and converted it into a gigantic dance hall, with the stage and stalls boarded over and a bandstand at either end. There, to 'In the Mood' and 'Chattanooga Choo Choo' and all the great Glenn Miller numbers, young men and women could jive away their precious, sometimes last, hours together, wearing the fashion of the day: battledress. But although the first-night ballet audience boasted the King and Queen, Queen Mary and the Royal Princesses, the Prime Minister, Clement Attlee, Ernest Bevin, members of the Diplomatic Corps and that gaggle of socialites referred to by Lord Keynes as 'the ancient hens of glory',[16] Mrs Hookham, who had worked so hard backstage, was disappointed by the front of house, which, despite being decked with fresh flowers, was let down by the dreary dress sense of its patrons. The atmosphere in the auditorium was a far cry from the gala night before the war when 'there had been such a flashing of real diamonds that the stage costumes were completely outshone'. Now, on 20 February 1946, the situation was about to prove the exact opposite. 'To me the only flaw was that many of the people in the stalls and circle [men] were very casually dressed since Labour got in . . . Since that day the standard of men's dress to go to the Opera, which used to be something of an occasion, has never recovered.' De Valois, however, had done her best to keep the old flag flying. 'I donned the evening dress I had not left in Holland,' she writes, 'and I presume Frederick Ashton was resplendent in the dinner jacket that I slept in on the straw of the cargo boat hold.'[17] The whiff of stale beer which had permeated the auditorium in the days of the Palais de Danse gave way to the strong scent of moth-balls. But the fustiness of the audience only lent more glamour to the scene which the parting crimson curtains revealed. A breathtaking £10,000 had been spent on this new *Sleeping Beauty*, but money could not buy the fanaticism with which the wardrobe department, led by the indomitable Mrs Hookham, had scoured the land for every scrap and bolt of brocade, and velvet and silk, that lay beyond the joyless grip of rationing. 'Many materials were impossible to find,' she writes, 'so some skirts of old Opera dresses were cut up, and friends of Messel who had big houses were asked to search their attics for velvet, in particular, as that was most difficult to get right. I remember the Queen's train was made of someone's red velvet curtains and someone else provided some furs . . . The endless cutting out, stitching and fitting of all those costumes made the work-rooms sound like a beehive.' But it was worth it. Oliver Messel's sumptuous designs requited, as no production has done since, not just the public yearning for romance, but the practical demands of those who had to contend with the sets and wear the costumes – the dancers themselves. Aurora's ravishing jewelled and sleeved tutu, and her stylishly lopsided headdress, were based on the Velázquez portrait, *La Infanta Margarita*; and, for de Valois, the sight of Margot, all shyness and grandeur, was the very mythological vision of which she had dreamed: 'She was the Sleeping Beauty whose role in real life was reversed – who was to awaken London's golden Opera House from its long sleep, a sleep which had lasted through the grimmest sequence of nights that it had known. But our Sleeping Beauty herself awoke to find overnight that she also, as other great dancers before her, could claim to be without rival. As she stepped on the stage that night . . . she was not a stage Princess celebrating her birthday but a great dancer celebrating her birthright . . . Fonteyn, who had never wavered in her integrity, her hard work, and her loyalty towards the institution that can proudly claim to have made her, was there to lead her companions to triumph.'[18]

More soberly, Mary Clarke admits that – although Helpmann, doubling as Carabosse and Prince Florimund, 'seemed not at all troubled by the enlarged frame he had to fill'[19] – Fonteyn 'had yet to take the measure of the auditorium and project her performance to its outermost areas. Always an artist of restraint, despising flamboyant tricks of presentation, she had to learn gradually how to adapt her performance, but when she did at last establish full mastery of her surroundings, her interpretation was all the richer for having been felt from within and not built up by a series of superficial additions.'[20]

Although, since first having been taught the role by Sergeyev in 1939, Margot had tried to refine her understanding of the lineage of the steps by consulting the memories of Preobrajenska, Karsavina and Volkova, she nevertheless lacked a visual guide, and, in her work with Ashton, was compelled to conjure her interpretation directly from her own imagination, just as she would have done in a ballet he was creating 'on her'. It is, perhaps, this deep originality of approach that has made her historical claim to the role so absolute. In an interview twenty years later she was to say: 'It seems funny to me that it is now accepted in the way that it is, with such high regard for certain familiar passages, because there is no valid basis for saying that the way I did it is the right way . . . In a way I suppose my position in *The Sleeping Beauty* is a unique one in our time, in that I have had to ferret out the overall shape entirely by myself. In Russia they have *always* had the example before them of dancers from preceding generations. For people coming after Pamela May and myself in *The Sleeping Beauty*, there has perhaps been something to watch and to criticize.'[21]

Pamela May danced the second performance, while, in faraway Shanghai, the man who was to be her second husband, Charles Gordon, sat at the famous English Long Bar with Margot's father. Together they raised their glasses to the two Auroras, for Felix senior had at last been released from his long internment. 'When the Japanese overran Shanghai,' Margot would later chronicle, 'he was among the enemy aliens taken into enemy camp, where on his arrival he wisely volunteered for kitchen duties and spent the next two and a half years boiling rice but remaining cheerful and adequately fed.'[22] By the time he returned to England, in the August of '46, bringing with him his new Austrian wife, Beatrice, the Sadler's Wells Ballet had just embarked on a long tour of the provinces: Newcastle, Aberdeen, Edinburgh, Glasgow, Leeds and Coventry. Felix had bought some land in Jersey where he planned to build a house, and he had the sense to leave Beatrice behind when he crossed to the mainland to see his daughter dance for the first time in ten years – a span during which not only had Margot become a prima ballerina, but his ex-wife, Nita, had been appointed Black Queen. BQ was magnanimous enough to throw a party in his honour, surrounding herself and Margot – as if to validate their independence of him – with luminaries from the ballet world. Annabel Farjeon was there, and described Mr Hookham as a 'plain English, reddish-faced man who'd been in the sun a lot. A bit shrivelled in a way from being in the wrong climate.' Leslie Edwards, however, who loved everything that pertained to Margot, had a much more favourable impression: 'We were on tour somewhere like Newcastle, and over came Dad. He was so jolly. Roaring with laughter. Looked very like Felix.' But neither mother nor daughter seems to have mustered much compassion for what Felix *père*, adequately fed or no, must have suffered at the hands of the Japanese during his years of captivity. 'We all rallied round Margot,' says Hassé, 'and buttered her up and paid great tribute to her to make him feel how much he had lost. Dull little man. Don't think she had any feelings for him. Don't think she cared at all.'

But Margot's father was a fixture in her life, and, whatever the nonchalance of her manner, her love for him was inviolate. It was her feelings for Hassé himself that were failing fast: Roland Petit had begun to visit her in London. Petit's first venture to Covent Garden was, he claims, 'organized by Margot like clockwork: a quick bath at Brown's Hotel, a little preliminary talk before the show in which she was dancing in Robert Helpmann's *Miracle in the Gorbals*. The ballet was quite ordinary. She divine, I in seventh heaven, sitting in the stalls next to two dream creatures, the young princesses Elizabeth and Margaret who were clapping as hard as they could. Supper after the show at Prunier's, French and English lessons during the oysters and smoked salmon. Margot and I, looking into each other's eyes, were very smitten with one another.'[23]

If Margot were considering an infidelity, this was not so much at Constant Lambert's expense, or even at that of Charles Hassé: the real threat was to Frederick Ashton's choreographic hold over her. Petit does not mince his words: 'We were together, in a London tea shop. And she was dressed like an English nurse: too strict. Not very feminine. We took tea together and she said, "Oh, I like so much to do something new because I do the same thing all the time." (You know, it is the dream of every choreographer to meet the ballerina, and of the ballerina to meet the choreographer.) So she said, "I like to come to Paris," and we started to be really close and to like each other very much.'

Margot's thoughts of defection, had he but known them, would have cut particularly deep with Ashton, because his talent, so painfully buried throughout the war, was about to break forth in full flower. *Symphonic Variations* was supposed to have its première less than a month after *Beauty* opened, but it had to be postponed until 24 April because Michael Somes, not long recovered from a spleen operation after a fall from an army truck, now tore a cartilage in his knee. The resulting extension of rehearsal time, Margot thought, accounted in part for the ballet's perfection.

What also doubtless contributed was Ashton's bitter determination to settle the score with his usurper, Helpmann. With the intensely dramatic *Miracle in the Gorbals* (so steeped in violent realism that patrons were advised in a programme note 'not to bring young children'), and now his latest, *Adam Zero*, a complicated allegory on the Life and Death of Man, Helpmann seemed to Ashton, and indeed to many critics, to be taking ballet, in the promotion of his own glory as actor-dancer, further and further from its true vocabulary – dancing. *Symphonic Variations* restored the purity of the form and established, once and for all, Ashton's incomparable mastery of it. Unlike de Valois, who felt the need to mask down the huge proscenium and stage area in an attempt to restore a more intimate scale to *The Rake's Progress* (succeeding only in making the dancers look like puppets), Ashton opened up the great Covent Garden stage, ridding it of all scenery save Sophie Fedorovitch's greenish-yellow backdrop, which was scored with sweeping lines, thus invoking a pastoral, yet abstract, sense of infinite space. The music, by César Franck, elicited the usual objections from Constant Lambert, who considered it 'complete in itself';[24] but Ashton was not to be swayed: he had listened to it incessantly throughout the war, and had formed 'a very elaborate idea of it, a kind of mystical marriage',[25] connected in his mind with the writings of St Teresa of Avila and St John of the Cross. But as work on the ballet progressed, any literary pretension and religious reference fell away, as did the originally envisioned large cast, until all that Sophie Fedorovitch had left to dress – and all in white – were six dancers: three men in tights and the barest of shirts, with touches of black at the waist and ankle, and three women in short, softly draped Hellenic tunics, so redolent of the uncluttered simplicity of the classroom that, in the late 50s, the design would become a prototype for the students' (black) uniform at the Royal Ballet School.

Symphonic Variations made unprecedented technical demands on its male dancers: Michael Somes, Henry Danton and Ashton's new eighteen-year-old lover, Brian Shaw. Somes pays characteristic tribute to the women: 'Fred was blessed with three marvellous girls – Moira, Pamela and Margot – and of course they *matched* so beautifully. The ballet was a great step forward for Fred, in that it has a particular Englishness about it: it epitomizes English style, which was developed very much on Margot's line.'[26] Despite the ensemble nature of the work, never had the rapport between the choreographer and his favoured ballerina been more pronounced. 'Even as one of the six performers,' Ashton would later explain, 'she was, on the one hand, able to submit with perfect ease to being an equal player in a sextet, yet within this context she still dominated . . . For that reason, if for no other, *Symphonic Variations* might be one of the greatest things she has ever done.' It is his way, of course, of acknowledging his own greatest work. For the 'mystical marriage' of Ashton's secret scenario had indeed taken place; and his original conceits (of which he had never spoken to Margot) of dedication and absorption in divine love, and the suggestion of 'a nun taking the veil into the ballet'[27] were all there, by instinct, in her performance. Marvellous and matching as May and Shearer may have been, they were but foils for a deeper and more touching grace. Study the photographs: if ever evidence of Margot's supremacy were needed, it is here, in this straightforward three-way comparison. And the evidence lies in the angle of the head, in the innate conviction that when the arms and legs are placed so, the head should be exactly . . . so. The auburn and the blonde look riveting enough, until you glimpse the perfect tilt of that dark head, which never forces the line, or presumes upon a step, but is somehow, as Goncharov had noted right back at the beginning of her training, *intent*.

And the intention is to preserve the integrity of the body's natural relation to movement and space. Like harmonious architecture, the sight of Fonteyn in *Symphonic Variations* was essentially calming. Calmness was what she conveyed, even though the twenty-minute ballet, in which no one leaves the stage, is such a test of stamina that I have seen dancers vomit in the wings at the end from sheer exhaustion. Margot was never even doubled over – never really seriously winded: that was the legacy of those gruelling war years, when she had danced harder and longer and more often than absolutely anyone. In *Symphonic Variations*, she is remembered, most of all, for her astonishing stillness when (for all practical purposes, catching her breath for a scherzo solo and skimming *pas de deux* to come), she stood downstage left, one foot crossed over the other, arms at her sides. 'This is where her submission came in as her greatest power,' says Violette Verdy, who, in her teens, saw the original 1946 cast. 'She was waiting for her turn to move, but not looking at the other dancers, or interfering with them, or stealing their thunder, but waiting *in the music*. She would fill her ears and her heart with it, and when the time came, she was forced to start because she was so full that it overflowed out of her.'

A decade later, the effect for a new generation of dancers would be just as potent. 'One couldn't tear one's eyes away from her,' says Antoinette Sibley, who first saw Margot in *Symphonic Variations* in the mid-50s. 'One wasn't watching the dancing that was going on in the centre. One was just watching that beautiful, beautiful woman on the edge of the stage. Moving the heart, but not moving in action at all. Just standing there. Motionless.'[28]

It was Margot's infatuation with Roland Petit that prompted her, at the age of twenty-six, at last to make the overdue break and find a home of her own, away from her mother's beady eye. 'Margot told me,' writes Mrs Hookham, 'that she found travelling up and down to the theatre by Tube all the time tiring, and had been told of a small vacant flat in Long Acre which she would like to take. I was somewhat shattered by this, which meant that now I would be alone in that big house, no husband, no son, and now no daughter . . . Well obviously I must get out and find myself a flat . . . After a short hunt I found a very nice two-roomed flat on the corner of Pont Street, on the ground floor.'

Margot's own new home was rather less salubrious and rather more of a climb – three floors above the smell of rotting cabbages and the wolf-whistles of Cockney barrow-boys which in those days lent such character to Covent Garden. But it wasn't always the sheer convenience that it sounds to live a stone's throw from the Opera House. Sometimes she would take a taxi round the block just to get back, lest fans, flocking nightly at the stage door, should be dispirited to discover that a ballerina returns home on foot, or worse, lest they be inspired to trail after her all the way to her front door.

In 1946, Petit brought *Les Forains* to the Adelphi Theatre with the Ballets des Champs-Elysées, starring, as well as himself, the voluptuous *danseur* Jean Babilée. London, according to Richard Buckle, had for a long time seen no male dancer as good as Petit, much less one with a spark of divine fire, like Babilée, and *Les Forains* was 'well calculated to whip us into a frenzy'.[1] Some members of the audience, however, took the French success 'as a personal affront to their beloved English company

. . . Even the broad-minded and sensible Ninette de Valois . . .
wore an air of chilly disapproval.'

The French were not the only threat to the supremacy of
the Sadler's Wells Ballet that season. The Opera House played
host to American Ballet Theatre and its abundance of virile-
looking, technically accomplished male dancers. 'The English
boys had been through a war, and it showed,' says Dick Beard,[2]
a member of the company whose own shining muscularity at
the age of twenty now put Ashton in a serious swoon. Most
embarrassing for de Valois was the dramatic impact made by
the choreographer Antony Tudor, whom, before the war, she
had allowed to slip through her fingers. Tudor's *Pillar of Fire*
starred Nora Kaye, and her psychologically harrowing and sexually explicit performance staggered Margot. But she chose to be
inspired rather than envious, and took up with Kaye in a way
that she had never before done with any woman, exchanging
gifts and imparting the secrets of her heart. Kaye was a vibrant,
sassy New Yorker of Russian extraction – 'a marvellous dame',[3]
according to Ashton – with a generous and candid spirit. Among
the silk stockings and blouses and hats that Kaye showered on
her new friend, she gave a silver fox stole to Margot, who,
though she would never have chosen something so showy for
herself, nevertheless wore it with delight. 'Nora admired Margot
extravagantly,' says Herbert Ross, who was married to Kaye from
1958 until her death in 1987. 'She thought she was the most
wonderful dancer with the most perfect body – an exquisitely
proportioned body. She and Margot were very close friends.
They admired each other's artistry without invading in any way
the area in which the other excelled. More than that, they just
understood one another. Nora did not have girl friends, and I
don't think Margot did either. But if Nora loved you, she was
totally yours.'

Nora was the first person to whom Margot admitted the
extent of her suffering over Constant, and his drunken violence.
She also told Kaye of her crush on Roland Petit, who came to
stay in the new flat in Long Acre and recalls: 'The fairy of

Covent Garden came to meet me on the morning I arrived on the Golden Arrow, to take me to her place, where a bright and welcoming room awaited me.'[4] Petit is at pains, though, to make clear that the relationship was, for him at least, not really physical in essence. 'Touch – touch – to have sex with someone is what, exactly? When I was living at Margot's she was coming in the morning to bring the breakfast. Coming close to me – but we hadn't been fucking all night. We had a passion, like a big flirt with lots of tenderness and love games, but for me it wasn't like with Zizi [his wife, Renée Jeanmaire], when I was for years and years in a very sexual relationship.'

Margot, after the life-and-death drama of Constant, and the unrelieved devotion of Charles Hassé, revelled, at first, in the levity of this new arrangement. Petit was four years her junior, and his effect on her was both invigorating and subversive. According to Richard Buckle, 'the academy of classicism meant nothing to him: he was a child of the boulevards, loving glitter and excitement.'[5] In February '47 Petit persuaded Margot to ask de Valois for leave of absence to study in Paris. De Valois agreed, so long as Mrs Hookham accompanied her. Petit is scathing of such nannying: 'Margot didn't need to be chaperoned, because she knew exactly what she wanted in life. She had a strong personality as an artist, and as a woman too, and she knew exactly what she was doing. She didn't need no mother, no anybody. The mother was strict, and probably a good help, and was giving her advice for sure, but Margot had already decided what she wanted to do, and she was pretending to listen. We were very young and we went together everywhere, doing the craziest things: we would take off our clothes and jump in the river and swim across and when we swam back our clothes were still on the bank. They could have been stolen – Paris was not like now with cars and police and everything. The river was clean like in the country. People were still washing their clothes in it.'

Margot could not have cared less what became of her 'austerity wardrobe'. The New Look – with its sloping shoulder-line, nipped-in waist, and lavish skirt swirling about the calf – was all the rage, and nowhere did it rage more potently than along the rue St-Honoré. Petit took her there to perform 'a spectacular metamorphosis' on her, but once inside the Maison Dior, the transformative magic was all Margot's own. Gone, in one stroke, were the endless hours spent treadling at her mother's sewing-machine, trying to update last year's frock, or sitting on trains between Hull and Manchester, stitching lace edging to the legs of cami-knickers so that her underwear might pass for French. High fashion and Margot were natural allies. Her hunger for extravagance was matched at once by Dior's sensible opportunism in spotting the advantage of having his designs modelled by this slim, dark-haired beauty on the brink of international fame. She emerged in a fabulous number from the new collection, and continued to be dressed at a *prix d'ami* until his death in 1957. In a foreword to Brigid Keenan's 1981 biography, *Dior in Vogue*, Margot would write: 'Like most people during the forties I happily regarded the square shoulders, skimpy skirts and platform shoes as very smart. Then along came Christian Dior's "New Look", with its feminine lines, small waists and full skirts that were much longer than anything we had seen for years. There were even some padded hips to accentuate the waistline. I was lucky enough to be more or less the same size as one of his favourite models, Vicki, and at the end of each season I was able to buy one of the model dresses made on her. From the first collection I had the simple black outfit called "Daisy".'[6]

Margot's attitude to her own looks was nowhere near as confident as Dior's. Late in 1946 she had made a film for children – *The Little Ballerina*, in which she played herself, adding an air of authenticity to an otherwise purely, and pretty puerile, fictional script, grinding resin into her *pointe* shoes in the wings, dancing a few excerpts from *Les Sylphides* with Michael Somes, and speaking in an extraordinarily plummy BBC accent to the young heroine of the film about the dedication required to enter the profession. She was dismayed by the sight and sound of herself, and more dismayed still when the film, which had been made for a limited audience, went out on general release.

As a screen-test it did her no favours, and put paid to an idea, mooted at the time, that a film be made of the full-length *Sleeping Beauty*: she was considered not photogenic enough. Although Margot had no real desire to be in movies, and was susceptible to de Valois's prejudice that the transposition of ballet to celluloid was a vulgarity, it nevertheless irked her that the film industry should be in hot pursuit of another, prettier ballerina: her titian-haired colleague, Moira Shearer.

Aware that most people in highbrow artistic circles considered a film contract to be little better than a pact with the devil, Moira at first turned down the chance to star in *The Red Shoes*. She held out for nine months against the blandishments of the director, Michael Powell: 'Wretched man – he was always hanging round the theatre. I didn't really want to do it – I was just at the beginning in the company. I kept saying no.' Moira thought that her principled and idealistic stance would earn her respect and support from de Valois, but this was far from the case. 'Ninette suddenly called me up to the office one day after rehearsal and for *once* she let me sit down. Usually one had to stand up while she blew one up, bawled one out, and so on. I sat down. I couldn't think what was coming. And then she actually said: "For God's sake just do this – this man is driving us all mad, Shearer, and it's going on and on and on. Why don't you just do it, get it over with, get it off your chest, get it off ours?" I was staggered. The only thing I asked her was, could I return to the company immediately the film was over and continue in exactly the same way? Or was this going to make some sort of difference?'

The difference which *The Red Shoes* made was, of course, all the difference in the world. Despite the corny backstage story, it took ballet out to a new mass market. 'Ninette laughed at it,' says Moira, 'called it "ludicrous, so bad", and spread that around.' But as Clive Barnes explained to Shearer years later, de Valois had harboured a long-term objective: 'My dear, she knew it would come out in '48, have an enormous showing all over America and be the perfect springboard for the company when you arrived in '49. She wanted you and Bobby as forerunners – for Margot.'

Great ruthlessness is born of immoderate loyalty, and despite her democratic spirit, which was pitted firmly enough against the star system where everyone else was concerned, de Valois's intense and tyrannical heart would always be bound to the original architects of her company – Lambert, Ashton, Helpmann and Fonteyn – branded by her favouritism in the eyes of the rest as 'untouchables'. Soon enough she herself would have a name which would make clear the isolation as well as the elevation of her position at the Opera House. In the New Year's Honours List of 1947 she was made a Commander of the British Empire; and in 1951 she would be made a Dame. But by then it would be too late for the dancers to learn to call her Dame Ninette. An Australian dancer, Gordon Hamilton, had already dubbed her 'Madam', and the tease, as well as the reverence of the title, had stuck, just as 'Black Queen' had stuck to Mrs Hookham. Good-naturedly, de Valois came to accept in all seriousness what had begun in jest, even signing her private letters, between quotation marks: 'Madam'.

But now, for the first time, Madam's loyalty was to be tested. One of her 'untouchables', the one whom she loved most, was coming under increasing professional fire. It was not the members of the orchestra who called into question Constant Lambert's efficiency as a conductor. His surpassing scholarship and musical intelligence remained their pride and inspiration, and they were happy enough to have him swaying about the podium if this meant that he was kept from keeling over in the street. Nor would the dancers have dreamed of complaining: although the tempi could sometimes be slower than usual, they dreaded to think what they would do without his unique sensitivity to their individual technical needs, and the discipline and flair which he could draw from their musical responses. But the Opera House had an administrator, David Webster, who felt no personal allegiance to Lambert's great wartime contribution, and did not see why the conductor's past achievements should exempt him from criticism. Not to put too fine a point on it, Webster thought Lambert 'drunken and unfunny'.[7] To Lambert, meanwhile, Webster was nothing but a 'musical businessman'. Webster, however, had a business to run, and he was running it for de Valois. And although it broke her heart to admit it, she was clear-sighted enough to concede that by 1946 Lambert, her great mainstay and adviser, that 'man of intellect and personality in our midst', was beyond salvation. 'You couldn't rely on him. We knew what was coming and there was nothing to be done about it, and we knew he didn't want anything to be done about it. All his friends knew this, but one hung on forever because he was such a wonderful man.'[8]

And still astonishingly productive. Half-way through 1946, Lambert had embarked on a mammoth collaboration which would celebrate the marriage of opera and ballet at Covent Garden, and, by bringing into the proceedings Shakespeare's words from *A Midsummer Night's Dream* (on which Spenser's poem is based), turn that marriage into a trinity, with Purcell's *The Fairy Queen*. Ashton and Malcolm Baker Smith were to help produce, while Lambert took on the adaptation himself. Michael Ayrton was to design the sets in the manner of Inigo Jones; Ashton to plan the choreography in his own inimitable manner; Helpmann to speak Oberon's lines to Margaret Rawlings's Titania; Michael Hordern to play Bottom, and James Kenny, Puck; Audrey Bowman, Constance Shacklock and David Franklin would lead the majestic plaints and choral set pieces, and Fonteyn and Somes would dance the Spirits of the Air in the second of three masques, the Masque of Love. Rehearsals for the dancers would take place during arduous tours of Scotland, northern England and Vienna.

The preparations lasted six months. But just before the first night, on 12 December, the whole cast was up in arms. David Webster had seen fit to oust Constant as conductor and to put Karl Rankl, a far less distinguished musician, in his stead. Fonteyn, Helpmann, Somes, Rawlings, Hordern and anyone else with any clout refused to set foot on the stage unless the production's presiding genius be restored to the pit. Webster was forced to capitulate. But the incident left Lambert more vulnerable to attack when it came. *The Fairy Queen* is five hours long, and Lambert had been obliged to cut it to half that length – injudiciously, some thought. Desmond Shawe-Taylor called the evening 'a fifty per cent success'.[9] The production had to bear the brunt not just of opera critics carping about the dancing, and of ballet critics taking issue with the singing, but also of the audaciously gifted young drama critic Kenneth Tynan, who sharpened the lethal rapier of his wit on the whole caboodle, with particular reference to the performance of Robert Helpmann (actually a rather restrained one by Bobby's standards): 'He speaks a good deal of verse in his thin ascetic voice, glowering all the time with his aghast little hatchet face.'[10] And, to the musical director, Tynan did not even pay the compliment of his humour. Mr Lambert had simply 'cut away much that was vital'.[11]

Helpmann had fared even worse with the critics in Ashton's latest ballet, *Les Sirènes* (1946), for which he made his entrance in a hot-air balloon blowing kisses and yodelling in a tinny tenor. The ballet world could no longer contain his diversity. His health, like Margot's, had broken down at the end of the war, and he was to find recovery over the next three years, not in rest, but in the redirection of his boundless energies into straight theatre and films, darting between Covent Garden and Stratford-upon-Avon, from Siegfried to Shylock, from Albrecht to King John. Not only did he undertake in 1947 to act and dance in *The Red Shoes*, but he had assumed, as well, responsibility for the choreography. He was only thirty-eight, yet the best of his contribution to English ballet was already behind him: he made no more works for Sadler's Wells. But Ashton was to find a fresh object for his hostility when de Valois invited Léonide Massine to Covent Garden, to stage and appear in two of his best-known ballets from the Diaghilev days: *Le Tricorne* and *La Boutique Fantasque*, plus a more recent work, *Mam'zelle Angot*. De Valois dismisses the inevitable slight felt by Ashton:

'It was necessary. I did it for the men who were madly weak after the war. It wasn't as if I'd brought in some little Englishman; I brought in a distinguished choreographer from the last generation. He [Ashton] was principally a woman's choreographer. I knew the girls were all right with Fred; I was worried about the boys.'[12]

Margot was left to fend for womanhood and herself. It was a new kind of challenge, as well as an honour, to appear opposite Massine as the Miller's Wife in *Le Tricorne*. Raised to a fever of expectation by the opening drumbeats of a thrilling de Falla score, the sedate London audience began to cheer like bullfighting *aficionados* at the very sight of Massine, still taut-bodied and fabulously self-obsessed at fifty-one, alone against Picasso's sun-drenched backdrop. It was the second time in succession that Margot had been given the chance to assume Spanishness (in *Les Sirènes*, wearing a black sombrero, she had played La Bolero), and much as she enjoyed the liberty of stamping about in high heels, it was hard for her to find an authentic flamenco style, never having laid eyes on an Andalusian gypsy. But the attempt so engrossed her – character-dancing having been, after all, her first love – that twenty years later the choreography was still, as Keith Money points out, 'safely locked away in her system',[13] waiting to be released by music. He has private evidence of this wonder, for 'once, when Margot arrived at my address unexpectedly one morning, it was just after I had put on a record of *Le Tricorne*, and upon hearing a theme filtering out into the hall, she positively flung her coat and very soon was whirling and dipping around the living-room (fortunately large) as the Miller's Wife of Massine's ballet . . . When the solo was ended, she dropped on to a sofa, slightly breathless, but in the highest of spirits. "Oh, I used to love doing that! I'm sure I was no good in it, at all, but it was such fun to do!" '[14] The fun of the original had been much intensified by the fire of her partner in the Fandango, and locking foreign black eyes with Massine, she was surprised, as she would be in so many instances to come, 'that my life at that time had more substance in the theatre than out of it. Only a fatal passion could have been more engrossing.'

Soon after the opening night, on 6 February 1947, she was obliged to seek her passion elsewhere. Only a few performances into the Massine season, Margot became ill and was unable to dance for nine weeks. Nowhere is the illness specified, although it was severe and protracted enough for her to suffer the sight of Moira Shearer dancing the Can-Can in her place on the opening night of *La Boutique Fantasque*. A strained ligament in Margot's left leg, which had first flared up in Vienna, and which was to bring her so much trouble eighteen months later, may have been the cause. Or was she brought low by coming face to face with Lambert's unequivocal defection from her? It is one thing to lose one's lover to the ravages of his own self-sabotaging nature. It is quite another to lose him to the arms of a rival woman. During the run of *Le Tricorne*, Isabel Delmer had encouraged Constant to move out of Ayrton's house and into a flat at Thurloe Square, the better to pursue their love affair. (In fact, Constant complicated the transition by having an interim affair with a Japanese soprano called Aki.) All his friends were aware of his new happiness with Isabel, and it must have been particularly galling for Margot, who had tried so long and hard to be his saviour, to hear that this 'heavy, stooped, prematurely aged figure, his breath usually smelling of drink, his eyes puffy and his clothes streaked with cigarette ash'[15] had actually stopped smoking, and given up drinking spirits, to please his new mistress. For all the safety that Margot had found in the number of her lovers, it was still – according to Judy Tatham, to whom she lent the flat in Long Acre for a fling with Donald Albery – a photo of Constant that Margot kept in a frame by her bed.

But it was to Petit that Margot now turned for solace. By June, she was again in Paris, this time with Vera Volkova as chaperone. The latter, being less redoubtable than Black Queen, was easier to shed; and what better remedy for injured muscles or an aching heart than a swim in the Seine? In the small hours,

Margot could be seen at the Balajo in rue de Lappe, stripped down to her underwear. 'It was summer,' says Petit, 'and she took off her dress and was just with the chemise in black satin. Today that wouldn't be shocking because girls are naked, almost, but at that period for a woman to take off her dress was something. Margot was above the situation. She was a lady.' At the Balajo, they danced the Java and practised the Carpet Dance. This, explains Petit, 'consisted of, while still dancing, putting a mat at the feet of the chosen girl, falling on your knees on it in front of her, where she joined you, and you kiss, to the applause of spectators. Farewell formalities. Margot was in my arms.'[16]

To what purpose? Despite Petit's inordinately happy marriage to Renée Jeanmaire – whom he wed in 1952 – he was not really (in Hassé's words) 'sexually available to women'. Petit describes the dynamic between himself and Margot as akin to her passionate friendship, fifteen years later, with the homosexual Nureyev. 'She did love me, and she did love Rudolf. What is an affair? How does it start? When does it finish? I didn't have a love affair to be in bed all the time. But it was like probably with Nureyev – I mean for a moment she has been the greatest woman in my life and I the greatest man in hers. If sex was in the middle somewhere, then she and Nureyev had it. For sure. They had been very close to each other and they loved each other closely. I don't think they have been in bed fucking all night. Probably they had sex a few times but it's not like phys- ical love. They had a sort of caress.'

How satisfying this lyrical embrace was to Margot, we cannot know. Especially as, by Petit's own admission, 'Margot was a woman who needed to have really sex. I heard that Constant Lambert was a good business in bed. I don't understand how she managed, because she was so beautiful and he was so ugly.' Many dancers in the company had felt the same sense of unease at the thought of Margot with Constant. 'I used to look at him,' says Julia Farron, 'and think, "How could she?" Physically, at that age, it was a bit off-putting. She liked to be adored by some- body – it didn't much matter whom. She was beautiful. Not pretty-beautiful, but ravishing, physically. She liked the intellectual man – she didn't really need to have beauty. She had her own.'

Margot was used to being desired. Up to this point, it had seemed to suffice. But now she found herself in the grip of desire itself, desire for a union that lay beyond her grasp. Petit was the first of her elusive young men – physical beauties in their own right, Dionysian by nature, bisexual at the least – who could cast her in the role of sexual instigator. Despite the implicit frustration, the experience liberated her emotionally, just as it would, in years to come, with Nureyev. It acquainted her with a recklessness which had lain dormant in her calm, biddable nature, and enhanced her capacity for joy. Dick Beard who, with Ashton and Nora Kaye, joined her in Paris that July, remembers her as the most enchanting of companions, able to smooth relations between everyone, and to simplify everything into 'dancers on a summer holiday', laughing 'from morning to night, through idiotic adventures'.[17]

And all of this despite news from London that the quarrel between Constant Lambert and David Webster had come to a head. Lambert had been forced to resign before he was dismissed. In acknowledging his resignation, Webster wrote: 'I remember hearing you many times in the early part of the war thumping on those pianos, and I cannot imagine any greater work and labour, nor can I think of anybody else in the country of your standing who would have been willing to give time to it.'[18] This was scant praise. It failed to take account of the huge personal sacrifice to Lambert's own career as a composer, a sacrifice made in the name of English ballet. Needless to say, he was drinking and smoking again – and with a vengeance. The tragedy was almost complete. And it was no longer in Margot's power even to attempt to avert it.

One act of rejection often invokes another; and, if Margot hardened her heart at the time, it was towards Charles Hassé. Every summer he had made it his business to take her and her entourage (Black Queen, Volkova, Pamela May, Charles Gordon, and a friend – 'not a sex friend' – called Fitz) to Cornwall, or, after the war, to the South of France. But, what with La Bolero and the Miller's Wife and the promise that Ashton's next-but-one subject was to be Don Juan, it was now Margot's whim – allied as ever to her artistic aspiration – to visit Spain.

Late that same summer, Hassé found a tiny hotel by the sea which was 'absolutely adorable. We hired bicycles and rode about the countryside.' They did manage to see some flamenco: Hassé took Margot to Barcelona where Pilar López was dancing. But his real ambition – that she should watch Manolete put a bull to death – was thwarted: the great Cordoban matador had been fatally gored the previous week. For Hassé, it was not a good omen. 'In Spain, Margot told me: "That's the end of our affair." A very sad last night. Because she'd fallen in love with Roland Petit. She'd got taken up by the French crowd. Dior was dressing her. Paris absolutely turned her head. She was very much wrapped up in herself after she left me. I so adored her, I don't suppose I was much of a challenge, really. I still spent time at her house – Christmas, and so on. I even slept there – alone, of course. Margot opted right out. It was rather painful, really. She'd come and kiss me goodnight in bed. Her character was strong when she'd made up her mind.'

She was to need all the strength that she could muster. In October, she received a blow every bit as shocking as the one which she had dealt to Charles Hassé. The company was on a gruelling autumn tour of Brussels, Prague, Warsaw, Poznan, Malmo and Oslo; and the dancers were in Malmo when the news from London reached them: Constant Lambert had married Isabel Delmer. 'Anyway,' he said of his new wife, to mollify his mother: 'She isn't coloured, she's half Welsh. Nor is she a ballerina.'[19] To the ballerina herself he offered no such palliative. She was merely left to find out by what means she might – like a dancer reading on a public notice board that she had lost a leading role.

Constant moved Isabel, along with one of his cats, Spalding, into a flat in Regent's Park, which, despite his wife's painterly tastes, he decorated with cryptic newspaper clippings and obscure cartoons. The couple got on, according to William Chappell, 'awfully well, leading the most appallingly slatternly life'.[20] Even Ashton, who at first regretted their union ('They were both terrific topers'), admitted that 'it might be better for them to drink together than alone'.[21] Isabel herself had no qualms. 'The house was an absolute shambles,' she said, 'but we were always dying of laughter.'[22]

What Margot – who was known to laugh as often from embarrassment as amusement – must have died of at the time would have felt horribly like humiliation. It was rumoured that Constant had once left her standing, if not at the altar, then at St Pancras Town Hall, the very registry office where his wedding to Isabel took place. That he should grant with such alacrity to someone new the compliment which he had for so long denied his Old Girl – how could it be borne? In utter silence, according to her anxious colleagues. All they noted was Margot's extraordinary capacity to close down completely on her feelings. According to Frederick Ashton she 'just cut out the whole episode. Sewed herself up and became virginal again.'[23]

It was to be nine years before anything which might be construed as anger surfaced in the presence of a friend. And even then, no words of passion were spoken, although the action was eloquent enough. Just before Margot's own marriage to Tito Arias, Michael Somes visited her flat. 'She was sitting on the floor,' says Wendy Somes, 'and she had all Constant's books around her. And she was tearing out the inscriptions. All the pages where he had written from Constant to Margot. It was like ripping out a heart.'

The strict necessity to conceal her private emotions rendered Margot's artistic expressiveness less reliable than usual. In the two new ballets which followed hard upon the news of Constant's latest marriage, she was accused of smiling both too little and too much. In Mam'zelle Angot, the third Massine piece, she could not find the fizzing dynamism demanded by the eponymous soubrette, and withdrew from the part after only five performances. And in the story-less, exquisite, though not popular *Scènes de Ballet*, which had its first performance on 11 February 1948, she was clearly ill at ease with the brittle Parisian veneer which Ashton had deliberately laid upon her, as if to pre-empt the thing which he most dreaded: that Petit should try 'smartening her up in a boulevard way'.[24] Her relative failure in *Scènes*, not to mention Moira Shearer's considerable success in it, only tempted Margot further to escape to the very boulevards of Ashton's fears. This time she planned, not just sessions with Dior, or classes with the fashionable Boris Kniaseff (who encouraged her to do the splits – 'and in second, too'[25]), but full-scale treachery. 'So finally,' says Roland Petit, 'we decided to do a ballet together. I found this Jean Anouilh story about a cat who, when she falls in love with a boy, becomes a woman. I had to ask the permission to Ninette and she said, "Yes, but be careful my boy, my dear, because she is my prima ballerina." And I promised I would be very careful.'

Carefulness was not exactly Petit's bag. 'One thing about Roland,' says Violette Verdy, 'is that he had to reveal the sexual identity of the dancers he worked with. Hence all the corsets that every one of his ballerinas was wearing – we all ended up in a corset of one kind or another. Because it's the epitome of French paintings – the idea that the man is allowed in the boudoir while the woman is in her corseting. It was almost childish, but it was also fetishist. Roland could be very loving and tender with women but, at the same time, mocking and cruel – I would say brutal. He always conceived that a woman only comes to full maturity if she's been mistreated by a man. He liked to see a kind of fallen angel. He wanted things to go through the mud a bit. Roland could have been one of the greatest classical choreographers of the time. In spite of his laziness in regard to the *corps de ballet* work, which he never bothered with more than as a salad round a lobster, he had the talent to make solid classical ballets such as we have only seen from Balanchine and Ashton. But Roland could not help being seduced by stars. He hated it when stars were not great dancers.

What he meant by a star was that she should be revealed in every one of her aspects. So, certainly with Margot, he must have enjoyed pushing her, taking her out of her retreat.'

Oddly, from Margot's point of view, Petit the great liberator proved surprisingly constricting to work with. She found almost at once that she was required to rein in her natural capacity to improvise, developed all those years ago in Shanghai, when she and June Brae had happily cavorted about in *plastique* classes, to the encouragement of plump Elirov. Ashton, who worked in a kind of 'what if? . . .' trance of suggestibility, had always valued her contributions and adapted them and made them his own; but Petit did not take kindly to an assertive muse. He had his own company now: Ballets de Paris. The Ballets des Champs-Elysées had broken up after only two years, which shocked Margot, to whom team spirit and respect for tradition were the staff of working life. Without the support and protection of what she and her friends called 'Old Mother Wells', she feared that her technique would collapse, and that her mystique would evaporate. Imagine her surprise, then, when she found herself suddenly shouting (and in French) in the middle of rehearsal, in a show of temperament and independence which left the members of the Ballets de Paris aghast.

Her fury had been provoked by a mask which the designer insisted that she wear. It was clever of Petit to be the first to make use of Margot's obsessional identification with cats. But to cover her feline features with a papier-mâché contraption, however realistic, was to obliterate any chance of her expressing that affinity. The tantrum worked, winning her not only a modified and much more flattering mask, but the enhanced admiration of the lesbian surrealist designer Léonor Fini, who adored female flare-ups, especially when the sparks flew in her direction. The rest of her costume for the cat-woman, Agathe, which, needless to say, incorporated a corset, Margot thought perfectly gorgeous, as did the Paris press, who breathed: 'Ah, le derrière de Margot!' and 'Elle a les jambes spirituelles',[26] which seemed odd, given the outrageous cut of

213

her dress at the back, until she found out that *spirituelles* can translate as 'witty'.

'That lovely white cat,' says Violette Verdy. 'I cannot tell you what an impact it had on us. You see, we thought Margot was a cool, crystal, almost unattainable dancer, but when we saw the sensuousness that exuded from her, without any distortion of her technique, it was overwhelming. Roland could never have harmed her. She was too well-schooled already. But in those days the woman in her was more free than the ballerina – available, experimental and wanting to be used and exploited. I realize now that there was a little romance with Roland, but you know, I was in love with Roland when I was eleven, so why not when you're older? That's more normal.'

There was, nevertheless, a child-like high-spiritedness to the affair. On stage with Roland, things tended to go riotously wrong: the set fell down as he chased Margot across the rooftops in the *répétition générale* of *Demoiselles* and, in *Sleeping Beauty* Act III *pas de deux*, her beaded costume, designed by Balmain, unravelled systematically, until the floor was a skating rink of seed pearls. In August Petit joined Margot on holiday in the south of France, where she was staying with Léonor Fini and a twenty-year-old American who was dancing in Petit's company, Joy Williams, who remembers: 'Léonor had taken a small villa overlooking the sea and set up an airy, light-filled studio for herself and Sforzino [Sforza], who was an amateur sculptor. Life there quickly fell into a lovely, hazy routine. Léonor and Sforzino worked in the mornings while Margot and I slept and read – Rosamond Lehmann's *Dusty Answer*, as I recall – and lazed about . . . All through this time, our little group of four felt absolute contentment. It was as though a film of gossamer protected us from any outside intrusion. Roland came down for a few days, which was fun, but we all agreed afterwards that we really preferred less energy around.'

Joy, who was to become a lifelong friend of Margot's, had, and indeed still has, a pale-eyed, gold-haired fragility which made Margot's gypsy colouring look positively swarthy beside her, a contrast that Léonor Fini was moved to catch on canvas. 'There was much experimentation,' writes Joy, 'of how and where we would sit or stand and a good deal of discussion about what we would wear. Many various head-pieces were tried out, as well as an unusual array of garments and draperies of one sort or another – where they came from, I can't imagine. They were unlikely to have been found in the rented villa. At the end of the month Margot and I left Le Brusc with our facial portraits completed and our figures more or less in place, with Margot standing and me seated. But we had no idea what the finished portait would look like. It was exhibited later that fall in Brussels and bought by Anna Magnani.'

Thirty-eight years were to pass before Margot and Joy would set eyes on a photograph of the painting, which turned up in a Christie's catalogue, priced at an estimated £40,000 to £50,000. And the image, as well as its title, came as something of a surprise to them. *Margot Fontaine* [sic] *et Son Amie* is an extraordinary piece of sub-Tretchikoff, featuring Margot dressed in a brief corselet, apparently wrought from the bark of a tree, with only a thong at the back, and a pair of rolled-down silk stockings. Her figure, swelled to provocative proportions, would instantly have relegated her to the back row of the *corps de ballet*. 'Son Amie', meanwhile, is seen clutching an arrangement of large twigs. One nipple winks through the black strands of the long hair-piece draped about her neck by way of collar. 'It seems a bit suggestive,' Margot would write to Joy in 1989. 'Léonor must have called it that to get more money.'

But even if Margot *had* knowingly partaken of the double-portrait's implication, it would not have been the first time she had entered into the Sapphic spirit of this kind of joke. Moyra Fraser, very much the company mimic, remembers an act which she and Margot worked up when she herself was only four-teen, and Margot not yet twenty. They gave each other camp nicknames: 'She was Evidge and I was Alice – pronounced Aylice. It sounds so silly now, but we would have these jokes where she would sort of chat me up. A sort of lesbian approach.

I suppose we must have met one somewhere – we didn't know much about it. But the idea of Margot pretending like that is so sweet. We used to shriek like teenagers.'

Margot, however, was now about to turn thirty, which for a shrieking single girl is pushing it, and for a dancer is definitely getting on. She can be forgiven for supposing that her career had already reached its peak and that, since her bachelor era was probably limited, she could afford the innocent hedonism to which, in telling contrast to the Fini portrait, a set of photographs from that same holiday attests. In these, she straddles rocks, or revels in the sand, or stretches voluptuously on the branch of a great tree, or rises unselfconsciously naked from a pool like the fore-glimpse of a mythic Undine from the deep. Yet this enchanted heedlessness marks not the dwindling of her fame, but the measure of the privacy which, until that summer of 1948, she had enjoyed. That she, who was to prove so fanatical and controlling where the camera was concerned, should let such carefree images loose into the world shows just how little, famous as she already was, she yet knew of fame. Or just how exposing would be the glare, the very next year, of the light that would be turned upon her.

The year of 1949, which was to mark the crowning moment of Margot's career, did not approach particularly auspiciously. Missed though Fonteyn had been at Covent Garden, her illustrious predecessor, Markova, had – in the spring of '48 – been invited back from America, to be acclaimed all over again for her Giselle, which one critic described as having 'a pathetic fragility and . . . a quality of intangibility that no other dancer has equalled'.[1] And while de Valois, in her sympathy with Margot's distress over Constant's marriage, had granted her a freedom which nobody else in the company, bar Helpmann, could possibly have commanded, Ashton's sense of grievance at her defection was not so easily assuaged. When the time had come, in September of 1948, for Margot's return to the bosom of Old Mother Wells, it was hardly likely that her truancy would go unpunished.

Indeed, she seems, at first, to have administered the punishment to herself. 'I went to the ballet,' said Annabel Farjeon, 'and I saw Margot in the audience, and I thought, "My God, what's happened to her?" And I said to some dancer, "What's happened to Margot's face?" And she said, "Oh, Roland Petit said, you're going to look very Jewish soon. You'd better have your nose done." So she did, and there was a big blob on the end. She had it re-done, and then it was this boring little thing. She'd had a lovely nose – elegant and sweet.' Annette Page couldn't agree more: 'It was a bit of a shock. She'd had a very distinguished nose before. Suddenly it was terribly scooped out in the middle and all nostrils.' Worst of all for Margot, Ashton was aghast: 'She came back with a *disaster*, and had to have it done again by the surgeon [New Zealander Sir Archibald McIndoe] who did all the pilots.'[2]

Though gallantry disinclines Petit to discuss Margot's recourse to the knife, he remains impenitent about his role in having recommended plastic surgery (which – as he is the first to admit – he himself had undergone). 'She was unhappy with her nose. She had a complex with it. I took her to the doctor who had done mine. He messed it completely. Then she had a second one in London to make it straight. The first one was a catastrophe. When I saw her after the operation I felt that it was my fault. But she was right to have done it, finally.'

Although the new nose, twice cut, took twice the usual time to settle, the final effect was perfectly natural and undetectable, and did not throw her huge eyes and wide, slim mouth into disproportion. Nor is there any doubt that its restructuring preserved the youth in her face, and would make girlish roles more accessible to her in her advanced years. Plastic surgery, during the war, had been developed into an art of high medical seriousness; but, now that peace had come, and with it the right to frivolity, its cosmetic benefits grew as fashionable as the New Look. To Margot, who worked every day for hours in front of a mirror to correct every aspect of her body, the refinement of her nose was no more drastic a step than the shedding of her puppy fat – just one more manifestation of a redefined Margot Fonteyn, the one who had returned from Paris more stylishly self-aware, less apologetic, and no longer content to accept the tag '*pas belle*'. This new European gloss would make one American critic, the revered Edwin Denby, later remark that she was like a one-woman revolution against 'the thinness and meagreness of temperament' which seemed to him to afflict Anglo-Saxon dancers.[3] But some of her colleagues at home were less convinced, and feared that her adventures in Paris had 'diminished her artistic integrity . . . After her nose surgery,' says Nadia Nerina, 'and her fanatical wish to be in films, she never came over in the same way. The most impressive photographs were taken before she had her profile altered.'[4]

Needless to say, we have no record of Margot emerging from McIndoe's clinic with dark sunglasses and a plaster clapped across her face. What we do have, however, is a woebegone photograph of her, taken on 26 November 1948, the day after the first night of *Don Juan*, with her leg in plaster. Yet there is plenty of evidence that this injury (a torn ligament in her ankle) was all too real – as real as had been her visit to Devonshire Place a month earlier for the removal of a small tumour, 'a ridiculous lump which pops out with a click on the side of my knee every time I straighten my leg', as she wrote to Guinevere Parry from the London Clinic on 19 October.[5] One's suspicions are aroused by a famous precedent in the 1830s of a ballerina trumping up an 'injury' to cover her tracks: visiting the virginal Taglioni (nicknamed 'Marie pleine de grâce'), who had been admitted for an operation to her knee, the composer Adolphe Adam was, some months later, surprised to find her nursing a new-born baby. 'What's *that?*' he asked. 'My knee injury,' she replied.[6]

A pathology bill for 300 guineas attests not only to the authenticity of the tumour story, but to Margot's willingness, by this stage in her career, to pull rank for the sake of frugality. In a letter to the Covent Garden treasurer, she makes plain: 'This seems a terrible lot to me, even if it is very little to him. Do you think you could ask him if it is the best he can do . . . ?'[7] Similarly, in relation to a subsequent rhinoplasty account, dated the following June, the relevant anaesthetist elects to waive his fee 'on condition you become a grateful patient and send him ballet tickets for performances in which you appear'.[8]

Meanwhile there was the torn ligament to contend with. Shocking and painful as this accident patently was, a psychological element, to which Margot herself admits, hung over the incident: 'Perhaps it was not wholly accidental . . . when I slipped and fell during that performance of *Don Juan.*' The sense of unease and insecurity which caused her, so uncharacteristically, to stumble was not due to the return of Markova who – at thirty-seven, with her technique in decline and her national reputation tarnished by a war spent in the safety of America – could dance *Giselle* as incomparably as she liked: Margot had learned that an artist flourishes best at the centre of new creations. And she was coming back from Paris to rehearsals of two new Ashton works: *Don Juan* and *Cinderella*. It was *Cinderella* which she most looked forward to – Ashton's first, much-vaunted, full-length three-act ballet, set to the beautiful, compulsively danceable score by Prokofiev. Despite the young blood that was baying at her heels for the classical roles – warm, generous-spirited Beryl Grey, with her long-limbed amplitude of movement and unforced technique; glamorous Violetta Elvin (Violetta Prokhorova) from Moscow, the shimmering grandeur of whose *port de bras* was a revelation; and South African Nadia Nerina, she of the light, high, buoyant jump – Margot had no need, so long as she remained at the centre of Ashton's poetic vision, to feel threatened. But while she had been away in Paris, there had been another Giselle at Covent Garden who had succeeded in rocking her confidence. Describing her most dangerous rival, Margot picks her words carefully, but her angst is concentrated in the last one: 'young, fresh, beautiful and – different'.[9] It was for that difference that the public now clamoured – as made manifest by the startling colour-scheme and sudden notoriety of Moira Shearer.

The film *The Red Shoes* had opened on 18 July, only five days after Shearer's début as Giselle, for which role the enterprising twenty-two-year-old had evinced the presence of mind to have herself privately coached by one of the great Giselles of the Diaghilev era. De Valois, infuriated by the decorative and dramatically radical changes which Shearer, without permission, had dared to introduce into the mad scene, demanded to know their source. The girl answered with one mythical name: Karsavina. Arrangements were swiftly made: Karsavina would be brought in to coach Margot in *Giselle*, and Margot alone. But the tide of publicity which engulfed Moira Shearer after the première of *The Red Shoes* could not so easily be turned either by de Valois or by Mrs Hookham. Says Nadia Nerina: 'The BQ entourage was in total disarray for the first time.' Shearer was besieged in her Kensington home, and had to escape to Switzerland, where, even on top of a mountain, she was hounded for her autograph. A vast new international audience of filmgoers now knew of only one English ballerina. And her name was not Margot Fonteyn.

This was the critical moment at which Frederick Ashton chose to exact his revenge on Margot for having earlier deserted him in favour of the novelty of Petit. For fourteen years it had gone without saying that Margot should be first-cast in Ashton's ballets, with other ballerinas taking over only when she was tired or overworked – seemingly as understudies. 'Any part,' she says, 'created for me by Fred belonged to me; or so I felt, with a possessiveness equal to jealous love.'[10] Now she opened *The Times* one morning and came across an item that hit her 'like a slap in the face'.[11] Apparently in Ashton's forthcoming *Cinderella* she was to share the title role, on alternate nights, with Moira Shearer.

This slight, and the manner of its delivery, clearly caused Margot greater distress than any hitherto suffered at the hands of a mere lover. 'I went to Fred almost in tears and asked indignantly why he had not even told me before it was announced in the press. He said calmly that the first performances had to run consecutively, and I had made it clear I could not dance a long ballet every night. He tactfully left it unsaid that younger dancers deserved some of the opportunities I had enjoyed at their age, and that I was too spoilt to have considered that aspect.'[12]

She would have plenty of time to do so. The Covent Garden stage surface was treacherous enough to induce an accident at the best of times. And *Don Juan* was made, frankly, at the worst. Ashton had tried to invest the abstracted and severely classical idiom which most interested him at that time with a hefty dose of sex, taking his inspiration from Luisillo, a sensational young flamenco dancer in Carmen Amaya's troupe. But, despite a garish costume and painted sideburns, there was no way that Helpmann, who, according to Moira Shearer, was 'bored to tears and spent the whole time sending everyone up, including Fred', could reproduce the mating fire of a Mexican gypsy. Luisillo and his partner, Teresa, were like 'two fierce and beautiful birds lovemaking'.[13] But Margot, as La Morte Amoureuse, was partnered by 'a glum, static figure which, even when the swelling music demands some virtuoso dancing, can do no more than run futilely across the stage'.[14] The baroque arcades of Edward Burra's darkly romantic designs were also pared down to what the wearied critics described as 'chi-chi ruins'.[15] The production's only mitigating factor was the return of Constant Lambert to the podium. After less than a year's absence he had been offered the post of artistic director by the shamefaced management – a vaguer post than his previous one of musical director. But just as his thraldom to Fonteyn had subsided, so his bond with the company had soured: his reception seemed to him to carry 'the mingled welcome and suspicion that greets a cat that has been lost for a week'. Even in his electrifying hands, Strauss's tone poem could not save the day. James Monahan does not pull his punches: '*Don Juan* was a failure pure and simple, the only specimen of [Ashton's] post-war choreography for Fonteyn which has died unmourned: here, for once, he did not cope satisfactorily with his music . . . And the ballet is chiefly remembered for its first-night disaster, when Fonteyn so hurt her leg that she was incapacitated for several months.'[16]

Though Margot fell half-way through *Don Juan*, Helpmann hauled her to her feet and she danced through to the end on a fast-swelling ankle. By the end of the next morning, it was in plaster – in which, she was told, it must remain encased for six weeks. *Cinderella* was to open in less than four. If Ashton had meant to punish her, he had only succeeded in punishing himself, for it was a bitter blow to him that Margot could not be his initial rags-to-riches heroine. He began by rehearsing in the role a young, dark-haired, dramatically gifted dancer: Anne Heaton. Heaton had been tipped by de Valois to be Fonteyn's successor, although patronage from Madam came at a price: 'I'm going to take that girl and break her,' she is said to have announced, 'and then build her up.'[17] But Ashton, who was systematically opposed to de Valois's taste in talent, dropped Heaton long before the first night. All the performances were to be danced (on consecutive nights, as Margot had protested she could not) by Moira Shearer.

'Through it all,' writes Pigeon Crowle, 'Shearer moved with lyrical enchantment. In the first act, she invested the part with a simple wistful humour as, with her broom for a partner, she danced in imagination at the ball. Her arrival at the Palace was the crowning moment of the ballet. Wearing a dazzling white dress with crisp foaming tutu, her coroneted head framed in a Medici collar of crystal and silver from which flowed a delicate jewelled train of pale lime green, she was the fairy-tale princess of everyone's dreams.'[18]

It was a vision that Margot did not hang around to glimpse. She fled, as fast as it is possible to flee on crutches, to – where else – Paris, this time without a chaperone. Not that she needed one: it was a time of constraint and introspection. Incessant, violent exercise raises the level of adrenalin in the blood, creating, metabolically, what is nowadays known as 'a high'. Deprived of daily classes, let alone of nightly performances, Margot's spirits plummeted like those of an addict going cold turkey. On the level of the body, classical ballet is as detailed and demanding a subject as are the great academic disciplines of the intellect. But entirely identified with the physical as Margot was, she had no idea how to find stimulation in the life of the mind. With so much time on her hands, she was left no option but to search her soul. And she did not like what she found – or rather, failed to find; for, without her dancing and the kudos and satisfaction which this gave her, what *was* she? Certainly no longer Roland Petit's mistress.

Their romance had been as impulsive and impossible as a first-night present from him which had once been placed at her feet on the stage of the Théâtre des Champs-Elysées, and which, at first glance, had seemed merely to be a basket of white orchids. But, underneath the flowers, there had been revealed a pure white kitten lying on a velvet cushion. Entranced though Margot was, she could not in all conscience commit so youthful and delicate a creature to six months' incarceration in quarantine, and therefore chose to give it up, leaving it behind, like the provisional life to which she had aspired in Paris with Petit. She had known all along it would be so. 'We were perfect oppo-sites in temperament. He told me I should leave the Sadler's Wells Ballet, where I was too restricted, and get out and dance new, exciting ballets. I told him he needed the stability of the Paris Opéra, from which he had broken away. Neither of us took the other's advice. I was not too swept off my feet to forget that my success was based on the position I held in the Sadler's Wells, while Roland knew he wanted complete freedom to create ballets in his own way.'[19] Now, as she spent her first Christmas away from the company that had created her, the independence which she had sought felt unpleasantly like exile. Despite all her romantic and sexual adventures, she could not wrest her deepest allegiance from Frederick Ashton. In her lone-liness and isolation, it became clear to her that 'The person I loved most and depended on most was Fred . . . I sought his opinion in everything I did to the extent that I thought I would never be able to marry anyone who didn't have his approval.'[20] Marriage – ah, there was the rub. In its banal way, *The Red Shoes* had hit upon a terrible truth, with its melodramatic story-line of earthly love versus spiritual vocation. For, yes, the choice for a gifted woman could still be as harrowing as that – she could be torn, metaphorically, in two, even if she didn't end up throwing herself under a train. Margot had witnessed this split assail her contemporaries. Cecil Tennant, when he had proposed to the divinely talented Irina Baronova, who was exactly Margot's age, had given her three days to decide between him and the theatre. (She never danced again. It was 1946, and she was twenty-seven.) As for those of Margot's friends who had tried to compromise, such as June Brae and Pamela May, she had watched their careers lose impetus under the pressures and distractions of a domestic other life. 'Marriage!' says an impassioned Nadia Nerina. 'When I arrived in England it was just unheard of that a ballerina should be married. You were supposed to be like a nun, dedicated to your profession. Of course Margot couldn't marry. It wasn't expected. I mean, I remember when Shearer got married – all the eyebrows went flying high.'

And none flew higher than Ashton's. His idol, Pavlova, although quite the concubine, had, after all, remained resolutely single and childless to the end. No doubt he had delivered his edict on the subject to Margot, just as, at the beginning of her career, he had snatched a lighted cigarette from her lips and crushed it underfoot, saying in the whispering hypnotic tone that she could never bring herself to disobey: 'Ballerinas do not smoke.'[21] And nor, most decidedly, did they reproduce. Margot and her mother were by now completely clear on that point, with the guilt and misery of two abortions behind them. Colleagues even think that it was probably around this time, while she was, in any case, *hors de combat*, that Margot took medical steps to ensure that, in that era of unreliable and clumsy contraception, she never conceived again. As far as the maternal instinct went, this was not something that Margot particularly believed herself to possess. Pauline Clayden is only one of many witnesses who remembers Margot shuddering when asked whether she would like a family: 'Ooh, no, she wasn't interested in the least.'

But during those stagnant weeks in Paris, Margot was forced to acknowledge that, despite the warm companionship of friends such as Joy Williams and Jacqueline Lemoine, Petit's right-hand woman and 'punching bag', she was, at the most profound level of her being, lonely. It is in rough times, not smooth, that character is forged; and now she was thrown back on her resources to discover where the strength of her true nature might lie. And what she came up with was that quality which, more than thirty years later, as Chancellor of Durham University, she would commend to the students on Graduation Day: tenacity – that same 'bulldog tenacity to complete successfully anything on which I have once embarked'. Others have put a less flattering name to her fighting spirit. 'She was incredibly competitive,' says Clive Barnes. 'The most competitive woman I have known. Competitive in every way.'

If so, then, given her public personality, which expressed itself so consistently in a serene equability and self-deprecating modesty, competitiveness was a hard characteristic for Margot to acknowledge and bring to conscious use. Her ambition had been slow to rouse itself, perhaps because, from the beginning, everyone had been so busy being ambitious on her behalf. This, after all, was the girl who was reported to have said in her teens that she could not bear to be a ballerina. Yet a prima ballerina she had become. Her life had been a blank page upon which others – her mother, de Valois, Ashton, Lambert – had all been feverishly writing their own story. But, now that she felt the plot which they had invented beginning to slip away from her, she was moved at last to pick up the pen for herself. And it was with the dark, hidden ink of her own competitive blood that she would imprint her indelible image upon Ashton's first full-length masterwork, *Cinderella*.

The ballet had not lacked success without her, least of all for Ashton himself, who was already giving the comedy performance of his life, playing addled and pathetic foil to Helpmann's more domineering and show-offy Ugly Sister. Despite the double drag-act, *Cinderella* was far from being a pantomime. Edwin Denby wrote lyrically of its 'grace of spirit', of its 'English sweetness of temper . . . To keep in a three-act ballet such a tone, to sustain it without affectation or banality shows Ashton's power . . .'[22] – a power which provoked Lydia Lopokova to exclaim: 'At last you have come into your triumph. My mind beams for you and my heart beats for you. You must have suffered before you achieved it.'[23]

In fact, Ashton had experienced nothing but pleasure working with the highly intelligent and spirited Moira Shearer, with her lightness and speed and that attribute which he most loved in a dancer: articulate feet. Where the process of invention was concerned, Ashton considered it just deserts for de Valois that the girl whom she had so underrated should be able to 'drag it out' of him, just as Margot had done. By now Shearer was sharing the title role with Violetta Elvin, who was bringing a positively regal glamour to the ballroom scenes. But who could rival the wish-fulfilling pink-and-white prettiness of Shearer's fairy-tale princess? Certainly not sallow-skinned, straight-haired Margot. The most handsome prince, Michael Somes, might be hers to reclaim, by divine right, as her partner. But the fans in the gods, primed for her return, expected their unswerving loyalty to her to be earned back. Margot had to find a new approach. Her solution was simple but inspired: she took the accent away from the ballroom and put it back in the kitchen. And, in order to achieve the desired humble effect, she did something uncharacteristically grand: she demanded a different costume for Act I.

Lilian Baylis would have turned in her grave. In all the penny-pinching and democratic history of Sadler's Wells, such a demand had been utterly unheard-of. 'Nobody else was ever allowed to change their costume at all,' says Moira Shearer. 'There was never any question of it. This charming Frenchman, Jean-Denis Malclès, had designed a brown-coloured dress – darkish brown – for the kitchen scenes. And he wanted the kerchief tied this way – in a very ordinary way. When Margot came to do it, suddenly she appeared in a black dress and a completely different hair-thing and all the rest of it. All those little changes were made. And I remember thinking *why?*'

One might just as well have asked why it had taken Margot so long – fifteen years of professional life – to develop the instincts of a star. The changes which she made were tiny but transformative, and Cinderella is the great transformation myth: without misery and squalor at the beginning, there can be no happy-ever-after. Shearer had followed the designer's instructions by tying the kerchief under her chin to (almost) disguise the luxuriance of her hair and the bloom of her cheeks, which were strategically dabbed with fetching streaks of grime. Margot took the same scarf and, pulling it tightly over her centre-parted hair, knotted it at the back of her neck like a skivvy. Her face, thus shorn of artifice and flattery, was all eyes – the eyes of a drab and frightened waif. With the black of her dress, she stripped the scene of warmth and colour and introduced an atmosphere of genuine deprivation. 'When Margot did it,' says Annette Page, 'suddenly it was a different ballet altogether. I mean, the poignancy of her just sitting there by the fireside. Little things she did, like polishing the grate and dusting – she suddenly became a real character instead of a ballerina pretending to be Cinderella.' And her scullery-maid pathos lent an unprecedented wonderment to the slow assumption of nobility in the famous testing moment when she must descend the ballroom steps, taking each stair on *pointe* without once lowering her eyes to check her footing. 'Only Fonteyn conveyed a sense of sustained ecstasy,' writes Julie Kavanagh.[24] David Vaughan agrees: 'No other dancer has been as exquisite in the variation in Act II, especially the magical moment when she balances in *relevé passé derrière* and looks back over her shoulder. Above all, there was an unaffected simplicity and sweetness of nature, which made her farewell to the stepsisters, especially Ashton, the most emotionally charged moment in the whole ballet.'

Margot could not have chosen a more important moment to reassert her leadership of the company. For what loomed ahead now was the greatest challenge so far posed to Sadler's Wells: the conquest of America. The plan had been a long time in the hatching. The charismatic impresario Sol Hurok, though he could conjure any name in international theatre, had spent forty years bringing high art to American show business, and had grown tired of ballet. But in 1946, having seen *The Sleeping Beauty* at Covent Garden, he announced himself 'reborn'.[25] His moment of rebirth had been Margot's entrance in Act I, when, for him, she bore 'the radiant gaiety of all the fairy-tale heroines of all the world's literature compressed into one'. But although he sent flowers and plaudits to her dressing-room the next day, Margot was not pivotal to his plan. 'The fact is, Hurok wanted to take us to New York in '47,' says Nadia Nerina. 'And he said to Madam he'd like Markova to lead the company – because she was known. She was a star. And Madam said, "No. When I go, it will be with my own dancers." Then, to show no ill feeling towards Markova, she asked her and Dolin to come to London.'

In the spring of 1949, Danilova was invited for much the same reason. She appeared at Covent Garden with fellow guest artist Frederick Franklin in *Swan Lake Act II*, *Coppélia* and *Giselle*, and with Massine in *La Boutique Fantasque*, following Hurok's second approach to de Valois. 'He asked her again because *Sleeping Beauty* was such a success and they didn't have anything like it in America – not in musicals – nothing. This time he suggested Danilova. And Madam said, "I'm not going to have Danilova, I'm not going to have any other star. I've got my own company." '[26]

By this time Fonteyn and Hurok had met. His impression of her was of 'a couple of black eyes like two great plums'.[27] Promising imagery, since Hurok reminded Margot 'of an old Russian peasant woman going off to market, basket on her arm, to pick out the best of the produce'.[28] And de Valois always made sure that, whenever Hurok chanced by, it was Margot's wares which were at the front of the stall. Alex Martin remembers an overwhelming performance of *The Sleeping Beauty* 'that took place some time in the spring of 1948. Her Act I was so absolutely stunning that one immediately asked oneself "*Who* is in front?" . . . It was, of course, Sol Hurok, casing the joint for possible American performances.'[29]

Although Hurok later professed to Margot that he had been in love with her at that time (and certainly he liked to encourage her to sit on his lap), the deal was struck for a more hard-headed reason. 'We went because of *Red Shoes*,' says Nadia Nerina. 'Otherwise Hurok wouldn't have taken the company. Pamela May, Margot Fonteyn – who knew *them* in America? Nobody. But they did know Shearer. He didn't have to find a star, he had one. And he wanted Moira on the first night.'

De Valois, for her own part, wanted a venue worthy of her company. Hurok's 1948 proposal that he should present the Sadler's Wells Ballet at the City Center Theatre as part of the Dance Festival was rejected after David Webster inspected it and pronounced the whole set-up too small. Not until Hurok came up with the Metropolitan Opera House (located, in those days, on Broadway – between 39th and 40th Streets) did she finally agree to his terms. Fond in the memory of that ancient victory, she later remembered Hurok as a worthy adversary. 'He was a character. He was very nice to us, you know. Very good to us. He said, "You and I could do vunderful business."' And so – in the wrangle over the programming – it proved. De Valois wanted to start the season with a triple bill which would include *Symphonic Variations* with its ensemble cast, thus featuring Fonteyn and Shearer in virtual unison. But New York had Balanchine, with his short abstract masterpieces. What America needed, Hurok insisted, was what they did *not* have: 'production miracles' – full-length, lavishly designed Russian classics performed in the meticulously schooled English style of sweet restraint. Round one, then, to Hurok: they would open with *The Sleeping Beauty*. But now came the sticking point: Hurok was determined to have Shearer as his first-night Princess Aurora. Jane Edgeworth, then the company's public-relations girl, came out of her office, which adjoined that of de Valois, to the sound of agitated voices. 'Madam was saying: "Moira is the star of *The Red Shoes*, and a most beautiful dancer, but Margot is our ballerina, and she has to open, and Sol, if you don't like it, we'll go to Coventry – we've been offered an Arts Council tour." He looked at me and said: "What do you do with a dame like this?" And I said, "Mr Hurok, you have to listen." Madam shouted something at me – like "Shut up, Jane" – and I went back into my office. And a few minutes later I heard her voice through the wall, saying, "Don't you glare at *me*, Jane Edgeworth." I *was* cross with her. Think of it: *Coventry* when we could go to New York. But she was dead right, and she got her way.'

Not, however, entirely without compromise. Before he left, the American impresario extracted from de Valois a private promise that, although the première would, agreed, be Margot's, she, Madam, would personally see to it that Shearer also appeared, in however minor a capacity, on that first night. Hurok's publicity machine revved into gear, and seats were already on sale in June, four months before the season opened (although prices were modest – top price $4.20, a good deal less than for *Oklahoma!* on Broadway). 'The Treasury wanted dollars,' writes de Valois, 'the manufacturers wanted trade and the English Theatre hoped for increased prestige. Every fashion house was determined to dress the Ballet, to photograph the Ballet . . . meanwhile the Ballet was thinking yearningly of T-bone steaks.'[30]

The carnivorous dancers were, at the time, in Florence, appearing at the Teatro Comunale. Seasoned travellers though they were, the prospect of America filled them with more than just culinary excitement. There was nothing war-torn about the distant and glamorous land of the free. Success there could yield money and luxury such as, in post-war Europe, were unimaginable. When, back in England, it was confirmed that Margot would be dancing Aurora on the New York first night, she 'started an attack of stage fright that must be the longest in history. It lasted three months.'[31]

Perhaps the thing that most truly characterizes a great performer is the capacity to experience adrenalin, not as a paralysing toxin, but as a stimulant to the psyche which can invigorate an audience by transmission. As hysteria in the company mounted around her, Margot tried to find a way of making her escalating nerves work in her favour rather than against. Day after day, as the dancers toured the insalubrious suburban cinemas of Croydon, Dulwich and Kilburn, grinding their way through ballets not chosen for the States, she practised, for two extra-curricular hours at a stretch, her *attitude* balances in the Rose Adagio, teaching her line-up of doughty Princes the art of daring not to approach her until she spoke aloud, like a ventriloquist through her dauntless smile, the urgent word: '*Now!*'

It was not her only venture into public utterance. The previous June, in Copenhagen, where she had appeared in a command performance with Helpmann, a dinner had been given in her honour. She was then expected, to her horror, to make a speech. The exaggerated over-development of one faculty in a person often renders other parts of the personality stunted; and dancers, so physically sophisticated and expressive, are often surprisingly inarticulate and baby-voiced, if not plain dumbstruck. It seemed at first as if all Margot's elocution lessons had failed her. A terrible shyness overcame her, and she glanced helplessly at Helpmann, who, with his uninhibited verbal skills, came to the rescue: 'Miss Fonteyn is too moved to speak,' he announced to the gathered guests. But . . . Not a bit of it. Miss Fonteyn now rose to her feet and, with all the ambassadorial charm into which she was soon to grow, spoke for six minutes.

Margot had always found in Helpmann's public fearlessness and irreverent humour a source of professional support; and it was a relief to her that although in April he had turned forty – the age at which he had vowed that he would stop dancing – he agreed to partner her on the tour of America and Canada. Even more reassuring (if infinitely more risky) was the inclusion of Constant Lambert as musical director. After the spontaneous ovation accorded to him (far longer and louder than the dancers had received) when he had conducted a revival of *Apparitions* at Covent Garden in March, even David Webster could see what folly it would be not to capitalize on 'the wonderful perform-ance issuing from the wrecked body'.[32] In the event, Lambert's chances of travelling with the company were nearly scuppered, not by the Sadler's Wells administration, but by American Embassy officials who harboured suspicions about the Com-munist implications behind his visit to Poland at the end of the war. Their enquiries seemed to hinge on what his father's initials, G.W., might stand for. 'George Washington,' he was able to roar without a word of a lie.[33] A visa was issued forthwith.

And so, with the girls togged out in the woollen sweaters and felt hats and checked rainwear that passed for high fashion in struggling, post-war Britain (the boys, mercifully, were left out of the couture campaign), 'the invasion', as de Valois was given to calling it, began. Unfortunately she, as their general, was not well enough to fly out with the first contingent, which included Helpmann, Ashton, Webster and Fonteyn. But Leslie Edwards took her place. 'I was Madam,' he said, 'because she had a migraine and couldn't go till Monday. I had the extreme pleasure of going first, with Margot. I flew across the Atlantic as Mrs Arthur Connell.'

Two days later, de Valois followed – as Leslie Edwards. She was the only woman on the flight. 'The planes were so small in those days,' says Alexander Grant, 'that instead of mixing us up they put the boys on one plane and the girls on another. Can you believe it? I mean – if we broke down!' But there may have been method in the madness, not to mention in the migraine, as it was bound to be the plane-load of girls that the New York press would be waiting to meet. 'Constant came with us boys, and de Valois looked after him on the great journey – because she knew he would drink all the way across. She literally carried him off.'

The planes had to touch down three times *en route* for re-fuelling, and the girls, who stripped down to their underwear the minute they were airborne, kept having to climb in and out of their designer outfits, which they were determined not to crease. The photographers thronging La Guardia airport, however, were not fashion-conscious, and were especially unsus-ceptible to the trend for calf-length skirts. 'Show us a bit of leg,' they yelled. A bunch of flat-chested toe-dancers in tweed and tartan was not their thing at all – a head of Titian hair was more like it. *The Red Shoes* had broken all records, running for fifty-seven weeks at the Bijou Theatre in New York, and they had come to point their cameras at a film star. '*Red Bush!*' they kept shouting. 'Over here, Red Bush.'

By ironic contrast, the arrival of the true stars of Sadler's Wells, two days earlier, had been a sadly low-key affair. Fonteyn and Helpmann's plane had been delayed for eighteen hours at Prestwick, and when the ordeal of the long flight was over, and Margot emerged in an austere dark dress, plain white jacket and head-clinging hat, there on the tarmac to meet them was a loyal band of but two: Sol Hurok and Nora Kaye. 'It was dark,' says Leslie Edwards. 'Who *were* we? We weren't international stars.'

Yet the faith of the devoted public which they had created

back in England followed them like a great searchlight across the Atlantic. And it sought to focus on one dark-haired girl in the final frightened hours of her obscurity. 'Just about now,' conjectured Richard Buckle, 'allowing for the spin of the earth, the Sadler's Wells dancers are preparing to face the first night audience of New York's Metropolitan in *The Sleeping Beauty*, and [the critic] cannot help hoping that the short-comings of the English company may on this occasion be overlooked and only its shining excellences be seen. He imagines the beating hearts of the dancers and he thinks especially of the great ballerina who has to face a sceptical new public in that most exacting of dances, the Rose Adagio. As she stands in open perfect *attitude*, her eyes raised modestly towards her upheld arm, she supports the honour and glory of our nation and empire on the point of one beautiful foot!'[34]

Nora Kaye, all too aware of the masochism that exists among ballerinas, knew perfectly well that Margot, however exhausted from her fourteen-hour flight, would be incapable of sleeping until she had set foot on the boards that could make or break her. Having shepherded her to the St Moritz, overlooking Central Park, Nora whisked her straight back out again, instructing the taxi to wait outside the Met on the way to supper at Reuben's. The scene dock was open on to the street, and Margot, kicking off her heels, stepped straight in from the pavement and walked out across the stage in stockinged feet, to gauge the space, and look the great red and gold auditorium in the face while its famous diamond horse-shoe tiers were still unpeopled. 'She took a deep breath,' writes Sol Hurok, 'and clasped her hands in front of her. "Thank goodness," she said, "it's old and comfortable and warm and rich as an opera house should be . . . I was so afraid it would be slick and modern like everything else here, all steel and chromium and spit and polish. I'm glad it's old."'[1]

Reuben's was also a venue best braved in advance, for like the more famous Sardi's it was one of the haunts where New York performers traditionally flocked in the small hours, ritually to await first-night reviews. But if Margot's presence was noted that initial evening, it was only because she happened to be dining, with Kaye and Helpmann and Edwards, as a guest of the playwright Garson Canin. And, in the days that followed, Margot was hard-pushed to command the attention which, for the sake of the company, it was vital that she attract. 'Everything was staked on her,' says Beryl Grey, 'everybody's hopes. Yet nobody had heard of her. Margot, Moira, myself, Pamela and Violetta were put in the best hotel by Hurok. And we were sitting having coffee or a milk-shake or something and some people came up and said, "Oh, are you with the Red Shoes company?" You can imagine how that went down with Margot. Moira was so embarrassed, as you would be. But no, Ninette was going to push Margot, and did.'

In fact, de Valois was in no immediate position to push anyone. The migraine from which she was suffering had presaged a virus, and she was laid low in her hotel room with a temperature of 104°. It fell to Bobby Helpmann to steer Margot through the press conferences that rendered her, by her own admission, 'as frightened as a mouse confronting a cobra'. And his heart was in the task, for, with his own dancing star on the wane, he recognized Margot as his own best bet with American audiences: 'I don't think anybody but I realized that Margot would be such an immediate success in the States. I think they thought that her dancing would be too pure, not showy enough to appeal widely. I knew that this would be precisely her big attraction.' It was Helpmann who contrived to keep Shearer out of the way, later saying to her: 'What a clot you were to fall in with it.'

'He wasn't the kindest creature,' says Shearer. 'But it's true I wasn't very clever at those sorts of things. If you don't think like that yourself, you don't see it at all. I didn't know there were tremendous press conferences going on. Ninette did something bad to me at the beginning of the season so that I would go down the drain, and I was just too confused not to do what she asked. Everyone had to be on on the first night of *Sleeping Beauty*. I at once thought I'd do my old roles of Fairy of the Crystal Fountain and one of Florestan's sisters which I'd done in 1946. But no: "I want you to do Bluebird with Alexis Rassine," Ninette told me. She promised me plenty of rehearsal. In fact I got two run-throughs in the basement of the Kingsway Hall. I'd never even had the costume on. She knew I'd go to pieces with nerves.'

'They were all so petrified of Ninette,' says Nadia Nerina, 'that Moira just gave in. I could never understand it. Bluebird wasn't her role. It isn't a role for a ballerina – it's the man's part. Moira had never danced it. But obviously Ninette had promised Hurok that she'd be on on the first night. Moira only had to say, "No I'm not doing it, I'll wait until I appear as Princess Aurora." But Ninette got her on . . . One can only speculate on what effect a Shearer first night would have had on Margot's career, and whether Moira herself realizes, to this day, the enormity of the error she made.'

Yet as Ninette de Valois, temperature still soaring, dragged herself to the Metropolitan Opera House, past the traffic which had come to a standstill outside the theatre and past the double queue of eager balletomanes which stretched round all four sides of the block, she knew, both as a visionary and a pragmatist, that she had made no mistake. There could be no successful invasion without casualties. What mattered was the inspiration of her troupe – that their hearts should be true to the cause. Shearer was not popular with the *corps de ballet.* 'I didn't realize how disliked I was,' she admits. But it was not just jealousy of the girl's film career. 'Her natural shyness (often mistaken for aloofness),' writes her husband, Ludovic Kennedy, 'combined with Scottish reserve and even puritanism (once, when we were engaged, she scolded me for watching two dogs rogering on the pavement), had never made her relationship with other members of the company easy.'[2] Fonteyn, by contrast, had earned, over the long and difficult years, nothing but the loyalty and affection of her peers. 'Margot was the perfect model,' says Annette Page, 'in the way she danced, the way she behaved, the way she dressed. In every aspect.' Even Beryl Grey, who might have had more reason than most to harbour resentment, cannot fault Margot's professionalism or sweetness of nature. 'She could have been prima-donna-ish, but she never was.' And never had Grey's respect for her colleague been more whole-hearted than in the hours leading up to the New York opening. 'She came to ten o'clock class. Went up to the wardrobe with the rest of us. And I thought, on a day like today, she could have been excused.'

For one thing, it was the hottest day of the year. It was 9 October, and India, as well as England, had come to New York. The unventilated theatre was like a tropical hothouse, and that was before the 3,459 seats had been filled by dignitaries and socialites, and the hoi-polloi had crammed themselves four deep into the allocated standing room. Margot was icy calm. Pamela May, knowing all too well how her friend relied on nerves to fire her up for a performance, was worried to see Margot in so peculiarly frozen a state. 'When she stood around beforehand in her dressing-gown,' recalled one of the Cavaliers, Alfred Rodrigues, 'she was white underneath the greasepaint – white, white, white.' The roses that eluded her cheeks had material-ized in her dressing-room – among them a bunch from an American GI she had met in London, Joseph Stuhl. Madam had come to wish her good luck; as had, by long tradition, her great friend Leslie Edwards, the only member of the company she could bear to have knock on her door in the two hours before curtain-up. Bobby Helpmann knew better than to be gentle with her: 'It's tonight or never,' he warned her. 'You're an unknown quantity; they *know* Moira and I are marvellous, and you've got to show you can leave us standing.'

But if Margot had a true champion that night, an invincible rock of support, it was the hulking figure in the orchestra pit who, though he no longer shared her bed, remained intimately connected to her in the sphere where they understood each other most sensuously and profoundly: the sphere of music. Still faintly feverish, de Valois had searched the Met for Constant Lambert. 'I went round the back in my usual state of agitation, particularly because of this wonderful bar they had there.' She asked the stage manager: 'Mr Lambert . . . er . . . have you seen him?' He knew what she meant. 'Dead sober, Madam,' he replied. Sober maybe; dead, far from it. 'Nothing was more wonderful,' swears Ashton. 'He stepped into the pit and started, and everyone was electrified.'[3]

The first appearance of Princess Aurora is delayed by Petipa until after Tchaikovsky's long Prologue, and the twenty-minute interval that follows it. But even from the tannoy in her dressing-room, Margot must have been aware that, as Lincoln Kirstein wrote to Richard Buckle: 'The hero of the occasion, according to Balanchine and myself, was Lambert; he had a fine band and the score never sounded so well . . . He whipped people up into applause, purely by sound; when nothing was really happening from a dancer he seduced everyone into imagining that she was divine.'[4]

Not that there was much need for sleight of hand. Some relics of amateur film, taken surreptitiously during that fabled 1949 season, still exist. And if one starts to watch in a spirit of conde-scension what threatens to be virtually a home movie, expecting to have to make allowance for the passage of time and the inevitable advancement in technique, then one is in for a shock. For even to the sophisticated modern eye, the flickering testi-mony makes clear that the company assembled by de Valois for America embodied standards of classicism and accomplishment and sheer ensemble style that, far from being surpassed in the intervening years, have sadly been lost. According to Pamela May: 'de Valois's casting for this performance was ruthless to a degree. She wanted only her top dancers in each role, which meant that the company's other ballerinas were doing solo roles from the Prologue onwards.' (The Fairy Variations were danced by Violetta Elvin, May herself, Anne Negus, Pauline Clayden and Avril Navarre, with Beryl Grey as the Lilac Fairy. Frederick Ashton was Carabosse and June Brae the Queen Mother.) May was 'determined, to put it mildly, to scintillate as never before . . . there was a very strong feeling that we would give the audi-ence a night to remember.'[5]

At the end of the Prologue the curtain fell to stirring applause, and Mayor O'Dwyer, in a box next to de Valois's, leaned perilously out of it to pluck her sleeve and bawl the most baffling thing: 'You're *in*, lady.'[6]

And this before her girl was even *on*.

Margot, when at last she ran out on to the stage, only remem-bers her reception as 'a burst of sound' which 'drowned out the music and also some part of my mind'. Once again, and at this most critical moment of her story, she makes no mention of her ex-lover's crucial contribution. Those on stage with her knew otherwise. 'Lambert understood she was like a racehorse,' says Alfred Rodrigues, 'and he altered the music just enough to make her forget to be nervous and just respond. Certainly I think he sort of pulled her up immediately, so that she just came on and did it. And then there was the incredible thing with the Rose Adagio where she just stood and lifted up her hand and *smiled*, and the audience screamed, and from that moment she was away. It was absolutely the most extraordinary night and I think Lambert had a great deal to do with it because he knew her so well – he knew, with his incredible musicality, how to raise her to that pitch.'

Legend has it that Margot's balances were on such perfect form that she chose to omit one of the Princes from the line-up altogether. In Pamela May's version: 'The last Prince, Jack Hart, stood smiling at the side of the stage with folded arms waiting for Margot to come off balance, and, after what seemed like an eternity, offered her his hand. The house went mad and the applause was unbelievable. The company members standing in the wings all had tears rolling down their cheeks with excitement – I was one of them and will never forget it.'[7]

Nor would Moira Shearer. She had to wait until Act III – the bitter end – to make *her* entrance, by which time, says Nadia Nerina, 'Margot had the audience in the palm of her hand. There she was, dancing at the height of her powers, in her best role: the jewel in the middle of this most fantastic production. By the time Moira came on, it was all over. Of course the audience was thrilled to see her – they stood up and shouted – I don't know how she finished her *pas de deux*, actually. But she'd had it. Because she was doing a short thing that didn't suit her, and Margot had already had two and a half hours.'

Not to mention the climax of the evening, which was yet to come. *The Sleeping Beauty* culminates in the breathtaking 'fish-dives' of the *grand pas de deux* with which Aurora's wedding is celebrated. And no classical variation was better suited to Margot's beguiling *épaulement* than the deceptively simple solo which ensues, to the plaint of a lone violin. And then there was just the coda to get through before the storm broke. Thunderous clapping. A tempest of flowers. Sweat-drenched faces coursing with tears of relief. Heaven knows Margot had been fêted often enough in England and Europe. But this . . . this was 'unimaginable success'.[8] Even the veteran Sol Hurok was hard-pressed to credit the degree of the response: 'I have had the privilege of handling the world's greatest artists and most distinguished attractions; my career had been punctuated with stirring opening performances of my own, and I have been at others quite as memorable. However, so far as the quality of the demonstrations and the manifestations of enthusiasm are concerned, the première of the Sadler's Wells Ballet at the Metropolitan Opera House, on 9 October 1949, was the most outstanding of my entire experience.'[9]

The curtain calls went on for half an hour. When Margot took hers, alone, the whole house rose to its feet and cheered. 'I thought they only did that in Hollywood films,' she was heard to remark[10] – ingenuously we hope, and out of Shearer's hearing. After the gold curtain had risen and fallen twenty times, de Valois felt moved to speak. And even in her hundredth year she could still be prompted to repeat the speech verbatim. 'I got her to tell that story a thousand times,' says Graham Bowles, 'because she so loved it and it got the adrenalin flowing when she was poorly at the end of her life. Once you got her on the Met opening night, you could hear her voice getting stronger with every syllable. "I felt I should say something," she would begin, "and I walked on and described how, during the Blitz, I'd crossed Waterloo Bridge with my umbrella up for safety, thinking to myself, as long as there's an America (if they come in) there'll always be an England." Then, of course I went on: "And I say the same tonight. As long as there's an America, there'll always be an England." I thought the roof would come off!' And de Valois, loath to let the reminiscence fade, would in later life return, as if invoking a litany, to her opening words, investing them with the gruff candour that had so charmed New York half a century before. 'Frankly,' she would repeat, as if to those 4,000 eager, ghostly faces, 'frankly we were terrified of you!'

Terror is the furnace, the *calcinatio* which purges ordinary mortals of irresolution. Margot's true reward that night, beyond the unprecedented adulation and sudden international recognition, was the fact that, in the extremity of her ordeal, she had found her courage. It felt, as these things strangely do, like loss. 'I realized that for the rest of my life I would never again be so nervous before any performance. Some small part of me had actually burned out.'[11] Meanwhile, there was the immediate delirium of victory to manage. 'With the weight of fear removed, I could have risen straight up to the ceiling. An overriding thirst made me almost inarticulate.'

Champagne flowed as freely as water, hydrating and re-animating the whole parched and stunned company at Gracie Mansion, the official riverside residence of the Mayor of New York. Like a clutch of wide-eyed Cinderellas, they were all to go to the ball – god-mothered by *Ambassador's Magazine*, in evening wear from top English couturiers such as Charles Worth and Norman Hartnell. The designer whose name Margot had democratically pulled out of a hat was Bianca Mosca, and now was the moment for the ballerina to don her tiered black brocade gown, which sported a huge bow at the breast and left her shoulders and neck bare, the better to display a borrowed diamond choker. In the way of beautiful women, she and Moira Shearer perpetuated the contest between them by taking longer to array themselves in their finery than they regularly did to dress and make up for the stage. To Hurok's gratification they 'were the last to be ready, each of them ravishing and stunning – the dark flashing beauty of Fonteyn in striking contrast to the soft, pinkish loveliness of Shearer'.[12]

The police formed a flying wedge to clear a path through the crowd for the stars. And as the cavalcade of buses, with motor-cycle outriders and squad cars as escorts, sped through the red traffic lights of Manhattan, a siren from the head of the fleet sent up a great wail, shocking the poor dancers who, reminded of the Blitz, began to scream with a hysteria they would never have permitted themselves in wartime Britain. 'It's all right, girls, that's the all-clear,' announced the calm, laconic voice of Constant Lambert.[13] 'I was with Margot,' says Pamela May, 'and we never stopped giggling and laughing until we reached the Mayor's party. This was held in his garden and was a beautiful sight – tables and chairs laid out on the lawns over-looking the river and a brilliant full moon shining down on us. Music was playing and there were flunkies in red helping everyone . . .'[14]

Toasts abounded, and it seemed that there was no one, from the President of the United States to the King of England, with whom the name Margot Fonteyn was not to be linked. There were two orchestras, and the dancers danced, as dancers, off-duty, tirelessly do. Except, that is, when they are busy eating. By 5 a.m. Margot, Pamela, Fred and Bobby were stoking up on coffee and bacon and eggs at Reuben's, while waiting for the first editions to hit the streets. 'Nora Kaye was in charge of us,' recalls May, 'and she was the one who dashed for the papers and came back shouting You're in! You're in! – which is exactly what the Mayor had said to de Valois!'[15]

'In' was an understatement – New York had taken English ballet to its heart. 'The Sadler's Wells has, let it be said, more than spectacle to offer. It . . . has manner, grand manner, and this is a quality we do not always find in our own ballet.'[16] So far, so fair. But then the *New York Herald Tribune* tired of impartiality and launched into the real news of the day. 'The admirable policy of having no stars can only go so far; when a star of the first magnitude appears before our eyes, it makes no earthly difference how she is billed. Margot Fonteyn is unmistakably such a star, a ballerina among ballerinas. London has known this for some time, Europe has found it out and last night she definitely conquered another continent.'

To the *New York Times* she was 'young and lovely to look at', and possessed of 'technical equipment so strong she seems to ignore it'.[17] A third publication deemed her 'simple and unaffected, as true greatness is', and could have written 'essays, or perhaps sonnets ... about her back, so classically straight in turns and poses yet so flexible and yielding when the occasion demands. Her legs sing out the beautiful phrases she is dancing and her head, radiant and demure at the same time, crowns a body designed by nature for the ballet.'

Success means nothing until the person who loves us best, and whose approval we need most, has been apprised of it. Margot's mother – either because of the astronomical cost of the transatlantic journey, or because her daughter, for reasons of independence and even superstition, vetoed it – had not come to New York. Whatever the case, in that era of telegrams, whose staccato style was conducive to hyperbole, the message sent by Margot to Black Queen was cautious and low-key. 'I think we made it,' was all the cable said.[18] Yet *how* that 'we' must have gratified Mrs Hookham, cut off, at this of all times, from the light of her existence. It was ambiguous of course: you could say that 'we' was supposed to mean the company, that Margot was generously deflecting the limelight away from herself and sharing the glory in the democratic spirit that de Valois as well as her mother had so fostered. Or you could read a more familial solidarity into the first person plural: an inference that, although the Atlantic lay between them, the powerful identification of talented daughter with aspiring mother had not been sundered.

But Margot did not share the cover of *Time* magazine with anyone. It was her face alone that looked out from newspaper stalls and kiosks all over the city. *Newsweek* soon followed suit with a full-length portrait of her adjusting the ribbon of a *pointe* shoe. These were serious, political publications whose front pages were usually reserved for world leaders and heads of state: to grant a dancer such pride of place was to raise the frippery of ballet to the level of an international incident. For Margot, it was the public accolade of a lifetime – the sort of acknowledgement that does not come without commensurate private disparagement. It was one thing for the English company to be proud of its leading ballerina, and glad for her, but, in New York, Margot was not without her detractors – among them the most eminent and respected commentators in the land. George Balanchine, for one, was distinctly underwhelmed by her: 'Hands like spoons, can't dance a step,' he would one day be heard to mutter.[19] Lincoln Kirstein, though primed by Richard Buckle on the subtleties of Fonteyn, found her Princess Aurora, of all ironical things, 'unawakened. She has a magical pall over her; she seems to breathe through a haze behind which there may be a brilliant presence, but it is not yet brilliantly announced . . .'[20] As for Balanchine's star ballerina, Alexandra Danilova, she was rumoured to have regaled a first-night party of stockbrokers thus: 'The music starts . . . this is Aurora's entrance. Where is prima ballerina? Where is prima ballerina? *This little girl* is prima ballerina? Ridiculous.'[21]

But America's other great star (and Balanchine's wife of the moment), Maria Tallchief, watching Margot in the daunting knowledge that the next première at the Metropolitan would be her own, as the Firebird, found the sight of the English dancer inspirational. 'At that time we hadn't seen anyone quite like Margot. I mean, when she appeared on stage in *Sleeping Beauty* it was like sunshine arriving – a true shining light. You felt you wanted to live up to a standard that she upheld.'

It took a star of another medium, however, finally to bring home to Margot herself the enormity of what had happened. Bobby Helpmann, who knew everybody, took her to meet his friend Katharine Hepburn. Margot stood excitedly on the brownstone doorstep, breathless at the prospect of being introduced to this goddess of the movie industry. And the door was opened, not by some flunky, but by Hepburn herself, who, just as breathlessly, exclaimed: 'Oh, I am so excited to meet you!'[22] This extraordinary reversal of awe shook Margot to the extent that she decided then and there to give up her blushes. 'It was ridiculous, if not grotesque, to remain so shy at the age of thirty.'[23]

And what better mentor could she find in her quest for self-confidence than that least retiring of all God's creatures, Robert Helpmann? 'He could stand up to anybody,' says Alan Sievewright. 'He could have looked into the face of the devil himself, and laughed.'[24] And lest earthly success, on the scale that had befallen Margot, should lead her into confrontation with the forces of darkness, what she now needed to invoke for her survival was a little of Helpmann's healthy audacity. According to both Anne Heaton and Moira Shearer, it was on this first American tour that the latent friendship between Margot and Bobby suddenly assumed the nature of a love affair.

Theirs was an unlikely coupling. Yet, for all the lionizing which the stars received, New York could prove a lonely place – as Constant Lambert, in a letter to Isabel, makes tangible: 'I am very alone and miss you more than I can say. Bobbie is at his *worst* and very sour at being overshadowed by Margot and myself. Margot in the beautiful but aloof world she has chosen.'[25]

Helpmann, at forty, remained a man of blazing theatrical ambition. So to find himself sidelined by the girl with whom he had once condescended to share his charisma, the girl who used to slip away unnoticed while he was mobbed by fans, must have been galling for him. New York – which could boast its own superb, virile, Balanchine-trained dancers, dancers who were nowhere near the dread age of forty – was not enamoured of Bobby's make-up box (he toned down his eyeshadow and shed his wig after comments overheard on the first night). Nor had New York a kind word to say for his contemporary works: '*Hamlet*,' wrote Lincoln Kirstein to Richard Buckle, was 'only to see once';[26] and as for the 'embarrassing' *Miracle in the Gorbals*: 'Well, mother. All is forgiven, but *never* do it again.' It was only when Helpmann, as Prince Florimund, led Fonteyn forward for their shared call that American audiences stood and cheered. So there was a roundness to the fate which now propelled him to seek consolation in Margot's arms. 'Helpmann is frank about his emotional make-up,' wrote his biographer, Elizabeth Salter. 'He is a narcissus who loves where he is loved; who responds to adoration from either sex. His world is the world of ballet where attraction flares quickly. Beauty and propinquity create the spark . . .'[27] Those, yes – and expedience. His penchant for men notwithstanding, Helpmann did not consider the love of women beyond his range – if they were beautiful and famous enough to advance his cause. After all, it had been Margaret Rawlings whom he had first prevailed upon to bring him to England; and at the height of his entanglement with Vivien Leigh (obsessive enough on both sides to cause Laurence Olivier considerable jealousy), the presents he showered upon the couple caused Ashton to snipe: 'That's not generosity, that's *investment*.'[28] But the women Helpmann adored saw beyond such opportunism: Katharine Hepburn found him 'Very sweet, and very tender and very nice and very thoughtful. *Very*.'[29] Margaret Rawlings could find no fault with him at all . . . 'He was so – oh dear – he was so attractive. A *magnet*.'[30] As for Vivien Leigh, who took her troubles to him as to no other, 'She *worshipped* Bobby. And Bobby worshipped her.'[31]

What probably drew Margot to Helpmann at this late stage of his dancing career was – as Leslie Edwards put it – more to do with her propensity for 'helping lame dogs over stiles'.[32] Her sympathetic nature was mobilized by the revelation that behind his dazzling wit and intimidating bravura lurked a fallible and ordinary being, in need of her encouragement and solicitude. Helpmann claims to have been taken as much by surprise as she was. 'Our partnership was perhaps one of the most extraordinary in my life, because I danced with Fonteyn for twenty-five years, and I don't suppose for the first nine or ten of those years I ever spoke to her at all outside the rehearsal room. I'd say, "Goodnight. What time's rehearsal in the morning?" but I never spoke to her. I think it was because I thought she was stand-offish, and she thought I was stand-offish, and we never bothered to enquire . . . I remember very clearly one day walking down the street and I looked at her and I said something and she laughed, and I remember thinking, my goodness, she's a friend. A great, close, intimate friend.'[33]

That this friendship, given Helpmann's clear orientation, should briefly develop an erotic dimension ought not, perhaps, to prompt incredulity. Margot had always preferred the company of what Nadia Nerina refers to as ' "the boys" – she was more relaxed with them'. Her perspective on heterosexual life may, in any case, have been distorted – by her absconding father, by the torment of her long affair with Constant Lambert, and, indeed, by her own, careerist suppression of the maternal instinct. Despite her healthy sexual appetites, she was not unused to feeling sexually extraneous, for homosexuals dominated the only world that she had ever really known. Al Khoner, describing himself as 'just an average guy from New York who didn't know a thing about the ballet', became, with barely an introduction, her escort to Coney Island and, indeed, her lifelong friend – simply by ringing her hotel and asking her where she'd most like to go. He maintains that she was cheerfully unfazed by his gayness. 'The first meeting she had with me I think she thought was going to be sexual. And when that didn't happen, that was perfectly all right with her. There was nothing ever said – I think she understood why.'

Margot had been understanding why – ever since her first crush, at the age of fourteen, on William Chappell. And if, with Helpmann, the question 'Why?' became 'Why ever not?' the answer lay in the overriding physicality of a dancer's daily existence. Margot and Bobby had been working together for fifteen years, and were already mutually possessed of an anatomical familiarity that a married couple might almost consider indecent. Dancers must breathe hard into each other's faces, bathe and slither in each other's sweat; she must split her legs for him without propriety and his hand must go wherever it will to gain the grip he needs to stall or haul or lift or propel or pivot her. Good partners can become so familiar with the smell and feel and sheer proximity of one another that sex can seem, in the event, a mere detail – something already half-enacted; something of limited bearing upon a wider and more compelling sensory experience.

'Were they in love?' Elizabeth Salter asks herself – and answers: 'For a while they thought they were. Or at least Helpmann thought he was. To create their stage magic they had to become part of it. Off stage they reverted to friendship.'[34] The blatant inseparability of those two old friends must surely have exacerbated Lambert's sense of isolation in New York. His gifts were all for instigation and initiation, whereas Margot's were for consistency and durability: while she went on, after the sunshine of her Aurora, to cast a further glow over the city with the moonlight of her Odette, his mood, in the wake of the elevation of that all-conquering first night, descended into boredom and depression. 'There are certain things in life,' he wrote to Isabel, adopting the tone of rash frivolity that his friends had come to dread, 'such as birth, fornication and death which have their ups and downs. The only thing in life which can maintain a continuous level is *cafard*. Talk about *cafard*! Fortunately I am getting acclimatized and can even distinguish between one street and another (which is more than most Americans do). I live rather symbolically between two avenues (both of which I have explored) – Park Avenue, which tries to be like Gloucester Gate without succeeding, and Lexington Avenue which is vaguely like Camden High Street, and quite frankly lets the whole fucking thing ride. I drink there rather gloomily after the show from time to time . . .'[35]

After the show, *and* before the show, and, as the season wore on, during it. At a performance of *Hamlet*, the final ballet of the evening, he fell, going into the orchestra pit, and had to be helped to his feet. The musicians did their best to follow his wavering baton, but, when his concentration gave out, the beat was lost and the orchestra ground to a standstill. Constant stood swaying on the podium in what the audience must have realized was a stupor.

Bobby Helpmann, lying prone at the front of the stage as Hamlet, tried to hiss to the prompt box: 'For God's sake, don't bring the fucking curtain down!'[36] Years later he told John Lanchbery: 'We could have managed somehow without music

– we could have done it with mime or something – not to shame Constant – but they brought the damn curtain down.' Next morning, Lanchbery relates, 'no less than four of the musicians went to the office of Bertie Hughes, the manager, and one of them said: "It was entirely my fault that Mr Lambert fell. I moved my stand and he caught his foot in the electric cord." And the others said, "Yes, we saw that. We had to pick him up because he tripped on the cord." '[37] The loyalty of the American orchestra was all the more heartening for being so recently won. But the confidence of the English management was long lost. Robert Zellor took over the musical direction for the rest of the tour, and Lambert returned to England, never to be invited to America with the company again.

His was not the only fall from grace. In Washington, in front of President Truman, Margot, along with just about anyone who set foot on the highly polished stage of Constitution Hall, found herself ignominiously flat on her face – an event which not only made its way into the English newspapers the next day, but into a subsequent parliamentary speech by Sir Stafford Cripps: 'My dear lady . . . I beg you not to take it too much to heart. It is not the first time – nor, I feel sure, will it be the last – when your countrymen will be obliged to assume that same prostrate position on entering that city.'

Washington was the first engagement on the whistle-stop tour which Hurok had arranged, involving dates in Richmond, Philadelphia, Chicago, East Lansing, Toronto, Ottawa and Montreal. And all in the space of five weeks. It was to ease this punishing itinerary that Hurok came up with his entrepreneurial masterstroke: a special train of six baggage cars, a diner, a drawing-room and seven Pullmans, to snake its way across the vast plains and dustbowls and rocky landscapes with the words 'Sadler's Wells Ballet' spelt out in huge letters along the length of its carriages. And to this train, after performances in those farther and farther flung venues, the dancers would return, sometimes as late as 2 a.m., to eat and sleep and lead their lives in what was, virtually, a travelling hotel, albeit a rather cramped and spartan one. Margot, at the age of ten, had crossed China and Russia on the Trans-Siberian Railway with her mother and a mere fourteen pieces of luggage. Now she shared a sleeping berth with Pamela May on a train which, speeding towards the blizzards of Canada, carried not just a full orchestra primed to serenade her every movement, but forty tons of scenery and props to create the various worlds which she nightly inhabited. On 11 December, the tour was to end, and Margot would fly home for Christmas – to her mother in Pont Street, and to her own tiny flat above the smell of rotting fruit in Long Acre. But who could say, any more, where home really was? The disappointingly restrained, stubbornly British reception for *Cinderella*, which opened the new season at Covent Garden on 26 December, confirmed Margot's sense of displacement and restlessness. Leslie Edwards writes: 'The house was packed to welcome us after our triumph in the States, where we had been constantly applauded to the rooftops, and now we awaited the possibility of the same treatment from our own loving public. We assembled on stage behind the familiar red velvet curtain, and, before Constant went into the orchestra pit, we all discussed with Fred how we were to react to prolonged opening applause: both he and Constant agreed that we should dance straight through it. Anyway, Margot, Freddy and Bobby, who were on stage when the curtain went up, would bear the brunt of it at first. The overture ended and the curtain rose. You could have heard a pin drop. Bobby and Fred as the Ugly Sisters, sewing away at the kitchen table, first looked at each other nonplussed and then broke out into helpless giggles: only the total professionalism of these artists prevented the audience from noticing this. Poor Margot, sitting woefully by the fireplace, pathetic and sad, had the worst of it: the giggling became infectious and she had to cup her face as she pretended to be gazing dreamily into the firelight. Not one pair of hands in the Opera House came together. The audience was going to behave just as they had always done, and applause would come at the final curtain.'[38]

To save the day, Margot was urged to make a curtain speech

and Kenneth Clark, who was in the audience with his family, remarked to his daughter Colette: ' "What an awful moment it must have been for her not to know what would come out" – so that is how bad her voice must have been. People were very snobbish in the past, so if you had any sort of accent you were considered odd. She came forward very shyly and opened her mouth and I only remember her saying: "And especially my dear ugly sister" – to Fred. We all thought that was very touching.'[39]

But class-conscious England was no longer the prime arbiter of Margot's worth. America, with the all-engulfing warmth of its embrace, had laid claim to her vagabond spirit. The Sadler's Wells Ballet had well and truly conquered New York – though at the price of an exclusive right to its own most valued possession. For Margot Fonteyn was no longer just an English ballerina. She was now an artist who belonged to the whole world.

One of the oddest cross-fertilizations spawned by the New York season was the collaboration between Constant Lambert and Roland Petit, whose Ballets de Paris had been wowing Manhattan at the same time as had Sadler's Wells. *Variety* wrote: 'That a dancing troupe from Paris would prove to be exhilarating and sexy was somewhat to be expected. But that a ballet company from stolid Britain, the land of mutton and ale, of tweeds and Scotch whisky, would prove to be exotic and glamorous, was a complete surprise.'[1] Yet, back in stodgy London, the attempt to mix divergent national styles was not so easily digested: Petit's choreography for the resulting ballet, *Ballabile*, was thought, when it appeared, rather lightweight and whimsical for the English dancers, and Margot's two ex-lovers clashed during rehearsal in the presence of Lambert's fourteen-year-old son, Kit. It must have been to Margot's immense relief that – exceptionally – she did not feature in the new production.

Just as exceptionally, she found herself cast in de Valois's first (and last) choreographic venture for Covent Garden, *Don Quixote* – in a dual role which demanded that she swoop between delicate refinement (the Lady Dulcinea) and peasant earthiness (Aldonza Lorenzo). As the latter, Margot 'was fascinating and shamelessly provocative', writes Elizabeth Frank, 'pulling her long black hair above her head with both hands, using her frilled petticoat as a matador uses his cloak, and flashing come-hither looks at the poor infatuated Don Quixote'.[2] But Helpmann, despite unprecedented recourse to Leichner sticks and bottles of spirit-gum, could make nothing of the name-part in this curiously dull work, and was dubbed, by a critic quoting Hilaire Belloc, a 'remote and ineffectual Don'.[3] Intellectually conceived but not imaginatively born, *Don Quixote* reflected, perhaps, the toll that the American adventure, with all its administrative responsibilities, had taken not just on de Valois's health but also on her creative energies.

It was left to George Balanchine, the Russian-born choreographic genius and founder, with Lincoln Kirstein, of the New York City Ballet, to light up the season with *Ballet Imperial* (first made in 1941), which he now mounted on the English company, while, in a hands-across-the-ocean exchange, Ashton choreographed *Illuminations* for the New York City Ballet, using, in one of the central ballerina roles, the long-legged Tanaquil LeClercq, who, in two years' time, was to become Balanchine's fourth wife.

But Balanchine, whose habit it was to fall under the erotic spell of talented female dancers, did not, even briefly, entertain the thought of Margot for his muse. 'Oh, you know Margot,' he said, years later, to Robert Gottlieb. 'What a nice girl. Very nice girl. Nice dancer. I take her to the movies once or twice. Nothing – you know? I had her in *Ballet Imperial*. Not very good in that. Other girl better.'[4]

'Other girl' was of course Moira Shearer, who was thrilled, at last, to find some appreciation – not just of her beauty but of her strength and musicality. She hurled herself fearlessly at Balanchine's intimidating inventions: 'Everything was off,' she explains. 'There was this extraordinary diagonal angling of the body, the whole time, and you had to appear to be falling. It had to look dangerous . . . He wanted you at an angle, and if you stayed too long at that angle, you would fall down. I could see him trying to get this, and quite honestly, Margot did not do it . . . She must have seen what he wanted, surely, but anyway she decided against it.'[5]

As far as Margot was concerned, no decision was involved – only a tacit admission, for the first time in her life, of technical defeat. 'The ballerina's first passage,' says Gottlieb, 'is unbelievably difficult. Unrelenting. And Margot told me, "I was never any good at it. I wasn't strong enough. Actually, Moira was better. I used to stand in the wings, thinking if only I can just get through this first passage. And you know, I never could." '

Charming – and typical – as her self-deprecation sounds, a certain ideological stubbornness (not to say private resentment) may have contributed to her inadequacy: the fact is that Margot was simply not, on any level, Balanchine's type. The whole point of her physique was its soft, unexaggerated femininity. Balanchine liked his women dancers to be leggy and athletic and stripped of all interpretative function. 'Choreographic movement is an end in itself, and its only purpose is to create the impression of intensity and beauty,' he wrote;[6] and certainly the incomparable emotional charge of his work depends, paradoxically, upon an almost mechanical observance of the steps and adherence to the beat, untrammelled by any sentimental attachment to meaning or melody. '*Ballet Imperial*,' writes Mary Clarke, 'admitted no subservience to the other arts . . . Throughout the ballet there was an exultance in movement, movement for its own beautiful sake, that was immediately communicated to the audience. How fresh, how joyous were the *sissonnes* in which Beryl Grey traversed the stage with up-raised arms!'[7]

Grey, dancing the secondary ballerina role, came closer even than Shearer to the Balanchine ideal, whereas Margot could not have been further from it – her confidence not exactly helped by an unflattering platinum wig. Technical accomplishment aside, Margot was no longer a blank enough canvas to please a second genius. Her style was too imbued with Ashton's romantic vision, which, over the years, had rendered her his supreme interpreter. Between them, she and Ashton had forged a new school of lyricism, and the emotional current and narrative line that ran through even the most abstract of his works now imposed their soft distinction on every step she danced. She could not – perhaps would not, not even for the great Balanchine – risk sharing the channel through which that private language flowed.

Margot was glad, after only two performances of *Ballet Imperial*, to escape with Robert Helpmann and Pamela May to La Scala, where they were to guest in *Sleeping Beauty*. But although Italy had been central to the development of classical dancing in the nineteenth century, ballet was now considered too 'Russian' to be popular – Tchaikovsky, in particular, was derided by Milanese audiences. Fitting into a foreign production demands intensive rehearsal, and the English dancers were astounded when, just as Margot happened to be suspended above Helpmann's head, a bell rang, and the orchestral players, as one, laid down their instruments and left the hall.

It was much the same on the first night. At the end of the performance, the curtains parted and the stars stepped forward graciously – to a smattering of applause led by a 'claqueur' and the sight of the audience making for the exits. Margot, Pamela and Bobby – unaccustomed as they were to public indifference – turned mutinous: they ate and drank whatsoever they fancied, not caring how bloated or tipsy they became, and, instead of rehearsing, took day-trips to Venice and Florence. After the show, they did the rounds of the clubs; and at one fashionable night-spot a band leader recognized them and launched into a jazz rendering of Saint-Saëns's *Le Cygne*. The dance-floor swiftly cleared of everyone save Margot and Bobby, who found themselves giving a 'hilariously corny ballroom exhibition'[8] of Pavlova's Dying Swan. And yet, suddenly, the Italian onlookers, so unmoved in the formal setting of the theatre, were in tears.

There was plenty of scope for sentiment back at Covent Garden, when Margot returned for a Gala to celebrate – a year early, by some administrative oversight – the Sadler's Wells Ballet's coming of age. Out-of-condition former members of the company (one of whom, Molly Brown, had five sons) came back to romp their way through the orgy scene of *The Rake's Progress* with such veteran verve that de Valois was heard to exclaim: 'Well, I shall *always* have that danced by married women in future.'[9] De Valois herself reclaimed her original part of Webster in *A Wedding Bouquet*, collapsing in exhausted, girlish giggles under the table at which Constant Lambert sat, reciting the words between slugs of undisguised champagne. Poor William Chappell, who was invited back to dance the Popular

Song in *Façade*, never even made it on to the stage, having thrown himself too strenuously into rehearsal and torn a calf muscle. But at least he had the consolation of witnessing from the stalls a performance which, as well as touching him to the core, seemed to him no less than an allegory of British ballet's evolution. For Margot Fonteyn appeared that night in the very first name-part she had ever played: the Young Treginnis in *The Haunted Ballroom*.

Whereas at fifteen she had been quite plump and heavy-featured and mature for her age, now, sixteen years later, frail-faced, and spare as a boy, she made an infinitely more convincing doomed child. It was as if the tender yet piercingly delineated creature in black velvet that now stood before the audience, commanding pity and horror with the merest nuance of a gesture or shift of expression in those huge dark eyes, had literally shaken off the skin of an earlier, less intense existence, and emerged from the blur of its chrysalis into the light.

In September the company was to return, by popular demand, for a nineteen-week tour of North America. This time they were to travel farther, and with a wider repertoire, than before, which meant that the sets and costumes of almost anything worth watching had to be packed up and shipped off well before the London season was due to close. Margot escaped the resulting doldrums that inevitably struck Covent Garden by joining Bobby Helpmann in June for a tour of the English provinces, dancing *Les Rendezvous*, excerpts from *Coppélia*, and a ballet by Alfred Rodrigues called *Ile des Sirènes*. The tour which Helpmann had instigated came to be nicknamed 'The Fonteyn Follies', a fact which may have triggered the new bout of restlessness which now seized Bobby; for, before the summer was out, he was choreographing a musical for Michael Benthall, *Golden City*, directing Elisabeth Schwarzkopf in *Madama Butterfly*, and contending with no less than four different roles in the film *The Tales of Hoffmann*. This flurry of diversification made him far too busy to be in New York on 10 September, and Margot had to start the season with Michael Somes as her partner. The ballet chosen for the première this time was *Swan Lake*.

Some Americans, notably Sol Hurok and Lincoln Kirstein, admired Margot's Odette/Odile even more than they did her Aurora. But despite the orchids and roses that carpeted her dressing-room, and the telegrams that covered its walls, one tumultuous reception is, ultimately, as deafening as another, and no second time can ever be as exciting as the first. Suffice it to say that it went well, and that the reviews were universally admiring. More interestingly, however, and less predictably, *Giselle*, which opened a week later (with Robert Helpmann back at the helm as Albrecht), met with serious criticism, Fonteyn's performance as the tragic peasant girl being compared unfavourably with Shearer's much gentler (Karsavina-coached) rendition. It was generally agreed – even back at home – that Margot, perhaps due to the toughening effect of success, was temporarily out of touch with the quality of pathos that had made her first-act *Giselle* so touching. Indeed, earlier that year – *and* in the presence of a silent Karsavina – Clive Barnes had made no bones about his disappointment: 'To my horror, I found myself telling Margot what I thought of her Giselle. It was coy, it was simpering – I really was very unflattering.' Nor had she much reason for confidence in her second-act interpretation, having not yet developed the aptitude for ghostliness which would one day make that scene properly haunting. But it was too late for fortune to reverse itself: far from threatening her now inviolable position with the press, those adverse reviews seemed only to confirm New York's adoptive attitude towards Margot – she was theirs now, to chastise as well as worship.

Adulation prevailed: on the last night at the Met, the management had to bring up the house-lights to put an end to the inexhaustible curtain calls. The company, after all, had to catch the Sadler's Wells Special first thing the following morning, 2 October. 'The train was classed as a freight train,' writes Margot, 'because there were five wagons of scenery, and it jolted and bumped so violently about in the night, that once, when we had a derailment, hardly anyone noticed the difference.'[10] Beryl Grey recalls that on that second tour, 'we lived in the train for three weeks without ever seeing a proper bed. And Madam was terribly strict about who went to what reception, because it was a goodwill tour . . . We had day clothes and evening clothes and cocktail clothes and she used to make lists . . . which was all very well . . . but the programmes didn't start until very late: 8, 8.30 . . . Then you got ready for a reception that probably didn't finish until 3 or 4, and you clambered exhausted along the rails and into the train at half past four or five in the morning and then you were rocketed along and shunted here and there. And I often wondered how dancers' bodies stood up to that. But they did.'

It was not just the social strain that kept the dancers from their rest. The intimacy of the sleeping arrangements was all too conducive to sexual intrigue. 'Romances,' writes Margot, 'serious and fickle, erupted and evolved in complicated patterns. Dramatic eternal triangles inevitably formed, bringing bliss to one compartment and tears to another.'[11]

Margot's own compartment was drier-eyed than most, since her mother had joined the American adventure this second time around, and was touring with the company through the Southern States, on the first leg of the journey: Philadelphia, Pittsburgh and Atlanta. Margot shared sleeping quarters with Pamela May, now married to Charles Gordon, whom May had met (along with her first, now dead, husband, Painton Cowan) during the Cambridge season of '37 – that unmatchable summer of youthful romance about which the two girls had never ceased to reminisce. In Atlanta, where the company appeared for two nights only, 'it happened,' explains May, 'that Margot and I were not in one of the programmes and we were up in the theatre manager's office, and the phone rang, and who do you think it was? Tito! He'd tracked down where she was. She answered it and said to me: "You won't *believe* who it is," and I said, "Oh, is it Tito?" I just *knew* by the look on her face.'

The look on Margot's face registered, as well as delighted astonishment, out-and-out alarm. 'He was talking as though we had seen each other last week, when it was twelve years since

I had heard a word.'[12] He was in New York; he was flying to Panama next day; he was calling her Darling. Without regard for her own pressing schedule, he declared himself ready to jump on a plane which would touch down in Atlanta if she would only rush to the airport to see him. Hypnotized as she always had been, and ever would be, by his hare-brained schemes and cavalier confidence, Margot agreed, provided he telephone her next morning with the exact time of his arrival. No such call came through. Was it relief or disappointment or just plain intuition that made her remark to Pamela May, 'I expect he is very fat by now, and has a wife and three children, too'?[13]

Margot was not at a time of life to indulge in heartache. Writing to her friend Guinevere Parry – in the whimsical guise of 'Fur Toes' – she describes herself as an ageing ballerina-cat who, though she will soon have to resort to tinting her fur and lifting her whiskers, finds the shelf upon which she seems destined to remain for life 'the gayest and most satisfactory place to be'. On tour it was the homesick, married, members of the company who tended to develop injuries that demanded their return to Blighty. Those who were fancy-free played as hard as they worked: Canasta on the train was not so much a game as a craze, and, at a swimming-pool in the grounds of their Houston hotel, the dancers swam and swallow-dived for Alexander Grant's home-movie camera like contenders for the crown of Esther Williams. In Los Angeles, film stars paid homage to them: Danny Kaye, Charlie Chaplin, Greer Garson, Laurence Olivier, Vivien Leigh – even Garbo. Sam Goldwyn was prompted by the escalating fashion for ballet to consider remaking *Grand Hotel* with a real dancer in the Garbo role, and it gratified Margot that it was she whom he approached – not Moira. But she knew, now, the folly of that path. 'I'm not a film star,' she told Goldwyn, 'I'm a ballerina.'[14]

And never was she more grandly that than with Sol Hurok, who, unaware of her inflexible rule about seeing nobody before the show, was foolhardy enough, one first night, to knock at her dressing-room door. No answer. Ten minutes later he tried once more, this time daring to peer in. She was sitting at her dressing-table. She did not raise her eyes, nor indeed her voice, but the two words that she uttered came from some wrathful and omnipotent depth that he would never have credited to her gentle and seemingly submissive psyche. In his own version of the story, he spells out those words for us lest we should fail to grasp the impact they had upon him: 'G-e-t O-u-t!'[15] And out he got. But at a party later that evening, Margot seemed to have quite forgotten his offence, and her own: ' "Are you angry at me?" [Hurok] asked her. "I?" She smiled an uncomprehending smile. "Why on earth should I be?" '

In fact, there was every reason for her to feel thrown off-balance. On 11 November, just before the end of the San Francisco run, the difficulties which had been brewing between Helpmann and de Valois came to a head, and Helpmann, who had in any case been planning to resign, stormed out. It was an unworthy end to a professional alliance full of humorous candour and mutually affectionate respect. 'I don't really know what the fuss is about,' de Valois made out to the press. 'Helpmann has to make a most important film and it is impossible to do this and also dance with us.'[16] But privately she wrote to Joy Newton: 'Bobby has resigned after much monkeying with his contract (a colourful packet of mixed lies), a dirty trick or two and the removal of any "character" from yours very truly. But never mind. He's down, now, and rather unhappy – I have refused to quarrel with him because I am fond of the old rogue and, now he is going down the ladder, I can't kick him. He'll bob up again – more so if he really makes up his mind to let younger dancers live (which is the reason he struggles on – he wouldn't mind dying if everyone else would also oblige!!). His influence on Margot is *very* bad – he and Fred hardly speak. It is all too devastatingly difficult and complicated, as Cecil Beaton would say.'[17] Helpmann, who admitted to being 'lost, homeless and adrift', drifted back to Hollywood, where the Oliviers, on their return from a tour of Australia, consoled him with snapshots of the house in Mount Gambier where he had been born.

Helpmann's petulant departure may not have been entirely unrelated to a new love affair on which Margot had embarked in San Francisco – with Bill Rafter, a local news editor. 'She and Bill really did have a great romance,' says Jane Edgeworth. 'She would disappear for long periods with him, and I covered for them a great deal, impersonating her for Room Service with my black hair tied up, answering the door, and signing her name, which I could do convincingly. Margot was no saint, but she was a luminary, and she had masses of men friends – masses. But we *longed* for her to marry Bill Rafter. He was a wonderful bloke. The simple thing was that he was committed to a great job in San Francisco, and she was the rising star of the whole world of ballet. What could they do? How could they sort it out?'

Sol Hurok's train could not hang about for an answer, and carried Margot away, via Sacramento, Denver, Lincoln, Des Moines, Omaha, Tulsa, Dallas, Oklahoma City, Memphis, St Louis, Bloomington and Lafayette, to Detroit. There, says Jane Edgeworth, 'Margot did *Sleeping Beauty* in a Masonic Ball ring, the size of the Albert Hall. Cadillac owned it, and they wanted to give her a party. Would she come in a Cadillac? "Well, you know, I'd love to," she said, "but there are seventy-three dancers, and all the musicians and staff, and we've all accepted your invitation, so I think I'll just go on the buses with the company." And at the end of the performance, there were 200 white Cadillacs waiting for us outside the theatre.'

So on again to Cleveland, and thence to Cincinnati. After Christmas in Chicago, the company travelled northward: to Winnipeg, White Plains, Toronto, Montreal and Quebec. The landscape flashing past the windows of the train froze over, as if to mirror the bleak state of Margot's heart. Not only did she miss Rafter, but Helpmann's abrupt defection had also proved an emotional – as well as professional – blow to her. Of course, her partnership with Michael Somes was firmly established, and had carried her through Bobby's absences before. But whereas Michael's was a reverent spirit, she had relied on Bobby's very irreverence to challenge her and take her beyond the confines of her nature. Not that she blamed Bobby for going – after all, he had stayed for her sake longer than he'd meant. They had often discussed retirement, and the wisdom of Karsavina's dictum: 'Leave the stage before the stage leaves you.' Margot had no doubts on the matter – 'I don't intend to be an old ballerina' – but Helpmann had given her an inscrutable look and an old Chinese proverb on which to ponder: 'Never name the well from which you will not drink.'[18]

But his wit and wisdom were lost to her now. And, just to complicate matters, she had to contend with a new room-mate. 'Pamela had this wretched knee-cartilage problem yet again, and had to be flown home,' explains Moira Shearer. 'Dressing-rooms being what they are, everyone had to move up one. It was a question of who would go in with Margot, and to my horror I saw my name go up (nobody *said* anything to me – you just saw it on the board). Obviously Margot must have agreed. Also, we had to share sleeping compartments on the train and the little drawing-rooms together at the end, and I thought this is *agonizing*, we don't *know* each other. It was terribly difficult to have a conversation with her – for years and years one had had no opportunity, and she could be enigmatic to the point of being quite chilly sometimes. However, after about two nights of dressing with her it struck me that she was feeling more uncomfortable and nervous with me than I was with her, and if one looked at it like that, then it became quite easy, and I thought, well, I'll just get to work now and be myself, and try and make her laugh. And you know, by the end of those months she was a totally different person – she even swore, once or twice, quite strongly, and I thought, my goodness, she's really loosened up.'

Shearer's effort seems all the more admirable given the degree of company prejudice which was pitted against her. Long before the first American tour, she had trodden on her colleagues' toes by daring to raise the subject of Margot's retirement. 'A few of us were discussing the problem of a ballet-mistress,' says Alex

Martin. 'We were going through names of various company members and discussing their possibilities, when Moira Shearer suddenly joined in and said, "What about Margot? She should be starting to think about what to do next." (This was in 1947 and Fonteyn was dancing like a dream.) Shearer's remark was greeted with a stunned silence, and her unspoken thought . . . "then I can take over" . . . was almost visible in the air.'

Since the fabulous first night in New York, any such thought had evaporated for the foreseeable future. Although Shearer was still only twenty-four (to Margot's thirty-one), it was she who would soon move on, refuting the Red Shoes myth with which she was so powerfully identified, by proving that it *was* possible to have it all: fame on the stage and screen, followed by enviable domestic and maternal fulfilment. Newly married to Ludovic Kennedy, she was, in the ordinary happiness that would soon wrest her away from the ballet world altogether, perhaps as much of a private torment to Margot as she ever had been a public rival. For the emptiness at the centre of Margot's emotional life was beginning to make her feel that most frightening of things: inauthentic. 'I had reached,' she tells us, 'the point where my identity was completely eclipsed by my idea of the image I should project to others: a glamorous, chic personage; gracious and a little aloof; but effervescent with gaiety after the performance – that bit, at least, came naturally. I even thought I ought to have a string of lovers, as many people believed I did. In truth I never had much aptitude for that life.'[19] But what need had she for such aptitude when her fans behaved like lovers anyway? Passing through New York on the way back to London, she was entertained by a slightly scary 'rich admirer' who gave her a mink coat. She had no trouble accepting it, since 'I had always thought that this was exactly the way ballerinas should be treated'.[20]

Although in those days a mink coat would have cost the princely sum of two or three thousand pounds, Margot did not declare it to Customs. 'She never told me where it came from,' says John Craxton, the next genuine lover in the ballerina's 'string' and the farthest thing imaginable from a sugar daddy, falling more into the category of beautiful boy. Five years Margot's junior, the neo-Romantic English artist was living on the Greek island of Poros when Ashton persuaded him to design his next ballet, *Daphnis and Chloë*. 'I had no money,' says Craxton. 'I fought hard to get the 500 guineas for *Daphnis*. And I spent most of it on Margot, going to restaurants and having fun and generally running around. No one seems to have understood the appalling financial situation that she was in when I knew her in '51. All Margot had was her not-exactly-expensive flat in Covent Garden. She couldn't afford to employ anyone: the pianist Jean Gilbert was helping her out, as was her brother and his wife, Idell. Margot didn't do much cooking. We ate out most of the time. She did get sent very nice steak-and-kidney pies from the Savoy Hotel, courtesy of Frederick ('Boy') Browning, a great fan of hers, who happened to be in love with her sister-in-law. Much more a would-be lover of Margot's was Boy Browning's wife, Daphne du Maurier. I sniffed a sort of feeling that she was rather keen on Margot. It was also through Margot that I met Graham Greene. He was quite fun – a very amusing man: I think he was in love with Margot too. There was a moment when they all went on a yacht and he and Margot disappeared for a few days. She was like any artist in her attitude to love: completely pagan. How she acted later when she became an ambassadress, I don't know, but certainly at the time I knew her she was a very grand bohemian. Yet, for all that, she was really a loner. Apart from being a very subtle, sensual person, she had very great personal control. She would cry her eyes out in private but no one ever knew. She never talked to me about Constant Lambert, but I did find in the cupboard of her flat a marvellous portrait (frightfully dirty – I had to put it in the bath to wash it) by Christopher Wood of Lambert, which he'd given her. I got it framed and hung it up, but a few years later when Tito arrived it went back in the cupboard. She was a model of discretion. She'd learned a lot from the people she'd been with: blotted it all up very, very young.'

Now, at the advanced age of thirty-two, Margot found herself, where the gifted, nervous young artist was concerned, in the heady position of teacher. 'I had fifty-five costumes to do,' says Craxton, 'and no time. The whole set-up at Covent Garden was so crummy. I painted the scenery myself. All the women's dresses were designed by Margot. The person who oversaw my designs had ideas to make them into off-the-shoulder cocktail dresses, and Margot came in and immediately saw that I was in a state and sweating with fear because my designs had been completely misunderstood. She said: "I think John really wants something more like this. Is that what you want, John?" And I said, "Yes, absolutely, I want something very simple, just a simple dress." And knowing a lot about costume she turned the skirts round underneath and pleated them outside and got this material that hung well and moved well. I would have been lost without her. I clung to her.'

At first, the clinging was purely metaphorical, for the creation of *Daphnis and Chloë* was an all-consuming pastime: there was no leisure left for love. Of all the ballets that Ashton had made for Margot to date, this was the most personal and gratifying. She had come to the music under Constant Lambert's tutelage at the age of seventeen, and, from the first moment of hearing it, had 'wanted the ballet desperately'.[21] After all, the score, commissioned by Diaghilev, was that rare thing: a symphony composed expressly for ballet. More rarely still, it was a musical masterpiece – one as yet unserved by any definitive, choreo-graphic interpretation, since Fokine's 1912 version had lapsed into obscurity after a spat with Diaghilev. Ashton, bored by 'Greek ballets with people running about in tunics and scarves', took the original Chloë, Tamara Karsavina, out to lunch and explained the contemporary treatment of ancient mythology which he had in mind: 'As though it could still happen to this day.' And thus, with the old ballerina's blessing, Craxton set about evoking the bare, sun-baked Mediterranean landscape of his own experience in which a modern-day Chloë could disport herself among her friends in an ordinary yellow dirndl skirt. But he was not prepared for the lighting, which, he explains, 'kills bright yellow. Suddenly everything stops at the dress rehearsal and Margot disappears with one of the shepherdesses, and comes back, wearing the shepherdess's dress which is pink . . . because she's discovered, very quickly, that pink shows up better than yellow. I just kept my mouth shut – it didn't matter – the overall colours remained the same. But psychologically it wasn't exactly what I'd wanted. What I did realize at that moment was how important it is for a ballerina to know how to present herself. She seemed to make the ballet work. The scene where she was subjugated, tortured and tied up by all those wild pirates was quite incredible.'

Bryaxis, the pirate chief, was played by Ashton's new lover, Alexander Grant. 'I used to have to rush on stage,' he says, 'pick Margot up with one hand and run off with her, and then on again for the pirate scene, swing her round and round, throw her on the floor and proceed to jump all over her.' The exciting aggression of Grant's performance was thrown into relief by the pastoral gentleness of Michael Somes's solo as Daphnis, where, with a shepherd's crook hooked under his arms and across his back, he became an almost martyred image of male submission. Never had Ashton's obsession with the theme of sacred-versus-profane love been more overtly explored. 'I enjoyed, almost more than anything, working on *Daphnis and Chloë*,' he has admitted, 'because it was all so very difficult, and I had to dig deeply into myself to do it.' But as with any artist working in any sphere, excessive joy or pain in the creative process are by no means the arbiters of great achievement. 'I have always thought this the most unrewarding of Ashton's works,' wrote Elizabeth Frank. 'Its many shortcomings and general air of tuppence-coloured Arcadia are only extenuated by the beauty of Ravel's score and the loveliness of Fonteyn's performance.' And although, after a subsequent success in America, *Daphnis and Chloë* eventually established itself as a great favourite both with the company and the public, the most perceptive English critics could never quite change their tune. Here is James Monahan in 1956: 'Even now there are times when the dance seems no more than a painstaking servant to the music rather than its equal partner . . . But there is one memorable passage in the final scene: Chloë's long dance of reunion with Daphnis in the course of which she springs up in his arms, then falls again, in movements which are almost purely classical and yet exquisitely reflect and enhance the music's ebb and surge. The image evoked is of a fountain, cascading, drooping, cascading again; and how delicately true in evocation it is, how fastidious in its understatement! It is a matter not only of Ashton's imagination but also of Fonteyn's line and taste and timing.'[22]

Not to mention her whole adaptation to womanhood. Despite his physical preference for men, Ashton's emotional identification was entirely with the female sensibility and its mysterious juxtapositions of Madonna and whore; and, whether in pink, yellow or tangerine, Margot as Chloë was the perfect conduit for his vision of human innocence. 'Of all dancers,' says Ronald Hynd, 'she was the only one who could portray virginity. As no one else. She was absolutely pure, although we all know that she wasn't. There was something . . . oh, just *stainless* about her.'

Margot may have been strapped for cash, but she was perfectly capable of cadging a free ride – not just for herself but for the members of her intimate coterie. One night, soon after *Daphnis and Chloë* had opened, John Craxton happened to be with her in her dressing-room when in walked the American choreographer Ruth Page and her husband, Tom Fisher, who had thrown a lavish fancy-dress party for the company in Chicago. Where – they wondered – would Margot like to be taken for her summer holiday? John Craxton saw no merit in holding back. 'I piped up: "I think Margot would like to go on a yacht round the Greek islands." Margot and Freddy said, "Tut-tut John, you shouldn't say things like that in front of these nice Americans." But Tom Fisher said, "It's a very good idea. I'll arrange it all." '

And so he did – although the *Elikki*, the only boat for hire in the port of Piraeus so soon after the war, was hardly, according to Ruth Page, 'what you would call a swank yacht. In fact it wasn't a pleasure craft at all, just a big fishing boat. There was only one toilet, which was just off Tom's and my cabin. It usually didn't work, and everyone had to go through our room to get there, and the smell would have been a little too much, had we not imbibed a good deal of ouzo and retsina.'[1]

Champagne and green chartreuse were brought aboard to cater for what Ashton called his 'tart's taste in drink'.[2] There was also the little matter of assembling a crew. Tom Fisher managed to hire a steward from the British Embassy and, from the Hôtel Grande-Bretagne, a cook. The latter, although ancient, was no mariner: he was bitten by a fish on the first day and took to his bed. Furthermore, communication was obviously a problem. 'Lucky thing was,' says John Craxton, 'that when we got to Athens we were in an open-air café in the main street, and I arranged for Paddy Leigh Fermor and Joan Raynor to turn up accidentally-on-purpose at our table, and they got on very well with the Fishers. When they got up to go and were fifty yards down the road, Tom Fisher said: "Oh, they're so nice, your friends – I wonder if I dare ask them to come on the yacht?" So I rushed after them and said, "Come back at once, they want you." '

As well as speaking fluent Greek and being blessed with famous good looks, the travel-writer Leigh Fermor was an erudite guide. 'Paddy told the captain where to go,' writes Ruth Page, 'and we went to all kinds of islands where no tourist had ever set foot. We usually had a donkey for Margot, and sometimes for Freddy and me, but mostly we walked and climbed and swam all day, then slept all night on the ship.'[3]

On the first morning, a stray wave came crashing through the porthole of Margot's cabin, drenching her where she lay, in her upper berth. Then, swimming in the sea, she sat on an octopus. 'We didn't care,' says Craxton. 'We were having the most hilarious fun. Greece at that time was magical beyond belief – Margot was in a state of total euphoria. At that stage, we weren't getting physically close; we were very fond of each other but there was nothing going on. There was nowhere we could have done anything anyway. She was in love with everybody on that yacht. She was having the time of her life. Sex was the least important thing to her. She would never have contemplated having children or anything – it would have meant giving up the freedom that she had.'

What her freedom yielded on that particular holiday was the thing for which Margot had striven all her grown-up life: the undivided adoration of Frederick Ashton. They danced together in waterside taverns, alongside local sailors who, with their teeth, could lift wooden tables into the air. 'She was marvellous,' said Ashton. 'If anything went wrong she always made light of it . . . She'd drink red wine and really be relaxed. But she'd still do her exercises every day. Even on a yacht she'd be hanging on the railings.'[4]

However improvised the *barre* or however rolling the deck, Margot at work was a familiar enough spectacle. What came as a revelation was the sight of her at play. Like de Valois before him, Ashton was transfixed by her unexpected athleticism in the water, a sea nymph in a checked gingham rag of a bikini, her long hair streaming out around her. And this was not the only portent of his Ondine that she brought. In the third week of that holiday, a violent storm brewed, threatening to plunge the leaky *Elikki* to the bottom of the Aegean. Ashton and Ruth Page clung to the mast and each other, but Margot showed no such respect for Poseidon's elemental rage. 'It seems,' she tells us with rare self-romanticism, 'that I rode the prow of the ship, laughing at the waves.'⁵ When, safely ashore the following evening at sunset, she did fall into Ashton's arms, it was not so much from terror as from rapture at the sheer excess of beauty: a school of dolphins flying through the newly calm sea.

Chastened by their near shipwreck, the group abandoned the *Elikki* in favour of seven donkeys who bore them to a regular passenger-boat bound for Athens. Margot amounted, after all, to precious cargo. 'It was,' according to Ruth Page, 'rather an ignominious ending for such an imaginative trip, but Marigoula reached London in time for her performance.'⁶

And it was by her Greek nickname, Marigoula, that John Craxton would call Margot when, back in the anonymity of the busy metropolis, he overcame his diffidence and the two at last found the privacy to embark on the affair that had been pending for so many weeks. 'Naked she was quite ravishingly beautiful,' says Craxton, whose artist's eye functions with an objectivity that discounts prurience. 'The figure of a swimmer. I used to watch from the wings, and one day I suddenly had a revelation. I realized what form in space was. It was like looking at a statue. A lot of statues are not good all the way round – they have a back and a front. But she had sides to her. There was a wonderful seamless beauty about her. My life-drawings of her were some of the happiest I ever made. Of course I was in love with her. What else could you be? She became part of my family.'

Just as Margot spent her Sundays lolling around John's parents' studio-house in Hampstead, so John found himself gathered into the domestic bounty of Black Queen. 'She taught me how to make mayonnaise.' He was aware, however, of how easily the mixture might have curdled . . . 'I had the impression that if she hadn't liked me, I'd have been out,' for it was clear that Mrs Hookham was becoming increasingly anxious about her daughter's marriage prospects. 'I thought Margot had terrible taste in people,' says Craxton. 'But, being a pragmatic person myself, I realized she was desperate to find some sort of security she hadn't got. She saw that she had a professional life and I had a professional life and it wasn't going to work.' And although Craxton could lay no claim to Margot's future, his romantic notions did powerfully evoke her past. 'Once,' he says, 'I went down to the East End of London. It was a lovely summer's day and I was walking, and, every telephone box I came to, I picked up the phone and rang her. And she said, "It's simply uncanny what you're doing. That's exactly what Constant Lambert did once. He picked up the phone on his way round London and said, "Hello; hello." '

And who knows that Lambert, lurching towards the end of his chequered life, was not, with his great reliance upon the supernatural, making some urgent covert bid for her attention? Ailing as he was, he had embarked, in July of 1950, on an ambitious new composition – his first original ballet score since *Horoscope*. It was titled *Tiresias*. And no work in the company's history was to have so damaging an effect on the reputation of British ballet.

In Graeco-Roman myth, Tiresias, originally a man, becomes a woman, and embarks on an erotic involvement with another man. Later, having regained his manhood, he is asked by the goddess Juno in which gender he, as the only living authority, has experienced the greater pleasure. Hearing his reply, she strikes him blind. Ashton was not at all sure that the central argument of this legend could be made intelligible by means of a dumb show. 'How do you explain in a ballet who enjoys sex more?'[7] he wanted to know. Like Tiresias, however, he did not doubt the answer: the woman. 'Of *course* she does. She gets penetrated.' But Lambert's less versatile predilections had granted him no such personal insight, and friends were privately mystified as to why an overtly bisexual theme should obsess him when, as Billy Chappell pointed out, 'he loved being with queer people, but there was not a sniff of it in him'.[8]

Lambert, as it happened, cared little either for the story's sexual ramifications or for its philosophical repercussions: it was the heat of the conjugal strife between Juno and Jupiter that delighted him, reminding him, as it did, of his first marriage. Although he was only paid £250 for the commission, the act of writing *Tiresias* brought him so much gratification that the facetiousness of his original concept fell away, and what had been meant to be a thirty-minute satire swelled into an hour-long work of brooding intensity. Margot, once more beyond his reach, had regained her fascination for him. The fact that his wife, Isabel, was designing the costumes and sets (among them a drop-curtain featuring a skeletal snake, mouth open, ready to strike at another skeletal figure) did not deter Constant from introducing a beautiful *siciliana* for the female Tiresias – an oboe solo which observant company members took to be a love poem: there was patently 'still something lingering between Margot and Constant – we all felt it'.[9]

The languorous music that followed for Tiresias and her lover recalled *Rio Grande*, and had Margot (supported by John Field) in meticulously angled profile to the audience, looking like a figure from a Minoan painting, and performing, with many a swish of her extended Cretan pony-tail, a sequence of slow-motion, high-stepping, trotting movements of fabulous equine elegance – although it is hard to conceive quite why a man-turned-woman should emulate a horse. But it was all just fore-play: the sounding of a gong ushered in a frenzied bacchanal, giving rise to 'an ecstatic, sexually ambivalent *pas de deux* . . .

273

that fizzed up into a kind of orgasm. After which the pair lay on the floor, in stylized post-coital stillness.'[10]

Lambert admitted to having set out to '*épater les bourgeois*', and, as rehearsals progressed, the dancers showed every sign of being suitably shaken. 'We thought it was a tremendously exciting ballet,' said Anya Linden. 'The stunning *pas de deux* wasn't at all Fred's romantic style: the sexy snakes and bare-bosomed designs by Constant's wild-looking wife . . . all seemed extraordinary to us.'[11] Most extraordinary of all was the energy which Lambert, in his inebriated exhaustion, found to complete the great task. Although it took no fewer than six friends – acting as 'extra pens for his tired hands' – to set the score to paper, the music was unmistakably not a collaborative effort, but his own; and, only hours before the first performance, he was to be found at the Nag's Head, still reworking the interludes. Denis ApIvor accompanied him to the dress rehearsal 'and stood with him on the huge stage as the men were unrolling the scenery. He stood looking half up at the roof, and then, tapping his stick in a gesture of mock vehemence, he explained with a grin, "Whenever I come into the theatre I feel like a tiger that has smelled blood." '[12]

Yet it was Lambert's own blood that was to be spilled that fateful night. And the predators were not just the critics but also the Establishment. *Tiresias*, commissioned by the Arts Council for the Festival of Britain, was to be premièred on 9 July 1951, at a gala in the presence of the then Queen and the two princesses. It was rumoured that deputations from the Palace were having the jitters about the work's suitability for royal sensibilities. Any notion that the watered-down programme-note (which made a nonsense of the story by replacing, at every possible turn, the word 'sex' with 'love') might lull the audience into smiling acceptance, flew out of the window the very second the proceedings opened with the violent cracking of two whips. But an erotic charge is one thing, and boredom another, so it may, in truth, have been the ballet's excessive length which accounted for the chill with which *Tiresias* was greeted. Although it was a hot summer's night, Margot, who only a month before had been made a CBE in the King's birthday honours, exercised the prudence to cover her transparent bodice with a cardigan when she visited the royal box after the performance – a courtesy which did not prevent the twenty-six-year-old Princess Elizabeth from averting her eyes and pointedly turning her back.

The press showed no such silent diplomacy. Richard Johnson, in the *New Statesman*, called the ballet 'a total loss', Lambert's music 'arid', and his wife's sets 'garish'.[13] But there was worse to come. The following Sunday, in the *Observer*, Richard Buckle did something which had never before been publicly done to de Valois: he attacked her acumen, her very judgement. The piece was headed 'Blind Mice': 'Did you ever see such a thing in your life? Sadler's Wells has three artistic directors. See how they run. Ninette de Valois is too busy to supervise every detail of production. Frederick Ashton is too easily reconciled to compromise; Constant Lambert, one imagines, looks in occasionally with a musical suggestion. Lambert cannot take all the blame for the idiotic and boring *Tiresias* . . . Ashton must have undertaken the choreography of such a work with reluctance and out of duty to his colleague, but de Valois should have forbidden it. Experimental risks must be taken even with the taxpayer's money – and this ballet must have cost £5,000 – but certain enterprises are clearly doomed to failure from the start. Such was *Tiresias*.'[14]

The company closed ranks. De Valois called a meeting in the girls' *corps de ballet* dressing-room, and forbade anyone to speak independently to the press. But the harm had been done. Although Constant instructed his solicitor to demand an apology from Buckle, his spirit was already broken. Within six weeks he would be dead. Isabel Lambert could only look on in horror as the tide of dissolution in which her husband chose to drown his sorrows carried him away. She knew that 'work would be the best help'[15] – not the endless conviviality he craved. At a party with Laureen Sylvestre someone spat in his face for keeping company with a black woman, but he was too drunk to defend her honour, or his own. He took Laureen and her daughter Cleopatre (whom it was falsely alleged he had sired) to the ballet. Luckily they were seated in a box, since he passed out on the floor. 'I was now alarmed,' said Isabel Lambert, 'frightened of the barrier that closed, separating us one from the other . . . He remembered nothing of his collapse.'[16]

On 15 August he conducted *Rio Grande* and Ravel's *La Valse* at the Proms, and later that evening collapsed again. Yet he lunched the next day with Edith Sitwell and, at the end of the week, attended a party given by Elizabeth Lutyens. The following Monday a delirium overtook him, fiendish visions assailed him, and he threatened to throw himself from a window. He was taken to the London Clinic, where, on 21 August, two days before his forty-sixth birthday, he died.

The official cause of death was certified as bronchopneumonia and diabetes mellitus – the undiagnosed condition which had made him appear sloshed even when he was relatively sober. But his friends were convinced that it was the condemnation of *Tiresias* that killed him. 'I must record my opinion,' wrote Osbert Sitwell in the *New Statesman*, 'that he would be alive today had it not been for the savage onslaughts of the critics . . . Such is the rage of the uncreative against the creative that nearly the whole body of critics, ignoring all Lambert had done, both for music and for British ballet, jumped on him as if he were a criminal. And they felled him just at the moment when he was unwell and seriously overworked. By this act solely will the critics responsible be remembered in future.'[17]

The company was in Edinburgh when the news broke. If the dancers had closed ranks before, now, in their collective shock and sorrow, they became a fortress, shoring up the reputation of the composer by dancing *Tiresias* as though it were the great work which, despite his dazzling ability and monumental labour, Lambert had never quite managed to bring forth. They took their lead, as ever, from their ballerina. Margot danced, according to Mary Clarke, 'as one possessed; she had a passionate intensity in this ballet which she has not equalled in any other role'.[18]

Too bad that such intensity was never transposed into words. In her autobiography, Margot does not even mention *Tiresias*, let alone her reaction to Lambert's death. Privately, however, she did write to 'Narby', her landlady in Cambridge, who had become a dear friend. 'Constant's death is the most miserable and ghastly shock, a lot of the time I still can't believe it. We were all paralysed by the news. Kit is at Lancing and the ballet will make provision for his education. It isn't yet decided how it will be done. Ninette rightly says that a sort of benefit performance, although it would no doubt raise a lot of money, might be hurtful to Kit and make him feel that he is just a public charity. I expect a subscription fund will be opened quietly without much publicity. Anyway, something will certainly be done. Poor Constant had probably had diabetes for years and must have felt terrible – as of course he did but was rarely credited with anything but a hangover.'[19]

It fell to Robert Helpmann to read the lesson at the memorial service which was held at St Martin's-in-the-Fields on 7 September. It was not upon Constant's musical genius so much as his unfailing verbal wit and social generosity that Helpmann had depended. Seated beneath the lectern in the packed church, and musing upon the irony of an atheist's music being played on the instrument its composer had most loathed – a church organ – Helpmann was not at all surprised to hear the vicar announce that something had gone wrong. The organ would emit no sound. A piano would have to be brought from Covent Garden. Helpmann relished the paranormal inference. 'I knew that Constant had somehow stopped that organ. Next thing, I thought, he will trip me on the spiral staircase . . . I did not trip and I read without a hitch. But as soon as I got home I telephoned the church. Ten minutes after the service the organ was all right again.'[20]

The Lambert whom Ashton mourned was a less jocular ghost. Although the choreographer had taken no part in Constant's

Fitzrovian life with Isabel – 'They were such drunks I couldn't keep up with them'[21] – Ashton still considered himself to have been Lambert's closest confidant. 'Every misery he went through I had to share. I saw him through it all with Margot.'[22] But the help had gone both ways, and Ashton had, in his time, been deeply reliant upon his friend's musical taste and judgement.

No one, however, was more stricken than that least dependent and sentimental of souls, Ninette de Valois. Earlier that year she had been made a Dame, and the honour exacerbated the forbidding quality that had always distanced her emotionally from her colleagues. To Ashton, in particular, with whom she had never been compatible, she would, essentially, forever be a schoolmarm. But with Constant she had retained the spirit of a schoolgirl. She had looked up to him, rated his intelligence above her own – 'revelled', as she put it, 'in his sagacious and virile company'.[23]

'His early death,' she writes, 'was a tragedy: doubly so because his life had a defiant, reckless quality that tended to interfere with the fine balance of his more considered judgements on all subjects and people . . . If the hand of destiny had been less wayward, Lambert would not only have fulfilled himself, but, equally important for this mundane, selfish world, he would have led and inspired the younger generation.'[24]

It is love speaking, of course, and love cannot see that genius in a life such as Constant's dare not fulfil itself, lest it prove as mundane as the very mortality which it aspires to transcend. If the more sordid details of his existence had obliged de Valois to place the interests of her company above her loyalty to Lambert, then his death set her free to return to her state of youthful adulation. Twenty-five years later, in her memoir, *Step by Step*, the critical attack on *Tiresias* could still draw from her an impassioned reaffirmation of that faith. Her reference is to Buckle's 'Blind Mice'. 'When' – she tells us ringingly – 'I am struck blind again, may it be in such equally worthy company.'[25]

Meanwhile, in the immediate wake of the *Tiresias* fiasco, the third blind mouse of the trio, Frederick Ashton, saw rather less of de Valois's solidarity. She, alarmed by dwindling audiences, set about pulling the repertoire back into shape, commissioning works by Massine and by a new, young, South African choreographer whom she admired: John Cranko. Ashton, left to lick his wounds, took himself off to arrange dances for a Hollywood film – *The Story of Three Loves*, starring Moira Shearer – and thence to New York, where he choreographed *Picnic at Tintagel*.

All this might have left Margot rather in the lurch, had she not pre-empted such an eventuality with a getaway of her own. It is tempting, in one who gave so markedly little expression to negative emotion, to interpret her outward injuries and illnesses as symptomatic of an inner turbulence. For, just as, at the time of Constant's second marriage, she had fallen and hurt her foot, so, now, in the wake of his death, that foot injury returned to plague her. As soon as the season had ended, she was forced, on doctor's orders, to take the longest break from the stage that she had ever afforded herself. She did not dance a step for the rest of the year. No *barre* work. No floor exercises. Nothing. Instead, she did something so amazing and unprecedented with her time that it made her laugh whenever she described it – 'frittering'.[1] She frittered with the glittering best of them, teaming up with Laurence Olivier and Vivien Leigh (hot from their season, at the St James's Theatre, of *Caesar and Cleopatra*). On 17 September 1951 they set sail, to brave yet another Aegean storm, on Alexander Korda's yacht, the whimsically-named *Elsewhere*. Also aboard was Graham Greene, who, according to his journal, seems, despite an all-consuming obsession with his married lover Catherine Walston, to have become wistfully enamoured of Margot: 'Only distraction from C to think of Margot. If I had stayed on the boat that might have developed . . .'[2] But the chance, apparently, was missed: 'We became close and the last night I had to leave to go off to Vietnam. And the last night we went out together and Vivien Leigh insisted on pushing herself in but then got hopelessly drunk and then we'd been drinking heavily and nothing happened, but we agreed to meet when I came back from Vietnam, which we did. We used to go greyhound racing together but by that time somebody had intervened . . . one of Korda's people. She was a very nice person and we had every intention – she wrote to me in Vietnam, but Peter Moore slipped in between us.'

From Margot's point of view, the problem seems to have been entirely logistical. She wrote to Greene: 'Now that you seem to be living in space it is very difficult to contact you by phone . . . Our season finishes in two weeks on 27th of this month [June] and I fly off to Spain early the next morning . . . I'm not really sure of my holiday plans but if I don't see you before I leave I will ring as soon as I am back – by which time you will probably have gone to Indo China! When I think of it, it is just as well that we never started that affair as we would have had very little chance to continue it.'[3]

Margot's extended absence from the Opera House happened to coincide with the exodus of a valuable batch of soloists who had all passed the witching age of thirty, and the *corps de ballet* was suddenly full of fresh young faces being pushed into parts for which they were under-prepared. The more experienced dancers, long starved of opportunity, did fall hungrily on the ballerina roles, and there were some notable performances: Nerina's first Swanilda, Elvin's Giselle, and Pauline Clayden's Chloë. For Beryl Grey, there was Massine's *Donald of Burthens*. 'That, at least, was created for me,' she says. 'That's the joy, isn't it – working with a choreographer from scratch – and I never had it until Margot wasn't there.' More joyous still for Grey was the chance to play muse to Ashton in an addition which he made to the Vision Scene of *Sleeping Beauty*. 'He, more than any other choreographer, actually let you have your head, show your responses: you could do what you liked and he tailored and trimmed it; no one ever knew how much of me went into that solo.' Despite her unique contribution (which can, with hindsight, be glimpsed in the sweeping legato of the Act II variation), January 1952 at Covent Garden became known as the season of the four Auroras: Grey, Elvin, Nerina and Rosemary Lindsay. Margot, the one-and-only, was all the more conspicuous for her absence.

Her return, so passionately awaited by the fans in the gallery, was scheduled for 9 February – in the relatively unexacting role of Chloë. Leaving the theatre after rehearsal at 6 p.m. on the 8th, Margot was aware that the queue down Floral Street was already fifty strong, and armed with camp-stools, blankets and thermos flasks of Ovaltine to see itself through the dragging, freezing small hours. Arriving back in the morning for ten o'clock class, she noted that the numbers had trebled. De Valois took care that all the leading dancers she still possessed should appear that night, and the judgement from the gods was made plain: the crisis had passed – not only was their darling back at the helm, but the company was at full strength once more. The Sadler's Wells Ballet now numbered sixty-eight, all of whom, in April, were included in the company's first visit to Portugal.

In the seductive Easter sunshine it was important not to partake too enthusiastically of the free-flowing local wine, for the stage of the San Carlos theatre sported a rake so vertiginous that a written warning had to be issued to the dancers 'not to touch, or even breathe on the scenery, owing to the difficulties presented by the steep stage'.[4] Nervously clinging to this cliff-face, *Le Lac des Cygnes* was much admired, as were *Checkmate*, *The Rake's Progress* and *Ballet Imperial*. But *Façade*, for some curious reason, offended Lisbon sensibilities; its knockabout humour was, according to the intelligentsia, beneath the dignity of a self-respecting opera house.

Back at shameless Covent Garden, a flippant confection by Cranko – *Bonne-Bouche*, about a flapper keen on diamonds –

was about to shimmy into production. It went ahead without Margot, who was being saved for the major event of the calendar: Ashton's new three-act ballet, *Sylvia*. Before this opened on 3 September, Margot, after a gala performance in Paris, managed to fritter for another month's holiday – this time at Rapallo, on the Italian Riviera, where the old gang from the *Elikki* were joined by a rather crotchety Donald Albery who, in his capacity as Margot's business adviser, was suspicious of her 'wild American friends'.[5] He was relieved to find the party on dry land, if only just: following the example of Greta Garbo and Leopold Stokowski, Tom Fisher had rented the Villa Cimbrone, whose wooded, terraced gardens hung 1,000 feet above the rugged Amalfi coastline. In no time at all, however, the friends were chugging out to sea in a small boat, in search of Gallo Lugo, the *Ile des Sirènes* which Diaghilev had talked Massine into buying – and which, one day, would belong to Nureyev. 'The island seemed absolutely deserted,' writes Ruth Page. 'We walked all over the enormous rocks and finally got up the nerve to enter the big house. We tiptoed all over it and finally found Massine fast asleep in his bed with his arms crossed over his chest, looking ascetic and severe but beautiful in this calm state of sleep.'[6] Ashton, for whom Massine, whether somnolent or waking, held little charm, simply wedged a visiting card between the Russian's toes, and the giggling band of intruders made their getaway, deaf to the cries of Mme Massine, who rushed on to the pier, frantically waving at them to return. Luckily, by the time the inevitable storm struck, they were safely ashore at Positano. Wherever Margot went, it seemed, she would 'Put the wild waters in this roar'.[7] Little wonder that, as he watched yet another ship founder, Ashton flirted with the idea of choreographing *The Tempest* for his inspiratrice.

Meanwhile, he was content to make her his Sylvia. Ever since Delibes had appeared to him in a dream, kissing him and saying, '*Vous avez sauvé mon ballet*,'[8] Ashton had felt a sense of mystical responsibility towards the honeyed score which, much as it attracted him, held his imagination in a kind of nineteenth-century vice. 'I try to be inventive,' he told Walter Terry, 'but I think I have a very adjusted sense of what the music is trying to say to me.'[9] Most wearisome to him were the large ensemble set-pieces intrinsic to a three-act ballet. According to Alexander Grant, 'The first thing Freddie did when he came into the studio was to go up to the piano and see how many pages he had to fill.'[10] But with the sequences involving Margot, he was anything but bored. Not since *The Wanderer* had he made such a showcase for her brilliance, which was now absolutely at its zenith. 'Her technique in the mid-fifties was phenomenal,' says Annette Page; 'her Black Swan left us breathless . . . She was all over the stage like quicksilver. Her feet may have been squidgy when she was a young woman, but they were not squidgy in the fifties. I always remember that supporting leg on *pointe* – the wonderful pulled-up knees.'

This 'pull-up', which operated like a rod, all the way from the knees, through the solar plexus, to the base of the skull, was, according to Violette Verdy, 'one of the most beautiful things Margot had, which we didn't have so much in France. That "pull" was the centre of her discipline, her reserve; and whatever came out of it – be it a glance, or a turn of the cheek, or an inclination of the head – could be read as something of great importance and value. Her moves were not as bold as I was used to from some of the French- or Russian-trained dancers. Nor were her extensions so high. But her connecting steps were light and quick, an expression of spirit, some burst of joy: little movements of the heart in the feet and legs. An *enchaînement* was never a series of steps, it was a *phrase*.' Verdy joined company classes in 1953 while visiting London with Petit's Ballets de Paris. 'Margot told me to stand behind her at the *barre* and I *loved* the outfit she had, with those pink silk tights and the pink sweater tucked in round the thighs – so clean and balletic – a uniform in a way, and yet so soft.'

The ballet studios at Barons Court, headquarters of the Upper School as well as the company, had a dusty, Degas-esque aesthetic of their own, and the students sought to emulate

Fonteyn's classroom look, scouring the underwear department at Ponting's for long-sleeved lisle vests which they would attempt to dye the subtle flesh-colour that was her trademark. What impressed the fifteen-year-old Antoinette Sibley about Margot 'was that she was in class every day looking stunning – from the moment she walked in, not a hair out of place. A gorgeous line in practice-clothes. Later on, I think someone in Brazil knitted them for her. She always promised my generation that she'd leave them to us, those lovely vests and silk tights. She always said, "When I stop, I'll give them to you," but the thing was she never *did* stop, did she? I mean, we'd all stopped before her, really.'

Margot's tireless capacity for practice was particularly evident during this era of collaboration with Michael Somes. Just as Margot had studied in Paris with Preobrajenska and Egorova, so Somes had recently crossed the Channel to work with Alexander Volinine – a one-time partner of Pavlova, and a teacher of renown – to return not only vastly more polished in schooling and style, but also altruistically determined to impart all that he had gleaned. Marriage to a beautiful girl in the company, Deirdre Dixon, had relaxed and steadied him, bringing him, from Margot's point of view, closer in real life to the noble, commanding figure he projected so effectively on the stage. The seriousness and industry of his approach played into Margot's natural humility, and the two rehearsed incessantly (with a doggedness which the more frivolous Helpmann would have scorned) under the fanatical eye of their favourite coach, Harijs Plučis. Plučis, a ragged and penniless displaced person from Latvia, had been a pupil of the great Asaf Messerer, and, according to Somes, 'took Margot and me over. For years we worked with him in the same way we had with Vera – every day. He was the one who taught me about strength in partnering; he was a great big man, and very, very keen on etiquette – if anyone walked across the stage with their hat on, he nearly had a stroke.' This almost obsessive emphasis upon good manners was intrinsic to the Fonteyn/Somes pairing, which, of all Margot's professional couplings, most exemplifies Lincoln Kirstein's edict that 'Dancers who, from habit or preference, have frequently danced together come to have a sense of each other's physical presence which, translated into terms of dancing, is revealed to an audience as an exquisite awareness or superhuman courtesy.'[11] Certainly, Margot's enhanced virtuosity owed a great debt to the steadfast reliability of Somes's support. 'I could do it blindfold,' he said. 'I knew exactly where her hand would be. She had that kind of musicality – the same as I had – where the end of the music is coming up, and it's accelerating, and you'd think she's never going to make it in time, never going to finish on the beat, but she did. In *Sylvia* she used to run and jump into a fish-dive with me and people would be thinking, My God, he's never going to catch her. We got it better and better and better until she had the confidence to fly over. I had to be exactly the right distance away from her – otherwise she'd have no teeth. And that's a great responsibility. I don't think I ever dropped her in my life – she never got hurt with me. I wanted her to look good and what I tried to be was invisible, as though she were doing things by herself which were impossible. And the more I could make that happen, the more I felt I had succeeded.'[12]

'Margot was partnered in her best years by Michael,' says Ronald Hynd. 'He presented her wonderfully. And *Sylvia* is a ballet people forget. Margot was glorious in it. An amazon, but touching – a bit girl-guidish. She was dancing at her peak.' The critics concurred. Clive Barnes wrote: 'The part has everything for Fonteyn. It exploits her imperiousness, her tenderness, her pathos, her womanliness, her bravura. It gives us Fonteyn triumphant, Fonteyn bewildered, Fonteyn exotic, Fonteyn pathetic, Fonteyn *in excelsis*. The range of her dancing is unequalled, the heart-splitting significance she can give to a simple movement unsurpassed. The whole ballet is like a garland presented to the ballerina by her choreographer.' And yet that, in a sense, was its very limitation, for *Sylvia* was not to survive unabridged, nor, until half a century later, to enter the Royal Ballet's annals on its own merit. Although James Monahan knew of 'nothing in the nineteenth-century classics or in the Ashton–Fonteyn repertory which excels the first act', he had to admit that 'the beauty dwindles when Fonteyn is not Sylvia'.

And all too soon that dwindling was to come about. In November 1952 – a mere eight weeks after opening night – Margot was suddenly neither Sylvia, nor Odette, nor Aurora, nor Giselle, nor Chloë, but simply a young woman fighting for her life. 'By this time,' writes Mrs Hookham, 'Margot had given up her Long Acre flat to Idell and had moved to a flat in a block just off Sloane Street called the Round House . . . I went to Ireland for a short visit . . . and . . . after I came back the ballet set off on another English tour. Four days later, I got a telephone message that Margot was ill and in hospital . . . Of course, I was very shocked and went down to Southampton immediately.' The illness that had attacked her was diphtheria – a word second only to polio for striking terror in the hearts of mothers of Mrs Hookham's generation. Pamela May suspects that the damage was, in fact, done a few days earlier, in Cardiff. 'We were due to rehearse on stage during the morning and they wanted to let down the black velvet curtain at the back. It wasn't controlled, and in coming down it suddenly fell and the cloud of dust that went up was terrible. Margot was on that stage practising and it choked her, practically, and I think that's probably where she got it.'[13]

The diphtheria bacillus causes a greyish membrane to grow over the tonsils, inhibiting the power to breathe. But even more insidious to a dancer than the threat of a tracheotomy is the danger of toxins, intensely poisonous to the heart muscle and nerve cells, entering the bloodstream and causing localized paralysis resembling the dreaded effects of poliomyelitis. To avoid the fatal spread of infection, it is vital that the patient lie flat, and Margot, in her ignorance, was incensed at what she took to be the carelessness of the hospital staff in failing to provide her with a pillow. The ambulance men who, a few days later, ferried her back to London, were no better, but by now she had lost the power of protestation. She could not make herself understood, what with the great numb plum in her mouth which had once been her tongue. Worse, she could not walk. Her feet could feel no contact with the ground, and dragged like lead weights. Mrs Hookham moved into Margot's spare room to look after her, and the doctor, who came every day, assured them that, although the nerves in Margot's feet and tongue were slowly dying off, they would, thanks to the miracle of penicillin, grow back within six weeks. But how was the waiting to be borne?

'She came to us for Christmas,' says Pamela May, 'with a selected few friends, because she couldn't really talk. It was very embarrassing for her – she hated it, and yet she felt all right. And her mother said one day: "I've got to go out and get my hair done . . . would you come and look after Margot? Make her some tea and toast, but don't let her get out of bed." '[14] No sooner had the front door slammed than Margot flung back the covers, slid from the mattress and tried to walk across the room. 'Can you imagine?' says May. 'She took three steps and was curled up on the floor. Her legs just gave out. Of course, instead of crying, she was screaming with laughter. And then, of course, I had to try to get her up, and back those three steps . . . Anyway we did it in the end, and her mother never knew.' The public was never allowed to know, either, how grave the situation had been, or the resultant, frightening extent of Margot's weakness. Baldly, a press-release stated that Miss Fonteyn would not be rejoining the company in January as advertised – her return had been 'postponed indefinitely'.[15]

It is hard enough at the best of times for a dancer to get back into practice, but when the doctors finally permitted Margot to resume daily class, she was so out of touch with her body that she had to look in the mirror to check the where-abouts of her feet. Her balance, which she was used to taking for granted, was a poor, rocky thing, while her jump, never entirely natural, had become a joke: she could hardly get off the floor. If ever her fabled ruling quality of tenacity was called for, it was now – through those five long months which it would take to regain her strength. George Goncharov, to her great sadness, had recently died, so Ailne Phillips, the new principal of teaching, now took her in hand. But Margot needed the attention of someone both harsher and more familiar, and she was prepared to travel to Copenhagen to work with her old friend and teacher – Vera Volkova – who had taken up a post with the Royal Danish Ballet.

The date finally agreed for Margot's reappearance, in *Apparitions*, at Covent Garden was 18 March 1953, but an interview which she gave that morning to the *News Chronicle* reveals her persisting nervous superstition about her health: 'I won't be looking in my dressing-room today, and I mustn't put in any of my pictures, or give the room the impression that I am really back to stay. If I do, I feel sure that I shall be carried off to rest again.'[16]

The role that put her to the test, the Woman in the Ball Dress, had been tailor-made for her by Ashton in 1936, when her technique had not been strong and he had wanted to smuggle her as discreetly as possible into Markova's shoes. Now, seventeen years on, Markova herself was in the audience that welcomed back the girl who had supplanted her. Markova, aged forty-two by this stage, had received a welcome of her own only two nights earlier – as guest artist with the company in *Giselle*. But between the two ballerinas there was no longer any question of rivalry or even comparison: nothing in the history of English ballet could equal the 'floodtide of emotion' that met the lone figure of Margot Fonteyn when she took her call at the end of *Apparitions*. Or rather: her fifteen calls. No one's standards were more rigorous than Margot's, and she knew that she had not danced particularly well. So, while the audience cheered itself hoarse, it was humbling for her to have to stand there for an interminable eleven and a half minutes in the growing realization that this was not an over-estimation by an under-informed public but something much more personal and heartfelt: a spontaneous outpouring of relief at the safe return of the ballerina who they had feared might be lost to them. The ovation came not just from the paying public, but also from fellow dancers, who crowded into the wings or slipped through the pass-door to the auditorium, while the front-of-house staff – programme sellers, barmen, commissionaires, cloakroom attendants – all gathered at the exits to join in the general, swelling, rhythmic chant of 'Mar-got! Mar-got!' Even David Webster, not known for his tender-heartedness, was seen to be in tears. Someone was fool enough to ask him what was wrong. 'If you don't understand,' Webster retorted, 'you certainly don't deserve to be told.'[17] Margot herself seemed as mystified as anyone. Finally, breaking both with convention and with her own conviction that dancers should be seen and not heard, she stepped to the front of the stage. 'I don't feel I deserve any of this,' she said simply, 'but thank you, all of you, very much.'[18]

Yet Margot's greatest sense of indebtedness would always be directed towards her mother; and, perhaps in order to consolidate the virtual marriage which existed between them, she agreed, as Mrs Hookham explains, 'that it would be very nice if we could get a little house for weekends not too far from London'. Amerden Bank, in Marsh Lane, Taplow, had originally been the stable-quarters of a fifteenth-century house, but, by the time that Mrs Hookham fell upon it, it had been joined to a huge barn which would, in due course, become a repository for Margot's memorabilia. The house, priced at £2,000, was flanked by a quarter-acre of neglected garden beside the Thames.

The suspicion that Margot's iconic status had begun to seed itself far beyond the narrow field of dancing was borne out two months later, when, to her astonishment, she was honoured with a Doctorate of Literature from the University of Leeds. 'But I'm illiterate!' she cried[19] – a cry which struck some, who knew the books that she had read and the French which she now spoke and the elegant expressiveness of her letters, as little more than affectation. Yet it was, nevertheless, a cry from the heart – the heart of that fourteen-year-old schoolgirl whose sense of academic inferiority had been set in stone twenty years earlier in Shanghai by the headmistress of the Cathedral School.

If Miss Fleet could see her now. On 2 June 1953, Coronation

night, Margot, cast as Queen of the Air in Ashton's *pièce d'occasion*, *Homage to the Queen*, seemed, with her practised royal smile (the trick was to press one's tongue against one's upper teeth, the better to sustain the rictus), almost interchangeable in the public mind with the young, newly-crowned Elizabeth II of England. That night the Queen's speech was broadcast to the audience, and really there was no place more patriotic to be than the Royal Opera House, where, earlier in the programme, a prodigal Robert Helpmann had returned, all differences forgiven – if not forgotten – to partner Fonteyn in Act II of *Swan Lake*, as he had done throughout the war.

The fledgling monarch, though seven years Margot's junior, had, crown jewels apart, one thing which the reigning queen of ballet sorely lacked: to wit, a husband, a consort – someone other than her mother to come home to. The subject of Margot's unwedded status never ceased to obsess the press, who photographed her as she proudly held the new-born babes of other dancers – elected godmother, as she was, to Gerd Larsen's daughter as well as to Moira Shearer's. Margot could be quite spiky with journalists, but she had learned to parry the inevitable marriage-question with cheery answers which fitted the bill. 'I suppose I have been too busy,' she told interviewer Iris Ashley, 'and probably, too, I have never met anybody whom I wanted sufficiently to marry. Ours is a wonderful way to see the world. We have everything arranged for us, we meet people every-where – and we are paid to do it. If I were married, I couldn't enjoy travelling like that unless my husband came too. Even then I'd be too busy to see him.'[20] But the truth is that the topic of wedding bells had acquired a contentious ring in the Hookham household. Not only had Margot's contemporaries long since taken their vows, but her brother had recently broken his – divorcing Idell after she had suffered numerous miscar-riages and lost a child at birth. 'After that,' writes Mrs Hookham, '[Idell] was not very strong for a long time and eventually the marriage broke up. In 1954 Felix married again. Needless to say he had not told me till about 3 or 4 days before. Anyway, I was pleased for him and liked the girl at once . . . I think that [Joan Alma Turner] had been married before. She had been a model and was very good-looking. During the war she had been doing secret work for the Government in Whitehall, I believe, but I don't know what. They were married in the Registry Office in Kensington and we had a nice little family party afterwards. A year later they had a daughter [Lavinia]. Over the years the names have changed and they have adopted Fonteyn, I being left as Hookham because I was too lazy to do anything about it, and Joan has become Feebee (Phoebe) from some private joke between them.' But it was typical of the moral and financial position which Margot, as virtual head of the family, now held that the jilted Idell should have been ensconced in the Long Acre flat, where she continued to live for the remaining forty years of her life, retaining the pre-war geyser over the bath, Margot's Edwardian armoire, and an unshakable affection for her ex-sister-in-law.

Margot, meanwhile, perhaps in a bid to settle her decorator's bill, allowed her new penthouse flat in Lowndes Street to be featured in a woman's magazine. *Everywoman* was granted access to the red walls and white paintwork in the ballerina's dining-room; the yellow figured wallpaper and carpet in her bathroom, the concealed cocktail cabinet and statue of the Three Graces in her living-room. Who could blame avid readers if they went on to conjecture what manner of man might finally lay siege to the 'mauvey-grey and pink-flocked'[21] recesses of Margot's bedroom? But even on matters aesthetic, she was not to be drawn: 'I don't have a favourite anything,' she told *Everywoman*'s Barbara Wace. 'Not a favourite role or a favourite composer or even a favourite food. Once you have a favourite you stay still and that is against my whole philosophy of life. I think everybody should change as they get older. What is my favourite today may not be so tomorrow – and certainly not next year.'[22] Famous last words. The next year would see her staring commitment in the face, locked for a lifetime into the unequivocal consequences of her choice.

It was not without significance that her closing days as a free agent should have been spent in the company of the man who, although he had smiled indulgently on her sexual adventures, had paradoxically guarded her heart as jealously as any father. If Frederick Ashton ever discussed with Margot the advantages which matrimony might bring her, this would always have been in terms of money and position – never of love. The virginity which she could portray 'as no one else' belonged, on a symbolic level, to him, since the depth of their artistic exchange had kept her frozen, Galatea-like, within the form that he had moulded. In early July, the two travelled together to Granada where, amid fountains and cypresses, Margot performed under an indigo sky in the beautiful Generalife Gardens of the Alhambra. Her dancing partner on this trip was Michael Somes, but her cherished companion and exclusive soul-mate was, for the last unfettered time, her beloved Fred. The boy from Lima and the girl with Latin blood sat until dawn in a house that had once belonged to Manuel de Falla, watching the gypsies who came from caves in the surrounding hills to dance their wild impromptu flamenco. Twelve years thence, in an interview with novelist and playwright Marguerite Duras, Margot would protest: 'I am not nostalgic for the past, you know, not even for my own past. Never, not for one second, have I wished to relive the days when I was younger. I've forgotten my past. It doesn't interest me. Things that don't interest you, you forget.'[23] Yet the depth and detail with which, in her autobiography, she dwells upon 'those hours of song and guitar, of dancing and wine, and of wandering the rough road to our hotel overlooking the misty plain in the early morning', and the sentiment with which she draws from this memory a metaphysical meditation upon the nature of time itself, give the lie to so pragmatic a claim, and betray just how much she would come to rue the passing of that era, and mourn her lost, unencumbered, single, pagan self.

The reappearance of Tito Arias in Margot's life took place on the sixth night of the third American tour. The season had opened rather uncomfortably, with a revised and not particularly popular production of *Swan Lake*, a ballet which, in any version, always made Margot 'unspeakably edgy until the third act [was] over'.[1] So it must have been of some relief that, on the night in question, 18 September 1953, the ballet in which she happened to be starring was *The Sleeping Beauty* – the familiar, adored production by Oliver Messel which New York had long since taken to its heart. But nothing could allay the anxiety induced by the words on the card which, just before curtain-up, was delivered to Margot's dressing-room: *Roberto E. Arias, Delegate of Panama to the United Nations*. The gentleman had informed the stage-door keeper that he would be back at the end of the show.

In fact, the gentleman did something much more outlandish and unnerving: he bowled up at Margot's dressing-room door during the second interval. Margot was pinning on her head-dress for the Vision Scene when Dr (as he now was) Arias presented, not just himself, but a complete stranger – a Chinese woman whom he introduced as Miss Gussie Chang. 'I decided not to wait till the end to see you,' was his explanation.[2]

Margot, famous for having shrieked 'Get out!' at the formidable Sol Hurok, invited the couple into her sanctum without a murmur. The visitors sat down, and Miss Chang chattered away for all she was worth. Tito, however, was entirely unforthcoming. Not one word of obligatory wonder at Margot's fabled Rose Adagio. Perhaps he had not been concentrating. Perhaps he did not intend to stick the evening out, for when Act II Beginners was called, he suddenly announced: 'I would like you to join us for supper at the 21 Club.'[3] Not even: 'If you are free.' Inevitably, she was not. But her unavailability proved no deterrent. 'Then I will telephone you in the morning,' he said, and left.

If there is one thing more rash than bursting into a ballerina's dressing-room during the interval, it is telephoning her next morning before nine. 'Darling,' said Tito, 'I have to leave for Panama at noon, so I want to have breakfast with you.'

'I'm not up,' said Margot. 'I can't see you . . .' But then she added the weakening words, 'so soon . . .'[4]

Half an hour later, Tito was sipping coffee in her hotel bedroom, sitting, as of old, cross-legged on the floor. It was a posture which no longer became him. He had grown stout. Even less becomingly, he had grown married. Margot's own words, spoken in jest to Pamela May ('I expect he is very fat by now, and has a wife and three children'), proved true in every particular: he was the unprepossessing, betrothed father of twin girls and a boy. Nevertheless, his ebullience amused her – it was cheering to see him. She answered his questions with a candour not available to *Everywoman*. No, she was not married. She had tried, many times, to fall in love, but it had never quite worked out. Not that she lacked offers: indeed, there was someone back in England whom she had promised she might marry next year (Peter Moore, whom she had met through Graham Greene). Then, in the voice that, even in those days when he could still speak properly, was soft and unemphatic enough to make you wonder whether you had heard aright, Tito murmured, 'Why don't you marry *me*?'[5] Margot laughed her embarrassed, cover-up laugh. What else could she do at a suggestion so preposterous? Had he not just explained that he was married with three children?

'My wife will divorce me,' said Tito blithely, and, next day, rang from Panama with the news that she had agreed to do just that.[6] 'I will be in New York tomorrow,' he promised. 'But don't!' implored Margot frantically. 'You can't do that. Don't be crazy.' Yet, even as she protested, long distance, that she hardly knew him, that she didn't love him, the immediate vicinity of her hotel room had already been invaded by an extravagance of flowers – a hundred red roses which she was made to count, lest there be one too few, by Tito's black chauffeur, Roosevelt Zanders, who declared himself under instructions to convey her, by limousine, to any destination that took her fancy. Thus began the great Latin courtship under pressure of which (the furs, the diamonds, the incessant dinners at El Morocco) Margot had to confess herself a divided spirit. Amused as she was by the karmic irony which decreed 'that the casual playboy was now the ardent wooer, whereas the lovesick girl felt nothing',[7] Margot was still daughter enough of her middle-class upbringing to declare, categorically: 'I don't like divorce, and I believe it is sinful to take another woman's husband.'[8] And although we may be inclined to take her word for it, we need to remind ourselves that this was not the first time she had found herself accepting (along with a 'beautifully simple'[9] diamond bracelet and a discreet sable) the compromising role of homebreaker. The first Mrs Arias, glamorous, feisty and, later on, a force of her own in Panamanian politics, had none of the propensity for victimhood of the tragic Flo Lambert. Yet this marriage was a Roman Catholic one, and Margot feared, if not for her soul, then at least for her reputation. Tito, however, remained nonchalant: 'You are going to marry me,' he insisted, 'and be very happy.'[10]

Margot could find no such blind faith in her heart – that heart which she describes as 'unused . . . crated up and stored away, forgotten inside the personage of a ballet star'. But if she could not recognize the power of her feeling for Arias, her friends most certainly could – and at first glance. 'She loved him,' said Leslie Edwards. 'Nothing to be done. I could say a lot. But you see, my adoration for Margot is such that I am going to tell you the things about Tito that I loved too. When he turned up out of the blue on that tour, he was kind and generous to all of us, and tremendously amusing. I said: "You know, you're so splendid now – what about this title? I mean: Ambassador-at-Large!" And he had his gig-lamps on, and he took them off and did a somersault on the pavement. And I said: "Oh, you haven't changed." I liked him.'

Edwards (along with Pamela May, whose second husband, Charles Gordon, remembered Tito from Paris with affection), was an honourable exception. Annette Page speaks with the weight of company opinion behind her when she says: 'It was unfortunate, really, that he was just not the kind of person that anybody took to.' Ashton went further, privately scorning 'the gold bracelets, pomaded hair and glib Latin charm'. John Craxton, although he did concede that Margot had 'a curious genetic link with South America', took 'an absolute chemical dislike' to Tito. 'He was desperate to get her. Wooed her hard as hard.'

In the course of his campaign, Tito threw a party which, though ostensibly for the visiting President Ramón of Panama, was actually for Margot and the ballet company. But, to the reticent English dancers, the invitations alone (thirty-word telegrams to every guest) struck not so much an impressive note as an ostentatious one. Ashton, in particular, was 'horrified'[11] – Ashton whose blessing Margot craved more desperately than anyone's. Despite his misgivings, however, he did go to the party and, perhaps in a spirit of competition, launched (after the drunken President had been steered away) into what Margot describes as 'the most sensational series of impersonations I have ever seen at one sitting. He showed us to the very life Pavlova, Isadora Duncan, Lopokova, Carmen Amaya, Pastor Imperia and I don't know who else . . . This firework display was climaxed by a flying leap into the arms of the head waiter . . .'[12]

If the inference was 'Beat *that*' – then Tito had the sense to refrain from resorting to one of his legendary somersaults. Even the impromptu rumbas of the Cambridge days seemed no longer in his blood: he was too diffident to dance. Next day, on the presidential plane, he disappeared back to Panama. For all the accusations of over-intensity, Tito's true romantic power lay in his elusiveness. His hold over Margot relied on her perverse delight at never being able to tell when next he might appear, or, indeed, vanish. Nor did he intend that the extravagance which was to mark their union should run one way: when he turned up in Boston, it was with a tray of gold cufflinks, borrowed from Cartier, so that Margot could choose the pair he wanted for his birthday, which fell on 26 October (rendering him, since he had been born in 1918, Margot's senior half the time, by half a year).

Daphnis and Chloë and *Sylvia* were both enjoying huge success in America (greater than in England) and Margot danced them gratefully, relieved to have a night off from the alternating rigours of *Swan Lake* and *Sleeping Beauty*, which she had to face every time the company train shunted into a new station. Arriving in Vancouver she was met by a letter from Tito, written on one of his interminable flights away from her, and running to twenty-three pages which Margot lays before us virtually uncensored.

It certainly is an astonishing document. Are we to credit that Margot, who had once been in receipt of love letters from the persuasive and discerning pen of Constant Lambert (and even, briefly, of Graham Greene), should esteem Tito's high-handed and self-centred phrases to be above all others conjured in her name? Yet Arias is, to be fair, not writing in his native tongue: when he rises to Spanish, in the one and only instance of the opening address, we hear, fleetingly but distinctly, what must have affected Margot so strongly – the sombre, heated voice of irrefutable passion.

Mujer de mi vida (Woman of my life). Then the letter, abbreviated, continues:

> Do not despair, my dear child. Do not be too terribly sad (for in the quality of your sadness is that same exquisite sensitiveness that makes you so unmeasurably lovable) . . . My heart and my mind had already travelled the whole route from Alpha to Omega . . . I must be patient – the first fourteen years are the worst! . . . When I was the young boy who kissed you with trembling lips and tightly shut eyes, I was crushed by what I believed then to be insurmountable odds, lack of confidence in

myself, sense of insecurity, geography, careers, and financial considerations . . . Careers – you have one – and destiny has given me a surprising multiplicity and flexibility in semi-careers. They, or a combination of whatever they are, can happily inter-mesh with the life of my love and her adorable one-track tastes, examples: the ballet, Dior, the Mediterranean, Cartier's and the best. The apparent problem was my wife and children. I had felt when in Panama that as long as neither she nor I were emotion-ally interested in other individuals we should try to keep the house running as best we could for the children, and perhaps to a certain degree for the public. She often said she didn't agree . . . You say only 'darling Tito, I am not ready, be patient' and it is clearly indispensable for your good and mine that I *be* patient. And so I will . . . There is no valid reason why to expect of you – much less demand – that you be suddenly ready . . . I *knew* that you loved me, but had been careful in the extreme not to tell you that I loved you. It is quite natural that you should have given up all hope long ago. It is just as natural that my vanity should have repeated to me from time to time deep in her heart is love for me and some day I will be with her again . . . This letter seems to be more for me than for you – yes, it is a need to confess that I have not recently allowed my better nature to guide my love. Unfortunately I do not always act as I write, but today my better nature needs to dialogue with you, without seeking promises by innuendo and without recoursing to shallow heroics. But all of Tito, the gentle and the violent, the good and the bad, the relaxedly serene and the emotionally tense, loves you most dearly.[13]

All of Tito seems, at this point, to have recognized but a fraction of Margot as perceived by Clive Barnes in his review of *Sylvia*. The letter may acknowledge Fonteyn bewildered, Fonteyn pathetic, eagerly enough. But where is 'Fonteyn triumphant, Fonteyn exotic, Fonteyn *in excelsis*'? It is as though the qualities which Barnes exalts – of imperiousness, woman-liness, bravura – qualities developed over thirty-four years of struggle and aspiration, had all been swept aside to reveal a timid, unsure girl, with spoiled 'one-track' whims. Yet it may be to this very infantilization that Margot, thrust as she had been into responsibility and obligation from such an early age, instinctively responded. If so, she was sorely mistaken, for Tito, like Constant Lambert before him, would prove to be the very antithesis of a father figure. If all love affairs have an under-lying parental dimension, then it was unquestionably the mothering nature of women that Arias was programmed to unloose. 'You could see the effect he had on them,' says his nephew Gabriel Galindo. 'This was a man who had an uncanny talent for eliciting the absolute devotion of some women. Not just Margot – I think there were a few others along the way. He would look shy and unassuming and he brought out the maternal or something. From a man's point of view, it was certainly enviable.'

From Black Queen's point of view, it was all too obvious: 'Tito is the child Margot never had,' she would say with a sigh.[14] Margot, meanwhile, was still havering over the adoption of a new name. A three-day train journey to the West Coast repre-sented blessed respite from decision-making. 'I thought "Thank God. He won't even be able to telephone. I shall just sleep all the way and try to think later." '[15] No such luck. The train broke down in the middle of nowhere and, along the tracks, from some remote junction, came a guard, brandishing a telegram, the very sight of which made Margot feel 'hunted and desperate'. 'See you in Seattle!' it read.

Sure enough, there Tito was to meet her, armed this time with ear-clips and a brooch. Margot's acceptance of these trib-utes, passive and reluctant though she claims it to have been, had begun to represent a tacit acceptance of the man himself. In Los Angeles, Tito enlisted his film-star friends – Red Skelton, Merle Oberon, Julius Stein and Danny Kaye – to help promote his cause. At last he came up with the perfect match-maker, in the politically questionable guise of John Wayne, who lent the couple his boat so that Tito could invite a group of Margot's friends to sail, on their day off, to Catalina Island. Margot, who always felt brave and carefree when confronted by the ocean, decided, as she stood on the deck with the wind in her hair, to take the marital plunge. 'I understood that I did love Tito, but that my love was not at all what I had expected . . . In Tito's company, I felt neither alone nor with another person, just fundamentally complete.'[16] And having arrived at that state of fulfilment, she began, in calculated stages, to break it to her mother.

'In one of Margot's rare letters she told me of the fantastic reception the ballet got, and the vying for the attention of the audience by some very eccentric men, the most successful being a bald elderly man wearing a tiara! She also mentioned that an old Cambridge acquaintance had turned up. [But] it was not till nearly the end of that tour that she told me [that] the Cambridge friend . . . was the one she had loved ever since those days 14 years ago . . . She was now 34 and had decided to marry the man she had liked best, but now [Tito] had come back into her life and loved her too and had followed her all through the tour and was determined she should marry him and of course it was her heart's desire to do so. Would I please get in touch with the man she had promised to marry and explain to him this unexpected turn of events? . . .' Mrs Hookham agreed to meet 'Mr M' (Peter Moore, presumably) for dinner at Wheeler's restaurant. 'He was very charming and had known Margot for some time and had flown to see her in many places whenever he could get away from his work which was filming and he loved her very much. I started talking about Margot and her eternal touring and the lack of time she had for writing letters, how rarely I heard from her on tour and her dedication to her work.' Finally Mrs Hookham got up her courage, and came to the nub, namely Tito. ' "Mr M" was shocked. His face froze for a moment, then flushed to a dark red. He was furious, and naturally enough said some nasty things about her . . . He was the second man I had had to try to console when she dropped him, though there had been no talk of marriage then.

I sat with [the first, Charles Hassé] in my car in St Martin's Lane for 1½ hours trying to soothe his very hurt feelings, she being away on tour again . . . When she got back I asked why she didn't treat her men more gently and explain to them herself. She said, "What is the use, they think I am softening and will go on trying to get me to change my mind which I know I shall never do, so it is better to make a clean break and that is all." I must say she is very strong for so kind a person and once she has decided, that is definitely the end.'

Though for Tito this was a new beginning, it was not necessarily one which Black Queen was inclined to endorse. She felt bound to warn Margot, from bitter experience – the abandonment experienced by her own mother – that Latin men were just not capable of fidelity. But, of Margot's two mothers, real and honorary, probably de Valois was the more dismayed by the news, relayed to her that Christmas in Chicago, of her protégée's intention to marry a man from Panama. Had she, de Valois, created the first great English ballerina only to have her abscond to South America? Running into Arias in the theatre foyer, de Valois put a brave face on it. 'I'm so happy to hear the news,' she said. 'Margot needs an anchor.' 'Damn it, Madam,' said Tito, 'I'm not an anchor.'[17]

He was, however, part-owner of a yacht, the *Edmar*, which he and his younger brother Tony kept in the Bahamas, and when the long tour was over he took Margot and her friends on a cruise along the coast of Nassau. 'We were an odd lot,' said Leslie Edwards,[18] who came aboard, as did the company pianist, Jean Gilbert, and Danny Kaye's wife, Sylvia. But the *Edmar*'s guest of honour was undoubtedly Frederick Ashton, who, despite the scathing remarks he still made about Arias behind Margot's back, accepted the freebie with alacrity. 'Fred adored every moment,' said Edwards. 'He loved being hot and swimming all day. We were lavishly treated by Tito; Mrs Kaye was charming and witty, with a great knowledge of the theatre; and there was a piano on board on which Jean played all Fred's favourite tunes.' While the Wedding March was hardly one of them, Ashton had, in principle, no objection to ballerinas marrying for money. Insatiably romantic on his own account, he was, where his friends were concerned, 'very practical. I'm so tired of seeing wretched dancers having to peel their own potatoes when they retire.'[19]

Not that it was any part of Tito's plan to have his wife-to-be quit the stage. His attitude might appear emancipated for an era when, as Margot rather wistfully points out, '[not] many men would have allowed me to continue my career'.[20] But in fact he was being cheerfully exploitative: 'It's difficult to retire a good racehorse,' was how he put it.

Reluctantly, Ashton gave the couple his blessing – 'I suppose only because she wanted it.' Touchingly, Margot allowed herself to be convinced. In the first edition of her autobiography, which came out in 1975, she writes: 'Fred loved the Bahamas and I felt that he *did* approve of the man who had chosen me as his wife.'[21] But the strange thing is that she, who in the later, revised version of her book, altered hardly a word (not even the shaming paean to the shamed Imelda Marcos), completely erased this sentence from the text. Instead, the chapter closes nebulously: 'It was a real holiday, and a time when I began to get used to the idea of marriage.'[22] So perhaps, in the end, she did come to accept the inevitable schism in her private and professional worlds, and to disown, if not Ashton's duplicity, then her own tender gullibility in believing that the people whom she loved should necessarily love each other.

19

Although Margot's decision to marry, reached in 1954, was absolute, Tito's divorce was not: the couple's wedding plans had to be deferred until February of the following year. Notwithstanding her newly-melted heart and gathering womanhood, Margot's thirty-fifth year was marked by her espousal of the most brittle and androgynous role that had yet come her way: the Firebird. As recently as 1949, Balanchine, in his great expatriate collaboration with Stravinsky, had discarded the initial Michel Fokine choreography, with its accent on pictorial drama, in favour of a much more metaphorical version of his own making, which, with Maria Tallchief in the title role, had cut a highly contemporary dash in New York. But de Valois's fond memory harked back to the original Diaghilev production, and in particular to Karsavina, whose creation of *Oiseau de Feu* had, according to the writer and critic, Gennady Smakov, 'resonated in the erotic twilight that enveloped Paris in the 1910s'.[1]

Neither the fact that this was now the prim mid-50s, nor, indeed, that the place should have been Scotland (the ballet was to open at the Edinburgh Festival), deterred de Valois from resurrecting Fokine's exotic choreography for her company. The season happened to coincide with the twenty-fifth anniversary of Diaghilev's death, and she had on hand the services of his *régisseur*, Serge Grigoriev (married to the ballerina Lubov Tchernicheva, whose recollection of the steps was photographic), not to mention Karsavina herself – although the latter was less reliable. 'She a little forget,' Tchernicheva would whisper to poor Margot,[2] who was obliged to learn opposing versions and produce her own amalgam in the hope that neither old lady would be miffed. But it was not so much that Karsavina had forgotten, as that she was still intent on invention. To be taught by her was, Margot explained to James Monahan, to be made aware of 'hundreds of details – little moments. One has to grasp them. They will change, every day. She'll teach you one thing one day, and you'll try to repeat it exactly the next day, and she'll change it. So you have to grasp from her the particular qualities that she has, as they go by. It's up to oneself, really, to get it. She gives me very much the sense that the role is still living in her and what she's teaching me is not exactly what she did herself on stage at all – it's as though the role is still in her mind, living and changing the whole time.'³

However, one thing she told Margot did come straight down the line, unedited, from Fokine. Sometimes a choreographer will say something which, beyond any physical or technical instruction, will illuminate the whole enterprise and render the perversity of the steps suddenly natural. And the words from the past which did the trick for Margot were these: *Here is no human emotion*.⁴ She, who could not help bringing poignancy and intelligibility to the least movement, was now being challenged to divest herself of her humanity, in order to reveal some fierce and primitive and hitherto unglimpsed side of herself. Michael Somes, whose rustic Ivan Tsarevich was easily the most perfect achievement of his career, remembers with awe how Karsavina whipped them on. 'She said: "You are a wild bird, Margot, you must use your arms, you must *beat* your arms . . . you've never felt a human hand on your body before, you've never been caught, and it's terrible – I will show you." I held Madame Karsavina like this and I thought, goodness, I must be careful, because I had to battle with her, she was fighting me and I had to hold her rather back because she was nearly seventy, and was slightly lame.'

Margot would be a mere fifty-eight, and, as yet, without an evident limp, when she would be called upon in her turn to hand down the guidance that it had been her privilege to receive. But faced, in 1978, with a plea from the then director of the company, Norman Morrice, she would prove to be as difficult to pin down as the very Firebird. And it is necessary, at this

25. On holiday in Greece with John Craxton, 1951.

26. Chloë.

27. As the female Tiresias.

28. Godmother
to Moira
Shearer's
daughter, Ailsa.

29. *Sylvia*, 1952.

30. With Tito in the Bahamas.

31. *Firebird* rehearsal, with Karsavina.

32. Family group, 1954: BQ, Tito, Margot, Felix and Phoebe.

33. *Birthday Offering*, with Michael Somes.

34. The wedding, 6 February 1955,
Panamanian Embassy, Paris.

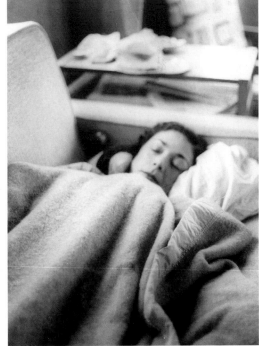

35. & 36. Aboard the *Edmar*.

37. *Ondine.*

38. Mother and daughter at the circus, 1956.

39. At the barre, 1962.

40. *Giselle*, with Rudolf Nureyev.

point, to stop and consider the sole yet persistent censure levelled at Fonteyn by her younger colleagues: her territorial attitude to what she considered to be her own roles, and her lack of generosity as a mentor. Monica Mason, who danced the Firebird in 1978, was desperate for some link with the past: 'I *knew* that Margot held the key for the Firebird because she had got it from Karsavina herself. And Margot, of course, as always, was so busy and couldn't be reached and wasn't available and then couldn't do it and then she'd be in the building and couldn't stay and all this. But I just couldn't accept the fact that she was not available for half an hour at some point in her life. And eventually one day I appealed to Norman. I said: "You know, I have a feeling that if I can't get some time with Margot, I don't really want to do it, because I can't do it without that." I was passionate about it. And so he had another talk to her. And one day, I suppose literally she gave us about forty-five minutes or an hour. It was wonderful. From the moment she started, I knew I'd been right – I had really, really needed her.'[5]

Despite her professed indifference to teaching, Margot proved a perfectly able and rather inspiring coach. She explained to Mason that in Russian folklore firebirds actually ate men, and that 'from the moment the Prince catches her, she hates him. She hates him for daring to touch her. Nobody dares to touch her. And another thing Margot said was that when you plead with him to let you go, you still retain this hatred for him, and there's no softening in your feelings. You hate him, and you even hate the fact that you have to ask him to release you. You have to plead, but you plead without losing any of your dignity or your feeling of self-preservation.'[6]

Margot must have uncovered exactly this ferocious sense of pride and hostility in the more flammable reaches of her temperate psyche: her own performance, wonderfully set off by Natalia Goncharova's glowing décor, had blazed with unprecedented fire. Although the conditions at Edinburgh's Empire Theatre were too cramped to give full rein to the breadth and splendour of the production, as soon as the ballet came home to Covent Garden the critics were frankly amazed that Margot, who had no jump to speak of, could make an impression of such vitality and vigour. So sharp was her attack, and so dramatic her interpretation (throughout the first *pas de deux* with the Prince, she actually bared her teeth) that one veteran critic, Cyril Beaumont, complained that she had exaggerated the aggression of the Firebird, whom he remembered as a much more tender, fairy-like being. 'Must she employ so exotic a makeup? ... Were the original arm movements so writhing?' But Karsavina sprang defensively into print: 'If Mr Beaumont doubts the accuracy of my memory,' she wrote in *The Times*, 'after twenty years of appearances in this part, he must perhaps concede me some knowledge of Russian folklore and enough integrity not to distort the ideas of Fokine.'

Most people, however, considered Fokine to be spectacularly well served by this new, alien creature who had once been their Margot, as glamorous under her plumed, coxcomb head-dress as some glittering film-star from the era of the silent screen: mouth meticulously over-painted to predatory proportions, eyes flashing blackly from beneath heavily false lashes. Equally dazzling was Ernest Ansermet's conducting of the complicated and ravishing score. Margot had been indoctrinated by Constant Lambert to be less than bowled over by the works of Stravinsky. But *The Firebird* changed all that. Ansermet was the first maestro to pay her the overdue compliment of consulting her as to which tempi she would prefer. Startled, she answered that whatever he had decided upon would be perfect. But his unexpected trust and respect encouraged her, in her autobiography, to dispense with her usual self-derogation regarding her musical responses ('merely rhythmic'), and to confide in us the depth of her affinity with the unfathomable genius of Stravinsky. 'I know nothing quite like *The Firebird* music. The overture is deep and mysterious, generating an atmosphere of magic so compelling that in my corner of the darkened stage, waiting for the curtain to rise, I was already lost, totally involved in the spirit of the proud arrogant creature.'[7]

Margot's personal triumph did not preclude plaudits for the rest of the company – particularly Michael Somes as the lumbering, none-too-bright yet always noble Ivan Tsarevich; Frederick Ashton, histrionically terrifying as the Immortal Kostchei; and, as the Beautiful Tsarevna, the twenty-one-year-old Svetlana Beriosova, whose grave and touching grace (had it hailed from England and not Lithuania) would have posed, perhaps, the most serious challenge yet to Margot's future supremacy.

'Margot – when she retire?' Clive Barnes remembers Violetta Elvin asking him in frustration as she herself approached the dreaded age of thirty. 'Violetta was *fantastic*,' says Barnes. 'One thing about her, though – she couldn't do first nights. She absolutely froze. But she could possibly have gotten over that, if she'd been given a chance.' Yet the chances had all gone – to Margot, who, as well as being paid a weekly £110 by comparison to Elvin's £40, had sailed so far ahead of the ballerinas even remotely of her own era that it was now dispiriting for them to attempt to stay afloat in her wake. It was the new recruits – a decade younger, as junior to her as she had been junior to Markova – who needed to be watched. Luckily for Margot, the most talented ones, rather than graduating, home-grown, from the Sadler's Wells school, tended to appear, fully-fledged, from far-flung dominions: Nadia Nerina from South Africa, Rowena Jackson from New Zealand, Elaine Fifield from Australia. The latter, as well as being endowed with a Vivien Leigh prettiness, possessed qualities of warm lyricism and cool classicism which came a little too close for comfort to Margot's own. Plus something else which, with her 'pats of butter', Margot had never been able to boast: a pair of gloriously arched insteps, reminiscent of Pavlova's, which had already seduced the eye of Frederick Ashton.

But to be favoured by him, to draw his attention even for an instant away from Margot, was often the quickest route, not to fame, but to a subtle form of persecution by de Valois. 'Ninette,' says Clive Barnes, 'was a savage, savage woman. She ruined careers. She ruined Beryl Grey's career, Moira's career, David Blair's career, because she would push people out of the way or into jobs they weren't fitted for. The number of careers that were lost − I suppose you might say from June Brae up until, and probably beyond, Antoinette [Sibley] − a whole generation of lost stars. All in the name of Margot. It was a love affair. An extraordinary love affair.'

If so, it was one conducted with more severity than sentiment. At the time of the engagement to Arias, de Valois was already on record as having said that Margot only had 'about three more years left in her'.[8] So, perhaps fearful that her beloved protégée might be snatched away by marriage to another continent, she devised a plan to pin the ballerina to her English heritage. In July of '54 she summoned Margot to her office and announced: 'Dame Adeline Genée is retiring from the Royal Academy of Dancing and it has been decided that you will be the new President.'[9]

Margot was appalled, and said as much. If there was anything more boring to her than the idea of teaching, it was the idea of administration. But, essentially, nothing had changed between the two women since de Valois had told her, back in 1936, that she would dance her first Giselle whether she liked it or not. Once again, everything was settled, and Madam would brook no argument: 'Margot,' she said, 'I have a lot of things to attend to this morning, so if you don't mind, I'd like to get on with them, now.'[10] Even as Margot left the office, there seemed no option but to start planning her formal acceptance speech, which was to be published in the *Gazette* in November of that year: 'I come with a fresh eye to the Royal Academy and cannot adequately express my admiration for all that has been and is being done. I am deeply aware of the responsibilities before me and will do my utmost to fulfil the trust which has been placed in me . . .'[11] Polite noises, one might think; but it was in Margot's nature, once a commitment had been extracted from her, to mean every word that she said. Her Presidency of the Academy, though not always informed by perfect wisdom, was to be utterly tireless, and truly devoted, and to last for the rest of her life. 'That she did impeccably,' says Clement Crisp. 'She would go round the world and all those madly demented dance teachers fell about with delight because she was simple, she was natural, she was absolutely charming, she was not a fool and they adored her. The perfect ambassador – she should have been the Queen.'

But reigning monarchs have been known to abdicate. And, despite an increasingly hectic schedule – in June alone, Margot appeared in Belgrade with the National Theatre Ballet, on BBC Television, in excerpts from *Swan Lake*, and travelled once again to Granada, where, dressed by Dior, she danced a short new concert-piece by Ashton to the music of Arthur Sullivan, called *Entrada de Madame Butterfly* – rumours of her imminent retirement gathered momentum. These had begun when the *Daily Telegraph* had picked up on a little joke she had cracked when pressured to make a speech: 'I'm not going to say anything now. I'm saving it for when I retire.'[12] When the article appeared, Margot, whose relations with the Opera House had always, to this point, been courteous and cordial, and the tone of whose business letters had often been rather beseeching, wrote with unprecedented temperament: 'I feel compelled to complain about the casual attitude of your Public Relations Department to the announcement in yesterday's *Telegraph* implying that I would retire next year.'[13] The *Telegraph* offered to publish a denial – but only if the Opera House undertook to send a formal letter of apology, should Miss Fonteyn, in fact, retire within the next year. Eventually, on 20 September, a compromise snippet appeared in *The Times*: 'The Royal Opera House stated on Saturday that it wished to deny reports that Miss Margot Fonteyn was to retire either within the next year or for some years to come.'[14]

One cannot help but sense, behind this scuffle, the litigious hand of Margot's lawyer-lover. Certainly, from the time she took up with Arias, she adopted a far less placatory tone with the press, brazenly lying to them if need be. In the *Evening News*, on 27 September, she categorically denied reports that she was to marry Roberto Arias. 'I'm tired of people asking me that question,' she protested. 'It's absolutely untrue.'[15] Nor was it true, according to the *Star*, 'that the ballerina had bought a £16,000 house in Thurloe Place, South Kensington. "Miss Fonteyn moved into a flat in Knightsbridge about a year ago," said Margot's secretary, "and she is remaining there." '[16] But journalists were quick to establish that it was a Miss Margaret Hookham who had closed the deal on the thirty-year lease of Amberwood House, a secluded Regency property in a cul-de-sac facing the Victoria and Albert Museum. The newsmongering about the buttercup-yellow doorway and black wrought-iron gates opening on to the thirty-yard gravel carriageway leading up to No.17a Thurloe Place was as nothing to the prurience which was trained upon its prospective co-occupant. 'These rumours,' confided the *Sunday Express*, 'of course concern Roberto "Tito" Arias, wealthy son of a President of Panama recently deposed by revolution. He it is, I hear, who sends her three dozen roses every time she dances. He it was whom she sat next to at her triumphal dinner party after the Covent Garden first night of *The Firebird*. With characteristic modesty she took the worst seat at the table, facing the wall of the restaurant. Arias is a few years younger than she is. He is shorter, more swarthy, and thicker built than the average Englishman: voluble and volatile.'[17]

Throughout her long career, Margot, like royalty, had seemed exempt from the more vulgar aspects of publicity; so it must have been strange for her to have to weather these snide articles about her husband-to-be, which, though their crude unpleasantness did not touch her personally, were full of a possessive resentment that *he* should have licence to do so: 'Who do you think is firing the legal cannon-balls on behalf of Aristotle Onassis in the battle between his whaling fleet and the Peruvian Navy? None other than Señor Roberto Arias, the sun-tanned Panamanian socialite who is spending a fortune making air pilgrimages to wherever prima ballerina Margot Fonteyn happens to be dancing. His papa, who may one day become La Fonteyn's father-in-law, is the brain behind the family law business and the most chucked-out dictator in South America. Papa Arias has twice been sacked as President of Panama. Still, that shouldn't worry him. Papa has a newspaper, handles most of the Panamanian oil company and shipping business, and he makes £2,000,000 a year.'[18]

La Fonteyn, however, was the undisputed Queen of Ballet, and in an era when the English press still saw it as its patriotic duty to propagate and protect the mystery and majesty of the reigning sovereign, Margot, with her regal smile and gracious aloofness, was in a position to rely on the restraint of leading journalists. One such, David Lewin, agreed not to break the marriage story on the understanding that she notify his paper twelve hours before going public. She did not call a press conference until 4 February, but, even then, Felix Fonteyn was still being vague on her behalf: 'My sister and Mr Arias have considered getting married in nearly every capital in the world. They even considered Panama. They decided not to marry in London because he is a big man and there are international reasons.'[19]

Just what those reasons might have been came to light when, in an interview in New York, none other than Tito's liveried chauffeur, Roosevelt, let slip that Panama had asked Britain to accept Señor Roberto Arias as its Ambassador to the Court of St James. The wedding ceremony, a civil one, would, much to the chagrin of British fans, be held in Paris, for the couple wished the proceedings 'to be quiet and dignified, in view of the recent assassination of the President of Panama'.[20] As the wife of an Envoy, Margot, beyond being entitled to a beflagged and specially number-plated car, not to mention immunity from prosecution for certain felonies, would henceforth be addressed as 'Excellency'. And most excellent she seemed as, frozen-faced and wrapped in mink, she glided into the bar at Covent Garden to meet the gathered press. It was enough to make you wonder if her prospective marriage had finally made a diva of her. But moments later the fur slipped from her shoulders, and, with it, all unapproachability. Her happiness was as modest and candid as Aurora's on her sixteenth birthday. 'Ask me anything you like,' she purred.

The press did not demur: what was so special about South American men? And could she cook? And did she want children? Well, she knew a girl from Moscow who'd married an Englishman and the Russians had said: What's so special about *English* men? There'd be a staff of three at the Embassy, one of these a cook. If she had married earlier and not been a ballerina, she would have liked six sons. Inevitably, someone asked her if, when she danced that night, she would be thinking about her husband-to-be. This was an inanity too many. 'When I perform,' she rebuked the reporter, 'there is no time to think of anything but dancing.'[21]

And she did not stint herself on the eve of her wedding, appearing at both the matinée and the evening performances – as the Firebird in the afternoon, and, at night, in the role which had lately grown dearest to her heart: that of Chloë. In the final moments, when Daphnis runs on, bearing his bride exultantly on his shoulders, the cast, who had been dancing with strangely scrunched-up fists, suddenly showered Margot with streamers and confetti. The audience clapped insatiably, with the tireless, heavy insistence of some former, wistful betrothed who will not let his beloved go without a valediction. At the umpteenth curtain call, Michael Somes led her forward to the footlights, where, weighed down by flowers and almost bedraggled by the paper and affection that had assailed her, she held her stance until the audience had composed itself at last. 'If,' she said, 'I am one tenth as happy in my future life as I am tonight, I shall be a very lucky girl. I thank you from the bottom of my heart for all your good wishes.'[22]

Her mother was not there to bask in the sentiment of the evening: 'Margot had asked me to go to Paris on the day before to buy some things for her including 1 kilo of best caviar which cost £9. The salesman looked at me to see if I really meant it, as I certainly didn't look able to afford such an expensive luxury, but concluded I must be some housekeeper, I think! I went to her suite at the Plaza Athénée next morning to see her before she was whisked off by her friends from Dior to their salon to be dressed in case anything needed to be adjusted as she had not had a final fitting, so I didn't even see her dress [but] stayed to answer the telephone and tidy up the chaos of the late arrival.' Leslie Edwards went with Margot to the salon, 'and there was Dior himself ... putting the final touches to the pale grey taffeta dress, making a stitch here and there and adjusting the head-dress, which was of small, grey, birds'-wing feathers'[23] – and not, in fact, the confection which Margot had chosen. Edwards, who had travelled from London that morning, along with David Webster, Michael Somes, Pamela May, Jean Gilbert, Ninette de Valois and Frederick Ashton, was told 'that the Consulate was far too small to accommodate all of us, and that we should wait for Margot and Tito to return and rejoin us at the reception. We were rather sad watching the car go off and waving her goodbye, until Fred suddenly rose up defiantly, declared that we had not got up at the crack of dawn to fly there and then not see her married, and called a taxi.'[24]

The tiny triangular office of Sr Jorge Royo, Panamanian Consul-General, four floors above the rue de la Paix, had no possibility of accommodating the 100 or more people – by no means all of them guests – who, on 6 February 1955, saw fit to squeeze into it. Margot arrived escorted by her father, who had travelled from his self-imposed exile in Jersey to give her away. But by the time she had fought her way to her bridegroom's side, the A-line of her skirt had been crushed as irreparably as her spirits. For someone who had hoped for a quiet and dignified ceremony, the din was quite unholy. Cameras whirred. Flashbulbs exploded. Huge bowls of lilac crashed wetly to the floor. She could see none of her intimates, not even her mother. And nor could her mother see *her*: 'When I got to the room,' writes Mrs Hookham, 'I was horrified. It was solid with people so that I could not get more than my shoulders inside.' BQ found herself wedged against a wall, beneath yellowing posters of past Panamanian presidents – some, violently deposed;

others, summarily assassinated. All of them knocked askew.

The service was brisk and in Spanish. The Consul-General, in accordance with Panamanian custom, tried personally to place the ring on the bride's finger. An eavesdropping reporter overheard Margot whisper to Tito: 'I don't want him to. Please put it on yourself, darling.'[25] But he could not oblige. She who, but the night before, had projected her voice to the back row of the gods could barely rally enough volume to legalize the proceedings by means of the small word 'sí'. As for signing the register, she deferred to her husband. 'Put your real name,' he told her, so she wrote 'Margaret Hookham'.[26]

The wedding party repaired for the reception to the Plaza Athénée, off the Champs-Elysées, where the press, interrupting Felix Fonteyn's attempts to photograph his sister and her husband formally, continued to be importunate, exhorting the couple at the top of the great staircase to kiss for the camera: 'Just one kiss, Señora.'[27] But Margot, who had kissed so many stage lovers, so publicly and suggestively, stamped her foot at this off-stage affront to her propriety. The most that she would allow was a peck on the cheek from the British Ambassador, who managed to graze his lips on her diamond earring. And when a camera, held aloft to capture the moment, clanged against a crystal chandelier, Margot could conceal her displeasure no longer. 'I've had enough,' she cried, 'positively enough,'[28] and dashed into a private room, swiftly followed by her mother, who slammed the mirrored door behind them.

Even the newlyweds' trip to the Caribbean got off to what seemed like an unpropitious start. Margot and Tito had to race across the tarmac to the plane. They further had to contend with headwinds, engine trouble, a missed connection, and an unexpected overnight stop in New York. But, in fact, Margot would come to understand that such last-minute dashes and changes of plan were intrinsic to the pleasure of travelling with her husband. Tito, dubbed 'the Globemaster' by his New York driver, courted unpredictability; and, where aeroplanes were concerned, liked 'to give them a sporting chance. Let them take off and then catch them.'[29] Not until 8 February did they finally board the *Edmar*, his 116-foot motor-yacht, for the two-week cruise of the Bahamas that would constitute their honeymoon. Margot was due to return to her old regime at Covent Garden on 24 February. She would then also step into her new role of Ambassadress. To say nothing of her role as a wife.

20

'In Panama,' Tito liked to remark, 'there are certain birds which run through mud, but when they come out, their feathers are white and clean.'¹ And it is true that Margot, despite her skittish past, was determined to enter into marriage behind a veil of reclaimed chastity. She had always possessed the capacity to expunge whole episodes from her personal history, and, in the months leading up to her wedding, she enacted various rituals designed to clear her conscience and the decks: the return of a gold watch to Peter Moore, the dispersal of her and Charles Hassé's china-cat collection, the excision of dedications from old books, and, most shockingly, the burning of some handwritten musical scores, composed and inscribed for her by Constant Lambert. She asked Ashton to be custodian of Lambert's letters to her, but he declined on grounds that he did not want the responsibility. In truth, he found her obsession to purge the past naïve and faintly risible. One instance, involving Kit, Lambert's son, particularly provoked Ashton's scorn. Patricia Foy relates: 'Kit was a great friend of Margot's and she used to visit him at school and take him out – it was marvellous for him when she came down. When he grew up, he had lunch once a week with her, and one day she said to him, "It's very sad but this of course will be the last time we can lunch together." He said, "Why?" and she said: "Well, I'm getting married next week: I'll be a married woman." Kit repeated this to Fred, who said: "Absolutely *bourgeois*." That, according to him, was Margot's trouble. He said that she was basically bourgeois.'

Even the much more strait-laced Ninette de Valois found this new-found sanctimony hard to take, especially when it came to Margot's refusal ever again to appear in Lambert's sexually explicit *Tiresias*, which the ballerina had once so passionately championed. De Valois wrote to her friend Joy Newton: 'Margot is taking her future very seriously. She has decided on a repertoire of six or seven works – and nothing more for eighteen months. She will not dance in *Tiresias* again (her future husband's wish) and has no wish to appear in Fred's new ballet. It may be the making of *him*. He is startled out of his complacency and insistence on her in every work – sometimes just to make sure of the success.'[2]

Ironically, Ashton's next three works, made to showcase the rising young stars of the company, were all deemed failures. *Variations on a Theme of Purcell* featured his lover, Alexander Grant, as a sort of master-of-ceremonies, conducting solos by Elaine Fifield, Rowena Jackson and Nadia Nerina, each embodying a specific instrument. Also premièred on 6 January 1955 was *Rinaldo and Armida*, which starred Svetlana Beriosova, of whom Richard Buckle had written: 'There is something in her arms, in her back, in the way she holds her head and uses her eyes, that cannot be taught, and for which technique is only a frame.'[3] And, perhaps because the gods already spoke so eloquently through the limbs of Beriosova, Ashton did not really feel driven to mould the ballerina to his own creative idiom. Both ballets were dedicated to Sophie Fedorovitch, whose mysterious death two years earlier had left Ashton bereft of her 'gentle bullying', which he missed even more sorely than he did the musical scholarship of Constant Lambert. When it came to the third ballet, *Madame Chrysanthème* (for which *Entrada de Madame Butterfly* had been a mere sketch), Ashton tried to redress his loss by commissioning a score from Lambert's friend Alan Rawsthorne, who, as it happened, had lately married Constant's widow, Isabel – the perfect designer for the delicate Kabuki look that Ashton envisaged. But although the sets and costumes were lovely enough, the score (which began and ended with 'an unaccompanied woman's voice wailing a wordless poem') was undistinguished. *Madame Chrysanthème* did not survive in the repertoire, any more than its star, Elaine Fifield, was fated, despite Ashton's pronounced interest in her, to last long in the company.

Fifield had become almost desperately dependent on Ashton's favour: her marriage to the conductor John Lanchbery was in disarray, and she had already given birth to a daughter – a masochistic move in the sadistically competitive world of the Sadler's Wells Ballet. Anorexic and psychologically fragile, Fifield was never to recover from a remark made by Ashton when, ten months later, she danced her first Aurora in *The Sleeping Beauty*. Bursting with elation as she came off-stage at the end, she blurted to her mentor: 'I enjoyed that more than anything else I've ever done.'[4] To her astonishment Ashton replied: 'Well, you shouldn't, you're a very naughty girl.' 'Why not?' cried Elaine. 'What was wrong?' And with his answer he put paid to her confidence at Covent Garden for ever: '*You* mustn't enjoy it – because *Margot* doesn't.'

Margot, for the first time in her life, took little notice of goings-on at the Opera House, so engrossed was she by her new duties at Thurloe Place. The property, which Tito described as 'early Valentino with Georgian overtones',[5] possessed a feature which he considered essential to any reputable embassy: a secret back door, several streets from the front entrance, through which friends could come and go without detection. But houses of this magnitude take some running, and Margot, accustomed to a bachelor-girl existence in a modest flat, confessed that she had no idea where to begin. 'It was the question of telling servants what to do that worried me most.'[6]

She might have made it easier on herself had she recruited her staff from a more orthodox source. Hitherto, Margot had employed no more than a smattering of devoted secretaries – Biddy O'Neal and Pauline Chasey in London, and Theodora Christon in New York. But it was typical of her strange combination of opportunism and thriftiness (she was long accustomed to being upgraded by airlines, and to having doctors, hoteliers and couturiers waive their fees) that she relied on the somewhat rum assumption of there being fans all over England who would enter her employ for love rather than for money. Two perfect contenders were Margaret ('Margot') Hewitt and her husband John. Margaret Hewitt had been a fan 'ever since I can remember. I got married in 1951 and we came to London on our honeymoon, so I wrote to Margot and said, do you think we could meet you for a few minutes? That would be *the* thrill of a lifetime. And she wrote back and said, Yes.'

Margot might not have responded with such alacrity had she known that she was not, in fact, Hewitt's original choice. 'My first ballerina was Moira Shearer. I knitted for all her babies as they came along. Anyway, I wrote to Moira Shearer first, and for some reason she couldn't see us. I thought, Right, I'll write to Margot Fonteyn. It was sheer fluke. After that, we used to come up for our anniversary every year, for two weeks, and we *lived* for those two weeks. And then, one day, out of the blue, I had this letter saying she was getting married and would we be interested in working as her personal maid and chauffeur/ butler. Everybody thought we were mad because we'd never done it before, and we'd got safe jobs in the Post Office, with pensions. John was carried along by me, and three months later we were with her. We had a sort of little flat in the Embassy. Our wages – for two of us – were eleven pounds a week, but it didn't matter. She was a very businesslike lady. Working for her was a real joy. But there was a slight barrier, which was right – I liked that. If you went and worked for the Queen, you'd know there'd be that. We were always a little bit in awe. We idolized her. *And* her husband. He had a marvellous sense of humour, but where everyday things were concerned, he just wasn't on the same planet. I mean, money to him was . . . five pound notes. Pound notes were small change to him, and silver was nothing. John'd be cleaning the car and he'd find money stuffed down the side of the seat where Tito had pushed it instead of putting it in his pocket. Margot obviously had to work very hard for every penny she had, but they were happy. Complementary. We used to take her orange juice, brown toast and cereal – never a cooked breakfast – at eight, and by nine she was on her way to rehearsal. She'd come back for a lunch of steak and salad. If she was dancing that night, she'd have two hours' rest in bed and then we'd wake her with tea and biscuits and she'd be off to the theatre. And then, after that, she'd probably have a big party, with actors and politicians, starting at eleven o'clock at night and going on 'til two in the morning. I don't know how she did it, but she never asked of us any more than she gave herself. I remember she'd been on holiday to Panama once, and she got home with this length of fabric and she said: "This would make beautiful curtains" – there was this long window – "perhaps some time you could make them up." She went to bed for two hours, and by the time she came down they were made and they were up. She commanded that sort of love.'

There was, however, a shadow-side to the Hewitts' adoration, which manifested itself in a loathing of the person who, for thirty-five unchallenged years, had been Margot's faithful stalwart: hand-maid, chauffeur and cook, rolled into one. 'Black Queen they called her, and Black Queen she was. She certainly queened it over everybody. We were frightened to death of her. She'd arrive at the front door and John would open it and she'd stalk in and say: "I want a large gin, and I want it now." She was sort of the *force*, you know? Oh, God, she was a formidable lady. She did make our lives hell – we had to be very fond of Fonteyn to stick it. I remember when Leo, the cook, left, and this other, professional cook came, and after two days he asked: "When do I get my afternoon off?" *Afternoon off?* We didn't have such things. Well, he lasted about a month I think – just scooted off, and we were terrified. What would we say if she rang down? And we didn't say anything – just got on and did it.'

At the end of the fourth American tour, in 1955–6, Tito had taken Margot home to meet his family for the first time. She remembered his brother, Modi, from the Cambridge days, and had recently met his sister, Rosario Arias de Galindo, in London. But it required an even subtler form of diplomacy than Margot showed at the Embassy to conquer the social scene in Panama. 'It was – let's not say difficult,' says Rosario, 'because Margot had the knack of putting you at your ease. But she was from a world completely different, and Tito had three children. The person who wouldn't have accepted her, for religious reasons, was Mother, because she was older. But whatever Tito did was all right with her, so she would always make excuses for him, and Margot never made a problem – she immediately got along with everybody. She was wonderful with the children and if there was any resentment from Querube [Tito's first wife], she never showed it. At least not to me. Relations were cordial, for the sake of the children. We had the impression, right from the beginning, that here in Panama Margot didn't want to be seen as a ballerina. She wanted to be seen as Tito's wife. So, to tell the truth, I kept rather to that separation. We were always informal with her, and allowed her her freedom. We never said: "Why didn't you call?" We didn't tie her down because, in her other life, she was tied down for every minute of the day. My father became extremely fond of her, and when Tito got involved in the politics here, and I got mad at him, Father didn't want me to put her in conflict with Tito. Father respected her. He said: "Don't lose sight of the fact that she is his wife."'

Margot returned from America determined to run her household with a firmer hand. 'Over there it's much more efficient,' says Margaret Hewitt, 'and I think she realized she needed experienced staff. You can be enthusiastic but it's no good giving your all if you've not got the expertise and are too emotionally involved. If we did anything wrong or not quite right it really upset us. John had all these jobs to do and she'd perhaps say to me: "Tell John to bring the car round in five minutes," and I'd go tearing all over the house frantically trying to find him so she could walk out of the door straight into the car. And if he wasn't there, I used to get all upset. We couldn't bear things not to be perfect. We wanted her life to be as smooth as it could possibly be. But it was at the expense of John's health, and I went as thin as a rail. So although it was terrible when we had to leave, it was a good thing. But, strangely enough, her staff kept changing – nobody stayed with her for very long.'

Therein lay another, more distressing, tale. Before Margot's seven years at Thurloe Place were done, there would come a day when she would sweep through the Embassy, dismissing every member of her staff: it had become common knowledge within the household that Dr Arias was bedding one of their number. The great torment and difficulty of Margot's marriage – Tito's philandering spirit, his refusal to toe the line of sexual fidelity – did not take long to surface; not even, rumour has it, as long as the length of the honeymoon. Rosario de Galindo tried, early on, to warn her sister-in-law about the pitfalls of having chosen a Latin American husband. 'When I met Margot, I wrote her a letter telling her to be sure not to love Tito more than he loved her. In a marriage a woman will always give more than a man. And if she gives him too much, boy, that man will certainly take advantage of it. Tito had been a man pampered by women. He had this softness about him. He was an attractive man and he was extremely intelligent and knew how to treat women. Any time he wanted to take a woman out he had no trouble, and that sort of forms a man. She laughed very much, but I could see that she had much more capacity to love than Tito did. *Much* more capacity.'

Colin Clark, son of the art historian Kenneth Clark, and brother of the politician Alan Clark, first met Tito when Margot brought her new husband to stay at Saltwood, the family home. In Colin's memoir, *Younger Brother, Younger Son*, a chapter headed 'Monsters' depicts Arias as 'the sort of monster for whom you gave your life . . . Until then, all the monsters I had known were loud, pushy and dominant. Tito was a monster of quite a different type. His voice was quiet to the point of being incomprehensible . . . He had the lazy charm of a baby who is so spoiled that he absolutely knows that he is going to get what he wants, and that he can toss it out of the pram again the moment he is bored with it.'[7] Tito's mental restlessness exacerbated Margot's intellectual and social insecurities. Since he held her profession in no great awe (according to his nephew Gabriel Galindo, 'Uncle Tito couldn't care less about ballet'), she often felt stripped of confidence in his company – his company, that is, when he provided it. She confessed to a friend that in those early months she rarely saw him from one day's end to another, and that he held her cognitive powers in such poor regard that he barely spoke to her except to introduce her at parties.

'Tito was extremely quiet,' says his sister, Rosario de Galindo. 'You never knew what he was thinking. He was private, like my father, but Father had more respect for discussing things with someone who he knew wasn't up to his intelligence. If Tito didn't respect somebody, he didn't think it worthwhile to waste time. He had a brilliant mind, but in practical matters there was a flaw somewhere. He could visualize things, but he didn't have the practical gifts to follow them through. He lived in the heights. Margot brought him down to earth. I was amazed the times I went to London when Tito was Ambassador. I don't know how she handled it. She had to cope with the running of the house, she had to cope with protocol, she had to cope with going to class, and after she danced would invite all these people back and have to remember who was going to sit where, and why.'

But Margot, like a performer for whom one bad notice will cancel out all the good ones, could only squirm at her mistakes. A particular source of anxiety was the business of introductions, and she would sometimes fail to recognize the ex-Viceroy of heaven-knew-where, despite having met him three times in the course of the previous week. Equally socially shaming was her inherent lateness. 'All my life,' she told *Woman* magazine, 'I had taken about two hours to get ready for anything.' But her husband, in his oblique and gentle way, soon had her trained to dress and make up in twenty minutes. 'One day,' writes Margot, 'when I found Tito, in evening dress, waiting, as usual, at the foot of the stairs, he told me a little story. "My mother," he said, "was very unpunctual. But she always knew when my father was becoming impatient." "How?" I inquired anxiously. Tito answered gravely: "He would put on his hat, indoors, and walk around with it on till she was ready!" "But you don't wear a hat," I told him triumphantly. "No," said Tito sternly, touching his bare head, "but metaphorically speaking *I've got one on now!*" '8

Hating to be an amateur at anything, Margot soon became, to her mother's further pride, an exemplary ambassadress. Yet if seeing her daughter raised so far above her station gratified Mrs Hookham, it must also have galled her to find her own London existence relegated, often as not, to the green baize side of the social door. The loneliness of her London flat was relieved by weekends spent at Amerden, the Taplow house where Pamela May's family was now installed in a separate wing. Leslie Edwards had been encouraged to buy a small weekend 'lean-to' abutting the main structure, and Gerd Larsen occupied a nearby cottage. Jolly as this riverside commune proved to be, and regularly as Margot and Tito visited it, there is no denying the social chasm which had opened between mother and daughter. This separation can be felt in the pages of Margot's autobiography, where, at the point of her marriage, she ceases to be 'I' and adopts the frustrating pronoun 'we'. Gone is the clarity of an undeferential point of view; and what, until now, has been a straightforward narrative line gives way to giggling anecdote, littered with famous names. The photographs, carefully selected earlier in the book for their sentimental or illustrative value, are now merely aggrandizing: Tito's parents with President Roosevelt, Tito himself outside Buckingham Palace, or aboard the *Christina* with Maria Callas and Aristotle Onassis; and Margot – in serial company with Errol Flynn, Bobby Kennedy, Winston Churchill – forever sporting her royal smile. A picture of Mike Todd and Elizabeth Taylor coddling their newborn baby is included for no other seeming reason than its dedication: 'To our dear Friends Margot and Tito with Love Liz and Mike'. That Margot, herself a lifelong prey to autograph hunters, should, from the vast array of representative images at her disposal, have elected to place such star-struck emphasis on this overblown irrelevancy is indicative of the profound alteration that had come over her.

It was an alteration which was to become manifest in her

professional signature: she now styled herself Margot Fonteyn de Arias. In the public domain, her name was about to grow more extended still, gaining a title that would rival any among her circle of dignitaries: Dame of the British Empire. On 7 February 1956, she attended the Palace for her investiture, a ceremony discharged by Queen Elizabeth the Queen Mother, who, standing in for her daughter, pinned one of the highest orders at the Sovereign's command to the self-same breast (demurely draped, on this occasion, by Dior) as had, five years earlier, in *Tiresias*, so offended palace propriety. Now that she was a married woman, Margot did, in fact, enjoy very cordial relations with the Windsors: Princess Margaret took tea at Thurloe Place, and the Queen, for her first visit to the ballet since her accession, had marked the occasion of Margot's return to Covent Garden by unexpectedly turning up to see *The Firebird* on the very evening that a party was to be thrown for all the dancers and stage-hands and friends who had missed the Arias wedding. This after-show reception, conducted very much in Tito's lavish manner, took place in a Chinese-lanterned, red-and-white marquee – the first marquee ever to be erected on an Opera House stage – and boasted a guest list of 400. Usherettes wept as they crossed the hastily constructed bridge between stalls and stage, because there was no time to go home and change out of their uniforms. But Margot, aglow in her grey silk wedding ensemble (minus the contentious hat), danced to the calypso band with commissionaires in their gold-braided, plum livery, and stewards in their white regulation jackets, fulfilling her promise to partner every male guest in turn. Prince Philip found himself robbed of this democratic opportunity, having been whisked back to the Palace by his wife before the shenanigans got under way. Nevertheless, word was that the Queen, sitting untiara'd in the thick of the grand tier, and 'gazing with shining eyes and lips parted at the stage', had been spellbound by Margot's red-feathered pyrotechnics.

The royal motif, which was to continue throughout 1956 with a flurry of galas and command performances, would culminate in a solemn document, handed, on 31 October, to the Governors of the Sadler's Wells Ballet, bequeathing upon the company the title: 'The Royal Ballet'. In the months that led up to the bestowal of this collective honour, Margot twice reneged on her decision not to accept any new Ashton works for the time being. On 15 February she and Michael Somes premièred *La Péri*, a new version of a short ballet based on Persian legend, which Ashton had first choreographed in 1931 for Markova and himself. Describing his own attributes as a partner in those days as 'pretty rickety', Ashton, this time round, had to contend with an even more severe stricture than the limitations of his own talent. The publishers of the music – by Dukas – insisted that the composer's capricious wish (that the male role in the ballet be confined to pantomime and partnering) should be obeyed to the letter of the law. So Michael Somes, whose speciality, in any case, it was to transport Margot about the stage so seamlessly that he almost melted into the décor, appeared, in this context, to be playing out not so much the story of Iskender the Shah, who steals the lotus of immortality from a fallen angel, as some unfortunate travesty of himself. Margot gamely reproduced the lateral, oriental head-shifting movements taught to her by Ram Gopal, but despite André Levasseur's costumes, which the two dancers, if not the critics, adored, *La Péri* did not make much impact in London, and came to be regarded as a mere display-piece for Fonteyn and Somes in their ever-increasing guest appearances away from Covent Garden.

Not so Ashton's next offering, which was exactly that: *Birthday Offering* – a tribute in honour of Ninette de Valois to celebrate the twenty-fifth anniversary of the company which, as the Vic-Wells, had given its first full evening performance on 5 May 1931, and which, now, as the Royal Ballet circa 1956, was to welcome back Robert Helpmann to dance the Tango in *Façade* with the 'little Chinese girl' who had grown up to be an English Dame. Ashton dashed off his new ballet (to a lushly melodic score by Glazunov) rather as a poet laureate might knock out a few catchy verses – more from duty than from any real inspiration. But, in fact, the result just went to show how inspired the choreographer *could* be when, instead of courting current intellectual trends and narrative complication, he allowed himself to submit to the rudiments of neo-classicism. The spirit of Petipa was upon him, and from the moment that the seven ballerinas and their partners began their sweeping, circling entrance to the first *Concert Waltz*, it became evident how consummately the company had imbibed Ashton's stylistic mastery of the grandeur and serenity that had characterized the great ballets of the nineteenth century. *Birthday Offering* made much of its female stars, but little of their cavaliers: hence its nickname among the dancers – 'Seven Brides for Seven Brothers'. But by that token, Margot was, needless to say, head wife – centre stage, gilded tutu, topaz spotlight. Even so, flanked as she was by so many of her younger colleagues – Svetlana Beriosova, Elaine Fifield, Nadia Nerina, Violetta Elvin, Beryl Grey, Rowena Jackson, all of whom had recently danced Aurora – Margot had her work cut out to retain her supremacy. And Ashton, as was his teasing way, saddled her with a solo which was all speed and sharpness and *petite batterie*, jibing: 'They're all going to have to look at Margot's feet.'[9] And, triumph though she did, the feeling was never stronger in the gods and on the boards that these were the last glorious days of a great artist who represented the company's golden past – a past which was about to give way to a shining, new-minted future. For who would have dreamt that of all the seven ballerinas in that line-up, the one who would be dancing when the others were long gone, the one for whom the brightest dawn had yet to break, was Margot Fonteyn?

Damehood seemed to have set the seal upon Margot's career. Her ambitions as a dancer were now so fully realized that the press felt obliged to invent a new destiny for her: MARGOT FONTEYN TO BE 'QUEEN' OF PANAMA, ran a headline in the *Daily Sketch*. 'Her husband, wealthy Señor Roberto Arias, now Ambassador in London, is to be the next President of Panama. When he takes over in 18 months' time, Margot Fonteyn will hang up her ballet shoes for all time. Señor Arias' move to the presidential palace is the talk of dinner parties in London's Latin American colony. The ambassador and his lovely wife blush every time the conversation switches to the future of their country. It's nothing unusual for a member of the Arias family to occupy the President's seat. His father was President in 1931 and 1935. His uncle was President in 1940 and from 1948–1951. But it's unusual enough for a ballerina to take over as First Lady.'[1]

Not even de Valois found the concept too far-fetched. In a letter to Joy Newton she confided: 'Margot still seems divinely happy and Tito gives no trouble – but what the future holds I know not. I suspect in two years time he will be running for the presidency in Panama like his forefathers – It appears that there are only three families that do this and they have pot shots at each other when a "change" seems like a good idea.'[2] But in October 1956, something happened that was to galvanize Margot in her true goal: the ambition to maintain her hold upon the world's perception of her as the greatest ballerina of the twentieth century. From behind the Iron Curtain, for its first London season, came the Bolshoi Ballet. And, at its head, Galina Ulanova, People's Artist of the Soviet Union.

Margot was already quite worked up about the prospect of seeing Ulanova dance. Back in 1951, Mrs Hookham had happened to be in Florence with her sculptor friend Fiore de Henriquez when the Russian star's début in the West took place at the Maggio Musicale. Though the setting was hardly worthy of the occasion, BQ had returned raving about the ballerina – not something to which Margot was exactly accustomed. But she knew, from films she had seen, that Ulanova, though more rhetorical and severe in style, was a dancer after her own heart: by no means one of technical bravura – indeed, almost timorous in the sensitivity of her approach – yet, nevertheless, a poet of understatement and a mime of genius. Ulanova was to appear in only three roles at Covent Garden: as Giselle, as Juliet, and as Maria in *Fountain of Bakhchisarai*, but, despite her advanced age (forty-six), she remained what the Soviet critic Vadim Gayevsky had once so poignantly called 'the ballerina of the morning'.[3] Gennady Smakov explains: 'Ulanova's smile, both bashful and radiant, and her body, high-strung, palpitating with anticipation and fright, could convey Giselle's or Juliet's morning of love as no one else. Her death scenes became legendary: no other ballerina could so potently express physical frailty in the face of death, and spiritual victory over it.'

London audiences were 'whipped into a state of hysterical adoration'.[4] Margot, with Tito by her side, was present at the opening performance of *Romeo and Juliet*; she wore a blood-orange dress and, on her face, the 'expression of a child taken to its first pantomime'.[5] As well she might. For Lavrovsky's transcription of Shakespeare's tragedy to the explicit Prokofiev score was, though emotionally full-blooded, little more than a dance-drama – choreographically impoverished by Western standards. Yet, however repetitious, what could be more hypnotic than the sorrowful, luminous *demi-arabesques* of Ulanova? Oh, and how she could run, 'leaving all behind her',[6] in the fabled Russian way that Ashton, for all his gifted mimicry, had never quite been able to convey. Now, at last, Margot understood. 'We were stunned,' she writes, 'by the revelation that was Ulanova.'[7]

The shock, Clive Barnes suggests, was not altogether a pleasant one. 'Given Margot's intense suburban competitiveness, it must have been incredible for her. She suddenly realized that there was something different. It completely reversed her and Ninette's revisionist view of history. Margot reshaped herself according to Ulanova. She didn't see her a great deal – only two or three times, but it had an enormous effect on her. Two effects, actually. One was the discovery that you could go on – to an older age than she had ever envisaged. That was the carrot. The whip was the incredible adulation that Ulanova received. Margot had beaten off Chauviré, she'd beaten off Alonso, she'd beaten off Nora Kaye. But now, here, everywhere, people were saying: *this is the world's greatest ballerina.*'

Not only did Ulanova prove that a dancer could be old. She also disproved the strange prejudice held by English dancers that a ballerina must be brunette. Fair-haired Antoinette Sibley, who had joined the company in January 1956, says that with the advent of Ulanova, 'we conceived of the idea that a ballerina could be blonde. Up till that time I honestly couldn't see that I was going to get anywhere. Markova, Pavlova, Fonteyn – everyone was dark. In fact, at one point, Margot told me I should dye my hair black. She said: "Theatrically, if your hair's black, you're already a dramatic dancer." But I'm fair. I'm not a dark person. *Her* skin was olive.'

Not that Ulanova, when Sibley first saw her, was blonde any longer. 'She was a mess. Like an old lady. She had a funny neck. We were dancing in Croydon while they were rehearsing to do their first ever performances at the Opera House, so we all came up in a coach to watch their rehearsal. I suppose we got back to London at 11.30 at night, and there they still were, doing *Romeo and Juliet.* They were just coming up to the balcony scene. Lapauri, or someone, was on as Romeo. Then the music stopped and he went up to say something to Yuri Faier, the nearly blind conductor, and this old woman got up from the stalls. We thought she was the ballet mistress. She was saying something to the dancers and then she went and stood on the stage up on the balcony and she still had these awful leg-warmers on and, well, she looked a hundred. And then she just suddenly started dreaming. And in front of our very eyes – no make-up, no costume – she became fourteen. I have never seen anything, in any sphere, as theatrical as Ulanova getting up in her scrubby old practice-clothes – the Russians didn't have pretty things like we did – with her grey, curly hair, and becoming Juliet. And our *hearts*! We couldn't even *breathe*. And then she did that run across the stage after the poison scene: well – we were all screaming and yelling, like at a football match. It was the turning point for me as an artist. From then on, I knew you could be a ballerina, an amazing ballerina, and be fair. *And* not perfect. Perfection was not part of Ulanova's scene at all. She was human. It was to do with transformation. The imperfections were what moved you. They made her so vulnerable.'

Poor, 'perfect' Margot. How could she compete? Yet to talk of competitiveness is to demean the profound influence of one great artist upon another. If one has pressed the point about Ulanova, it is because Margot, who even at the age of six could watch Pavlova with detachment, had, since childhood, been given scant opportunity to feel overwhelmed by a fellow performer. Not since Markova's departure from Sadler's Wells in 1935 had there been any suggestion that Margot should model herself on anyone. She had, of course, been impressed many times, and was humble in the face of her own inadequacies; but she was fundamentally possessed of that strange inner authority, peculiar to genius, which remains blithely uninfected by the gifts of others. Ulanova awoke in Fonteyn, perhaps for the first time, a desire for contagion. She wanted to be, not better than the Russian, but equal to her – akin to her – so that the two might meet upon that lonely, elevated plane where so few are chosen to go. When Margot first saw Ulanova in person, sitting on a suitcase in the foyer of Covent Garden, she rushed ahead of the interpreter and threw her arms round the bewildered ballerina, pressing into her hand 'a little Victorian locket that I had picked up as I left the house. I had the impression that people were not usually so forward when they met her, but I think she understood that it was a spontaneous action on my part.'[8]

Ulanova, as it happened, was deeply suspicious of spontaneous Western ways, her iconic status at home having been, according to her compatriot Gennady Smakov, 'related to her conformist, obedient behaviour [and to] her support of oppressive political actions of the Soviet Government'.[9] The Bolshoi had arrived in London under a public relations cloud, having almost cancelled the entire trip due to a petty incident in Oxford Street – the arrest of a Soviet Olympic discus thrower, Nina Pomonerova, accused of stealing five 32s 11d hats from C&A Modes. Ulanova had put her signature to a letter questioning whether, 'while the provocation against Nina is not suppressed . . . the troupe will be able to perform in London under normal conditions without being exposed to some kind of persecution'. It was an atmosphere absurd enough to make even the gift of a Victorian locket seem like a plant, and Ulanova, who had few off-stage social graces, made no effort to return the compliment of Margot's passionate interest. Indeed, not once did she trouble to visit the Davis Theatre in Croydon where Fonteyn was dancing. But, as in all unreciprocal exchanges, the person who expends the emotional energy is the one who stands to gain: Ulanova's visit proved a landmark in Margot's development – a precursor, perhaps, of the forthcoming love-affair between the restrained English ballerina and the wild Russian soul. And its influence came to permeate all her existing roles, broadening and loosening her neat, contained style, and paving the way for the revelation of *Ondine*, the germ of which was already taxing Ashton's imagination.

Competition was a godsend to Margot. When she saw something greater than herself, rather than be crushed by it, she hauled herself to meet it. This she managed not by some sudden, superhuman effort of will, but by the steady application of the skill most prized by Ninette de Valois: 'an incredible facility for learning. Margot had it from the start and she never lost it. Her attention, if she saw or heard something that impressed her, was absolute. Not at all spectacular. You hardly realized she was concentrating. But if you knew her, you came to recognize that sudden, rooted attention.'

Margot's attention, however, was far from rooted by the prospect of her next port of call, which should have been Moscow but turned out to be Sydney. A shipload of equipment and scenery had already reached the docks in Leningrad, and the Sadler's Wells Ballet, with its impending Royal Charter, was all set to fly to the Soviet Union as part of the exchange agreement with the Bolshoi. But on 4 November, just one day after the Russians had left London, an incident – rather more serious than the alleged theft of a few hats – halted the English dancers in their tracks: Soviet tanks were rolling into Hungary. Three days later, David Webster cabled Moscow: 'In view of public opinion in this country which strongly condemns the renewed suppression by Soviet forces of Hungarian liberty and independence . . . it has been unanimously agreed that in the present circumstances the projected visit of the Sadler's Wells Ballet to Moscow cannot take place.'[10] In fact, British outrage at the crushing of the Hungarian revolution by the Red Army might have carried more moral weight had Anglo-French forces not tried (and failed), less than a week earlier, to wrest back control of the Suez Canal from Colonel Nasser by bombing Port Said. But Margot, whose husband harboured every political intention of one day presiding over the world's other vital canal zone, devotes not one autobiographical word to these grave developments. Instead, she takes us waltzing (Matilda) straight off to Australia – a country whose vitality and candour she would, in due course, come to adore, but which, at the time, she held in the supercilious contempt of a stereotypical 'Pommie'. 'It was a place,' she confesses, 'I had no wish to visit. My preconceived notion was of a thoroughly dull place, full of stodgy people.'[11]

One person who did – and desperately – want to be included on the tour was Elaine Fifield. After eleven years' absence from her native Australia, she longed to show her compatriots what she had achieved abroad, and, knowing how much publicity her homecoming would excite, confidently expected to be chosen. But when the four names went up on the notice board, hers did not figure among them. Those elected to travel with Somes and Fonteyn were Brian Ashbridge and Rowena Jackson. Jackson was a champion technician, who could spin like a top without ever veering into Margot's hallowed, poetic territory. She also happened to be a New Zealander – although the major tour was bound only for Sydney and Melbourne. Fifield, miserably disappointed, eventually decided to go home under her own steam, and handed in her notice. But de Valois did not tolerate displays of independence unless one happened to be Bobby Helpmann, and could deal with ingrates who broke company ranks as chillingly as any KGB commissar. 'My child,' she said, 'you're going to regret this all your life. You have burned your boats.'[12] And so it proved. Less than two years later, when Fifield meekly enquired whether she might return to Covent Garden, de Valois replied: 'It is out of the question. I never take dancers back when they leave of their own accord.'[13]

Actually, the management need not have feared for Margot's interests. Australia's colonial sense of inferiority decreed that no locally born artist would ever be favoured above an English one – especially one as identified with 'the old country' as Fonteyn. Margot may have felt devoid of any connection to Australia, but Australians could not have felt more connected to *her*. (I, for one, kept a framed photograph of her – the one on the cover of this book – on my bedroom wall.) Geography notwithstanding, Australian culture in the 1950s was overwhelmingly British, and, to those who loved theatre and the arts, the face of Margot Fonteyn was almost mythical in its connotation: immemorial, Shakespearean – the 'Queen of the Swans' of Avon. It was not just balletomania that greeted her when she arrived in Sydney, but a kind of flag-waving outburst of loyalty and patriotism; and it was from astonishment, perhaps, that she behaved, initially, as royally as she was treated.

'When I first met her, I didn't like her,' says Bill Akers, then stage manager of the Borovansky Ballet, with whom the four stars were to guest. 'I thought, "You're cold and you're haughty and you're proud and you're English" – everything, I suppose, that I didn't understand. Our dancers were so relaxed. And

Margot arrived cool and elegant in a beautiful, formal black frock. Someone must have preconditioned her, I think, because she seemed very wary and Michael [Somes] was being terribly lordly. Everybody had to call her Dame Margot, which drove me mad. Mr Borovansky was a god to me, and I thought, "Why does he have to go around making all this obeisance?" If I'd been her I would have said: "Enough, we don't want any more of *that* – we're *working* together." The company was a good company. Boro had created, *per capita*, the biggest ballet public of any country in the world. I thought him a genius of a man, and I still do.' But in her book, Margot dismisses the Czechoslovakian émigré as a 'smallish, bald-headed man who had been a character dancer and sometimes confused the names of ballet steps, saying "port de bras" when he meant "pas de bourrée". He tried to keep discipline by shouting all through rehearsals in his cracked voice and Russian accent. He even, to our surprise, gave instructions to the *corps de ballet* from a down-stage wing during performances. Dancers in Ninette de Valois's company knew what they were doing by the time they got on stage, and didn't need coaching as they went along. We asked him to go away from the corner while we were dancing, as he distracted us.'[14]

By the time they opened in Melbourne, however, Margot, because she learned so quickly, had become chastened by the informality of her new surroundings. 'I had to take the flowers on,' says Bill Akers, 'and this *vast* basket was waiting to go on. I always took the cards out so they could be replied to by letter, and I read this one, and it said – I still have it – "To this wonderful company who've treated me so kindly, thank you so much. Yours, Margot." And then, at the bottom: "No Dame *please*." So she redeemed herself. On the last night of the season, Boro had arranged to have ninety dozen roses delivered to the theatre – they were out of season, so he'd had to send all over Australia for them – and between the matinée and the evening performance, he and I and the property boys tore the roses to pieces. We put them on a plarch in the flies, and when at the

335

end of Aurora's wedding they do that *révérence*, down came all the petals. The only other person this had ever been done for was Pavlova. You couldn't see the stalls for the streamers thrown from the circle on to the stage. While the speeches were droning on, Margot bent down and picked up a roll and tucked it into her cleavage. When her turn came, she walked forward, took the microphone, put it to one side, and addressed the whole of the Empire Theatre, saying: "Ladies and Gentlemen, microphones make me nervous," and that's when I fell in love with her. She made a very short speech, and then at the end – I've never forgotten the words – she said: "As the warmth and richness of your applause has bound you forever to my heart, may this streamer" (taking it out of her bodice) "bind me to yours." And she threw it. And you could have got a thousand pounds an inch for it.'

A company party thrown by Margot followed, at the Windsor Hotel. 'We smashed the stems off a couple of champagne glasses and put the flutes in Margot's *pointe* shoes, and we stood on the tables and drank the champagne. Then the girls insisted that we do it out of Michael's – so we had to drink out of his clammy old ballet-flats. Margot was wonderful at parties – we all had a wow of a time.' All, that is, except Edouard Borovansky. 'He had gone to a great deal of trouble to have the repertoire of his company photographed, and he'd had these beautiful books bound – I think there were five – and he gave them as a present. And she went without them. Left them behind in the dressing-room. He was terribly wounded.'

It was not the first time that Margot's carelessness had caused distress. 'She was actually the most charitable person,' says Patricia Foy, 'and would never have deliberately hurt anyone. But she was the worst person in the world to give a present to. She never bothered to open them. Once, looking in a wardrobe, she found bags of old Christmas presents. She began unwrapping them, and amongst them was a silver spoon that had belonged to Taglioni. It was a great treasure of Karsavina's, who'd given it to Margot at Christmas. Margot had noticed that Karsavina was being distant with her, and hadn't been able to understand why.'

Margot's casual attitude towards people's kindness was hardly consistent with the scruples of the girl who, during the war, had faithfully acknowledged, by letter, every piece of steak, and pound of sugar, and even carton of hated eggs left by fans for her at the stage door. But times had changed, and so had the company she kept. Her highly principled, sensitive nature was now diverted away from its ruling sense of duty to the public, and directed solely towards her husband; and she no longer cared to draw his attention to her own massive celebrity. 'She was a bit frightened of him,' says Foy, 'and she didn't want to make him jealous.' And it is true that Margot did cancel her press-cutting service at this point. Her linen-covered scrapbooks, kept up meticulously until the first year of her marriage, stop abruptly at Volume 29. Tito, on the other hand, did not shy from invoking Margot's jealousy. 'He behaved very badly to her,' says Annette Page. 'He would grab the youngest, prettiest little *corps de ballet* dancer at a party and sit her on his knee, with Margot standing there, pretending to laugh it off. She laughed all the time, but I'm sure she was very hurt by it.' But at least, on such occasions, she had him in her sights, for, during his time as Panamanian Ambassador to London, he became, according to Colin Clark, 'a seducer on an international scale. Margot would give wonderful first-night parties after each new ballet, never knowing if Tito would turn up or not. On one occasion I met him in her dressing-room before the performance, and later he phoned to say he couldn't join us for dinner because he was in Paris.'

But Tito had coined a mollifying phrase, 'Our separation is only geographical', which, for a couple always flying off in separate directions across the world, proved a motto apt enough for them to vow that, one day, it would adorn their shared grave-stone. And during her month in Australia, Margot had missed her husband so dreadfully that, on her return, she opted, at every opportunity, to dance at the theatre in the Casino at Monte

Carlo, where Onassis kept his offices. Tito's activities there remain something of a mystery, although Margot is at pains to tell us that he specialized in marine law. 'Once,' writes Mrs Hookham, 'I asked him what his business was, though I knew he was an international lawyer, and the reply was "Helping rich men to keep their money in safe places." Onassis was one of his clients and several other shipping men who only ever talked in millions.' Colin Clark writes: 'This was possible because the Onassis fleet was registered under the Panamanian flag, but I think Tito was really more of a "fixer", someone who could smooth things over with government officials. When he married Margot, his prestige with Onassis increased dramatically. Onassis was having an affair with the opera singer Maria Callas, and suddenly the two men had something in common.'[15] Margot found Onassis's way of life 'intelligent and civilized'. Asked, years later, by an incredulous friend, how Callas (whose celebrated affair began in 1959) could have found Onassis attractive, Margot, who was as much the Greek shipping magnate's type as he was hers, protested: 'But Onassis was very sexy.'[16] She turned to her husband for support, and he could not have endorsed his wife's predilection for millionaires with greater relish. 'Most sexy man I ever met,' he decreed.[17]

The same could not be said for Arias himself, who, according to Jane Edgeworth, 'wasn't someone you'd fancy. But he could be very funny; and he was a marvellous ballroom dancer. And a quite brilliant international lawyer. Multilingual. He had enormous qualities that Margot must have admired. I learned a lot from Tito, and Margot trusted me because she knew what a male whore he was and she needed someone who would understand. I was leaving Covent Garden and going to the British Council and she asked me as a favour to go with him on a trip to buy Japanese ships for Onassis. But Tito was awful in many ways. He was jumping all round and over my bed – it was disgusting. I said, "Will you sod off, you silly, ugly person," and he just thought I was hilarious. I would never have discussed with Margot how difficult it all was, but I'm sure she knew.'

'There is no doubt that Tito thought about sex a bit too much,' says Colin Clark. 'When Tim Willoughby and I were invited by Onassis to a lunch party at Monte Carlo's Sporting Club – I suppose because Timmy was the grandest young milord available – Tito and Margot were there, and so was Callas, but Tito was taking no part in the conversation. "Come and see what I can do, Colin," he said, beckoning me to sit beside him. He took an orange from the table, got a little penknife out of his pocket and started to carve. After a few deft strokes, he turned it inside out and converted it into a huge phallus. I was so convulsed with laughter that the whole table stopped talking. "What are you doing, Tito darling?" called Margot. "Show us what you've got" . . . Poor Margot was really very prim and conventional. "Oh, Tito," she sighed.'[18]

Also high on Arias's list of types to be cultivated was 'dynamic, amusing, generous and attractive' Mike Todd.[19] In September 1957, he would come to see Margot at the Met in *Petrushka*, which, in its eerie Russian barbarity, was rather beyond the range of the Royal Ballet. Margot, meanwhile, as had long since been proved in *Coppélia*, was not at her lyrical best as a doll; but that was not Mike Todd's point when he railed at her: 'Why are you *dancing* that ballet? It's called *Petrushka*, isn't it? Are *you* Petrushka? No? Well, get out of it then.'[20]

No worries on that score about *Cinderella*, which Margot, as the eponymous heroine, had found time to record for NBC during the New York season of '55. Television, still in its black-and-white infancy, lacked the flattering finesse of film. Editing was a hit-and-miss process which had to be achieved live, in the studio, by means of cumbersome cameras, wheeled about at the will of the producer, who often had scant knowledge of the fundamentals of ballet; so it is little wonder that the *Cinderella* close-ups don't flatter Margot: in some shots she looks tired and strained and, frankly, her age. Yet at thirty-eight she was still a matchless urchin, and a few passages – notably the poignant sequences with the broom in the kitchen, where her mood sweeps delicately between playfulness and despair – remain as truly representative of her genius as anything that we possess on celluloid. Exhausted as she evidently was, there were still five months of touring to go, across the length and breadth of the United States and Canada, in Hurok's special train, dancing in a new town every few days, and spending Christmas, yet again, in Chicago. It was not until 25 January that the company returned to England.

During the next Covent Garden season, which ran from February to May 1956, the Ariases continued to entertain at Thurloe Place in their customary high style. At one of these parties, the new Brazilian Ambassador to London, Sr don Francisco Assis de Châteaubriand de Melho (more reasonably known as Château), had the inspired idea of inviting both Margot and her mother on a pilgrimage to the country of their ancestors; and certainly, in their respective accounts, the prose of both women rises to embrace the thrill of the whole adventure. Margot writes movingly of the plans for the still fledgling capital, Brasília, marked out, high on a plateau in a great sunbaked expanse of red earth, 'as though someone had scraped a great stick in the sand'.[21] Similarly Mrs Hookham tells of how 'the whole city was planned out in the shape of an arrow with a half-moon-shaped lake near the Palace' and of a church in Ouro Puerto, where 'the Virgin had a heavy-looking crown of jewels, diamonds and rubies and other stones, and pearls on her gown, and the whole Church just glittered with gold everywhere even to the nipples of the angels, which amused me'.

As Margot alights, in the middle of a tropical storm, from the President's plane on the island of São Luis, she cannot conceal her ironical amusement when, having caught her heel on the final step, she falls to her knees on the soil of her grandfather's birthplace. BQ, making a more careful descent from the presidential plane, notices '50 or 60 people standing holding photographs as tall as themselves of my father, the frame wreathed in flowers! It was a nice photograph of him, I imagine taken when he was in his mid-40s. Very good-looking and presumably rich.

He had done a lot for the little town and its people, apparently, and they loved him for it . . .'

Mother and daughter were taken to a small cottage a few miles from the airport, where, as BQ writes, 'Château ordered everybody except the reporters out . . . In a corner, sitting beneath a crucifix with candles burning all around was a very old lady who I believe had been the family Nanny. Margot ran to her and knelt at her feet and kissed her and the old lady with tears running down her cheeks said a few words and blessed her' – presumably unaware that Margot, though long-lost, was no legitimate descendant.

So taken was Margot with this whirlwind trip that, in June 1960, she would agree to join Ballet de Rio in a sparsely cast version of *Giselle*. To the twelve English dancers who were to tour with her, Margot would prove a revelation on two counts: her cheerfulness in the face of improvised and sometimes squalid working conditions, and the unexpected grandeur of her antecedents. 'She loved the gypsy life,' says Leslie Edwards. 'But when I saw the way her relations lived, I understood for the first time the formidable side of Margot, the side that could play the princess to the hilt.' Jill Gregory was also among those invited to lunch with Margot's autocratic widowed aunt, Macissi, widow of Mrs Hookham's half-brother, Ernest. 'We stopped somewhere to pick up two guards, and they got in with these large guns and we went quite a way up, to this large beautiful house over-looking a lake with mountains all around. Margot's aunt was seated at the head of the table and her servants all wore white gloves and, my goodness, she looked down the table and made some gesture and in a flash one of these gentlemen rushed round. She didn't like the way the knife and fork had been placed beside the plate – they weren't straight. It was a scene from a day-dream. And I thought: if this is what the family is like, no wonder they thought it was terrible to have someone on the stage. No wonder they wouldn't let her use the Fontes name.'

Whether Arias, whose name Margot now so proudly bore,

felt pleased or eclipsed by his wife's newly discovered cachet in his own neighbouring territory is a matter for speculation. His ventures, a dozen at once, in all parts of the world, were not going well. The power of the Arias family – one of the most elevated and influential in Panama – had waned. The brother of the then president, Don Ernesto de la Guardia, was in dispute with Tito's father over the country's bauxite resources, a dispute which was developing into a political confrontation between de la Guardia's authoritarian regime and the supporters of the more liberal branch of the Arias family. It was this quarrel that persuaded Tito, in March of 1958, to resign his ambassadorship. Not for the first time did his mind seethe with plans for revolution – plans which he discussed with all and sundry. Colin Clark remembers how, on visits to Saltwood, 'he would walk round the grounds telling me all about his problems in a series of almost incomprehensible grunts and mumbles . . . "It's so expensive," he would complain. "No one realizes how much a revolution costs. The telephone bills from London alone are incredible. Margot never makes a fuss" – guess who was paying? – "but one day they will bankrupt us. I swear that this will be my last revolution. As soon as my uncle is back in power, I'm going to stop plotting against him, and get him to give me a job." "How many revolutions have you had?" I asked. "This will be my seventh," said Tito in an absent sort of way. "But I've promised Margot it will be my last." '[22]

His wife was, by this stage, stumping up for rather more than the odd telephone bill. Tito's resources were not what they had appeared when he had wooed her with furs and diamonds, and chartered yachts to win Fred Ashton's blessing. Indeed his shipping company, after the building of his very first vessel, was on the verge of bankruptcy. Margot's quietly spoken, sleepy-eyed husband had only one ship to his name. And he called that ship the *Ondine*.

Ondine was supposed to be Margot's swan-song, or, at the very least, her chance to phase out further performances of the dreaded *Swan Lake* – the more dreaded given the trouble which her left foot was currently causing her. After all, Ulanova, who had not donned a tutu for years, nevertheless remained, even on the strength of her non-classical repertoire, unrivalled in the affection of the Russian public. A major new three-act ballet, specifically tailored to display Margot's interpretative strengths and to disguise what she believed to be her fast-diminishing technical prowess, was what Ashton had promised her as early as 1956, when he had considered adapting *The Tempest* or *Macbeth*. But (perhaps on the Mike Todd principle of never playing heroines who are not eponymous) neither Lady Macbeth nor Miranda had appealed to Margot. She did, however, consider 'ideal'[1] the notion of Undine, the water sprite – a sort of Teutonic Little Mermaid who emerges from the sea, falls in love with a mortal, and ends up killing him with a kiss.

Ashton had wanted to commission a score from William Walton; but the composer, being otherwise committed, recommended Hans Werner Henze. Ever since *Scènes de Ballet* had been shown in Berlin in 1948, Henze and Ashton had sustained a heightened correspondence of the passionate yet sublimated sort which steams towards artistic collaboration: 'To me,' wrote Ashton, 'you are Berlin & the whole charm of Germany – your blondness, your sentiment, your forthcoming warmth.'[2] For his own part, Henze extols Ashton's 'sense of elegance in human relationships . . . He was for me like a rope to climb up from the sea.'

But it was Ashton's converse inclination to descend to those imaginative depths which were his *Ondine*'s watery element: 'I wanted the movement to be fluid, like the rhythm of the sea, rather than a set of ballet steps . . . I spent hours watching water move, and have tried to give the choreography the surge and swell of waves.'[3] In the absence of da Vinci, whose sea drawings obsessed him, Ashton took Diana Cooper's advice and hired Lila de Nobili, famous for her beautiful monochrome 1955 version of *La Traviata*, directed by Visconti and starring Maria Callas. The designer, regardless of her shabby shawl and laddered stockings, seemed, to Ashton, the most aristocratic of women; her Sapphic bohemianism and high visual standards (she hand-painted her own backdrops) beguiled him utterly, and offered him some compensation for the loss of Sophie Fedorovitch. So potent was the rapport between designer and choreographer, and so unashamed their shared nostalgia for nineteenth-century Romanticism, that the much younger twentieth-century German composer, whose instinct it was to push the venture towards a more modern treatment, could not help feeling sidelined, not to say starved of the encouragement he needed in order to produce inspired work. 'A decision was taken that did not go in the direction the music went. The amount of discrepancy did not become obvious until the last rehearsals. The first act I wrote in Battersea and the rest at home in Naples, but, by then, the style had been established. It became a kind of ritual that Freddie would come to Battersea in the evening and listen to what I had done in the daytime, and then we would go over to Yeoman's Row and have some kind of dinner in the base-ment – Alexander Grant usually being present – and Freddie would criticize what I had done. Boxing me, hitting me, saying: "Give me a tune – I want a *tune*." He didn't recognize my tunes. The score is very tuneful.'

Time has proved the composer right: the score of *Ondine* is perfectly accessible to us now. But either Margot was as deaf to its melodies as Ashton, or she had been conditioned by the choreographer's reactionism. Certainly Henze found Ashton alarmingly possessive of his ballerina. 'I think she was kept away from me, like a secret I wasn't quite up to. She had difficulties with the music which, for a year or so, was from the piano score – a very insufficient informer of what is going on in terms of colours, rhythms, counterpoints, all that. And so Margot, it seems, was saying: "I can't hear it, I can't hear it." I would have rushed to London and explained the music myself and played it to them, but I was never asked. In the end, I found a sympathetic orchestra and recorded it from beginning to end, and the dancers worked from the tape. I had the impression she didn't want me to come nearer than I was.'

But Fonteyn and Ashton were long accustomed to a hermetic method of working. Frustration and limitation pressed them to shared feats of inventiveness. In an interview with Peter Brinson, Margot explains: 'Sometimes Henze's score . . . just didn't seem to say the same things as the scenario. Take, for example, the little mime about Palemon's heart in the first act. Ondine comes out of the water. Palemon sees her and loves her. After this, in the original version, Ondine was attracted by Palemon's amulet and snatched it away. When he took it back she became petulant and angry. But when we did that scene it seemed false, especially musically. So now Ondine replaces the amulet round Palemon's neck because she is newly interested in him rather than the amulet. At that moment he presses her hand to his heart. She is frightened by his heartbeat (Ondines don't have hearts, you know) and jumps back with surprise. Then, overcome by curiosity, she puts her hand over his heart to feel it beat again.'[4]

Of exactly such detailed and delicate moments was Margot's portrayal of Ondine constructed; and the ballet, which, even in its own mythological terms, is a virtual allegory of the compulsive, elusive bond between artist and muse, marked the apex of collaboration between Ashton and Fonteyn. 'Things you've been trying to get me to do all my life,' she confessed to him in rehearsal,'I'm at last beginning to understand.'[5] Take, for instance, the way he made her use her eyes. Never had she widened them to more eloquent effect than when she rose through the fountain as Ondine taking her first, hesitant steps on dry land. 'Dancers today don't understand what eyes are for,' Ashton persistently complained. 'With your eyes properly used you can distract everybody from your technique. You draw the public to you with your eyes.'[6] *And* you reduce your colleagues to sobbing wrecks. 'At the first full rehearsal,' says Annette Page, 'when we saw Margot for the first time as Ondine, the whole room was in tears, not only because she was so wonderful and moving, but because we all felt that this was going to be her last thing.'

Ondine was premièred, after several postponements, on 27 October 1958. 'From the moment the watery nymph steps timidly out from the waterfall,' wrote the *Sunday Times* reviewer, 'feeling with wonder the texture of dry rock and foliage, her character is established. The solo which follows, as she darts around, a delicious sex-minnow, shaking drops delightedly and flirting with that delicious acquisition a shadow (this is Ashton's version of Cerrito's famous *pas de l'ombre*), is enchanting. From then on Fonteyn hardly leaves the stage. Whether she is luring the hero into the magic wood, trying to soothe the storm which threatens their ship, or – finally – reappearing from the depths into which she has been snatched, to give her faithless lover the kiss of death, she never loses for a moment the shy grace and little-girl tenderness which are her special qualities. Her part, largely written in variations of *arabesque* and *attitude* which flow liquidly across the music, requires acting and an effortless smoothness. It gets both. This is a fine performance.'[7] But a performance executed in a vacuum. 'Gone,' continued the *Sunday Times*, 'was all pretence to democracy within the company.' The *Observer* agreed. 'The hero, Palemon (Michael Somes) is a handsome dummy; Berta, the land-based Other Girl (Julia Farron) is a conventionalized hard nut, whose relationship with Palemon is not explored (she doesn't even have a *pas de deux* with him, while Ondine has no fewer than five – one of them of inordinate length). Tyrrenio the Sea-God (Alexander Grant) and the Hermit (Leslie Edwards) are understandably impersonal.'

Ondine was Ashton's 'Fonteyn-concerto',[8] and she (according to Henze) 'his violin'. Music-making apart, there was the astonishing *sheen* of the instrument. Margot's thirty-nine-year-old body, openly on show beneath the transparent bluish-green wisps of costume (unashamedly designed along the high-waisted lines of Bolshoi practice dresses), had never looked more beautiful: pared down, yet still softly girlish in every flesh-tinted contour. The visual impact evinced an almost fetishistic response from Cyril Beaumont: 'With her pale, intensely expressive features framing her dark trailing hair like floating sea-grass, her spume-coloured dress spotted with dew, she creates the illusion of a being from another sphere, infinitely curious about the strange world of mortals . . . Fonteyn owes Ashton much, but Ondine is perhaps his greatest gift.'[9] And indeed Margot, who had once professed not to 'have a favourite anything', came to love *Ondine* more than any other Ashton role. 'It was the ballet I had dreamed of, and worked for, and waited for him to create. It was the perfect character for me, naïve, shy, loyal and loving, and a creature of the sea.'[10] She even preferred it to Chloë, on account of its directness and simplicity. 'Chloë's innocence is a human innocence,' she said in interview. 'Ondine is innocent in a different way, for she has no knowledge of the perfidy and deceits of Man.'[11]

But innocence was fast losing fashionable sway. As the 50s drew to a close, a new moral atmosphere was afoot – a transformative sexual climate in which Margot's abiding air of purity risked proving, at the least, inapplicable, and, at most, obsolete. May 1956 had seen the opening in London of John Osborne's *Look Back in Anger*, a play destined to wipe the middle-class smugness from the face of British drama. *Ondine*, despite being a welcome star-vehicle for a revered ballerina, provoked among the intelligentsia considerable disquiet regarding the artistic strategy of the Royal Ballet. The notion that modern emotions could be roused by ancient myths struck Alexander Bland as 'aesthetic taxidermy. The nymphs of the nineteenth century are as dead as the shepherdesses of the eighteenth. Only the violent twist of a Picasso or Cocteau can revive them. In spite of the superimposition of contemporary music, Ondine, with her grottoes and amulets, is rooted in the dead past. To have her displayed before our eyes so exquisitely is an extraordinary achievement for sputnik-year. But one day ballet will sink altogether if it does not shed its cargo of Victorian clichés.'[12]

In a letter to Cecil Beaton, Lincoln Kirstein was contemptuous of the conventions espoused by Ashton. 'My private opinion is that he works under conditions that cannot produce really great work. He should refuse to do three-act ballets; they are not in our tempo. He is not Petipa. Margot is a marvellous dancer, but she should be shown as herself, not as some echo of a 19th century star. Ninette is not Nicholas II. Today is 1958. The Maryinsky Theatre is not Covent Garden and Henze is not Tchaikovsky . . . The Royal Ballet has no intellectual direction, no contact with necessity, that is WHAT IS ACTUALLY NEEDED for its public . . . it has a great theatre, a subsidy, and it is a national object of veneration, and Ninette is a combination of Montgomery of Alamein and Mrs Bowdler. If I had anything to do with it, I would blast the place open.'[13]

That blast was coming. The Royal Ballet now comprised two distinct institutions: the major company, based at Covent Garden, and a smaller, more junior one, which still had its London season at the Sadler's Wells Theatre, and undertook the less illustrious provincial tours. This latter troupe, confusingly called 'The Royal Ballet, formerly the Sadler's Wells Theatre Ballet', was emphatically *not* to be known as the second company, which of course, by the dancers, it instantly and incorrigibly was. And, even by nature of its forbidden, steerage-class appellation, there was an alternative flavour to its activities: under the direction, initially, of Peggy Van Praagh, and next, John Field, it harboured dancers of a certain stroppy waywardness, toughened and emancipated by the necessity to perform more often and in less favourable circumstances than their more cosseted colleagues at Covent Garden. To members of the second company, Ashton and Fonteyn and their immediate entourage were known as the Royal Family. And into this potentially revolutionary atmosphere there had come, in July 1957, a shy, unsophisticated Canadian girl, who considered her round, sweet face to be 'like a full moon . . . so ugly',[14] and whose name – Berta Lynn Springbett – de Valois was bound to write off as 'preposterous'.[15] Enter, then, Lynn Seymour.

If Margot's physique was, even by her own admission, perfectly right for ballet ('The secret of my lasting so long is probably a simple one: it lies in my well-balanced proportions, which distribute the stresses evenly over the whole skeletal structure'[16]), then Lynn Seymour's was perfectly wrong. Christopher Gable, her most trusted partner, has said: 'She was fighting with an appallingly difficult body which, to a greater or lesser extent, she has been fighting with [throughout] her whole career. It is an amazingly fluid, flexible body that would express, even then, almost every nuance that she was thinking; and this, of course, is a glorious asset for a dancer to have. But the price you pay for this kind of fluidity is that the muscle structure is not built to take the stress. Consequently the technique was weak at this stage.'[17]

Oh, but the way she moved! 'When Lynn dances,' Nureyev was later to claim, 'heaven descends into your lap'[18] – 'lap' being the operative word, for there was something visceral about her approach, something raw and authentically voluptuous that made her contemporaries, so many of them faithful reproductions of Margot, look arch and cosmetic. Kenneth MacMillan, whose dark, brooding choreographic talent had been fostered in the second company, spotted Seymour in a *corps de ballet* rehearsal. 'She did one movement, and it struck me that I had never seen a dancer do a movement so beautifully before. It was a *temps levé* in *arabesque*, which is one of the simplest steps in the whole vocabulary of dance. Yet it had a freedom that young dancers then didn't possess.'[19] On the strength of that fleeting revelation, he cast her as the female adolescent in his new one-act ballet *The Burrow*, based not on any ancient classical myth but on a searing account of shocking modern history: *The Diary of Anne Frank*. And thus began a new professional love-affair which would come to rival the mystical bond between Ashton and Fonteyn. MacMillan said of his rapport with Seymour: 'It was as if we shared the same brain. She would come to the same conclusion as I would about a movement at exactly the same time. It was uncanny. I don't know how it happened, and I still don't.'[20]

Like Margot before her, Seymour, at the tender age of seventeen, had to struggle to understand that the almost frightening degree of intensity between muse and mentor was artistic rather than carnal. Of her relationship with MacMillan she wrote to a friend: 'I discovered my joy in being with him was really due to his way of transmitting *his* world to me and greatly appreciating what *I* had to offer him. You can imagine how my heart soared with that realization.'[21]

But youthful hearts that soar stand, in the harsh fullness of time, to be broken. And, just at the time when the MacMillan/Seymour alliance was being forged, Margot was beginning to suffer the rejection which so often follows upon deep affinity, be it of body or soul. Ashton, after *Ondine* had been perceived as Fonteyn's success and his honourable failure, resolved never to build a full-scale ballet around her again; and although, eventually, his stance would weaken, he held to it for five long years. No less reprehensibly, he silently stood by – even as the directorship of the Royal Ballet was passing into his hands – while the management began to treat Margot with a shabbiness which her twenty-four-year loyalty to the company should have made unthinkable. Speaking with hindsight, at the end of her own career, Lynn Seymour says: 'Fred was getting sick of her. She was getting all the kudos and maybe he thought he wasn't getting enough. The choreographers Ashton, Cranko and MacMillan all had dancers they worked really, really closely with, and had success through. Ashton thought he could manage without Margot. Cranko did the same thing to Marcia Haydée: once she'd done the business and was his person, he started giving her very awkward roles and bringing in weird people and giving her unfriendly things to do. MacMillan did the same thing to me. There was something about their insecurity that made them want to dump those ballerinas who were their original inspiration. All three of us were treated with equal cruelty.'

Whether the souring of relations between Margot and the administrative board at Covent Garden was really the result of Ashton's growing disenchantment with her as his Terpsichore is doubtful. To judge from the timing, a more likely explanation would be the management's resolve to distance itself from the embarrassing political activities of Arias. Margot had never seriously believed that her husband's revolution would happen. 'It came to be a sort of romantic jaunt in my mind, an idea that we lived with for quite a long time.'[22] Whenever the plans were discussed she would collapse into schoolgirl giggles, egged on by Tito, who would invent fanciful scenarios for her amusement: 'Tito's favourite plot, never alas carried out, was the idea of a masked ball at which all the male guests would be invited to go dressed as the President – who had a distinctive small moustache and smooth hairstyle. When the party reached full swing the real people would be unobtrusively hustled away, and taken out of the country aboard a yacht, preferably Errol Flynn's to add colour to the coup.'[23]

However, her naïve stance must have become tricky to sustain when, early in January 1959, while headed for a week's holiday in Acapulco, Tito suddenly announced that 'it would be interesting to go to Havana'.[24] It was a move that horrified both his father, Harmodio, and his sister, Rosario, whose own sister-in-law happened, ironically, to be the *primera dama* of Panama – the wife of President de la Guardia. 'Tito did many things politically that Father and I didn't agree with. He went with Margot to Cuba. They played with the Left, for what purposes I don't know. He was unwise politically. It was strange because he could be so intelligent in other ways.'

What had happened was that another Caribbean revolution had suddenly come to a triumphant conclusion. The hated Batista had fled Cuba on New Year's Eve, and Castro, with his *barbudos* (bearded ones), had come down from the hills to claim the running of the country. Castro's party was left-wing but not

Communist, and, before it was delivered by the Americans into the arms of the Russians, seemed to herald a new era of freedom. Tito had gleaned that Castro was ideally placed, both politically and geographically, to assist his own revolutionary plans; so, within two days of Castro's entry into Havana, he had re-routed himself and Margot from New York to Cuba.

The couple took a room at the Havana Hilton, which was teeming with young men in green overalls and bushy black beards, all heavily armed, since Castro had established his head-quarters on the top floor. Thanks to Tito's friendship with President Urrutia's secretary, Dr and Mrs Arias were taken to meet the head of state, who was still in the process of settling into the palace. Tito and Margot were made to wait in one of the bedrooms, where Urrutia's wife, along with some of her friends, was ransacking the wardrobes of Mme Batista, who had left rack upon rack of clothes. The new president organized a meeting for Tito and Margot with the Paramount Leader – Castro himself; and in due course they were ushered into the top floor of the hotel. Flanked by a bevy of whiskered officers and surrounded by the remains of half-eaten meals, a very tall figure with a deep and mesmerizing voice rose to greet them. Castro and Tito held a lengthy discussion, in Spanish, of which Margot professes to have understood not a jot. Irrespective of this claim, she can hardly have failed to interpret the tone of the meeting, which, she would have us believe, was cordial. In point of fact, Castro is known to have screamed: 'What do you, Tito, an old man, know of politics and government? It takes youth, man, youth!'[25]

The youthful beauty of the 'bearded ones', with their 'candid soft eyes looking out from their would-be ferocious faces', certainly captivated Margot, who, back in 1940, had shown such marked animation in the company of the Dutch soldiers at Velsen. She seems to have succeeded in overlooking the reali-ties of war by immersing herself, with the obsessive attention to detail of a costumier, in the trappings of conflict. The boy in charge of them 'wore a green cotton battle-dress, and the soft army cap, so familiar now in photographs of Castro. Several hand-grenades and a knife decorated his trim waistline, and he held a menacing firearm, which he looked much too young to control. I was enchanted by the idea of this picturesque youth guarding my baggage and helping me into a taxi.'[26] Later, passing through New York on the way home, Margot took the fashion-story further when she and Tito lunched with Judy Tatham, an English friend who happened to be working in the Manhattan rag trade at the time. Tatham, who coincidentally went on to marry one of Margot's former lovers, Charles Hassé, was recruited to drum up 500 Kelly-green shirts, with short sleeves and pockets, 'for cartridges and things'. Nora Kaye, visiting Margot at her hotel, was astounded to find her friend in the basement, engaged in a spot of gun-practice. 'It was so outside Nora's experience of her,' said Herbert Ross, 'that they drifted apart after that. Nora couldn't cope with Margot as President-ess, painted by Annigoni in Panamanian dress.'

The portrait in question – by the artist who had so contro-versially flattered the Queen – now graced the drawing-room at Thurloe Place, whither Annigoni had come a year earlier to familiarize himself with his subject. 'We were told that a guest was coming for lunch,' says Margaret Hewitt, 'and this man turned up and I thought he was a tramp, he looked so scruffy and disreputable. He painted the hands and face at his studio, but for the actual dress he could do without Margot being there.' Maurice Lambert (brother of Constant), who had made a sculp-ture of Margot at around the same time, also had to contend with an elusive model: the legs on the finished work are those of Georgina Parkinson. It is almost impossible for someone who is not Degas, or has not been a dancer, to capture the subtle musculature peculiar to ballet training, but the eyes are very much Margot's, with their theatrically-enhanced lashes made of strands of wire. The tutu, of metal gauze, is arrayed with the signs of the Zodiac – a reference to Constant Lambert and *Horoscope*. Like his dead brother before him, Maurice Lambert fell madly in love with Margot, and, in 1956, when the life-size figure was exhibited in the octagon of the Royal Academy, took to sleeping, revolver in hand, beside his creation, lest any intruder should cause it harm. The statue now poses on *pointe* in the foyer at White Lodge, where the young ballet students, before exams and demonstrations, habitually touch forefingers with their heroine for good luck. The bronze has visibly worn. Yet Margot's hands, according to Fiore de Henriquez, who, in the mid-40s, made the most accomplished head of Fonteyn that exists, were not easy to sculpt. 'She had ugly hands. She managed to do something with them so you never noticed. Maybe I make a mistake, but, to me, she was not beautiful. In repose, without dancing, she was like a flower, something gay, something laughing. But, to me, beautiful is another thing.'

Rosario de Galindo, bred to appreciate the delicately boned, natural elegance of South American women, reiterates this discrepancy between's Margot's onstage and offstage attractiveness. 'If you saw Margot at an airport or on a bus, and you didn't know who she was, you wouldn't have looked at her twice. She wasn't a person who struck you as extraordinarily graceful. Her hands were rather ugly. Her feet – my God – well, they *had* to become that way.'

'The ugly little frog that she is becomes a beauty through the quality of her spirit,' Cecil Beaton would later write,[27] in unkind echo of Karsavina's '*Pas belle, mais belle pour la scène.*' No wonder that the film director Patricia Foy tells us that 'Margot never believed that she was pretty.' And it may have been this self-doubt – the fear of how her face would appear in close-up – that had kept her for so long from the screen. But now that she had been depicted for posterity in statue form, it was inevitable that – too late, perhaps, for expediency, and against her own better judgement – she should allow her moving image to be preserved on film. Dr Paul Czinner, an admired director from Vienna, who had propelled to fame, and married, the actress Elisabeth Bergner, had already produced the feature-film *The Bolshoi Ballet* in 1957. He was now set to repeat that success in English terms for the Rank Organization, with a cinematic record of Act II *Swan Lake*, *The Firebird* and *Ondine*. The film was to be called *The Royal Ballet* – a title which suggested the broadest possible airing of individual achievement within the company. The three proposed works might well have been specifically selected to accommodate the varying and contrasting gifts of the three senior ballerinas: Fonteyn – being of course indelibly identified with Ondine; Nerina – whose spectacular attack and *ballon* (bounce) cast her as an obvious Firebird; and Beriosova – acclaimed by now as a legendary Odette. But although Czinner's film of the Russians had featured Raisa Struchkova and Lyudmila Bogomolova as well as the great Ulanova, *The Royal Ballet* was to star – in red, white, and eau-de-nil – Margot, Margot, and Margot.

The film which, by orthodox methods, would have taken three months to commit to celluloid in the studio, was shot over three days (two Sundays and one all-night session) at the Royal Opera House, using eleven cameras, each with four positions, these dotted around the stalls, boxes and gallery to achieve forty-four different angles. Mrs Hookham, a lone figure in the circle, watching the Firebird stop and start to the frustrating tempo of movie-making, admitted to the *Daily Mail* that Margot was loathing every minute of it, and not just on account of all the hanging about. 'She hates making films because times change. Famous people in old films are only made fun of in later years. But I thought she ought to make this one film, if only for the future. She is the purest exponent of this style of dancing, and it is only right that up-and-coming generations should have a chance of seeing her.'[28] The reporter asked, as well he might, whether, on this issue, Margot had been in receipt of motherly advice. 'Nothing of the sort,' snorted the redoubtable BQ. 'Wouldn't do any good. Did *you* take notice of *your* mother's advice?'[29]

Once the film was in the can, Margot's next stop was Japan. She rather dreaded this trip, for her Chinese childhood had caused her to resent the Japanese, who, after all, had interned her father in Shanghai. But her prejudice was confounded by a people whom she and Michael Somes discovered to 'have such a refinement of manners that Westerners feel gauche and boorish, and tone down their strident ways to mingle better with their hosts'[30] – only to have to tone them up again when, after guest appearances in Tokyo, Kyoto, Nagoya and Takalazuka, the pair travelled southwards to join up with the touring company in strident Sydney. She and Michael were old campaigners by now – she, nursing that ever-troublesome left foot; he, still battling with his old war-time knee injury. Gone were the days when, on those far-flung, protracted tours, they would occasionally banish loneliness by toppling into bed together in a spirit of camaraderie as much as of carnality. 'The old girl needs servicing sometimes,' Somes is reported to have said,[31] while Margot had told Nora Kaye: 'Michael's a poppet. It doesn't mean anything.'[32] But they had grown beyond such light-hearted frolics – Margot because of her marital status, and Somes because of the sudden, shocking death from meningitis of his young wife, Deirdre Dixon. Yet they still played faithful consort to one another on social occasions, honouring the responsibilities of their partnership off-stage as well as on – this despite their great differences of temperament: 'There were so *many* parties and receptions,' says Somes, 'and what used to madden me about her was that she would say, "We'll just go for twenty minutes," and then she'd be off like a bullet. She was very strong. She could restore herself, recharge her batteries very well. You'd be finished rehearsing by twelve o'clock, so you'd go and have lunch, and then she'd go to bed, and she'd be able to sleep until five o'clock and that was another day for her. She'd get up, prepare for the performance which went on until late, and then she'd want to go out and giggle with local friends or dancers or whatever. I'd be dying, longing to go home, but I felt I couldn't leave her. And then, what was worse, she'd finally say, "Class at ten, must go home," etc., and *finally* we'd get the taxi, *finally* get back to the hotel and there'd be two or three people still with her and she'd say, "Darling, come up and have coffee or a drink," and I'd think, "Oh no!" And on it would go again. She was one of those people who just can't say goodnight.'

But as the tour moved on to New Zealand, taking in Christchurch, Wellington and Auckland, Margot was beginning to feel that the effort was all uphill. 'We had rather a posh do,' says Anne Heaton, 'and I said to Margot: "Oh God, I wish I'd bought some shoes to go with my new dress," and she said: "I've got some shoes," so we went up to her room and looked through and I borrowed some. I was very tired at the time because I'd done the whole tour, and we got to commiserating with each other about how hard a dancer's life was, and she said to me: "You know, I can't go on very much longer. It takes such push, such drive. If I can't do it as well as I used to be able to, I don't want to do it any more. I really am thinking very seriously about packing it in." '

An old friend was on hand to make her think again – or at least think more broadly about her sense of duty to posterity. Bobby Helpmann, now aged forty-nine, had returned home to a more tolerant Australia than the one which he had left, and, between performances of Noël Coward's *Nude with Violin*, was gracing the touring company with the odd guest appearance. It was he who persuaded Margot that the time had come for her to rise above her lifelong antipathy to teaching and hand down a few pointers to a young ballerina whose dramatic gifts he passionately endorsed. The dancer he had in mind was Lynn Seymour. Here is her version of the story: 'Margot had arrived in Christchurch to guest on the last two dates of what had been a six-month antipodean tour. I had debuted in *Swan Lake* on my nineteenth birthday, some five months earlier. And in the interim had danced around forty performances. During that time, John Field had asked the other visiting stars – Robert Helpmann, Svetlana Beriosova and Rowena Jackson – to take me and my partner, Donald MacLeary, through our paces, passing on tips, knowledge, and making suggestions. We were thrilled and not a little nervous to hear that Margot had agreed to do the same. The rehearsal was inauspiciously and cruelly scheduled at 10 a.m., necessitating a 9 a.m. warm-up, after having performed the night before. Margot asked me to begin, with Odette's entrance into the enchanted forest. I ran on two or three steps, and was stopped. Not for running clumsily or executing an ungainly *jeté* but for looking back over my shoulder as I ran. Now, this "look" wasn't a random gaze, but something I had thought long and hard about. And felt it indicated I had momentarily left a dreadful Rothbart behind me for a moment's respite. I became utterly demoralized, as, one by one, my carefully considered "moments" were summarily given the chop. I was in such a turmoil that I became clumsier and clumsier until I could scarcely dance. Here was I, an absolute beginner, in complete disagreement with the world's greatest ballerina! The other stars respected the interpretation I had been developing, and had concentrated on technical execution – which in my case was unreliable . . . Margot's approach left me utterly demoralized and it all ended in tears. I never wanted to dance again. Oh youth! Poor Margot. I was led to understand that this episode caused her to make a silent vow never to coach again which, thank God, she didn't keep. Nor did it cause me to stop dancing. Even with the benefit of hindsight, though, I think my reaction would have been similar, for I utterly believed, and still do, that it is each dancer's right and responsibility to seek and find their own way. Indeed, it is how you become an artist. This search was, for me, the reason to dance and why it remains a passion. I know that Margot came to understand and respect this. And was probably happy to know that I had no intention of challenging her territory.'[33]

But another territorial dispute was developing thousands of miles from the strains of Tchaikovsky. And Margot was about to take centre stage in a drama that would leave her colleagues gaping.

Dispirited as she was by her work, Margot craved, more than ever, that thing for which marriage, beyond the propagation of children, is designed: consolation. She looked forward to a well-earned holiday with her husband, and flew, straight from Auckland to San Francisco, towards what she believed would be his equally impatient arms. It was 9 April 1959. No sooner had the plane landed than she rang Tito in Panama to find out where, after their two-month separation, they could be reunited. But, despite his claims that things were 'a bit strained here . . . it might be rather uncomfortable for you',[1] his eager wife was not to be discouraged: Margot insisted that she would be taking the first morning flight out, and Tito, after his initial misgivings, was finally won round. Next, Margot telephoned Judy Tatham in New York, who, having recently returned from 'some mysterious mission' in Panama, regaled her with a long description of goings-on out there, highlighting her account with the snippet that, trusting in the Customs' 'sense of decorum', she had succeeded in smuggling two boxes of emblematic brassards past the officials, by secreting them in 'packets of [sanitary] napkins'.[2] (In Margot's autobiography, she claims that 'the whole thing sounded like *Modesty Blaise*, and about as believable' – which might explain why, in that very paragraph, she elects, with her consummate belief in 'modesty', to spare the reader's blushes over matters menstrual by converting the objects of concealment into 'Teddy bears'.) But Margot had no time to chatter.

Beyond her wish to recover from the long trip from Auckland, her overriding concern was 'not wanting to look terrible . . . next day'.[3] Which meant: rising early, rushing to the hairdresser for an overdue tint, and on to the beauty salon, before boarding her flight to Panama. Attention to such details would pay dividends, for, unbeknown to Margot, this was the eleventh hour of Tito's simmering revolution, which would have to take place in advance of the notorious rainy season. The plan of action, though simple enough, had much to recommend it. Two bands of students were to be sent, with the purpose of fuelling discontent among the peasantry, to strategic locations in the mountains overlooking the country's richest agricultural regions – near the Costa Rican border (coffee), and in the central provinces (sugar and cattle). The underlying rationale was that the Guardia Civil should thus be distracted away from the densely populated areas, notably Panama City and Colón, and the seeds of apprehension be sown among provincial landowners. Once these objectives had been achieved, Tito, ostensibly fishing in the Bay of Panama, was to alight at Caimito, an obsolete fishing harbour, proceed overland to the neighbouring provincial town of Chorrera, and block off Panama's sole highway to the interior.

At this point, further groups of students were to emerge from their urban hideaways and sever the capital in half, thereby splitting the rich from the poor, the well-heeled from the downtrodden; and, confining the activities of the police to the needless part of town, limit its protection to Panama's past, rather than to its burgeoning future. The final stage of Tito's scheme was that Cuban-trained guerrillas should make a sea-landing on the Atlantic coast of the Isthmus and take control of a key checkpoint on the road from Colón to Panama, separating the two terminus-cities – after which the various groups of rebels could join forces, march jubilantly into the capital, and proclaim their victory.

But events did not quite go according to plan. A twenty-strong faction of students in the provinces, too eager by half, burst into a village store in Santiago a week before time, seized a shotgun and some shells, and proclaimed that the revolution had come – thus providing President de la Guardia and his government with premature intelligence of Tito's intended bid for power. To exacerbate matters, Rubén Miró, a cousin of the

Arias family, was simultaneously broadcasting in Cuba that he was at the head of a revolutionary uprising in Panama – presumably with the intention of earning himself, in the instance of the plot's success, some nepotistic advantage.

When, next day, Margot stepped off the plane, her husband was nowhere apparent – neither on the runway tarmac nor in the arrivals lounge. Friends eventually hustled her through to his closed car outside; but, despite Tito's distracted countenance and 'noncommittal replies', Margot, relieved to be 'free of all the worries about preparing *pointe* shoes and practice clothes and getting to the theatre on time . . . put everything out of [her] mind and felt utterly carefree'.[4] The couple were driven to the El Panama Hotel, because their own apartment, overlooking the picturesque bay, with its shrimp-boats and fishers and nets, was not yet adequately furnished. But, once at the hotel, Tito kept switching rooms – in case, he explained, they should have to make a quick getaway. By midnight he had grown so uneasy that they transferred to an entirely strange apartment, seemingly surrounded by Guardias Nacionales – this, Tito assured Margot, only because they were next to the house of the Assistant Chief of Police. 'No one,' he reasoned, 'would think of looking for me so close.'[5] But, by daybreak, they were on the move again – to their own, ill-equipped, apartment. Although Margot spent a few days here, she and Tito never slept at the same location twice: 'Once it was a disused retreat in a tower above the family's newspaper office; [another] sitting in the car in a country lane, and another . . . calming some young rebels who were getting impatient in their hideout.'[6]

At mid-morning on Wednesday the 15th, Margot was fluttering around the new apartment when Tito rang to suggest a fishing trip. She duly packed a bag, and, as instructed, went to meet him at the family's newspaper office. But when she arrived, although she ran into two of the Arias brothers, Modi and Gilberto, both in a state of high Latin excitement, Tito seemed to have vanished. It eventually transpired that a warrant had been issued for his arrest, and that he had bolted down a staircase, shouting orders that Margot should be driven by Gloria, the company secretary (and, according to Margot, the only level-headed person in the place), to the Yacht Club in Balboa, which, being located within the Canal Zone, wasn't under Panamanian jurisdiction and therefore provided a safe haven.

Here Margot waited in the blistering sunshine at the end of a long pier, until, an hour later, Tito, driven by a friend, Moreno Góngora, came rolling up to describe how he had escaped from the newspaper offices – bundled in the back of a company van which had been speeding off to deliver the noon edition. The van had been tailed by Góngora, who, as soon as Tito was within the Canal Zone, had picked him up. But, from this point on, the revolution was doomed to descend into farce.

Tito hurried Margot aboard a small launch, the *Nola*, which, having cast off, headed out into the bay, for all the world as if the suggested fishing trip were a reality – Margot, carrying her cine-camera and dressed in a crisp, white *piqué* shirtwaister; Tito, briefcase in hand, looking as if he were merely taking a break from work. Margot describes the time she spent on board during the next five days as 'idyllic'. Most of the 'business' (making contact with twenty-one confederates who were supposed to be awaiting them on a shrimp-boat, the *Elaine*) took place at night; and, during the day, the couple were able to enjoy 'long snoozes' while the boat lurked in hidden coves and inlets along the coast.[7]

Once Tito had located the shrimp-boat, he discovered that there were only eight, somewhat anxious, revolutionaries aboard. Of these, Margot seems particularly to have been struck by the sinister 'expressionless face'[8] of one Alfredo Jimenez. At any rate, Tito and Margot joined the gang and set off on their mission: to track down a small speedboat being driven by Bill Sutra (captain of their honeymoon yacht), which was carrying an arsenal of weapons concealed under a false bottom. The boat was found, but, being unnaturally heavy, sank while being towed behind them, with the result that the group was compelled, at dusk on the following day, to return and haul it aboard the

Elaine; whereupon the eight youths decided to prise open the cases of arms, and festoon themselves with rifles, hand-guns and decorative grenades.

It was next discovered that the steering of the *Elaine* had been damaged; so when the sun rose she dropped anchor and Tito and Margot returned to their original yacht, the *Nola*. That evening they met up with a second shrimp-boat, in order that the revolutionaries and their arms could be transferred; and while the *Elaine* slouched back towards Panama, the *Nola* and the new vessel set off for the Pearl Islands, fifty miles out in the Pacific. Margot admits that she viewed the whole enterprise 'in *Boys' Own Paper* terms'.[9] The smell of the shrimp-boat, and the swell of the ocean, and the very dangers that they were running, seem to have filled her with a juvenile excitement.

But by the following Saturday, events had grown graver. Having learned from the radio that the crew of the *Elaine* had been arrested, it became clear that a search was now under way for the remainder of the rebels. During the night, a boat without lights could just be made out, and, at dawn, a light spotter-plane began to swoop low over the *Nola* and its fellow shrimp-boat. Everything pointed to the fact that the revolution had collapsed. Tito clambered across to the shrimp-boat and held a conference with the young rebels. It has been suggested that, had they had enough fuel, they would have taken the shrimp-boat to Costa Rica. It has also been suggested that Tito wanted to land back in Panama, in order to deflect the Guardias' interest from other friends and arms-caches on the Isthmus. But what was, even then, beyond doubt was that Margot could not accompany Tito. She understood that 'a woman would be too much of a liability'.[10] Instead, she was to remain aboard the *Nola*, sailing, by way of decoy, in great circles along the coast, and, in due course, return ashore. Tito leapt on to the shrimp-boat, while Margot, at their parting, is said to have stood with 'her chin . . . high and her shoulders back in an expression of brave encouragement'.[11]

Not until Tito's boat had disappeared from view did she

permit despair to overcome her; but even her tears, when they came, were decorously shed – for the sake of the captain, 'black, poor and compassionate'[12] Aguinaldo Dawkins, whose lamentations about his wife knowing nothing of his whereabouts, and, what was worse, being short of housekeeping money, Margot assumed to be his discreet attempt to take her mind off worrying about Tito. Discretion notwithstanding, Dawkins would later fasten a painted commemorative sign to the *Nola*: MARGOT LLORÓ AQUÍ (Margot Wept Here).[13]

But when the captain and Margot finally reached the harbour of the Yacht Club, they discovered that the royal yacht *Britannia* was about to set off after an official visit by the Duke of Edinburgh. Margot had 'half a mind to go alongside and ask for admittance',[14] but, even if the 'special' status which she is rumoured to have enjoyed with the Prince would have prompted him to haul her aboard, her sense of duty seems to have overcome her coquettish desire for succour. Instead, she telephoned her sister-in-law and was collected in due course. After very little sleep, she rose early to meet with Tito's mother, 'a kindly, imperturbable lady [whose] features clearly reveal[ed] the beauty of her youth',[15] in order to confess her 'negligence at not holding Tito back'. But the family matriarch, whose husband had twice been President of the Republic, and whose brother-in-law had thrice been overthrown, was philosophical about political farragos. 'Putting her head back a little and half-closing her eyes, as though recalling memories, she said, "Never mind, never mind. Tito always comes back."'[16]

On the night of Monday 20 April, Margot, wearing up-to-the-minute Dior, was a guest at La Cresta, the house of Tito's sister and brother-in-law, the Galindos. As she dined beside a turquoise pool on a paved courtyard dripping with orchids, the comedy of Caribbean skulduggery spiralled into a saga of family errors. Señor Galindo's sister happened, somewhat inconveniently, to be married to President de la Guardia, who, claiming not to 'believe in "sacred cows"', wanted Margot arrested; but his wife, the *primera dama*, would not hear of it, not *here*. 'No. To seize

[Margot] while at the table of my brother cannot be. To do so would be in the worst tradition of the Borgias. She must be lured elsewhere!'[17] And lured she was. The President's chief of secret police, Señor Valdez, made a quick call to La Cresta, and, claiming that Panama was in such turmoil that Margot could not be assumed to be safe in her hotel, suggested that she sleep at his house, two doors away from the Galindos – a ploy for which Margot fell: 'At last, I thought, I will get a good night's sleep!'[18]

But ten minutes after her weary head had hit the pillow, she was roused by a distressed Señora Valdez and told that she was wanted for questioning by the District Attorney. In a limousine outside, looking so jittery that Margot didn't recognize him, Max Heutermatte, formerly Panamanian Ambassador to Paris and a guest at her wedding, was waiting to ferry her for her interview with the Fiscal. She was duly driven through the enormous gates of the Cárcel Modelo (Model Gaol), and, once within the compound, delivered to the charge of the Major on duty, Araúz. 'Several Guardias,' says Margot, 'were standing around, jack-booted and battle-helmeted, hung about the waist with guns and truncheons . . . They looked at me with curiosity, and I held my head high in disdain.'[19]

The Major expressed surprise that, while she waited to be interrogated, Margot should not appear nervous. But Margot, who had been musing about 'resistance fighters . . . taken in by the Gestapo', snapped: 'Why should I be nervous? I haven't done anything wrong.'[20] When, after having repeatedly refused the Major's offer of a room in which to rest, she discovered that she might be kept hanging about until the next afternoon, she finally decided: 'In that case, I will lie down. Thank you.'[21] She was ushered up to the third floor and led into what she took to be the suite for VIP prisoners – because her sheet, though 'not exactly white',[22] was at least clean, and the roses on display had, according to the Major, been grown by the Governor himself. Even when the Major informed her that she was being locked in 'for her own protection', her composure did not desert her: 'How very kind,' she smiled.[23]

But sleep, yet again, did desert her. Every hour, on the hour, the guards, in order to prove that they had managed to stay awake, blew piercing whistles from their high turrets, and, by 5 a.m., the inmates were already being drilled in the courtyard outside. At 6 a.m. the Major brought her some tea, which she accepted; and, 'so that [she] would have music to dance to',[24] a radio, which she declined. After what she describes as 'verbal minuets'[25] regarding whether she was a guest or a prisoner, she was left, in the absence of newspapers, to ponder Tito's fate. In the afternoon, the Arias family, being 'familiar with the routine of revolutions',[26] sent her clothes and food – but Margot, feeling not exactly hungry, 'shared the chicken with the Major'.[27]

That evening, at long last, the interview took place. Margot 'got the impression that it was designed for [her] to prove [herself] innocent'.[28] Even when the officials quizzed her as to the identity of one of the men on the *Elaine*, they gave the wrong surname and nationality – thereby furnishing her with a means to deny any knowledge of him. Meanwhile, in an adjacent room, an exhausted British ambassador, Sir Ian Leslie Henderson, hardly recovered from the state visit, was waiting. And after a further two hours' delay – to do with red tape about her papers – Margot was finally scuttled out through a side entrance and driven directly to the airport. Simultaneously, the wives of the British Embassy staff had been despatched to the El Panama Hotel in order to pack her belongings post-haste, so that these might be taken to her before she caught her flight to Miami. But, in a vignette bearing uncanny echoes of that earlier scene, witnessed by Tito and Margot – where Urrutia's wife and her friends had ransacked the wardrobes of Mme Batista – now the British ladies took a few minutes to scrutinize the finer details of the fugitive's boldly printed up-to-the-minute trapeze-line creations, so that Mme de Hahn, the local dressmaker, might run up for them accurate replicas of the latest Parisian fashions. 'The frocks were positively lovely,' admitted one of the dames. 'I've had dozens of calls to find out just how they were made. But, of course, I won't tell.'[29]

Margot changed planes in Miami, and, after a further four-hour flight, arrived in New York at 2.15 the following afternoon – wreathed in smiles and neatly coiffed, wearing a white woollen coat, a pink and white cotton dress, and beige shoes. A double strand of pearls set off, according to the *Herald Tribune*, her 'serene, though understandably fatigued' countenance.[30] Greeted on the tarmac by battalions of the world's press and photographers, Margot told herself: 'This kind of thing only happens to visiting Prime Ministers, so you had better make the most of it; it will never happen to you again.'[31] Judy Tatham, who was there to meet her, reminisces: 'It was a wonderful, warm, sunny spring day . . . The plane landed on schedule, and Margot was the last passenger to leave. Looking calm and poised, and amazingly well after all she had gone through, I remember thinking that I did not know another woman who would have looked so well-groomed after such an experience; even her dress gave the impression of having just been put on.'[32] Margot describes the mob-scene from the plane to the airport newsroom as 'fantastic, with journalists and photographers fighting for a picture or a quote',[33] and seems, during the half-hour conference, to have acquitted herself 'like a diplomat long-tested under fire'.[34] In reply to some particularly pointed enquiry, she replied: 'You can read the answer to that in the papers.'[35] And 'with that one heavensent phrase', she adds, 'the atmosphere changed in my favour. I learned an invaluable lesson about keeping good-humoured relations with the press.'

Following the conference, Margot went into a private room to telephone her mother but, having failed to get through to Mrs Hookham, was ushered by Judy outside, where friends Joy Williams and Michael Brown were waiting to drive them to Judy's apartment on First Avenue. Safe at last in Judy's small sanctuary, the women settled down to chat, ate a light supper, and opted for an early night. But at four in the morning, the ring of the phone startled Judy out of her slumbers. A female reporter from the United Press informed her that the Panamanian police had found Tito's briefcase at a cottage in

Santa Clara Beach, and inside it, along with details of his financial transactions and particulars of such high-profile names as John Wayne and Aristotle Onassis, a couple of unguarded letters from Judy to Tito and Margot respectively – thereby incriminating Judy in the whole drama. Reading aloud, the reporter treated Judy to a few excerpts of her epistolary remarks: 'How I love the Latins after these antiseptic Americans, they really make me feel a woman again'; 'Love Tito dear, and do take care, think what fun we should miss if you got knocked off!'; 'The plot thickens very much. It has been an endless source of amusement to me.'[36]

Fearing a visit from the press, or even the police, Margot now decided that she and Judy had better bolt; so they took refuge in the house of Trumbull ('Tug') Barton and John McHugh, who happened to be away. From there, on the following day, the women sought the protection of Sir Pierson Dixon, UK Ambassador to the United Nations, who, after giving them tea at the British Consulate, smuggled them out of America. That night, Margot and Judy, under the aliases of Miss White and Miss Lane, took off from Idlewild Airport.

But during the time that they were airborne, the press cottoned on to the ruse. Tatham recalls their landing at Heathrow: 'As the plane taxied past the airport building, I saw . . . that the verandas and roof were black with people. I saw cameras set up on tripods and on top of lorries; I saw the gentlemen of the press waiting, notebooks in hand.'[37] Shielded by dark glasses, Margot and her 'mystery companion . . . walked down the steps into the bright sunshine of a Friday afternoon in spring' – to be met, not just by reporters, but also with roses of welcome. English newspapers that day were carrying banner headlines about Margot's conference in New York, and the hacks were hoping for a repeat performance. She did not disappoint them: 'Britain's prima ballerina,' reported the *Manchester Guardian*, 'subjected herself with good grace to an hour of intense questioning . . . She smiled as radiantly as ever she smiles at the curtain call at Covent Garden.'[38] 'Miss Fonteyn said it was likely her husband's life was in danger and that he might be shot if found by Panamanian authorities. She sidestepped a question about letters the Panamanian Government claims to have found linking her and Arias with the purported plot. "They would have to say that," she shrugged.' Did she look like 'a sheep in wolf's clothing'? The press had to admit that she looked like 'the essence of chic'.

Once through the barrier she was reunited with her mother and a friend, tin millionaire Jaime Ortiz Patino, who were waiting impatiently to take her to Amerden. On the following afternoon, the chief of the Associated Press Office in London rang to say that Tito had been found – at the Brazilian Embassy in Panama. It was already six days since Margot had heard news of him, and it would be a further two months before she saw him again – Ortiz Patino arranged his safe conduct to Brazil. But what had happened in the interim was this: soon after the shrimp-boat had sailed away from the *Nola*, Tito and his eight men, being short of fuel, had carried out a precarious landfall in high seas on a remote beach near Tito's father's ranch, where they had buried the cache of arms. The group had then dispersed, and Tito, with two others, had headed for the mountains. Before long, however, the Guardias had caught up with them and opened fire, whereupon Tito and a youth called Baquero had fled one way, and the other youth, Delgado, another. Baquero was killed, but Tito managed to get away. After hiding for several days in the homes of local gentlewomen, he was eventually driven, in the boot of a friend's car, back to Panama City, delivered to the Brazilian Embassy, and granted asylum.

Margot, back in London after her weekend in Berkshire, was making light of the whole episode, as if it amounted to yet another comic scene from the long-running opera of Latin politics. She was not alone. John Profumo, then Minister of State for Foreign Affairs, dismissed the drama – and he was qualified to know – as 'a regrettable incident'. And Aneurin Bevan, the Shadow Foreign Minister, told the House of Commons that 'The British public did not appreciate – having seen [Margot] in the role of the swan – seeing her in the role of a decoy duck.' The upshot was that even such distinguished lampoonists as Osbert Lancaster, Nicolas Bentley and Giles whooped it up with cartoons of armed ballerinas and farcical Latin policemen, and captions about *Le Ballet Militant* – gags which, when they filtered through to the Panamanians, did not exactly meet with hilarity.

Tito's sister, Rosario, remembers 'being extremely hurt by those caricatures that they made in England. But of course [Margot] never saw our point of view. She only saw Tito's. And she couldn't grasp, for instance, the humiliation it brought to our relations with the United States. We were looked upon as a joke. She turned it that way in protection of herself and Tito. From her point of view it may have been an adventure, but not from ours. Our whole stability in Panama was threatened. It was a very uncomfortable and dangerous situation. Margot made a joke of it. To us it was no joke. Some people died. Some people lost their lives.'

24

Tito's revolution may have ended in disarray; but from that disarray sprang the serious changes for which his revolutionaries had campaigned. Washington and Moscow were suddenly alerted to a new arena for their tug of cold war. 'Arms and spies began to pour into the little Isthmian republic,' writes Tito's friend from Cambridge, the political historian Paul Kramer. 'Whereas previously Panama had had neither a navy nor an air force, now it got both. Meanwhile scholarship and travel grants to Eastern Europe began to rain down on semi-talented impoverished Panamanian youths. And while Panama's police was enlarged into an army beyond its own wildest dreams, the country even got a ballet mission.'[1]

But, if Panama's fortunes were inadvertently enhanced, so the aborted coup undermined the Arias marriage: Tito's *machismo*, at a loss for an outlet in affairs of state, seems thenceforth to have been poured, undiluted, into his life as a Don Juan. According to Kramer, 'Tito had not only to show that he had as a wife the most famous ballerina in the world, but also that he was irresistible to Panamanian women. Thus began an extramarital series of relationships with other women. It did not matter that some of them were frumps. What did matter was that he appear irresistible. Ultimately Margot learned of some of these relationships. In the beginning she dismissed them as derived from their frequent separations due to her various dance engagements. Later, during what she herself described as their "bad period", they became both depressing and mortifying. Ultimately, however, there was always a favourite ballet to fall back on. Daphnis had *not* been faithful to Chloë during his captivity. Quite the contrary, there had been a *violent love affair*. But once reunited, they found they still loved one another and were encompassed by a greater happiness than ever.'[2]

However, Margot was deluded if she imagined that ballets like *Daphnis and Chloë*, with their nymphs and shepherds, could lead the Royal Ballet into the 1960s – a decade which, in its first year, could yield a work as sexually explicit and emotionally audacious as Kenneth MacMillan's *The Invitation* (inspired by Colette's *The Ripening Seed*) and feature Lynn Seymour as an underage virgin being graphically and savagely raped. Indeed, audiences, once initiated to such sights, would be unlikely to bemoan the fact that Margot had quietly ceased to dance *Swan Lake*, when instead they could watch, as Odette/Odile, that first pure product of the English classical school, Antoinette Sibley – tipped (fair hair notwithstanding) to be Fonteyn's long-awaited successor. Michael Somes certainly thought her The One – he coached her for *Swan Lake*, partnered her at her début, and, soon afterwards, married her. 'He was in a shocking state over Deirdre's death,' says Sibley, 'and Madam immediately picked up on him and gave me to him to rehearse, as something to focus on. I didn't really know Michael apart from his normal flirting about, which he did of course with everybody – any pretty girl caught his eye.' Being partnered by Somes was a revelation: 'You literally did nothing. Oh, I mean nothing. He would take you through the ballet. All you had to deal with were the acting and the musicality – he did the rest for you. I have never known anyone like that – not even my darling Anthony [Dowell].'

De Valois had offered Somes a job as *répétiteur* which he was impatient to accept, but, in his loyal way, he struggled on for Margot's sake. 'I told de Valois, as soon as Margot gives up, I'll give up, but it would be too hard for her to have to start with another boy now.' The boy under consideration, David Blair, was the nearest thing to a *danseur noble* that the Wells had lately managed to produce. But not noble enough for Margot. She, sweet and charitable though she strove so hard to be, could not conceal her irritation with Blair whenever he deputized for Somes. 'David was a Yorkshireman, and brash,' says Antoinette

Sibley. But it is an odd form of snobbery that would tempt Margot to look down on someone whose northern accent was no more broad than her own mother's. Yet ballet does have its own inexplicable hierarchy, and de Valois, with her sweeping dictums about straight-haired versus crinkly-haired ballerinas, saw the mismatch in simple terms of category: 'David Blair excelled in bravura roles. He wasn't meant to be used in the romantic work. He was a demi-character virtuoso. It was not the right partnership for Margot. No one's fault. Just not right.'[3]

De Valois had nevertheless led Blair to believe that he stood in direct line to take over as leading dancer of the company, and his assumption that this would automatically mean becoming Margot's partner went down badly with Somes: 'I mean, he's dead poor darling, and it was a shame because he was a wonderful artist, and wonderful with Nadia, but with Margot he was just a little bit . . . not right. He was a good dancer and a good boy but he was young and just a little bit bumptious and thought he was going to step straight into my shoes and be equal with her, which he couldn't be.'

Yet, as Sibley says of Blair, 'his arrogance was what was marvellous about him'. Audiences certainly thought so: London theatre had lately been invaded by a surge of raw working-class talent from the north – Peter O'Toole, Alan Bates, Albert Finney – and Blair was their balletic counterpart. What Somes might have regarded as effrontery, the younger generation saw as an overdue lack of deference, and Blair countered the clique of the Fonteyn/Somes/Ashton 'Royal Family' by starting up a club of his own, 'to which the entrance fee was the ability to execute eight pirouettes, later increased to twelve'.[4] Frederick Ashton had the sense to appropriate this exuberant exhibitionism for his next project – his first full-scale work *not* to star Margot Fonteyn. The ballet was *La Fille mal gardée*, and it would come to be regarded as his masterpiece.

The ballerina whom de Valois insisted he use for his heroine, Lise, was the one with whom Blair, as Colas, enjoyed perfect and proven chemistry – Nadia Nerina; and, as rehearsals progressed, so excitement mounted not only among members of the company, but also among students of the Upper Royal Ballet School in Barons Court, who, crowding to spy through the glass in the practice-studio door, gasped at the technical feats which these two were achieving. The fantastically strong Nerina could actually prance on *pointe*. And Blair, at the end of his swaggering solo, dropped straight from a double *tour* to a crouch, no sooner touching the floor than bounding back up again to a dauntless finish. Nerina, bolder than Margot, was lifted so high that she sat above Blair's head in the palm of his hand. Unrolling a great length of pink satin ribbon, Ashton asked the dancers to work out how, with the entwinements of their own bodies, they could construct, on a human scale, a cat's cradle. This tender and witty ribbon-motif would flutter and thread its poetry through the entire action. *Fille*, which to Ashton's surprise 'went like the wind',[5] was completed in four weeks. Released from having to accommodate the diminishing capacities of Fonteyn and Somes, and inspired by a humble and infinitely hummable score (a hybrid of Hérold, Rossini and Donizetti tunes, arranged by John Lanchbery), Ashton's inventiveness broke free and soared into a new and rapturous realm. His theme was pastoral: 'At some time or another every artist pays tribute to nature,' he wrote;[6] and having recently bought a house in Suffolk with his legacy from Sophie Fedorovitch, the moment was perfect for him to make manifest 'the thrill of arrival in the country and the days of contemplation and distant, endless staring and dreaming to a *musique concrète* of farmyard noises, all to end in a storm . . .'[7] It was Ashton's vindication that, in re-creating the most archaic and seemingly most trivial of ballets (with a libretto by Dauberval and an anonymous score dating back to 1789), he had at last made a work of profound humanity and unarguable contemporary validity.

And he had made it without Margot. More gravely, he could not have made it *with* her. She was unimaginable as the madcap Lise: she just did not have the athleticism or the bucolic flounce for it. The euphoria which the new ballet brought to the whole company ('Whatever you felt like, after a few minutes of *Fille* you forgot everything'[8]) was denied to Margot. And if, as a result, she felt sidelined and dispossessed, this was only part of the pattern which had begun on her return to London after the failed coup.

Walking past the Opera House one summer's day in 1959, she had chanced upon a poster advertising the forthcoming ballet programme, across which had been slapped a banner proclaiming that seat prices were to be raised for all future Fonteyn performances. Margot was outraged. That such an announcement should be made without consultation with her seemed extraordinarily high-handed of the management. Had she been asked, she would have refused to allow her name to be associated with a demand for special treatment from a public which had faithfully struggled to support Sadler's Wells throughout the war. The higher cost of a ticket to see her – *her* in particular – would subject her to heightened expectations, just at a time when she feared that the standard of what she could offer was inexorably dropping. She guessed that David Webster, whose treatment of Constant Lambert she had never forgiven, was the culprit, and she marched straight into his office to complain: 'This is the sort of thing they do for guest artists, and I'm *not* a guest artist.'[9]

Returning two weeks later from a trip to Rio de Janeiro, she discovered that a guest artist was exactly what, in her brief absence, she had been made. Again, no one had warned her, or asked for her opinion on the matter. She merely happened to notice a headline in the social column of *The Times*, through which she was leafing in her taxi from the airport: 'Dame Margot Fonteyn has become a guest artist with the Royal Ballet.'[10] Webster was the author of an official – and categorical – press release: 'While Dame Margot's artistic home will remain with the Royal Ballet, her special position is now marked at the top of the company with the word "Guest". "Guest" means simply that she appears with the Company when she is available. In recent years Dame Margot has been more and more in demand for performances all over the world – a right and fitting tribute to her supreme position. It is also right that Dame Margot's time should be completely at her own disposal and not subject to the demands and policy of the Royal Ballet. This arrangement also clarifies her post in relation to the foreign work of the company which can no longer be assumed to include Dame Margot. This arrangement has been made at the suggestion of the company and with the consent of Dame Margot.'[11]

As coups went, this one was all too successful. Margot had no option but to accept her new status. Where else, but with the Royal Ballet, could she appear in her accustomed repertoire? What other tone could she adopt (in a written response, dated 20 July) but a meek one: 'Thank you for making me a Guest Artist. I feel it is better from all points of view and will make no difference so far as I am concerned to my feeling for the company and my desire to dance with it as much as possible.'[12]

Her colleagues, naturally, imagined the step to be voluntary – a bid for the right to negotiate higher fees. But to Margot, who had been a company girl all her life, this loosening of what were virtually family ties seemed designed not so much to free her as to cast her adrift. The grandiloquent description 'guest artist' did not fool her. It reminded her of the last, sad days of Markova. And what other title had Beryl Grey settled for when, only a year before, she had absented herself from Covent Garden in final frustration at the cruel neglect of her talent?

Yet the situation for Margot was not comparable with that of any other ballerina. Ever since her activities on the international political stage, she had moved beyond mere theatrical fame towards something more broadly compelling: notoriety. People wanted to catch sight of her now not just for what she did but for who she was. Inflated prices notwithstanding, the box-office takings on the nights when she danced were now hard evidence of a one-woman business.

With her horror of 'airs', Margot had never entertained the services of anything so conspicuous as an agent. In the early days it would have been unthinkable – she had been indoctrinated by Lilian Baylis and de Valois in the repertory company ethos of vocational frugality, which preaches that one must be grateful to scrape a living for the privilege of doing what one loves. De Valois herself, issued with money for personal expenses by Sol Hurok on the first American tour, returned the unspent change, claiming it to have been 'too much'. But that same tour had opened Margot's eyes to her own worth, and throughout the 50s she would occasionally 'rearrange' her salary with David Webster, whenever she needed, as she put it, to 'keep the wolf from the door – an ever hungrier wolf'.[13] Salary, however, was hardly the word for it: a memo from 1952 stipulates 'no perform-ance, no rehearsal: no payment', and 'no payment for holidays'. Her rehearsal rate at the time was £100 a week, and, beyond that, she was paid, per performance: £100 for full-length ballets – *Beauty, Lac, Giselle, Coppélia, Sylvia* – and £50 for short ones. In 1956 these sums were doubled; but now that she was a guest artist, much more frequent negotiation would come into play. Retirement seemed too imminent to justify an agent, but luckily Tito, the lawyer, was on hand to interest himself in Margot's earning capacities. God knows her money was needed. He instructed his secretary to set up an offshore company in Jersey (under the enigmatic pseudonym 'Diana'), which was to be 'en-titled to the exclusive services of Dame Margot Fonteyn de Arias outside the United Kingdom of Great Britain and Northern Ireland'.[14] In other words: Margot was now empow-ered to negotiate her own foreign contracts.

Whatever her official status, Margot's appointments until Christmas 1959 were all scheduled in London. On 26 November there was a Gala Performance for the Royal Academy of Dancing at which not only did she waive her fee but, as President, persuaded everyone else to do likewise. If Ashton ate his earlier words and made a *pas de deux* for her and Somes, it was only as a test-piece, in advance of a concert version of Glazunov's *Raymonda* which he planned for Beriosova. *Rêve d'Amour* (later retitled *Scène d'Amour*) depicted Raymonda's emotional leave-taking of Jean de Brienne on the eve of his departure for the

Crusades; and Margot, according to Ronald Hynd, who was later to dance it with her, 'was heaven in it', throwing herself into the long farewell with a tearing passion. 'It's easy,' she would explain to Hynd. 'It's the story of my life. Saying goodbye to Tito.'

At Christmas she had the chance to say hello to him, since she was working in Monte Carlo. Back at the Opera House on 29 December, she danced the Firebird in a gala to commemorate the fiftieth anniversary of Diaghilev's company. In that same week she performed both *Scène d'Amour* and the *pas de deux* from *Casse-Noisette*, and, at a midnight matinée, starred in an extract from *Birthday Offering*, in aid of the victims of the Fréjus flood disaster. But Tito was conspicuously absent from the first showing of Margot's film *The Royal Ballet* on 7 January 1960. Princess Margaret, however, did attend the première at the Columbia Theatre, which the *Evening Standard* described as 'more discreet than afternoon tea in a vicarage . . . The first bars of *Swan Lake* tinkled out into the foyer. Several people looked in vain for Dr Arias. "He's been fogged down, I'm afraid," said Dame Margot.'[15] The film, though hardly ground-breaking, was warmly received, and its world-wide release set Margot up for a lucrative year of 'guesting'. 1960 reads like a whirlwind: January, Brussels; February, Milan; March, a gala in aid of the Benevolent Fund at the Opera House; April, a further gala for the state visit of General de Gaulle; May, Finland and Belgium; June, a trip with Somes to South America, where they appeared as guest artists with the Ballet de Rio. In July, at last, she and Tito took a break – with Aristotle Onassis and Maria Callas on the yacht *Christina* – but in August Margot was back with the company at the Edinburgh Festival for *La Péri*; and the following week, on 6 September, she flew to New York for yet another mammoth American tour, the Royal Ballet's sixth.

After a month in New York, the company set off once more, weaving its way by rail from state to state. Margot managed to escape in December, returning to England for an appearance in the *Firebird* at the RAD's annual gala. By dint of some convoluted chain of events in South American politics, Tito had once again been appointed Panama's Ambassador to London, and was due, five days after the gala, to present his credentials to the Queen. But, for all that Tito had missed Margot's film première, nothing in the world would have 'fogged' *her* down on the occasion of her husband's investiture. 'Everyone who worked at Buckingham Palace was tickled to death that she turned up,' says Rosario de Galindo, 'and they were all hiding behind curtains, trying to get a look at her. She had to come in after Tito to do the almost-kneeling thing you have to do, and Margot being Margot, and having that sixth sense, did this wonderful curtsey: half the protocol one and half her own dancing one. The Queen, after-wards, told Tito that she was afraid people would start clapping.'

After a further week in London, Margot flew off to Chicago and rejoined the tour. And it wasn't until the end of January that the dancers played their last American city and were able to take a month off before the London season began on 2 March. At Easter, Margot made her second trip to Japan, this time with the Royal Ballet's own touring company. Tito, so often abroad when she was dancing in London, was now ensconced at Thurloe Place. 'I used to be invited to parties and receptions at the Panamanian Embassy,' says April Olrich, then a particularly fetching twenty-two-year-old, who had just left the company, 'and I received a gold-edged invitation. So I went along and, to my surprise, Tito opened the door. "Hello," he said. "How lovely to see you." I said, "Where's Margot?" and he said, "She left today for Tokyo." I said, "Oh?" and he said, "Let me give you some champagne." We went into one of the enormous reception rooms. He said, "I must show you my collection of gold Aztec jewellery – it's all on blue velvet behind frames." So of course, when I got there, this happened to be in the bedroom. He said something about my having a bosom – because I did have a bosom: in the ballet I had to have it flattened – and then he came up close behind me. I was used to skipping out of people's way, and, when I did, he said, "Oh, you stupid little girl." He took me off to the Café de Paris – I'd never been there in my life. He said, "A terrible couple is joining us." The "terrible couple" turned out to be Maria Callas and Onassis, who sat on the banquette shouting at each other all through the evening. Nobody took the blindest bit of notice of me. When it got past coffee time, I escaped to the ladies', and got the No. 19 bus home.'

Meanwhile, during Margot's fortnight in Japan, the touring company went on to appear in three different theatres, one of which had a stage nearly two-and-a-half times the width of Covent Garden's. Specially large scenery had to be constructed in Japan, based on photographs mailed from London. The audience had not forgotten Margot's previous visit with Michael Somes, and proved as adulatory as ever. One critic likened her performance to a Noh play, and another, after comparing the sets to 'a Christmas card from the Royal Family, rich beyond expectation', concluded that her interpretation of Giselle 'symbolized with extreme purity and beauty the memory of a maiden who disappears from everybody's mind leaving only a sweet scar'. As well as in Tokyo, they danced in Osaka, and, on the homeward lap, in Hong Kong and Manila.

It was a punishing régime for a woman now in her forties, and it took a particular toll on Margot's troublesome left foot. To increase her anxiety, a new hurdle now loomed – one almost as testing as the first American tour of '49, namely the Company's long-postponed visit to Russia, scheduled for June–July 1961. Margot knew that she could not perform in the country which, in effect, was the birthplace of her classical repertory and fudge certain steps in order to allay the pain. A doctor suggested manipulation under anaesthetic, and she decided to take the gamble. Although the procedure proved a success, part of her would have been relieved if it had not done; for, as well as dreading exposure to Soviet scrutiny, she felt little inclination to sample the questionable delights of Communism. The Eastern European states which she had visited after the war had depressed her, and de Valois, who had done a reconnaissance trip to Moscow in 1955, had further reported: 'Never have I seen so many ugly women, bad taste, dreariness, fear, apprehension of everyone and everything – it would get a rat down.'[16]

Margot, like many artists of her era, feigned blithe disregard for politics, but the fact is that, though intellectually uninformed, she was by no means emotionally impartial. Ever since her father had seen it as his patriotic duty to support the Establishment by driving a bus during the General Strike of 1926, Margot, like her mother before her, had been implacably right-wing. It was a stance which had never really been challenged by anyone whom she had admired. De Valois and Ashton were both staunch Tories, and even Constant Lambert, despite his subversive brilliance of mind, was as instinctively anti-Communist as he was occasionally anti-Semitic. According to Peter Brinson, 'one of Margot's problems was this tremendously narrow ideology. She was politically naïve, certainly to a point which was dangerous and almost to a point where it was tragic. And that, of course, led her into unfortunate alliances.' Marcos and Pinochet were to come. Meanwhile she had Tito, who, for all his flirtation with Castro, was, both by temperament and upbringing, a natural member of the far right. 'He, himself, was a very reactionary gentleman,' says Brinson, 'with very reactionary views.'

These were views that could only be of advantage to him in the social milieux where he currently found himself. Harold Macmillan's Conservative government had raised not an eyebrow at Tito's ambassadorial reinstatement, and the publicity that had attended his piratical antics had done nothing but endear him to Winston Churchill, who, now in his dotage, invited the Ariases to lunch at Chartwell. Sitting on the terrace with Sir Winston while Margot played croquet on the lawn with Lady Clementine and Viscount Montgomery, Tito confided in the old warlord that he still had every intention of taking Margot back to Panama. '"In that case," said Churchill, "I must warn you not to use Montgomery in any of your revolutions . . . If you do, you will be bankrupt before you start . . . Do you know . . . that man over there needs a minimum of thirteen divisions before he'll make a move."'[17]

'Diana' demanded that Margot be paid a minimum of £2,000 for the month-long Russian tour – a fee which placed her, at last, on a par with Maria Tallchief, then the highest-paid ballerina in the world. An exchange was planned, this time with the Kirov rather than the Bolshoi, whereby the Soviet dancers would take over Covent Garden while the Royal Ballet appeared in Leningrad, moving on to Moscow. This reciprocal arrangement resulted from months of negotiation at the height of the Cold War. Early in May, the Soviets had shot down an American U2 plane which they claimed had been spying, thus furnishing Khrushchev with a pretext to dismantle his summit meeting with Eisenhower, Macmillan and de Gaulle. Despite the tension between Russia and the West, the Royal Ballet managed to arrive in Leningrad on 14 June. Most members of the Kirov company were in Paris, heading to London, but those who had been left at home came to meet the English dancers at the airport. Formal speeches about friendship between the two countries struck Margot as extraneous. 'If everyone danced,' she writes, 'we wouldn't have time for political problems!' Nevertheless, she does not refrain from voicing her disappointment with Russian life, noting that the Royal Ballet stage crew – 'the British workers' – were the ones who most missed their comforts and most disliked the Soviet Union. The dancers themselves were scandalized to encounter female officials sleeping on every landing in their hotel. 'You just knew,' says Nadia Nerina, 'that the minute you left for the theatre your room would be searched.' It takes two sides, however, to make a Cold War, and, to everyone's horrified bewilderment, when the costume baskets from London were opened by the Soviet backstage staff, a great stash of anti-Communist pamphlets fell from the folds of velvet cloaks and layered tulle skirts. Only the diplomacy of Michael Wood, right-hand man to de Valois, saved the company from being sent straight back home in disgrace.

This was the season of the long summer 'white nights', and the thrilling sight of the eerily lit Winter Palace and the Neva River reminded the visiting dancers that Leningrad was the

Petersburg of Anna Pavlova, and that the Kirov Theatre was the Maryinsky of Karsavina's peerless memoir, *Theatre Street*. Their opening night in the beautiful blue-and-gold opera house was, in the natural course of things, handed over to Margot – as Ondine. Her foot was much improved, and, for once, a sense of history seems to have banished her nerves: 'As I stood, with Michael, on the bulwark of the ship in Act I, I remembered Karsavina writing about her first performance in the ballet *Corsaire*. She described how elated she became in the scene of mutiny and shipwreck with the crescendo of music augmented by storm effects and the firing of cannons. Such moments on the stage are heaven.'[18]

Unfortunately, it is a truism among artists that the moment they feel themselves to be soaring is often the moment at which the effect falls flat. *Ondine* was politely enough received, but Soviet audiences were not flabbergasted, as English audiences had been by the Bolshoi's first visit to London. It took the freshness and brio of *La Fille mal gardée* to elicit a properly gratifying reaction. Nadia Nerina had visited Moscow and Leningrad a year before, and the public already adored her for her Cecchetti-trained un-Englishness: after the first night of *Fille*, fans bore her back to her hotel on their shoulders.

Margot received no such triumphant ride. But she did have her own private admirers among the dancers, notably the shy and sensitive Alla Shelest, who, for the first three days of the Leningrad run, came to Margot's dressing-room and seemed content simply to sit at her feet. From the fourth day, however, she appeared no more. The reason was political fear. Nadia Nerina explains: 'My husband telephoned me to say that there was a fuss in the newspapers about the defection in Paris of a Kirov dancer. His name was Nury-something. As I couldn't hear, I asked Charles if he could turn off the music. Of course the line was being jammed. I told Nikolai Sharigan, a great friend of Constantin Sergeyev, that I had just learned that a dancer had run away from their company in Paris by the name of Nury etc. "Nureyev?" he asked. "Yes, that's what it sounded like." "Well, the West can keep him," replied Nikolai. "Why?" I asked. "He is a good dancer and an exciting artist but no one speaks about homosexuality here. Nureyev talks openly about it. He is very brave but he has got quite a few of us into dreadful trouble." [19]

Even on a clear line, the name would have meant nothing to Margot, who, at that stage, would doubtless have presumed the defector to be yet another of those thunderously-thighed Slavs, any one of whom could leap and spin and beat poor Michael Somes and the rest of the English male dancers into a cocked hat. Margot could not help feeling that the Royal Ballet had some gall to be presenting *The Sleeping Beauty* at the very theatre in which it had been created, and, fearing the judgement not of the public but of the Kirov dancers and teachers, she gave, as Aurora, what she describes as her 'worst performance ever'.[20]

But the unexpected support of one esteemed fellow artist was awaiting her as she stepped off the plane in Moscow. Ulanova, perhaps in reparation for her aloofness in London, was on the tarmac to greet the company and to drive Margot to her hotel. Just as Margot had once pressed a Victorian locket into the hand of the Russian ballerina, so Ulanova now pressed into Margot's a small box containing 'a beautiful antique oval ring, with several little diamonds set in gold'.[21] She explained that, once again, she would be unable to see Margot dance, because her health was poor, and she was due to enter a sanatorium. But she invited Margot to her flat near the Kremlin, overlooking the river. They dined early – at 4.30 – and Margot noticed that her hostess hardly touched her food. Afterwards Ulanova took them in her chauffeured car to the country, and they walked together, gathering wild flowers, among the silver birches. 'It was a lyrical day,' writes Margot, 'the happiest of the tour.'[22] In fact, Ulanova did turn up for the last performance at the Bolshoi Theatre, coming into the dressing-room before *Sleeping Beauty*, and taking a great practical interest in English *pointe* shoes. 'I did the same with Soviet shoes,' says Margot;[23] and indeed it was on this basic, almost mundane, level that the two dancers were mutually drawn, as if to a soul-image in a mirror. Ulanova's characteristic modesty and restraint chimed exactly with Margot's own quintessential simplicity: 'I felt that the warmth she showed me broke through her natural reserve, and I appreciated it all the more.'[24] Yet the soul seeks not reassurance, but transformation; and if Margot imagined that the lessons to be learned from the Russian temperament resembled, even remotely, anything she had ever absorbed before, she was in for a rude shock. Profound change was afoot: its harbinger had already broken free of his stony-faced guards and bolted, wild-eyed, across the airport lounge at Le Bourget, to commit his undoubting genius into the custody of the French police. And neither modesty nor restraint figured in his fierce agenda.

Rudolf Nureyev did not, in fact, consider himself to be Russian in the strict sense of the word. He thought of himself, first and foremost, as a Tatar: 'I can sense the difference in my flesh. Our Tatar blood runs faster somehow, is always ready to boil. And yet it seems to me we are more languid than the Russian, more sensuous; we have a certain Asiatic softness in us, yet also the *fougue* of our ancestors, those lean superb cavaliers. We are a curious mixture of tenderness and brutality – a blend which rarely exists in the Russian.'[1]

According to Nureyev's passport, he was born on 17 March 1938 – a date that falls neatly between Margot's first full-length *Swan Lake* and her nineteenth birthday. But mythological creatures cannot be ordinarily incarnated, and Rudolf, by his own account, had to be 'shaken out of the womb feet first', on a Trans-Siberian train 'dashing along the banks of the Baikal Lake not far from Irkutsk'.[2] No amount of self-dramatization, however, can overstate the harshness and privation of a childhood which spanned not just the war but Stalin's Great Terror, under which an estimated 1,000 people a day were put to death – children over twelve not exempted. From the age of five, Rudolf lived three families to a room in Ufa, on the eastern side of the Ural mountains, a place so godforsaken that soldiers who died there were found with their spinal fluid frozen. The Nureyevs were Muslim, but Rudolf's only god, before he found dancing and Dionysus, was the potato. Whereas Margot had been faddy about food, he would sometimes faint from hunger: 'Only potatoes mattered to me – they were worth their weight in gold let alone their weight in prayers. The whole country was like a ravenous wolf.'[3] And indeed, real wolves did, once, surround his mother as she trudged through a darkening wood in search of food: she had to rip the blanket from her shoulders and set fire to it in order to frighten the predators away. But in the words of a Russian proverb which Nureyev would often cite: 'If you are born to live with wolves, you have to howl with them as well.' 'I came to consciousness,' he writes, 'in a world caught up in the throes of an apocalypse . . . I knew no other values. It takes a long, long time to counterbalance a child's initial ugly impressions of horror and to accept them in their right perspective . . .'[4]

Following his 'leap to freedom', Nureyev, penniless, was immediately entrapped by the Marquis de Cuevas company in Paris; and although the French press followed him wherever he went, and Richard Avedon was commissioned from New York to photograph him for *Harper's Bazaar*, the boy's existence did not at first impinge upon Margot, who, on her return from Russia, was all over the map herself, dancing in the Lebanon, Damascus and Athens. The Temple of Bacchus, at Baalbek, is a ruin of extraordinary pagan historicity into which, Margot rhapsodizes, 'that most artificial of arts, the ballet, fits . . . with an aptness that can only be explained by the fact that dance itself is as old as time'.[5] Here, in the exaggerated heat which her bones so loved, she found the courage (albeit partnered by David Blair) to take on *Swan Lake* again – 'in halves',[6] dancing, on alternate nights, the white swan and the black.

She needed to work – not just for the money but also to distract herself from the loneliness of her marriage, a loneliness which she would admit to no one, not even her closest female friends. Colin Clark's twin sister, Colette, who, as a child during the war, had, like her brother, been happy occasionally to forgo her ration-card 'so that Margot could have a good steak',[7] worked with the ballerina from 1958 to 1968, helping her to run her RAD galas. 'She took the whole thing on,' says Colette. 'Obsessive attention to detail. Fantastically slow going. She could talk on the telephone about those galas *by the hour*. And she would write to me from all over the world about people she'd seen who might be good for this or that reason. She was a great girl for mad schemes. We became huge friends, and she did depend on me for those ten years, but in all that time I never heard her say a malicious thing. She was never cross, never irritable, never vain. The only great artist I've ever known who was utterly selfless. She wasn't a great intellectual, you know – she was practical, she talked about very superficial things. I think her deep emotions were reserved for her artistry. We used to like gossiping about men – who was the most attractive and so on. We used to lie side by side on her great big double bed, roaring with laughter and waiting for a phone call from Tito.'

And waiting. And waiting. 'What is really etched on my heart,' continues Clark, 'is the way Tito abandoned her during those last years before Rudi appeared. She was always longing to go on holiday while she was working herself to death and making all this money for his gun-running and stupid political things. I remember her saying: "Oh, by the way, I won't be here in June or August because I'm going on holiday with Tito." And then when it came to it, she'd say with a very light laugh: "Oh, it can't be helped – Tito can't get over, so I'll be here now. He's terribly busy in Panama so it'll be September instead." And then September would come, and the same thing would happen. And then she'd *really* start to look unhappy. Eventually Tito would ring and say, "Meet me in Nice in an hour," and she'd drop everything and go. And then, a week later, she'd reappear, and I'd say: "You're back." And she'd say, "Well, yes, Tito had to leave." Oh, she was so disappointed. That really was heartrending to the degree that you could say she couldn't stand the marriage any more. So Rudi's arrival must have consoled her a lot."

Margot, on her return from Baalbek, had hoped to receive confirmation that Ulanova would dance at her forthcoming RAD gala, scheduled for 2 November 1961 at Drury Lane. But the news was gloomy: Ulanova could not come – perhaps because relations with Moscow's Ministry of Culture were particularly strained, owing to the defection of Nureyev. There was nothing for it but to try to inveigle the culprit himself into filling the bill. Tracking him down took some doing, but rumour had it that Maria Tallchief had fallen in love with him and taken him to Copenhagen to meet Erik Bruhn, with whom Rudolf, in his turn, was infatuated. It transpired that the two male dancers – the one so coolly elegant, the other so hotly exotic – were taking classes with none other than Margot's old teacher, Vera Volkova.

From that very first phone call to Volkova's flat, the Fonteyn/Nureyev exchange was characterized, as it would be onstage, by the jostling for supremacy of two opposing forces: his audacity and her condescension. Their separate versions of the call do not tally. According to Rudolf, Margot came on the line in person: 'I knew nobody in London. Who could it be? It was a small voice – nothing imposing. "It's Margot Fonteyn here. Would you dance at my gala in London?" '[8] But in Margot's account the conversation is conducted second-hand, with Colette Clark and Volkova as mouthpieces.

COLETTE: He says he wants to dance with you.

MARGOT: I've never set eyes on him, and anyway I've asked John Gilpin to dance *Spectre of the Rose* with me. Ask Vera if he is a good dancer.

COLETTE (the next day): Vera says he's adamant about dancing with you, and that he's marvellous.

MARGOT: He sounds rather tiresome to me.

COLETTE: No, they say he's extraordinary. They say he has such a presence he only has to walk on stage and lift his arm and you can see the swans by the lake. I think it would be wonderful if you could dance with Nureyev as well as Gilpin.

MARGOT: The more I hear of him the worse he sounds. I don't mean as a dancer, but why should he decide to dance with me when he's only twenty-three and I've never even met him?

COLETTE: Well, Vera thinks he's a genius. She says he has 'the nostrils', you know what I mean? People of genius have 'nostrils'.[9]

Rudolf happened, as a child, to have given genius a helping hand by shoving pencils up his nasal channels. But Margot, having not yet witnessed their irrefutable flare, remained unconvinced. Maria Tallchief, who was with Nureyev when Margot turned him down, describes him as 'devastated. He came to my room and showed me the telegram. It said, "Delighted to have Nureyev come to London but I can't dance with him. I already have a partner." In the few months I'd known him, I'd never seen him so dejected . . . I tried to cheer him up. "Don't worry, Rudy. The instant Margot meets you she'll want to dance with you. You'll see." I meant it. Rudy was only about five foot eight . . . they were a good match. But that was only part of it. I knew she'd find him irresistible.'[10]

The first meeting got off to an unpromising start. Rudolf came to London on a secret three-day visit, posing as a Polish dancer, Zygmund Jasman. He was to stay at Thurloe Place, and Margot planned to send her chauffeur to meet him, as she was due to go to a cocktail party. Two hours earlier than expected the telephone rang and she heard his voice for the first time. 'Here is Nureyev,' it announced. 'I am one hour at London airport.'[11] She exhorted him to wait where he was: she would send the car post-haste. Forty-five minutes later, the phone rang again: 'Here is Nureyev.' But *where?* Lindley, the driver, could not find him. Rudolf resorted to a taxi, 'as simply as an ordinary tourist', and arrived on Margot's doorstep shortly before she was to leave for her party. 'I was bowled over,' he has written, 'by the warm, simple way she welcomed me, without any fuss.'[12] Margot was less immediately smitten. She had expected him to be taller. 'He had a funny, pinched little face,' she says, 'with that curious pallor peculiar to so many dancers from Russia. I noticed the nostrils at once.'[13]

And *he* noticed what she was wearing – to the extent that he commented a year later, after the dry-cleaners had done their worst: 'What happened to ribbon? Looks different.'[14] His close scrutiny could not have been more gratifying to Margot, whose own detailed recall of the dress in question ('it was navy pleated chiffon and had a satin ribbon round the hem and a white camellia at the neck'[15]) reveals the heightened sensory perception of a woman romantically roused. There was just enough time for tea before she had to rush away. They had strong Earl Grey, without milk – a brew which they would drink together, over the years, in huge quantities; he set the immoderate tone by helping himself to five sugars. It was all very decorous until Margot 'said something light and silly. Suddenly he laughed and his whole face changed. He lost the "on guard" look, and his smile was generous and captivating. "Oh, thank goodness," [she] said. "I didn't know Russians laughed. They were all so serious when we were there." '[16] She left him in the capable hands of Colette Clark, to whom she later admitted that despite 'a steely glint in his eye', she 'liked him nine-tenths'.[17]

It was a ratio which, when she saw him dance, she would quickly revise. He had agreed to appear at the gala in a classical *pas de deux* with Rosella Hightower, on condition that he also be given a solo specially choreographed for the occasion by Frederick Ashton – who made the unprecedented concession of letting Rudolf himself choose the music: Scriabin's *Poème Tragique*. Margot and Colette watched his first rehearsal on the Drury Lane stage: 'Rudolf was a riot – not intentionally, but his character revealed itself through his dancing and everything was there, including his sense of clowning. He was actually desperately serious; nervous, intense and repeating every step with all his might until he almost knocked himself out with the effort. From time to time he stopped to take off his leg warmers before a very difficult step; after the exertion he stopped again, let out a breath rapidly and forcefully with a sound like a sibilant "Ho." . . . He was working like a steam engine. Colette and I couldn't help laughing. At the same time, I thought he would never get through the solo if he put so much effort into each movement . . . Afterwards, when I suggested he should save something in the middle so as to finish the long solo strongly, he said with what sounded like pride, "In Paris, I never once finish variation!" I said, "Wouldn't it be better if you did?" He considered the point as if it were an original idea.'[18]

What, actually, was a new idea to Margot was that someone

391

should wear such passionate commitment on his sleeve. 'Dedication' had been an immodest concept to her generation. You might have it, but that was no reason to flaunt it. Diffidence had been the order of her day. All her life she had been taught to disguise the difficulty, to make what was complex and agonizing seem simple and effortless. And now, here was this boy who seemed intent on demonstrating that the smallest movement, done from the heart, could cost you blood. Laughing at Rudolf was something you soon learned to do on the other side of your face. Violette Verdy, who had already seen him dance in Paris, 'could not get over his intensity, his focus, and of course, his beauty. He was not so much wild as he was untamed and unpolluted.'[19]

Ashton, 'like a ringmaster wondering whether this beautiful animal would perform his tricks, or whether I would be mauled in the process',[20] had approached the arrangement of Rudolf's solo with trepidation. In fact, he found the young man 'rather reticent, rather suspicious',[21] and, beyond swathing him in a red cloak and making him rush from the back of the stage headlong towards the orchestra pit, was so in awe of the boy's superior classical heritage that he left him fairly much to his own improvisational devices. In the event, Nureyev, having flung off the cloak, to reveal, above grey-streaked tights, a bare torso crossed by a red-and-white sash, 'hurtled round the stage to such effect that the detail did not matter'.[22] *Poème Tragique* was over in four minutes, and Keith Money goes on to say: 'We all clapped and cheered and wondered exactly what we had just seen.'[23] Enough, it would seem, to make Cecil Beaton swear that his 'very bloodstream had altered',[24] and for Diana Cooper to hiss in his ear: 'Better than Nijinsky!'[25] Richard Buckle wrote shrilly of 'tragic clutching arms, falls to the knee, hair all over the face – thrilling!'[26] while, for Alexander Bland, Nureyev's performance 'produced the shock of seeing a wild animal let loose in a drawing-room'.[27] Ninette de Valois found the whole thing a bit overwrought: 'The solo had been done very quickly for him and didn't show to great advantage the man that I saw standing in front of the cloth.'[28] What did convince her of his genius, however, were the ensuing curtain calls. 'I saw an arm raised with a noble dignity, a hand expressively extended with that restrained discipline which is the product of great traditional schooling. Slowly the head turned from one side of the theatre to the other, and the Slav bone-structure of the face, so beautifully modelled, made me feel like an inspired sculptor rather than the director of the Royal Ballet. I could see him clearly and suddenly in one role – Albrecht in *Giselle*. Then and there I decided that when he first danced for us it must be with Fonteyn in that ballet.'[29]

De Valois would always protest that her invitation to Nureyev to join the Royal Ballet (as 'a sort of permanent guest artist') was made for the general benefit of the company which she had constructed: 'One must be prepared to risk toppling something over, to find out whether it has been built securely.' But in truth, if, at the moment of witnessing the defiant young Tatar make his soft-armed *révérence*, de Valois decided to break with her own lifelong policy and open the nationalistic doors of her institution to a foreigner, it was for the single sake of her ageing favourite, whose personal advancement had always taken precedence over more collective concerns. The crowning achievement of de Valois's directorship had been Fonteyn. 'Once you've produced a Pavlova, as we did, you have to live it out. Rudolf came at a time when we were afraid that Margot would disappear. I couldn't find a partner for her. It was very, very worrying – the partner means so much. I saw at once that he would add five years to her career. I don't remember ever having had such an ambition as to see those two together. Age gap of nearly twenty years, of course. But it didn't matter.'[30]

Margot took some convincing. Nigel and Maude Gosling, who had already befriended Nureyev, had tried, up to the last minute, to persuade her to relent and let him dance with her in *Le Spectre de la Rose*. But Margot told them firmly: 'I'd look like his mother.'[31] She was startled, however, by the hysteria of the reception that greeted Rosella Hightower (only one year her junior) later in the programme, for the honour of having been Rudolf's foil in the Black Swan *pas de deux*. Margot had herself made a second, more classical appearance – in a *pas de deux*, with Michael Somes, from *Birthday Offering* – but audience response had been, by comparison, muted; and when the matinée was over, she was able to walk from the stage door, unmolested by autograph hunters. They were too taken up with mobbing Nureyev and Hightower – Rosella's costume, which she was carrying, was almost rent in two – and Margot was obliged to assume the role not so much of mother as of minder, forcibly dragging the couple to their car.

If Margot regretted her decision over the gala, she did not have long to repent. De Valois's ambition was overtaken by Nureyev's own. He asked Madam out to lunch (what upstart since Robert Helpmann had dared to chance *that*?) and the two, according to Margot, 'got on like a house on fire. The Irish and the Tatar understood each other at sight. Her wit, shrewdness, humanity and intelligence delighted him, and he has revered her ever since. Of course, he was just the kind of rebellious talent and engaging *enfant terrible* that she loved.'[32] The *Giselle* that de Valois had dreamed up was in the bag. But when she rang Margot to tell her that Nureyev had agreed to give three performances with the company the following February, the ballerina remained sceptical about becoming involved. She famously told her mentor: 'Oh my goodness. I think it would be like mutton dancing with lamb. Don't you think I'm too old?'[33] De Valois, in her own version of events, snapped: ' "Margot, you are *not*" – and that was the end of the argument, and we all know the result.'[34] But in fact there was now a higher authority than Madam in Margot's life, one to whose opinion the ballerina utterly deferred. Whatever Tito advised, would be done. And that evening, it was he who spelled out the stark choice that lay before Margot: 'Get on the bandwagon, or get out.'[35] So, on to the bandwagon, at the age of forty-two, she gamely jumped. And Madam, for once in her life, turned out to be wrong. Partnership with Rudolf did not add five years to

Margot's career. It prolonged it by eighteen. Not until 1979 would Fonteyn and Nureyev appear together for the last time: in, as irony would have it, that same old die-hard ballet considered most suitable for ballerinas on the brink of retirement: *Le Spectre de la Rose* – by which stage Rudolf, as the petal-clad replica of Nijinsky, would himself know the strain of struggling against a body past its spring, as he launched himself, not just through the open window of Bakst's mandatory set, but into his own forty-second year.

But then, Margot's long professional history is a geometry lesson in full circles, inscribed by the wheel of time on a career ordained. *Giselle*, for instance, had been the rite of passage through which, when she'd been all of seventeen, her ballerina status had been born. Now, as she approached what would come to be regarded as her veritable rebirth, that gothic ghost story of wronged maidenhood and the redemptive power of remorse would again provide the backdrop for her ordeal. She had three months' grace in which to prepare herself: Rudolf had to honour his contract with the de Cuevas, while she was committed to a winter visit to Monte Carlo, where she was to appear with David Blair in John Cranko's *Beauty and the Beast*, and a matinée of *The Sleeping Beauty* on Christmas Day. Rudolf, flanked by Hightower and Bruhn, came over from Cannes to see her dance at the Casino. 'He stood in my dressing-room,' writes Margot, 'looking like a little boy, and said, "Tell me. I must be in London long time for rehearsals. I cannot stay so long in hotel. What you think I do?" I said, "I don't know. I will think about it and tell you tomorrow." He had stayed in our Embassy on his short incognito visit to London, and I told Tito: "It's very funny. I'm sure Nureyev really wants to stay with us but I'm rather suspicious. Supposing the Russians have made a deal allowing him to remain in the West on condition he does some spying or something. What do you think?" Tito thought my imagination was over-working.'[36]

It would be Tito's own speculative fantasies that, before long, would spin into action – as, for ever after, would the public's.

That Margot and Rudolf should rehearse together was one thing, but for Rudolf to live under her roof, as he did for the duration of his stay in London, was another entirely. The unrelieved social intimacy might easily have undermined their professional interaction, and yet it seems to have enhanced it: they were, from the start, wrapped up in one another, whether in the studio or out of it. Margot, pre-empting our censure – or worse, our mockery – self-deprecatingly assures us that she was no more than 'the London nanny',[37] adding in the process that 'he had another in Monte Carlo, one in Paris, and gradually acquired them in almost every city in the world'. But when it came to helping Rudolf explore 'London and London life',[38] there was nothing of the nursery about the manner in which she conducted herself. 'I do remember looking at her,' says Colette Clark, 'and thinking, "Oh my God, Margot's fallen in love." I just knew the signs.'

Yet how could her true friends be anything but glad to witness the great renewal of joy and spontaneity which now broke like a tide through the barriers which Margot's pride had erected around her unhappiness? In the darker days of her marriage, she had, according to Heather Albery, grown 'rather hard and remote'. Now the sun shone for her once more, melting the ice that had blocked her emotional responses. 'She did transform,' says Colette Clark. 'She and Rudolf were absolutely adorable together – sweet and gay and giggly: it was like being with two young lovers. Really, genuinely, happy. They never stopped laughing and holding hands – you know, in a sweet sort of way. Of course she wasn't incredibly young, but they didn't look a bit odd together. She looked so beautiful.'

Nureyev could not have felt less compromised by the difference in their ages. It suited the dynamic that he instinctively set up with women – of little-boy-lost – and, besides, Margot was a baby compared to Dudinskaya, his frequent erstwhile partner at the Kirov, who had been born in 1912. For all Ninette de Valois's 'vision' of him as Albrecht, it was by no means his first stab at the role – he had made a great success of it in Russia

– and he had strong ideas as to the manner in which the whole ballet should be interpreted. He may have despised the political régime from which he had escaped, but he held the Kirov tradition which had fostered him in the highest esteem, imposing its virtues and values upon Western methods wherever he travelled. During his first, incognito, visit to London, he had been to Covent Garden to see Margot dance: in (it just so happened) *Giselle*. And although he managed the diplomacy of professing to be 'moved by Margot's wonderful smooth and musical performance, and impressed by the high standard of the company',[39] he could not suppress his loyalty to the Russian way. 'In our Kirov version everything is expressed more or less in terms of the dancing. This is how I think it should be. Even the long "mad scene" should be a sort of variation. The Covent Garden arrangement is often perhaps more dramatic, but the acting seemed to me that night to be separated from the dancing.'

The changes that he tried to wring in rehearsal were all very confusing to Margot, who, having been coached by Karsavina, had every reason to believe that her mime scenes were perfectly authentic. But, after the first *Giselle* rehearsal, she admitted to a friend that she had been wrong not to dance with Rudolf at the gala. And it is to her great credit that never once did she stand on her dignity or treat the suggestions of someone half her age as presumptuous. Indeed, she found that she gleaned 'a great deal simply from watching him in class. Never had I seen each step practised with such exactitude and thoroughness.'[40]

Nureyev, whom abject poverty and an obstructive father had prevented from entering the Kirov school before the age of seventeen, had good reason to think that he must keep slaving away in the classroom. Nadia Nerina elucidates: 'Rudi's driving force throughout his career, his paramount priority, was to make up for the lost years of his early training. It has always surprised me that this was not more evident to those persons, including critics, who knew him well. He was conscious that he had started his serious ballet training too late and he was too intelligent not to be conscious of it. Those years were lost irredeemably: they could never be recovered. To my mind, much of his eruptions and tantrums derived from a deep-seated anxiety and frustration, his insatiable desire to perform, to be on stage being an endeavour to overcome "the lost years".'[41]

Something about Margot's way of working allowed the down-to-earth side of Rudolf's high-flying sensibility to flourish. 'She was very businesslike manner. She laughed a lot. She was noisy. She said, "Get on and work and get it over and get out." I sort of liked that. Then, most extraordinary I thought, one of the things which makes her apart is the willingness to learn. I mean, there is young boy comes and tells her, well, your Giselle is not that good, and do this, do that, and do this differently or something, and she let me do that. She was always ready to take any knowledge which passed in front of her.'[42]

The ordinary members of the *corps de ballet* were by no means as taken as Margot with this studious new interloper. Susan Carlton Jones remembers the first combined company class that Nureyev attended: 'We were in the middle of *barre* work – Gerd Larsen was teaching – and the door opened and in came this figure covered in green wool, with long hair, which, in a man, just wasn't on. It was before any of us had all-in-ones – we used to wear pink tights, leotards, and maybe leg-warmers – and here was this sort of animalistic frog standing next to Margot, who, as usual, was in her pale pink vest. When it came to centre practice, we girls went first, but when Gerd said, "Now the boys," there was this terrible atmosphere because David Blair, who was kingpin at the time, was suddenly elbowed aside. I thought David jolly nice, one of the boys – I was too young to understand about alcoholics and all that – and I resented this creature grabbing the middle of the front row. He was doing some kind of weird turn with an extension – *pirouette, dégagé à la seconde* – and I can remember thinking, "He's not keeping his *heels* on the floor. Spinning like a top, of course. But taking off from ¼ *pointe*!"'

Yet for all such scandalous impurities, Nureyev had huge technical knowledge, and enough patience and generosity to impart it. While rehearsals for *Giselle* were under way, Margot was also in the process of resuming the full-length *Swan Lake*, partnered by David Blair. Seeing her in the studio one day, struggling to master the step she most loathed, Nureyev asked her, 'What is your mechanic for *fouetté*?' 'I was dumbfounded by the question,' writes Margot. 'I had never thought of "the mechanic". I just did them with determination. I faltered in my answer and tried the step again. "Left arm is too back," he said, and with that simple correction, I recovered my old form . . . It was paradoxical that the young boy everyone else thought so wild and spontaneous in his dancing cared desperately about technique, whereas I, the cool, English ballerina, was so much more interested in the emotional aspects of the performance.'[43]

And, in this meeting of shadows, Rudolf, for his perverse part, was delighted, not with her acquiescence but with her stubbornness. 'Dancing with Fonteyn is always exciting . . . There's a face and there are brains – one has something to argue with . . .'[44] Dissent was, in fact, like a breath of fresh air to Margot. Christopher Gable, speaking as someone who was himself to partner her, explained: 'People were always terribly respectful of whatever Margot wanted. Suddenly, Rudolf wasn't. Suddenly, she had a *hugely* demanding, passionate man wanting an equal share in every stage moment. I think it was probably the most stimulating and wonderful thing for her that there was someone arguing with her and shouting at her, and telling her that she was rubbish. And she would also argue with him.'[45]

Margot puts a characteristically calm complexion on these early altercations: 'With a new partner there is some carpentry necessary to fit the two different versions together. Usually each does as he or she is accustomed to do, until there comes a section that doesn't match. Then one says, "What do you do here?" And the other says, "What do *you* do? *I* do this." Most of the men say, "I will do it your way, how does it go?" Rudolf, however, said, "Don't you think this way better?" We entered into some negotiations and each altered a few steps here and there. What mattered to me most was the intensity of his involvement in the role . . . He literally *became* Albrecht, and there was an extraordinary harmony between our interpretations. I was deeply impressed by the unexpected felicity of working with him, and I forgot my complexes about mutton and lamb. We were happy with each other over *Giselle*.'[46]

There is something about that last sentence which implies that the pleasure would never be quite so unalloyed again. Rudolf was, after all, still on his best behaviour – although, even before the first performance of *Giselle*, Margot seems to have had to overlook certain shortcomings in his manners: 'Among his boyish characteristics was an inability to say "I am sorry," and a difficulty in expressing standard social phrases like "Thank you for your help." They apparently struck him as stilted or false.'[47] He, however – and with extraordinary consequences – would find his own, wordless, way of making his contrition and his gratitude plain to her.

No sooner had the three performances of *Giselle* been announced than there had been frenzy at the box office; 30,000 applications for seats – an oversubscription of 800 per cent, leading to a black-market bonanza: no wonder ticket holders for 21 and 28 February and 7 March were primed to discover a partnership which – in a phrase originally coined by Mary Clarke – was 'made in heaven'.[48] That trinity of performances seems, in the retrospective public perception, to have been rolled into one, or to have swollen to encompass all the renderings of *Giselle* that Fonteyn and Nureyev were ever to give, such was the sense of privilege engendered by having actually *been there*. The editor of *Dance and Dancers*, present on all three occasions, was keen to throw his magazine's lofty weight behind 'some of the most memorable performances in the history of the Royal Ballet. I would like to think also that they herald a new era in which the company reaches even greater heights of hospitality to the world's great dance stars. Nationalism is a fine thing but internationalism should be ballet's ultimate horizon.'[49] Yet, for ordinary Londoners, the thrill was the much more personal one of beholding their beloved ballerina in the arms of this most ardent and tender of strangers. The *New York Times* would speak for them when it came to describe 'a confluence of dancers where the chemistry, the times and most of all, the artistry, all were right. To see Fonteyn was one thing. To see Nureyev was another thing. But to see Fonteyn and Nureyev together, on the same stage, with their particular love and assurance, was almost indescribably special.'[50]

Like all decent success stories, this one did not get off to an entirely untroubled start. Certain quarters were appalled by Nureyev's innovations: his naturalistic 'Stanislavskian' acting, his appropriation of centre stage at the ballet's end, and, in particular, the thirty-two *entrechats six* which he tore off at the climax of Act II. 'All tragic quality, and pathos,' railed the *Daily Telegraph*, 'had been removed from the plot. What we saw was a nicely calculated piece of balletic fireworks in which Mr Nureyev coruscated at the expense of everyone else . . . He and Fonteyn might have been creatures from different planets.'[51] But the *Observer*'s Alexander Bland was close to besotted: Nureyev, to him, was 'a great artist greatly taught . . . When he makes one of his great loping runs round the stage like a cheetah caught behind bars, he seems to be made of more elastic material than normal humanity . . . [His] streak of post-adolescent instability . . . arouses mixed feelings of anxiety and protectiveness. It is the James Dean charm of a boy who will always be in trouble, and always be forgiven.'[52]

And there, of course, we have it. To that charm, that boyish trouble, Margot's maternal nature, so long suppressed, now rose and sprang to flower like a bloom raising its face to precious rain. Just *look* at the photographs of *Giselle*. People talk of the ballerina's rejuvenation, but what those pictures reveal is a sudden, heart-breaking maturation. With Rudolf, Margot gave up all claim to coquetry; she danced, not like a girl, but as a woman. The change was not so evident in Act I, although Nureyev's feckless, infatuated Albrecht drew none of the usual coyness from her in the peasant scenes. But it was in Act II that the real transformation showed. Margot had never really had the measure of Giselle-as-spirit, not being possessed of an effortless jump or the asceticism implicit in a shadow. Yet, even in the short time that she had known Rudolf, the earthly limitations of their bond – her marriage, his homosexuality, their disparate ages – had taught her about transcendence, and now she could base her interpretation on her own spiritual resources, drawn not from the nebulous air, but from the vast, unfathomable sea of maternal passion. Keith Money writes movingly on the 'haven of calm peace emanating from [Fonteyn's] Giselle. Here was this creature who had really become the thought in Albrecht's mind, so he was sustained by a glow of ideal love . . .'[53]

If, at the end of the first performance, when the curtain fell – to pin-dropping silence, followed by pandemonium – de Valois felt vindicated in the unorthodoxy of her professional match-making, she was about to witness an even more gratifying moment, one which would launch the partnership she had championed into the realms of legend. It had been in front of the curtain that she had first glimpsed Nureyev's 'genius', and now, as he and Margot took their call, he did something so nearly ludicrous and yet so extraordinarily affecting that she knew she had not conjured that word in vain. *Dance and Dancers'* special editorial elucidates: 'As the two stars of the evening came out to take their bow, a roaring was heard from above and was gradually caught by all those other more expensive and usually less demonstrative parts of the house. The ballerina curtseys to the public with all the humble grace which comes so naturally to her, then she presents a rose from her bouquet to the boy who up to this point has been looking rather dazed. In a gesture that appears to be spontaneous the boy sinks to one knee, grasps the ballerina's hand and covers it with kisses . . . It may be fanciful, and far-fetched but not impossible, that when Nureyev kneeled to kiss the hand that offered him the rose it could have been a gesture that, unbeknown to anyone at the time, heralded a new ballet boom for Britain.'[54]

We must not forget that those roses would have been from Tito – sent, albeit by standing order, from wherever on earth he might be. But it does put a crimson complexion on Rudolf's gesture, which, in our full view, clearly imprinted itself on Margot's heart: 'It was his way of expressing genuine feelings, untainted by conventional words. Thereafter, a strange attachment formed between us which we have never been able to explain satisfactorily, and which, in a way, one could describe as a deep affection, or love, especially if one believes that love has many forms and degrees. But the fact remains that Rudolf was desperately in love with someone else at the time, and, for me, Tito is always the one with the black eyes.'[55]

Are we to doubt her? Certainly we are. For, despite Margot's last-minute equivocation, those 'forms and degrees' of love were the true constituents of passion.

26

In deference to Margot's sense of propriety, people try to moot the question delicately – the question which, despite its implicit prurience, none of us can, in the end, quite refrain from asking: did Fonteyn and Nureyev sleep together? In the context of dancers, flaked out in lonely hotel rooms, such euphemisms seem almost ludicrous: of *course* Margot and Rudolf would have lain together. After all, what close companion of Margot's did not, at one time or another, stretch out beside her, since any respite that she was granted from her unnatural exertions she was sensible enough to spend flat on her back? But Rudolf was not a girlfriend, with whom to giggle and discuss men and doze off when Tito, yet again, failed to make that promised call. Even according to Tito's own daughter, 'there was a sexual element to all [Rudolf's] relationships . . . he saw himself a sexual being'[1] – one for whom Margot, married or not, made no attempt to disguise her blatant longing. Yet Margot herself does her best, with clever use of the sad truth, to throw us off the scent and place the accent back where she is determined that it should belong: firmly with Tito. 'As I was obviously very fond of Rudolf and spent so much time with him, it was food for scandal to those who liked it that way. I decided there was little I could do but wait for it to pass. The truth will out eventually, I thought. Meanwhile, I worked with Rudolf and often went out with him. But I hardly ever saw him go home. He always walked off into the night, a lonely figure diminishing in perspective down a desolate street. There was something tragic in his departing step after the uproar of laughter and gaiety over supper. It is frequently so with stage people, who pay for coming out in the limelight by going home in the rain. Is it that we are stage people because we can never really live normal, settled lives?

And isn't Tito one of us in his inability to settle, which explains why he understands me so well?'[2]

Arias certainly appears to have understood that great philanderers are not immune from cuckoldry. He took himself, and sharpish, to Covent Garden, where, for once, Margot seems to have been less than delighted to see him. 'Tito came bounding back,' says Colette Clark. 'Only time I've ever seen Margot look cross. I went round after a performance to find Tito sitting there, four square. "Oh heavens, Tito, good Lord, are you here?" He said: "I read in the newspaper about Nureyev moving into the house. I thought it was time I came back." Margot, in the mirror, had a very set face.'

But did Arias really have grounds for sexual jealousy? There are those who swear not. Joan Thring, who was Rudolf's assistant for years and was sometimes herself mistaken for his girlfriend, insists that anything more than close friendship was 'completely out of the question. A love affair would have destroyed some part of it sooner or later. Margot wasn't that silly. She wouldn't have jeopardized it. I was with them so much I would have seen something, and there was never any sign of anything like that.'[3] And Theodora Christon, New York secretary to 'the Dame', as she calls Margot, attests to her employer's calm acceptance of Rudolf's promiscuity. 'Go next door,' Margot would tell Christon, 'and find out what the Boy is doing. And be careful to knock.'[4]

But neither Thring nor Christon was around at the beginning, when the thrall between the two dancers was at its most potent. And it was the Boy's great strength – his guiding morality, you might say – that he always did exactly as he chose. Although his sexual preference was for men, he is known to have taken female lovers when it suited him (the first had been the wife of his revered teacher, Pushkin). The trouble was, as he complained to Violette Verdy: 'It's a job with women. It takes such a long time to make them satisfied. I get it done in the end, but it's not the same as with a boy . . . With men it's very quick. Big pleasure.' Nureyev's misogyny was at a pitch in 1965, when he told *Time* magazine: 'Women are silly, every one of them, but stronger than sailors. They just want to drink you dry and then leave you to die of weakness.'[5] His horror seems emotional as much as sexual: 'It is a big prison, when you are in love or are loved,' he told *Esquire* in 1968. 'Jesus! Love is what you look for all your life, every second, every day. But when it is somebody there with love pouring out of them, it kills you when it's unwanted, it kills you. Why ruin my life, some girl's life? I don't want to marry.'[6]

'I'm sure it never occurred to Margot to marry Rudolf,' says Georgina Parkinson. 'She had him where it really mattered. I think she was the dearest thing in his life without any doubt. Just knowing that she was in the world was sufficient for Rudolf. Towards the end of his life I went with him on one of his gigs in LA and he started talking about Margot. He said to me – so it's first hand – that he wanted to marry her but that she would never leave Tito.'

This is borne out by a last interview with *Esquire* in 1990, where he confessed to having loved only three people in his life – Erik Bruhn, Margot Fonteyn and (to general bewilderment) Frederick Ashton. 'Rudi was in awe of Margot,' says Violette Verdy. 'He always talked about her and certain things she'd said. We know how impressed he was with Erik Bruhn, and men seemed to have some priority with him, to do with power. But Margot was the epitome. She was the woman he loved most and forever to his death.'

Are we, then, honestly to believe that the love between these two extravagantly beautiful people whose shared idiom was the language of bodies did not at some point come to carnal expression – if only in the rumoured 'one terrible abortive bang in Vienna', which Clement Crisp remembers from the time? 'Just imagine,' says Jane Herrmann, erstwhile director of American Ballet Theatre, 'what it's like to be a forty-five-year-old woman who's got this absolute bastard of a husband and you discover there's this most beautiful man that's ever been born in love with you, young enough to be your son and a genius to boot.

I mean, who's going to turn *that* down, even if you've only got it for one year?' Yet it is equally hard for us to comprehend how a woman of Margot's romantic sensibility could have sustained herself in the harsh reality of Rudolf's phallic world. While there should be no underestimating her sexual sophistication – bisexuality in a partner was, as has been seen, no deterrent to her, and it is Rudolf himself who, 'though he said it a lot more crudely',[7] is supposed to have confided in his friend Genya Polyakov that 'Margot liked the physical side of their relationship' – it is likely that the promiscuity intrinsic to his style of homosexuality would have been, from a female point of view, distasteful, not to say dispiriting. Maria Tallchief remembers finding Margot weeping in her daughter's bedroom in Chicago, and although Margot never admitted the reason, Maria, having loved Rudolf herself, hardly needed to ask: 'If she adored him – look, I don't blame her. There was never anyone more attractive. Sexy, wild – it was all there.'

But not, in the final analysis, on offer to women. And nor would women have been wise to pursue such desires to the limit. Violette Verdy, in whom Rudolf chose to confide, and who, with her markedly compassionate intelligence, sometimes 'got more than [she] wanted out of him', shudders somewhat at Rudolf's visceral take on man-to-man copulation, which she recalls as 'something barbaric left over from an animal world. They need it for their survival, almost like a piece of raw meat. We [women] would hesitate. But they know it's good for them.' Yet to women who do not shrink from the thrill of taboo (and Margot had risen to it in her time), homosexuals can present an irresistible challenge. 'A lot of women,' says Maryon Lane, 'seem to imagine you can change a man. I do think Margot waited and hoped. Of course she suffered, but when you're in love, half of it is suffering and half of it is happiness, isn't it?'

A bargain well worth striking, concludes Verdy. 'Maybe on the personal level, Margot might have made herself a little bit unhappy over Rudolf, but I can imagine that the relationship must have been just unbelievable on the human level. To be honest, I don't think the physical was the primary thing. It would have happened almost irresistibly, with an enormous amount of tenderness, but it's a detail.' A detail, however, which continues to elude us. Alexander Grant saw the couple disappear together late at night into a Melbourne hotel room. And although, in New York, Clive Barnes noticed them emerge from another shared room in the morning, he cannot but admit: 'If I were to be asked on oath did Margot and Rudolf fuck, I would have to say I don't know. But on what possible grounds would they not?'

And for all his admirable straight-talk, Barnes leads us straight into the most baffling territory of all: the innate subjectivity of witnesses. There is something about this 'did they/didn't they' enigma which appears to turn people inward. They simply voice what they themselves would have done. Lustier characters, whom nothing would have held back, can see no obstacle; more squeamish homosexuals, preferring to claim Rudolf for their own fraternity and Margot for Madonna-hood, will not stand for the possibility of penetration; but some of Rudolf's numerous other women – perhaps themselves scorned by him – scorn the idea that Margot might have made headway where they made none. So when I admit that – based on what Rudolf-told-Fred-told-Kenneth-told-Deborah-told-me – yes, I *do* believe that Margot and Rudolf were lovers, you must also understand that I, like the rest, am telling you more about my personal prejudices and predilections than ever I could about what really went on between those two people who, as if sharing some complicit laugh, took their secret, undivulged, to their separate graves. And the frustration which they have bequeathed to us endures for a very good reason – in order to lead us to the real question, and to its true answer: namely the fact that rapture has a realm beyond the bedroom, and that whatever took place behind closed doors, out of our sight, was as *nothing* compared to what happened on the stage, in front of our eyes.

The joy of professional exchange is a curiously undersung hymn. Perhaps we despise the bargain, central to the concept of mutual advantage – yet what is marriage, essentially, but a contract? For great practitioners of the arts, whose lives are at the mercy of a vocation, the discovery, on that long and lonely road, of a fellow aspirant both willing and worthy to give and take support along the way, is a blessing of almost mystical proportions. Since the goal, which is perfection, lies beyond human reach, such people are wedded to the endless rigour of the search; and perhaps the most intimate union that an artist can ever forge will be with someone who shares, not his bed, but his dreams.

Collaborative work has its own, alchemical effect; and, while it is fair to argue that a woman, however much she might hope to, cannot change a man, the fact remains that Rudolf, in the process of working with Margot, did, miraculously, undergo a transformation. 'She civilized him,' says Violette Verdy. 'It was not just Beauty and the Beast. It was civilization versus primitive strength. For him, it was the beginning of a taming of sorts. She was everything to him, because she was *in the dance*. And she belonged to a company. She was Home. I really felt that he created through her a whole family of women – the sisters and the mother he had lost. He came to some other, more humane and restful aspects of himself thanks to her.'

And Margot changed too. 'He helped her to prepare for that long chapter she was going to have to live again in even more vital terms since she was no longer so young.' Ninette de Valois summarizes: 'He brought her out, and she brought him up.' Yet although they were patently trading with one another – the childless, middle-aged woman and the boy who'd forsaken no less than his motherland – it would be misguided to define the dynamic between them simply as 'Oedipal'. The potent romantic appeal of Fonteyn and Nureyev's artistic coupling owes a greater debt to the tradition of courtly love, as immortalized by the medieval troubadours – a tradition which, far from being dead, persists in the collective imagination. 'The central motif of courtly love,' writes Liz Greene, 'was the knight who selflessly worshipped an unobtainable lady as his ideal. She was his muse, the embodiment of all beauty, goodness, and grace, who moved him to be noble, spiritual, and high-minded. Courtly love demanded . . . a non-physical relationship between the lovers . . . She usually had a noble husband . . . to whom she was bound for life . . . Courtly love could not exist *within* marriage, for the woman would then become a mere mortal, and no longer a symbol of the man's eternal aspiration.'[8]

Just as the public was mesmerized by the archetypal nature of what it saw, so the two protagonists were mystified by what was going on between them. Asked how it was to dance with Margot, Rudolf would one day attempt to explain: 'It's not me, it's not her, it's the sameness of the goal. She convinces me.' No wonder, then, that Erik Bruhn, watching that first performance of *Giselle* from the wings, should have grown visibly distressed and, the moment the curtain was down, have fled. For all of his sexual supremacy with Rudolf, Bruhn must have realized that, on the level that most mattered, he was facing defeat – twice over. Not only would he never, now, be instated as *premier danseur* at Covent Garden, but he had lost his lover to a more signifi-cant partner – a woman able to personify Rudolf's beloved in that place where no man could: the theatre.

It would, in fact, be some months before Margot could dance with Rudolf again, since she was due to tour Australia with David Blair, whom she had filched from Nadia Nerina, his regular partner. Nerina, in Blair's absence, had been given *carte blanche* to invite whomever she liked to Covent Garden, and, when Fedeyechev proved unavailable, she asked Bruhn. So Bruhn *did* appear at the Opera House in the spring of 1962 – but among a whole plethora of guest artists, including Sonia Arova and Yvette Chauviré – and there were many in the Royal Ballet who would have chosen the princely Dane with his impeccable placing and noble bearing in preference to Rudolf, who, according to Peter Martins, was what the Bournonville-trained élite called 'a dirty dancer'. 'Not clean, not finished. Russian . . . rough, rough, rough . . .'[9] But English audiences had spoken, not only through the vulgar mouthpiece of the box office, but with a petition of 2,000 names: Nureyev was their man. 'He was the obvious one to go for,' says John Tooley, then Assistant General Administrator under David Webster. 'Margot needed a new partner and made it quite clear, rather to her surprise, that she was going to find a new life with a young person. It all fitted, there wasn't much debate, though Erik certainly was not happy about it.'[10] To put it mildly. 'Erik did not finish the season,' says Nadia Nerina. 'Rudi demoralized him to such an extent that he had to go into a nursing home in Denmark . . . He never did recover completely. One can date the beginning of the sad decline of this superb dancer from the beginning of his relationship with Nureyev.'[11]

Margot, on her return from Australia, was alarmed to find the tables turned: the partner to whom she was hurrying back had been nabbed, in turn, by Nerina. 'I had been invited,' says Nerina, 'to appear at the top of the bill in the most popular television programme of its time, *Sunday Night at the London Palladium*; the house was always filled to the rafters with an invited audience. I telephoned Erik in Copenhagen to ask whether he would like to dance with me in the *Black Swan pas de deux*. He declined, saying he was still indisposed. He then telephoned me back and begged me as a special favour to invite Rudi, explaining that he was dying to dance with me, and that incidentally, he desperately needed the money. It was Rudi's first television performance in England, perhaps his first in the West. Just before the show, the stage-manager came to tell me that Fonteyn, who had only just returned from her Australian tour, was in front with her two stepdaughters. What was he to do? I asked him to see that she was given the best seats in the house. After the performance, she came backstage. Rudi was still changing, we were enjoying a glass of champagne. When Rudi appeared, Margot took him by the arm and said: "You're coming with me, we're going." Rudi, surprised, explained that he couldn't as he was expecting to speak with his mother in Leningrad from our house later in the evening where we were to have supper. "Never mind," she said, "I will have the call transferred." She asked him to get his bag and, to my astonishment and that of my husband, the four of them left. From that night Margot virtually never let Rudi out of her sight. Next day Charles [Charles Gordon, Nerina's husband] sent a note to Margot taking her to task for her manners. She was most upset and apologized. The incident reflects her early panicky possessiveness of Rudi.'[12]

Margot was by now juggling a breathtaking diversity of roles — not just those of ambassadress and ballerina, wife and putative adulteress, but also that of stepmother to Tito's children — Querube, Rosita and Roberto. Querube remembers Margot taking both her and her fifteen-year-old twin sister to that show at the London Palladium: 'We took a train. A regular train. These things were sometimes at the weekend and Margot had no one to leave us with. Her family was in France and my father wasn't in London, so we were left with just her, and the chauffeur, Mr Lindley, to take care of us. School in Panama ended in January and we didn't have to start boarding school in the States until September, so we had a long time with her. Nureyev used to come too — he didn't speak English.'

'He may not have known much English,' says Susan Carlton Jones, 'but he could swear — in *any* language.' And to the horror of the company — which was rehearsing *Giselle* for a second run of performances, plus a television transmission in the summer — he unleashed his repertoire of expletives for the first public time upon Margot. 'We Wilis were all lined up, behaving ourselves,' continues Carlton, 'when suddenly Rudi let fly at Margot. He swore at her. He was *evil*. And she just stood there and took it, and then quietly left the studio. Jack Hart, who was taking the rehearsal, didn't quite know what to do. Nobody else had ever behaved like that. We'd never known such a display of temperament.'

It was a scene to which the dancers would grow, if not inured, certainly accustomed. Nerina reiterates: 'Rudi played the fool, treated Margot with disdain, was rude and frequently showed he was the dominant sexual partner in that relationship, to the embarrassment of members of the company, who would turn away pretending not to have noticed how she was being humiliated by him.'[13] And yet, according to Georgina Parkinson, throughout these tirades, Margot 'never lost a scrap of dignity. We didn't always like the way he treated her. We'd only seen her treated like gold-dust by her partners, and here he was screaming at her and dropping her and not taking care. But for Margot there was just so much else in that relationship which sustained her. She was terribly private, and what she was feeling was never displayed in front of us. One had to assume that she must have loved him very dearly to put up with some of the stuff he dished out to her, because he was quite brutal.'

Violette Verdy sees Nureyev's obnoxious behaviour as a syndrome: a punishment meted out to any female who drew too close. 'All the women who helped him he both adored and hated because of that. He was always resentful of what you did for him, just like a bad child. He needed it, you did it, and then he insulted you for it. We were all used to it.' Georgina Parkinson is equally accepting. 'The man was so great that you had to put up with all that shit. Underneath, he was just a struggling dancer. But he loved those of us who were struggling too. The person as a whole was challenging and inspiring and energized and generous, not with his money, but his spirit.'

Yet of all the women to be undone by Rudolf's unpredictable charm, the least likely was, without a doubt, de Valois, in whose forbidding lap the Russian was seen, at one point, actually to bury his unruly head. 'During rehearsals,' says Nadia Nerina, 'he would sit cross-legged at her feet, gazing up at her, chatting away and teasing her as one would a naughty child. On one occasion he cajoled her into getting up and demonstrating for him variations on the *pas de bourrée*, which she did in high spirits; she was proud of the intricate, quick, neat footwork of the English school which she founded. She was proud of her own prowess. Only Rudi could have got her to "perform". Her discipline over dancers was rigid. No one would have dared to carry on as Rudi did. She behaved as if she were a doting mother with her favourite spoilt child, and Rudi played it for all he was worth. If he arrived late for rehearsals, a rare occurrence for any dancer, he would teasingly mimic her, completely disarming her. During the years that he was with the company, his wayward behaviour, and Madam's inability to come to terms with him, not only demoralized the company, especially the male contingent, but put Madam in a somewhat equivocal position, to the extent, in my view, that, feeling compromised, she felt it necessary to retire far sooner than was necessary . . . If you question whether I believe that Rudi was to blame, the answer is yes.'[14]

De Valois excused Nureyev's tantrums thus: 'When it happened, it was like watching a panther at bay – so much at bay that even the pride of self-control was no more. Such outbursts were, I know, as painful for him as for us. They were also confusing – never could one forget that he had, fundamentally, a true sense of humility about himself and his art. At this stage of his career, his integrity, dedication and exuberance were allied to a youthful innocence that animated his dancing with something of the concentration of a child in its own special world.'[15] In so far as de Valois was in love with talent, her capitulation seems inevitable. 'At his height,' she privately confessed, 'he had the same memory and effect on me as Pavlova. Nothing to touch them. Great dancers. He and Pavlova had a world thing. No good bothering about what they did or what they didn't do. It happens about twice in a century.'

And it had happened to the Royal Ballet. 'We'd never had guest artists,' says Georgina Parkinson. 'And all of a sudden it was like Margot and Rudolf were the only two dancers in the company. We all hated it, in a way. If you were trying to make a career in that company, it was devastating. A good number of aspiring ballerinas, who were no mean dancers, were put, constantly, constantly, constantly, on back burners. Their careers were changed because of Margot and Rudolf. As for the men – forget it. They simply couldn't deal with it – all killed themselves or died of alcohol or whatever. It was just too much for them to take on.'

Parkinson exaggerates, of course; but the fact remains that there *were* casualties, and these, in years to come, would be attributed directly to the effects of this internecine upheaval. David Blair's widow, Maryon Lane, says: 'Cats and dogs were in love with Nureyev. We were all perfectly blinded by him. Even Ninette de Valois lost her reason. And so it was a very sad time for the ballet in lots of ways. You don't just drop your own people and forget them, ignore them because you've got a brilliant new dancer. We lost all trust in Madam and Ashton whom we'd always adored and looked up to. They were so overwhelmed by Nureyev that they didn't seem to notice whom they trod on. Quite a few dancers were badly hurt by it. David was about to take over from Somes, and de Valois had even promised him that he would one day be Director of the Royal Ballet, and all that just went flying out the window. It was a hard time. Very hard. I adored Margot. I thought she was the most wonderful girl. But she was terribly in love, and when you're in love you don't see much else, do you?'

Margot, who, with David Blair, had danced her 'last' *Swan Lake* in 1959, took it up with him again in 1961, because she knew, she says, that 'dancing the most taxing of all the ballets would give me more strength for the *Giselle*'.[16] But from the moment she took her first steps with Nureyev, it seemed inevitable that he would graduate from her Albrecht to her Siegfried. 'Rudolf came to my dressing room after *Swan Lake*,' she writes. And 'although he marvelled at the way in which I did the mime scene (dating from the original production and no longer done in Russia), he thought he would not be able to do the scene himself, when we danced it in the summer. He thought he would feel silly standing about doing nothing while I told the story in gesture, and added, with a touch of embarrassment, "I am afraid I will ruin your *Swan Lake*." I looked him straight in the eye and said amiably: "Just you try." '[17]

He *did* try, and, to some extent, succeeded, since Margot was persuaded, at least on a temporary basis, to drop the contentious mime sequence which had been such a feature of her interpretation. 'I did not mind learning his danced version, but I objected to some of the other changes he proposed. I said, "Rudolf, I have been doing this ballet since 1938." He giggled a bit, and I quickly added, "I suppose that was before you were born?" He replied, "No, just exact year." It broke us both up completely. As our rehearsal progressed we came to loggerheads. Neither of us was prepared to give an inch. Finally, I said, "We had better go and have some tea, otherwise this will ruin our friendship."' [18]

Both Margot and Rudolf were what Keith Money describes as 'tea junkies', and the 'copious draughts' which they drank in the canteen, throughout the bare two-and-a-half-day rehearsal which they managed to snatch in London before the Nervi Festival in Italy, bore witness to a struggle for compatibility which, on both sides, took some swallowing. The challenge, however, was, as always for Margot, a springboard; according to Money, during this volcanic rehearsal period, Nureyev made a far-reaching discovery: 'that Fonteyn's security in the bravura sections of Act III was quite at odds with her own diffident view of her technique. With her degree of control, he could not understand why she should not push it all further, and in a moment of premeditated devilry, he said to her one day, "So – you are Great Ballerina. Show me!" It was just what she needed, this flick of the whip, and from that moment something extraordinary, in ballet terms, took place: a ballerina, past forty, proceeded to improve several elements of her basic technical armoury. Nureyev was admiring – and fascinated by the possibilities to which this renaissance could lead.' [19]

Despite the confusion and compromise and shortage of time, the performances, Margot marvels to relate, 'came out beautifully'. [20] Rudolf says: 'We worked out version and when we went on stage all arguments, all differences, were forgotten, and we become one body, one soul, removed in one wave where it was very complementary, every arm, every head-movement. There were no more cultural gaps, or age difference. We been absorbed in characterization. We become the part, and public was

416

enthralled – I think only because we were enthralled with each other.'[21] A decade later he would tell Roland Petit: 'At the end of *Lac des Cygnes* when she left the stage in her great white tutu I would have followed her to the end of the world.'

But it was one thing for Margot to appear as Odette/Odile with the touring company in an open-air, unpublicized Italian festival – where a poster announced the appearance of RUDOLF NUREYEV, partnered by a 'famous ballerina' – and another thing for her to lay herself open to the hothouse scrutiny of London critics. She had a few months to gather herself, because Rudolf – jumping off a London bus – had injured his foot, and not until 7 February 1963, the following year, did the Fonteyn–Nureyev *Swan Lake* reach Covent Garden. Notwithstanding some carping among the critics about the choreographic changes – in particular the languorous solo which Nureyev had created for himself in the first act – the actual dancing was rapturously received. And the strange thing was that those who had rushed to book seats in response to the clamour which surrounded the new boy found themselves, ironically, forgetting to watch him, so transfixed were they by the quiet sight of Fonteyn, at once familiar and reborn. 'I'd been on stage,' says Georgina Parkinson, 'as a *fiancée* in Margot's farewell performance of *Swan Lake*. She did it with David Blair, and we all knew it was her last – she was not going to do that ballet any more. And she did her usual twenty-three and a half *fouettés*, and everybody cheered and the audience went nuts and we all shed a suitable tear. And now, two years later, here she was, practically out-dancing Rudolf in this ballet. It was absolutely extraordinary for us.'

David Blair was not the only one to have felt himself professionally jilted. Michael Somes, although he'd given up appearing in the classics, had not yet formally retired, and was wanting to take his final bow with Margot in some sedate duet appropriate to long-term associates, over the hill and descending gracefully, hand-in-hand. 'At the next gala,' says Antoinette Sibley, who had, by this stage, become Somes's wife, 'he was terribly upset because Margot danced with Rudi when she was supposed to dance with him – it was one of the last things they were due to do together. She didn't write to him or speak to him about it, which was unusual, because Margot was very proper in her dealings with people – she was like the Queen: she didn't ever put a foot wrong. Michael had danced on so gallantly to see her out, and it was a really bad thing, the way she dealt with him – he was just taken off the programme and not even a phone call. What he was hurt about were the early years – the way they were wiped out by this new theatrical animal which was Margot-and-Rudi.'

In November 1962, Nureyev taught Margot something which he had brought, committed to memory, from Russia: the famous *pas de deux* from *Le Corsaire*, an eight-minute show-stopper from an old Petipa ballet, set to a not overly refined score by Riccardo Drigo. It was in this exotic fragment that Nureyev, bare-chested and harem-panted, had catapulted to fame and the first prize in the students' competition in Moscow. Margot, never at her happiest in concert pieces taken out of their context, was particularly uneasy about the programming, which isolated the excerpt, like a circus act, between two intervals. She took her distress to Ashton; but the latter's reply sounds as embittered as it does comforting: 'Well,' he told her, 'it will be all right. Ten minutes of *Corsaire* and twenty minutes of applause. What are you worrying about?'[22]

It *was* all right – for a more laudable reason: Margot's sheer intoxication at sharing the stage with a performer of such infectious braggadocio. 'The first step of his variation, when one clearly saw him sitting high in the air with his feet tucked under him, exactly as though he were flying on a magic carpet, was beyond description . . . It was so exciting to watch him from the wings that I lost all nervousness for myself and danced with a glow of exhilaration and joy.'[23] The *Observer* observed that Fonteyn 'sparkled and spun like a filly loosed out to grass', while Nureyev, 'lithe and hungry-looking in silver trousers, stunned the audience . . . leaping and turning like a salmon, soft as a panther, proud and cruel, never for a moment relaxing his classical control'.

Ashton preferred not to watch. 'Nureyev was yet another person who had taken Margot away from him,' says Anthony Russell-Roberts. 'He'd sit out *Corsaire* in the crush bar, saying, "Let the Sacred Monsters drink in their applause – *we'll* stay at the bar."' Inevitably – and just as Ashton had predicted – the ovation lasted longer than the item itself, and heaven knows that Margot was the absolute mistress of the call. It was an area in which Nureyev, for all his competitiveness, had to bow, as it were, to her supremacy, exclaiming once: 'How she *do* it? I go out. I do big gesture. She only go on one knee . . . and they go crazy. *How* she do it?'[24] With humility, one might have ventured. Yet one would also have had to admit that the applause grew most rapturous when she placed her hand in his. For better or worse, ballet, once so esoteric, had contracted the common touch, and suddenly was less about movement and drama and musical expression than about the cult of personality – a cult which drew to Covent Garden a class of audience, and, for that matter, of critic, less stirred by the specialist medium than by the popular phenomenon. 'In her own way,' wrote Kenneth Tynan of Fonteyn's *Giselle* in 1963, 'that dark-haired girl signalling madness while spinning so prettily, was every bit as poignant as Mary Pickford at her peak . . . but what moved me more than anything else in her performance was the fact I knew she was Margot Fonteyn. As for Rudolf Nureyev, I mistimed my emotional response, owing to the pressure of thrilled expectation in the house, and began to be moved just *before* he made his entrance . . . his face, which is that of a wide-eyed mutinous orphan with a shock of ungoverned hair, reminded me throughout of the youthful Johnnie Ray, who had the same kind of delinquent pathos . . . I defy anyone not to be affected by the curtain calls . . . here, more than anywhere else, romantic ballet justifies its existence. Embracing bouquets, Dame Margot curtsies; Nureyev bows deeply from the neck, while the other men bow from the waist; Dame Margot proffers a bloom or two; Nureyev accepts them and kisses her hand; solo calls alternate with dual calls; and applause, the incessant obbligato, rhythmically swells and subsides. The more one claps, the more one's eyes mist with tears – tears of gratitude, perhaps, that art can be as undemanding, and at the same time as status-spawning, as this.'[25]

If something in Margot's wildly oversubscribed lifestyle had to give, what gave was her untarnished reputation as a company member. Annette Page compares and contrasts two concert tours – what she calls the Happy Tour (to Australia, New Zealand, Manila and Hong Kong in February 1962), and the Unhappy Tour (to Greece, Athens, Israel, Japan and Hawaii in the summer of '63). 'On the Australian tour, Margot was just wonderful to us. She would order supper for us in her suite after the show. Buy us endless drinks. Take us out. And at the end she gave us all the most lovely presents. Then, only one year later, she suddenly became a very difficult person to work with. Kept changing her mind about the programme. Became possessive of her roles. Behaved badly for the first time, like a sort of temperamental ageing ballerina. She began to be late – something she'd never been. I remember even her mother, who was travelling with us in Japan, saying: "I don't know *what's* got into her." To me, those two tours illustrate the difference between Margot's early self, which was warm and generous, and what she later became. She'd been "Our Margot" – I've heard Ashton call her that. She was the head of a company, the perfect model – up to a certain point. And that point was the arrival of Nureyev. I think she was infected by his narcissism. With his advent, the company became background – a montage. We no longer felt her support.'

That support was, indeed, directed elsewhere, but Nureyev was by no means its sole recipient. For all her childlessness, Margot now found herself with a family – not just Tito's son and twin daughters, but his nephew, Gabriel Galindo, who spent his holidays with the Hookhams at Amerden. 'Margot had a phenomenally all-encompassing heart for that family,' says

Galindo. 'I never got the feeling that she wanted children of her own. She really became my surrogate mother – she adopted me, as she had done the others. Here was Black Queen, and Felix, and all of a sudden I had this enormous family. Absolute *adoration* she had for her husband. She thought him fun and roguish. I think to some extent she was a bit contaged [*sic*] with his jokey spirit, but it didn't come naturally to her. She was brought up in the solid, middle-class, English tradition, so she did have a strong ethical background. She pulled me by the ears and the hair when I was naughty – she was very gentle about it but quite clear. But she had to put up with worse pranks from Uncle Tito.'

Scope for pranks at the London Embassy, however, was limited. Hardly had Tito expressed a wish to sell up than a canny estate agent had found a buyer for Thurloe Place, and, in a trice, he was off to Panama to buy a new house, on the perfectly natural pretext that his father was old and frail and in need of him. Margot was left with two weeks in which to pack up 'the accumulated chaos of seven years'.[1] Secreted in the cellar she found a suspicious-looking wooden crate, unopened and unmarked. Once again, in her autobiography, she sees wifely ignorance as her best means of protection both against the authorities and our moral censure. 'I guessed it was not the kind of thing I should discuss over the telephone with Tito in Panama, so I put it in a tin trunk under some curtains and shipped it off with the furniture, hoping for the best. By the time the stuff was delivered to our new home in Panama the government was less friendly to Tito, and the customs inspector was on the look out. All day long the big containers were being unpacked and our possessions carried into the house. When I saw the tin trunk my heart sank. I directed the unloaders to one room, and Tito distracted the inspector's attention in another, while the wooden crate was dispersed innocently among the glass and china already checked. It was a tense moment because Tito had told me that it contained hand grenades – a leftover from the revolution days.'[2]

Another version of the story has Margot actually sitting on

the trunk, and swinging her comely legs for the delectation of the susceptible customs officials; and it was at nonchalant moments such as this that she most lived up to Tito's dreams of perfect partnership. 'You have to understand,' says Gabriel Galindo, 'that Uncle Tito didn't hold as sacred the things that most people hold sacred. I rather suspect that he thought the whole of creation was one big joke perpetuated by the everlasting you-know-what at the expense of hapless man. What tends to be perceived as eccentric behaviour – however polished and witty – has to be perceived in that context. I don't think he considered himself bound by the normal rules. His coup comes in here – his whisky smuggling – all these things.'

The three-roomed house that Tito had bought outside Panama City was unassuming, with blue-tiled floors and a lawn running down to the beach. Margot felt wonderfully ordinary there, in the company of two puppies given to her by a friend. For all the rarefied pets which she had owned in her youth, Margot had never possessed anything so domesticated and responsive as a dog, and these two, Bona and Otoque (named after the islands where she and Tito had sheltered during the revolution), transformed her overnight from elusive cat-woman to overt dog-lover – a significant reversal, according to Tito, who believed that there exist two distinct categories of human being: cat-lovers, who need to love, and dog-lovers, who need to be loved. 'It was funny,' says Rosario de Galindo, 'because there were these little creeks which you had to wade through and Margot would carry the dogs across. It was difficult for her to accept that dogs knew naturally how to swim. The dogs were so heavy she finally put them down and decided to try it, but it gives you an idea of how much everything to do with the countryside amazed her. She found things here that, in life, she'd never had, or had only ever seen from afar.'

But that Christmas in Panama was not destined to be a care-free one for the Arias family. Margot and Tito shared a belief in the power of premonition, and, in the early hours of 23 December, Tito awoke in a state of inexplicable panic. A few hours later, his sister rang to say that their father, Harmodio, had died of a heart attack at 3 a.m. It was the second death to strike the clan in a matter of months – less than a year earlier, Tito's younger brother, Tony, had been killed in a plane crash. Once again Tito sought distraction in the only admissible pastime that he knew: passionate involvement in the convoluted politics of his country. Any pretence that he could live as Margot's consort in England went out of the window. Two years earlier, Margot had bought a Burne-Jones studio house for Black Queen, in Barons Court – the one next door to the Royal Ballet School. But on her return from Panama in January 1963, Margot came less as a visitor to number 149 Talgarth Road than to seek refuge, once more, under her mother's roof.

She flew home, not just to dance *Swan Lake* with Nureyev, but to resume rehearsals for a new ballet – one which would shamelessly exploit the public appetite for the erotic innuendo of her new professional liaison. The choice of subject-matter was not, in fact, as calculated as it might have seemed. Five years had passed since *Ondine*, and Ashton, despite having made *Fille* for Nerina, *Two Pigeons* for Seymour, and *Persephone* for Beriosova, had not been able to shake off his habit of keeping an eye out for yet another perfect Fonteyn vehicle. An insistent image of her had come to him in 1961 – 'before Rudi Nureyev had been invented'[3] – while watching Vivien Leigh rehearsing *La Dame aux Camélias*. But an existing score based on the Dumas play – by the French composer Henri Sauguet – had left the choreographer cold. It was not until a year later when, as he lay steaming in his bath, he heard Liszt's Piano Sonata in B Minor on the radio, that the ballet flooded, of its own volition, into his mind. 'Almost immediately, I could visualize the whole thing,' he told the *Observer*'s Alexander Bland. However, that visualization had come, not chronologically, but as 'a kind of tabloid, a pilule. But I would like it to be strong enough to kill.'[4]

Not too tall an order, perhaps, given the casting that he had planned. It was, by now, April '62, and Rudi Nureyev had well and truly 'been invented'. The Russian's foot injury, plus his commitments abroad, meant that the much-publicized date in December for *Marguerite and Armand* (as the ballet was to be democratically titled) had to be postponed. Ashton, however, did manage, before Margot and Rudolf respectively disappeared across the Atlantic and Pacific, to snatch a few rehearsal sessions, not to mention a glimpse of the heightened temperature which his latest work was destined to fuel. Michael Somes had been cast, none too kindly, in the unsympathetic role of Armand's father. Ashton told Bland: 'Michael was standing with Margot, very stern and stiff, and I saw the door open a crack and Rudi looking in very cautiously, in his scarf and everything. I could see him tiptoe round behind me as we went on working and when we began to come to the end of the scene he started stripping off his coat and things, and just at the right moment he flew out from behind me into Margot's arms.'[5]

This incident very nearly overwhelmed Margot. 'As Michael and I played the scene over, an electrical storm of emotion built up in the studio. We came to the end and Rudolf tore into his entrance and the following *pas de deux* with a passion more real than life itself, generating one of those fantastic moments when a rehearsal becomes a burning performance.'[6] Yet, for all his headlong intensity, it was Rudolf who, in later rehearsals, would be the one to try to bring order to the proceedings. 'It was so exciting,' says Maude Gosling, 'and they got so carried away that Rudolf had to stop and pull the thing together, saying, "Let's get down to basics, what steps are we actually *doing*?" '[7]

Basically, what Ashton was, as ever, trying to do was re-create some ingrained image of Pavlova – crossed, in this instance, with the spirit of Garbo, 'head flung back, hands half in prayer'.[8] 'Pavlova was radiant from *here*,' he would say,[9] indicating the upper part of his body. The steps in *Marguerite and Armand* were subsidiary to what he called 'the impact of personality . . . People now think it's camp. How stupid they are. Everyone wants to be stirred – personality is so utterly important.'[10] Where his stirring choice of music was concerned, he had chanced upon an unexpected felicity. Having dispensed with the play in favour of Dumas's original novel, on grounds that 'it was stronger; for instance the bit where Armand has Marguerite's body dug up just to look at it again, and it's all wormy',[11] he discovered, to his delight, that Marie Duplessis, a courtesan on whom the character of Marguerite Gautier was based, had, in the last two years of her life, been sexually involved with Franz Liszt. 'This seemed to be a marvellous thing . . . that somehow this music had fallen into place . . . one doesn't know how much of the piece was Liszt's memory of her. It may not have been so, possibly not in the least. But you see, it *could* have been.'[12] For once, Ashton took Margot into his intellectual confidence, quoting Marie Duplessis's declaration to Liszt: 'I will be no trouble to you. I sleep all day, go to the theatre in the evening and at night you may do what you will with me.'[13] This went deep with Margot: it opened up her understanding of the character of Marguerite. 'The words were particularly touching – I don't know why. I think they contain something of that vulnerability of the feminine woman, like Marilyn Monroe.'[14]

There was a limit, however, to how far Margot was prepared to go with the looser aspects of womanhood. She refused – 'for reasons of modesty connected with the novel'[15] – to wear on her costume the red camellias stipulated by Cecil Beaton. 'Without liking to explain, I insisted on wearing white flowers.' What she found embarrassing to articulate was this: courtesans of Marguerite Gautier's era were known to deck themselves in red corsages as a sign that they were menstruating. 'I could have kicked her,' wrote Beaton,[16] whose impatience with Margot's lady-likeness had already caused him to record in his diary: 'She gives maternal dignity to all the natural functions I am sure.' But Margot was, in fact, the least of Beaton's troubles. Nureyev had taken a pair of scissors to the tails of his frock-coat and torn two of his high-collared shirts to shreds. He was about to embark on a third when de Valois intervened. 'I said to him, "This can't go on, if you tear that shirt you'll have to wear it. What's worrying you?"'[17] 'I am *not* waiter,' Rudolf retorted, although what was *actually* worrying him was the relative shortness of his legs, which he categorically refused to have other than on full display. 'It was no use my pointing out,' writes Margot, 'that Bobby had looked elegant and poetic in *Apparitions*. Rudolf chopped the coat-tails to a length that satisfied his keen sensibility to his own proportions, regardless of what might suit anyone else or what the designer thought.'[18]

No flies on Rudi. Notwithstanding the glories of Pavlova's upper half, he was well aware that it was the proportions and contours of his white-hosed lower body that would get the audience going – that, and the publicity which inevitably resulted from such shirt-ripping scenes. An article in the *Daily Express*, headed 'Tearaway Nureyev',[19] provoked a further outburst.

'Dear Cecil,' wrote Bruce Beresford to Beaton. 'What a day of . . . storms, rage, hysterics, drama and alarm! . . . As it was the photo-call day and we had 50 photographers here I prayed for calm seas. In vain. I went to Rudi's dressing-room at 10 a.m. to see how he was. He said: "Do you have anything to do with publicity?" Upon my short "yes" he gave a sort of pantherine snarl, threw a tray of cups of tea across the room, tore off his shirt [yours] and stamped on it . . . The ballet started at 10:30 and on his first entrance we knew we were in for some fun . . . He made no attempt whatsoever to dance, he treated Margot abominably, flung her about, tore his shirt off and flung it into the orchestra, shouted at Lanchbery, fixed us all with the evil eye, flung the riding stock at the stage manager and generally gave such an exhibition of bad manners that we quailed and sank from sight with terror and sheer horror. Fred *must* have been in tears. I didn't dare look at him. Ninette sat clutching my arm in a vice and just moaned. The photographers . . . were struck dumb . . . Ninette strode up and said, "Rudi, I've never told you a lie, the Opera House did *not* give this story to the press." He managed a wan smile, was helped back into his shirt and suddenly the storm was over. We took the pictures . . . Margot, ice calm, behaved . . . as though nothing had happened.'[20]

Where the issue of photographs was concerned, Rudolf's fury was, for once, exacerbated by Margot, who, with her phobia about cameras, had instilled in her new partner 'the idea that cameramen should arrive pleading and depart bleeding'.[21] According to Keith Money, 'The general situation had all the elements of war photography or a tiger-shoot: you might get the beast, but then again the beast might just get you.' Yet Zoë Dominic, another respected photographer, finds Margot's attitude understandable: 'When I first started, there was very little control over who attended photo-calls, so that dancers like Margot would be doing the dress rehearsal, which is the moment of needing to find your way, and perhaps not being absolutely perfect, and there might have been thirty or forty photographers in the stalls – some fairly skilled, others totally *un*skilled. Once through those portals you could shoot what you liked, and a lot of material was published where dancers were wearing their leg-warmers, which I thought was simply a disgrace. In the early days, Margot was always photographed in the studio, and there was one set of Beaton pictures that were posed in that particular style as a way of marketing *Marguerite and Armand*. But by the early 60s we were all into action stuff, and the film was probably not quite fast enough and therefore some pictures did show movement. I think that's what made Margot very, very defensive. She was, I found, completely unpredictable. So that when you submitted a set of pictures, and you had in your mind the ones that were going to be passed, you could never be sure. She might pick some you thought were not right. Performers need photography but they fear it. And there are only a limited number of people that they trust.'

The approved pictures were projected, Brecht-style, on to a cyclorama – blown-up portraits of Margot and Rudolf hovering above the 'gilded cage' which constituted Beaton's set. There was a tacit agreement among the critics that, given the 'orgy of star-worship'[22] which surrounded *Marguerite and Armand*, it was pointless to bring artistic judgement to bear upon it. Though James Kennedy (James Monahan) personally found it 'a "Reader's Digest" version' of *La Traviata*, he maintained that 'so long as both of them are to perform it, it is likely to remain the darling of the multitude – no matter what the critics think of it'.[23] Richard Buckle considered that, since 'it is less of a ballet than a series of psychological close-ups, its choreography is not important enough to make it worthwhile giving without these two powerful personalities. But this is OK by me. I am all for *pièces d'occasion* which exist only for the artists who inspired them.'[24] Buckle, having been banished from Ashton's esteem over *Tiresias*, redeemed himself with his review of *Marguerite and Armand*, which Ashton told him was 'just what ballet criticism should be'[25] (i.e. unbridled adulation): 'I don't know how much of a ballet *Marguerite and Armand* would be without Fonteyn and Nureyev,' wrote Buckle, 'and don't much care. What is *Le Spectre de la Rose* without Karsavina and Nijinsky? And without Pavlova *The Dying Swan* is absolutely disgusting. Fonteyn and Nureyev . . . in Ashton's ballet . . . are . . . altogether beyond praise. From the wild opening wood notes of Humphrey Searle's subtle arrangement of the Liszt sonata we recognize that we are due for a bout of all-in romanticism; and fine frenzy is what we get . . . Marguerite loving Armand before renouncing him – a white battle. Next the party: Fonteyn coughing in black with camellias in her hair and a new diamond necklace. Nureyev comes in and yearns . . . With a change of mood he seems to try to sweep her off. But no, he flings banknotes at her and wipes his hands down his sides with a grimace of repellence . . . Turning again to the sobbing Fonteyn, he seems to relent, then points at her with dagger derision and backs out, fiendish, laughing. To her death-bed, cloak swooping, a desperate nightrider, he soars. Whisks her up, whirls her round, cuddles her on the floor, smothers her with smiling, mocking sympathy. Mad embraces. She is lifted, diving to the sky; then falls. She raises a hand, touches his brow, gazes wildly. Her hand drops. Death. Sour chords.'[26]

Sour indeed. 'Frankly,' confided Ninette de Valois, 'I don't believe in ballets that can only live through certain artists. It's like writing an opera that only Melba can sing. Well – there's something wrong with the opera. I mean you can do it, and it's great fun to do it, but it's not serious. I would think it wouldn't work without them. Ashton said he didn't want anyone else to do it and he allowed himself to be completely influenced by them. That's not the essence of choreography. It should have its own essence.'

Members of the company were equally cynical. 'A dreadful ballet,' says Ronald Hynd. 'But seeing Margot crumple was supreme.' This 'crumple' had the dancers lining the wings to watch, every time Margot performed it: a kind of staggering exit made on *pointe* after her renunciation of Armand – 'bourréeing off', as Buckle puts it, 'broken by duty and coughing'.[27] It was in the unballetic realism of such moments that the innovation lay. 'This hectic choreography,' wrote Clive Barnes, 'with all its plunges and grapplings, still bears traces of classical elegance, but it is far wilder than anything Ashton has created before. Nureyev seems to have prompted the same revolution that he earlier prompted in Fonteyn . . . He has challenged both of them to discard their inhibition . . . Fonteyn acts with every nerve naked and with every emotion exposed . . . the last shred of artificiality has been cast aside.'[28]

But the transformation that had come over Margot was not one which made Ashton happy, since it was not he who was responsible for effecting it. His resentment of her marriage to Arias was as nothing to his jealousy of Nureyev's hold over her. As Maude Gosling says: 'Margot gave herself so utterly to Rudolf that Fred felt deserted.'[29] During rehearsals, Ashton, 'brought up to believe a ballerina is a sacred being',[30] had been horrified by Rudolf's 'biting remarks . . . Margot never minded in the least, it was only me with that exaggerated sense of courtesy, I suppose you could call it.' Ashton envied Nureyev's ability to impart technical knowledge to Margot. 'She was in a state where she was willing to be refructified. She accepted from him.' That curious word, 'fructified', had been the one which Ashton had used to the women in *Symphonic Variations* when Margot had been his talent's mystic bride. But she now had a new fructifier. After the première of *Marguerite and Armand*, the drama guru

Peter Brook wrote: 'When Fonteyn curtsied before a stamping and cheering house, it could have been Duse. And when she and Nureyev stood together, tired and tender, a truly moving quality was experienced; they manifested to that audience a relationship graver, paler and less flesh-bound than those of everyday life.'[31]

The cast around Margot was changing in more ways than one. Her new artistic dependency upon Rudolf had been spawned just in time, since the great stalwart of her cause was about to bow out, leaving her, for the first time in her long career, professionally unmothered. Three days after the première of *Marguerite and Armand* came a shock announcement: Ninette de Valois was to retire. At the end of the company's seventh New York season, she would bequeath the directorship to Ashton – a dubious honour which made him feel 'like James the First succeeding Queen Elizabeth'.[32] And if Ashton were crowned Director, with all the toll on his creative energies that this administrative work would take, then the choreographic opportunities would fall to Kenneth MacMillan, who had no interest whatsoever in making ballets for Margot.

Nor dared she continue to fool herself that she could rely on Tito for support. He had flown in for the opening night of *Marguerite and Armand*, only to fly straight out again the following morning – the brevity of which visit did not go unnoticed by the press. 'It was very sweet,' Margot chirruped to the *Evening Standard*. 'He came over from New York for the day.'[33] But it was becoming painfully obvious that the only role available to Margot in her husband's life was a supporting one. And it would not be long before she was called upon to play it. On 22 March, Arias was arrested in Panama, along with ten other men, in connection with the seizure of 1,000 cases of whisky which the National Guard intercepted on 'a remote Pacific beach'[34] – not a million miles from the bottom of Tito's garden. The £35,000 cargo had been towed there by no less a vessel than the *Elaine* – the very shrimp-boat which had served as warship in Tito's revolution. Once again Margot's name was plastered all over the papers – this time as the wife of a suspected smuggler. She put up a brave front, laughing off the accusation as 'a silly Panamanian farce'.[35] 'My husband would have nothing to do with this sort of thing,' she protested to the *Sunday Express*. 'It is clearly a manoeuvre to throw discredit on the good name of the Arias family. My husband has continued his father's work in fighting poverty in Panama. Any connection with the contraband whisky would be quite ridiculous. I am not all that worried. Roberto's family are all in Panama. Obviously they will be trying to clear his name. I hope justice will be done and that he will be released before any harm comes to him.'

He was released on £2,500 bail, after being held in solitary confinement for seventy-two hours. His treatment, he told the *Daily Express*, had been 'brutal – absolutely savage. After my arrest, the National Guard commander, Bolivar Vallarino, and his second and third in command all conveniently disappeared for the weekend so that they could not be found to sign my release.'[36] The same article claimed that he had phoned Margot in London, warning her 'not to be surprised at anything that happened to him during the opening stages of the coming presidential elections'.

This was not the kind of scare a ballerina needs in the run-up to a New York opening night. Although, on 17 April, Tito attended the gala performance of (what else but) *Sleeping Beauty*, Margot's Aurora failed to light up the Metropolitan Opera House as it had done in each of the seven seasons since 1949. 'Dame Margot Fonteyn was not at her best last night,' wrote the *New York Times*. 'She got off to rather a rocky start with the Rose Adagio and never seemed to get back the totally winning ways we remember from her first performances.'[37] The lukewarm reception may have owed something to the fact that Margot's partner on the first night was Blair rather than Nureyev. There had been an attempt on the part of the management to field the home team rather than let a guest artist steal all the plaudits. Some hope. A new word had to be coined to convey the excitement engendered by the Russian: 'Rudimania'. He had, as it happened, made his début in New York a year earlier at the

Brooklyn Academy, to somewhat cautious reviews. But news from London of the mythical partnership had driven caution to the winds, and when, on 3 May, he did finally appear with Margot – unadvertised, as second cast, in *Giselle* – the audience stood and screamed orgasmically like idolatrous pop fans. Suddenly, according to Walter Terry of the *Herald Tribune*, Margot was dancing 'more beautifully than ever before. The youthful Nureyev, almost twenty years her junior, has given her new theatrical inspiration. Combine the smoulder, the mystery, the dynamic presence, the great streaks of vivid movement which Nureyev gives us with the beauty, the radiance, the woman-liness, the queenliness and the shining movements of Dame Margot, and the cheers that have shaken the old Met to its foun-dations are explained . . . This, rightly or wrongly, was the Royal Ballet; this, while Fonteyn and Nureyev were representing the most ephemeral, the most fleeting of all arts, was ballet itself.'[38]

On nights when the two did not dance, or danced separately, the theatre was far from full. On nights when they did dance together, mounted police had to be called to protect them from the fans who had slept in the subway tunnel under the Lincoln Center to secure tickets which were changing hands at black-market prices: a $15 seat could fetch as much as $75. Fonteyn and Nureyev were 'the hottest little team in showbiz'.[39] And the hottest tickets of all were not for the staple Royal Ballet *Giselle* or *Swan Lake*, but for Nureyev's own, imported fragment: *Le Corsaire*. This time, it was no mere matter of 'ten minutes of dancing, and twenty minutes of applause' – the clapping went on throughout the entire interval, refusing to subside until the curtain rose on the next ballet.

But although Rudolf, like Margot before him, made the cover of both *Time* and *Newsweek*, not everyone was in thrall to his Tatar cheekbones. Chief among the unbelievers was John Martin, seventy-year-old doyen of American ballet critics, who vented his spleen in the *Saturday Review*: 'It was a black day for the Royal Ballet when [Nureyev] arrived in London as a roving *cause célèbre* and moved on to the company . . . To see him as

Fonteyn's partner is an unhappy experience ... Some of us have tried putting a hand over one eye and trying to look only at her but it is no good. She is, after all, an exquisite part of a legend, and it is difficult not to feel somehow embarrassed ...' And then Martin delivers the punchline which, to this day, balletomanes quote with a mixture of horror and mirth: 'She has gone, as it were, to the grand ball with a gigolo.'[40]

28

If a speck of rueful truth made John Martin's preposterous comment stick like mud to the archives, this was because the ballet world tacitly acknowledged that a woman of Margot's quality would never have gone 'to the grand ball with a gigolo' had she not been, deep down, alone. It was obvious to those around her that, despite her impregnable loyalty to her husband, Margot's marriage was headed for the rocks. She intimates as much in her autobiography: 'The death of his father had left Tito profoundly at a loss for direction in his life. At a time of uncertainty he did not want to ask me to retire but, as I continued dancing with Rudolf, who grew stronger daily, the effort took all my resources and I had little time left over to help Tito. It was a critical time for him, and for me too . . .'[1]

The grand ball, meanwhile, rolled on. Princess Grace, Greta Garbo and Jacqueline Kennedy all flocked to those New York performances. The latter was prevented from going backstage by a nervous Sol Hurok who, lest the Russian dancer and the American First Lady ignite some incident with the KGB, locked Rudolf into his dressing-room. Undeterred, Mrs Kennedy sent a private plane to fly Rudolf and Margot (with Ashton, Somes and Lanchbery as entourage) to Washington for tea. The United States and the Soviet Union were poised to sign the first nuclear testing ban – 1963 being the year which marked the instal-lation of a White House/Kremlin hot-line – and in the Cabinet Room, while Jackie's back was turned, Rudolf did his fleeting best to defrost international relations by warming his prized buttocks in the President's chair – 'to find out what power really felt like'.[2] Yet for Margot, the pleasure of that tea-party was derived not from any rich feast of compliments about her dancing, but from a few crumbs which fell her way, concerning

Tito: 'The President received us and astonished me by saying, "I remember your husband, Dr Arias, told me something about sugar that I did not know. I was very grateful for the information" . . . It was more than flattering to have the incident recalled so clearly by the President without apparent prompting. I couldn't wait to report it to Tito.'[3]

Chance, however, would have been a fine thing. Arias had disappeared back to Panama, where he was now seeking power by more orthodox means: as a candidate for the National Assembly 1964 election – scheduled for 17 May – to be Deputy for the Province of Panama. Margot and Rudolf, after dancing their gruelling way round the States and Canada, embarked, in the summer, on their Mediterranean and Far Eastern itinerary: the 'Unhappy Tour' of Annette Page's recollection. Apart from *Birthday Offering* and *Symphonic Variations*, which Margot danced with Royes Fernandez, and *Scène d'Amour*, in which she was partnered by Ronald Hynd, the repertoire for this particular batch of 'Fonteyn Follies' came courtesy of Rudolf. As well as *Corsaire*, it included *Gayané*, a Kurdish-style *pas de deux* which Margot had already performed in London and Washington with a young Hungarian dancer, Victor Rona. But entirely new to her was a third piece from the Kirov canon: the *Grand Pas Hongrois* from *Raymonda*.

Early in their partnership, Margot had been able to handle Rudolf's outbursts with cool diplomacy. 'He would scream, "Shit, shit, you dance like shit," ' says the conductor John Lanchbery, 'and Margot would turn to him and say in the sweetest voice, "Well, tell me how I am like shit, Rudolf, because maybe I can change it." '[4] But now her confidence seemed to have been eroded to the point where she could no longer humour him. 'An awful lot of door-slamming went on when he was staging *Raymonda*,' says Ronald Hynd. 'He spoke to her and she just rushed out – left the rehearsal in floods of tears. There was a big pause while we all tried to look the other way and then she had to be coaxed back to continue rehearsal.' 'Either that,' chimes in Annette Page, 'or they were always giggling. Margot

got out of an enormous number of awkward situations by giggling, and they were quite silly – you wanted to bang their heads together and say, "For goodness' sake let's get on with the rehearsal – we're all standing here while you muck about." Because she'd never mucked about. Never ever. She started wasting time and fooling around and not being very funny about it either. On that tour she behaved in a way which made us all say, "I'm sure it must be the menopause." She was a bit flushy, too. No Hormone Replacement Therapy then. You had to live through it. She never spoke about it. I'm sure she had very conflicting emotions to deal with. Enchanted by Nureyev and disenchanted with her husband at the same time.'

Margot's emotional conflict may not have been helped by the presence of Erik Bruhn, whom Rudolf had roped in to stage an extract from the Bournonville classic *La Sylphide*. Bruhn, though not invited to perform himself, travelled with them for the early part of the tour, and he and Nureyev were inseparable. 'Even people who didn't know who they were,' says the French dancer, Hélène Trailine, 'would turn to look at them because they were so sublimely handsome. You were struck by their beauty.'[5] It made Margot long for Tito's company. But he, of course, was nowhere to be found. 'Tito travelled extensively in South America,' she protests, 'and at times it was difficult to locate each other for days on end which added to our unhappiness. Then Tito developed a serious attack of shingles, but despite this insisted on crossing the Atlantic for a reunion while convalescent.'[6]

Not exactly. According to Ronald Hynd: 'We were rehearsing in Monte Carlo and Tito was supposed to be flying over from America. Things were not going terribly well – awful rows between Margot and Rudi, and I was the ballet master trying to hold it together for this small group – it was all very difficult. Daily came the news: Tito can't make it. Now he's got shingles. Finally – on the last day – he turned up. Margot said, "Come over to the hotel and let's go through tomorrow's calls," and we went, and there was a message from him saying he'd already arrived. I was in her room when he came in and I felt rather awkward. The first thing she said was, "Oh, let me see," and she pulled up his shirt – almost as if to prove before a witness that he'd got shingles. It was all very shaky, that. I just wondered whether what was *really* going on in her marriage didn't make her want to prolong her career.'

In the first bloom of Nureyev's rejuvenating influence, Margot confessed to John Tooley: 'God! I've never done the things I do now.'[7] But, as time went by, the effort, at forty-four, of keeping up with a twenty-six-year-old was proving a mammoth strain. 'I struggled to regain a technique which had been eroded during the years with the bad foot. Muscles that had grown lazy did not take kindly to coming out of retirement. Subsequently, on tour in Israel, where we danced somewhat unsatisfactorily in football fields, I damaged my left calf muscle but managed to continue for another three weeks, with difficulty and in pain.'

But the pain in her body reflected, as ever, the inner suffering which she would not voice. On his flying visit to Monte Carlo, Tito had done something which had filled Margot with superstitious foreboding. 'He'd taken off his wedding ring,' says Ronald Hynd, 'and, rather symbolically, left it behind. Margot wore his ring over the top of hers. We were travelling from Tel Aviv to Haifa and we stopped *en route* to bathe in the evening. It was hot and there were these wonderful ruins down by the sea, and we all went in. Suddenly, there was a shout from Margot. Tito's wedding ring had dropped into the sea! We were all diving and trying to find the damn thing on the sandy bottom and we never found it. We got back into the cars and Margot was absolutely stricken. I was sitting next to her, and I just wanted to put my arm round her. Here was Margot and in this awful situation, and somehow the fact of losing the ring when he'd been so tardy in coming made it seem that something really serious had gone wrong. And for the rest of the tour she seemed very much disturbed.'

Joan Thring, who was handling the travel arrangements, had booked Tito in wherever Margot was to stay, but he did not join the tour again until Honolulu. Margot always rested in the afternoon before a performance, and Thring heard her 'begging him to come back to the hotel. He refused. He was having too much fun in the sea.' That fun included flirting with Joan, who was horrified as well as unresponsive. 'It was so humiliating for Margot.' But the ballerina, in her autobiography – that volume known by Keith Money as 'Margot's best-case scenario' – described those ten days in Honolulu as 'a small oasis in which I could once more hold Tito's hand'.[8] And there was no denying her spectacular capacity for denial. 'Margot's way of getting through life,' says Money, 'was to have sort of steel bulkheads like a ship, and if she couldn't cope with something . . . a relationship, a problem, whatever, if she didn't solve it by dusk, it went into a box, the box went into the cupboard, the cupboard was locked and the key was thrown away.'[9] This coping mechanism was perfectly conscious and had served her well since her twenties, when she had told Volkova: 'I'm determined to be happy. If an unhappy thought comes into my head, I suppress it. I put it at the back of my head.'

And nothing kept the dogs of depression at bay more effectively than the challenge of a new work. Ashton's first tactic, when, in September, he officially took over as Director of the Royal Ballet, was one of passivity rather than initiation: he acceded to Nureyev's ambition to mount *La Bayadère* Act IV, the Kingdom of the Shades, at Covent Garden. For Nureyev, *La Bayadère* represented unfinished business: the role of Solor was one which he would have danced in London with the Kirov, had he not made his dash for freedom in Paris. The Kirov production, with its famous repeated-arabesque entry of the entire female *corps de ballet*, had made an indelible impression on London audiences, and the English dancers would now have to raise their game – not to mention the height of their working leg *en penchée* – to compete. For the solo roles, Nureyev cast three already proven luminaries of the company: Lynn Seymour, Merle Park and Monica Mason, and was amazed to find that this, and his automatic assumption that Margot would dance the show-case central role, was met with 'open distaste'[10] by Ashton and his two assistant directors, Michael Somes and John Hart, who felt that 'the company itself should become the "star"'.[11]

But Margot more than justified Nureyev's faith in her, which, if anything, had grown stronger through familiarity. 'I had my donation, you know,' he said. 'My vision of her. I was amazed by her ability to do things. I thought, she's not what's called a robust ballerina in Soviet style. But there she was – she did all the steps. I guess introducing her to *Raymonda*, to *Bayadère*, to *Corsaire*, made her pull her socks up, no? – *and* compete with me. I think there was excitement. I think every performance we did together, each one was treasured. I love her company, I love her presence, I love being with her. She was very cheerful and concerned for me that I be too grim and gruff and miserable, and she make great effort to shake me out of my miseries.'[12]

Margot approached the role of Nikiya, which involves a lot of symbolic business concerning a draped muslin scarf, with her usual creative practicality, showing great interest 'in the shapes made by the scarf itself, so that she endlessly reappraised this aspect at rehearsal, working out the exact spots at which she had to clasp the muslin, in order to produce the nicest effect'.[13] Though she found the Minkus score dull, Petipa's choreographic structure, as remembered and augmented by Nureyev, was 'really pure Bach, so I cling to that'.[14] As producer, Nureyev subdued his romantic fire in favour of a disciplined severity. 'Petipa has never been better served,' wrote de Valois. 'Nureyev has given the artists of the Royal Ballet the very spirit of the great French choreographer. He got the very best classical work out of our dancers . . . In fact, I afterwards found the Kirov production disappointing by comparison.'[15] The Shades scene from *Bayadère*, set against a featureless backdrop, was, wrote Alexander Bland, 'as cold and clear as crystal, a distillation of dancing . . . The long white lines of girls acquitted themselves valiantly and the soloists – Park, Mason and Seymour – spun through their exquisite variations with a newly blossoming verve. At the radiant centre Fonteyn – neat, quick, poised and fluent – shone like a diamond.'[16]

The Kingdom of the Shades has no story other than the theme of an Indian prince searching for the spirit of his beloved, and it was Nureyev's tribute to his adored partner that, in presenting her framed by his own inherited tradition, he sought, like that prince, to uncover the last vestiges of her potential, and thus reveal her in a newly polished and multifaceted light. 'We expected Nureyev to shine,' wrote Clement Crisp in the *Financial Times*, 'but it was Fonteyn who dazzled even more. This was Fonteyn the superlative stylist, and also Fonteyn the amazing technician, dancing with extraordinary speed and superb assurance.'[17]

Clive Barnes was similarly bowled over. 'Ballet may have previously known a career that followed the curious path of Margot Fonteyn's, but if it has I cannot recall hearing of it . . . For here she was dancing a bravura role with considerable distinction, in a way that would, I think, have been beyond her fifteen, five or even two years ago. Of course, Fonteyn's balances have for many years been outstanding, and *Bayadère* exploited them. But the ballet also exploited a whole technical armoury that one hardly knew she possessed. Her turns, both supported and unsupported, have never been stronger or faster, and surely she has never jumped so high or danced so effortlessly. The placing of her body looked glorious. Here she was contrasted with three very strong young dancers – [all] probably rather stronger than Fonteyn was at their age. But Fonteyn's authority over them was never for one instant in doubt.'[18]

Nor was there any doubt that it was to be Margot who, on 12 December, would open in Ashton's new production of *Swan Lake*. In the event, she was partnered by David Blair, since Nureyev, who had been knocked down by a motor-scooter, had needed stitches in his right ankle. Much was made in the press of Margot, 'in chunky sweater and thigh-length jack-boots', collecting 'the injured Nureyev, in striped pyjamas' from the hospital in Chelsea and taking him to her mother's house. ' "He often comes here, to my mother's," ' Margot told the *Daily Sketch*, "for meals after practice at the Royal Ballet School (it's just round the corner). I have just had a word with him. He is very direct about wanting to be left alone. He's not temperamental, just direct." At this point Dame Margot's mother, Mrs Hookham – Dame Margot always stays with her mother – came in and announced: "He has refused his pudding." [20]

This last remark has such humorous overtones of Black Queen's early culinary struggles with her daughter that it is tempting to let it stand for the general tenor of Mrs Hookham's good-natured and practical dealings with Rudolf. As BQ explained to Rosario de Galindo: 'When I was a very young girl and I misbehaved, my grandfather used to say, "You're behaving like a Tatar." I never knew what he meant. *Now* I know what a Tatar is! And I realize I must have been horrible!'

Rosario, Tito's glamorous and worldly sister, who was now running their dead father's newspaper, *Panamá América*, understood, when Margot managed to snatch a few days in the spring to join Tito's Panamanian campaign trail, that all was not well with the Arias marriage. 'I sort of grasped that there was something wrong between them, which to me was quite normal. I mean, it's difficult to keep a marriage like that – extremely difficult – with those kinds of pressures from both sides. You know: Tito running to meet her here, or her running to meet him there, and by the time she got to where he was, she was exhausted, and by the time *he* got there, he was thinking he could have been doing something else, or had left something hanging. She really was torn between her profession and her marriage.'

On this particular trip Margot found herself in the unaccustomed role of camp-follower, steered around the hustings by Buenaventura ('Ventura') Medina, whom Tito had taken into his employ for the specific purpose of guarding his famous wife. Deprived of Tito's company, Margot clambered in and out of cars, and on and off helicopters, with a young Austro-Panamanian friend, an acolyte bright and glamorous enough to have enjoyed a lengthy affair with Nureyev: Louis Martinz. With Martinz acting as interpeter, Margot was witness to that sight so dear to a woman's heart: the sight of her man in the throes of a great adventure. 'This time I saw a different side of Panama,' she writes, 'the slums, the villages, front porches, farm houses and the little corners where people came to hear Tito speak. His electioneering personality was so different from his normal contemplative demeanour. I had never heard him talk so much or with such vehemence, and everywhere there were throngs of people, people of all shades from café au lait to black, with hundreds of squirming, healthy, black-eyed children with laughing faces. The old ladies doted on Tito, and the young ones worked with fervour for his election.'[21]

She makes Tito's connection with these fervid womenfolk sound innocent enough, but it was during this trip that Margot finally came to despair of Tito's loyalty to any concept of marriage as she understood it. If, in London, he had made a vague effort to avoid flaunting his dalliances, here, on his home turf, not only did his reputation as a heart-throb matter more to him than his wife's sensibilities, but it also seemed to earn him political kudos. Despite Margot's presence, he made no attempt to conceal the affair which he was conducting with his new secretary, or to discourage the youthful flatteries of a neurotic social beauty called Anabella, who attached herself to him with sycophantic ardour, and whose surname, sinisterly enough, was the same as that of his arch-enemy, the Chief of Police: Vallarino. Later, it would be rumoured that Tito had played with fire even closer to home, by involving himself with the wife of one of his political allies, and Margot's reference to this supposed cuckold is tight-lipped: 'Campaigning with [Tito] every day was Alfredo Jimenez, the expressionless one whom I had last seen sailing away on the shrimp-boat in the revolution. He was hoping to be at least a substitute deputy, to stand in for Tito during his absences abroad. That position, however, legally depends on the number of votes gained by each candidate in the ballot.'[22]

Her husband's conjugal neglect in the very public arena of her newly adopted country seems, for Margot, to have been the last straw. She had looked for salvation in marriage, away from the heavy demands of her career, only to find that, for all the physical strain which dancing placed on her, ballet was now a veritable haven compared with the grim reality of marital disappointment. By the time the elections were held – on 17 April – Margot was thousands of miles from Tito's side: appearing with Rudolf as a guest of the Australian Ballet, now run by Peggy Van Praagh following the death of Borovansky. Bill Akers was amazed by the change that had come over Margot. 'When she first came here in 1957, she was at the peak of her career, a *grande dame* on the way out. By 1964, she was totally transformed, as if she were a young dancer. There was joy in what she was doing. When she and Rudolf arrived, the first person they asked for was the *maître* (ballet master), Leon Kellaway. For class. For tradition. It was the time of the Beatles, and Rudi had this terrible blond mop. A photograph of him appeared doing an *entrechat* on the front page of the *Sun*, up in the air with his hair out to *here*. And I said to Margot, "Jesus, they're going to think he's a screaming queen." She said, "Well, if you can induce him to have it cut, dear, good luck to you." So I called in a barber, and Nureyev walked in, with his hair all beautifully cut. I said, "Oh, don't you look wonderful." He said, "Don't be ridiculous. I look like lesbian. And it's your fault." And Margot walked behind him and gave me a big wink. If she told him to do something, it was sacrosanct. He was not Europe's spoilt darling in those days. He had this incredible reverence for her, and she was still in thrall to his fantastic, raw talent. You only had to watch them on the stage and it was like satyrs and nymphs having sex all over the place.' The Australian press certainly speculated with salacious glee on the intimacy between the two stars, and, whatever the ambiguity of *that*, its converse was undeniable: the ballerina's separation from her husband could no longer be termed 'only geographical'. For the first, serious, time, Margot was contemplating divorce.

But where would divorce leave her? Battling her way through three *Giselles* or three *Swan Lakes* a week, at the emotional mercy of a homosexual young enough to be her son? 'I was exhausted at the end of the tour,' she writes, 'and anxious to see Tito, who I hoped would be able to meet me in Miami on my birthday.'[23] Faint hope. The votes from the election were not yet counted. Margot flew to Panama, only to feel 'lost in the political jabbering'.[24] The most she could do before she left was to extract a promise from Tito that he would meet her in Rome to discuss divorce proceedings. The idea, peddled in Peter Watson's *Nureyev*, that her decision to divorce was influenced by the discovery that she was pregnant by Rudolf meets with derision from her friends, who believed her to have been long since sterilized, and utter scepticism from the doctor to whom she would eventually be obliged to confide her gynaecological history. But Margot did join Rudolf in Stuttgart in a particularly sombre state of mind, knowing that a crisis could no longer be averted, any more than nature, in the face of exhaustion, can continue to be cheated. At the deepest level of her being, she had run out of resources, rather as a dancer might suddenly find herself devoid of breath. And to that dancer, whirling in the spotlight, abrupt cessation would be tantamount to physical death. But fate, when it struck, deflected its blow. It was not she, but her husband, who was brought to a standstill.

'We were in Rome,' says Joan Thring, 'and Tito was supposed to join us to discuss the divorce, and he didn't turn up. We were running about like hairy cats, because Rudolf, wherever we went, had to see everything, and Margot kept wanting me to leave him looking at things and go back with her to the hotel every hour, on the hour, to ring Panama to see where Tito was. And he wasn't there. Where was he all that weekend?'

From Rome, on Monday 8 June, Margot and Rudolf flew to the English spa town of Bath, where they were to open its festival with *Divertimento* – the one and only *pas de deux* which Kenneth MacMillan was ever to create for them – to Bartók's Sonata for Solo Violin. Keith Money was there to take photographs. The dancers went straight to the theatre to rehearse with the violinist, who happened to be Yehudi Menuhin. 'On paper,' writes Money, 'this was a grand confluence but the hectic schedule of all the participants meant that the piece itself had to be constructed before both dancers left for a series of perform-ances in Australia, two months before the première, and there was no time for any further polishing until the very eve of the event. Rather surprisingly, the dancers had somehow remem-bered most of the work during the interim, and the first stage rehearsal was progressing satisfactorily, when Menuhin suddenly stopped playing, waved his bow at the two dancers, and said: "I think, here, something a little lighter, more cheerful, perhaps." '25

The great violinist's cheery notion that ballets were made up as they went along should have kept the group in stitches over dinner at 'some frightful old run-down café somewhere on the "wrong" side of the city'.26 But Margot was still distracted over Tito's whereabouts, and her powers of premonition were working overtime. 'She kept talking about this friend of theirs who was shot,' Money recorded in his journal. ' "It couldn't happen again? It couldn't happen again!" she said over and over again.'27 And it is tempting to surmise that the 'friend' was none other than President Kennedy, for, only seven months earlier, on the eve of the première of *La Bayadère*, Frederick Ashton had stepped in front of the curtain after a performance of *Marguerite and Armand*, and announced to an aghast audience that the American President had been assassinated. Certainly Modi Arias had tried to persuade his brother not to stand for election, warning him, 'You'll be next.'28

'We all had a premonition,' says Joan Thring, 'because when we arrived back at the Lansdowne Grove Hotel at about midnight, there were too many photographers around. I said to Rudolf: "Don't you think this is a bit odd?" They were only there for two nights, doing this five-minute dance of Kenneth's, and we thought, "What's all the fuss about?" Then Yehudi and Diana Menuhin came out of the hotel and Diana came up to me and said what had happened. I said to Rudolf, "You disap-pear," because the press was doing its thing of putting Margot and Rudolf together, and it was getting a bit stupid. I said, "Just go to your room, and I'll come and tell you what's going on later." We still didn't know everything, but I was given a number to ring, and Tito's brother Modi said that if Margot wanted to see Tito alive, she'd better come now. So I had to go and tell her. She was in a room talking to Kenneth and the designer, Barry Kay, and I thought it would probably be easiest for her if I told her in front of them. Afterwards she said she wished I hadn't told her in front of other people. She screamed and ran out the room, and that hotel is full of corridors. She ran into a ballroom, so I went after her, and then I called Rudolf and he cuddled her for a bit. She just wanted to scream, so she screamed. When I told her who had done the shooting, she said: "It can't be. You must have it wrong. They're our best friends in Panama." I told her: "Everybody has spelled out the name for me [Jimenez], and I don't have it wrong," but she ran away from me again. Margot was very odd in that way – she didn't want to hear things that she didn't want to hear. She'd take a little bit at a time. After an hour or two she came back to me and said: "You can tell me a bit more now." I said: "Well, the bit more is that I have to get you on a plane straight away if you want to see him alive." And she said she wouldn't go. "No, I'll do tonight's performance, it'll be all right." I said: "I don't think that's a good idea, Margot. I can get Lynn [Seymour] to come and do it." But she stayed.'

In all the annals of Show (must-go-on) Business, this instance must surely take the biscuit. The press hardly knew what to make of a heroine who danced on, while her husband, on the other side of the ocean, lay at death's door. Had she donned the Red Shoes, or what? 'It looked so heartless,' says Joan Thring, 'but Margot could be very stubborn. She'd geared herself up to leave Tito and she was three-quarters of the way there. The timing was bad. It was all out of sync.'

John Field was in Bath to help stage *Divertimento*, and his wife, Anne Heaton, was privy to Margot's dilemma. 'Tito had set up with another woman, and Margot told John, "I'm not going." I don't think she expected Tito to live, anyway. It was her mother who got on the phone and said, "What's the world going to think if you don't go?" ' By morning, Margot had been persuaded to let Joan Thring book her on a flight – but not until after the première. Black Queen herself stepped in to deal with the press. 'This has been a terrible shock to Margot,' Mrs Hookham told the *Daily Sketch*. 'She was so looking forward to being reunited with her husband this week. She saw him in Panama about three weeks ago on the way home from her Australian tour . . . If only there had not been a delay in votes coming in for the Panama election Dr Arias would be in London today – safe and well.'[29]

But the *Sketch* was not altogether convinced. On 10 June, in a front-page story, headlined 'AGONY OF ARIAS', Aubrey Chalmers wrote: 'Dame Margot decided yesterday that she would dance, then fly to her husband, Dr Roberto Arias, lying wounded in Panama. So she prepared for last night's première of *Divertimento* with Nureyev at the Bath Festival – and planned to catch a plane out of London Airport this morning. After five telephone calls to Panama, she had heard that her husband, shot four times in a political row, was out of danger. It was then that she made up her mind to dance and to be back for her next performance at Bath on Saturday. Pale and weary after a night without sleep, Dame Margot said: "I will only go to see my husband if I can get back by Saturday." Later, following four hours' rehearsal before the new ballet, Dame Margot went back to her hotel for a rest. Violinist Yehudi Menuhin said: "She is standing up to it very well. She is very courageous . . ." A spokesman of the Bath Festival said: "Since Dame Margot heard that her husband was out of danger she has brightened up considerably. She has started laughing and joking again." Dame Margot, who married 46-year-old Dr Arias in 1955, said this of her husband's career: "Of course, things have become intense out there but I am not normally a pessimistic person. Whatever he does I fully appreciate the situation." She said it was "absolutely ridiculous" to suggest that their marriage was in danger. "I do not see him often enough – but still, I do see him. I cannot stop dancing for six months at a time. However, when I do stop, I hope to be able to spend more time with him." '[30]

To dampen speculation in the press, David Lewin of the *Daily Mail*, whom Margot had previously entrusted with exclusives, was mobilized to present the ballerina's version of events in an article titled 'MY CALM'. 'One cannot live in terror,' Margot asserted. 'I always knew the risks of Panamanian politics and there have been other occasions in the past when I have been more scared. But it is like my mother who is worried every time I fly anywhere; she has learned to control her fears. So have I with Tito. In a crisis such as this I tend to reduce things to their simplest: is my husband in danger or will he recover? I was assured three times by phone from Panama during the night and the morning that his condition was not critical; that he was not paralysed and that he would recover. The simplest thing, therefore, was to continue dancing and fly to him after the performance. The simplest thing was just to get on with it. I deal with problems as they arise. If, when I get to him, he is all right then I can come back. If he is not I will decide then what to do next . . . There is a risk in everything – even being run over by a car in the street. One cannot think of it all the time. When it is all over I get a secondary reaction – a realization of how bad things might have been. That secondary reaction is still to come.'[31]

Margot's superhuman power to banish unhappy thoughts to the back of her mind had, in this case, rather disastrous repercussions for what went on in the front: namely, her immediate ability to concentrate. During the actual performance of *Divertimento*, she suffered a prolonged memory blank – not that the audience noticed, demanding, as it did, an encore of the entire work (which must have seemed bafflingly unfamiliar the second time around). Earlier that day, Roberto, Tito's sixteen-year-old son, who was studying at Millfield School in nearby Somerset, had turned up in Bath; and, after the performance, Margot and her stepson travelled to London for dinner at Barons

Court with Black Queen, before setting out, at last, for Panama. Only once airborne did Margot have a chance to read what the newspapers had to say about her husband's condition. But she forwent the opportunity, kicking the papers under the seat, lest Roberto should become anxious during the long journey. Roberto, equally protective of Margot, did not mention what he could hardly have failed to see at the airport: accompanying the 'MY CALM' story, which featured a bravely smiling picture of his stepmother, flanked by Menuhin and Nureyev, was a much larger picture of his father, in shocking disarray – glasses knocked sideways, tie yanked askew, shirt splattered in blood – lying unconscious on a stretcher. Of the other headlines, Margot had glimpsed but one word – but that alone was enough to freeze her blood: the word was 'Paralysed'. She chose, however, not to believe it. 'I was confident,' she writes, 'that I knew better than the journalists after my conversation with Tito's brother . . . at that point, and for a long time to come, my mind refused to conceive the possibility of permanent, serious injury.'[32] But, by the time she was next photographed, in the Arrivals lounge, now flanked by Panamanian heavies, the news which Tito's brother was whispering in her ear had wiped from her face all semblance of a smile. Marlene Worthington was also at the airport, and, for the first time in her life, Margot, previously so cold and suspicious, fell into the secretary's arms. Outside the hospital waited a gathering of Arias supporters, who had kept vigil around the bulletin board for two days. As she hurried arm-in-arm with Roberto down the hospital corridor, someone muttered: 'We expected you yesterday.' 'I felt reproved,' writes Margot, 'but nothing anyone said could have prepared me for the sight in store.'[33]

Tito, naked under a sheet, was lying strapped to a Stryker bed – a narrow table, rather like an ironing-board – which revolved at measured intervals to relieve the pressure of weight from immobile limbs. His right arm, cast in plaster, was winched aloft. Tubes sprouted from his ankles, pumping nourishment into his veins and waste product out. Even his breathing was effected via a hole in his neck. 'I was appalled,' writes Margot, 'shocked beyond measure. At last I understood that he was more than desperately ill, and that I should not risk tiring him even by my presence.'[1]

That this sudden confrontation with human frailty should have provoked Margot to such a volte-face – from prospective divorcee to wifely martyr – has struck some sceptics as hypocritical, or, at least, typical of her propensity for role-playing. 'There was an awful lot of pretend in Margot's head,' says Joan Thring. 'There's no knowing where it began or ended.' Yet, surely, all pretence must have ended *there*, in that darkened hospital room, as compassion for her felled husband overwhelmed Margot's heart – that heart which, in its natural state, was so unswerving. No need, any more, to suffer the pain of not knowing where, or with whom, Tito might be. Gone, too, the agonizing split between marriage and profession, husband and stage lover – resolved, at a stroke, by the sudden clarification of the one thing which she had ever needed to know: where her duty lay. That duty, she now understood, involved not only standing by her man, but continuing with her dancing – *for his sake*. Buenaventura Medina, Margot and Tito's loyal manservant, later recalled: 'When she saw him on that bed, in his situation, I think she said to herself, "I'm going to make you happy – doesn't matter how." Everyone thought when he became paralysed that she would just pay someone to take good care of him and that's that. But she said, "No, I'm going to show the world that I can dance *and* I can take good care of my husband." And she did it – right up to the end. That was my fight with her. She wanted to take better care of him than of herself. I said, "No Madame, no." But it was her character to be like that.' Colette Clark agrees. 'It wasn't a role in the end. She was absolutely herself – did everything beautifully and tirelessly. People said it was such a tragedy, his being shot. Of *course* it wasn't a tragedy, because she got what she wanted. Someone to look after and love and lavish with all the devotion and strength of her marvellous character.'

If being shot was a tragedy for Tito, he refused to acknowledge it as such. In 1980 Margot would write: 'I cannot remember hearing him complain in all the sixteen years. He just says, "A tragedy isn't a tragedy if you don't make it one." He ignores it, and gets on with his life.'[2] Certainly Tito's philosophical style of detachment never became him more than in his own cheerful recounting of the attempt on his life, which took place as his chauffeur-driven car drew up at the traffic-lit intersection of Calle 50 and Via Brasil: 'I was under the impression that "Yinyi" Jimenez, the would-be assassin, was firing an automatic. After deciding he had done the necessary he turned his attention to my driver, Nato Medina. "I will kill you, too, if you get in my way," he threatened. Then he tried to finish me off by emptying what was left in his automatic into me.

'The first shot had been the most effective. I felt a sharp pain in the back of my neck. It is odd to smell gunpowder and know that you are the victim. I had often wondered what people about to die really think and I did quickly think of my wife and three children. I also realized that most of the bullets went through my arm, and I was smiling or laughing at the thought of what a bum shot Jimenez must be. Then I was lying on the front seat of the car feeling rather helpless as it was manoeuvred violently to turn left towards the hospital. After that I lost consciousness . . .'[3]

Coming round, Tito was greeted by the face of Dr Octavio Vallarino, father of Anabella. Next, there appeared a nurse, who introduced herself as Gloria, sister of Marlene, Tito's secretary. It was explained that a specialist, Dr Crespo, would be performing a tracheotomy without delay. The last rites were swiftly performed. On the way to the operating theatre – though this next detail is suppressed from Margot's book – Tito 'could recognize two girls who had been helping me with legal work earlier and who had spent most of the political campaign with me. One is quite tall, so I could make out an outline that was recognizable.'[4]

According to Louis Martinz, who personally brought the tall girl to the hospital, this was Anabella Vallarino, who was distraught at the news that Tito had been shot. Martinz was dismissive of the rumour, repeated in Peter Watson's *Nureyev*, that the wife of Jimenez had been in the car with Tito on that fateful journey through Panama City. Only in England, Martinz sighed, could the story of a *crime passionnel* have taken such hold. 'People always want more,' says Rosario de Galindo. 'Sex stories are more interesting than political stories.' Certainly Jimenez bore a political grudge against Arias, who had reneged on his promise to register Jimenez as his substitute deputy. But both Tito's sister, Rosario, and his daughter, Querube, insist that it would be a simplistic view of Panamanian politics to regard the socially rather downtrodden Jimenez as anything other than a front-man for a much more complicated conspiracy – probably by the police itself – to rid Panama of the powerful Arias influence. Neither of these women shows the least interest in denying Tito's propensity for adultery, but both become impatient with the unsophisticated Anglo-Saxon insistence upon marital triangles. 'Let me give you one little bit of advice,' Querube confided. 'Don't look for *one* mistress. There were lots of girls infatuated with my father – all the little "Miss Panamas" and so on. He was like any of these men who run around when they're alone. But the running around was never really that serious. Once or twice it got enough so that it hurt Margot's feelings, and then we would worry. It was worrying where Anabella was concerned and it must have been very upsetting for her family. You couldn't really call her a mistress, because no one had to support her – she had a comfortable home with her parents and a chauffeur to drive her about. But there was something wrong with her. A beautiful society girl, but screwed-up in the head. It wasn't really my father looking for her – she went after *him,* and she would say to people that she loved him even more after he was shot. But look at her last name: *Vallarino.* This is what I think must have caused the confusion in London, because Vallarino, which is a very common surname in Panama, was also the surname of my father's greatest enemy, the head of police, who hated my father for getting the votes and being the next likely one after Arnulfo, politically speaking. Arnulfo had no children, so his good grace fell on my father. Vallarino was the Number One general in Panama, but he knew that if Arnulfo got elected, the military would be pushed out in a second. At the time of the shooting, many people believed that "Yinyi" Jimenez was only a front, and that the assassination had been ordered by the police. And, sure enough, a few years later, when Arnulfo *did* win, the police took over in the form of Torrijos (who had Noriega for *his* main general) and Panama went through twenty years of military rule.'

Certainly if Margot feared further reprisals, it was not from the bungling Jimenez, but from the armed guards who now stood watch outside Tito's private room. So anxious was she for her husband's safety that she organized a rota of friends to stand guard over the guards. She was relieved to find that Tito's lungs had drained and that he could speak – provided one closed the aperture in his throat. However, she refrained from tiring him while he was comfortable, and instead collected anecdotes in her head, so that, when his Stryker bed was upended, she could lie on the floor and amuse him with stories while he endured his half-hour face-down. She took to sleeping in the hospital beside him, so that she might be there each morning when Dr Gonzalez-Revilla, armed with hammer and pin, came to test whether, as the swelling subsided, Tito's mobility showed any signs of recovering. But although Margot was stubbornly optimistic, Dr Gonzalez-Revilla was not. His version of events is matter-of-fact. 'An opponent shot Dr Arias three times. Once in the chest, once in his right arm and once in the neck. The bullet in the neck produced a little pressure on the spinal cord. That's all. I operated on him two hours after the accident. I removed the bullet and placed him in intensive care. He was quadriplegic. Paralysis of the four extremities. He had an infection of the urine because he had a catheter, as his bladder was paralysed as well. Still, his speech was all right. In order to start developing mobility, what I advised Margot Fonteyn was to take him to Stoke Mandeville Hospital in England, which was a very good hospital for rehabilitation.'

This plan made sense to Margot, for Stoke Mandeville was only an hour from London, and she, with every day that went by, was breaking her contract with the ballet: a contract for money which would now be sorely needed to cover medical bills. Not for another two weeks would Tito be well enough to travel, and she asked Dr Gonzalez-Revilla if she might fly on ahead to resume rehearsals. 'You husband is getting on well,' said the doctor, 'but I must warn you there is one danger in cases such as his. At any moment he could suffer a thrombosis.'[5] Gonzalez 'In that case, I would fly back immediately,' Margot retorted. The doctor told her gravely, 'You would be too late.'

But Margot hardened her heart, put the Panamanian bungalow up for sale, and flew to England to rehearse Nureyev's full-length production of *Raymonda*, which was to open in Spoleto on 10 June. On the 4th, Tito arrived at Stoke Mandeville, accompanied by Modi, Marlene, Gloria, and five teddy bears. 'I sent my assistant with them,' says Dr Gonzalez-Revilla, 'and he in particular told the hospital *not* to stop the antibiotics. They did.'

Raymonda, meanwhile, in Spoleto, was having its own melodrama – what with the choreographic notes having been smuggled out of Leningrad in a thermos flask by a Canadian pupil of Pushkin, and the fact that, in order to get the go-ahead for the production from Covent Garden, Margot and Rudolf had to pay for the costumes out of their own pockets, costumes which, when the Italian designer delivered them, turned out to be almost amateurishly underadorned . . . 'It was the nightmare of all time,' says Joan Thring. 'Margot didn't know whether she was coming or going, and Rudolf was in a temper because he had to teach the ballet to Doreen Wells. Margot was there on and off, which drove us completely crazy. I rang her all the time. Eventually she said, "Now that I've got Tito into Stoke Mandeville, I can come." When she got to Spoleto she asked if she could stay in my room because she didn't want to be by herself. In the morning, she went down to the theatre to rehearse with Rudolf, and no sooner had she left than the phone rang and it was Stoke Mandeville saying that Tito had gone into a coma. I had to get her back – *that* wasn't easy. Thank God her mother had come with her.' Mrs Hookham, luckily not yet unpacked, was bundled into a taxi with Margot. It was twelve noon, and their plane was due to take off at 2:00. 'Poor Margot was almost grey-faced and remote,' writes Mrs Hookham, 'so we sat hand in hand in silence for about an hour, when suddenly she said, "God, he is on the wrong road for the airport." . . . She shouted to [the driver] to stop at the next crossing where she flung some money to him and started dragging our suitcases out on to an island and looking for another, more modern taxi, but it was lunchtime and there were [none] . . . Suddenly a private car drove up . . . and Margot obviously told the driver what had happened and so he drove us to the airport. The plane was just about to leave and I think we left without a ticket . . . but we got on at last . . . Margot sat with her eyes closed, willing her love and strength to [Tito] that he should not die and I prayed for them both.'

A car was waiting for them at the steps of the plane and they were the first passengers to get off. Leonard Lindley, their chauffeur, who had tuned into the radio five minutes earlier, told them that according to the latest news bulletin, Tito was still alive. But when Margot and her mother reached Stoke

Mandeville, the situation could not have been more grave. Tito, freed at last from his Stryker bed, was now packed in ice. Dr Revilla is convinced that the English hospital staff made an error in ceasing to treat Tito's urinary infection. 'They stopped the antibiotics, and all of a sudden, four days later, Tito's temperature had risen to 108 degrees – a temperature not compatible with human life. He had convulsions and he lost the capacity to speak.'

The German doctor who 'pulled [Tito] back from heaven by one foot'[6] was Sir Ludwig Guttman. In all his forty years of practice, Dr Guttman had never seen a man survive such an exaggerated fever, so he could offer Margot no clue as to what, were Tito to survive, the effect might be. Margot kept such unstinting vigil at Tito's bedside that Dr Guttman had to order her to rest. 'But he underestimated,' she writes, 'the advantage in times of stress of a long ballet discipline.'[7]

Panicked as she had been on leaving Spoleto, Margot did not omit to scribble a lipsticked scrawl on Rudolf's dressing-room mirror: YOU ARE GREAT I WILL MISS YOU.[8] She would now have hours and hours and hours to contemplate the truth of those carmine words. 'The interminable hospital days were a period similar to the war, that I knew would eventually terminate and be like another book on the shelf.'[9] But when Tito's coma finally did abate, the sounds which issued from him could not be discerned as words. The viability of his brain was in question. It was amid these doleful developments that Margot returned to Spoleto to pick up the last performance, and battle on to Baalbek, with *Raymonda*. Blessed with a reassuring score by Alexander Glazunov – that composer whose swinging rhythms no dancer can resist – *Raymonda* was, despite a tedious story-line (medieval knight rescues Hungarian lady from Moorish villain), a ballet which suited Margot every bit as much as *La Bayadère* had done, sweeping her back, in its spirited finale, to the character-dancing which she had so loved in her youth. Audiences cheered her courage as well as her performance, and, if footage of her rehearsing is anything to go by, she was – when the rictus of her smile, which was particularly strained at the time, fell away – the very model of a tragic heroine: too thin, wild-eyed, and dancing with a certain new violence, as though to lose herself in some more viable existence.

Back in the reality of Stoke Mandeville, there was a glimmer of improvement. 'When Dr Guttman held up his hand showing three fingers in front of Tito's face, and asked, "Arias! How many fingers have I?" Tito struggled to control his diaphragm, his larynx and his tongue and finally brought out the word, "Eleven." '[10] Nothing could have been better evidence of Tito's intellectual survival than this irreverent return of his propensity to tease. But it would take more than a sense of humour to effect the huge act of acceptance which Tito would have to make. Sir Ludwig Guttman's daughter, Eva Loeffler, met many of her father's patients, but few as severely afflicted as Tito Arias. 'He was terribly, terribly disabled. My father started the treatment of spinal paraplegia in the mid-forties, and without it, someone like Arias would certainly have died. When you're paralysed, the blood supply becomes very poor and the skin breaks down much more easily. He would have had to be turned regularly – every half-hour. When he was in a chair, you would have had to be very, very careful that everything was very soft, and there could be no damage. The level of his disability was such a high one. He couldn't even, if a fly landed on his nose, sweep it away. He was extremely well looked after. But it was like that play *Whose Life Is It Anyway?*'

And, at first, like the protagonist of that as-yet-unwritten tract, Tito did find the prospect of life intolerable. 'Not a day went by without his begging me to let him die,' Margot writes. 'I concluded privately that, being his wife, I was the one who would have to help him. I further resolved to do it, if it became necessary.'[11] But conversations with other patients encouraged her to believe that the death-wish would pass. 'Please wait a little longer,' she would implore Tito. 'I don't think you should take a decision when you are still so weak and ill.'[12]

Tito was in hospital for two years. Margot's attendance upon him was almost maniacal in its devotion. 'Every day,' wrote Barry Norman in the *Daily Mail*, 'she has commuted between Buckinghamshire and London. At first when [Arias] was critically ill, she lived in a private room at Stoke Mandeville. Later, when he came off the danger list, she moved to a hotel in nearby Aylesbury. Not that she lives there. She merely sleeps there, keeps her clothes there. Her free time – all her free time – is spent at the hospital with her husband. For Dame Margot, the day begins with a call at 6.30 a.m. and a short drive to the hospital for breakfast with Dr Arias. Week by week his condition improves but his movements are still limited and he likes to have her around. Five months ago his wife could not drive at all, and was not particularly interested. Then, because having a car would give her more time with her husband, she took lessons, and within a few weeks had passed her L test.'[13]

The press made much of this feat, photographing Margot giving graceful indications of left- and right-hand turns, bare arm extended from the window of the Mini Minor – black, with trendy basketweave bodywork – in which she had been chauffeured since 1961. It seems to have slipped the newspapers' attention, however, that, within a short space of time, the ballerina was involved in an accident. 'She'd only had the licence about a week,' says Keith Money, 'and she was going down a long, straight hill, and she had a blow-out. Terrible thing to happen to a new driver – fighting, fighting for control. Ninette was in the front with her, and finally they ran off the road. Ninette smacked her knee against the dashboard. A passing policeman had to get them out. Margot was all right, but Ninette's knee was a mess, and she had recurrent trouble with it after that – sometimes she'd walk with a very stiff leg. That really damaged Margot's confidence hugely – she felt so guilty. She never drove later in Panama.'

While he was at Stoke Mandeville, Margot tried to get her husband to re-engage with life by persuading him to dictate notes to her for a prospective autobiography, and to let her set down the business plans which were always crowding into his head. But her determination to be an angel of mercy while also running a hard-headed career struck Keith Money less as saintly than as evidence of an accelerating divide between her honest and her crowd-pleasing selves. 'The side of her that made you terribly protective,' he says, 'was a marvellously simple, rare creature. But there was this doppelgänger which had been manufactured by a million other people. All that nonsense about going up and down to Stoke Mandeville. I used to go up with her occasionally. We'd go by train and get a taxi at the other end. She and I would sit for hours taking transcriptions from Tito about this plan that he was working out, and I swear to God it was a pipeline to pump maple syrup from one side of Canada to the other. And we had to draft and re-draft the letter, just to make him feel important. And we're sitting there – she, fifteen times more than I – faint with hunger, cross-eyed with weariness.'

Yet who can say that these bouts of self-abnegation did not sustain Margot, and inure her against the rampant egotism which might otherwise have overtaken her as she clung, at the age of forty-five, to her position at the top of the tree – that tree which now had many precarious branches, a long way from the safety of her roots at Covent Garden? When the Royal Ballet had recently revived Robert Helpmann's *Hamlet* for Nureyev, she, who had created the role of Ophelia/Gertrude, was not included in the cast; it had only been later, at Baalbek, that she was invited to dance it. And now she was to do *Swan Lake* in Vienna – on film as well as on stage – in Nureyev's own production, one in which he would take the brooding self-absorption of Hamlet and invest it into the character of Siegfried, swelling the role that traditionally was something of a cipher, in an attempt to make it dominate the ballet which Margot had long regarded as her own. That she could survive his shrieking obscenities in rehearsals, and still retain the essence of her fabled Odette/Odile while absorbing his radical innovations (which incorporated some unaccustomed music in Acts III and IV), attests to the extraordinary depth of concentration and sheer self-belief which her job now required of her. Indeed, thanks to the embargo which she put on any close-ups of herself, she emerges from the film with rather more dignity than does Nureyev, who, in too much make-up and a Beatle wig, seems something of a casualty of his own choreographic invention. We see him, at the end, drowning and drowning in waves of navy muslin, while Margot is borne loftily back into the clutches of von Rothbart, who, in Rudolf's Soviet-flavoured version of the story, appears – like Tito – not only to have survived, but to have won the battle for the Swan Queen's soul.

The accumulated number of curtain-calls (eighty-nine, according to *The Guinness Book of Records*) that Margot and Rudolf received over the four acts of *Swan Lake* on its last night in Vienna can only have exacerbated the problem which now beset Margot in her dealings with the Royal Ballet. 'Margot had entered that bleak period,' writes Keith Money, 'wherein the management with ill-grace occasionally pencilled her into the big classics, to appease the box office, while slicing away at the majority of the Ashton works which really sustained her own interest in the London repertory.'[14] So it was that, in the autumn of 1964, Margot found herself carrying a heavy burden of *Swan Lakes* and *Giselles*, unrelieved by the chance to perform ballets she loved such as *Daphnis and Chloë*. This was partly because, even by her own reckoning, Nureyev was unsuitable for the role of Daphnis, but mostly because Ashton, ever-protective of Michael Somes's feelings, was pitted against her dancing Chloë with somebody new. Money, however, was convinced that Lynn Seymour's regular partner, the fresh-faced and romantically feasible Christopher Gable, would make the perfect Daphnis; so Margot, having met with a wall of managerial refusal, confronted Ashton directly. 'Oh – it was awful,' Margot reported to Money. 'I said to Fred, quite simply, that I wanted to do *Daphnis*, and I wanted to do it with Christopher, and I didn't want to have a fight over it. Fred was absolutely *furious*. Finally he shouted, "Oh, very well. *Do whatever you want to!*" and then walked out of the office.'[15]

The dispute, although it resulted in a spate of memorable

performances of *Daphnis* in both Europe and America, further strained the bond between Fonteyn and Ashton; so that the line which he adopted in what happened next was all the more disconcerting. The only new parts coming Margot's way these days were Rudolf's reconstructed offerings from the old, Russian, Petipa repertory. At the RAD gala, in November 1964, she danced yet another *grand pas* – this time from *Paquita*. The real creative energy in the Royal Ballet was now emanating from a quarter which had never included her: the inspired artistic collaboration between Kenneth MacMillan and the twenty-four-year-old ballerina Lynn Seymour. These two had honoured their apprenticeship, and were now about to storm into the mainstream with a major three-act work to Prokofiev's most popular score, scheduled to open on 9 February at Covent Garden and on 21 April at the new Met in New York. So, just as 1949 had been Margot's year, surely 1965 would see a new world star in the firmament – the dancer born to be Shakespeare's Juliet: Lynn Seymour.

But events were not to concur with natural justice. *Romeo and Juliet* got off to an entirely unexpected start. And though its launching would propel the public's perception of Margot even higher into the stratosphere, it would bring her, in the eyes of her colleagues, morally low.

30

No sooner had the dates for *Romeo* been announced than Lynn Seymour discovered herself to be pregnant. The abortion cost £500, which she had to borrow against her weekly salary of £40. Her marriage – to dancer and photographer Colin Jones – did not survive the brutality of the sacrifice, but a talent such as Seymour's has no choice. 'Juliet was mine,' she states simply. 'Juliet was the bonding of my partnership with Christopher Gable . . . Juliet, the classic heroine of the theatre, was the culmination of all my fantasy roles as a dancer.'[1]

Three days after her abortion, Seymour was back at rehearsals, which proved to be nothing less than 'exclamations of wonder at every step – a joyous exchange of insights and motivations'.[2] MacMillan was having to follow not only Lavrovsky's fabled 1940 production for the Bolshoi, but also two admired Western versions: one, in 1955, by Ashton for Copenhagen, and another, seven years later, for Stuttgart by John Cranko. What MacMillan planned to offer, as well as unprecedentedly lush passages of dancing, was a much more modern, psychological approach. Seymour writes: 'We had seen Franco Zeffirelli's stage production co-starring Judi Dench and John Stride, and Kenneth was determined that his ballet, full of slashing vigour, should overflow with the same vital accent on youth . . . Because Kenneth was creating the ballet on Christopher and me – dancers he knew and trusted – he allowed us tremendous freedom . . . He seldom wanted straight pretty-pretty lines. Working with Kenneth . . . I realized that I could move my body in oddly extended shapes that might otherwise have seemed impossible or improbable.'[3]

MacMillan had conceived his Juliet as a randy, headstrong teenager after Lynn's own heart: 'a modern free spirit who knew what she wanted and would risk all to get it'.[4] Imagine his despair, then, when he was informed that the role was to be showcased by the demure doyenne of the company, Margot Fonteyn, a woman twice Seymour's age and three times Juliet's. Seymour's first intimation of doom came from Christopher Gable, who had read in the newspaper: 'Nureyev and Fonteyn as Romeo and Juliet. That is the top attraction for the new season announced by Sir Frederick Ashton today.'[5] Seymour and Gable tried to reach MacMillan for an explanation, but the choreographer had fallen into a mute depression. His excuse, when it surfaced, was that Sol Hurok had insisted that Margot and Rudolf open in New York, threatening to cancel the tour if they did not. Ashton, whose own agenda may have been governed more by jealousy of, than concern for, MacMillan's success, agreed that the London opening also be given to Fonteyn and Nureyev, establishing *Romeo and Juliet* as their new 'star vehicle'. Seymour, meanwhile, was assigned a humiliating task: that of teaching the role to Margot and three other ballerinas: Merle Park, Annette Page and Antoinette Sibley. Rumour has it that 'MacMillan wickedly encouraged her not to give [Margot] much help', but Seymour magnanimously writes: 'Margot wisely, understandably, wanted to create her own Juliet. Her position was vulnerable. She was expected to learn the highly individual movements specifically shaped for another dancer. I gave her the gist and she instinctively made adjustments. She did not choose to die with her legs askew or sit quietly on the bed during a long musical passage. These decisions were absolutely right for Margot.'

When the sequence of performances was finally posted on the notice board, Seymour had a further shock to withstand. Though Gable was down to partner Annette Page on the second night of *Romeo*, Lynn's name was at the bottom of the list: fifth cast – for the ballet which she had created. It was a fantastic piece of cruelty. 'I had lost the première,' she writes. 'I had taught the role to four Juliets. My reward, or perhaps more accurately my *punishment*, for falling in love and getting married and then

41. Rehearsing *Marguerite and Armand* with Nureyev.

42. As Marguerite Gautier.

43. *La Bayadère.*

44. *Divertimento* rehearsal shortly before hearing of the attempted assassination on Tito.

45. With Rudolf in the company canteen at Barons Court.
Vergie Derman and Georgina Parkinson in the foreground.

46. Tending to Tito.

47. Work goes on.

48. 'Ballerinas never smoke.'

49. Tito in Margot's dressing-room, BQ looking on.

50. Photographed for *Vogue* in Cecil Beaton's St Regis Hotel apartment,
New York, 1968.

51. Rehearsing *Romeo and Juliet.*

52. Carrying John Gilpin in *Night Shadow*.

53. With Frederick
Ashton after a
performance of
*Marguerite and
Armand*.

54. In *Floresta Amazónica* with David Wall.

55. With Tito and the cows at La Quinta Pata.

56. With Ninette de Valois at the fund-raising gala, Covent Garden, May 1990.

57. *'¡Más polvo, más polvo!'*
Last days at La Quinta Pata.

being careless enough to get pregnant – a greater offence for a young dancer than an abortion – had been primitively and publicly printed on a sheet of paper and pinned to a bulletin board.'[6]

In the event, however, Seymour would appear – due to Page's indisposition – at the second performance, but what, for Lynn, nevertheless remained a mortal professional blow is glossed over, with a couple of sprightly sentences, in Margot's autobiography. 'I was lucky to have had the chance to add Juliet to my repertoire of love-lorn females. Kenneth MacMillan created his own version of the ballet that had bowled me over when I saw Ulanova and the Bolshoi and, despite my usual misgivings about my age and ability, I grabbed the role enthusiastically.'[7]

'Grabbed' would seem, according to Clement Crisp, the operative word. 'It's the only time in Margot's life that she ever snatched anything. She'd seen Ulanova triumph on that first night of the Bolshoi season, and she wasn't going to have her aces trumped by some elderly Russian lady. Ulanova had opened her eyes – not only to how *long* you can go on, but to *how* you can go on. Hurok wanted her anyway, and it was consistent with Margot's life that she should get what she wanted. You can't blame her for having taken it. She was forty-six and here was a cracking great role that she'd always wanted, and she had to have it. She knew she had a duty to keep herself performing, and she did.'

Yet Keith Money, fierce in Margot's defence, swears that she was all too ready to take a back seat. He was present at a lunch in New York where Margot, though professing herself willing to try out Juliet later in the season, struggled to persuade Hurok to let her off the hook of responsibility. This is how Money's record of the conversation goes:

'No, Sol, I can't. I really *can't* do any more of these openings. You've all those other dancers to present. And it isn't as if Rudolf can't do something with one of the others.'

'Margot, Margot, how can you desert me? After all our years! Why you must do this to me?'

'Because I'm not as young as I was, after all our years!'

'What about Pavlova? What about Ulanova?'

'Well, I'm not Pavlova, and I'm not Ulanova.'

'Of course, of course. You're Margot! That's why you have to open in New York!'[8]

This is all very self-effacing – as far as it goes. But Margot's vague references to 'all those other dancers' and 'one of the others' will not suffice. Where is the specific, passionate endorsement of a young artist by a mature one, the generous acknowledgement that genius, when it strikes, must have its day? Lynn Seymour had *created* the role of Juliet. And no one knew better than Margot what it was to be a participant in that numinous intercourse, how it felt to have movement dragged out of you like something alive from your entrails. There comes a moment in all our stories when we are called on to give back some element of the blessings which we have received. And Margot had received more than most. When de Valois, in 1949, had faced down Sol Hurok ('Margot is our ballerina, and she has to open, and Sol, if you don't like it, we'll go to Coventry'), she had done so in all honour – for the honour of her company and the right of its best dancer to be seen. Perhaps because Margot's plea lacked any such breadth of vision, her case with the impresario did not prevail; and by the time she arrived back in London, Hurok had already telephoned Covent Garden, demanding that Margot do the opening night – or else. 'It was a desperate business,' writes Money. 'Margot was appalled, yet she dared not provoke a total stand-off if the management did want her to dance, since she was paying huge hospital fees for her husband and had no such amounts of money if she did not keep dancing. Rudolf queried the plans for his own reasons: not wanting to be seen as third or fourth cast in an important ballet.'[9]

Like Margot, Rudolf changed MacMillan's steps to suit himself. As Christopher Gable told Nureyev's biographer, Diane Solway: 'If he felt that the audience wanted to see an explosion of his skill at a certain point, he'd put something in. And if he felt that a lift was going to make him tired for his first solo, he'd cut it out.'[10] No wonder MacMillan sank into a 'semi-nervous breakdown of misery'.[11] According to Georgina Parkinson, 'Kenneth hated Margot in it, but he let them do what they liked and thought of Lynn and Christopher as his first cast.'[12] Meanwhile, the real first cast remained woefully under-rehearsed. Nureyev was nursing a bad ankle and refused to dance full-out, denying Margot – who had learned her part in three weeks – a straight run. 'She knew,' says Money, 'she was being used purely as a safety net for a financial enterprise, and she felt desperately unsupported in what was, by any reckoning, an enormous challenge – for *any* dancer. Launching a three-act ballet in which she had barely received the framework of the steps, she was also expected to cope with insidious layers of pressure, yet still pull the rabbit out of the hat, on the vital night, for MacMillan.'[13]

Even at the dress rehearsal, however, it became abundantly clear not only that Margot's professionalism had triumphed, but that MacMillan's majestic ballet would become, with the sweep and vigour of its inventiveness, and its confident, allusive homage to the inspiring versions that had gone before, the definitive interpretation of Prokofiev's emotionally charged score. It is only perhaps for those who were present at the dress rehearsal the day before – at which Lynn Seymour and Christopher Gable gave their own rendering – that the heartbreak and sense of injustice must surely persist. The extraordinary speaking rapture of Seymour's dancing took ballet beyond its narrow perimeters, and set her Juliet alongside any in the history of theatre where words instead of steps are the means of expression. That we have no record of her performance (except a television snippet, danced ten years too late, with Nureyev rather than Gable) and, instead, have Paul Czinner's predictable film with Margot and Rudolf as the star-cross'd lovers, amounts to little short of a crime for those who had the good fortune to witness what MacMillan had really intended to be seen. In Fonteyn's performance, even the costumes (by Nicholas Georgiadis) were changed.

Gone was Seymour's high-waisted, Renaissance shift in corrupted shades of flesh, for the sake of something purely white, moulded low on the hips, to flatter Margot's less decadent line. Gone, too, were all Seymour's most daring touches: the nerve to sit stock-still throughout the most turbulent of musical passages, for which Margot substituted a flurry of agitated turns; the foetal position which Lynn adopted after swallowing the potion, for which Margot substituted a decorous arrangement of limbs, like some Sleeping Beauty. And, at the final moment of Juliet's suicide, Margot chose to stab herself through the heart, whereas Seymour had driven a dagger into her womb.

The wound which *Romeo and Juliet* caused the Royal Ballet is an old one now, and it might seem churlish to keep worrying the scar, since it would be ridiculous to pretend that Margot, in her own way, did not have, as Alastair Macaulay points out, a 'huge impact in the role',[14] or that, with the passage of time, the ballet itself would not become invested with her particular magic. Macaulay was one of the new generation of discerning theatre-goers whose first sighting of Fonteyn, as late as 1976, happens to have been in *Romeo and Juliet*, and even though, by then, she was all of fifty-six, the revelation of her greatness came to him untarnished. He returned to Cambridge haunted by the rapture with which she had reacted when Nureyev kissed the hem of her dress. Later, he would write: 'She could still seem to shine with the brightness of youth; and she knew – none better – how to shape a ballet, scene by scene, and build it to a climax.'[15] But other, old critics, present on the first night, were less forgiving, among them Clement Crisp. From the beginning, Crisp had adored Margot in all her guises, but, as Juliet, he '*loathed* her. I thought she was totally detestable and artificial and insecure. Do you remember that bloody silly stole she had, and all that writhing on the bed? I hated her performance.' Yet such voices of dissent were lost in the general roar of approval which reached a pitch when Margot dropped a specific curtsey to Box 36, where Tito, on his first outing from Stoke Mandeville to Covent Garden, could be seen watching his wife from his wheelchair. As Keith Money makes plain, 'forty-three curtain calls do not attend a disaster'.[16] The success of MacMillan's ballet was assured; albeit that, next day, the *Telegraph* attributed its success, first, to the sumptuous sets of Nicholas Georgiadis, 'who with these remarkable designs can take his place by such ballet immortals as Bakst and Benois',[17] and then to a production which had 'showed us at last a portrayal many of us had long awaited – Dame Margot Fonteyn as Juliet . . . Dame Margot's Juliet, consciously cast perhaps in the heroic mould of Ulanova, yet with an ecstatic radiance of its own, had a memorable personal victory in choreography not ideally shaped to her image. Mr Rudolf Nureyev, injured, but dancing with half a foot better than most men with two, gave a mocking yet ardent Romeo . . .' MacMillan's choreography comes bottom of the critical list: 'the Royal Ballet might have done better to have waited a couple of years until it could have mounted the definitive Lavrovsky production. But, in all conscience, this new MacMillan should serve us well enough.'

Serve it has, to the present day, outlasting all other versions and boasting a whole panoply of glorious Juliets down the ages – Antoinette Sibley, Merle Park, Natalia Makarova, Gelsey Kirkland, Alessandra Ferri, Sylvie Guillem, Viviana Durante, Darcey Bussell, and, most recently, Alina Cojocaru. So why continue to carp about the ancient damage to its creators? On the grounds that Margot herself found the topic impossible to ignore. The company's collective grievance – that it was being extinguished by its own stars – was confirmed on the ensuing American tour. Hurok gave up advertising Fonteyn and Nureyev's appearances and adopted a policy of forcing audiences to take pot-luck, lest no tickets be sold for other dancers' performances. Such was the potency of Margot and Rudolf's fame that audiences felt cheated to be offered an alternative. On one occasion, in Chicago, the two were replaced at the last minute by – of all the ironies – Gable and Seymour as Romeo and Juliet. Gable encountered patrons 'crying in the lobby because they'd got these terrible understudies. We worked our asses off and by the end of the show we *got* the audience. But next day, the gist of the reviews was "If the understudies were this good, can you imagine what the *real* thing would have been like?"[18]

Little wonder that, within two years, Gable should have given up dancing to become an actor. As for Seymour and MacMillan: they handed in their notices, and left England to work in Berlin. And although each would return – Macmillan to direct the company, and Seymour (having given birth to three sons) to light up British ballet in the 70s, something in the betrayal which they had suffered soured both their careers, and conspired to undermine the creative trust that once had bound them. Although Margot, endowed as she was with tenacity, can hardly be held responsible for others' lack of staying power, the handling of these unique artists was a disgraceful episode in the Royal Ballet's history, and one to which Margot – however passively – had been a party. So it is important to know that it preyed, as it did, on her conscience. At the very last gala of all – a performance of *Romeo and Juliet*, starring Sylvie Guillem, given, after Tito's death, to raise funds for Margot – the latter was overheard, at a private dinner, desperately asking Lynn Seymour for forgiveness. Lynn, with customary largesse, was conducting herself as if there were nothing to forgive, while Rudolf kept interjecting: 'Drop it, Margot, drop it.'[19] But it redeems her in our hearts that she could not.

Romeo and Juliet changed all the rules for Margot, and would compel her to rely heavily on her new MacMillan role, since all her old, Ashton, ones were being systematically stripped from her repertory. She had stopped *Symphonic Variations* in 1963, and, after Gable left the company, she was no longer cast as Chloë; as for *Ondine*, it would cease to be danced by anyone until three years before her death. Ashton's creations had been the stepping-stones of her career, and without them, or others to replace them, her autobiography seems suddenly denuded: nine years of her life roll away in the space of one chapter. She could no longer count on support from any source, and must fend, not just for herself but also for Tito. Of paramount concern was earning money – a priority which invariably paves the way for compromise. If she had doubted the wisdom of appearing in the Royal Ballet film of 1959, imagine how sceptical she must have felt, six years down the line, about the making of Paul Czinner's *Romeo and Juliet*. She confided in her friend, the actress Ann Todd, about her horror of being caught – recent tucks to her face notwithstanding – in hard-breathing close-up. The physical renaissance wrought in her by Nureyev had receded, and although the mutual joy which (between screaming matches) they took from their passionate friendship was still conspicuous, the romantic element of their attachment had given way to a greater realism – a realism which acknowledged both Margot's renewed emotional commitment to her husband, and the escalating seediness of Rudolf's lifestyle.

Joan Thring remembers an episode which took place in her Earl's Court house, after Rudolf and Margot had a tiff: 'I had to do a sort of *pas de deux* in the back garden, to get her on my shoulders, so that she could climb through my bedroom window to get us freed, because, just when I'd got dinner ready, he threw a wobbly with her and said, "I have to go and find boy." I said, "What, on an empty stomach?" so, before he left, he locked the door on us. We couldn't get out.'

Joan Thring had, in fact, recently found Rudolf a house, which he went on to buy, in East Sheen, adjoining Richmond Park. Susan Carlton Jones recalls a party he threw there during the filming of *Romeo*. 'There was one hell of a shindig going on at Rudi's house, and by dawn there were bodies all over the place – they'd all passed out in various states of drunkenness. Apparently Rudi's bedroom had this great big Elizabethan four-poster bed. Suddenly a very dainty, beautifully dressed lady could be seen, delicately stepping over the debris to open the double doors and there was Rudolf Nureyev lying naked between seven tattooed matelots from the East End, dead to the world. Margot took hold of Rudi's big toe and waggled it and said: "Rudolf, dear, it's time to get up. We have to film the balcony scene." '

But, in truth, Margot's detachment was due less to cool realism than to the heat of a new distraction: her private life had recently taken a romantic twist of its own. Charles Hughesdon, 'pilot, entrepreneur and favourite of the showbiz élite',[20] a man who confesses his life to have been ruled by two passions – 'for aeroplanes and for elegant women'[21] – set about notching the initials of the world's most famous ballerina on his extramarital bedpost. 'I have often wondered to what extent aeroplanes and elegant women might be connected. Both are objects of beauty. Both need skilful handling. Both offer unique thrills and the satisfaction of conquest. Both carry dangerous risks and, to me, risk-taking has always been exciting and still is.'[22]

The risks, of course, were the usual ones associated with adultery. Hughesdon, an East End boy who had made a fortune from aviation insurance, was married to the actress Florence Desmond, star, with Gracie Fields, of *Sally in Our Alley*. He had first met Margot in 1958, when he and his wife had invited her, along with some mutual friends, to lunch at Dunsborough, their house in Surrey. The Hughesdons and Ariases became friends and, over the years, were to entertain each other both in England and Monte Carlo; but after Tito had become paralysed, Hughesdon 'telephoned [Margot] in London and suggested dining that evening – just the two of us. She said she already had a dinner engagement but we could have tea if I could meet her at Idell's [her sister-in-law's] flat in Long Acre. When I arrived she was alone . . . Our physical attraction was mutual and within a short time we started an affair. Two hours later Idell arrived. We were dressed and happy and we three had tea. Margot's dinner assignment went out of the window and we spent the rest of the evening together, dining at a local restaurant.'[23] But, unlike his brief dalliances with Ava Gardner and Marlene Dietrich, Hughesdon's attachment to Margot seems to have stood the test of time. 'From then on over the next ten years we met (with Idell's blessing) at the flat until Margot took an apartment in the Grosvenor House Hotel in Park Lane. There our trysts were always in the early morning – I would visit her

472

for breakfast. Margot's dancing life was hectic during that period of her legendary partnership with Rudolf Nureyev and involved much travel abroad. I was kept up to date with her itineraries and contrived to make my foreign travel coincide with hers wherever possible. We met all over Europe, in South Africa, the USA and Australia . . . On our meetings abroad I would usually watch the performance, then the three of us would dine and Rudolf would disappear into the night and we would be left to ourselves. Our happiest times together were on those overseas meetings where we did not need to be so secretive. Almost to the time she retired to Panama she relied on me for love and advice and help when it was needed. I kept in touch even at arm's length.'[24]

The undemanding and cheerful nature of the affair sustained Margot, while at the same time forcing her to further compartmentalize an existence which was already dangerously disjointed: her dealings with Tito became tinged with that exaggerated air of conciliation which so often accompanies sexual guilt. It had been to ingratiate Tito with his friends that, on 19 November 1964, she had agreed to appear on television in circumstances which could only compromise her. It was Churchill's ninetieth birthday, and the great man conceived a whim that Margot should rekindle his reminiscence of Pavlova by dancing the *Dying Swan*. This was a concert-piece that could veer close to melodrama, and one which, in serious circumstances, Margot would not have dreamed of appropriating. It went deeply against her artistic grain to *bourrée* into the spotlight that had been Pavlova's. Yet it pleased Tito that she should please Churchill, and, in a way, the impersonation was apt enough, since Margot was, by now, pretty much the same age as Pavlova had been when Peggy Hookham had been taken to see her at the Palace Theatre. Would children taken to see the ageing Fonteyn for the first time, Margot wondered, regard her with the same nonchalant dispassion as she herself had viewed Pavlova in the mid-20s?

Pavlova, travelling to any far-flung outpost so long as she could keep on dancing, had become a slave of her own cult; she had refused an operation to her ribs which would have halted her career, and, six days before her fiftieth birthday, died of pleurisy. And it was, eerily enough, incipient pleurisy that Margot, unable to shed a cough which had settled on her lungs, was now diagnosed as harbouring. But she took herself straight from the New York doctor's surgery to her dressing-room at the new Met to do her make-up for *Giselle*, only to be faced with a prospect infinitely more horrifying than the onset of any mere life-threatening disease: news that Anton Dolin was bringing Olga Spessivtseva – newly released from a mental institution, and the greatest exponent, ever, of Giselle – to see the performance. As if that were not enough, Dolin, not content with having unnerved Margot by dint of a warning note, now saw fit to bring Spessivtseva, 'a trim little figure in a plain, wool coat and a small fur hat',[25] backstage to Margot's door – *before* curtain-up. After the curtain had come down on the ordeal, Margot admitted to Keith Money that 'for much of Act I, she could not feel anything below her knees. "I had *no* idea where the floor was. I was just guessing where my feet might be" . . . After this, by degrees, the pleurisy was somehow shrugged off, and she never missed a scheduled performance.'[26]

Joy Williams, by now Mrs Michael Brown, who witnessed that *Giselle* from the wings, was touched by a scene enacted immediately after the calls. 'Dolin was round very quickly – he must have brought Spessivtseva through the pass-door – and I saw Margot cross the stage and, like a student, drop a curtsey of absolute obeisance before what looked, from where I was standing, to be an ordinary little old lady. The humility of it caught my heart.' Margot was rewarded by a message from Spessivtseva, who, though clearly moved in her turn by Margot's own personal plight, seems to have got muddled between Adam's *Giselle* and Chopin's *Sylphides*. 'Dear Margot,' she wrote in a letter which Margot would keep among her treasured possessions all her life, 'I would like to divide with you your sorrow and hope to the best. I received big pleasure in seeing you in the ballet "Sylfids". You were like a cloudy vision good luck to you. Olga Spessiva.'[27]

Even from so far away as the United States, Margot fled the now standard cries of 'Nureyev! Margot! Nureyev! Margot!' (a chant which betrayed the curious disparity of intimacy felt by American audiences for the two stars) and returned for a brief visit to Stoke Mandeville. Tito was in better spirits. Marlene Worthington, whose secretarial ministrations had so unsettled Margot before the shooting, had now become an indispensable stalwart in his life, keeping him abreast of the political manoeuvrings in Panama which were his life-blood. His physiotherapist, Ida Bromley, was teaching him to bang the table with a wooden gavel, so that despite his lost capacity for speech, he would be able to vote at the National Assembly when he returned, as he vowed he would, to Panama. Margot could only be grateful to see him once more full of plans — however unrealistic — since her own working schedule was so consuming: Milan, Rome, Naples, Bologna, Birmingham. This last venue was where she and Rudolf would team up with the Australian Ballet on its first international tour, for a revised and redesigned production of *Raymonda*. Off they would trundle again all over Europe before the première in London at the New Victoria Theatre.

By Christmas Tito's health had improved to the point where Margot felt able to accept an invitation to take him sailing in the New Year on Sam Spiegel's yacht. Despite Tito's irreversible paralysis, he coped so well that it was decided he should continue his rehabilitation programme as an outpatient at the Ludwig Guttman Centre in Barcelona. But, on phoning his hotel there one day, Margot was astonished, she writes, 'to be told by the long-distance operator that Dr Arias was not available — he had gone away and left no address. Thinking the operator had misunderstood me I tried again the next day to be told, "Dr Arias has gone away for two weeks. He has left no address." At first I felt very aggrieved and then I started to think how marvellous it was that he was once again able to take off impulsively on a journey without even knowing his destination. In this case he had gone on a tour of Spain in the car with his secretary

475

and the Spanish chauffeur.' With bills mounting, Margot gave a series of performances at Covent Garden which left those critics who had long loved her groping for an explanation as to her enduring power. Seeing her as Cinderella on 23 December 1965, Peter Williams could only write: 'So far, amazingly, after 17 years, she remains without equal in the part.'[29] And, on 7 February [when she danced with Donald MacLeary rather than Nureyev], Clement Crisp found himself at a similar loss: 'Last night Fonteyn danced *Swan Lake*; superlatives will not do, analysis is impossible; what can one say that will do justice – if not honour – to such an interpretation? It needs the pen of Valéry, Levinson, Edwin Denby, to capture something of its greatness. I must content myself with recording that it was magnificent on all counts, faultless in style, immensely touching in its tragedy and poetry . . .'[30]

Donald MacLeary had been coached in *Swan Lake* by the greatest ballet-mime of all – Robert Helpmann – so Margot was able to reinstate the dumb show in Act II, which she loved for its direct communication of the strange Teutonic myth behind *Swan Lake*. When dancers are not camping the whole thing up with alternative lyrics ('I'm a Swan Queen, You're a fairy, Go away from me, I don't like fairies') the words which a ballerina must sing in her head to the music are these: 'Over there is a lake made of my mother's tears. And over *there* is one who's wicked; he me makes a Swan Queen. But if one me loves, swears, marries, I, Queen of the Swans no more.'

Despite Margot's outward excuses about continuing to dance in order to make money, the 'one who's wicked', that tyrannical demon who was to keep her entrapped in a white tutu and feathers for a full forty of her seventy years, can only be judged, with hindsight, to have been ballet itself, which claimed her, body and soul, and barred all routes of escape into any ordinary form of human existence. But if she was doomed, Odette-like, to weep unrelievedly at the lakeside, she was also, by way of compensation, granted licence, in the guise of Odile, to perpetuate her life as a coquette. Now that Nureyev had begun, increasingly, to follow his own star, Donald MacLeary was but one of a dozen new dancing partners with whom Margot began to commit on stage what she jokily calls 'infidelity'.[31] Listing these cavaliers as if they were conquests – Attilio Labis, Egon Madsen, Richard Cragun, Anthony Dowell, David Wall, Donald MacLeary, Desmond Kelly, Ivan Nagy, Heinz Bosl, Garth Welch, Karl Musil, Mikifumo Nagata – she would often pick up a partner, according to Desmond Kelly, in whatever country she happened to be dancing, only caring to enquire beforehand: 'Is he handsome?' and requesting a photograph. Nureyev, meanwhile, when asked the whereabouts of his famous partner, would assume a mock-tragic expression, and reply: 'Dancing with younger man.'[32]

The young men in question were only too flattered to play occasional consort. For Donald MacLeary it was the fulfilment of a childhood dream. 'When I was at the School we were all terribly in awe of her. Sometimes there were passes to matinée performances and eight of us would go. And I can remember telling a lie. The woman who organized it said, "Has anybody never seen Fonteyn?" and I pretended I hadn't, I was so keen to see her in *Swan Lake*. She was an icon. She was very sweet to partner, very professional. It was easy because she was so well-placed – you knew you weren't going to have to push her round on pirouettes and things. She had beautiful balance because her sense of gravity was in the right place. She didn't sweat much. If you work hard you get beyond sweating. But she confided to me how nervous she got. I'd no idea.'

While touring with MacLeary behind the Iron Curtain, Margot received a telegram from Tito, dated 12 October 1966. JURY FOUND LAST NIGHT THAT JIMENEZ DID NOT APPEAR AT TRIAL WAS GUILTY OF INTENT TO MURDER STOP DECISION IS APPEALABLE TO SUPREME COURT WHICH NORMALLY CONFIRM WITHIN SEVEN WEEKS STOP BELIEVE IT IS POLICE PROBLEM NOT MINE TO FIND JIMENEZ AND REALLY CARE VERY LITTLE WHAT IS DONE IN PANAMA REGARDING THIS MATTER STOP . . . LOVING HO

Tito's lack of concern about the fate of his would-be assassin was a matter of wonderment to Margot, who writes: 'At no time have I ever heard him say a bitter word about Jimenez.'[33] Her own bitterness on her husband's behalf, however, was uncontainable, and the fact that Jimenez was allowed to elude justice came to anger her over the years, to the point where her usual diplomacy and decorum deserted her. 'At receptions,' says Joan Thring, 'Margot used to attack ambassadors, and say: "Why haven't you arrested that man?" She didn't seem to be able to get it into her head that they had no *right* to arrest him. He had a right to do what he did because Tito had slept with his wife.' But Nitzia Embiricos, who grew up close to the situation, was fed a more pragmatic explanation for Tito's apparent placability: 'In Panama they say that Tito didn't want Jimenez prosecuted because he had too much dirt on Tito. He had spent four years doing everything that was necessary to get Tito elected, and when he was made to eavesdrop on a phone conversation where Tito was tricked into saying that he was having second thoughts about who to make his alternate, Yinyi picked up a gun and went straight out to get Tito. If I know my country, Tito wouldn't have chucked his marriage to Margot Fonteyn for an affair with the wife of Jimenez. He might have chucked it for Anabella Vallarino. But Jimenez was not of the same social class.' Tito's sister Rosario agrees with this assessment. 'When you hang around with people who are not from the same cultural background, you can expect the unexpected from them. The one Tito made his Man-Friday shot him. We feared it, and it happened. They tell me that Jimenez is in a wheelchair now. It takes time, but justice is done in the end. One thing Father taught us: just turn the page around. Plenty of people came to me wanting to help avenge Tito, and I always said: "No, no, no, no, no. I will not take part in a plot to spill anyone's blood."

If anybody's primitive passions were roused to seek retribution, they were Margot's own. Tito was determined to return to Panama to get himself sworn in as the Deputy which he still, legally, was; and, in early 1967, she was given brief leave of absence from Covent Garden to see him safely back to his homeland. Her own heart-stopping victories notwithstanding, she writes: 'It was the most moving and triumphant moment of our lives as Tito was lowered from the plane on a fork-lift at Tocumen Airport, in Panama, two and a half years after he had been flown out on the Stryker bed. A colossal crowd of well-wishers swarmed across the tarmac to greet him, and to follow in a two-mile motorcade to the city . . . A few days later I was full of pride as I watched him raise his own hand to take the oath at his swearing-in ceremony in the Panamanian National Assembly.'[34] But, soon enough, she would have to return to Covent Garden, leaving her husband behind to embark, despite his frailty, on a new election campaign. And such was her anxiety at abandoning him there, with only the manservant, Buenaventura, for protection, that the time would come when, to the astonishment of her sedate English friends, she would resolve to take the law of common hoodlums into her own uncommon hands.

The last bastion of Margot's classical repertoire had been infiltrated on Boxing Day, 1966, when she appeared with Nureyev at Covent Garden in *The Sleeping Beauty*. The critics were not particularly taken with his textual innovations to what, for twenty years, had been the company's most cherished showpiece. A. V. Coton wrote in the *Telegraph*: 'Dame Margot uses a delicately refined movement technique as unconsciously as she breathes, but too often in this performance it was obvious that she was unable to project the character of Princess Aurora fluently because of faulty partnering by Mr Nureyev.'[1] Margot had long since given up arguing the toss. Six months earlier she had told Susan Barnes: 'I don't always agree with Nureyev on the way steps should be done. But he is so forceful and feels so strongly and makes such a fuss that it's easier for me to change and do it his way. This makes other people angry. They may be right. But I don't think the actual *steps* are the important thing: it's the way one does them . . . He's much more set in his ideas than I am in mine. Although he admires what he calls my "*progressive mind*", he's not willing to change himself. If I do what he wants, I'm progressive. If I don't, I'm retrogressive.'[2] (It is interesting to note that Nureyev eventually came round to the mime scene in *Swan Lake*, incorporating it, exactly as Margot had shown him, into his own production for the Paris Opera Ballet.)

Meanwhile, rejigging the classics was not enough to keep the Russian's lust for western modernity at bay. With the world at his feet, he longed to work with the one person who showed no interest in him: Balanchine. So Margot, lacking any influence with Mr B, conjured as best she could, and came up with her old friend Roland Petit, who, though lying in a hospital bed when she approached him, agreed to lend his choreographic services. It was a brave move to team her old paramour with her new one. But, in the 'two is company, three is none' stakes, it was *she* who stood to find herself vaguely excluded. 'I had just undergone a serious operation,' writes Petit, '. . . and, in spite of the warm friendship of Margot and the young barbarian . . . I was thrown into a depression you could cut with a knife . . . Margot had warned me: "If you let Nureyev get the upper hand you won't finish the ballet. A word to the wise." At the first rehearsal of the moujik's solo, I demonstrated a reverse step for him which showed off his muscles and gave him an athlete's physique. He liked the step, but when I asked him to do it three times, he replied that once was enough. I left the rehearsal, and when I returned the next day, he performed the notorious step three times, with no bad temper, and even gave me a wink of approval. Nureyev and I became great friends . . . Together we did the rounds of the London antique shops and the sleazier pubs where great toothless dockers sang in drag. Nureyev loved to play the dirty old man, the kind that opens his coat to frighten little girls and turn on the naughty boys around him. He did it for me one day in Soho to make me laugh.'[3]

Between these two reprobates, vying with each other for the lower moral ground, Margot seems, in a filmed record of Petit's rehearsal, to be – more exaltedly than ever – the lady, assuming in interview an air of exaggerated gentility at hilarious odds with the crotch-splitting angularities demanded of her harmonious limbs. Rudolf, with the reporters, is monosyllabic; his love affair is entirely with the camera lens, into which he gazes with a teasing candour, winking at it brazenly whenever Petit looms behind him with some suggestive experiment. 'Margot was playing shy,' says Petit, 'but she was laughing, really, because everything looked, not pornographic, but sexual. Nureyev was laughing and I tell you she was *not* shy. Private, yes, but not shy.'

Petit's ballet, based on a poem by Jean Cau, had a modernist score, punctuated with twanging gongs and thumping drums, by the composer/conductor Marius Constant, who addressed

481

the bemused orchestra thus: 'Gentlemen, I expect you have all heard of Milton's *Paradise Lost*. Well, I just wanted you to know that this ballet has nothing whatever to do with Milton's *Paradise Lost*.'[4] It did, however, have everything to do with the space-age pretensions of the Swinging Sixties. 5-4-3-2-1, flashed a neon sign, as a blazing white primeval egg gave birth to Adam, who was soon joined by Eve, the latter attired in a plastic mini-dress. The pair cavorted beneath a pop-art Tree of Knowledge, tempted by jump-suited snakes, until the set itself, two huge eyes and a lipsticked mouth, seemed to cause Eve to succumb. Frenzied Adam tore round the stage and dived head-first through the parted lips, only to be dragged back on by Eve.

Carnaby Street had come to Covent Garden: the first-night audience of *Paradise Lost* included Princess Margaret and Mick Jagger. Margot's instinct to engage Petit had been a sound one: whatever the merits of his actual ballet, he had, once again, presented her in a new and fashionable context. Her gratitude, however, had its limits. Marguerite Porter, limbering up for a performance next to Margot, was witness to an odd conversation between ballerina and choreographer: 'Margot was doing forward kick-steps (her favourite warm-up method), when Petit approached her from behind, and said, "Margot, I do love you." "I love you, too, Roland," she replied breezily. "But I *really* love you, Margot," he persisted with Gallic intensity. Even more breezily she said: "And I really love *you*, Roland." '

For his part, Petit was confused by the martyred power with which Margot now wielded her married state. 'I had always the feeling half-and-half. One feeling was: what is she doing with that man? She's a real witch. A witch with him and a witch with herself. She's terrible – she laughs like a witch. She's got him at her mercy – like Carabosse. And then, immediately, I would go to the other side, thinking: She's a saint. She's really making a hell out of her life to help him, and she's wonderful and unhappy and sad and she's doing everything she can to be honest with herself.'

No sooner had the curtain come down on the first night of

Paradise Lost than Margot was hot-footing it back to Tito's side – and very publicly. Having missed the last plane to Paris, where she was to pick up her flight to Panama, she threw herself on the mercy of Air France, who knew a good photo-opportunity when they saw one. They boarded her, like cargo, on to a Breguet freighter, and had her pictured among crates of early morning newspaper editions in the belly of the plane, smiling the sacrificial smile of a woman whom the airline had enabled to spend two days with her husband instead of one. Adventurous days, at that.

'A long day's ride over almost impassable roads in a jeep would have exhausted the healthiest of men, but Tito thrived on it and I finally stopped worrying about him when I watched him lowered over the side of a launch in his wheelchair and rowed ashore in a dinghy to be landed on an island beach. My heart was in my mouth lest the little craft should overturn, but Tito said reassuringly, "Don't worry about me. Paralysed people always float. That's one of the advantages!" '5

On her forty-eighth birthday – the night when the New York audience first took it into its head to sing 'Happy Birthday' to her, an annual tradition which was to endure for as long as she kept dancing – Margot found herself crawling thirty feet under a steep rostrum in order to wait in the cramped position from which she made her entrance in *Paradise Lost*. 'This is a hell of a way to spend your forty-eighth birthday,' she giggled to Rudolf. But he, with more wistfulness than wit, answered: 'I wish I could think I am dancing still on forty-eighth birthday.'6 (And how, when the moment came, we wish that he had *not* been.)

Margot, dressed, since the death of Dior, by Saint-Laurent, was far too neatly groomed to pass for a flower-child. But she did raise her hems well above her fairly sturdy knees, and was photographed at a nightclub wearing 'an African-style dress of grass fringing and wooden beads . . . with a psychedelic dot on her tummy'.7 When Leslie Edwards grumbled to her that he found the whole hippy culture scruffy and irksome, she said,

'Oh no! I think it's fascinating. I can't take my eyes off those people!'[8] So it was as a sightseer, perhaps, that, even without Tito to lead her astray, she became involved in events which, once again, were to land her in gaol. Coming out of the stage-door in San Francisco one night, she was accosted by a tall, bearded hippy, a philosophy graduate from Trinity College, Dublin, who introduced himself as Paul Wesley and asked if she'd like to come to a 'freak-out'. She was on her way to dinner with Rudolf and other friends, but took the address regardless; and, after a midnight supper at Trader Vic's, she persuaded her entourage to move on in a white Cadillac to Haight-Ashbury, the heart of the hippy district, 'just for twenty minutes'. When they arrived at the squalid fourth-floor venue, there was nothing whatever to drink: the only thing on offer was a 'half-lid' which the dancers declined. Two record-players competed, pitting classical music against pop. The room was in blackout, and someone was trying to approximate a psychedelic effect by switching a flashlight on and off. Suddenly there was a commotion and a girl shouted: 'It's the fuzz, everybody buzz,' and the hitherto lethargic guests rushed up the fire escape on to the roof. There the police found Rudolf, sprawled face-down in his 'double-breasted black pea-jacket, tight pants and Western boots',[9] and Margot, crouching patiently behind a low retaining wall with her white mink, folded inside out, over her knees.

Next day, the fiasco made headlines on both sides of the Atlantic. 'DRUGS PARTY: FONTEYN AND NUREYEV HELD', expostulated the *Evening Standard*. 'Dame Margot Fonteyn and Rudolf Nureyev were among 19 people arrested by San Francisco police today when they raided a party in the section of the city known as Hippieland. Police said the Royal Ballet Company stars and other party guests were charged with "being in a place where marijuana was used or kept". It was a "wild" party, stated the police, and they alleged that Dame Margot and Nureyev tried to flee . . . Dame Margot they said was found hiding on a nearby rooftop. So was Nureyev, who was "lying prone". They were taken to Park Station police headquarters.

There, Miss Fonteyn sat on a bench and declined to give her age.'[10]

In the morning, Vernon Clarke, the Royal Ballet Manager, arrived at the Hall of Justice cells and the dancers were released on bail of $330 each. 'They came straight from gaol to class,' says Wayne Sleep. 'Not a word to anybody. Didn't look anybody in the eye.' Charges were dropped, and the Royal Ballet itself was 'more titillated than ruffled by the affair'.[11] The English press quoted Mrs Hookham as saying: 'The whole business is the result of sheer stupidity and curiosity.'[12] Two days later, on the evening of 12 July, 700 hippies, with daisy-chains round their necks, staged a 'love-in' outside the San Francisco Opera House, ringing bells and playing wooden flutes. Police were brought in as a precaution, but the only aggression they suffered was to be strewn with petals. It took fifteen minutes for Rudolf to steer Margot through the crowds from the stage-door to the waiting car. 'She may wear ermine,' said a jangling girl in a rainbow dress, 'but she's one of us now. She played it so cool.'[13]

It may have been the fantastical element of an incident such as this, and the eagerness of the press and public to condone it, that led Margot to imagine that she had reached a point of fame which somehow placed her above the law. For she was soon to command the headlines in a more sordid capacity: that of would-be kidnapper. Her plan, Operation 'Loving Ho' (the code with which members of the Arias family always signed off), was hatched with the help of Tito's son Roberto and a private detective by the name of John Merry. With the elections in Panama looming, Margot's fears for her husband's safety had reached a pitch where she was prepared to enlist help from any source, however dubious. 'John Merry,' says Joan Thring, 'was a trickster. I tried to talk Margot out of seeing him. He sort of appeared on the scene wanting to be a bodyguard for me and Rudolf, and, as he was leaving, Margot said: "Do you ever do mercenary work?" and he offered to do a bit of shooting around the place for a certain amount of money. I said, "Look, Margot, this is England, you can't do things like this." And later he came and demanded money from her, even though he hadn't done what he was supposed to do."

It was this financial wrangle which dragged the whole business into the papers. 'London solicitor Mr David Jacobs, who acted for the four mercenaries who claimed to have been arrested by police in Panama following an alleged plot to kidnap Panama's police chief, said today that a writ had been issued against Roberto Arias, stepson of Dame Margot Fonteyn, claiming £1,000 alleged to be outstanding from a £5,000 sum . . . Private detective John Merry and Associates, of Oxford St, said several days ago through his solicitors the cheque was for his services in a plot by Dame Margot Fonteyn and her stepson to kidnap Gen. Bolivar Vallarino, chief of the Panama police.'[14]

But, once again, Margot's cronies in the press smoothed things over for her. Her old friend David Lewin interviewed her for the *Mail*: 'Dame Margot said last night: "Ten days ago when there were bullets flying again in Panama and it seemed pretty much a police state, a man claiming to be a private detective in London told me that my husband had been arrested. I said to him: "Is it possible to kidnap – just to get him out of the way – the chief of police, Brigadier General Bolivar Vallarino, in case my husband should come to any harm?" I was told that it would be possible for mercenaries to be sent from England and at the time it seemed a good idea because it was the only way in which my husband would have some protection and some safety. In fact my husband was not arrested and the plot never came to anything. Looking back I suppose it all seems a bit fantastic . . . But the point was that with Tito's brother under arrest at the time and Tito still paralysed I just had to think of some way in which he could be safeguarded . . . Tito flew to Miami the other day and I telephoned him there and told him all about it. He laughed – you know what Tito is like – and said to me: "But I don't think your plan would have got anywhere. [The chief of police] has a bodyguard of about forty around him all the time and I don't think your men would have got anywhere near him." '[15]

Margot had a date to dance at the new Met, after which she hoped to fly to Panama for the elections on 12 May. But the British Embassy warned her off. Michael Field, for the *Daily Telegraph*, wrote on 11 May: 'Opera officials in New York, where Dame Margot is at present, also asked her not to go. The warnings follow the attempted assassination yesterday of Dr Arnulfo Arias, Roberto's uncle, who is standing for election as President for the Opposition National Union. Shots were fired at the candidate and three American journalists who were accompanying him on a canoe trip to an Indian village. A ricochet grazed one journalist on the arm. Dr Roberto Arias, who remains almost paralysed from the incident in which he was shot in 1964, told me he did not now consider himself in particular danger . . . Sunday's election, he insists, "cannot possibly be fair". To guard against destruction of ballots and to help the poorly educated, "extra" ballot papers already being marked in his uncle's favour are being prepared. Dr Arnulfo Arias has been deposed twice as President. But experienced onlookers here predict violence if he fails to win a sweeping majority.'[16]

In private, Margot received a warning which was rather more physical and specific. Keith Money says: 'She and I got locked in a car with this crook who said he was going to break her legs.' But Margot was not to be deterred: not only did she turn up in Panama, but she did so with a suitcase full of guns. 'She was as mad as Tito in the end,' says Joan Thring; and Keith Money agrees. 'If you put any of this stuff down as a sort of stupid *Woman's Weekly* story, people would say: "How ridiculous." You can laugh, but it wasn't funny. Everybody has to understand that Margot had a very passing grip on reality. Her life was never normal. She was not like other people. No matter how scared she was, she just went on into the eye of the tornado. Once, she and I were in a small, tinny green car in Panama, trying to get to our hotel with a very nervous driver. Round the corner came a whole mob, and the driver tried to get through. All these faces were peering in and somebody recognized Margot and said, "That's Mrs Arias" – they were from the

Opposition. So they started smashing the car with poles. The driver was petrified, but Margot was saying, "Keep going, keep going," and I was pretty scared, thinking she's going to be in big trouble if the glass goes. But Margot could just tough things like that out. She thought it was funny.'

Around this time, Money was shooting a documentary to commemorate Margot's fiftieth birthday – the locations for which took them, in early 1968, to Venice, Naples and Turin with Festival Ballet, and thence to Panama, New York, Paris, and a great barn of a theatre in Bournemouth, commandeered by Money for a weekend to shoot precious footage of Margot as Aurora. This account of Act I, *Sleeping Beauty*, featured the touring section of the Royal Ballet and Messel's well-worn sets and costumes, which had lately been dropped by Covent Garden.

The touring company always felt reassured when Margot travelled with them. 'Many dancers seem to be particularly scared of flying,' says Gail Monahan, 'but when Margot and Rudi were with us on the plane we felt safe – as though fate would *have* to look after us.' But increasingly the stars had other plans. Due to fly from Oporto to Granada, on a tour organized by Julian Braunsweg, Nureyev announced to the portly, pint-sized impresario: 'I don't like flying charter. It makes me nervous . . . Margot and I don't like travelling with the company.'[17] Joan Thring undertook to escort the leading dancers on a scheduled flight to Lisbon and then to rent a three-seater biplane to convey them to a military airfield in Granada. When Braunsweg baulked at her demand for £140, Thring warned: 'You'd better let Margot do what she likes.'[18]

Travel arrangements were, in fact, the least of Braunsweg's headaches. 'Nureyev had once been duped by an impresario who did not pay him his salary. Naturally he was on his guard. He and Fonteyn insisted that before each performance, I pay their secretary, Joan Thring, their fees in dollars . . . I had to sleep in great discomfort with bundles of dollars stuffed beneath my pillow.'[19] The grandest tantrum, however, was thrown not by Nureyev, but, to everyone's astonishment, by Fonteyn. The

Royal Ballet opened in Granada with *Giselle*, in the presence of Don Juan Carlos, the pretender to the Spanish throne, his wife, Princess Sofia, and sundry other local mantillas. Fonteyn and Nureyev had refused to allow a photo-call during rehearsal, so Braunsweg provided facilities for the press to take pictures, during the performance, from the orchestra pit – on condition that no flashbulbs be used. 'Half-way through the first act,' wrote Braunsweg, 'Fonteyn stopped dancing and stormed down to the orchestra pit. Staring angrily at the photographers, who with professional aplomb continued to take pictures, she shouted: "Get out. I will not go on with the performance unless you leave. You are not supposed to be taking pictures" . . . Nureyev walked down to the photographers and gave them a piece of his mind. If the Spaniards had understood him they would have lynched him. The embarrassed *corps de ballet* quietly left the stage while the stars continued to argue. Officials asked the photographers to leave. "Start from the waltz," Nureyev called, as he and Fonteyn moved back to their positions. The orchestra struck up. The *corps de ballet* made their entrance and the performance continued. However, Fonteyn had made a major mistake. She had stepped out of her character of the gentle, vulnerable peasant maid who dies for love. The make-believe spell, so essential to ballet, had been broken.'[20]

Margot is the last to condone her own action. 'My belief in the sanctity of theatre is gravely wounded by such behaviour,' she writes.[21] But the sound of a shutter clicking during a performance was genuinely intolerable to her. Once, in Paris, during the same ballet, *Giselle*, Bill Akers had to restrain her physically as she rushed off the stage at the end of the first act, shouting: 'I'll kill him! I'll kill him!' about a photographer who, snapping from the wings, had interrupted her concentration and caused her to fall off *pointe*. David Wall, who, three years after the Granada incident, when a similar confrontation occurred in New Mexico, walked off the stage in solidarity with her, can understand her phobia all too well. 'It wasn't so much the distraction as the fact that she didn't trust the press. At her age, she was very conscious that the media might pick up the worst possible photograph and slap it on the front of the newspaper.'

But nothing could have been worse than the *Mail*'s headline: 'MARGOT FLOUNCES OFF.'[22] To the consternation of her fellow dancers on that 1968 Continental tour, the ballerina seemed to have committed the most cardinal of all theatrical sins: the sin of unprofessionalism. How, in their minds, could they identify her with the paragon she had once been – the unassuming, compliant performer who, during the war, before some of them had even been born, had continued to dance calmly on, bringing courage to the terrified audience when, one night, a bomb had fallen fell perilously close to the New Theatre just as she made her entrance as Aurora?

It was at this very theatre, the New, a quarter of a century after her wartime triumphs there, that Margot, with Festival Ballet, now made a rare appearance in a Balanchine work: the beautiful and romantic *Night Shadow*. This time the newspapers chose to print a (literally) staggering shot of her: in the act of carrying John Gilpin, as the dead Poet, bodily off the stage in her arms. Gilpin, who weighed ten and a half stone, told the *Evening News*: 'It's done by my being placed in her arms and then putting most of my weight on my own arms, which are round her neck. The ballerina leans a little backwards and the extra weight is taken on her hips. The whole thing lasts for half a minute or so and, of course, has to be carefully rehearsed. It is all a matter of careful balance.'

The balance with which Margot now sustained her outlandish existence was every bit as precarious as that representation of Balanchine's sleepwalker implied. Childless, Margot might have been, yet a maternal symbolism permeates this shocking photographic image of her: a woman of uncertain years with the fragile frame and long tresses of a girl, supporting, with a superhuman strength, the dead weight of a fully-grown man-turned-baby.

32

'The theatre,' quoth Stanislavsky, 'is a second home' – and just as well, for Margot was now no longer in possession of a first. Her suspicions regarding Tito's real foe were confirmed when, eleven days after the inauguration of his uncle Arnulfo, the latter was overthrown – not by the Opposition, but by the National Guard. Tito was forced to hide in a friend's house, until, next day, the resourceful Marlene and Buenaventura managed to smuggle him into the safety of the Canal Zone. This latest coup meant that Margot and Tito had no house to call their own, in any country. 'We were gypsies,' claims Margot, taking the opportunity to add: 'Not the best moment for me to retire.'[1]

When would it ever be? Margot had always imagined that the moment would take her, as much as anyone else, by surprise. Before Nureyev's advent, she had said to John Tooley: 'I will phone you after breakfast one morning, John, and tell you this is it.'[2] But, like an athlete who has come up against the limits of his strength and run on through the pain-barrier and out the other side, Margot was now operating on what amounted to a 'second wind'. She had also turned something of a psycholog-ical corner, whereby she 'felt like a concert artist who has played the printed programme and reached the encores. So late in life, I thought no one would expect too much of my dancing, and I was able to enjoy the performances instead of dreading them.'[3] And never had her services, with or without Nureyev, been so much in demand. 'Margot was genuinely surprised,' writes Keith Money, 'at the level of interest which persisted, and at the some-times elaborate levels of persuasion which flowed from foreign managements.'[4]

With Tito's medical and travelling bills to foot, Margot's way of conducting herself sometimes struck these managements as mercenary. 'She would always insist,' says Bill Akers, 'that the money for the performance be placed in an envelope on her dressing-table before she went on. She was ready, she was fulfilling her side of the bargain, but you had to fulfil yours. She was quite charming about it, but there it was. That was the cold-hearted side of her.' The warm-hearted side danced on because she could not bear to let her public down. But genuine as both her sense of obligation and her desperate need of money might have been, these were essentially excuses. The truth about Margot and her over-extended career is at once simpler and harder to grasp. 'What some people failed to recognize,' Money writes, 'was that she was, heart and soul, a performing animal.'[5]

Just when Margot might also have been withdrawing from her responsibilities at the Royal Academy of Dancing, she seems to have redoubled her efforts there as well – though with mixed results. Peter Brinson, founder of the Royal Ballet's educative programme, Ballet for All, recalled: 'I used to say to her, "Isn't this a terrible burden for you, Margot?" and she'd say, "No, I must do it, mustn't I, it's my job." I came in at a time when she had recruited two teachers to introduce a new syllabus, and it reflected her judgement as Director. I had to sit with her often when she used to attend community occasions. There was one Saturday which was open to the public when there was going to be a prize for the best mover and I wondered how Margot would handle it: would she go for the shape that was closest to the classical ideal? I'd spotted a rather stout teenager who had an extraordinary quality of movement – rather like a big black Momma – and to my delight Margot chose her. What Margot was not so good at was planning ahead. But she was very respon-sive to the big idea, and the thought that the RAD might move from its rather dreary location in Holland Park to premises in Knightsbridge was very attractive to her. Never mind that the building in question was totally inappropriate – it only had potential for four studios with ceilings so low that if a boy lifted a girl she'd hit her head. Margot's reliance on the people she knew socially just about shipwrecked the RAD. She was blinded by the circles in which she moved and those were very much established circles – very much the court. We would all be lined up in the crush bar to meet the Royal Family and Margot would wheel in Tito and pull the Queen over to talk to him, and I realized that the two of them had a kind of rapprochement which was perhaps a little unusual – I mean the Queen is rather reticent normally, but she very much unfolded to Margot who interpreted for Tito.'

In late October 1968, Margot flew to Iran with Nureyev for a special performance in honour of the Shah's birthday; and one can't help but speculate whether, given her suspect fondness for dodgy dictators, it was not Margot who, when, eleven years later, the Shah was overthrown, suggested to him that Panama might provide a handy bolt-hole. Although Fonteyn and Nureyev were now following their own paths to opposite ends of the globe, it still behoved Covent Garden to feature the famous pairing on gala occasions for which they could charge inflated prices. Such an occasion cropped up around the thirty-fifth anniversary of Margot's first appearance with the company. And, once again, Roland Petit was brought in to devise a new vehicle for the stars. The piece which he came up with – based on Schoenberg's symphonic poem *Pelléas et Mélisande* and essentially a three-hander for Fonteyn, Nureyev and Keith Rosson – was debuted at the Opera House on 26 March 1969; but although, on account of its excessive length and narrative impenetrability, it left the public underwhelmed, critics seem, given the commemorative nature of its première, to have resisted the urge to pan the piece in general, and, instead, to have trained their judgement on Margot in particular. Richard Buckle, of the *Sunday Times*, led the pack. 'There are times,' he wrote, 'when I could willingly strangle Margot Fonteyn, the hundredth anniversary of whose first appearance on the stage is now being celebrated . . . She has been so well brought up either by her Mum or by that potent pedagogue Dame Ninette de Valois that she has perfected the art of answering questions at length and saying absolutely nothing. She would never, even under torture, admit that pink was her favourite colour for fear of offending orange and mauve. This quality of old-school decency is allied to another of her outstanding characteristics – her loyalty. She is disgustingly loyal. She is not just loyal to her friends, and the Royal Ballet and the Queen: she is loyal to everyone. If she had a flop in a new ballet by an old friend, you could be sure that he would be asked to do her next ballet for her. It is maddening.'[6]

The New York season at the Met opened on 22 April 1969, but, although *Pelléas* fared little better across the Atlantic, the tour itself proved a personal triumph for Margot. As Clive Barnes put it: 'Margot Fonteyn is not just the world's ballet superstar, but much more simply the very heartbeat of what is, after all, still her company.'[7] And the heartbeat of her country too. On Margot's fiftieth birthday, Alexander Bland wrote: 'This kind of quiet, restrained, but scrupulous excellence is something we like to think of as especially English. You could call her the Rolls-Royce of the dance – but if you did she would laugh and say she preferred her little Mini.'[8]

Having driven herself so long and so hard, Margot's own bodywork was beginning to show distinct signs of wear and tear. 'I was in New York,' says Donald MacLeary, 'having treatment in the physio room, and I rolled over and there was another bed, and I went, "Oh my *God*, whose feet are *those*?" And they were Margot's. They looked raw and lumpy and disfigured. She giggled and said, "That's where I've had my nervous breakdown."' She had also begun to suffer from arthritis, which she bore with fortitude, shedding in the wings the pain that often caused her to limp, before running out on to the stage. 'I have one very vivid memory of Margot,' writes Charles Hughesdon. 'In the US with Rudolf, she had performed a particularly arduous role. The following morning she said she would accompany me to the airport to see me off. I told her that it wasn't necessary but she insisted and clearly wanted to do it. It was almost like the role she wanted to play. An announcement came over the speaker system stating the boarding gate for my flight – it was a long way from the lounge where we were waiting.

494

She said that she would walk with me and despite my protests she insisted. It was a painful journey for her, her legs were always bruised and aching from the battering she gave them. At the gate we said goodbye and I watched her hobbling away alone, never looking back. That was Margot, very brave and very often alone.'[9]

Arthritis decreed that incessant practice become more and more of a necessity, and she undertook it at all hours. When Galina Samsova and André Prokovsky started their own small company, the London Ballet, Margot went, along with Attilio Labis, to dance at the very first Hong Kong Festival. Samsova and Prokovsky had already checked in at their hotel, and, when they heard that Margot had arrived, they went down to welcome her and to ask what time she wanted to rehearse the next day. But the man at the desk told them that she had gone to the theatre. 'And there,' says Samsova, 'we found her, doing a *barre*. She said, "I have to do it, the minute I get off a plane. Otherwise I seize up completely."'

Ivan Nagy, who partnered her on a long tour with Scottish Ballet, likewise remembers how Margot roped him in to do class with her on Sundays, claiming that she couldn't practise alone. 'So,' says Nagy, 'I work every day with her. Me, who born lazy!' Nagy, at the time exactly half Margot's age, fell, as did all her younger partners, under the ballerina's particular, no-nonsense, spell. 'She put you in the place to relax and get on with it. We were doing *Cinderella*, *Swan Lake pas de deux* and *Gayané pas de deux*, and at the first rehearsal I was never so nervous in my life, I was shaking. We did *Cinderella*, and we had to do the kiss. And she said, "Oh darling, I'm so sorry. I just had lunch and I had the most fabulous garlic." She was the most human, down-to-earth person I ever met in the dance world. She said, "Look, Ivan, you're so polite, but we have so many performances, you have to drop the Dame." I said, "Yes, Dame Margot." "OK," she said, "I'll call you Sir." "No no no, you can't." "Why not?" "It's very unfortunate in Hungarian." "What's the meaning?" "Pubic hair." That was the biggest mistake because the rest of my life she always call me "Sir".' But, emboldened by their growing intimacy, Nagy was foolish enough to speak his mind. 'When we went to Melbourne, just before we opened, I said to her, "Maybe we are not doing *Romeo* together [the George Skibine *pas de deux* staged to music by Berlioz]." She said, "Why?" I said, "I just thought maybe we should do something else." She said, "No, but I want to know why you're thinking we can't do *Romeo*. I want a straight answer." I said, "Really, I think age difference is a little, you know . . . maybe it's better if we choose something else." "No," she said, "I think it will be all right."'

But then his words begin, eerily, to echo those of Antoinette Sibley when she first saw Ulanova as Juliet. 'Came the dress rehearsal,' continues Nagy. 'There was Margot, showing her age, no make-up, pain everywhere, face tortured. I felt so sorry for her. And then the orchestra started and I have never seen such a transformation. Completely virginal, sixteen years old. I was in tears. When it was over, I apologized. I was so taken aback. I really loved her. She was constant. She wasn't just nice when she needed me. She was constantly nice. I loved her unconditionally.'

It was exactly this kind of archetypal, youthful adoration for an ageing diva that John Cranko chose to exploit in his *Poème de l'extase*, made in March 1970 for Stuttgart. Cranko had always wanted to create a ballet for Fonteyn – in particular, *Onegin* – and had in fact, years before, choreographed the enchanting *The Lady and the Fool* with Margot in mind, even though de Valois had insisted that he use Svetlana Beriosova instead. Margot could only spare a week from her tight schedule to rehearse *Poème*, which, inspired by Colette's novel *Break of Day*, and arranged to a score by Scriabin, involved, as well as five comely young men, a complex set in the mosaic style of Gustav Klimt by Jürgen Rose, featuring metre upon metre of silk which parachuted down from the flies – a breathtaking effect when it worked. But on the first night the mechanics played up, and the curtain had to be brought down. Margot, far from being fazed, immediately allayed the panic of the German company by rounding up the five boys to take her through the Rose Adagio. And yet, something of this exercise in distraction must have filtered through the closed curtain. For, after the ballet had been repeated from the beginning, this time successfully, Arlene Croce was later prompted to write for the *Dancing Times* that Fonteyn's role 'trades on her legend without adding to its lustre. She's supposed to be a great lady contemplating the prospect of a last affair while reliving four former ones, but all that happens on the stage is a series of acrobatic adagios in which she is lifted and swung in turn by Egon Madsen (as a Nureyev–Armand figure) and four exceedingly implausible males (as the ghosts of the former lovers) who are harder to tell apart than the four princes in the Rose Adagio. Perhaps the whole thing is a send-up of the Rose Adagio; when the curtain falls and Fonteyn presents roses to each of her partners, it's hard to resist the feeling that things have been going in reverse since the start of the ballet.'[10]

On 7 April, Margot performed the real *Sleeping Beauty* with Attilio Labis at the National Opera of Finland and then flew straight to Washington to appear in a new production of *Cinderella* with the National Ballet. But by the end of the month, the Royal Ballet was back in New York, preparing for the now imminent departure of Frederick Ashton as Director, news of which had recently been made public. 'We were absolutely in shock,' said Antoinette Sibley. 'Everyone was in tears, crying their hearts out, and Anthony [Dowell] and I had to hold the company together during a performance. We had to keep it all going. Fred was very much our mentor. Our love for him was boundless.'[11]

The situation, according to John Tooley, had been extremely badly handled by David Webster, who was bowing out himself and was determined to take the recently knighted Ashton with him. But at the back of the manoeuvre there lurked, as always, the hand of de Valois, who, still regarding the succession as her prerogative, had grabbed the chance to reclaim Kenneth MacMillan, now aged forty-one, when his Berlin contract was up. Ashton, perfectly sprightly at sixty-six, had fully expected to be persuaded to stay. But his diffidence had long irritated de Valois, who saw him as the architect of his own bitterness. 'Fred knew he was going to be Director, but he did nothing but say he didn't want to be. He was always boasting that he was off as soon as his time was up. To such an extent that we believed him. He'd pretend that he didn't want to stay on, and he rather overplayed it and misled a lot of people. Very childish. It was an extraordinary act he was putting on.'[12]

But the affection which he had inspired in his dancers was far from feigned. For Ashton's New York farewell Margot had only been asked, rather impersonally, to dance *La Bayadère*, but for his London farewell her position at the centre of his creative universe could not have been more pointed. This farewell gala, devised by John Hart and Michael Somes with the help of Leslie Edwards, was perhaps the most intimate and emotionally charged ever to be presented at Covent Garden. It was a retrospective of his entire career, with excerpts from thirty-six ballets, secretly rehearsed and with so strong a surprise-element that the audience – who had paid ordinary prices, so that his true following might be represented – were only issued with programmes as they left the theatre. Billy Chappell wrote the commentary, Bobby Helpmann narrated it, and during the last excerpt, in which everyone danced the waltz from *A Wedding Bouquet*, in whatever costume they happened to be wearing, Ashton was led backstage. 'They incline to oblige only one,' intoned Helpmann, quoting Gertrude Stein. 'Only one,' he repeated, whereupon Ashton descended on a lift from the flies to take his bow. He tried to speak but broke down. For, by his side, dressed in her Chloë costume, stood his ballerina. 'Of all Ashton's dancers,' wrote Clive Barnes, 'Margot Fonteyn has always been his jewel. Here miraculously – for unlike anyone else time has stopped for Dame Margot – she blithely danced some of the roles of her youth . . .' (*Apparitions, Nocturne, The Wise Virgins,* and, inevitably, *Marguerite and Armand*) '. . . Then, almost unbelievably, as the lovers themselves (in *Daphnis and Chloe*) came Fonteyn and, yes, her old partner Michael Somes . . . and the audience cheered and cheered.'[13] Earlier in the evening, some elderly members of the audience had wept to see revived the ravishing intricacy of Margot's arm-movements in *The Wise Virgins*, and her touching solo from *Nocturne*, danced in the original costume, which had been tracked down in some fusty wardrobe and still fitted her, without one altered seam, as perfectly as it had done in 1936.

Ashton would return to make more ballets for the company, but it was inevitable, Margot knew, that under a MacMillan regime the Fonteyn–Nureyev monopoly would be phased out once and for all. Nevertheless, when she and Rudolf did *Swan Lake* together at the Garden in June 1971, the *Daily Telegraph* deemed her 'in magnificent form, dancing with her unique, enigmatic and exquisite finesse, making every movement seem created especially for her . . .'[14] A mere matter of days later, she was performing the same role in Munich, now opposite Richard Cragun (one of her partners in *Poème de l'extase*), but to similarly rapturous plaudits. On 28 June she appeared in a fund-raising gala at the London Coliseum, organized by Richard Buckle, during which, although she made, as might befit a woman in her fifties, two discreetly long-skirted appearances (as the Nymph of the Garden Party in a piece by Peter Darrell, and as the Poet's Muse in *C.1830*, newly choreographed by Ashton), she then defied any suggestion that she should be taken out of tutus by dashing off a perfectly creditable performance, with Nureyev, of *Aurora's Wedding*.

Although committed to dancing twenty-six three-act *Raymonda*s with the Australian Ballet later that year, for which she rehearsed in London with Garth Welch, she joined up, *en route* to Perth, with the Stuttgart Ballet at the Met in New York for six performances of *Poème de l'extase*. Once in Australia, she danced *Raymonda*, the second act of *Swan Lake* and the *Gayané pas de deux*; partnered in all by Garth Welch. Welch had come a long way since Fonteyn had guested with the Borovansky Ballet in 1957, when, to his boyish pride, he had played Benno in *Swan Lake*, standing by to catch Odette as she swooned. Now he was a dancer in his prime, upon whom she relied to haul her to her feet. 'When she finished the *Gayané* solo, she had to go down on her knees and she said, "You're going to have to take my hands and really pull me, otherwise I'll never get up." She had the heaviness that comes into your body as you get older. You could see that she was treading on her heels when she was running and stepping heavily to get up into the air. You'd see her and think, "You're not going to make it." And then suddenly something would happen, and she'd be a girl again.'

While in Darwin with the Australian Ballet, Margot received a telegram from Imelda Marcos, inviting her 'and her maid and hairdresser' to stay when the company came to Manila. On her way from the airport to Malacañang Palace, Margot stopped off, as was her unvarying ritual, to check out the theatre, and, when she emerged, a message awaited her to say that the President, having waited up for her, had now retired to bed. ' "Oh dear," [she] thought, "that's hardly the best way to start off my visit." ' Would that she *had* offended the Marcoses. But no such luck. 'The First Lady received me the next day and, in response to my expression of delight with the lavish rooms I occupied, she said, "Yes? You see that is called Suite 1. It is reserved for people of Prime Ministerial rank. But I said, 'It is only reasonable that there should be Prime Ministers in the arts as well as in politics, and Dame Margot is a Prime Minister in the arts, so she is entitled to Suite 1.' " ' Thus began the friendship which, morally, was to prove perhaps the most compromising of Margot's life. 'I understood,' she informs us, 'that I was with a person of high philanthropic ideals, laced with a dose of good common sense.'[15]

This spectacular piece of bad judgement was compounded in April the following year, 1972, when, much to the horror of her colleagues, Margot broke ranks with the United Kingdom's stance on Apartheid by agreeing to dance in South Africa. David Poole, a former member of Sadler's Wells, was directing the CAPAB Ballet Company in Cape Town, and was keen to establish its right to funding from the South African Government. Poole played a major part in persuading Margot to go over, and although she did voice all sorts of reservations, he finally persuaded her that only by means of her presence could the government be won over. 'She was trying to help the profession to which she owed so much,' says Peter Brinson, 'but, at the same time, she was endorsing the Apartheid régime, and consequently raised enormous protests here. And I have to say that I was one of the protesters. She simply didn't understand.'

Accustomed as she was to being mobbed, and to receiving impassioned fan-mail, Margot was astonished when angry demonstrators pitched up outside the stage-door at Covent Garden and the United Nations Special Committee in New York wrote asking her specifically not to go to South Africa. But, with characteristic bullishness, she was not to be deterred – although, to pour oil upon the political waters, she did at least stipulate that one performance be given before a non-white audience, and that her fee for the whole tour be donated to a fund that would benefit black children. 'If they want to demonstrate against me, that's fair enough,' Margot told the *Evening Standard* on 13 April. 'It's my bad luck. I think it would be cowardly and wrong of me to cancel after I'd accepted just to retain the admiration of my fans who had not thought it all out. I'd be rather ashamed if I did that. I think the people who want to make protests are trying to use me and I don't feel it is my place to make the actual protest. You either accept or not. I accepted for ballet reasons. The real point is that if I had turned them down in the first place who would have known? There would have been no headlines. And what difference would it have made to the South African government? An empty gesture.'[16] But a week later the demonstrators were still following her – all the way to Heathrow. *The Times* noted: 'A rescue operation for Dame Margot Fonteyn: setting off for South Africa on the visit which has aroused some anti-apartheid controversy, she was faced with the problem of getting to the airport on time, through the traffic jams. Mr Charles Hughesdon, the company director and husband of Florence Desmond, lent her his helicopter to fly her from Battersea to Heathrow. "I don't think she would have got there otherwise," he tells me.[17] And when she landed in Cape Town she found herself, yet again, accosted by demonstrators, and heckled by agitators brandishing placards proclaiming: 'Dame Margot Dances to Apartheid Tune' and 'Shame on You' and 'No True Christian Accepts Apartheid'. Bracing herself with her staple smile, Margot approached the bearer of this last banner, and told him: 'I agree . . . But doesn't it make more of a point if I come here and you can demonstrate like this?' To which someone pointedly replied: 'Then why don't you go back now?'[18]

Despite telling the press that she thought the demonstrators 'absolutely right', she nevertheless gave a week of performances at the Nico Malan, and, after this, one further performance for non-whites at the Three Arts Theatre. In the circumstances, however, this last event was largely boycotted, and, instead of the expected blacks, whites who had been unable to obtain tickets for earlier evenings 'blacked up' with pancake make-up and, wrapped in saris, inveigled themselves into the theatre. To Margot, who had been through so many political skirmishes with Tito, it was perhaps just a further, crazy adventure. But it was one that made her seem to the public not dashing and hare-brained, but misguided and reactionary. Yet an aberration that might have cut short many another career did nothing to hamper hers. 'You had to make allowance for her,' says Peter Brinson. 'People forgave her these inconsistencies because of her artistry, her generosity, her professionalism and her shining love for Tito. And anyway, there was no impresario in the world who would say, "I'm not going to invite Margot Fonteyn to dance."' Least of all Sol Hurok. Margot's reception in New York, when she flew straight from Cape Town, had never been more open-armed. 'Many classic ballerinas outstay their welcome by a few years,' wrote Clive Barnes, 'and it is a critical custom – not upheld, I think, by myself – to lie a little about their prowess . . . I hasten to assure posterity that Dame Margot needs none of this. She is not just the best 53-year-old ballerina in the business, she is still, without qualification, the greatest ballerina in the world.'[19]

Unchastened by the violent disapproval which her South African jaunt provoked, Margot, with Tito's encouragement, would later merrily accept an invitation to dance before General Pinochet, thereby 'getting [herself] into hot water again with those who like to tell others their business'.[20] This time Peter Brinson could find no extenuating circumstances. 'Pinochet, after all, was someone whose human rights record in Chile had been condemned world-wide, and her presence there was used by the Pinochet regime, without any doubt, to give that regime a certain amount of extra clout.' Margot's excuse was the age-old one of artistic exemption. 'She had strong feelings,' continued Brinson, 'about the approach of the artist as opposed to the intellectual — that the artist's approach is towards people and inevitably subjective. She didn't particularly believe that the artist had a duty to the public other than as a performer.'

And there is something of this defiant self-justification in the interview she gave John Gruen of the *New York Times* during that 1972 season. 'I only think of what I must do tomorrow — that I must dance *Swan Lake*, that I must dance *Sleeping Beauty*. I go from day to day. I don't clutter up my mind with a lot of externals and things I have no control over. Perhaps I survive by not thinking about all these things. All I'm concerned about is concentrating more and more on what has to be done, and I feel I must work continually harder . . . I suspect I'll go on dancing until I can't any more. But, I assure you, I don't think about it. I only think about doing things well.'[21]

Locked into this deeply uncontemplative mindset, she now approached a new challenge, spurred on by no less a literary figure than the First Lady of the Philippines. 'On my first visit Mrs Marcos talked to me about my writing my autobiography. She was quite insistent and added, "You know that I am very determined when I believe that something should be done." That was the impulse for [the] book's existence. It is my own way of expressing respect to a woman of great courage and imagination who cares about people.'[22]

Various accounts of Margot's life and work had appeared between hard covers in the 50s, notably William Chappell's impressionistic hymn to his adored colleague, with a text as poetic and studied as the early Beaton portraits which graced its pages; Elizabeth Frank's short biography, mostly gleaned, if its lively and wholesome tone is anything to go by, from conversations with Margot's mother; and, above all, James Monahan's masterly appreciation of her character and work: *Fonteyn – A Study of the Ballerina in Her Setting*. To say that Margot had remained aloof from these publications would be to put it mildly: she did not even open them. 'Dear James,' she wrote to Monahan in November 1957. 'Thank you so very much for sending me the book. I have not yet had the courage to read it, not because I think I won't like it but because I find it terribly hard to read about myself. Short articles are one thing, but a whole book – I would feel ashamed to sit down and solemnly read a whole book about me!'[23]

Now, however, she was to embark on the production of just such a tome – and in her own hand. Margot was used to controlling every detailed aspect of the presentation of her stage persona, and the book, as well as being, she hoped, a lucrative venture, was to be a further exercise in that control: better her personal, if edited, version of events than the impertinent conclusions of some prurient stranger. How much editorial help she received in the writing of the autobiography is a moot point: Money, a passionate believer in her all-round intellectual capability, swears none at all, while the actress Ann Todd – an intimate at the time – claimed a great deal; certainly Robin Duff, who is acknowledged in the front pages, presented the finished product to Dadie Rylands as 'my book on Fonteyn'. But also acknowledged is David Scrase, who says that Margot simply rang him incessantly for help on times and dates and places. What is indubitably Margot's own is the authorial 'voice', the sheer vitality and charm of which mitigates powerfully against any irritation one might feel about omissions and distortions in the text. Quite how she found the time to work on it is another matter. Querube Arias says that it was written 'mostly on planes, on very long flights to Australia. If Margot was to enjoy time with my father, she couldn't be writing when she was with him. He'd say, "Come and read your book to me, so that I can fall asleep." We learned quickly that books give you very little money. But I can't tell you what learning to write did for her – her greatest sense of pride was when she bought a new hat because she was invited to a literary meeting.' After the camaraderie of the theatre, Margot apparently found the act of writing weirdly lonely. Sitting at the dining-table in Amerden with her papers spread about her, she would say to her sister-in-law, Feebee, 'Oh, darling, please won't you come and sit beside me and talk to me while I'm doing this?'

But *anything* is a walkover compared to dancing *Swan Lake*, and Margot, one way or another, was so prolific in the end that her manuscript had to be cut by 40,000 words. Robert Gottlieb was the book's prime editor and publisher in America. 'I was not there at the time of its commission but, because no one else involved had any ballet background, I naturally did all the pictures and brush-up work and I prodded her in certain areas – I'd say, "Can you tell us how you approach a role? Let's take, for instance, Giselle." "Well, you know, Bob," she said, "I would stand behind the door of the hut listening to the music and waiting for my cue and I would just come out and dance." Now that was just a *faux naïf* tale – Margot was much too sophisti-cated not to have given some thought to Giselle – how she saw this girl, how she saw this drama – but she was not going to discuss those things. She didn't think they should be discussed – I think she thought it would be inhibiting to her art. There was no getting it out of her. Another kind of person would have tried to give an editor what he wanted. But she wouldn't say, "I won't do it"; she'd just say, "I don't know." She combined extraordinary modesty with extraordinary wilfulness. You could not budge her. Certainly not by argument or confrontation. The only thing that would budge her would be her own good nature.'

In fact, a decade earlier, Margot's good nature had prompted her, for friendship's sake, to open up a little to Keith Money, the text of whose *The Art of Margot Fonteyn*, the first volume of his reverent and sumptuously illustrated tetralogy, relies to a considerable extent upon the ballerina's own slant on her roles. And although the unpretentious practicalities she comes up with may seem – now that 'Dance' is deemed a subject worthy of a degree – less than satisfying to the academia of today, her comments nevertheless convey all that an actual dancer will ever need to know about the delicate business of performing, where mental analysis serves only to dim the illuminating power of gut reaction. 'In any ballet, a certain amount comes out in rehearsals for me, then when I start performances it is advanced one stage further. As I go on doing performances, in some strange way these things form themselves. I never spend a lot of time thinking about the characters during the day; I cannot work in that practical way, but suddenly, during performances, one will come to some moment in the choreography – perhaps a simple arabesque or position. Then for the first time one senses a deep reason for that particular step; that she should, for instance, turn her head slightly at that point rather than look straight ahead. One suddenly knows more of what she would be thinking at such a moment. The new discovery is added to one's perform-ance, and this slight variation might then be retained for the next two years before it is discarded again. So many of one's moves are entirely instinctive that it is often dangerous if anyone tells one of particular moments that have "worked"; one becomes overconscious of their importance and the spontaneity is imme-diately in danger of being lost.'[24]

But Margot did not see it in her remit to clutter her own book with artistic insights. She planned to deliver something much more to the general public's taste: an out-and-out love story. Embarked no further than page twenty, she already begins to invoke what she feels to be the nub of her subject. 'So it was really all there by the time I was six. I had won a pink sash for dancing the best polka in my class. I had encountered the sea and travel. I loved to laugh and dress up, and I knew devotion as well as the rudiments of flirting. I believe too that from the age of six I sensed the existence of just such a person as my husband. Had we met then, a silent, black-eyed little boy, and a round-faced, solemn little girl, we would have had a wordless understanding as deep as the deep blue sea.'[25]

Yet, for all those who dismiss as pure fiction this incessant extolling of Tito, there are others who attest to the tangible fact of her love. Nitzia Embiricos, who, as Margot's young guest, studied at the Royal Ballet School while helping to type parts of the book from the longhand, recalls the atmosphere in the apartment which the couple were renting at that time – Flat 7, No. 1 Princes Gate. 'They had a dark brown study, a bluish-grey sitting-room, and a dark dining-room with the Annigoni in the middle. There was a black-and-white photograph of Tito in a bull-fighting ring, with him in his wheelchair and the bulls staring at him. Tito needed typing done – letters in Spanish – but what Margot really wanted me to do, I realized immediately, was keep him company. She'd say, "Tito gets so bored with me," always putting herself down, "at least he can talk to you about Panamanian politics. If you don't get nervous you'll understand everything he says. It's just that the sound level is so low." It was a matter of relaxing and making the atmosphere natural. That was what Margot was so magnificent at – she would put everybody at ease immediately, and the atmosphere would be very pleasant and friendly and warm, and things would go well. I think it was the happiest period of my life, mainly because, if you had a problem, you'd only have to think, "Do *I* have a problem? Look at *him*. He's in a wheelchair. And she's running to work, and between him and the work and the letters there's no time, and yet she's always smiling and she's always happy." Of course, she'd have bad moments when someone didn't deliver *pointe* shoes on time or something, and she'd be furious for a moment, but then she'd snap out of it. Margot had this way with people – people that she cared for – she would *give* so much. She had this talent of laughing at misfortune – it was the secret of her happiness that she could laugh at the most incredible moments and make them disappear. Even if Tito was nearly on the floor, because so many times they nearly dropped him, she would laugh, and Tito would be laughing and in tears, and of course he would contract as soon as he laughed and in order to stop this spasm we had to stop laughing. I used to stay sometimes until eight o'clock in the evening because I didn't want to leave them. It was like living in another world. You would come out floating. There was so much – I think the word is *goodness* – between them. Something I cannot explain.'

Tito countered all this undiluted female virtue with whatever
vices a man in a wheelchair can still muster – which, according
to his manservant, Buenaventura, were not few. 'He like to prove
he can still do what he wants. The only difference is he can't
walk.' The location of a particular penthouse party posed no
obstacle to Arias: he simply had his wheelchair hoisted up the
fire escape. 'If he decided he wanted to go swimming,' said New
York publicist Donald Smith, 'a car would have to be hired to
take him to the New York Athletic Club round the corner.
Then someone would have to be hired to help him in the pool.
An afternoon could end up costing $600 or $700.'[1] But Tito
continued to derive his greatest pleasure from eluding his wife,
and, for his disappearing acts, he relied on the discretion of
Buenaventura. 'Sometimes,' says the latter, 'he's not with another
lady, but just in the car. He says, "Margot, I have to go see some
person." And then when we're in the car he makes another
decision. I drive him hours and hours, sometimes six hours
before we come home. I get angry with him when he says,
"Margot, I go to the airport now," and then at the airport he
decide to go somewhere else – not the place where Margot
thinks we're going. Once, we were in Spain and we supposed
to meet her in Paris. But we miss our plane and fly straight to
London. We go to a hotel close to the airport and I put him
to bed and hours later we call her. "Ventura, where *are* you?"
"We're in London." "But I was waiting for you *here*! What am
I going to do now?" And next morning at seven, there she is,
waiting for us at Heathrow airport. Happy to see him, you
know? Happy that her husband can still do what he wants. He's
the person she likes. He's not like the ballet people, soft. She
want something different. Always he knew where she was, but

she never knew where *he* was — because he keeps moving in his wheelchair. It was the life she wanted for him. It was expensive — good salary for me, best clinics all the time for Dr Arias, best hotels, best suits. He was the best-dressed paralysed person . . . If there's something wrong with his suit, she say, "Ventura, don't you see? This is not correct." And so we must take off his suit and put him in another one. She fight with any person who don't take good care of him. If Dr Arias is having dinner, and a girl — any girl — say, "Hi, Tito, how are you," you know what Dame Margot say to that girl? "Why don't you come here and take care of Tito, please?" He's happy to have some girl help him with the spoon. Dame Margot didn't mind, not with those things. She was an English lady . . . He used to cry, you know, when she was up on stage, but later, when he go to her dressing-room and she ask, "You like the performance, my love?" he say, "You know I not like ballet." '

Ballet, however, facilitated Tito's return to his beloved Panama. Colonel Noriega, as yet only Chief of Intelligence under President Torrijos, had a weakness for girls in tutus, and Tito's exile was effectively ended when Margot began to champion the National Ballet of Panama. 'She agreed to appear with us,' says Nitzia Embiricos, 'and we danced in the stadium of a boys' school — no lights, no orchestra, only tapes — *Bayadère* and *Swan Lake* Act II. She managed to get *Swan Lake* costumes for us from the Royal Ballet for 50p each. They were going to be thrown away. Then, in 1973, she was with us when we re-opened the theatre which had been abandoned, and finally the Government redid it. It has frescoes on the ceiling — a little jewel. Only thing is, it takes no more than 500 people. So when you bring someone of prestige, it's difficult to charge the amount of money you need to cover your costs. And the stage has a bit of a rake. But Margot did *Sylphides* with us, and she brought Ivan Nagy.'

Nagy was not best pleased to find himself dancing for the delectation of 'that hideous drug-dealer', but even though, at the end of the performance, Noriega demanded that they repeat the entire ballet, Margot betrayed no glint of temperament. 'Margot loved the whole Noriega thing,' says Colette Clark. 'She *would*, because Tito loved that sort of intrigue and drama. People would say, "How dreadful for Margot having to deal with General Noriega," and then you'd see a picture of her having him to lunch or dinner or something. She always did what Tito said. That's what you have to realize. It's nothing to do with what she thought; she wouldn't consult her own thoughts. Margot didn't use her judgement – which was extremely good – in anything related to Tito. If he'd said, "Run down naked into the Thames and swim to the other side and bring me out that stone," she'd have done it.'

The novelist Richard Koster and his wife, Otilia, an ex-dancer, were invited to Margot and Tito's for dinner. 'General Noriega was there,' says Otilia, 'talking business with Tito. Margot told us over dinner that General Noriega was the most cultured man in Panama. I nearly choked. I said, "*What?*" I knew Noriega – he used to hang around the ballet in the early years, '68, '69. By no means was he a cultured man. He admired dancing and he admired Hitler. Those were his two passions . . . "Well," I said, "tell me the latest book Noriega has read." And Tito said, "The Marquis de Sade." '

Nitzia Embiricos takes a more tolerant view of the friendship. 'Noriega and Tito did see each other and they did talk to each other, because Noriega admired Tito's mind. Tito was not the kind of person who gave up on his ambitions – otherwise he would have shot his brains out. He was in a wheelchair – he lived off his dreams. That's what kept him going – his imagination. Anybody who would pay attention to him and spend time with him was welcome. People forget he was a crippled man who could hardly talk, and a man like that will cling on to anything that gives him excitement. And so these conversations with Noriega, like his conversations with Marcos, would keep him alive – keep him thinking that he was still a human being who could have some interest in his country.'

Margot and Tito were now living by the coast, close to the

ruins of Old Panama in the ground floor of an apartment building. 'The sea would come storming in,' says Embiricos, 'and she had a little bit of a pool where they would put Tito to do his exercises.' A year or so earlier, Margot had bought a London house in Rutland Gardens Mews, which she was kitting out with handrails and low-level fittings for Tito. But the builders took ages, and, eventually, preferring to stay where she was, in Princes Gate, she let the house to Jacqueline du Pré, who lived there until her death in 1987. Margot, after all, never stayed at any one address for more than a few nights.

'She used to call my father,' says Querube Arias, 'and say that sometimes when she woke up she didn't know where she was. One hotel was the same as another, and that sort of gave us the hint that she was getting tired and lonely and miserable on those tours. So when I was nineteen or twenty, my father would quite often send me to take care of her for him.' Even when Fonteyn was with Nureyev, guesting with the Ballet de l'O de Marseille in 1971, Rosella Hightower, who was directing the company, became worried about Margot. 'I saw that she was not happy in Marseilles and was feeling sort of lonely and down, so I went to talk to her. She said, "Yes, well, of course I am lonely because Rudolf is busy and he's rehearsing or he's doing this or that, and I don't see him very much." And I said, "He doesn't come and dine with you?" She said, "Well, not particularly." "Oh," I said, "we'll have to fix that." I had a very handsome boy who was doing the King in my *Sleeping Beauty*, so I asked him. I knew he needed money, and so I said, "Would you like to earn some extra money? Because she needs somebody to escort her when she goes to the restaurant. She needs somebody to pick her up at the hotel, bring her to the theatre, be a real cavalier for her." He said, "Well, I think that would be easy and I'd love to do that." I saw her being very gay and very cheery and she did some wonderful performances because she was happy, and she didn't have to wait and hope that Rudolf was going to come and pick her up or something. She had her escort.'[2]

Of all Margot's latter-day cavaliers, perhaps the most protective was David Wall, three decades her junior. 'My main concern was looking after her,' he says. 'We had a wonderful relationship, the two of us. Totally platonic. I think she felt very safe with me.' On a tour of South America in 1973, Margot danced what would prove to be her last full-length *Sleeping Beauty*. 'It was Kenneth MacMillan's production, and she didn't have a lot of time with the company, so it was quite a traumatic experience for her, and we ended up with her being in a bit of a state about it. I dismissed the company and just kept the four Princes back and took her through the balances which were worrying her. And the apprehension of the rehearsals was set aside when she actually came on for the performance. It was a magnificent Rose Adagio that she did, and the audience in Rio went absolutely wild.'

The classical ballet which Margot found hardest, *Swan Lake*, was the one to which, with typical obduracy, she clung longest. But when she danced it in London in December 1972, James Kennedy (Monahan) for the *Guardian* had taken a leader article to say: 'I cannot endure it that a new image of diminished, studiously economical dancing should oust the memories of unanxious greatness.' Clement Crisp told in the *Financial Times* of an evening that found Margot 'below form . . . [with] a technical constraint that dulled the impact of much of the ballet. If it seems ungracious to carp at a muted Fonteyn performance . . . let me add that my standards are of the highest because established by Dame Margot herself.'[3] And in the *Sunday Times*, Richard Buckle, however complimentary about her performance in the short George Skibine version of *Romeo and Juliet*, could not prevent himself from saying of her latest *Swan Lake*: 'Adoring her as I do, I should not wish her to embark on the ordeal of Act III ever again.'[4]

Although Margot soon ceased to appear as Odile, she claims that these reviews – the first truly disenchanted ones of her life – did not impinge on her, and until 1976 she continued to announce Act II of *Swan Lake* in her touring repertory. 'So long as my services remained in demand I thought it wiser not to read any of the notices and just get on with the show.'[5] And thus she persisted with her frenetic round of travels and guest appearances, much of the time dancing with Nureyev, who, when asked what he was doing next, was now apt to jibe: 'I have to go and push that old woman around.'[6] He, for his own part, was currently bringing his powers of professional seduction to bear upon a woman racked with arthritis and twenty-five years Margot's senior, namely the eighty-one-year-old Martha Graham, whose studio, known by her students as 'the temple of pelvic truths',[7] he religiously attended in the hope of convincing the high priestess of modern dance that – should she be persuaded to make a work for him – he could absorb the raw, unballetic style which she had pioneered. What did, in fact, persuade Graham of the wisdom of working with both Nureyev and Fonteyn were the huge box-office returns – with tickets ranging from $50 to $10,000 – which the famous pair could generate for a benefit gala in aid of her own company. Graham, to the horror of her friends, also appeared with Margot and Rudolf in a series of full-page advertisements for Blackglama Furs, receiving, as well as a sizeable donation for her school, a complimentary floor-length mink. 'They are helping me to get money which I badly need,' she protested haughtily. 'The dancers will no longer work for nothing. Costumes cost, sets cost, musicians cost, and, God knows, stage-hands cost. Will *you* give me the money?'[8]

The real cost of the enterprise – a ballet called *Lucifer* (1975) – was probably, in the final analysis, an artistic one exacted at Margot's expense. Whereas between Nureyev and Graham, both hungry for innovation, there existed a genuine attraction ('not since the lion and the lamb did their fabled bedtime act has there been such an unlikely but happy merging of differences'[9]), Graham had pitted her whole life against the decorous classicism for which Fonteyn stood. Yet Margot gamely attempted the contractions and knee-crawls assigned to her, even though her role of Night, the Temptress, had, for reasons of scheduling, to be created on another dancer, Janet Eilber. When the part

514

was restaged to accommodate Margot, Eilber remembers: 'Fonteyn was having a great deal of trouble with a side fall next to Nureyev. It was a completely Grahamesque movement, and she just couldn't get it right. She wanted to stay upright, and Martha agreed to change it for her. "All right," Rudolf told Fonteyn with a sniff. "Be comfortable." And so she did the fall exactly as it was supposed to be done.'[10]

Falling was, actually, the least of Margot's worries. Long gone were her days of barefoot abandon: arthritis was beginning to affect her ability to flex her toe-joints – it was particularly painful for her now to stand on half-*pointe*. 'My biggest problem was what to wear on my feet. One imagines that ballet *pointe* shoes are not ideal, but bare feet are no better. They present their own disadvantages, but the other dancers sympathetically helped me to overcome them.'[11] Graham, however – arrayed in kaftans, gnarled hands gloved, face lifted to a thin, colourless tissue of skin over skull – reserved her creative fire for her sessions alone with Nureyev. Seeing him as 'someone she could instil with her own persona',[12] she 'flirted with him eagerly and openly'. *Lucifer* was grandly conceived to represent 'the end of a war which possibly only took place in the battlefields of our imagination: the war between classic ballet and modern dance';[13] and, if it did not exactly take its place in history as such, at least Rudolf – despite a jewel-studded jockstrap, designed by Halston with the assistance of Elsa Peretti from Tiffany's – was deemed by the critic Arlene Croce to be 'not ridiculous. The element of camp in his personality frees him from incongruous undertakings such as this; he gives to the bizarre a touch of authority . . . It wasn't good Graham dancing, but it was good Nureyev.'[14] Yet it was also, by general admission, sub-standard Fonteyn. Clive Barnes commented: 'What is certain is Nureyev's ability to relate creatively to the Graham repertory. About Fonteyn I am more dubious. She looked young and gorgeous, and although she does not yet dance Graham with anything like confidence, let alone authority, she might still be able to contribute something if she worked on the style.'[15]

But Margot, having just received news that her own beloved teacher, Vera Volkova, had died in Copenhagen at the age of seventy-one, was hardly inclined to open her mind to an entirely new discipline at this late stage in her professional life. Equally upsetting had been the death, from leukaemia at twenty-nine, of the engaging Heinz Bosl, who had regularly partnered her in Munich and America. So, if Rudolf was disappointed in her failure to live up to his restless quest to move forward, perhaps the time had come for him to look for a partner to rejuvenate *him*.

The *Corsaire* which he danced at Ballet Theatre on 28 July with the prodigiously gifted twenty-two-year-old American Gelsey Kirkland made the performances which Margot gave with him at Washington's Kennedy Center – of the same *pas de deux*, in the same month – look positively ill-advised. But Kirkland had another partner, the newly defected Russian Mikhail Baryshnikov, with whom she was embroiled in a troubled affair. And Baryshnikov, in his turn, was intrigued by the seasoned English ballerina, partnership with whom had made his Russian precursor so renowned. In 1976 when Margot crossed from Washington to New York with the Australian Ballet to appear in *The Merry Widow*, Baryshnikov faked a finger injury so that he could take time off to watch her dance. Keith Money, who accompanied him to the Uris, 'an uncompromising concrete barn of a place',[16] was anxious as to what the young man in his prime might think of the woman so long past hers. 'When the curtain was due to go up, I was hugely nervous and of course the clever, slow musical build to the Widow's entrance wound the nerves to a higher pitch. Finally Margot appeared at the top of the ballroom stairs. Under the applause I could hear Misha gasp. I thought Margot seemed all right, though she had barely moved more than her fan, so far. Then she started to descend the stairs, acknowledging two or three admiring men as she went, and Misha let out another gasp. I still couldn't interpret his gasp, but he was clutching my upper arm in a vice-like grip which did not slacken. Finally, Margot reached the floor of the stage and went into some supported lifts, looking astonishingly glamorous in the doing. Misha then said, "Oh – *amazing!*" and I realized that things were probably going to be all right . . . And when Margot did a quick change in the wings, to run straight back on again as the young Hanna, in a peasant girl's dress, with all her hair blowing free, and looking all of seventeen, Misha said, very loudly, "Incredible!" I don't think he let go of my arm all through the act . . . By the second interval, he was on air. This is what one great performer can do for another great performer.'[17]

The Merry Widow was as traditional a vehicle as any old-fashioned star could have wished for. Ronald Hynd says: 'I'd done it in Australia for a young girl, Marilyn Rowe. A year later it was decided that Margot should come into it. I started teaching it to her and it was kind of difficult – even though she's in a long dress she's got some very difficult stuff. But you know, she learned absolutely every step. A couple she modified, but she actually had a go at the whole damn thing. After I taught it to her in Barons Court, she went to San Francisco to work with John Meehan, who was partnering her, and then we all coalesced with the Australian Ballet in Washington. And then suddenly I think she realized what she was taking on – a big new full-length ballet with a partner half her age, and me a not particularly experienced choreographer. And she got a little bit uptight. But she got over it and did a wonderful performance. She ran it for a month in New York immediately after Washington and apparently it was a wow. What was fascinating was to see a fifty-seven-year-old woman take over from a girl of twenty-six – the difference that thirty years can make: all that know-how.'

John Lanchbery concurs: 'She wanted to have a hand in the emotional control of the whole thing, and was grateful when you were with her on that. For example, *The Merry Widow*, which she did quite near the end of her life. The musical quality is frequently not very high – it's my own arrangement, based on the Lehár, so I'm at liberty to say that. In the last scene she put in a tiny touch of business that made such sense that Ronnie

Hynd, once he'd seen it, taught it to all succeeding Widows. It's set in Maxim's, and she's arrived wearing a wonderful ostrich-feather cloak designed by Desmond Heeley, which she's given to the head waiter. But there's a row, and all her friends go off, including Danilo, her lover. She's left, quite alone, at a café table and she signals that she wants her cloak, and the head waiter goes off to get it. He comes back with it a moment later, but meanwhile Danilo has come back too, and he takes the cloak from the head waiter. She hears footsteps and puts her hands back to get the cloak and, as she touches the man's hands, she realizes that these are in fact the hands of her lover, and not of the head waiter. And the *look on her face*. She placed it on just the right note. The music, rather cornily, goes from that mushy middle section of the waltz back to the A tune and of course they waltz together starting slowly and tenderly, and up to a whirling finish as the curtain falls . . . The last eight perform-ances she gave of that, in '77, were in Tasmania of all places, and at this very moment that I've just described I heard sobs and I looked up and she was crying – crying quite hard, on the stage. Someone had told me, a few days before, about her arthritis – apparently she'd said, "Oh, I just take some aspirin and get on with it." So I went to her dressing-room and asked, "Is your arthritis playing you up, because I noticed you were upset." She said: "No, I was crying because I suddenly realized what a wonderful moment in the story that is, and I'm afraid the tears just took over." '

Whenever Margot's heart was stirred in this metaphysical way, her thoughts would invariably turn to Ashton. 'Darling Fred,' she wrote on 24 July 1977. 'Don't ask me why, suddenly, in the middle of an Australian tour, I have time to write when I usually hardly have time to sneeze. But London is the most difficult for some reason. There is always someone to telephone, something to arrange, silly little things to be done which, put all together, eat up my life and I am tired all the time . . . Anyway, sitting by myself in a coffee shop in the Melbourne Hotel on Sunday, here is my chance to tell you that you are the most marvellous person in the world, the wisest, most sensitive human and that I regret so much I never seem to do anything for you. From way back during the war when I did not write because I thought my stupid letters would bore you, I still have a silly hidden complex that no one is good enough to invite to dine with you and you would have a miserable evening with us. But when I am away, I think of you so often and with such great love, but how will you ever know if I don't tell you?'[18]

And how would *she* ever know if he shrank from telling her the brutal truth? Ashton had long ago made a pact with Margot: that when he thought she should stop dancing he wouldn't beat about the bush. But, as he later admitted, 'when the time came she made it impossible for me to say anything'.[19] Ashton had more than bitten his lip – in 1975 he had made a new *pas de deux* for her which was to form part of a longer ballet by Margot's Brazilian friend Dalal Achcar, by then Artistic Director of Ballet do Rio de Janeiro. It was called *Floresta Amazónica*. 'Dalal created all the *corps de ballet* work,' says David Wall, 'and Frederick Ashton worked in London with Margot and myself on the *pas de deux* and solo variations.'

Nothing had really changed between the choreographer and his muse. 'As always,' writes Margot, 'Fred was early for rehearsals. He lit a cigarette and stood up nervously, saying, "I don't know what we're going to do. I haven't an idea in my head." Less than one hour later, David and I had a dreamy new love *pas de deux*, which I find an unbelievable bonus at this late stage of my ballet life.'[20] In fact, Ashton, in his kindness, had ensured that Margot's sequences involved a lot of rolling about on the floor with David Wall, or being hoisted aloft in his strong arms, so that her painful feet need hardly take any weight. It was a ploy which ended in tears on the first night. Delayed at various airports, Wall only arrived in Rio on the morning of the performance. 'Margot could see I was a bit jet-lagged, so when we'd got it all slotted together, she said, "I don't want to tire you – let's just mark the *pas de deux* and save it for tonight." It finished with a horizontal lift above my head, with her just lying flat, like a board. I ran around the stage with her, and then we went down into the last position. You could always rely on Margot to perform, and when I got her up there on the night she decided that she needed to do an extra thing. Just a little flourish – so minimal – but it was enough to propel her out of my hands and she fell flat on the stage. And the whole audience, who'd come to see their goddess, just *stood*. All I could see were these sudden sparkling jewels. And there was this terrific gasp. Margot could tell I was terribly upset, but she just laughed it off.'

Nothing – still less in the land of her forefathers – was going to mar Margot's pleasure in dancing a work once again tailored, as only Ashton knew how, for her true talents. The music, by Heitor Villa-Lobos, was adapted from the score of a film based on W. H. Hudson's novel *Green Mansions*, the theme of which (nature-spirit in love with a mortal) carried with it nostalgic shades of *Ondine* – so much so, that Ashton, the most reluctant of travellers, who had not been back to South America since his Peruvian childhood, made the trip to Rio for the opening and followed the dancers on their tour of the interior. Margot's own delight in her Brazilian roots was palpable – especially when she managed to find the actual railroad built there by her English paternal grandfather in 1900. 'It was seventy-five years, perhaps to the very day, after my father arrived there by rickety coastal boat – my grandmother dreadfully sea-sick and distressed by the cockroaches – that I landed by light plane (also a rough journey) in a field outside Imbituba, fully expecting all traces of that remote seaside paradise to be obliterated by concrete promenades and neon-lit hamburger haunts. I could hardly believe it true that the dirt roads, the deserted beaches, the little painted cottages, the single-track railway and the old engine sheds were exactly as I had always imagined them. The town is extended, of course, and now has a fine church, but with every step I took, I was sure my father had trodden the same dust and gravel while the soft breeze ruffled his boyish hair.'[21]

Margot's deep attachment to Brazil was returned to her in kind by the Brazilian audiences, who treated her with an almost dangerous possessiveness. 'There was a performance in Brasília of *Bayadère,*' says David Wall, 'in a huge auditorium, with something like 30,000 people watching. I think they must have sold an extra 20,000 black market tickets. So there were enormous riots outside and the performance actually had to be stopped. Riot police came in and cleared everybody with double-sold tickets away.' Such scenes filled Margot with guilt rather than elation. In these final years, when she felt that she had little but her legend left to offer, her sense of duty to her fans could swell to masochistic proportions. David Wall recalls that after a particular performance in Vancouver, 'she was really feeling terribly tired. These tours were one-night-stands. I think she had something on her mind – she was slightly agitated, and I sensed this and said, "I'll take you back to the hotel." There were a lot of people waiting outside, wanting autographs. I said, "What we'll do is just clear a path through and I'll put you straight into the car and explain to them the situation and we'll drive away." Which we did. But she suddenly got guilt pangs and made us go round the block, back to the stage-door and she got out and signed all those programmes.'

Inspired, perhaps, by her Brazilian great-grandfather's mercantile spirit, Margot now embarked on a business venture with Dalal Achcar. Not since the 60s had she taken such an unballetic step, when, with Donald Albery, she had launched the warehouse theatre which they had named the Donmar. On the same principle of merging abbreviated first names, Margot and Dalal called their enterprise Mada. It was to be a brand-name for ballet-wear, with designs based on the lovely silk tights and knitted vests that Margot herself always wore, and which dancers all over the world were known to covet. 'We sold a lot for a while,' says Achcar. 'We made them in Brazil and I sent them to her, and someone wanted to market them in America. She gave me power of attorney. We were like sisters.'

This powerful sense of kinship was something which those whom Margot allowed close felt driven to declare. 'Personally,' Keith Money told the congenitally impersonal Ninette de Valois,

'I must say that in many respects I feel as strongly about Margot as I do about anyone in this world.'[22] And Nureyev, on camera, once announced simply: 'To me she is part of my family. That's all what I have. Only her.'[23]

In so far as Covent Garden had been 'home' to the great partnership, 10 January 1976 marked a sad but inevitable leave-taking. Since Margot's first appearance there with Rudolf, in *Giselle* fourteen years earlier, she had discouraged him from falling to his knees at her feet, lest his obeisance place extra emphasis on their age-gap – and on the mother/son dynamic so inherent to their coupling. But when, after this particular performance of *Romeo and Juliet*, she passed him the usual long-stemmed red rose from her bouquet, he repeated that original act of homage, kneeling to her and impulsively kissing her hand. For this was an occasion of high sentiment: their last appearance together in a full-length ballet at the Opera House.

They gave their final *Marguerite and Armand* not on the London stage, but in Manila, at a gala for President Marcos's birthday – a celebration which moved the First Lady to ply her guests with rich gifts. Bill Akers was squiring Margot at a reception on the night before opening at the Cultural Centre, and happened to admire the President's embroidered, buttercup-yellow shirt. 'And at eight o'clock the following morning,' says Akers, 'there was a knock at my door, and standing there was a youth with a copy of the shirt – in pink. Somebody had stayed up all night to make that shirt. The same afternoon, at five o'clock, we went into the theatre so that Margot could do her *barre*, and in the mail was a green velvet box about seven inches long. Margot took it to her dressing-table and suddenly I heard her scream *that word*. I turned round and she said, "Well, what would *you* say?" And she was holding up a bracelet. If I remember correctly it had seven rows of jewels across it – rubies, diamonds, pearls, emeralds, and then back the other way. She said, "What can I *do*? I can't give it back."' (It is interesting, for the moral record, to note Nureyev's reaction when, three years later, at the end of a Thanksgiving party thrown by Imelda Marcos at the Waldorf

Towers in New York, he found himself in receipt of a similar offering. He was on his way home in a limousine with Monique van Vooren when he unwrapped the present: a pair of diamond cufflinks which, without a word – least of all *that* one – he instantly donated to the anonymous driver. ' "Rudolf!" said Monique. "What are you doing? Don't you like them?" "I love them," he replied. "But I don't like the source." '[24])

It was not only to her great roles that Margot must now bid farewell. Her father had, all his life, been hale and hearty. 'Totally solid,' according to Keith Money. 'Heart of oak.' But Mrs Hookham writes: 'Sadly, in 1976, while still apparently well and active as ever, he had a heart attack and died at once. Beatrice was ill with shock for a long time as she had been totally dependent on him for everything and was a naturally emotional person in the continental manner.' 'Margot kept in touch with Felix's wife when he died,' says Nitzia Embiricos. 'Nice lady. Different from BQ who was a very determined, self-sufficient woman. Beatrice was more dependent on Margot's father. They came to the house when Margot was launching her autobiography. He was correcting her spelling in the proofs. I think Margot doesn't talk much about her father in the book out of loyalty to her mother. He was quite passive when I met him, a normal, down-to-earth man, kind. And Margot was very kind to Beatrice – I know she had to help her economically when her father died.'

The plight of her father's widow only served to provide Margot with yet another spur to battle on. Her erstwhile disdain for the Antipodes had been thoroughly cut down to size, for she now depended upon the brash flair of the Australians to keep her show on the road. Bill Akers, the stage director who she was convinced could light her more charitably than any other, remembers: 'Michael Edgely, during the European holidays, would assemble ten couples from the top international companies and bring them out to Australia for a show called *Stars of World Ballet*, and we'd do knock-'em-down, carry-'em-out programmes. Bobby Helpmann would come and put it all together, and you'd start off with something like the opening of *Birthday Offering* and they'd all come on, as they do, the ballerinas and their partners. And then they'd do their *Don Qs* and their *Corsaires* and all their trick numbers, and at the end they'd do the finale to *Birthday Offering* so that it was a production rather than just a circus night.' Leslie Edwards was also on the tour as Helpmann's assistant. 'In the opening, Margot did not appear in this ensemble but entered from the back of the stage, bursting through the dancers to take her position in the centre to perform the famous solo from *Raymonda* . . . It was a real *coup de théâtre* on Bobby's part . . . To relieve the tedious repetition of dancing the same role night after night for the six weeks of the tour, operation "all change" was put into effect, giving rise to some interesting variations of partnering; we all enjoyed seeing Margot with Liepa in a very turgid Russian *pas de deux*.'[25]

Maris Liepa, a People's Artist of the Bolshoi, had, as a child, dreamed of dancing one day with Margot Fonteyn, and it was on his forty-second birthday that Margot surprised him by presenting herself on stage – instead of Marina Kondratieva, his usual partner – as a birthday treat. But a more momentous anniversary was looming: on 18 May 1979, Fonteyn herself would, unbelievably, turn sixty.

You could hardly blame the Royal Ballet, with Norman Morrice now at its helm, for staging her gala evening as if it were a formal send-off. Fittingly, it consisted of a quadruple Ashton bill – which included one item that had never been seen before – *Salut d'Amour*, described in the programme as 'A grateful and loving tribute from Frederick Ashton to the great dancer, in which she recalls moments from the ballets he created for her in a long and rewarding collaboration. (F.A.)' Alastair Macaulay wrote for *Ritz*: 'The curtain rose in silence on Dame Margot. The huge roar of applause soon subsided at the sight of her, quietly seated, dressed in calf-length evening-dress of oystershell-pink and heeled shoes, all stillness and beauty. As she had always been. The frock was by William Chappell . . . There she was, just gazing off into the wings, remembering . . . and then she rose and started to dance. It was all tender, all the fleeting memories of a galaxy of Ashton parts created upon her . . . so extraordinary to have these conjured up without the appropriate music or costumes or set, but made there and then in a moment by Dame Margot: unforgettable . . . Then she turned to see . . . walking towards her a man in a dress-suit with white hair . . . who came to kneel at her feet and kiss her hand . . . Sir Fred himself, of course. He rose, folded her arm about his, and together they began to leave the stage, dancing a phrase known as the "Fred step".[26]

In less expert hands, *Salut d'Amour* could have proved horribly embarrassing, but in the event the three-minute ballet created such a storm of sentiment that it had to be enacted all over again. It wasn't the audience's last sight of her: Margot would return with Robert Helpmann at the end of the programme, to do the Tango from *Façade*. 'Only Fonteyn,' continues Macaulay, 'could dance a deb at the age of 60 and make it triumphantly and unforgettably hilarious . . . There's a moment when the Dago should pick her up and flip her right over like a tiresome piece of baggage . . . Sir Robert isn't young, of course, and Fonteyn's simple gesture to him not to *dare* to try the lift was far funnier than the lift itself . . . I can't ever forget the fun of it.'[27]

At Margot's behest, there were no speeches. The rapturous calls were all about flowers. They rained down from the balcony until Margot was ankle-deep. And then began a procession, led by Michael Somes, of the men in the company, who, one by one, brought her a single red rose, placing each, when she could hold no more, on the floor at her feet. It was left to the last and youngest boy to gather up those roses and deliver them into her arms, so that Margot, when Ninette de Valois came on to the stage, could, in turn, present the great welter of blooms to the woman who had, from the beginning, watched over her career with such singular ferocity and love.

It was an evening designed to gratify the faithful. Margot's last, shining glance, as she made her (second) exit in *Salut d'Amour*, was trained unequivocally up towards the amphitheatre. But, after Somes had turned his back on the audience to conduct the company in a chorus of Happy Birthday, the curtains swished closed for the last time, and the fans were relegated to Floral Street, where they would wait until 1 a.m. for a final fleeting glimpse of their heroine as she emerged from the stage door. She, meanwhile, in flame-red chiffon, was cutting her cake with the dignitaries in the crush bar, where, at long last, the title of Prima Ballerina Assoluta was conferred upon her by Princess Margaret, and where John Tooley presented her with a silver medal for distinguished services to the Royal Ballet. And now she *did* speak: of the tears which she had shed during the evening, and of her family, and, most pointedly, of her eighty-four-year-old mother. 'No ballerina,' she acknowledged, 'has ever been so blessed in her life.'[28]

News of the evening claimed the front page of the *Standard*: 'FONTEYN'S FAREWELL. Dame Margot Fonteyn, 60 (and looking 40), took her leave of London in the gentlest and most enigmatic way at Covent Garden last night.'[29] But had she *really* gone? There had been no formal announcement. And what was her true legacy? James Monahan, by now Director of the Royal Ballet School, found himself wondering 'how much good she has done the cause of ballet . . . I want ardently to remember her as she used to be until, say, 1957, and the Margot of the years since then has made it ever more difficult to do this. Also, I ask myself: how does she herself want to be remembered? Which brings me to the inevitable question: why does she do it?'[30]

But it is a question which rebounds upon him; for, at the end of his long 'elegy on the Fonteyn I worshipped of yesteryear', he goes on to admit: 'On May 23rd 1979, I am in the audience at Covent Garden for the celebration of her sixtieth birthday – a performance by her successors in the Royal Ballet of three works by Frederick Ashton in which she used to shine, *Birthday Offering*, *Symphonic Variations* and *Façade*, and, on this sixtieth birthday, she dances the *Tango* with that irrepressible comedian Robert Helpmann . . . and a delightfully mocking account they give of it, this sexagenarian with her septuagenarian cavalier. There is also a performance of *Salut d'Amour* (Elgar music – and how appropriate a title for the occasion!), a marvellously tactful, tasteful, nostalgic concoction by Ashton in which, by posture and gesture, by personality and lovable stage-presence, rather than by dancing in any full sense of the term, she evokes this and that role out of the many which he (*her* choreographer) created for her down the years. I witness this, also the unassuming yet regal little address she makes to us at the party afterwards and, along with everyone else, I am altogether re-conquered. I am made to feel that all reservations about her latter-day career and about the sum of her contribution to the well-being of ballet are, when all is said and done, mere niggling curmudgeonliness; that such reservations are nothing when set against our, my, joy and pride in Britain's first *prima ballerina assoluta*.'

Margot's so-called last performance was almost immediately followed by a flurry of further finales. A fortnight after the farewell gala, she surfaced at the London Coliseum, dancing with Rudolf for the concluding lap (16–23 June) of the Nureyev Festival, appearing every week-night and twice on Saturday as the leading Nymph in Nijinsky's *L'Après-midi d'un Faune*, and – God help her – as the Young Girl in *Le Spectre de la Rose*. And then, as if on a whim, she danced no more. Overnight, she broke with the sacred ritual of class – except that (and there always had to be an exception with Margot, who continued to tease her fans by describing herself as '90 per cent retired') she would go on to make two further appearances in the early 80s. The first was in the mime role of Lady Capulet for the Ballet of La Scala, Milan; and the second, at a centennial gala in New York, where seventy-nine-year-old Ashton became her cavalier again, in another evocation of the past, *Acte de présence*. 'Because Margot had had such a success there as Aurora,' Ashton told Julie Kavanagh, 'I thought why not do something to do with that. She was lying on a chaise-longue in Saint-Laurent red taffeta wearing a hundred thousand pounds' worth of diamonds from Harry Winston . . . And there she lay looking *wonderful*. I stood away with four roses in my hand and went over like the Prince and kissed her awake. Then she got up and I gave her a rose and she did a turn and I gave her another and so on . . . Then we did a little bit of nonsense. Then what everyone calls my step, but it's not mine at all – it was Pavlova's step and I always put it in as a kind of signature. So then we went off. To *roars* of applause, I must say. They had told us we were only allowed one call, and I said, "Yes, we'll see." So when we finished we took one curtain call, and I said, "Come on, let's go through," so we went through twice . . . Then I said to Margot, "let go of me, I'm going to carry on." They adore it you see – the ludicrous aspect – they think it's outrageous. No one would *dare* do it there, and I play up to it like mad.'[1]

When people had the temerity to ask Margot what she would do when she stopped dancing, her stock reply had always been, 'I'll sit beside Tito and grow fat and happy.'[2] But contented idleness was not to be her lot, for, as Rudolf once wickedly told the press: 'Margot never sits full-arse on the chair.'[3] And so, no sooner had she left the stage than, thin as a reed, she was invading our living-rooms. *The Magic of Dance*, a television series which she devised and presented herself, was aired at prime-time in November and December of 1979. She had conceived of the programme years earlier with her brother and her friend David Scrase, but nothing had come of the project until 1975, when her brother Felix mentioned the idea to Frank Muir, who arranged a lunch with Aubrey Singer, then Director of BBC2. Patricia Foy, Margot's producer-friend, also came along, surprised though she was by the ballerina's interest in television, a medium which – unsurprisingly – she had never had time to watch. But Margot, who, since her acceptance into the Sadler's Wells School, had never suffered the indignity of having to audition for anything, made an impressive pitch for the job of presenter, seducing Aubrey Singer over lunch with her animated and heart-felt anecdotes of tragic Nijinsky. 'Put an outline on paper,' Singer advised. 'So I went to Harrods,' writes Margot, 'and bought six large sheets of thick drawing paper in different colours, ruled them up, and, basing each one on a star name of a different period, filled them in with names of dancers, ballets, choreographers, famous theatres. I added aspects of the social life of the times. Ana Cristina Alvarado from San Salvador, who had been responsible for my performances there with Heinz Bosl, helped me to make the presentation. We put the sheets in a large handsome folder with *The Magic of Dance* flourished across the front in thick black letters; we thought it looked quite attractive. It was delivered to the BBC and we waited.'[4]

The rest, as they say, is history – a charming, if potted, history of dance as filtered through Margot's highly subjective, sometimes oddly pedantic, but always generous-spirited sensibility. After the penny-pinching ways of the ballet world, she was astonished to find that the BBC was prepared to fly her and the camera crew to, say, Greece, just for one shot of her at dawn, holding forth beneath the Parthenon about Isadora Duncan. And Margot certainly gives the programme-makers their money's worth, sweeping the blue skies beneath the monolithic pillars with the arc of her bare arms and using her eyes like the first *ingénue* of antiquity. It was, in fact, quite difficult for her, given the magnification of a stage manner which had for so long projected effortlessly to the back row of the gods, to shrink her expressiveness to suit the unnaturally close scrutiny of television; but, after the first few items, in which she is apt to over-dress, or to waggle her head, or to pose hand on hip, foot neatly crossed behind ankle, she gets the measure of the medium, like the true pro that she is. And we – despite the gentility of her tone, and the visual confirmation that she cannot, indeed, sit 'full-arse on the chair' – find ourselves captivated by her shirt-waisted, tea-party company.

Having invoked the concept of 'magic', not just in the title of the series but also in that of the accompanying, commissioned book, neither commentary nor text seems able to desist from harping on the word, as if in populist sop to readers' and viewers' supposed taste for escapism. Yet Margot, under the erudite influence of her editor, Robert Gottlieb, and her producer, Patricia Foy, entered into the programme research with pent-up intellectual fervour, surprising herself, as the book's high-flying section-headings make clear – 'Dance Universal', 'Dance Experimental', 'Dance Imperial', 'Dance Aerial', 'Dance Mythological', 'Dance Traditional' – with a latent philosophical bent. 'It may seem strange for me to say that during the forty-some years of my career I read very little about dance; the activity itself was totally absorbing. I knew the general history from my student days but I had no desire to delve more deeply until those years of experience on the stage began to press on my mind and odd questions would crop up . . . As I looked for answers, I came to sense, rightly or wrongly, that I have a "back-stage" understanding of many of the people and how they felt in certain situations.'[5]

So innate is this power of identification that, when interviewing the great luminaries of her field, from Nureyev to Fred Astaire, all she has to do is sit and smile for them to open up to her. And she is broad enough in her tastes to be able to honour two just such disparate personalities simultaneously: 'Astaire's charisma is relaxed, Nureyev's is tense. They are both geniuses, yet Astaire is at ease in retirement whereas Nureyev will guard his passion until his last breath.'[6] Nureyev's continued grip upon her loyalty is made all too evident in the programme's major hobby-horse – that the man should share fully in the ballerina's limelight. She virtually hands over the interview to him. 'Well,' he tells her, 'I never thought of man in balletic terms being inferior to woman. I always thought that he could be just as subtle and as fine and delicate and forceful and whatever as woman could be. Somehow in Russia he look like he's being only heroic and being lifter and being generally in backwaters.'[7] Margot credits Rudolf with having changed, single-handedly, the public's perception of men in tights, and suggests that before his 'leap to freedom' male dancers could only claim centre stage if attired in top hat and tails. She commends to us the people about whom she has written, and trusts that we will 'look searchingly into their pictures'.[8] Yet, obediently studying the stills sequence of Fred Astaire, dancing in *Top Hat* with Ginger Rogers, we are struck by a perverse phenomenon: we can't stop our eyes from wandering, away from the svelte male figure clad in black tails, towards the twirling, lissom girl in the frothy white dress. In shot after shot, Ginger Rogers, like Margot herself, cannot make an ugly shape. And the revelation is that Margot's own vivacious, unaffected style may well have owed as much to a 30s film-star's high-heeled grace as ever it did to the classical *pointe*-work of Markova.

Of the other bee in Nureyev's bonnet – his ideological reverence for what she had always regarded as the more pseudo side of modern dance – Margot is less indulgent. In interview, he goes on to say: 'When I came to the West, idea was not just "Here I am, the best, the greatest . . . let me show you." I came to learn. All modern choreographers, what they aim is really to discover new way of moving, new language, because that language allows one to delve into one's inner being. More complex things could be portrayed on stage.'[9] There is a break in the tape, covering – maddeningly for us – what is clearly some frank exchange between them. For the cut leaves Rudolf laughing into his lap and then raising his head in mutinous defiance of her smiling, tight-voiced answer: 'Some modern ballets,' she ventures, 'seem to me a little unemotional compared to the sort of excitement of *Corsaire*.'[10] It is a prejudice which her film proceeds to endorse, for the footage of Rudolf, revolving, earnest and muscle-bound, on the strung-out ropes of Glen Tetley's *Pierrot Lunaire* makes us long for the return of his irreverent, troubadour spirit, as demonstrated by her introductory item. It is truly sad to contemplate that Rudolf, though twenty years Margot's junior, was, by the time that she finally released him from their partnership, virtually as washed-up as she. In 1981, the first cases of AIDS would be diagnosed in America, and his accelerated decline would begin. Already in the ascendant was Baryshnikov, who may be seen, in a later episode of *The Magic of Dance*, partnering Margot for the one and only time, in *Le Spectre de la Rose*. Her performance with him is a miracle of deception: even through the lens of an ungovernable camera, she remains utterly in control of where she wants our eye to be – *not* on her lax, decrepit feet, but on the still-taut glory of her upper body, her speaking *port de bras*, and lovely face.

The Magic of Dance was only the latest offering in Margot's literary œuvre: a year before, she had published *A Dancer's World* as part of the two-book deal which she had struck with W. H. Allen at the time of her autobiography. Though somewhat hurried in its execution, *A Dancer's World* is a sensible little tome for children and parents, which includes a chapter called 'The Mother', by Mrs Hookham, and which offers such a fund of sound and practical advice to students that it is hard to believe that Margot felt no impulse whatever to teach. But, in fact, she was actually quite offended by the suggestion that she should owe any further debt to the collective. Had she not given her life-blood to the profession? Was her visual example not enough? Why should she be expected to tell people what she'd already shown them? According to Roland Petit, 'If you ask her to teach it's as if you ask Greta Garbo if she wants to teach. She's irreplaceable. What she had she cannot teach.'[11] Dancers, however, continued to take a fairly censorious view of what appeared to be not just a lack of respect for the tradition of handing down, but a denial of the joy that the imparting of such knowledge can bring. 'She'd just retired,' recalls the American dancer Isobel Browne (mother of Leslie Browne, the young star of the ballet film *The Turning Point*), 'and I said, "Margot, why on earth aren't you coaching the kids?" And she said it right out: "I'd be jealous of the person I was working with, because I can't do what they're doing any more." This was Margot's problem − not so much that she lacked confidence but that she knew it wasn't going to be good for her head. She didn't want to destroy herself in that way.'

Before the 80s were out, hard times would dictate that Margot succumb to the financial lure of coaching. But 'she didn't think', says Jane Herrmann, 'that she'd have the patience. She'd say to me, "All right, you can send me in six girls. But out of the six, who's good?" I said, "About three." And she said to me, "Then *don't* make me look at the others." She really felt, "Don't waste my time. What good am I going to do if they're not talented?" It's hard to be generous when you're a great dancer. Erik [Bruhn] told me that it took him five years to be able to bear looking at the dancers who weren't as good as he was.'

Georgina Parkinson was Ballet Mistress with American Ballet Theatre when Margot finally agreed to do some coaching sessions there. Georgina's own history with Margot on this front had been chequered. 'At Barons Court, Antoinette, Merle and I used to share a dressing-room with her, which is where I got closest to her. She used to do the most incredible Prélude in *Sylphides* and since I was going to do it, I remember saying to her one morning: "Margot, I don't know if you have any time, but I would really appreciate it if you could run through the Prélude with me." She categorically refused. She said: "I don't think I do anything different from anyone else. Just learn it, and do it." I thought it was strange. I didn't think, "Oh, Margot's so ungenerous," because you never thought that, but I was cut short, definitely. She did not want to get into a rehearsal studio and discuss things like dancers do today and some of us did then: Lynn [Seymour] and I used to work together and help each other – on a technical level – but I never saw Margot in that kind of situation. Never. That was not what interested her about the art. She knew she had to have sufficient technique to express whatever she wanted to, but it didn't appear to us that she liked to analyse much. I think she was very smart, actually, the way she stayed within her limits. I'm not saying she didn't work hard, but in class she was very much at peace with herself, somehow.'

However, when Margot did eventually capitulate to coaching American Ballet Theatre – for *Birthday Offering* – she became very quickly what Jane Herrmann describes as 'gung ho',[12] exhorting the dancers to develop an overview of each musical phrase. 'She gave you the most incredible pointers,' says Georgina Parkinson, 'such as "The most important thing is the last step, and maybe the first." She taught you about pacing yourself, about steps that you show and steps that you give away. It was all about the construction of a variation, and all done in a very matter-of-fact, black-and-white sort of way. If you were having a technical problem with turns or something, she would never help. Whether she *could* or not, I don't know, but she never did. It was all about the bigger picture."

Margot's vision was, in fact, global. 'She had a dream,' says Querube Arias, 'this great idea that a whole new style of dance could be developed from the music and movement of South America – a sort of Caribbean equivalent of the Russian style. She didn't think it would be like the Tango; she really thought it would be a new kind of classical ballet. But she needed the auspices of someone in Panama: that's how she got into the whole Noriega thing. And she wrote to all the First Ladies in North and South America, and she began this scheme. Dancers from all over the continent would meet and work together for three months of every year. We had some setbacks, because a whole group of these South American dancers were killed in a plane crash, and Margot arranged a benefit for all their families.'

No pension had been put in place for Margot herself despite her long services to ballet; and her decision to live away from England further cut her off from any hope of state support. Nor could she really conceive of a day-to-day life which lacked some sort of project. There was no question in Margot's mind as to where she proposed to spend her post-dancing years: in Panama. But now that Tito's political ambitions had come to nought – and put paid to any possibility that she might herself ever be a First Lady – in what capacity? 'They were looking about for a house,' says Buenaventura, 'and I said to Dr Arias, "Why don't you buy a farm?" Dr Arias and myself went first quite a long way from the city and we found a big piece of land with nothing on it. Dame Margot called from London and I explained to her there is a farm and we're waiting for her to have a look.' Arias, however, as always reserved the right to change his mind. 'I telephoned the flat in Panama,' writes Margot, 'and Buenaventura answered and said, "The Doctor has found another farm and has gone to buy it." I said, "Oh my goodness. What's wrong with the one by the lake?" Buenaventura replied, "This one is much nicer, and it has a kilometre of beach." I was won over immediately. A farm with a kilometre of beach on the Pacific! What more could one ask?" '[13]

Well, a roof over one's head, for a start. With nothing but the remnants of a mud-hut on 600 acres of wilderness through which roamed wild horses and cattle, Margot and Tito initially had to rent a house twelve miles away, and commute back and forth to the ranch. But, to Margot, their own plot of land, near the humble settlement of El Higo, at the end of an unnamed, rutted road, was as enchanted as the forest through which Prince Florimund had hacked his way to waken his princess. 'I think our farm is the most beautiful place in the uncivilized world,' she wrote to Ashton. 'The beach is one kilometre long, and empty. Two rivers wind across it to get to the sea, sometimes making nice calm swimming pools of fresh water. There are fresh-water shrimps, too, if someone catches them. The sea is always warm – but not, alas, as clear as in the Bahamas. We plant fruit and flowering trees all the time. Of course I might not see them all but I like to know that someone will enjoy them one day. Luckily the avocado will be ready in four years and the grapefruits, too. The corn only takes ten months. We already have limes, lemons, guavas and other tropical fruits as well as papayas. The mandarin trees haven't given fruit, perhaps I should talk to them kindly. Fresh coconuts are opened every day when we get hot and tired. I keep thinking that as soon as we have a house you could come and stay, there is a flight that goes all the way to Panama without changing . . . I am wondering how to plant our cliff top when we build our house because I don't want to block the view of the sea or of the distant mountains. On the slope going down to the sea I want lots of oleander.'[14]

It would be four years before their own house – set a long way back from the exposed clifftop – was finally built: of grey colonial-sized bricks made up by hand from a mix of cement and horse-dung, topped with a roof of corrugated iron which overhung the structure to form a veranda. Tito refused to engage an architect, and designs drawn up by his new son-in-law, Carlos Brillenbourg, proved too costly to be practicable, so Margot eventually bequeathed the job to an elderly and half-blind local builder, who promised: 'Just tell me where you want the rooms, and I'll do it.'[15]

The resulting four-roomed dwelling, without ceilings or air-conditioning, was unpretentious to the point of being ramshackle. But Margot loved it and never once apologized for its simplicity. Although she and Tito had wanted to call their estate Reina Negra, Black Queen seemed less flattered than she might have been. 'It may *sound* beautiful,' she wrote to Margot, 'but it could be a pub.'[16] She suggested 'something more realistic. A descriptive name of some kind I think is best to help visitors find it.' The farm, eventually to be named La Quinta Pata (which translates variously as 'Duck Farm' or 'The Fifth Leg') was nowhere near ready when, in 1980, Mrs Hookham had visited Margot and Tito in Panama. Nor could her trip have been described as a runaway success. 'We were driving the car from the country,' says Buenaventura, 'and BQ was sitting in the back. I said, "Don't open your window, Madame." "That's OK," she said, "just for a minute." And in that moment the people in the street threw a jug of water over her.' The tropical climate, in any case, struck Mrs Hookham as little better than 'an agreeable warm shower bath', and during her six-week stay she was plagued by insect-bites.

'All insects love my blood,' she wrote afterwards to Margot, 'and for some incomprehensible reason they don't like yours.' The land of her daughter's choice seemed full of poisonous plants and snakes: 'I must say I think I should be a bit nervous walking about unless I had rubber boots on.'[17] Not that she *could* walk much any more. Essentially, Mrs Hookham, ever since that first trip to China, had loved travelling, possessing what she had always described as 'hot feet'. But now the knees above them were being turned, by arthritis, into stone. 'Here,' she writes ('here' being a flat at 27 Onslow Square), 'I get very bored because I don't get many visitors and can't go out shopping because of my accursed knees. When I am on two feet I can walk short distances on my good days, but sometimes I have to ask passers-by to give me a hand.'[18] Patricia Foy, during the making of *The Magic of Dance*, had been called upon to give just such assistance. 'I had to take Margot all over the world,' she says, 'and sometimes her mother came along, and really it was such a nuisance. We had to wheel Tito in a chair *and* we had to wheel the mother in a chair through airports. And we were pushing the chairs and Margot was walking ahead. Margot sort of did it to make her mother feel better. But the mother was very pushy. It was the same with Menuhin – he had that sort of mother. People like that have to have a mother with the intelligence to direct them correctly. And I do think Mrs Hookham was a very wise woman in many ways.'

But it is difficult, when you are nearly ninety, and half the world away from your beloved child, to make your wisdom felt. 'Dearest of daughters,' Mrs Hookham wrote to Margot, 'You slightly worry me, you are doing too much and not getting enough sleep . . . Why do you let the dogs on to your bed and wake you up, not to mention putting their paws on your face? Somewhat unsanitary I would think. I am sorry to hear you have been slightly in the wars yourself with having had your toe broken and now getting stung with the nettles or whatever they are . . . Is it the nice-looking young man who is stealing the prawns? I think it must be very sad to have so few people you can trust.'[19] But sometimes Mrs Hookham, sounding less like a concerned mother than a grieving lover, would confess the sadness to be all her own. 'I am in a poor way myself, and cannot shake off the gloom of loneliness though I despise myself for it. If you, who are so busy, miss me, who has nothing to do, you can imagine how much I miss you – every morning when I hear the postman I am out of my bed within seconds, hoping it is from you. I read it over and over, if it is . . . Darling Margot, I miss you more and more as I get more and more stupid and forgetful . . . I really am horrified at my mental condition and pray I don't go completely dotty . . . I have a kind of malaise about doing anything except reading and gazing into space and thinking of the "good old days". Does Feebee tell you how vague I am?'[20]

In fact the family talked of little else. Feebee, who was driving to London daily to cook and care for BQ, had long been trying to persuade her mother-in-law to give up the flat and live full-time at Amerden. But by the time Mrs Hookham agreed, her condition had deteriorated to the point where it was thought best that she be admitted to a home 'for Distressed Gentlefolk' in nearby Ascot. Margot, in a letter to Frederick Ashton, confided her anxiety about her mother: 'I don't like to leave her too long between visits to see her as she seems to feel that she is getting near the end. It's not that she minds going but that she gets upset about the idea that she's seeing me for the last time. She is supposed to come to Panama for Christmas, so I told her to hang on.'[21]

But although Mrs Hookham hung on in body, she was fading all too fast in mind. 'To the dearest and best of daughters. Excuse please. Can not write properly. I am sorry I am writing blindly holding a magnifying glass. Obviously must go to opticians.'[22] And yet her eyesight did not fail her, nor her lucidity entirely desert her, until she had seen her daughter bestowed with one last and unexpected honour. In 1982, to a 'specially composed fanfare of trumpets',[23] Margot was installed as Chancellor of Durham University. Tito accompanied his wife to the 'breath-taking'[24] ceremony of installation at the Cathedral, and to the subsequent lunch, during which she was handed a telegram of congratulations from the Prince of Wales, and a message from de Valois, which read: 'With all my love and everlasting pride in "Little Hookham".'[25] Margot had never known 'such a glorious day',[26] and must have performed a mental cartwheel at the thought of her headmistress in Shanghai, Miss Fleet, who 'would have been dumbfounded'.[27] Sir Frederick Holliday, the university's former Vice-Chancellor, later recalled that Margot had made her installation speech unprompted by notes, and that she had surprised most of the academics as she 'seemingly plucked from the air . . . passionately fluent'[28] sentiments in the cause of education: 'I believe that every child is born with a talent which we should seek out, encourage, value and respect. What wealth of talent lies untapped among the millions of under-nourished and under-educated children of this world.' 'That speech, the first of many delivered impromptu within the university,' Holliday was to write, 'set the tone for her period

of office. She brought grace, dignity, commitment, professionalism and a sense of international presence to the many congregation ceremonies over which she officiated. Her stage training
and excellent memory added to these occasions; she listened
carefully to each name called by the deans as students came
forward for their degrees; she then greeted each student by first
name and congratulated them. She had a special word for any
handicapped students, always with Tito's situation in mind.'

In her quavery hand, Mrs Hookham wrote to Margot: 'I am
amazed that you have all these gifts. You give good lectures,
write splendid books, were the world's best dancer and everybody gives you Honours and admires you and you are a very
unspoilt remarkable woman and my darling daughter.'[29] As for
de Valois: in the last, long twilight of her life, she kept but one,
framed, photograph on her mantelpiece: of 'Little Hookham',
dressed not in tutu and tiara, but in full academic regalia, as
Chancellor of Durham University. Yet on the occasion of the
investiture, de Valois had been unable to attend on account of
a broken toe. A year later she would write to Margot, 'I paid a
visit to Durham to give a lecture and I was filled with an undying
shame for not turning up at your event – the first time I have
failed to "be there" for an honorary degree. Wonderful to think
the ballet world has given us a Chancellor . . . Do you remember
how Constant, during the wartime days, would always make us
come out into the corridor to look at Durham Cathedral as we
went past?'[30]

Perhaps it was her admission into the groves of higher learning
that persuaded Margot to take part in a new literary venture –
a collaborative effort, this time, with Roberta and John Lazzarini,
on a book titled *Pavlova Impressions*, with a text gleaned mostly
from press-cuttings contained in three albums kept by Pavlova
herself which the Lazzarinis had acquired at a Sotheby's auction.
'Fonteyn's function is defined as "presenter",' wrote Nadine
Meisner in the *Dancing Times*. 'In her commentary she might
have helped flesh out the picture . . . She supplies the bare facts
necessary to our understanding of the quoted texts . . . Yet rarely

does she question what Pavlova says. For example, there is no reference to Pavlova's probable illegitimacy and Jewish father; Pavlova's claim that her father died when she was two is allowed to pass without comment.'[31]

John Percival, however, found it 'illuminating' to hear one great ballerina speak of another. 'When Dame Margot remarks that Pavlova "could never be completely aware of the impact she had on people because she could never see herself on the stage", you realize the full poignancy of that. Equally authentic is the remark on ballet shoes, "the bane of every ballerina's life", that precedes an account of Pavlova's dealings with Nicolini, her shoe-maker in Milan.'[32] Margot, after all, had, for the first three or four years of her career, favoured Nicolini shoes. 'After the old man died,' she writes, 'I always dreamed of the absolute perfection of Nicolini's shoes, compared to which all others seemed to lack some secret magic . . . We do all know the despair of going through the available shoes and finding barely two that are "right". It is one of the curses of tension which is often described as "temperament".'[33]

The need to publicize the new book in England, plus her annual visits to Durham University, served as pretexts for returning regularly to see her mother. For a while Margot kept a flat in Ovington Square, but as time went on she found it easier, on her trips to London, to take a suite at a hotel.

'When Margot Fonteyn stayed at Claridge's with Roberto Arias,' says Michael Bentley, 'her accommodation was paid for by Nancy Oakes, the Baroness von Hoyningen-Huene. We had a combination of rooms at Claridge's, with a twin-bedded room and a bathroom and a single room all behind one front door. Margot and Roberto used to go down for lunch quite frequently, and she was so attentive to that man, cutting up his food, giving him dignity, never hiding him. The most touching thing of all was what always happened on the day they were leaving, when she'd call me up to the room. Roberto would be out with the manservant taking a breath of fresh air, and she'd say, "Would you bring the bill up with you," so up I'd go. We'd sit on the bed and she'd say, "Now, I know Nancy's paying for this accommodation and she's very, very kind, but I have to pay for all our food and drink and telephone bills." So I'd give her the bill for extras, and we'd go through it, and then she'd pay me – in five, ten and twenty pound notes: probably three or four hundred pounds. And we'd sit on the bed and she'd count all this money and then she'd make *me* count it. I don't know whether she had it under the mattress, but I always thought it funny that she never gave me a cheque. I know she was very hard-up.'

Margot's straight and unembarrassed way with cash went back to her early pay-packet days at Sadler's Wells. She had been brought up by her mother to cultivate a kind of piggy-bank mentality, and her father had devoted whole books to the meticulous enumeration of every penny spent on the petrol and oil and nuts and bolts that serviced his passionate love affair with motorcars. In her latter years, Margot herself kept a series of leather-bound diaries as full of minor expenses as they are devoid of personal revelations – 'Fish: 3.5, Grapas: 4.25, Flashlight: 7.60, Thermometer: 5.00, Trousers press: 2.00, Gasolina: 22.75, Dog meat and bones: 8.00.' At the top of each page, the diaries chart the births and deaths and sex-lives of cows: 'Parto Simbra (M) de Vaca Amarilla. 2? Insemination Novilla Blanca 20.14. Parto Vaca Glauca Simbra (H) Amarilla. Sold to Celso from VMS Novillos 11 Vacas. Sr Juan came at 5.30 a.m. to start looking for a cow about to give birth who had been lost for several days and no one able to find her. We drove down the road outside La America and eventually, in Camino Bujo de Jobo, found another cow who had given birth yesterday. Came back to QP to find that the lost cow had been found but had gored Jupiter in the top of the thigh. Adelino, Juan, Chan and Javier put him to the ground and Adelino sewed up the wound, applied iodine and oil to protect it from flies. We went to consult Pieruano – about drying the physio pool – now out of action for several days – enough to seal and paint it.' 'Tito poorly – did not go into the physio pool.' 'Tito still with little problem of retention. Slept badly. Was better after shampoo, bathroom, physio pool etc.' 'Tito had bad night with retention. Felt ill all day with slight temperature.' Tuesday 20 November 1984: 'Tito very unwell with kidney stones and also bad chest.'[34]

Tito grew desperately ill just as La Quinta Pata finally became ready for occupation. 'The illness came upon him very suddenly,' writes Margot, 'and we rushed him to the city by ambulance. He was almost unconscious when we reached the hospital, and soon appeared to be on the point of death. His children flew in from America, and the archbishop tried to administer the last rites, but once again Tito did the unexpected, and survived. I was determined that when he was eventually able to return to the country it would be to live in the new house right on the farm, so I gave up the lease on the rented house, and did my best to get everything ready. We had less than a minimum of furniture, and only candles for lighting, but there we were on the first night having dinner on our own terrace with a full moon above, Tito was alive and almost well and the dogs obviously happy that we had settled down all together at last.'[35]

Was she contented? She swears blind that she was. And how comforting it would be to believe that she had reached a place of respite – some brief, God-given time of happiness-ever-after between the exhaustion of her dancing years and the medical ravages to come. It had taken two years from the point of her retirement, Margot tells us, for the last vestige of fatigue to leave her body; and it would be a mere two years before the first signs of illness would begin to erode that long-delayed, much-deserved, sense of physical well-being. She was, in her mid-sixties, moving into her first non-provisional home, to become unreservedly what she yearned to be: first and foremost a wife. 'Margot could be wistful about her friends' homes,' writes Keith Money. 'In many of these her own possessions were quartered in old corners, as overflow from her mother's packed cupboards . . . And all the while, Margot, I know, had this sweet dream about retiring, and gathering all these things together, and sitting at the centre of a *real home*. It never quite happened. When she did retire, and went to live in Panama, the circumstances had altered, the climate was different, and the imperative for being surrounded by the trappings of a successful life had faded. So, all her "bits and pieces" just slumbered on, elsewhere.'[36]

Let them sleep. Margot had awoken to a new and uncluttered spiritual existence. 'She was very Spartan with herself,' says Ana Cristina Alvarado. 'Simple in her eating habits; austere, even, in the way that she and Tito lived. She was just so happy that she didn't have to go to class, never had to lift her legs again. She had come back to a life that was so simple and unmaterialistic. She found such great inner harmony by being in contact with nature that she could manage with next to nothing, like a monk. She was back in reality, taking care of the chickens and hens and cows.'

Margot certainly embarked upon her agricultural duties with astonishing enthusiasm. The glamorous, curl-horned cattle which she and Tito bred from sperm provided by Nelson Rockefeller's herd wandered on to the veranda and even into the house, the pale hide of their rumps branded with the initials MF. 'I had never seen the birth of a calf,' writes Margot. 'Gradually I discovered that cows don't necessarily get pregnant and give birth regularly each year as I had presumed, so I try to keep a record of their laziness. One doesn't expect them just to lounge around the fields eating a lot of grass and not producing. The genetic aspect of cattle cross-breeding fascinates Tito, and is another source of solace to him . . . He has developed some exceptional animals which carry off the top trophies in all the provincial cattle fairs. It is nice to have our house decorated with medals, cups and ribbons instead of the ballet pictures that some people expect.'[37]

Yet a journalist, Beverly McFarland, who visited Margot at La Quinta Pata in 1985, paints a more sinister picture of this home-sweet-home. 'Where Margot Fonteyn now lives there are boa constrictors and coati-mundis in the jungles and wild parrots as big as loons and people have recipes for paloma pie and nikki stew (wild pigeon and giant rat). A short trek by Land Rover up the lone road from her farm is a place where you can see square trees and pre-Columbian stone carvings on boulders as big as buildings and tiny golden frogs so poisonous that the most infinitesimal trace of their bright skin can be used to kill a man instantly. Some of the beaches near hers are fine black sand that will scorch your feet at midday. In the shanty bars strung out in the dusty towns along the highway the men swig clear moonshine called *seco* from carefully saved glass bottles. The bars are called "Jardín de Paraíso" and the Pacific current is so strong that it is often dangerous to swim. The humidity eats satin toe shoes and yellowed press clippings. The termites eat carved wooden furniture. It is a raw, powerful, all-consuming country.'[38]

As is the country of love. Gabriel Galindo is convinced that if Margot embraced her existence at La Quinta Pata with the fervour that she did, this was entirely for Tito's sake. 'They lived in something akin to destitution. Her only consideration was his welfare. Whatever projects she undertook towards the end of her life were in contemplation of the fact that it would make my uncle's life in some way more comfortable. She would see beauty in things in Panama which – gosh – you would really have to have a trained eye to notice. I think what drew her to Panama obviously wasn't Panama – *Tito* was the epicentre of her life. That a woman of her stature should be so unassuming and unpretentious as to go off and live in those rather primitive conditions – I'm not even sure they had a telephone – it's staggering.'

It certainly staggered her friends back in England, whose only means of contacting her was by letter to a PO box an hour and a half's drive from La Quinta Pata, on the outskirts of Panama City. But on a visit to London Margot told John Tooley: 'If anyone questions my happiness, will you please reassure them. I'm the happiest woman in the world. I'm doing exactly what I want to do, which is to be with Tito, in Panama, on our farm, looking after the cattle, learning how to keep the stock records and everything else, and just thoroughly enjoying myself, wearing shirts and jeans and not having to fuss about anything.'[39]

Wearing jeans was certainly an innovation. Never in her life had she allowed herself to appear publicly in trousers – except, of course, for the inevitable exception: the Puss–in–Boots outfit by Saint-Laurent which she sported in the late 60s. Once, filming in freezing temperatures in China, she had put a rug over her lap rather than let the camera crew see that she was wearing woollen slacks for warmth. But now she could let her absurd standards drop under the unjudging eye of simple country people, and in the all-forgiving company of her dogs. 'There were about six or seven dogs at the farm all the time,' says Buenaventura, 'and two of them preferred to stay in Margot's bedroom. At ten o'clock when she was sleepy, the dogs would start to scratch the door and Dr Arias, who was awake, would say, "Margot, Margot, the dogs want to get in." She would get up and put them in the bed – inside, you know, with the pillows. She was in love with everything – dogs, horses, cows, and the people around. She's thinking our town was *her* town. On the farm, we had to move quickly – she was always in front of us. She was a farmer, a Panamanian farmer. *Una ranchera*. A Cow Lady.'

Margot circumvented the concern of her old friends by making new, much younger ones. During the last decade of her life, her closest female intimates might well have been her daughters. Dark-haired beauties all – Ana Cristina Alvarado from El Salvador, Nitzia Embiricos from Panama, Dalal Achcar from Brazil, and Christina Berlin, an American heiress – they were, indeed, contemporaries of Margot's stepdaughters, Querube and Rosita. Margot would lend this clutch of glamorous surrogates her couture dresses and play matchmaker and confidante in their love-lives. 'She adored to be with young people,' says Ana Cristina. 'The world was changing, and she had *such* curiosity. She'd say, "You're young, I'm not – what's going *on*?" She liked pretty, intelligent girls near Tito to make him happy, girls who were funny and entertaining and understood Tito when he spoke, girls who didn't need an interpreter and would amuse. In fact, *I* loved it because Tito amused *me* so much: I had such a good time with him. Because his brain was trapped in his body, he was a great observer and he would watch things nobody else knew were going on, and then he'd relay them back to you like a story-teller. He was wicked – *malo!* That's what makes Latin men so charming. The best of lovers and the worst of husbands. I could see why Margot loved him.'

But there was one pretty and intelligent woman – a blonde, interestingly enough – who, though she hung on Tito's every slurred word, did so very much *without* Margot's blessing, and (let us hope) without her knowledge. Anabella Vallarino, the Panamanian socialite with whom Tito had been sexually involved at the time of the assassination attempt, had never left his life, and became, over a period of more than twenty years, his 'shadow wife'. 'When Fonteyn had to leave Tito to perform around the globe to support them financially,' the *Daily Mail* reported in 1991, '[Anabella] would move into his home. She would take Fonteyn's place, feeding, comforting and caring for the stricken husband as if he were her own. When she knew Fonteyn was returning, she'd go back to her own home. There, living with her own parents, she would wait for the next time.'[1] None of Margot's friends or family even attempts to deny the story. Indeed, Arias's son, Roberto, contributed to the *Mail* piece: 'Despite the situation I liked Anabella. I think her feelings towards my father amounted to hero-worship. Because of his paralysis, of course, there could be no physical relationship; but you must realize that even after the shooting my father still had a magnetic personality. She was unbalanced, yes, but we are all unbalanced or obsessed in one way or another. She chose my father.'[2]

Louis Martinz, Rudolf's sometime lover and Margot's long-term friend, had other – split – loyalties for Anabella. 'I knew her very well. We used to date – both of us for "convenient" reasons – and when, after Tito was shot, her involvement with him continued in its own very bizarre way, I asked Anabella: "Tell me, what *is* this?" and she said: "Yeah, I'd been having an affair with Tito, but I didn't fall in love with him until *after* the incident" – which is a very strange answer. The relationship got very intense and continued for the rest of Tito's life. Anabella, from being a wild, show-off girl, became a total recluse. She wouldn't go out of the house unless it was for Tito. And she was a beautiful, beautiful woman. I don't think that Margot was really conscious of the situation. She may have known about it vaguely – like there's something unpleasant in your life or mine and we just decide that it doesn't exist. Margot was very good at blocking out. Ventura said, for instance, that she would find a note or a lipstick in the house and say, "Ventura, who left this?" And by the time Ventura had thought up an answer, she'd be talking about something else.'

It could, of course, be that Margot, having adopted both Tito's family and his country, had further adopted the classic role of Panamanian wife. 'She was like a wonderful Latin woman,' says

Ana Cristina. 'In Latin America, I don't know a man who understands the word Fidelity. Is it something genetic in them? Or is it culturally ingrained? Latin women have been trained for hundreds of years to ignore adultery. They choose not to see it. They refuse to suffer by it. They're very much in control – queens of the home. And the husbands *never* leave them. Anabella was mentally deranged, so she would have found it strangely appealing to sneak into the farm when Margot wasn't there. But Buenaventura would hide anything that would hurt Margot. Men in Latin America will cover for each other. All of them. You might say, "Please tell me the truth, you are my brother." And the brother would say – even to his own sister – "Didn't happen." ' But according to Buenaventura, Margot was well aware that it *did*. 'Dame Margot didn't mind, not with those things. She was too clever. People talk about that girl, but what about the others? There were so many. People just want to put the blame on *that* one. But why? She was a nice girl. She never try to interfere between Dame Margot and Dr Arias.'

Margot had, in her time, been grateful for the discretion of the men in *her* life – most notably Charles Hughesdon – so the need to assume a complaisant attitude towards Tito's peccadilloes (unconsummated as these could not but be) may well have felt as natural to her as a well-deserved penance. Or perhaps a certain, old-fashioned acceptance had been fostered, in Margot's youth, by a mother who could admit about her own husband: 'I knew enough to be prepared for him to have had some affairs while we were apart . . .' But the trouble was that Margot and Tito were now almost incessantly together. 'After Margot retired,' said Louis Martinz, 'Tito found her possessive in a way that sort of asphyxiated him, and he would do anything he could to get her out of town so that he could have his girlfriend over. He was so desperate to have time on his own that he would get Margot to commit herself to several engagements in London, saying he was going with her, and then, at the last minute, he would withdraw. Much as I liked Anabella, I would never go to the farm if Margot was out of town.'

It wasn't as though Margot didn't enjoy the pageantry of Durham or having tea with Jackie Kennedy in New York, but she had convinced herself that Tito needed her at home. And even if the atmosphere, when she got back to the farm, was less than harmonious, she would pile the blame on her own shoulders. 'When they fight,' says Buenaventura, 'it was because of him, not her, but still she always say *he* was correct.' 'Poor Tito,' writes Margot. '. . . He must have hoped that one day he would have a perfect wife by his side. Unfortunately, I was not an instant perfect wife. I was too inclined to make decisions I thought were for the best. Tito didn't always agree. He needed a wife who would accept things the way he wanted them: he didn't want to ask for everything and explain everything.'[3]

Margot, in order to meet her husband on the intellectual plane where his energy had so long been dammed up, kept abreast of political developments. 'She had this little radio,' says Ana Cristina, 'which she was always listening to. She knew the news before anybody, and not just the local news. She would tune that radio into world-wide stations, and would know what had happened that morning in Asia or Australia. She would say, "Tito is interested." No! She was making life interesting for *him*. And my God, when people came to the house, she would be leading the conversation. Her questions were so intelligent – she was truly and genuinely interested in world affairs.'

Domestic affairs were another matter. If Margot *could* be faulted as a wife, it was in the contentious area of housekeeping. 'She left everything up to Buenaventura, including the cooking,' says Louis Martinz. 'She always expected people on Sundays. There was no way of reaching her by phone, so one just simply went. Margot practically didn't know what we were going to eat. But, my God, what a small failing. I would go to the house and bring someone with me who I knew would amuse her, such as the Indian Ambassador, and the people I took along were always flabbergasted. They would watch her cutting up Tito's food while her own got cold, always being so gay and carefree. And when we left, those people would say, "Oh my

God, that woman, she's incredible, she's a saint. Yet she never makes herself look like one." Saints don't, you know.'

Margot's impulse to shed the trappings of earthly vanity had lately been signalled by the fact that she let her hair – dyed black for so long that she no longer had a clue as to its true colour – gradually reveal its faded pigment. 'She didn't care,' explains Querube Arias. 'To her, worrying about her hair was like getting ready for a performance. There was a terrible point where it had grown out half-way. I said, "We must do something." She gave me one chance. It was for some gala or other. I had a colourist come to the hotel. They put some yellow in, and she looked like Mae West. But we finally found a formula which was like a golden rinse, and I bought her many bottles. But later, when she was away in hospital, I went to Panama to see my father. And he had these two little girl-nurses who used to come in and shower him outside in his wheelchair on the terrace, and I said, "What shampoo are you using?" And I realized they were using Margot's dye.'

Margot sent a photograph of herself – minus the blonde rinse – to Frederick Ashton: 'Darling Fred. Here is the new "me" with grey hair and the cows. Tito doesn't change much and still has far less wrinkles and bags. I long to see you . . .'[4] But she did not make it to London for the première, on the Queen's sixtieth birthday, of his latest, and last, ballet, *Nursery Suite*, which featured scenes from the childhood of Lilibet and her little sister. 'I had written to Princess Margaret,' Margot told Ashton in a further letter. 'She sent me a reply headed "Darling Margot". I thought that was very sweet of her and she said of your ballet, "It was charming and avoided being sentimental or twee – clever old him." Without exception they all said it was superbly done with your touch and genius for getting things right . . . There is really NO ONE like you. How incredibly lucky I was in my career to fall into your magic hands. Imagine where I would have been otherwise with my no elevation, no extension, no instep and feeble pirouettes! It is nice to be retired and have time to think about people one loves – especially you, you, you.'[5]

But she, she, she also had cows to consider. 'The Queen and Princess Margaret had invited her to tea,' says Querube, 'and Margot really didn't want to leave Panama, because she had a cattle sale coming up.' Margot told her stepdaughter, 'I don't think the Queen liked it when I said, "I can't come because I've got to buy semen!"'

Margot's own status, however, remained as virtually royal as ever. 'We had a big, big gala of *The Sleeping Beauty* in Miami,' says Peter Wright, who was directing the 1986 Sadler's Wells Royal Ballet tour, 'and Princess Anne couldn't come. We'd been tearing our hair out and had tried every member of the Royal Family without success. I said, "What about asking Margot to come? That might do it, because you know Fonteyn's name will live forever in the States. Maybe we could even get her to appear as the Queen in *Beauty*." So I phoned Margot and she hummed and hah'd but eventually said, "All right, I'll do it. But you know, if I come I'll have to bring Tito and all the entourage." It meant taking a huge suite at the best hotel in Miami, plus all the fares, but I didn't care. What was so impressive was the way that she approached the role. In my production there's some wonderful music that's usually left out. After Aurora's pricked her finger and seems fine, there's this bit for the Queen – I think that's what attracted Margot to the part. She insisted on having a lot of rehearsal and wanted to know, exactly, every move. And she was quite adamant about the costume – a beautiful gold one by Philip Prowse, which she wanted something done about at the front. She loved the costume, but she said, "My bosom looks dreadful," and she sort of heaved it around and worked out how it could be lifted. Every single detail was given her utmost attention, and when she got on and did it, the company were all in tears. At the end of it, the audience went completely wild. But Margot wouldn't take any more applause than the other dancers. I said, "Maybe now you should go on and take a solo call," but she said, "I wouldn't *think* of such a thing. This is Aurora's ballet."'

Clive Barnes knew perfectly well whose night it really was.

'She was an Aurora's mother who got more applause on entrance than some Auroras get on exit. She behaved impeccably. Her acting proved studiously unexaggerated, completely attuned to the suave authority of her King – himself a long-time dancing partner, Desmond Kelly. She accepted her roses with the moist eyes of pleasure. She still walked in beauty, the way a star danced at her birth.'[6]

But that birth, when all was said and done, had been in England. A certain uncharacteristic disillusionment with things foreign had begun to creep into Margot's letters, especially those to her 'Darling Fred': 'I feel like writing to you, not to get an answer but because I want to send you my love. Here we are always busy with silly little things to do with the farm or the car – which always breaks down – or the dogs which are our distraction from the other niggling things. I try to help the Ballet Nationale, but if ever anything was "pushing treacle upstairs", that's it. I also cherish the pig-headed and extravagant ambition of raising the art of ballet up in the eyes of Latin American governments to the position of prestige in which it deserves to be held. I once discussed the matter with Mme Pinochet in Chile at a meeting I had requested for the purpose. You can imagine that the concept of ballet as a prestigious and highly respected source of national pride is not one which govern-ments in this part of the world take to easily. Maybe it will happen one day, but meanwhile talented dancers are wasted and that upsets me terribly. My English blood comes to the fore, living in a village. Now I understand why all those ladies in the English country organize their village women's community groups or whatever. I can't bear to see the opportunities for people to get together and make mango chutney or tamarind jam, straw hats and heaven knows what else, all going to waste. Dozens and dozens of children in the area don't go to school after they are twelve because their parents can't afford the uniforms and books. If the village would make an effort they could teach the children all kinds of trades instead of school, but no one does anything. And that is something I really don't

553

have the time or energy to push. I just observe and wish I could help. Thank you so much for rehearsing Nicola in the Baiser variation. Does she look a bit like I did – only prettier and dances better?'[7]

The handing-on of the *Baiser* solo to Nicola Katrak was effected at long distance, by means of an amateur film – shot in Panama and subsequently mailed to Ashton – in which Margot, looking drawn and weary and a tiny bit bored, takes a local dancer through her paces. As it happened, Katrak was learning the variation so that it could be demonstrated in a film planned by Patricia Foy to commemorate Margot's own seventieth birthday. But it suited the Royal Ballet to ask for the ballerina's help where it was felt that she could give it. Sir John Tooley, who retired as General Administrator of the Royal Opera House in 1989, says, 'I arranged for Covent Garden to pay her an annual sum of money. This was done with the genuine intention of getting her back to work, but equally, as a way of dealing with her financial problems, because she said to me when I was about to leave, "What on earth am I going to do? – I've got nobody there I can talk to any more." And I said, "Well, look, I've organized this so that you get regular money." Then, as she became less and less well, she used to say to me, "This is dreadful, I'm taking money under false pretences. I'm not doing *anything*." And I said, "Look, if you're well enough to work with the Royal Ballet, that's wonderful, and if you're not, everybody is going to be very sad for you, but the money goes on." She couldn't come to terms with that. She was quite uncertain about taking money for nothing. It was an attitude attributable to the early impact on her upbringing of Lilian Baylis. It's the same kind of attitude you would find with Ninette de Valois, who would send a cheque back saying, "Please make sure I'm only paid what I was paid last year. I don't need it and you can't afford it." I used to have terrible trouble with Ninette, getting her into taxis. She'd say, "I can't bear to sit in the back and see the meter clocking up." '

Margot herself, these days, often resorted to public transport.

'Panama is a small place,' said Louis Martinz, 'and she would be seen walking from the farm to the highway in her straw hat to take the bus into the city. They only had one car at the farm, which needed to be kept available for Tito in case anything happened.' By now, Margot had a portable phone on which she could make outgoing calls as far as Panama City; but, to speak long-distance, she would have to climb the steep cliff road to a small, beach-front hotel four kilometres away, run by a wild Russian émigré, a whiskered, maverick, former merchant seaman whom she longed to introduce to Rudolf.

Nureyev, for reasons of his own, eventually made a trip to Panama. He had grown frustrated by Margot's increasing insularity. 'She's such great company,' he told the dancer-turned-writer Luke Jennings, 'but now she won't let us play with her. I'd like to spoil her, oh, take her here, there. We don't have to be in the theatre or see the theatre ever again.'[8] He had hoped to persuade her to take his house in Monte Carlo. 'He'd thought since she liked hot weather, it would be perfect for her. But obviously he didn't succeed in talking her into it.' (Instead, much to Rudolf's consternation, she talked *him* into meeting General Noriega.) Martinz was unsure as to how she would react to a visit from Rudolf. 'I'd noticed,' he said, 'how, since her retirement, she hadn't wanted to talk about ballet. I'd asked once if she'd seen the book *Fonteyn and Nureyev*, and she'd said, "No, I'm not really ready for it." On one of her birthdays, I'd started telling all the anecdotes, the funny parts of my experiences with her and Rudi, and she said, "Louis, can we change the subject?" I stopped mid-sentence.' But he also remembers one happy, impromptu night when 'we went out to dinner – Margot, me, Rudolf, Jane Herrmann and Tito. In the lobby, Margot said to me, "Louis, I want to pay the bill." I knew Margot well enough not to argue. She gave me some money in an envelope. But suddenly in that restaurant Margot and Rudi got into this terribly intense conversation about *Swan Lake*, something about ballerinas who *would* flap their arms, forgetting that Odette was also a woman. I started to feed Tito so that Margot wouldn't be distracted. She was so full of joy to be with Rudolf again. That night was a catharsis for her.'

David Wall was also someone in whose company Margot could unwind and be her old coquettish self. When he told her that a rich sponsor, Cartier, would lay on a trip to the Far East with limousines and luxury hotels, if she, as President of the Royal Academy, would join him in a flag-waving exercise to introduce an RAD syllabus into the Pacific Rim, she readily agreed – on one condition, of course: that Tito come too. Wall's friend, advertising executive Christopher Lawrence-Price, was in the lobby of the Mandarin Hotel in Hong Kong on 14 December 1987 to meet them. 'The whole staff lined up – about fifteen of them – from the manager down, and two white Rolls Royces pulled up outside the door. Out gets David. No Margot!'

Wall takes up the story. 'She phoned me just as I was leaving London to say that she was still in Panama. Tito wasn't very well. Apparently he loved Lea & Perrin's sauce and the cook had put virtually the whole bottleful into their dinner and Tito was poisoned. I'd been told that *she* wasn't well.' Having missed her plane, Margot had to be re-routed and helicoptered about: the journey took forty-eight hours. 'She arrived the following day around lunchtime,' continues Christopher Lawrence-Price. 'By the time she got up to her suite, she was very, very tired. As soon as she was inside the room, this bit of a wreck collapsed into a chair. And then she looked round and suddenly realized – and it was the funniest moment – that in this room were just her and eight men. She rose to her feet, and smiled and giggled and did a whole number with the manager. She had the entire room entranced. David said, "Margot, we've got a huge press conference at three o'clock – what do you want to do? Lie down?" And she said, "No, no, I've got to get to the hairdresser's." Her hair was completely white. Scraped back. But, lo and behold, at 2.30 we're sitting there and in walks this fabulous-looking woman with a blonde rinse in her hair, looking ten years younger. And off we went.'

Margot was pictured the next day on the front page of the *South China Morning Post*, 'hair swept back in a classic French roll, and dressed in an elegant blue and green sheath frock . . . Cameras clicked ceaselessly as the 68-year-old prima ballerina assoluta, still looking every inch the dancer, captivated a packed press conference with a speech that owed nothing to prepared notes and everything to devastating charm . . . "In my mind's eye Hong Kong is still as it was when I first came here at the age of eleven. I think I was almost crying – to tell the truth I *was* crying when I arrived here this morning." '9

The emotion carried her on into the early evening, when they had an appointment at the hotel in Repulse Bay where she'd actually lived as a child. 'At eight o'clock,' says Lawrence-Price, 'there was a sponsored dinner on the other side of the bay, so on we went, and, once again, she was the life and soul. I was shattered. David was pretty tired. But she was raring to go. Eventually we went back to the hotel in different cars – she was ahead of me with David. And that's when I saw her in the back seat go from the left side straight over and, in an absolutely magical moment, I saw her lying in David's arms, spread out across the car, like a tired little girl. She trusted David. She told him privately that she'd been to Houston and that she hadn't had great news there. And she said a couple of strange things, like: "You never know how long we'll be able to do things like this." She alluded to the fact that life could change.'

Margot's intimations of dark times to come were not unfounded. Already, in the preceding year, two of her dearest friends, Robert Helpmann and Nora Kaye, had died. But in 1988 there followed two further deaths which, for Margot, made the world begin to feel like the sort of party where, now that the most important people had left, her own presence was redundant. The first to go, on 27 January, at the age of ninety-three, was the person who, more faithfully than any husband, had been Margot's lifelong ally and accomplice: her mother, Black Queen. Yet, at the funeral, which was held in Slough, it was not Margot who broke down, but her brother Felix. Margot, perhaps honouring the quality which, from the start, Mrs Hookham had prized so highly in solemn little Peggy – self-control – remained poised enough to deliver the address, which culminated with *Said the Child*, a poem by Ninette de Valois, from her collection *The Cycle*.

Margot's second eulogy, for Frederick Ashton, who died on 19 August, was so 'remarkable for its lack of pretension – the very qualities that had defined her own art', that Julie Kavanagh chose it as an ending for her laudable biography. 'It would take a poet of equal genius to do justice to the genius of Frederick Ashton. In ordinary words I can only say that he was a rare artist, comparable in his field to Shakespeare for his extraordinary understanding of the human heart and mind and his ability to illuminate them through his own art form . . . He once said that he could not remember innocence, that he had always seen through people to their hearts, their motives and their characters, since he was a child. How he came to be able to translate that insight into movement is a mystery which must be explained only by the word genius . . . As a man I see a paradox: on the one hand sophistication and finely developed taste in all things, yet on the other a very simple person at heart. One might expect a highly sophisticated person to make an effort to conceal some emotions. Not Ashton; like a child, if he was hurt, angry or even jealous, he made no pretence. He was, above all, a very *human* human being, and for that, as much as for his extraordinary talents, he was beloved by all . . . Today, knowing, loving and remembering as I do, I cannot help but feel strongly that he is looking down on us all and saying to himself, "Ah, a packed house, much better than I expected." '[10]

But Margot was not present at the crowded Service of Thanksgiving on 29 November in Westminster Abbey. It was left to Michael Somes to read out her tribute. No excuse was given, but whisper had it that Margot had been unwell for some time. 'Fred died when she was in hospital,' says Querube Arias, 'and the first thing she asked, which I couldn't answer, was, "How did he die, and where?" She had me call again to find out. Apparently Fred had been afraid of dying alone. I said, "Why does that matter, Margot?" And she said that Fred was always worried that no one would close his eyes.'

It comforted Margot greatly to know that Ashton had, in fact, died at the end of a perfect day after a lobster lunch with friends – Alexander Grant having come to stay with him in the country to cut the topiary. Fred, in the words of Princess Margaret, simply 'climbed into bed and went to heaven'.[11] But Margot had already, by this time, become aware that her own end was not destined to be so gentle. 'I first met her for hormone replacement in 1986, when she was sixty-seven,' says London gynaecologist Basil Appleby. 'She'd had menopause when she was fifty-one, and, as a dancer, she'd be asking for osteoporosis. She'd never had a miscarriage, but she'd had two terminations of pregnancy. She was very reticent – she had this rather regal attitude. Normally patients tend to relax with their gynaecologists, but although she was always very friendly and moderately warm, you couldn't really get close to her. And then I saw her again, in June 1988, when she was complaining of sciatica, which was obviously this nasty business. When I examined her under anaesthetic, I found that she had a very advanced growth. The uterus was normal, but there was this large mass behind it. I got her to see a colleague of mine, and he concluded that it wasn't vulval, it wasn't anal, it wasn't uterine and it wasn't ovarian, so we really don't know where it started. It was a sort of rogue cancer that one unfortunately sees from time to time. One suggested to her that she have pelvic radiotherapy in conjunction with chemotherapy, but she didn't carry on with it. She went back to Panama. No reaction, really, at all. She didn't get alarmed, she didn't cry, she accepted it. She was terribly stoic about it. One didn't feel that it was going to be all right. I referred her on to the chemotherapy people, and I would assume they would have made that quite plain. But I spoke to them afterwards, and they said that it was absolutely as if you'd told her that she had a nasty cold which was going to last for some time. Quite amazing. She wanted to go home. I think the fact was that she realized that she wasn't going to get any better and whatever time she had left she wanted to spend with Tito.'

Astute as this assumption may have been, Margot did not return directly to Panama. With her death-sentence fresh in her mind, she stopped off in New York to be part of a parade of Rudolf's peers at a celebration, on 27 June, of her former partner's fiftieth birthday. That evening at the Met she was seated next to Maria Tallchief, who recalls: 'Against all expectations, Rudy was still dancing and appeared in a piece [*Songs of a Wayfarer*] that had been choreographed in his honour. Seeing him dance, however, was upsetting. He was too old to be on stage as a *premier danseur*. After his solo I turned to Margot. "Oh Margot, dear, it's so painful watching Rudy like this." She shook her head. "Oh, no, Maria. I thought he was wonderful." I was shocked that she couldn't see him objectively. He was still her Romeo, her Armand. But I believed it would have been far better to let Rudy know that he wasn't being fair to himself letting the present generation see him perform when he was so long past his prime.'[12] During the curtain-call, when Margot joined the line to greet him, the audience leapt to its feet at the sight of her. Nureyev embraced her. As he led her into the spotlight, confetti rained down.

Back in the suite at her New York hotel, Ana Cristina was shaken to note red stains on Margot's clothing, but Margot claimed breezily that the blood was merely menstrual – a likely story, as her sister-in-law, Rosario, whom Margot telephoned on returning to Panama, confirms. 'She was having this terrible pain, and she wanted to see a gynaecologist. She asked me to go in with her. The doctor ordered some X-rays, and took her for a physical examination. He wanted more examinations but she refused, right there. He said, "There's very little I can do for you if you don't take these examinations." I said, "Margot, you can't refuse." She said, "I'm not going through that. That's a horrible examination." I didn't think I had the right to force her. She refused to be ill while Tito was alive.'

Although Margot had a horror of predeceasing her husband,

she certainly had no intention of dwelling on her own ill-health while she still had his to consider. And his condition was deteriorating. Politically indefatigable as ever, Tito had, that summer, decided to run for national deputy as a candidate of a party sympathetic to Noriega. He was roundly defeated. Margot wrote to Querube: 'The political situation in Panama is eerie and I don't like the look of it. No one really knows what Noriega is up to. Days and weeks pass and nothing happens, although the government has no money and the US have stopped the payment that was expected. Is Noriega waiting until nobody gets paid any more because the government is flat broke? We struggle with the farm, but your father is worried because we are undercapitalized for this size of operation to make an acceptable profit.'[13]

It may be that Tito's sense of loss – both political and entrepreneurial – contributed to his decline. 'Ventura and his brother took turns,' says Rosario, 'because every three hours they had to move Tito. Margot went to bed in the bed beside him, and woke them up to turn him, so she always had to be dressed. One day they brought Tito from the country to see the doctor, and when they decided to keep him in hospital, I said to the doctor, "Check Margot," because she had a very bad cold, the beginnings of pneumonia. And the doctor wanted her to stay in hospital too. Margot refused. I said, "All right, I'll take her home and see to her myself." My room had an electric bed and TV, so I settled her there and took some nightgowns for her right away to wear. And next day she said to me, "You've no idea how much I'm enjoying this." I said, "That's funny, you were complaining you didn't want to come." And she said, "No, what I'm enjoying is wearing your clothes, because, you see, I never get the chance to wear lingerie. I stopped buying it long ago." Twice, when I wasn't at home, she got dressed and walked to the hospital to see Tito. It was six blocks.'

But Margot's left foot, when she walked, now dragged pronouncedly; in a horrible irony for one whose physical frame had proved so nearly superhuman, she was at the mercy of a disease which was attacking her very bones and muscles and tendons. 'She knew she had to go to a cancer clinic,' says Querube Arias, 'because, by that time, it was clear that she was going to be in great, great, great pain. She went to the Houston Ballet to do some coaching for Ben Stevenson, and there she met a small, old ballerina who had taught her in Panama. The old lady said, "I've been ill, but I have this wonderful doctor who's made me better and is an incredible fan of yours. He's young and he loves ballet, and the nicest thing you could do for me is to write a note or call him." And Margot said, "I'm not going to call him. I'm going to come and see him with you." So she went along and thanked him in person. And when they were going out to the elevators to leave, she said to her teacher, "Could you wait here just a moment?" She went rushing back and said, "Doctor, I need to see you. Will you take care of me? And will you take care of me with absolute and total anonymity?" '

Appraising the frail woman before him – more spirit than flesh – Dr Robert Benjamin gently told her: "Yes. But I need your *body*." '

Margot Fonteyn was admitted to the Anderson Center in Houston, Texas, under the alias of Jane Arias. 'Margot was very popular as "Jane",' says Querube. 'People who didn't know who she was loved her anyway. She was on the fancy floor, so the nurses were there in two seconds. Dr Benjamin used to come in every morning and kiss her, and every afternoon as well, to check her out, most of the time bringing his portable disc player. He'd say, "I don't want you to be sad. Today you're going to listen to this opera." There were a great many phone calls and we were afraid the press would get the number, so we decided to let everything go through the nurses' switchboard. And every Sunday they would come to the door and say, "The Madame is calling." The *Madame*! As in the head of a whorehouse!'

De Valois was one of the few people to whom Margot admitted the truth of her illness. 'I naturally respect your wishes,' Madam wrote. 'Your health will not be mentioned to anyone who does not already know.' 'Tito and Ventura knew about it,' says Ana Cristina, 'but Ventura had strict orders not to mention it. The word cancer was never mentioned. So we talked about a hip replacement and sciatic nerve problems. Dr Benjamin and all the people at Houston also played the game, because that was the way Margot wanted it.' The weight of hospital visiting fell heavily on Querube's shoulders. 'I said to Margot, "We have to tell one more person. I want that person to share time here with me." So we asked Lita Legarda. Lita was a Filipino doctor, a paediatrician who would do anything for Margot – she spent her own money on air tickets. Angie Novello, who had been Bobby Kennedy's secretary as well as my father's, was also asked to help, and that's how we covered the whole time. Between treatments, Margot would get a little better and go and see my father.'

Despite having endured three operations, Margot was determined to make her annual pilgrimage to Durham University. 'On these visits,' writes Leslie Edwards, 'she would find time to go to the Royal Ballet studios to coach the young principal dancers. When I heard Phoebe bringing the car round from the garage, I would come out of my cottage to wave goodbye. She was walking now with a stick, and to counter any reaction on my part she would wave and smile and say, "I'm incapacitated," as if this were a perfectly ordinary state of affairs.'[1] On these trips, Margot was often too ill to stay at Amerden, and would book herself into a hospital in Slough. 'I used to tour theatres,' she told Rudolf's masseur and Italian manager, Luigi Pignotti. 'Now I tour hospitals.'[2] It was on one of these 'tours' that she met up with Patricia Foy, with whom she was to raid the barn at Amerden in search of old photographs to serve as stills for *Fonteyn: A Tribute* (1989), a television documentary of the ballerina's life which, over a period of five years, Foy had been researching, and which Margot, despite her infirmity, would manage to complete, appearing elegant and radiant on the screen, and astonishing Foy by delivering her script entirely without the use of a tele-prompter. But the filming had to be confined to Panama. 'The plan was,' says Foy, 'to film her in places which had played a special part in her life . . . She showed me a photograph of [her and Tito] sitting on the river bank with King's College in the background. I suggested that she should be filmed walking past the same place. "I'm afraid I won't be able to do any walking because my foot is paralysed," she said quite casually . . . The implication shattered me . . . I asked her if her foot would get better. "No, it won't, but when I think of all the *fouettés* it has done for me I don't think that I can really complain."'[3] Margot ostensibly left for Panama, but three days later she telephoned Foy. ' "I'm not in Panama. I'm in hospital in Houston," she said. "I have cancer. I know you guessed."'

But in 1989, the word cancer was to surface in a way that forced Margot to take it seriously. 'Dame Margot was in Houston having treatment,' says Buenaventura, 'when we called her to explain about Dr Arias having some problems, and she came home immediately. They did an operation on him and everything was fine. Dame Margot said, "Oh Ventura, you can go home and rest." And she went to Rosita's house. When I came back, very early in the morning, the nurses said, "Please go to Dr Arias soon – he has been calling the whole night." As soon as I saw him he said, "Please turn me." And he was on his back when the nurses ran into the room to push his heart and give him some oxygen. Dame Margot had just arrived. She didn't make it to his room.'

Querube was in New York when news of her father's death reached her. 'Margot called me and said, "But I didn't see him. I wasn't with him." I said, "He did see you at the door." They decided to bury him the next day, so by the time I arrived Margot had made all decisions. The big thing was the knot on the tie – the tie he was to wear in the coffin. She said, "Well, you know how to do it." I said, "I won't. I can't." Then she said, "Well, won't you come in and give him a kiss with me?" So I said, "All right. I will go after you." So I let her in first. And when she came back she said, "Have you ever heard how cold people are when they die?" And I said, "No" – I really hadn't seen anybody die. And she said, "Darling, he's very cold, so unless you really want to see him, don't." She'd changed her mind. And then Buenaventura went in and started to cry and came out and she said to him, "Please do the tie, and give him that Cambridge knot." She wanted him smart. I don't think he would have cared at all.'

Tito died on 22 November 1989. Within weeks of his death came what Gerasimos Kanelopulos, proprietor of Margot's favourite book-store in Panama City, describes as 'the sweetest sound I ever heard'[4] – the roar of American bombers, come, at last, to rout the corrupt regime of Noriega. But Margot, ever stubborn, just as she had been over the deposed Imelda Marcos (to whom, to Bob Gottlieb's horror, she had actually wanted to dedicate *The Magic of Dance*), could not bring herself to condemn the General outright. 'You can be clever without being wise,' she told *Vanity Fair* in 1990. 'I think General Noriega was clever but not wise . . . At least [he] gave the impression that he knew that such things as art existed. Nine times out of ten, foreign invasions are not justified, but this time I think the US did the right thing. There was no other way.'⁵ Meanwhile, as the jets swarmed overhead, Margot was holed up at La Quinta Pata with Lita Legarda, who read to her, non-stop, from the Bible. But Margot needed no such spiritual reassurance: she, who had once conquered New York, no longer knew fear. The people whom she loved most had 'left' – for what should *she* stay, other than to get on with the protracted business of dying? 'I can still scarcely believe I have lost Tito forever,' she wrote to David Scrase. 'I need him too much.'⁶ Rosario de Galindo says: 'When Tito died she just gave up. It was her choice. She had her own private relation with Tito and if she felt she didn't want to live without him, and she had this thing that would take her, it was her right.'

Margot's heightened notion of lovers dying for love – and simultaneously, at that – had been fostered by the mythological world which she had inhabited as naturally as the real one. In 1989 she had published yet another book – written, presumably, in hospital – and had recorded it, too, in the deep, incisive tones that her recent film appearances had taught her: an illustrated version for children of *Swan Lake*. Lavishly presented, and featuring a blonde, wavy-haired Odette, the text nevertheless offers a vivid and moving insight into the compelling power of such fairy tales over Margot's passionate imagination.

'What will become of us now, my beloved?' asked Siegfried.

'Alas, my noble prince, there is no longer any hope for us. The wicked von Rothbart has used all his cunning to keep me in his power. If I can never be yours in life, I will die rather than live as a swan-maiden. I will throw myself into the lake and remain yours alone for eternity.'

'No, no, stay with me!' he cried. 'I love you, and only you. Stay with me, I beseech you!'

Odette embraced him most tenderly, as if to leave her heart and soul in his keeping. Then, quickly slipping out of his arms, she threw herself into the dark waters and was seen no more.

Siegfried hesitated not a moment before following her, and he, too, vanished below the surface at exactly the same spot as his love.[7]

No sooner had she found herself widowed than Margot's obsession – that she and her husband should be reunited in the grave – began. Tito's brother Gilberto had died before him; and, as Rosario points out: 'Gilberto and Tito were fresh in the tomb, so there was no room for Margot. She put her ring in with Tito when he died. Then she had second thoughts and asked the doctor, "Could I have my ring back, and Tito's?" He gave them back and she wore them both. She told me, "When I die, you cremate me, but you take these rings out and you put them into the urn, and you put the urn into the tomb where Tito is."'

Yet, unbeknown to Margot, someone else had already leapt into that metaphorical lake, in a dramatic bid to be Tito's 'alone for eternity'. Upon hearing of Tito's death, Anabella Vallarino had carried out her vow: to kill herself on the day that her beloved died. Locking herself in the bathroom at her parents' house, she swallowed a bottle of chlorine meant for the swimming pool, and died in agony. In deference to Margot's feelings, the Arias family closed ranks and kept any hint of the scandal under wraps until after the ballerina's death. But in June 1991, the *Femail* section of the *Daily Mail* blazoned a picture of Anabella on its cover, with the headline: 'MARGOT FONTEYN'S HUSBAND BETRAYED HER FOR THIS WOMAN.'[8] Anabella's funeral was conducted within hours of Tito's. The *Mail* went on to say: 'In the tight little circle of the Panamanian upper class it meant that one group of people were in double mourning. Some attended both funerals. "It was strange," says one friend of both families. "I went from one service to the other in the same clothes and saw the same faces. Most of us knew what was behind it all."'

Anabella's tragedy stole the emotional centre stage, even in the minds of those most strongly aware of Margot's grief. Louis Martinz travelled with her to the service. 'I seated her behind the driver and, as I went to get in the other side, Buenaventura came round and whispered to me, "Is it true that Anabella committed suicide?" And when I said "Yes," he brought his fist down on the roof of the car, which must have startled Margot.' But Margot's position, despite the sympathy which surrounded her, remained that most piteous, not to say invidious one for a cheated wife: a position of ignorance. 'I hate to say it,' Martinz later told the *Mail*'s correspondent Tony Burton, 'but yes, it was a betrayal. It was so unfair to Margot . . . It was not easy for her, first Tito's paralysis and then her cancer. It was a strain looking after him. But she never complained. Never . . . Noble, that is the only word for her.'

Yet it is a word which tended to get up the notorious nostrils of Margot's most uncompromising friend. 'Trouble is,' said Rudolf, who, by this stage, was fighting for his own life – a life which he would never knowingly have laid at the altar of any lover – 'trouble is Margot wants to go down in history as a saint.' And if there lurked, in Margot's aspiration to prove herself morally unimpeachable, even a hint of hubris, then the gods most certainly saw to it that she suffer the fate of martyrs. 'You have no idea what Margot went through,' says Ana Cristina. 'There were moments when I would go to the end of the corridor and I would listen to those screams and start perspiring and think, "Why doesn't she die? This is not a life." '

Yet, by April of 1990, Margot was, once more, back at La Quinta Pata, writing to Querube: 'I'm progressing inch by inch [but] I only put in about an hour's housework every day, instead of six or seven. I want to get it all to the point that I can leave everything organized when I go away.'9 In order to meet her hospital bills, she sold an abridged version of her autobiography to *Hello!* magazine, claiming in interview: 'I want to stay here till the end . . . in the place I chose to live with my husband. But I don't fall back on nostalgia to get away from my loneliness, because I don't feel alone. I have a lot of work, and I'm surrounded by good people. I still have my family in England, but I also have my Panama family, Buenaventura Medina, Señora Zoila Perez, and Oderal de la Cruz. Sometimes I go to swim at the beach. It isn't far to walk, though it isn't so easy now since I fell and broke my hip. I love going there, even though it makes me sad because, whenever we could, Tito and I used to go there together at twilight to bathe together.'[10]

There is an image to illustrate this assertion: of Margot lying on that very beach, photographed by Lord Snowdon for *Vanity Fair*. 'The last time I saw her really happy,' says Louis Martinz, 'was when Snowdon came to the farm. He was livid because Rudi hadn't shown up, but Margot was just delighted by Tony. In one of the pictures, he wanted the cattle to move, so that there would be more dust. And he would say, "Tell them, Margot." And she would yell at the cows, "*¡Más polvo, más polvo!*" She'd had a few glasses of sangría. Oh, she was so giddy, so happy.'

There were also moments of light-heartedness in Houston. Ana Cristina kept some of her Valentino dresses at the hospital in the hope that Margot, with whom she had been in the habit of swapping outfits, would think, should she ever feel up to going out, that there was always something glamorous there for her. 'When she was drugged, she would love to see me wearing beautiful clothes, so I would deliberately change three or four times and she would say, "Show me this one, show me that one."' And in May 1990 the chance presented itself for Margot to wear her own beautiful multi-coloured, many-sequined dress by Saint-Laurent one final time. News had reached John Tooley that, the previous summer, Margot had been reduced to auctioning off some of her jewellery at Christie's. It had transpired, after Tito's death, that La Quinta Pata had been heavily mortgaged. Tooley, dismayed, proposed that the Opera House stage a benefit evening for Margot. But Margot was not easy to help. Ana Cristina recalls: 'She said to me, "What do you think of this gala? I *can't* accept it. It's so denigrating." She was such a proud person. And then John Tooley came up with a brilliant idea to help her save face.' The proceeds of the gala were to go into a trust to help talented young dancers, or old disabled ones. While Margot was alive, the interest from that trust could be hers; beyond that, however, she would be contributing towards a fund for posterity.

But what, given Margot's emaciation, could she possibly wear? Ana Cristina was aghast at the initial choice: 'She'd picked out something that looked as if she'd been brought up in Queen Victoria's day – like the governess of a school – a black skirt, straight, with a white silk blouse. Long sleeves. I mean, *totally* unlike Margot. I said, "It's not bad, but the one I *really* love is that magnificent one that Saint-Laurent made for you, the one you were wearing when Felix took that lovely picture of you. That will look wonderful if you have to come on the stage." She said, "I'm not coming on the stage." I said, "Well, even if you don't, it would give you colour, and Saint-Laurent is going to be so happy if you wear that." So, of course, out of loyalty to Saint-Laurent, she said, "Let's try." And it looked perfect. But there was no way she was going to come on the stage. Little did she know that Plácido Domingo was organizing this sere-nade and that the only thing he was doing in the dress rehearsal was worrying about the lights going on her in the Royal Box and the champagne being brought to him on a tray so that he could raise a glass to her. The Royal Ballet was waiting for hours, and never got to rehearse because he was so concerned that the light should come right on her. She didn't know any of this was happening, and I thought, "Oh my God, the shock that she's going to get." But Margot was a woman of the theatre. And at the last moment, when she got to Covent Garden, *and* the pictures, *and* Madam, *and* the flowers, *and* the crowd waiting for her, she gathered herself together. And she walked on to the stage *without limping*. And she took a curtain call. And Madam was there, and, above all, Rudolf was there.'

Rudolf had, in fact, put in rather more of an appearance than had been anticipated. The ballet given that night was *Romeo and*

Juliet, with Sylvie Guillem and Jonathan Cope in the leading roles. Rudolf had been invited as Margot's consort for the evening, the idea being that he should *sit* with her. But, as Anya Sainsbury told Diane Solway, 'He took it for granted that we wanted him to dance. It was his idea to dance Mercutio. We couldn't very well say, "Well, actually, we had something else in mind." '[11] Seat prices that night were astronomical (the gala raised £250,000, of which Margot only lived to enjoy one tenth); yet, for the audience, which included Princess Margaret and Princess Diana, it was obviously gratifying that Nureyev should have been performing for Fonteyn, and that Fonteyn should have been sitting there, watching him. 'But in terms of his dancing,' Monica Mason admitted to Solway, 'it was heartbreaking.'[12]

The night before the gala, when, at a dinner hosted by Jacob Rothschild, Margot had been unable to walk down the stairs, Rudolf had simply gathered her up in his arms, as he had so many times on stage, and carried her down into the dining-room. But, at the crush bar party after the performance, his pity turned in upon himself. According to Diane Solway, Anya Sainsbury found Margot desperately searching for Rudolf. ' "He was here a minute ago. Now he's gone." '[13] Sainsbury caught up with him at the stage door, where he was waiting for a cab. "He was upset about something and in one of his moods and I had to beg him to stay. I just went on and on and when I told him how distressed Margot was that he was unhappy, he said, 'She doesn't need me.' Finally, he relented." '[14]

In fact, Margot needed him greatly – and not just because, despite his reputation for 'sewn pockets',[15] he was, by now, paying some of her hospital bills on the quiet. She needed someone for whom to rally the last remnants of her tenacity, that quality which, in her final June address of 1990, she had commended to the students of Durham University: 'If, like a fairy godmother, I could give each of you one gift, I think, after long consideration, I would choose *Tenacity*, because that is what has helped me most in those times of adversity that come even to the luckiest, like me.'[16]

Rudolf was the person for whom she had tried hardest, pushed herself beyond her perceived capacity, transcended the tiresome limitations of her body. And he, beyond all others, now understood her need to rise above her illness – he who had many symptoms of his own to deny. As early as 1984, Rosenbaum, a pioneer of AIDS research, had tested Nureyev at his laboratory in the Pitié-Salpetrière hospital in France, and the results had suggested that the dancer had been HIV-positive for some three or four years. In September 1983, Nureyev had assumed the ballet directorship of the Opéra, by which time, according to biographer Otis Stuart, 'his physical problems were assuming an ominous pattern, such as the weight loss, unexplained fevers, and recurrent night sweats that were already synonymous with the onset of AIDS. By the time Nureyev went with the Opéra for guest performances at the Edinburgh Festival in the summer of 1984, he was, according to Patrick Dupond, "not well at all. He had pneumonia and then, on top of that, he had hepatitis too. He was green and he couldn't breathe, and we all said that he should go back to Paris, go to a doctor. But he did all of his performances anyway, every single one of them. It was beyond courage." '[17]

Margot, having heard rumour of these alarming bouts of ill-health, made an unannounced trip to Paris to check up on Nureyev. 'She arrived without telling him,' says Ana Cristina, 'so that he couldn't put up a good show. She must have known that Rudolf was a very good candidate for AIDS. And she finds him all right. And she comes back and says, "It's perfectly all right, he just had a slight cold. I don't know why they were making such a fuss." And the man had been in hospital with a horrendous pneumonia.'

Rudolf's 'slight cold' was the equivalent of Margot's 'hip replacement'. 'They were exactly the same,' says Ana Cristina. 'He knew he had AIDS. He refused to accept it. You've got two twin souls there. For them it was almost degrading to talk about it. You don't demean yourself by talking about these gross illnesses. Between them they had this extraordinary relationship whereby they would both know the reality, but each one would tell the other what the other wanted to hear. So they would sustain each other. We would say, "Rudolf is coming to see you next week," so that she would hold on.'

When Rudolf came, which he often did by long-distance taxi, keeping the car waiting outside the hospital for the hours that he spent with Margot, she would insist upon donning her make-up and sitting up at a table, wrapped in the antique shawl which he had given her and from which she would not be parted. He would bring with him armfuls of teddy bears and *I Love Lucy* tapes to make her laugh. Denial reached a pitch when all treatments had failed and talk began of Margot's leg having to be amputated. 'She was resisting the operation,' says Ana Cristina, 'because, you know, for a dancer to have the body mutilated is worse than death. Rudolf said, "What's wrong with crutches? You lose one leg? You have another leg. It's not difficult. You hop." Margot laughs and says, "All right," and picks up the phone to Doctor Benjamin. "Rudolf thinks it's a very good thing that I should have this operation." Rudolf goes out. Starts crying like a baby in the corridor. Rudolf was afraid of death. Margot was not. Rudolf was a brilliant, extraordinary child. Margot was a grown-up – a very wise woman.'

Margot did not undergo the amputation. 'You can go so far with these things,' says Christina Berlin, 'and then it gets stupid. Margot had her cut-off point. She and Tito were the same age, and she'd suffered the irony of him sitting in a wheelchair for twenty-five years while she'd been moving like no woman ever moved. The irony was not going to go full circle with her. She was too proud to let that happen. And she was particularly proud of her legs. If there was one thing she'd say if you asked her – and I did ask her what part of herself she most liked – she'd say, "Well, I have good legs – for a dancer." ' Needless to say, when Rudolf came to Houston next, he did not mention that she was still in possession of both her pins. Instead, he distracted her with a new idea of his own. 'He tells her that he's fed up with the dance,' says Ana Cristina, 'and Margot's so happy to hear this, because she thinks he's gone on too long. He says, "I'm going to become a conductor." And she says, "Brilliant, darling! You know the ballets inside out. You won't even have to study. You're absolutely right to become a conductor." So he became one, and it gave another dimension to his life. These two extraordinary souls understood each other at another level. Most people are on level A. They were on level Z. Things that could not be faced alone, they could face together.'

For those who had known Rudolf in his pantherine prime, he was now, in his own right, a tragic vision: shuffling gait, moth-eaten hair, and the hollow, haunted eyes that epitomize AIDS. Perhaps it was for his sake that Margot, despite her impatience to join her departed husband, lived on for twenty-seven months after Tito's death. Or perhaps her heart, given the great physical stamina which she had worked so hard to develop, was simply too strong for its own good. 'Margot's cancer was the worst I've ever seen,' says Ana Cristina. 'Her body was completely distorted. The only things that kept beautiful were her breasts, which were still like a fifteen-year-old's. I can't tell you how much the nurses loved her. But once, when Plácido called, I heard her say to him, "They've got me trapped here. I want to go home." And I said, "You're not imprisoned. You want to go home? Let's go home." '

Margot made it back to La Quinta Pata one more time, in November 1990. Louis Martinz went to the airport to welcome her, and to ensure that her drug supply got through Customs. 'I walked on to the plane and I couldn't believe what I saw. If there was one thing Margot always did, it was use lipstick. And to see her without it, still smiling, but so pale, and having to be carried – it was awful, awful.' But Margot still had unfinished business at the farm. 'The last thing she did for the town,' says Buenaventura, 'was ask the English Ambassador to get some sewing machines for the ladies there. And the very nice Ambassador say, "Oh yes, we can get those things." And then she promise to the people, "I'm going to get five machines for this town so everybody can learn." And the Ambassador gave me the five machines and I put them in a house, and they got a teacher from somewhere, and all those people now know how to sew because of Dame Margot.'

When, the following January, Margot finally gave up the fight, she did so in her own calm but powerfully disciplined way. 'I called the hospital,' says Querube. 'They said, "You'd better get over here because she's not answering the phone." I got to Houston. I hadn't seen her since before Christmas, I guess. I walk in and she says, "Querube, I want to talk to you," as though she hadn't noticed I'd been gone. She said: "I've decided not to have any more treatment. That means I'm going to die, so I want you to call Felix and tell him." I called him up, and there was no answer, only the phone-machine, so I said, "Margot, he'll be back later this afternoon." She said, "Well, give me the phone." And she said into the answer-machine, "Felix, this is Margot. Querube and I are here and I've decided that I'm going to die. She's going to make all the arrangements. I'm going to Panama and she wants Feebee to come." I asked for that, because Margot loved Feebee, and she was accustomed to Feebee handling her. I went on ahead to Panama and had a chat with Rodrigo, the head of the hospital. I said, "Look, I don't have a penny, but I know you'll be paid. I need a room where Margot can be and where we can be constantly there." And he said, "No problem. You just get her here." And when we got her there, she'd been given a suite. It was crazy to go back to Panama, but she got there through the grace of Buenaventura, who basically carried her just like he had my father. We had to stop him from giving her juice. He said, "If we could just make her strong." He got the dropper like we used for the cattle – the baby cattle – and he would give her juice. From the *dropper*. "Gracias, Buenaventura," she would say. But it was all nonsense.'

There remained one more ritual to be carried out. If Margot's wish that her ashes be placed in the Arias grave was to be fulfilled, she must convert to Roman Catholicism. 'We found an American priest for her,' says Rosario de Galindo. 'Such a beautiful priest. He looked like Santa Claus. He came to the hospital and we did the conversion there. It was nothing. She was totally lucid that day, and she embraced the Catholic Church without any problem. She had never been a religious person. But she was a believer in God – in her own way. And that's how she managed to have the funeral service in the San Francisco Chapel where Tito had his, and have her ashes put into his tomb.'

Everyone wanted to be in at the last. 'The British Ambassador would come every day with greetings from the Queen,' says Querube. 'Every afternoon he would have a different greeting. And the President of Panama would send her flowers every day.' Because Margot had been so distressed at missing Tito's death, Querube was determined to be there when Margot's own moment came. 'I drove the pain specialist crazy, wanting him to assure me that her death would be nice and peaceful and pleasant. Finally he sat me down and said, "Look, Querube, I've been in this business a long time, and if you've been a good person and you've had a nice life, you usually die very well." Having not seen anyone die before, I didn't know what to expect. But the death was terrific, to tell you the truth. She wasn't scared or anything. It was like having a baby – you know how it starts and there's no stopping it. And she was lying in that same position, looking up and holding on to us.'

Legend has it that when Pavlova was dying she asked, in her last breath, for her swan-costume. And then her arms are supposed to have fluttered up, and to have come down to rest as they did when she danced *The Dying Swan*.

But Fonteyn did not die like a bird – especially not one which drowns in a lake. If Margot did appear, in death, to move from one element to another, it was from the dark gloom of water to the daylight of dry land. 'She died like a fish, you know. A little fish. A fish receiving air.'[18]

Epilogue

Dame Margot Fonteyn de Arias died on 21 February 1991. A Service of Thanksgiving for her Life and Work was held at noon on 2 July at Westminster Abbey. Readings were given by Sir John Tooley and Dame Antoinette Sibley, the latter speaking from the nave, so that those not invited into the Abbey proper would still feel part of the service. Addresses were made by Sir Frederick Holliday, former Vice-Chancellor of Durham University, Mr John Macdonald, British Ambassador to Panama, Mr David Wall, Miss Patricia Foy, and, after a musical interlude, Dame Ninette de Valois. Madam did not speak extempore; instead, standing high in the church under medieval lectern light, she read, for the first time in her life, from notes, perhaps fearing that her focus at the age of ninety-three would fail her, or grief cloud her words, as it might those of a mother who has outlived her child. She concluded her address with an oddly terse little poem by George Meredith – one which she had once brandished in defence of the adolescent Margot, when the critics could not yet understand what was staring them in the face:

> Faults of feature some see, beauty not complete,
> But, good friends [*sic*], what makes holy earth and air,
> May have faults from head to feet.[1]

The crux of her tribute, however, had come earlier: 'Music was the root of Fonteyn's dancing. She submitted herself to it wholly, not just in part. Thus, Fonteyn was the perfect example of fusion in an artist. Such people portray to perfection, but never impose . . . What of the music? Again, she was dedicated simply through her inborn musicality.'

And it was the music at that service, performed by the Orchestra of the Royal Opera House under the baton of John Lanchbery, that instantly reeled us back to the image which we so prayed would be invoked – of Fonteyn at her apogee. In fact there had been quite a fuss about what numbers should be featured. 'Margot was so controlling,' de Valois would later tell me. 'She even controlled her own memorial service from the grave.' Felix, in deference to his sister's wishes, refused to let the Rose Adagio be played, despite its historical closeness to the congregation's heart; so, by way of compromise, the rhapsodic Panorama from *Sleeping Beauty* was given in its stead. But where the introductory programme was concerned, Jack Lanchbery fought his emotional corner – or rather, Constant Lambert's. Lanchbery was adamant that Lambert's music should be represented, and that Fonteyn should be unlocked from her marriage long enough for the composer's spirit to be coupled with hers once more; and he conducted the beautiful Sarabande from *Horoscope* ('dedicated to Margot Fonteyn', as the Order of Service defiantly made plain) with tears streaming down his face. Despite the inclusion of an excerpt from *Marguerite and Armand*, Lanchbery's other choices further managed to disengage Margot from her Fonteyn-and-Nureyev era, and to return her to us in the limpid purity of her youthfulness as imaged in the *Rake's Progress* solo, Faithful Girl, and moving celestially through our minds to a passage from the Bach/Walton *Wise Virgins*: Lord hear my longing.

Friends travelled from every corner of the globe to be there. But two of the people dearest to Margot did not. The first of these was Nureyev, whose absence raised many eyebrows. He was, after all, only in Paris, and could have flown to London; but, as Maude Gosling said, 'He couldn't come, because he was facing his own end.' He later left a message, versed in the third-person, at Querube's hotel, saying: 'Rudolf is afraid of dying and he misses Margot terribly.' But when Querube tried to return his call, the caller was no longer there.

The second absentee was Buenaventura Medina, for whom

no one seems to have thought of buying a plane ticket. Yet, even if England appeared, in all its circumstantial pomp, to have reclaimed Margot, it was Buenaventura who was bequeathed the privilege of being able to visit her final resting place. There are those who feel strongly that Margot's remains should have been taken to Westminster Abbey, and are shocked by the modesty of plot 6-18(A) at the wire-fenced, tin-shacked edge of the Jardín de Paz on the outskirts of Panama City, where Fonteyn's ashes are interred – not, as promised, within Tito's tomb, but at its foot. A square, greenish, bronze slab, the smallest in the cemetery, marks the spot, and merely bears the name: Margot Fonteyn Arias. Yet I recall Querube Arias, who was to prove Margot's most generous witness, calling after me at our first meeting, when I was embarking on this biography: 'If you get stuck, just remember: the word which best applies to Margot is "simplicity".'

Keith Money brings some rigour to this mantra: 'I think Margot was a mystery to herself in a number of ways, and although her "simplicity" of style and nature was widely remarked, it always seemed to me that she was an extremely complex – indeed almost split – personality. It is doubtful if she could have survived some of the extremes of pressure which frequently descended upon her, had she been otherwise, and it surely requires a great complexity of resource to suggest simplicity, without appearing merely simplistic; a rare art, in fact.'[2]

To celebrate her mother's ninetieth birthday, Margot had written a story for Black Queen to read out to her great-grand-children, Amy and Jack. It is a fanciful tale about bears, perhaps too full of private family jokes to be of serious public interest. And yet, coming from someone who kept the secrets of her heart even from herself, it does reveal a fascinatingly confessional undertone. For, as any writer will tell you, truth shines more plainly through fiction than ever it did through fact. The story is called *Grizelda*, but it is in the minor character of Moussia that the reader can detect both the joy and the resentment which

Margot must have felt about the lifelong burden placed upon her by her great talent.

Moussia was a performing bear whom the villagers of the Northern Steppes loved to watch 'cavorting a bit as her owner coaxed her this way and that to show off her prowess. Indeed it was impressive to see how she could dance on two legs, with her front paws held at a rather elegant angle just below the level of her chin . . . She enjoyed dancing and she made a lot of money for her owner – not that he was very generous to her considering all she did to better his life . . . When [the crowds] saw Moussia dancing so elegantly and gracefully with little steps, a half turn here, reverse and go round to the left – one, two; one, two, three – and back again to the right, the women would start singing gently with their warm creamy voices. Moussia would be quite carried away with the pleasure of it all and dance even better than usual – perhaps balance for a moment on one leg, the other stretched out in "arabesque".'[3]

After Moussia's death, her ursine descendants make a long, intrepid pilgrimage to her grave. And although the tomb which they find replicates Margot's, both in its farawayness and its modesty, yet it carries a very different epitaph from the one which so mattered to Margot in real life, the one which is to be found engraved on her husband's tombstone: 'NUESTRA SEPARACION ES SOLO GEOGRAFICA' (Our Separation is only Geographical). The epitaph which Margot's subliminal wisdom yields up speaks of a far lonelier, more singular being, a woman free of any 'owner' but her art.

'There was a tiny garden round the hut and Moussia's grave was there with a very simple tombstone. On it were the words:

MOUSSIA
GRACE AND BEAUTY
SOOTHE THE SOUL.'[4]

Notes

When not otherwise stated, it can be assumed that all unattributed quotations with named interviewees are from conversations with the author which took place between 1991 and 2003. All quotations attributed in the text to BQ (Hilda Hookham) are from her unpublished memoir.

Prologue

1. Robert Helpmann, speaking on *Birthday of a Ballerina*, BBC documentary produced and directed by Patricia Foy, 1969.
2. Maude Lloyd married Nigel Gosling; their joint writing name was Alexander Bland.
3. James Monahan, *Fonteyn – A Study of the Ballerina in her Setting*, A. & C. Black, 1957, p. 28.
4. Margot Fonteyn, *Autobiography*, W. H. Allen, 1975, p. 218.
5. ibid., p. 121.
6. ibid., p. 77.
7. Ninette de Valois, interview, 29 April 1991.

Chapter 1

1. Margot Fonteyn in interview with Esther Rantzen, BBC radio transcript, 1973.
2. Grace Bosustow, quoted in Elizabeth Frank, *Margot Fonteyn*, Chatto & Windus, 1958, p. 13.
3. ibid.
4. ibid.
5. Margot Fonteyn, *A Dancer's World,* Alfred A. Knopf, 1979, p. 39.
6. ibid., pp. 39–40.
7. Margot Fonteyn, *Autobiography*, W. H. Allen, 1975, p. 22.
8. ibid.
9. Nita Hookham, in Keith Money documentary, *Margot Fonteyn*, London Weekend Television, 1969.

10. Keith Money, *Margot Assoluta*, Fair Prospect, 2000, pp. 34–5.
11. Fonteyn, *Autobiography*, p. 15.
12. Zoe Dominic and John Selwyn Gilbert, *Frederick Ashton: A Choreographer and his Ballets*, Harrap, 1971.

Chapter 2

1. Margot Fonteyn, *Autobiography*, W. H. Allen, 1975, p. 31.
2. Elizabeth Frank, *Margot Fonteyn*, Chatto & Windus, 1958, p. 18.
3. Audrey King, speaking on *Birthday of a Ballerina*, BBC documentary produced and directed by Patricia Foy, 1969.
4. Frank, *Margot Fonteyn*, p. 18.
5. Margot Fonteyn, *A Dancer's World*, Alfred A. Knopf, 1979, p. 43.
6. Fonteyn, *Autobiography*, p. 38.

Chapter 3

1. The General Committee of the Camargo Society was composed of: Mme Adeline Genée, Chairwoman; Lydia Lopokova, Choreographic Director; Arnold Haskell, Art Director; Edwin Evans, Chairman and Musical Director; Alfred Tlysser, Treasurer; Marie Rambert, Phyllis Bedells and P. J. S. Richardson. Grace Cone, Ninette de Valois, Tamara Karsavina, Penelope Spencer, Anton Dolin and Stephen Thomas on advisory committees.
2. Ninette de Valois, interview with Meredith Daneman, 'Call Me Madam', *Sunday Telegraph*, 2 February 1992.
3. Ninette de Valois, *Come Dance with Me,* Hamish Hamilton, 1957, p. 59.
4. ibid., p. 62.
5. ibid., p. 112.
6. Mary Clarke, *The Sadler's Wells Ballet*, A. & C. Black, 1955, pp. 68–70.
7. ibid., p. 81.
8. Pamela May, interview, 27 October 1992.
9. ibid.
10. Ninette de Valois, *Step by Step*, W. H. Allen, pp. 19–20.
11. Margot Fonteyn in *Margot Fonteyn, a Tribute*, BBC documentary produced and directed by Patricia Foy, 1989.
12. Margot Fonteyn, *A Dancer's World*, Alfred A. Knopf, 1979, p. 46.
13. ibid.
14. De Valois, *Come Dance with Me,* p. 102.

15. Margot Fonteyn, *Autobiography*, W. H. Allen, 1975, p. 43.
16. Ninette de Valois, quoted in Keith Money, *The Art of Margot Fonteyn*, Reynal & Co., 1965, no page numbers.
17. Margot Fonteyn, 'My Dancing Years', *Woman*, September 1961.
18. Fonteyn, *Autobiography*, p. 43.

Chapter 4

1. Elizabeth Salter, *Helpmann*, Angus & Robertson, 1998, p. 69.
2. Elizabeth Frank, *Margot Fonteyn*, Chatto & Windus, 1958, p. 21.
3. Parmenia Migel, *The Ballerinas: From the Court of Louis XIV to Pavlova*, Macmillan, 1972, p. 8.
4. Ninette de Valois, interview, 29 April 1991.
5. Salter, *Helpmann*, p. 57.
6. Ninette de Valois, *Come Dance with Me*, Hamish Hamilton, 1959, p. 103.
7. Salter, *Helpmann*, p. 53.
8. ibid., p. 71.
9. ibid.
10. Margot Fonteyn, *Autobiography*, W. H. Allen, 1975, p. 47.
11. Fonteyn, 'My Dancing Years', *Woman*, September 1961.
12. Robert Helpmann, in Alan Sievewright documentary, *The Tales of Helpmann*, LWT, 1990.
13. William Chappell, *Fonteyn: Impressions of a Ballerina*, Rockliff, 1951, p. 4.
14. ibid.
15. ibid., p. 7.
16. Fonteyn, *Autobiography*, p. 51.
17. ibid.
18. ibid.
19. ibid., p. 43.
20. ibid., p. 53.
21. Frederick Ashton, quoted in Julie Kavanagh, *Secret Muses: The Life of Frederick Ashton*, Faber and Faber, 1996, p. 181.
22. ibid., p. 182.
23. Chappell, *Fonteyn*, p. 12.
24. Margot Fonteyn, quoted ibid.
25. Constant Lambert, quoted in Anthony Powell, *Messengers of Day*, Heinemann, 1978, p. 122.
26. Andrew Motion, *The Lamberts: George, Constant and Kit*, Hogarth Press, 1987, p. 186.

27. Angus Morrison, quoted in Richard Shead, *Constant Lambert,* Thames Publishing, 1973, p. 54.

Chapter 5

1. Margot Fonteyn, *Autobiography*, W. H. Allen, 1975, p. 41.
2. Elizabeth Frank, *Margot Fonteyn*, Chatto & Windus, 1958, p. 29.
3. Ninette de Valois, quoted in Maurice Leonard, *Markova: The Legend*, Hodder & Stoughton, 1995, p. 57.
4. ibid.
5. ibid., p. 129.
6. *Evening News, 27* March 1935.
7. Ninette de Valois, quoted in Leonard, *Markova.*
8. Frank, *Margot Fonteyn*, p. 28.
9. Ninette de Valois, interview, 29 April 1991.
10. Frederick Ashton, quoted in Julie Kavanagh, *Secret Muses: The Life of Frederick Ashton*, Faber and Faber, 1996, p. 184.
11. ibid., p. 183.
12. Fonteyn, *Autobiography*, p. 53.
13. Frank, *Margot Fonteyn*, p. 31.
14. Kathrine Sorley Walker, *De Valois, Idealist without Illusions,* Hamish Hamilton, 1987, p. 52.
15. Frederick Ashton, quoted in Kavanagh, *Secret Muses*, p. 389.
16. ibid., p. 127.
17. Frederick Ashton interview, broadcast in *The Absolute Ballerina*, written and presented by Jan Parry, BBC Radio 3, 3 January 1992.
18. ibid.
19. ibid.
20. Frederick Ashton, quoted in Fonteyn, *Autobiography*, p. 52.
21. Frederick Ashton, quoted in Keith Money, *The Art of Margot Fonteyn*, Reynal & Co., 1965, no page numbers.

Chapter 6

1. James Monahan, *Fonteyn – A Study of the Ballerina in Her Setting*, A. & C. Black, 1957, pp. 14–15.
2. Gordon Anthony, *Margot Fonteyn,* Phoenix House, 1950, p. 24.
3. Lambert/Ashton correspondence, Royal Opera House Archive.
4. ibid.

5. Frederick Ashton, quoted in Julie Kavanagh, *Secret Muses: The Life of Frederick Ashton*, Faber and Faber, 1996, p. 191.

6. Margot Fonteyn, *Autobiography*, W. H. Allen, 1975, p. 60.

7. Anthony, *Margot Fonteyn*, p. 28.

8. Fonteyn, *Autobiography*, p. 61.

9. Robert Helpmann, quoted ibid.

10. Anthony Powell, interview, September 1992.

11. Andrew Motion, *The Lamberts: George, Constant and Kit*, Hogarth Press, 1987, p. 121.

12. Patrick Hadley, quoted ibid., p. 132.

13. Anthony Powell, *Messengers of Day*, Heinemann, 1978, p. 57.

14. Tom Driberg, quoted in Motion, *The Lamberts*, p. 214.

15. Powell, *Messengers of Day*, p. 61.

16. Ninette de Valois, *Come Dance with Me*, Hamish Hamilton, 1957, p. 112.

17. ibid.

18. Ninette de Valois, interview, 29 April 1991.

19. Fonteyn, *Autobiography*, p. 64.

20. Keith Money, *The Art of Margot Fonteyn*, Reynal & Co., 1965, no page numbers.

21. Lambert/Ashton correspondence, Royal Opera House Archive.

22. Molly Brown diary, Royal Ballet School Archive.

23. Lilian Baylis, quoted by Mary Clarke, *The Sadler's Wells Ballet*, A. & C. Black, 1955, p. 126.

24. Frederick Ashton: source withheld.

25. P. W. Manchester, *Vic-Wells: A Ballet Progress,* Victor Gollancz, 1946, p. 35.

26. Undated cutting.

27. Fonteyn, *Autobiography*, p. 63.

28. Ninette de Valois, quoted ibid.

29. Lynn Seymour with Paul Gardner, *Lynn*, Granada, 1984, p. 120.

30. Edward Denby, quoted by Dale Harris in *Ballet Review*, Vol. 4. no 5.

31. Fonteyn, *Autobiography*, p. 57.

32. Monahan, *Fonteyn*, p. 68.

Chapter 7

1. Margot Fontyen, *Autobiography*, W. H. Allen, 1975, p. 68.

2. ibid., p. 69.

3. Fonteyn, 'My Dancing Years', *Woman*, September 1961.

4. Harmodio Arias, interview.

5. Fonteyn, *Autobiography*, p. 55.

6. ibid.

7. Fonteyn, 'My Dancing Years'.

8. Molly Brown, diary, Royal Ballet School Archive.

9. Alexandra Danilova, quoted in Mary Clarke, *The Sadler's Wells Ballet*, A. & C. Black, 1955, pp. 121–2.

10. William Chappell, quoted in Julie Kavanagh, *Secret Muses: The Life of Frederick Ashton*, Faber and Faber, 1996, p. 220.

11. ibid., p. 227.

12. Frederick Ashton, quoted in Andrew Motion, *The Lamberts: George, Constant and Kit*, Hogarth Press, 1987, p. 191.

13. Ninette de Valois, quoted in Fonteyn, *Autobiography*, p. 55.

14. William Chappell, *Fonteyn: Impressions of a Ballerina*, Rockliff, 1951, p. 30.

15. Margot Fonteyn, *Swan Lake*, Gulliver Books, 1989, storyteller's note.

16. Fonteyn, *Autobiography*, p. 61.

17. Elizabeth Salter, *Helpmann*, Angus & Robertson, 1998, p. 84.

18. Lilian Baylis, quoted in Fonteyn, *Autobiography*, p. 42.

19. Audrey Williamson, quoted in Salter, *Helpmann*, p. 84.

20. Ninette de Valois, *Come Dance with Me*, Hamish Hamilton, 1957, pp. 78–82.

21. Lilian Baylis, quoted in Fonteyn, *Autobiography*, p. 42.

22. ibid., p. 70.

23. Tangye Lean, quoted in Keith Money, *Fonteyn: The Making of a Legend*, Collins, 1973, pp. 58–9.

Chapter 8

1. Alan Carter, quoted in Julie Kavanagh, *Secret Muses: The Life of Frederick Ashton*, Faber and Faber, 1996, p. 230.

2. William Chappell, quoted ibid., p. 230.

3. Frederick Ashton, quoted ibid., p. 231.

4. ibid.

5. Richard Shead, *Constant Lambert*, Thames Publishing, 1973, p. 114.

6. Constant Lambert, *Music Ho!: A Study of Music in Decline*, Faber and Faber, 1936, p. 328. There is a marked similarity in melody between Lambert's 'Saraband for the Followers of Virgo', and the opening movement of Sibelius's 6th Symphony.

7. Margot Fonteyn, quoted in Andrew Motion, *The Lamberts: George, Constant and Kit*, Hogarth Press, 1987, p. 212.

8. ibid.

9. Limerick by Constant Lambert, quoted in Tom Driberg, *Ruling Passions,* Jonathan Cape, 1977.
10. Frederick Ashton, quoted in Fonteyn, *Autobiography*, p. 94.
11. ibid.
12. ibid., p. 70.
13. ibid.
14. Ninette de Valois, quoted ibid., p. 75.
15. Serge Diaghilev, quoted in Boris Kochno, *Diaghilev and the Ballets Russes,* Harper & Row, 1970, p. 172.
16. Serge Diaghilev, quoted in Fonteyn, *Autobiography*, p. 75.
17. ibid., p. 77.
18. Mary Clarke, *The Sadler's Wells Ballet*, A. & C. Black, 1955, p. 143.
19. ibid.
20. Elizabeth Miller, diary, Royal Ballet School Archive.
21. In fact, Lambert wrote an appreciative essay on Tchaikovsky in Gordon Anthony, *The Sleeping Princess, Camera Studies*, George Routledge & Sons, 1942.
22. Kochno, *Diaghilev*, p. 173.
23. Serge Diaghilev, quoted ibid., p. 174.
24. Margot Fonteyn, quoted in Elizabeth Frank, *Margot Fonteyn*, Chatto & Windus, 1958, p. 47.
25. Clarke, *The Sadler's Wells Ballet*, p. 145.
26. Kavanagh, *Secret Muses*, p. 244.
27. Fonteyn, *Autobiography*, p. 80.
28. Pamela May, speaking at *The Fonteyn Phenomenon*, Royal Academy of Dancing conference on Margot Fonteyn, September 1999.
29. Ninette de Valois, quoted in Kavanagh, *Secret Muses*, p. 256.
30. Frederick Ashton, quoted ibid.
31. ibid., p. 258.
32. ibid.
33. P. W. Manchester, *Vic-Wells: A Ballet Progress*, Victor Gollancz, 1946, pp. 45–6.
34. Frank, *Margot Fonteyn*, p. 49.
35. Attributed to Keith Money.
36. Gordon Anthony, *Margot Fonteyn*, Phoenix House, 1950, p. 72.
37. ABCA: Army Bureau of Current Affairs; CEMA: Council for the Encouragement of Music and the Arts; ENSA: Entertainments National Service Association.

Chapter 9

1. Robert Helpmann, quoted in Annabel Farjeon, *The Dutch Journal*, unpublished memoir, broadcast on BBC Radio 4 as *Ballet Behind the Borders*.
2. Farjeon, *The Dutch Journal*.
3. ibid.
4. ibid.
5. ibid.
6. Robert Helpmann, quoted ibid.
7. Farjeon, *The Dutch Journal*.
8. ibid.
9. ibid.
10. Leslie Edwards with Graham Bowles, *In Good Company*, Dance Books, 2003, p. 87.
11. Margot Fonteyn, *Autobiography*, W. H. Allen, 1975, p. 83.
12. Farjeon, *The Dutch Journal*.
13. Ninette de Valois, quoted ibid.
14. ibid.
15. ibid.
16. ibid.
17. Fonteyn, *Autobiography*, p. 95.
18. Vera Volkova, quoted ibid.
19. ibid.
20. Pamela May, quoted in Julie Kavanagh, *Secret Muses: The Life of Frederick Ashton*, Faber and Faber, 1996, p. 274.
21. Dyneley Hussey, *Spectator*, 31 January 1941.
22. William Chappell, *Fonteyn: Impressions of a Ballerina*, Rockliff, 1951, p. 31.
23. ibid.
24. ibid., p. 32.

Chapter 10

1. Margot Fonteyn, 'My Dancing Years,' *Woman*, September 1961.
2. Margot Fonteyn, *Autobiography*, W. H. Allen, 1975, p. 87.
3. ibid.
4. Andrew Motion, *The Lamberts: George, Constant and Kit*, Hogarth Press, 1987, p. 220.
5. ibid., p. 221.
6. Fonteyn, *Autobiography*, p. 87.
7. Mary Clarke, *The Sadler's Wells Ballet*, A. & C. Black, 1955, p. 151.

8. Undated press cutting, Neil Ambrose collection.

9. Shakespeare, *Hamlet*, act 3, scene 1.

10. Elizabeth Salter, *Helpmann*, Angus & Robertson, 1998, p. 118.

11. ibid.

12. Gordon Anthony, *Margot Fonteyn*, Phoenix House, 1950, p. 9.

13. Motion, *The Lamberts*, p. 224.

14. Anthony Powell, interview.

15. Motion, *The Lamberts*, p. 222.

16. Elizabeth Frank, *Margot Fonteyn*, Chatto & Windus, 1958, p. 62.

17. Herbert Farjeon, *Sunday Graphic*.

18. Ninette de Valois, *Come Dance with Me*, Hamish Hamilton, 1957, p. 104.

19. John Lanchbery, interview.

20. William Chappell, *Fonteyn: Impressions of a Ballerina*, Rockliff, 1951, pp. 20–22.

21. Constant Lambert, quoted in Julie Kavanagh, *Secret Muses: The Life of Frederick Ashton*, Faber and Faber, 1996, p. 288.

22. Maude Lloyd, quoted ibid., p. 124.

23. Annabel Farjeon, 'Dancing for De Valois and Ashton', *Dance Chronicle*, 1994, p. 201.

24. William Walton to John Warrack, quoted in Kavanagh, *Secret Muses*, p. 290.

25. Frederick Ashton, quoted in Kavanagh, *Secret Muses*, p. 289.

26. ibid., p. 292.

27. Source withheld.

28. Motion, *The Lamberts*, p. 178.

29. Fonteyn, *Autobiography*, p. 89.

30. Constance Tomkinson, *Dancing Attendance*, Michael Joseph, 1965, pp. 22–3.

31. Motion, *The Lamberts*, p. 226.

32. Lambert/Ayrton correspondence, Royal Opera House Archive.

33. Clarke, *The Sadler's Wells Ballet*, p. 182.

34. Frank, *Margot Fonteyn*, p. 63.

35. Tamara Karsavina, quoted in Pigeon Crowle, *Enter the Ballerina*, Faber and Faber, 1955, p. 112.

Chapter 11

1. Margot Fonteyn, *Autobiography*, W. H. Allen, 1975, p. 91.

2. ibid.

3. Margot Fonteyn, 'My Dancing Years', *Woman*, September 1961.

4. Roland Petit, *J'ai dancé sur les flots*, Bernard Grasset, Paris, 1993, pp. 296–7.

5. Leslie Edwards, interview.

6. Isabel Lambert, quoted in Andrew Motion, *The Lamberts: George, Constant and Kit*, Hogarth Press, 1987, p. 236.

7. Michael Ayrton, quoted ibid., p. 230.

8. Ninette de Valois, *Come Dance with Me*, Hamish Hamilton, 1957, p. 156.

9. Michael Ayrton, quoted in Motion, *The Lamberts*, p. 230.

10. Fonteyn, *Autobiography*, p. 94.

11. ibid.

12. Lord Alfred Tennyson, 'The Day Dream'.

13. De Valois, *Come Dance with Me*, p. 154.

14. Frederick Ashton, quoted in Julie Kavanagh, *Secret Muses: The Life of Frederick Ashton*, Faber and Faber, 1996, p. 308.

15. Frederick Ashton, interview with Alastair Macaulay, *Dance Theatre Journal*, p. 6.

16. Maynard Keynes, quoted in Mary Clarke, *The Sadler's Wells Ballet*, A. & C. Black, 1955, p. 201.

17. De Valois, *Come Dance with Me*, p. 156.

18. Ninette de Valois, *Step by Step*, W. H. Allen, 1977, p. 69.

19. Clarke, *The Sadler's Wells Ballet*, p. 203.

20. ibid.

21. Margot Fonteyn interview, Keith Money, *The Art of Margot Fonteyn*, Reynal & Co., 1965, no page numbers.

22. Fonteyn, *Autobiography*, p. 90.

23. Petit, *J'ai dancé sur les flots*, p. 297.

24. Constant Lambert, quoted in Kavanagh, *Secret Muses*, p. 310.

25. Frederick Ashton, quoted in David Vaughan, *Frederick Ashton and His Ballets*, A. & C. Black, 1977, p. 204.

26. Michael Somes, interviewed on Margot Fonteyn obituary documentary, produced by Julia Matheson, 1991.

27. Frederick Ashton, interviewed by Richard Buckle in *Ballet Magazine*.

28. Antoinette Sibley, interviewed on Julia Matheson documentary.

Chapter 12

1. Richard Buckle, *The Adventures of a Ballet Critic*, Cressnet Press, 1953, p. 71.

2. Dick Beard, quoted in Julie Kavanagh, *Secret Muses: The Life of Frederick Ashton*, Faber and Faber, 1996, p. 319.

3. Muriel Bentley, quoted ibid., p. 320.

4. Roland Petit, *J'ai dancé sur les flots*, Bernard Grasset, 1993, p. 297.

5. Buckle, *Adventures*, p. 87.

6. Foreword by Fonteyn to Bridget Keenan, *Dior in Vogue*, Octopus, 1981.

7. Andrew Motion, *The Lamberts: George, Constant and Kit*, Hogarth Press, 1987, p. 238.

8. Ninette de Valois, quoted ibid.

9. Desmond Shawe-Taylor, *New Statesman and Nation*, 21 December 1946.

10. Kenneth Tynan, *He That Plays the King – A View of the Theatre*, Longmans, Green, 1950, pp. 57–8.

11. ibid., p. 56.

12. Kavanagh, *Secret Muses*, p. 335.

13. Keith Money, *Margot Assoluta*, Fair Prospect, 2000, p. 66.

14. ibid.

15. Motion, *The Lamberts*, p. 235.

16. Petit, *J'ai dancé sur les flots*, p. 298.

17. Dick Beard, quoted in Kavanagh, *Secret Muses*, p. 343.

18. Letter from David Webster, quoted in Motion, *The Lamberts*, p. 239.

19. Constant Lambert, quoted ibid., p. 240.

20. William Chappell, quoted ibid., p. 241.

21. Frederick Ashton, quoted ibid.

22. Isabel Lambert, quoted ibid.

23. Frederick Ashton, quoted in Kavanagh, *Secret Muses*, p. 343.

24. ibid.

25. Fonteyn/Parry correspondence, Jennie Walton collection.

26. Margot Fonteyn, *Autobiography*, W. H. Allen, 1975, p. 110.

Chapter 13

1. Mary Clarke, *The Sadler's Wells Ballet*, A. & C. Black, 1955, p. 226.

2. Frederick Ashton, quoted in Julie Kavanagh, *Secret Muses: The Life of Frederick Ashton*, Faber and Faber, 1996, p. 343.

3. Edwin Denby, 'New York City's Ballet', *Ballet*, August 1952; reprinted, *Dance Writings*, Dance Books, 1986, p. 428.

4. Nadia Nerina, written account.

5. Fonteyn/Parry correspondence.

6. Taglioni story quoted in Jean-Louis Tamvaco, *Les Cancans de l'Opéra*, CNRS editions, Paris, 2000, Vol. 2, p. 1107.

7. Fonteyn papers, Royal Opera House Archive.

8. ibid.

9. Margot Fonteyn, *Autobiography*, W. H. Allen, 1975, p. 114.

10. ibid., p. 115.

11. ibid.

12. ibid.

13. Richard Buckle, *Ballet*, Vol. 5, No. 7, July 1948.

14. P.W. Manchester, *Dance News*, 19 November 1953.

15. Annabel Farjeon, *New Statesman and Nation*, 4 October 1948.

16. James Monahan, *Fonteyn: A Study of a Ballerina in Her Setting*, A. & C. Black, 1957, p. 84.

17. Anne Heaton, interview.

18. Pigeon Crowle, *Moira Shearer, Portrait of a Dancer*, Faber and Faber, 1949, p. 69.

19. Fonteyn, *Autobiography*, p. 101.

20. ibid. p. 116.

21. Elizabeth Frank, *Margot Fonteyn*, Chatto & Windus, 1958, p. 33.

22. Edwin Denby, 'Ashton's Cinderella', *Ballet*, February 1949; reprinted, *Dance Writings*, p. 362.

23. Lydia Lopokova, quoted in Kavanagh, *Secret Muses*, p. 366.

24. Kavanagh, *Secret Muses*, p. 366.

25. Solomon Hurok, *The World of Ballet*, Robert Hale, 1955.

26. Nadia Nerina, interview.

27. Hurok, *The World of Ballet*.

28. Fonteyn, *Autobiography*, p. 118.

29. Letter from Alex Martin, Alastair Macaulay collection.

30. Ninette de Valois, *Come Dance with Me*, Hamish Hamilton, 1957, p. 186.

31. Fonteyn, *Autobiography*, p. 118.

32. Andrew Motion, *The Lamberts: George, Constant and Kit*, Hogarth Press, 1987, p. 246.

33. Richard Shead, *Constant Lambert*, Thames Publishing, 1973, p. 146.

34. Richard Buckle, *The Adventures of A Ballet Critic*, Cressnet Press, 1953, p. 212.

Chapter 14

1. Solomon Hurok, *The World of Ballet*, Robert Hale, 1955, p. 212.

2. Ludovic Kennedy, *On My Way to the Club*, Fontana Collins, 1990, pp. 200–201.

3. Ninette de Valois, quoted in Andrew Motion, *The Lamberts: George, Constant and Kit*, Hogarth Press, 1987, p. 247.

4. Lincoln Kirstein, letter to Richard Buckle, quoted in Buckle, *The Adventures of a Ballet Critic*, Cressnet Press, 1953, p. 169.

5. Pamela May, dictated to Gail Monahan.

6. Margot Fonteyn, *Autobiography*, W. H. Allen, 1975, p. 120.

7. Pamela May, dictated to Gail Monahan.

8. Fonteyn, *Autobiography*, p. 120.

9. Hurok, *The World of Ballet*, p. 213.

10. Elizabeth Frank, *Margot Fonteyn*, Chatto & Windus, 1958, p. 77.

11. Fonteyn, *Autobiography*, p. 121.

12. Hurok, *The World of Ballet*, p. 214.

13. ibid., p. 215.

14. Pamela May, dictated to Gail Monahan.

15. ibid.

16. Walter Terry, *New York Herald Tribune*, 10 October 1949.

17. John Martin, *New York Times*, 10 October 1949.

18. Fonteyn, *Autobiography*, p. 120.

19. George Balanchine, quoted by Gelsey Kirkland in *Dancing on My Grave*, Doubleday, 1986, p. 70.

20. Lincoln Kirstein, letter to Richard Buckle, quoted in Buckle, *Adventures*, p. 169.

21. Source withheld.

22. Fonteyn, *Autobiography*, p. 122.

23. ibid.

24. Alan Sievewright documentary, *The Tales of Helpmann*, LWT, 1990.

25. Constant Lambert, letter to Isabel Lambert, quoted in Richard Shead, *Constant Lambert*, Thames Publishing, 1973, p. 149.

26. Lincoln Kirstein, letter to Richard Buckle, quoted in Buckle, *Adventures*, p. 171.

27. Elizabeth Salter, *Helpmann*, Angus Robertson, 1998, p. 61.

28. Frederick Ashton, quoted in Julie Kavanagh, *Secret Muses: The Life of Frederick Ashton*, Faber and Faber, 1996, p. 287.

29. Katharine Hepburn, interviewed on Sievewright documentary.

30. Margaret Rawlings, interviewed on Sievewright documentary.

31. Stewart Granger, interviewed on Sievewright documentary.

32. Leslie Edwards, interview.

33. Robert Helpman, interviewed on Sievewright documentary.

34. Salter, *Helpmann*, p. 49.

35. Constant Lambert, letter to Isabel Lambert, quoted in Shead, *Constant Lambert*, p. 148. (*Cafard*. Avoir le cafard: to be down in the dumps.)

36. John Lanchbery, interview.

37. ibid.

38. Leslie Edwards, *In Good Company – Sixty Years with the Royal Ballet*, Dance Books, 2003, p. 141.

39. Colette Clarke, interview.

Chapter 15

1. *Variety*, quoted in Mary Clarke, *The Sadler's Wells Ballet*, A. & C. Black, 1955, p. 244.
2. Elizabeth Frank, *Margot Fonteyn*, Chatto & Windus, 1958, p. 85.
3. ibid.
4. Robert Gottlieb, interview.
5. Moira Shearer, interviewed in Barbara Newman, *Striking a Balance: Dancers Talking about Dancing*, Houghton Mifflin, 1982, p. 107.
6. George Balanchine, informal 'notes on choreography', quoted in Clarke, *The Sadler's Wells Ballet*, p. 248.
7. Clarke, *The Sadler's Wells Ballet*, p. 249.
8. Elizabeth Salter, *Helpmann*, Angus & Robertson, 1998, p. 149.
9. Alexander Bland, *The Royal Ballet: First Fifty Years*, Doubleday, 1981, p. 100.
10. Margot Fonteyn, *Autobiography*, W. H. Allen, 1975, p. 123.
11. ibid.
12. ibid., p. 126.
13. ibid.
14. Frank, *Margot Fonteyn*, p. 89.
15. Solomon Hurok, *The World of Ballet*, Robert Hale, 1955, p. 233.
16. Salter, *Helpmann*, p. 151.
17. De Valois/Newton correspondence, Royal Ballet School Archive.
18. Fonteyn, *Autobiography*, p. 169.
19. ibid., p. 127.
20. ibid., p. 125.
21. ibid., p. 135.
22. James Monahan, *Fonteyn – A Study of a Ballerina in Her Setting*, A. & C. Black, 1957, p. 82.

Chapter 16

1. Ruth Page, *Page by Page*, Dance Horizons, 1978, p. 180.
2. John Craxton, interview.
3. ibid., p. 177.
4. Julie Kavanagh, *Secret Muses: The Life of Frederick Ashton*, Faber and Faber, 1996, p. 389.
5. Margot Fonteyn, *Autobiography*, W. H. Allen, 1975, p. 136.
6. Page, *Page by Page*, p. 180.
7. Kavanagh, *Secret Muses*, p. 390.

8. ibid.

9. ibid.

10. ibid.

11. Anya Linden, quoted in Kavanagh, *Secret Muses*, p. 391.

12. Denis ApIvor and Constant Lambert, quoted in Richard Shead, *Constant Lambert*, Thames Publishing, 1973, p. 156.

13. Richard Johnson, *New Statesman and Nation*, 12 July 1951.

14. Richard Buckle, 'Blind Mice', *Observer*, 15 July 1951.

15. Isabel Lambert, quoted in Andrew Motion, *The Lamberts: George, Constant and Kit*, Hogarth Press, 1987, p. 256.

16. ibid.

17. Osbert Sitwell, obituary for Constant Lambert, *New Statesman and Nation*, 31 August 1951.

18. Mary Clarke, *The Sadler's Wells Ballet*, A. & C. Black, 1955, p. 265.

19. Fonteyn/Narborough correspondence, David Scrase collection.

20. Robert Helpmann, quoted in Elizabeth Salter, *Helpmann*, Angus & Robertson, 1998, p. 157.

21. Frederick Ashton, quoted in Kavanagh, *Secret Muses*, p. 393.

22. ibid.

23. Ninette de Valois, *Come Dance with Me*, Hamish Hamilton, 1957, p. 112.

24. ibid., p. 111.

25. Ninette de Valois, *Step by Step*, W. H. Allen, 1977, p. 57.

Chapter 17

1. Elizabeth Frank, *Margot Fonteyn*, Chatto & Windus, 1958, p. 94.

2. Letter from Graham Greene, quoted in Norman Sherry, *The Life of Graham Greene*, Vol. 2, Jonathan Cape, 1994, p. 499.

3. Letter from Margot Fonteyn, quoted ibid., p. 500.

4. Frank, *Margot Fonteyn*, p. 95.

5. Ruth Page, *Page by page*, Dance Horizons, 1978, p. 180.

6. ibid., p. 181.

7. Shakespeare, *The Tempest*, act 1, scene 2.

8. David Vaughan, *Frederick Ashton and His Ballets*, A. & C. Black, 1977, p. 226.

9. ibid.

10. Alexander Grant, quoted in Julie Kavanagh, *Secret Muses: The Life of Frederick Ashton*, Faber and Faber, 1996, p. 404.

11. Lincoln Kirstein, quoted in Alexander Bland, *Fonteyn and Nureyev*, Orbis, 1979, p. 7.

12. Michael Somes, interview, 16 May 1991.
13. Pamela May, speaking at the *Fonteyn Phenomenon* conference.
14. ibid.
15. Frank, *Margot Fonteyn*, p. 96.
16. Margot Fonteyn, quoted by James Thomas, *News Chronicle*, 8 February 1952.
17. David Webster, quoted in Keith Money, *Fonteyn: The Making of a Legend*, Collins, 1973, p. 145.
18. Frank, *Margot Fonteyn*, p. 96.
19. ibid., p. 97.
20. Interview with Iris Ashley, undated cutting, Neil Ambrose collection.
21. Interview with Barbara Wall, 'Top of the Tree' no. 3, *Everywoman*, November 1953, p. 87.
22. ibid., p. 85.
23. Margot Fonteyn, interviewed by Marguerite Duras, *American Vogue*, 15 January 1968.

Chapter 18

1. Michael Somes, interview, 16 May 1991.
2. Margot Fonteyn, *Autobiography*, W. H. Allen, 1975, p. 141.
3. ibid.
4. ibid.
5. ibid.
6. ibid.
7. ibid., p. 142.
8. ibid.
9. ibid.
10. ibid.
11. ibid.
12. ibid., p. 143.
13. ibid., pp. 144–6.
14. BQ, quoted by David Scrase in conversation with the author.
15. Fonteyn, *Autobiography*, p. 147.
16. ibid., p. 149.
17. ibid.
18. Leslie Edwards, quoted in Julie Kavanagh, *Secret Muses: The Life of Frederick Ashton*, Faber and Faber, 1996, p. 412.
19. Frederick Ashton, quoted ibid., p. 411.
20. Fonteyn, *Autobiography*, p. 149.

21. ibid., 151.
22. Fonteyn, *Autobiography*, 1989 edition, Hamish Hamilton, p. 142.

Chapter 19

1. Gennady Smakov, *The Great Russian Dancers*, Alfred A. Knopf, 1984, p. 191.
2. Margot Fonteyn, *Autobiography*, W. H. Allen, 1975, p. 153.
3. Margot Fonteyn, speaking on Margaret Dale BBC documentary, *Tamara Karsavina: Portrait of a Ballerina*, written and presented by James Monahan, 10 March 1965.
4. Fonteyn, *Autobiography*, p. 153.
5. Monica Mason, interviewed in Barbara Newman, *Striking a Balance – Dancers Talking about Dancing*, Houghton Mifflin, 1982, pp. 300–301.
6. ibid.
7. Fonteyn, *Autobiography*, p. 154.
8. De Valois/Newton correspondence, Royal Ballet School Archive.
9. Fonteyn, *Autobiography*, p. 155.
10. Keith Money, *Margot Assoluta*, Fair Prospect, 2000, p. 106.
11. *Royal Academy of Dancing Gazette*, November, 1954.
12. Undated cutting, Neil Ambrose collection.
13. Fonteyn papers, Royal Opera House Archive.
14. ibid.
15. *Evening News*, 27 September 1954.
16. *Star*, 20 July 1954.
17. Undated press cutting, Neil Ambrose collection.
18. Simon Ward, *Daily Sketch*, 29 November 1954.
19. ibid., 4 February 1955.
20. *Evening News*, 4 February 1955.
21. Undated press cutting, Neil Ambrose collection.
22. Margot Fonteyn, quoted by Cyril Beaumont, *Sunday Times*, 6 February 1955.
23. Leslie Edwards, *In Good Company – Sixty Years with the Royal Ballet*, Dance Books, 2003, p. 159.
24. ibid.
25. Margot Fonteyn, quoted in Peter Stephens, 'Margot Weds – But Not So Quietly', *Sunday Mirror*, 7 February 1955.
26. ibid.
27. Simon Ward, *Daily Sketch*, 7 February 1955.
28. ibid.
29. Fonteyn, *Autobiography*, p. 164.

Chapter 20

1. ibid., p. 147.
2. De Valois/Newton correspondence, Royal Ballet School Archive.
3. Frederick Ashton, quoted in Julie Kavanagh, *Secret Muses: The Life of Frederick Ashton*, Faber and Faber, 1996, p. 414.
4. Elaine Fifield, *In My Shoes*, W. H. Allen, 1967, p. 94.
5. Margot Fonteyn, *Autobiography*, W. H. Allen, 1975, p. 158.
6. ibid.
7. Colin Clark, *Younger Brother, Younger Son*, HarperCollins, 1997, p. 199.
8. Margot Fonteyn, 'My Dancing Years', *Woman*, September 1961.
9. Frederick Ashton, quoted in Kavanagh, *Secret Muses*, p. 422.

Chapter 21

1. Simon Ward, *Daily Sketch*, 2 September 1955.
2. De Valois/Newton correspondence, Royal Ballet School Archive.
3. Vadim Gayevsky, quoted in Gennady Smakov, *The Great Russian Dancers*, Alfred A. Knopf, 1984, p. 37.
4. Smakov, *The Great Russian Dancers*, p. 38.
5. Elizabeth Frank, *Margot Fonteyn*, Chatto & Windus, 1958, p. 108.
6. Margot Fonteyn, *Autobiography*, W. H. Allen, 1975, p. 52.
7. ibid., p. 166.
8. ibid., p. 165.
9. Smakov, *The Great Russian Dancers*.
10. Cable from David Webster, quoted in Alexander Bland, *The Royal Ballet – the First Fifty Years*, Doubleday, 1981, p. 118.
11. Fonteyn, *Autobiography*, p. 168.
12. Elaine Fifield, *In My Shoes*, W. H. Allen, 1967, p. 116.
13. ibid., p. 125.
14. Fonteyn, *Autobiography*, p. 168.
15. Colin Clark, *Younger Brother, Younger Son*, HarperCollins, 1997, p. 200.
16. Margot Fonteyn in conversation with David Scrase.
17. ibid.
18. Clark, *Younger Brother*, 201.
19. Fonteyn, *Autobiography*, p. 173.
20. Mike Todd, quoted ibid.
21. Fonteyn, *Autobiography*, pp. 175–6.
22. Clark, *Younger Brother*, p. 200.

Chapter 22

1. David Vaughan, *Frederick Ashton and His Ballets*, A. & C. Black, 1977, p. 292.
2. Frederick Ashton, quoted in Julie Kavanagh, *Secret Muses: The Life of Frederick Ashton*, Faber and Faber, 1996, p. 426.
3. Frederick Ashton, interview with Peter Brinson, quoted ibid., p. 438.
4. ibid.
5. Margot Fonteyn, quoted ibid., p. 437.
6. Frederick Ashton, quoted ibid.
7. Alexander Bland, *Observer*, 2 November 1958.
8. ibid.
9. Cyril Beaumont, undated cutting, Neil Ambrose collection.
10. Margot Fonteyn, *Autobiography*, W. H. Allen, 1975, p. 206.
11. Margot Fonteyn, interviewed by Peter Brinson, 'Creating Ondine', *Sunday Times*, 8 March 1959.
12. Alexander Bland, *Observer*, 2 November 1958.
13. Lincoln Kirstein, letter to Cecil Beaton, quoted in Kavanagh, *Secret Muses*, p. 438.
14. Lynn Seymour, quoted in Richard Austin, *Lynn Seymour*, Angus & Robertson, 1980, p. 41.
15. Ninette de Valois, quoted in Lynn Seymour with Paul Gardner, *Lynn*, Granada, 1984, p. 60.
16. Margot Fonteyn, *Autobiography*, W. H. Allen, 1975, p. 183.
17. Christopher Gable, quoted in Austin, *Lynn Seymour*, p. 50.
18. Rudolf Nureyev, interviewed on BBC documentary, *When the Dancing Had to Stop*.
19. Kenneth MacMillan, quoted in Austin, *Lynn Seymour*, p. 56.
20. Austin, *Lynn Seymour*, p. 57.
21. ibid., p. 68.
22. Fonteyn, *Autobiography*, p. 186.
23. ibid.
24. ibid., p. 179.
25. Fidel Castro, quoted in Paul Kramer, 'Swan Lake', *Latin American Panorama: An Anthology*, Capricorn Books, 1969, p. 309.
26. Fonteyn, *Autobiography*, p. 180.
27. Cecil Beaton, unpublished diaries.
28. BQ, quoted by Douglas Marlborough, *Daily Mail*, 26 January 1959.
29. ibid.
30. Fonteyn, *Autobiography*, p. 205.
31. Source withheld.

32. Herbert Ross, interview.

33. Lynn Seymour, written account for the *Fonteyn Phenomenon* conference, later published in *Dance and Dancers*.

Chapter 23

1. Margot Fonteyn, *Autobiography*, W. H. Allen, 1975, p. 187.

2. Judy Tatham, unpublished memoir.

3. Fonteyn, *Autobiography*, p. 188.

4. ibid.

5. ibid., p. 189.

6. ibid.

7. ibid., p. 190.

8. ibid.

9. ibid., p. 192.

10. ibid.

11. Kramer, 'Swan Lake', p. 313.

12. Fonteyn, *Autobiography*, p. 193.

13. Dawkins, in fact, later denounced Zito and told the press that Margot was a 'busybody' who had given him two twenty-dollar bills for his wife.

14. Fonteyn, *Autobiography*, p. 194.

15. ibid., p. 193.

16. ibid.

17. Kramer, 'Swan Lake', p. 314.

18. Fonteyn, *Autobiography*, p. 194.

19. ibid.

20. ibid., p. 195.

21. ibid.

22. ibid., p. 196.

23. ibid.

24. ibid.

25. ibid., p. 197.

26. ibid.

27. ibid.

28. ibid.

29. Kramer, 'Swan Lake', p. 315.

30. Undated press cutting, Neil Ambrose collection.

31. Fonteyn, *Autobiography*, p. 199.

32. Judy Tatham, memoir.

33. Fonteyn, *Autobiography*, p. 199.
34. Undated press cutting, Neil Ambrose collection.
35. Fonteyn, *Autobiography*, p. 199.
36. *Manchester Guardian*, 24 April 1959.
37. Judy Tatham, memoir.
38. *Manchester Guardian*, 24 April 1959.

Chapter 24

1. Paul Kramer, unpublished appended pages (8 January 1992) to 'Swan Lake', *Latin American Panorama: An Anthology*, Capricorn Books, 1969.
2. ibid.
3. Ninette de Valois, interview.
4. Julie Kavanagh, *Secret Muses: The Life of Frederick Ashton*, Faber and Faber, 1996, p. 446.
5. Frederick Ashton, quoted ibid.
6. Frederick Ashton, 'My Conception of La Fille mal gardée', *Dance and Dancers*, June 1966.
7. ibid.
8. Nadia Nerina, interview in Barbara Newman, *Striking a Balance – Dancers Talking about Dancing*, Houghton Mifflin, 1982, p. 141.
9. Fonteyn, quoted in Keith Money, *Margot Assoluta*, Fair Prospect, 2000, p. 145.
10. David Webster, quoted in *The Times*, social pages, August 1959.
11. ibid.
12. Fonteyn Papers, Royal Opera House Archive.
13. ibid.
14. ibid.
15. Margot Fonteyn, quoted in *Daily Mirror*, 8 January 1960.
16. De Valois/Newton correspondence, Royal Ballet School Archive.
17. Kramer, 'Swan Lake', p. 319.
18. Margot Fonteyn, *Autobiography*, W.H. Allen, 1975, p. 208.
19. Nadia Nerina written account.
20. Fonteyn, *Autobiography*, p. 209.
21. ibid.
22. ibid., p. 210.
23. ibid.
24. ibid.

Chapter 25

1. Rudolf Nureyev, *An Autobiography with Pictures*, introduced by Alexander Bland, Hodder & Stoughton, 1962, p. 23.
2. Peter Watson, *Nureyev*, Hodder & Stoughton, 1994, p. 14.
3. Nureyev, *Autobiography*, p. 26.
4. ibid., p. 29.
5. Margot Fonteyn, *Autobiography*, W. H. Allen, 1975, p. 212.
6. ibid.
7. Colin Clark, *Younger Brother, Younger Son*, HarperCollins, 1977, p. 199.
8. Nureyev, *Autobiography*, p. 103.
9. Fonteyn, *Autobiography*, pp. 213–14.
10. Maria Tallchief with Larry Kaplan, *Maria Tallchief: America's Prima Ballerina*, Henry Holt, 1997, p. 286.
11. Fonteyn, *Autobiography*, p. 215.
12. Nureyev, *Autobiography*, p. 104.
13. Fonteyn, *Autobiography*, p. 215.
14. Rudolf Nureyev, quoted ibid.
15. Fonteyn, *Autobiography*, p. 215.
16. ibid.
17. ibid.
18. ibid., p. 216.
19. Violette Verdy, quoted in Diane Solway, *Nureyev, His Life*, William Morrow, 1998, p. 171.
20. Frederick Ashton, quoted in John Percival, *Nureyev: Aspects of the Dancer*, Faber and Faber, 1975, pp. 161–2.
21. Frederick Ashton, quoted in Julie Kavanagh, *Secret Muses: The Life of Frederick Ashton*, Faber and Faber, 1996, p. 459.
22. Keith Money, *Fonteyn and Nureyev, The Great Years*, Harvill, 1994, p. 10.
23. ibid.
24. Cecil Beaton, unpublished diaries.
25. Lady Diana Cooper, quoted ibid.
26. Richard Buckle, *Sunday Times*, 5 November 1961.
27. Alexander Bland, *Observer*, 5 November 1961.
28. Ninette de Valois, speaking on Margot Fonteyn obituary documentary, produced by Julia Matheson, 1991.
29. Ninette de Valois, *Step by Step*, W. H. Allen, 1977, p. 104.
30. Ninette de Valois, interview.
31. *Margot Fonteyn, A Tribute*, BBC documentary produced and directed by Patricia Foy, 1989.

32. Fonteyn, *Autobiography*, p. 217.

33. ibid.

34. Ninette de Valois, speaking, on Julia Matheson documentary.

35. Fonteyn, *Autobiography*, p. 217.

36. ibid., p. 218.

37. ibid., p. 220.

38. ibid., p. 219.

39. Nureyev, *Autobiography*, p. 105.

40. Fonteyn, *Autobiography*, p. 219.

41. Nadia Nerina's written account, quoted in Otis Stuart, *Perpetual Motion. The Public and Private Lives of Rudolf Nureyev*, Simon & Schuster, 1995, p. 169.

42. Rudolf Nureyev, in *The Absolute Ballerina*, written and presented by Jan Parry, BBC Radio 3, 3 January 1992.

43. Fonteyn, *Autobiography*, p. 219.

44. Rudolf Nureyev, quoted in Alexander Bland, *Fonteyn and Nureyev, The Story of a Partnership*, Books for Pleasure, 1979, p. 58.

45. Christopher Gable, quoted in Solway, *Nureyev*, p. 256.

46. Fonteyn, *Autobiography*, p. 218.

47. ibid., p. 220.

48. Mary Clarke, *Sunday Times*, 25 February 1962. (This quotation has hitherto been erroneously attributed to Richard Buckle.)

49. Editorial in *Dance and Dancers*, April 1962.

50. Undated cutting, Royal Opera House Archive.

51. Updated cutting, Royal Opera House Archive.

52. Alexander Bland, *Observer*, February 1962.

53. Keith Money, *Margot Assoluta*, Fair Prospect, 2000, p. 36.

54. *Dance and Dancers*, April 1962.

55. Fonteyn, *Autobiography*, p. 220.

Chapter 26

1. Querube Arias, quoted in Diane Solway, *Nureyev, His Life*, William Morrow, 1998, p. 294.

2. Margot Fonteyn, *Autobiography*, W. H. Allen, 1975, p. 230.

3. Joan Thring, quoted in Solway, *Nureyev*, p. 300.

4. Theodora Christon, quoted ibid., p. 301.

5. *Time*, 16 April 1965.

6. Leon Harris, 'Nureyev Uptight', *Esquire*, 1968.

7. Genya Polyakov, quoted in Solway, *Nureyev*, p. 301.

8. Liz Greene, *The Astrological Neptune and the Quest for Redemption*, Red Wheel/Weiser, 2000, pp. 180–81.
9. Peter Martins, quoted in Otis Stuart, *Perpetual Motion. The Public and Private Lives of Rudolf Nureyev*, Simon & Schuster, 1995, p. 106.
10. John Tooley, quoted in Solway, *Nureyev*, p. 249.
11. Nadia Nerina, written account, quoted in Stuart, *Perpetual Motion*, p. 150.
12. Nadia Nerina, written account.
13. ibid., quoted in Stuart, *Perpetual Motion*, pp. 129–30.
14. ibid., p. 174.
15. Ninette de Valois, *Step by Step*, W. H. Allen, 1977, pp. 104–5.
16. Fonteyn, *Autobiography*, p. 219.
17. ibid.
18. ibid., p. 221.
19. Keith Money, *Fonteyn and Nureyev*, Harvill, 1994, p. 104.
20. Fonteyn, *Autobiography*, p. 222.
21. Rudolf Nureyev in *The Absolute Ballerina*, written and presented by Jan Parry, BBC Radio 3, 3 January 1992.
22. Fonteyn, *Autobiography*, p. 226.
23. ibid.
24. Keith Money, conversation with Alastair Macaulay, 1997.
25. Kenneth Tynan, *Tynan Right and Left*, Longmans, Green & Co, 1967, pp. 134–5.

Chapter 27

1. Margot Fonteyn, *Autobiography*, W.H. Allen, 1975, p. 221.
2. ibid.
3. Frederick Ashton, quoted in Alexander Bland, 'Birth of a Ballet,' *Observer*, 10 March 1963.
4. ibid.
5. ibid.
6. Fonteyn, *Autobiography*, p. 224.
7. Maude Lloyd, quoted in Julie Kavanagh, *Secret Muses: The Life of Frederick Ashton*, Faber and Faber, 1996, p. 470.
8. Kavanagh, *Secret Muses*, p. 469.
9. ibid.
10. ibid.
11. Vaughan, *Frederick Ashton and His Ballets*, A. & C. Black, 1977, p. 330.
12. Frederick Ashton, quoted in Kavanagh, *Secret Muses*, p. 468.

13. Fonteyn, *Autobiography*, p. 224.
14. ibid.
15. ibid., p. 225.
16. Cecil Beaton, quoted in Hugo Vickers, *Cecil Beaton*, Weidenfeld & Nicolson, 1993, p. 459.
17. Ninette de Valois, quoted in Kavanagh, *Secret Muses*, p. 467.
18. Fonteyn, *Autobiography*, p. 225.
19. Michael Wale, *Daily Express*, 9 March 1963.
20. Bruce Beresford, letter to Cecil Beaton, undated.
21. Keith Money, *Fonteyn and Nureyev*, Harvill, 1994, p. 41.
22. James Kennedy (James Monahan), *Guardian*, 21 November 1963.
23. ibid.
24. Richard Buckle, *Sunday Times*, 17 March 1963.
25. Richard Buckle, *In the Wake of Diaghilev*, Holt, Rinehart & Winston, 1982, p. 277.
26. Richard Buckle, *Sunday Times*, 24 November 1963.
27. ibid., 17 March 1963.
28. Clive Barnes, *Dance and Dancers*, April 1963.
29. Maude Lloyd, quoted in Kavanagh, *Secret Muses*, p. 471.
30. Frederick Ashton, quoted ibid, p. 467.
31. Peter Brook, 'The Writing on the Wall', 17 March 1963.
32. Frederick Ashton, quoted in Kavanagh, *Secret Muses*, p. 474.
33. *Evening Standard*, 14 March 1963.
34. *Sunday Express*, 24 March 1963.
35. ibid.
36. Roberto Arias, quoted by Robin Stafford, *Daily Express*, 25 March 1963.
37. *New York Times*, 19 April 1963.
38. Walter Terry, *New York Herald Tribune*, 26 April 1963.
39. ibid.
40. John Marlin, *Saturday Review*, 25 May 1963.

Chapter 28

1. Margot Fonteyn, *Autobiography*, W. H. Allen, 1975, p. 229.
2. Diane Solway, *Nureyev, His Life*, William Morrow, 1998, p. 275.
3. Fonteyn, *Autobiography*, p. 275.
4. John Lanchbery, interview.
5. Hélène Trailine, quoted in Solway, *Nureyev*, p. 278.
6. Fonteyn, *Autobiography*, p. 230.
7. John Tooley, interview.

8. Fonteyn, *Autobiography*, p. 230.

9. Keith Money, quoted in Solway, *Nureyev*, p. 300.

10. Keith Money, *Fonteyn and Nureyev, The Great Years*, Harvill, 1994, p. 66.

11. ibid., p. 65.

12. Rudolf Nureyev, in *The Absolute Ballerina*, written and presented by Jan Parry, BBC Radio 3, 3 January 1992.

13. Keith Money, *Margot Assoluta*, Fair Prospect, 2000, p. 65.

14. Money, *Fonteyn and Nureyev*, p. 66.

15. Ninette de Valois, *Step by Step*, W. H. Allen, 1977, p. 106.

16. Alexander Bland, *Observer*, 1 December 1963.

17. Clement Crisp, *Financial Times*, 29 November 1963.

18. Clive Barnes, *Dance and Dancers*, December 1963.

19. *Daily Sketch*, 10 December 163.

20. ibid.

21. Fonteyn, *Autobiography*, p. 230.

22. ibid., p. 231.

23. ibid., p. 232.

24. ibid.

25. Money, *Fonteyn and Nureyev*, p. 136.

26. ibid.

27. ibid.

28. Harmodio Arias, interview.

29. Mrs Hookham, *Daily Sketch*, 9 June 1964.

30. Aubrey Chalmers, *Daily Sketch*, 10 June 1964.

31. Fonteyn, quoted by David Lewin in *Daily Mail*, 10 June 1964.

32. Fonteyn, *Autobiography*, p. 238.

33. ibid., p. 239.

Chapter 29

1. ibid.

2. Unpublished Arias memoir, Querube Arias collection.

3. Margot Fonteyn, *Autobiography*, W. H. Allen, 1975, pp. 233–4.

4. Unpublished Arias memoir.

5. Fonteyn, *Autobiography*, p. 241.

6. ibid., p. 244.

7. ibid., p. 246.

8. Film footage of Spoleto tour.

9. Fonteyn, *Autobiography*, p. 246.

10. ibid., p. 247.

11. ibid.
12. ibid.
13. Barry Norman, *Daily Mail*, 11 February 1965.
14. Keith Money, *Margot Assoluta*, Fair Prospect, 2000, p. 172.
15. ibid., p. 173.

Chapter 30

1. Lynn Seymour, *Lynn*, Granada, 1984, p. 182.
2. ibid., p. 181.
3. ibid.
4. ibid., p. 185.
5. ibid., p. 187.
6. ibid., p. 191.
7. Margot Fonteyn, *Autobiography*, W. H. Allen, 1975, p. 252.
8. Margot Fonteyn and Solomon Hurok, quoted in Keith Money, *Fonteyn and Nureyev, The Great Years*, Harvill, 1994, p. 210.
9. ibid.
10. Christopher Gable, quoted in Diane Solway, *Nureyev, His Life*, William Morrow, 1998, p. 319.
11. Georgina Parkinson, quoted ibid.
12. ibid.
13. Keith Money, *Margot Assoluta*, Fair Prospect, 2000, p. 148.
14. Alastair Macaulay, *Margot Fonteyn*, Sutton Publishing, 1998, p. 85.
15. ibid.
16. Money, *Margot Assoluta*, p. 148.
17. *The Times*, 10 February 1965.
18. Christopher Gable, quoted in Solway, *Nureyev*, p. 324.
19. Source withheld.
20. Publicity handout for *Flying Made It Happen* (see next note).
21. Charles Hughesdon, *Flying Made It Happen*, Book Guild, London, 2003, p. vii.
22. ibid.
23. ibid., p. 215.
24. ibid., p. 215–16.
25. Money, *Margot Assoluta*, p. 62.
26. ibid.
27. Letter from Olga Spessivtseva, Royal Opera House Archive.
28. Margot Fonteyn, 'Roberto My Love', *Woman*, September 1968.
29. Peter Williams, *Dance and Dancers*, February 1966.

30. Clement Crisp, *Financial Times*, 8 February 1966.
31. Fonteyn, *Autobiography*, p. 135.
32. ibid., p. 228.
33. ibid., p. 241.
34. ibid., p. 251.

Chapter 31

1. A. V. Coton, *Daily Telegraph*, 28 December 1966.
2. Margot Fonteyn, interviewed by Susan Barnes, *Sunday Mirror*, 29 August 1965.
3. Petit, *J'ai dancé sur les flots*, Bernard Grasset, Paris, 1993, pp. 151–3.
4. Marius Constant, quoted in Margot Fonteyn, *Autobiography*, W. H. Allen, 1975, p. 252.
5. ibid., p. 253.
6. ibid.
7. *Daily Express*, 18 July 1967.
8. Leslie Edwards, interview.
9. Jack Fincher, *Life*, 21 July 1967.
10. *Evening Standard*, 11 July 1967.
11. Jim Hicks, *Life*, 21 July 1967.
12. David Lewin, *Daily Mail*, 12 July 1967.
13. Jeremy Blyth, *Daily Mail*, 13 July 1967.
14. *Evening News*, 23 April 1968.
15. David Lewin, *Daily Mail*, 27 April 1968.
16. *Daily Telegraph*, 11 June 1968.
17. Rudolf Nureyev, quoted in Julian Braunsweg, *Braunsweg's Ballet Scandals*, George Allen & Unwin, 1973, p. 256.
18. Braunsweg, *Braunsweg's Ballet Scandals*, p. 256.
19. ibid., p. 255.
20. ibid., p. 257.
21. Fonteyn, *Autobiography*, p. 105.
22. *Daily Mail*, 26 June 1968.

Chapter 32

1. Margot Fonteyn, *Autobiography*, W. H. Allen, 1975, p. 255.
2. Margot Fonteyn, quoted by John Tooley, *In House: Covent Garden: 50 years of Opera and Ballet*, Faber and Faber, 1999, p. 140.

3. Fonteyn, *Autobiography*, p. 261.

4. Keith Money, *Margot Assoluta*, Fair Prospect, 2000, p. 118.

5. ibid.

6. Richard Buckle, *Sunday Times*, 30 March 1969.

7. Clive Barnes, *New York Times*, 2 June 1969.

8. Alexander Bland, *Observer*, 15 May 1969.

9. Charles Hughesdon, *Flying Made It Happen*, Book Guild, London, 2003, p. 217.

10. Alene Croce, *Dancing Times*, undated.

11. Antoinette Sibley, quoted in Julie Kavanagh, *Secret Muses: The Life of Frederick Ashton*, Faber and Faber, 1996, p. 501.

12. Ninette de Valois, quoted ibid., p. 500.

13. Clive Barnes, undated cutting.

14. *Daily Telegraph*, undated cutting.

15. Fonteyn, *Autobiography*, p. 264.

16. Sydney Edwards, *Evening Standard*, 13 April 1972.

17. *The Times*, 21 April 1972.

18. Michael Knipe, *Observer*, 19 April 1972.

19. Clive Barnes, *New York Times*, 6 June 1972.

20. Fonteyn, *Autobiography*, p. 261.

21. Margot Fonteyn, interviewed by John Gruen, *New York Times*, undated cutting.

22. Fonteyn, *Autobiography*, p. 265.

23. Margot Fonteyn, letter to James Monahan, Gail Monahan collection.

24. Keith Money, *The Art of Margot Fonteyn*, Reynal & Co., 1965, no page numbers.

25. Fonteyn, *Autobiography*, p. 19.

Chapter 33

1. Donald Smith, quoted in Maureen Orth, 'Private Dancer', *Vanity Fair*, May 1990.

2. Rosella Hightower in *The Absolute Ballerina*, written and presented by Jan Parry, BBC Radio 3, 3 January 1992.

3. Clement Crisp, *Financial Times*, undated cutting.

4. Richard Buckle, *Sunday Times*, undated cutting.

5. Margot Fonteyn, *Autobiography*, W. H. Allen, 1975, p. 255.

6. Michael Wishart, quoted in Diane Solway, *Nureyev, His Life*, William Morrow, 1998, p. 301.

7. Solway, *Nureyev*, p. 399.

8. Martha Graham, quoted in Agnes de Mille, *Martha*, Random House, 1991, p. 400.

9. Clive Barnes, *New York Times*, 21 June 1975.

10. Janet Eilber, quoted in Otis Stuart, *Perpetual Motion – the Public and Private Lives of Rudolf Nureyev*, Simon & Schuster, 1995, p. 201.

11. Margot Fonteyn, *Autobiography*, Hamish Hamilton edition, 1989, p. 257.

12. Peter Sparling, quoted in Solway, *Nureyev*, p. 400.

13. Clive Barnes, *New York Times*, 21 June 1975.

14. Arlene Croce, *New Yorker* magazine; reprinted in Arlene Croce, *Afterimages*, Alfred A. Knopf, 1977, p. 161.

15. Clive Barnes, *New York Times*, 21 June 1975.

16. Money/Macaulay correspondence.

17. ibid.

18. Fonteyn/Ashton correspondence, Royal Opera House Archive.

19. Frederick Ashton, quoted in Julie Kavanagh, *Secret Muses: The Life of Frederick Ashton*, Faber and Faber, 1996, p. 567.

20. Fonteyn, *Autobiography*, 1989 edition, postscript.

21. ibid, p. 258.

22. Keith Money, *The Art of Margot Fonteyn*, Reynal & Co., 1965, no page numbers.

23. Rudolf Nureyev, speaking on *Margot Fonteyn, A Tribute*, BBC documentary produced and directed by Patricia Foy, 1989.

24. Monique van Vooren and Rudolf Nureyev, quoted in Peter Watson, *Nureyev – A Biography*, Hodder & Stoughton, 1994, p. 375.

25. Leslie Edwards, *In Good Company – Sixty Years with the Royal Ballet*, Dance Books, 2003, p. 198.

26. Alastair Macaulay, *Ritz*, June 1979.

27. ibid.

28. Sydney Edwards, *Evening Standard*, 24 June 1979.

29. ibid.

30. James Monahan, Zsuzsi Roboz, *British Ballet Today*, Davis Poynter, 1980, pp. 79–80.

Chapter 34

1. Frederick Ashton, quoted in Julie Kavanagh, *Secret Muses: The Life of Frederick Ashton*, Faber and Faber, 1996, p. 580.

2. Margot Fonteyn, *Autobiography*, Hamish Hamilton edition, 1989, p. 274.

3. Rudolf Nureyev, interviewed by Jane Slade, 'Margot My Love', *Sunday Express, Weekend*, 21 April 1991.

4. Fonteyn, *Autobiography*, 1989 edition, p. 270.
5. Margot Fonteyn, *The Magic of Dance*, BBC, 1980, p. 10.
6. ibid., p. 61.
7. Rudolf Nureyev, interviewed by Margot Fonteyn in *The Magic of Dance*, BBC Television 6-part documentary, 1979.
8. Fonteyn, *The Magic of Dance*, p. 10.
9. Rudolf Nureyev, interviewed in *The Magic of Dance* documentary.
10. Fonteyn, *The Magic of Dance* documentary.
11. Roland Petit, quoted in Maureen Orth, 'Private Dancer', *Vanity Fair*, May 1990.
12. Jane Herrmann, ibid.
13. Fonteyn, *Autobiography*, 1989 edition, p. 274.
14. Fonteyn/Ashton correspondence, Royal Opera House Archive.
15. Fonteyn, *Autobiography*, 1989 edition, p. 278.
16. BQ/Fonteyn correspondence, private collection.
17. ibid.
18. ibid.
19. ibid.
20. ibid.
21. Fonteyn/Ashton correspondence, Royal Opera House Archive.
22. BQ/Fonteyn correspondence, private collection.
23. Fonteyn, *Autobiography*, 1989 edition.
24. ibid.
25. Fonteyn Papers, Royal Opera House Archive.
26. Fonteyn, *Autobiography*, 1989 edition, p. 281.
27. ibid.
28. Professor Sir Frederick Holliday, Tribute to Margot Fonteyn, February 1991, reproduced in *Dancing Times*, April 1991.
29. BQ/Fonteyn correspondence.
30. De Valois/Fonteyn correspondence, private collection.
31. Nadine Meisner, 'The Elusive Ballerina', *Dancing Times*, November 1984.
32. John Percival, 'Next Best to Seeing Her Dance', *The Times*, 25 October 1984.
33. Margot Fonteyn, *Pavlova, Portrait of a Dancer*, Viking, 1994, p. 56.
34. Fonteyn diary, private collection.
35. Fonteyn, *Autobiography*, 1989 edition, p. 278.
36. Keith Money, *Margot Assoluta*, Fair Prospect, 2000, p. 193.
37. Fonteyn, *Autobiography*, 1989 edition, p. 276.
38. Beverly McFarland, 'The Uncommon Retirement of Margot Fonteyn', *Tropic*, 3 February 1985.
39. John Tooley, interview, November 1991.

Chapter 35

1. Tony Burton, *Femail Magazine*, *Daily Mail*, 6 June 1991.
2. ibid.
3. Margot Fonteyn, *Autobiography*, Hamish Hamilton edition, 1989, p. 279.
4. Fonteyn/Ashton correspondence, Royal Opera House Archive.
5. ibid.
6. Clive Barnes, 'Radiant Fonteyn', *New York Times*, 24 February 1986.
7. Fonteyn/Ashton correspondence, Royal Opera House Archive.
8. Luke Jennings, quoted in Diane Solway, *Nureyev, His Life*, William Morrow, 1998, p. 514.
9. Zelda Cawthorne, *South China Morning Post*, 16 December 1987.
10. Frederick, Ashton, quoted in Julie Kavanagh, *Secret Muses: The Life of Frederick Ashton*, Faber and Faber, 1996, p. 598.
11. Princess Margaret, quoted ibid., p. 596.
12. Maria Tallchief, *Maria Tallchief – America's Prima Ballerina*, Henry Holt, 1997, p. 329.
13. Letter from Margot Fonteyn, Querube Arias collection.

Chapter 36

1. Leslie Edwards, *In Good Company – Sixty Years with the Royal Ballet*, Dance Books, 2003, p. 237.
2. Luigi Pignotti, quoted in Diane Solway, *Nureyev, His Life*, William Morrow, 1998, p. 51.
3. Patricia Foy, 'Margot Fonteyn – a story of Courage and Dedication', *Dancing Times*, April 1991.
4. Maureen Orth, 'Private Dancer', *Vanity Fair*, May 1990.
5. ibid.
6. Fonteyn/Scrase correspondence.
7. Margot Fonteyn, *Swan Lake, as told by Margot Fonteyn and illustrated by Trina Stuart Hyman*, Gulliver Books, 1989, no page numbers.
8. Tony Burton, *Femail Magazine*, *Daily Mail*, 6 June 1991.
9. Letter from Margot Fonteyn, Querube Arias collection.
10. *Hello!*, 2 March 1991, p. 62.
11. Anya Linden, quoted in Solway, *Nureyev*, p. 515.
12. Monica Mason, quoted ibid.
13. Margot Fonteyn, quoted ibid.
14. Anya Linden, quoted ibid.
15. Brian Masters, 'Margot Fonteyn', *Harpers and Queen*, 14 March 1991.

16. Durham University Address, 1990.

17. Robert Tracy quoted in *Vanity Fair*, March 1993.

18. Querube Arias, interview.

Epilogue

1. George Meredith, 'Love in the Valley'. At Fonteyn's memorial service de Valois substituted the word 'friends' for the word 'gossips'.

2. Keith Money, *Margot Assoluta*, Fair Prospect, 2000, p. 5.

3. Margot Fonteyn, *Grizelda*, unpublished children's story, 1984, kind permission of Lavinia Exham and Phoebe Hookham.

4. ibid.

Bibliography

Writings by Margot Fonteyn

Anna Pavlova: Impressions, presented by Margot Fonteyn, Weidenfeld & Nicolson, London, 1984.

Autobiography, W. H. Allen, London, 1975; revised edition, Hamish Hamilton, 1989.

A Dancer's World, W. H. Allen, London, 1978.

The Magic of Dance, BBC, London, 1979.

Swan Lake – As told by Margot Fonteyn and illustrated by Trina Schart-Hyman, Gulliver Books, Harcourt Brace Jovanovich, 1989.

Other works

Anthony, Gordon, *Margot Fonteyn*, Phoenix House, 1950.

Austin, Richard, *Lynn Seymour, An Authorised Biography*, Angus & Robertson, London, 1980.

Beaumont, Cyril W., *Ballet Design Past and Present*, Studio, London, 1946.

Beaumont, Cyril W., *Ballet to Poland*, A. & C. Black, London, 1940.

Beaumont, Cyril W., *Ballets of Today* (2nd Supplement to *The Complete Book of Ballets*), Putnam, London, 1954.

Beaumont, Cyril W., *The Complete Book of Ballets*, Putnam, London, 1937.

Beaumont, Cyril W., *Dancers Under My Lens*, C. W. Beaumont, London, 1949.

Beaumont, Cyril W., *The Sadler's Wells Ballet*, C. W. Beaumont, London, 1946; revised and enlarged 1947.

Beaumont, Cyril W., *Supplement to the Complete Book of Ballets*, C. W. Beaumont, London, 1942.

Beaumont, Cyril W., *3rd Supplement to The Complete Book of Ballets*, Putnam, London, 1955.

Beaumont, Cyril W., *The Vic-Wells Ballet*, C. W. Beaumont, London, 1935.

Bland, Alexander, *Fonteyn and Nureyev*, Orbis Publishing, London, 1979.

Bland, Alexander, *The Nureyev Image*, Studio Vista, London, 1976.

Bland, Alexander, *The Royal Ballet – The First Fifty Years*, Doubleday, New York, 1981.

Brahms, Caryl, *Robert Helpmann, Choreographer*, Batsford, London, 1943.

Braunsweg, Julian, *Braunsweg's Ballet Scandals*, as told to James Kelsey, Allen & Unwin, London, 1973.

Brinson, Peter, and Crisp, Clement, *Ballet for All – A Guide to One Hundred Ballets*, with contributions by Dan McDonagh and John Percival, Pan Books, London, 1976.

Buckle, Richard, *The Adventures of a Ballet Critic*, Cressnet Press, London, 1953.

Buckle, Richard, *Buckle at the Ballet, Selected Criticism*, Dance Books, London, 1980.

Buckle, Richard, *In the Wake of Diaghilev*, Holt, Rinehart & Winston, New York, 1983.

Buckley, Kevin, *Panama: The Whole Story*, Touchstone, New York, 1991.

Chappell, William, *Fonteyn, Impressions of a Ballerina*, Rockliff, London, 1951.

Chappell, William, *Well, Dearie! The Letters of Edward Burra*, Gordon Fraser, 1985.

Chujoy, Anatole, *The New York City Ballet*, Alfred A. Knopf, New York, 1953.

Chujoy, Anatole, and Manchester, P.W. (eds.), *The Dance Encyclopaedia*, revised and enlarged edition, Simon & Schuster, New York, 1967.

Clark, Colin, *Younger Brother, Younger Son*, HarperCollins, London, 1997.

Clarke, Mary, *The Sadler's Wells Ballet*, A. & C. Black, London, 1955.

Clarke, Mary, and Vaughan, David, *Encyclopaedia of Dance and Ballet*, Pitman, London, 1977.

Coward, Noel, *Diaries*, ed. Graham Payne and Sheridan Morley, Weidenfeld & Nicolson, London, 1982.

Crisp, Clement (ed.), *Ballerina – Portraits and Impressions of Nadia Nerina*, Weidenfeld & Nicolson, London, 1975.

Croce, Arlene, *Afterimages*, Alfred A. Knopf, New York, 1977.

Croce, Arlene, *Going to the Dance*, Alfred A. Knopf, New York, 1982.

Croce, Arlene, *Sight Lines*, Alfred A. Knopf, New York, 1988.

Crowle, Pigeon, *Enter the Ballerina*, Faber and Faber, London, 1955.

De Mille, Agnes, *Martha – The Life and Works of Martha Graham*, Vintage, New York, 1992.

De Mille, Agnes, *Portrait Gallery*, Houghton Mifflin, Boston, 1990.

De Mille, Agnes, *Speak to Me, Dance with Me*, Little, Brown, Boston and Toronto, 1973.

Denby, Edwin, *Looking at the Dance*, Pellegrini & Cudahy, New York, 1949.

De Valois, Ninette, *Come Dance with Me – A Memoir 1898–1956*, Hamish Hamilton, London, 1957.

De Valois, Ninette, *Invitation to the Ballet*, Bodley Head, London, 1937.

De Valois, Ninette, *Step by Step*, W. H. Allen, London, 1977.

Dominic, Zoë, and Selwyn-Gilbert, John, *Frederick Ashton – A Choreographer and his Ballets*, Harrap, London, 1971.

Driberg, Tom, *Ruling Passions*, Jonathan Cape, London, 1977.

Edwards, Leslie, with Bowles, Graham, *In Good Company – Sixty Years with the Royal Ballet*, Dance Books, London, 2003.

Fifield, Elaine, *In My Shoes*, W. H. Allen, London, 1967.

Fisher, Hugh, *The Sadler's Wells Theatre Ballet*, A. & C. Black, London, 1956.

Forbes, Bryan, *A Divided Life*, Heinemann, London, 1992.

Frank, Elizabeth, *Margot Fonteyn*, Chatto & Windus, London, 1958.

Franks, A. H., *Ballet – A Decade of Endeavour*, Bark Publishing, 1955.

Gage, Nicholas, *Greek Fire: The Story of Maria Callas and Aristotle Onassis*, Alfred A. Knopf, New York, 2000.

Greene, Liz, *The Astrological Neptune and the Quest for Redemption*, Red Wheel/Weiser, London, 2000.

Gruen, John, *The Private World of Ballet*, Viking, New York, 1970.

Haskell, Arnold, *Ballet*, Penguin, London, 1938.

Helpman, Mary, *The Helpman Family Story, 1796–1964*, Rigby, London, 1967.

Henze, Hans Werner, *Undine – Tagebuch eines Ballets*, R. Piper & Co. Verlag, Munich, 1959

Hughesdon, Charles, *Flying Made It Happen*, Book Guild, London, 2003.

Hurok, Sol, in collaboration with Goode, Ruth, *Impresario*, Macdonald, London, 1947.

Hurok, Solomon, *The World of Ballet*, Robert Hale, London, 1955.

Karsavina, Tamara, *Theatre Street*, Dutton, New York, 1931.

Kavanagh, Julie, *Secret Muses – The Life of Frederick Ashton*, Faber and Faber, London, 1996.

Kersley, Leo, and Sinclair, Janet, *A Dictionary of Ballet Terms*, 3rd edition, A.& C. Black, London, 1973.

Kirkland, Gelsey, with Lawrence, Greg, *Dancing on My Grave*, Doubleday, New York, 1986.

Kirstein, Lincoln, *Ballet: Bias & Belief*, Dance Horizons, New York, 1983.

Kirstein, Lincoln, *Movement and Metaphor, Four Centuries of Ballet*, Praeger, New York and Washington, 1970.

Kirstein, Lincoln, *The New York City Ballet*, Alfred A. Knopf, New York, 1973.

Kirstein, Lincoln, *Nijinsky Dancing*, Alfred A. Knopf, New York, 1975.

Kochno, Boris, *Diaghilev and the Ballets Russes*, Harper & Row, New York, 1970.

Kramer, Paul, *Latin American Panorama*, Capricorn Books, 1969.

Lambert, Constant, *Music Ho! A Study of Music in Decline*, Faber and Faber, London, 1934.

Lambert, Constant, *The Sleeping Princess, Camera Studies by Gordon Anthony*, George Routledge and Sons, London, 1942.

Legat, Nicolas, *Ballet Russe*, translated by Sir Paul Dukes, Methuen, London, 1939.

Lester, Susan (ed.), *Ballet Here and Now*, Dobson Books, London, 1961.

Mandinian, Edward, *Purcell's The Fairy Queen as presented by the Sadler's Wells Ballet and the Covent Garden Opera*, a photographic record by Edward Mandinian; with the Preface to the Original Text; a Preface by Professor E. J. Dent, and articles by Constant Lambert and Michael Ayrton, John Lehmann, 1948.

Manchester, P.W., *Vic-Wells: A Ballet Progress*, Gollancz, London, 1942.

Markova, Alicia, *Giselle and I*, Vanguard Press, New York, 1960.

Martin, John, *American Dancing – The Background and Personalities of the Modern Dance*, Dance Horizons, New York, 1968.

Maurice, Leonard, *Markova – The Legend*, Hodder & Stoughton, London, 1995.

McDonagh, Don, *Martha Graham – A Biography*, Praeger, New York, 1973.

Migel, Parmenia, *The Ballerinas: From the Court of Louis XIV to Pavlova*, Macmillan, New York, 1972.

Monahan, James, *Fonteyn – A Study of a Ballerina in her Setting*, A. & C. Black, London, 1957.

Money, Keith, *Anna Pavlova – Her Life and Art*, Alfred A. Knopf, New York, 1982.

Money, Keith, *The Art of Margot Fonteyn*, Reynal & Co., New York, 1965.

Money, Keith, *Fonteyn – The Making of a Legend*, Collins, London, 1973.

Money, Keith, *Fonteyn and Nureyev – The Great Years*, Harvill, London, 1994.

Money, Keith, *Margot Assoluta*, Fair Prospect, London, 2000.

Morris, Jan, *Destinations*, Oxford University Press, 1980.

Motion, Andrew, *The Lamberts: George, Constant and Kit*, Hogarth Press, London, 1987.

Newman, Barbara, *Antoinette Sibley − Reflections of a Ballerina*, Hutchinson, London, 1986.

Newman, Barbara, *Striking a Balance − Dancers talking about Dancing*, Houghton Mifflin, Boston, 1982.

Nijinska, Bronislava, *Early Memoirs*, translated and edited by Irina Nijinska and Jean Rawlinson, Holt Rinehart & Winston, New York, 1981.

Nureyev, Rudolf, *An Autobiography*, Hodder & Stoughton, London, 1962; reissued 1993.

Nureyev, Rudolf, *Nureyev*, E.P. Dutton & Co., New York, 1963.

Page, Ruth, *Page by Page*, Dance Horizons, New York, 1978.

Percival, John, *Nureyev*, Granada, London, 1979.

Percival, John, *Nureyev − Aspects of the Dancer*, G.P. Putnam & Sons, New York, 1975.

Perlmutter, Donna, *Shadowplay − The Life of Antony Tudor*, Limelight Editions, New York, 1995.

Petit, Roland, *J'ai dansé sur les flots*, Bernard Grasset, Paris, 1993.

Powell, Anthony, *Messengers of Day*, Heinemann, London, 1978.

Rambert, Marie, *Quicksilver − The Autobiography of Marie Rambert*, Macmillan, London, 1972.

Roboz, Zsuzsi, *British Ballet Today*, with text by James Monahan, Davis Poynter Ltd, London, 1989.

Salter, Elizabeth, *Helpmann*, Angus & Robertson, London, 1998.

Seymour, Lynn, with Gardner, Paul, *Lynn*, Granada, London, 1984.

Shead, Richard, *Constant Lambert*, with a Memoir by Anthony Powell, Simon Publications, London, 1973; revised edition Thames, 1988.

Shearer, Moira, *Ballet Master − A Dancer's View of George Balanchine*, Sidgwick & Jackson, London, 1986.

Sherry, Norman, *The Life of Graham Greene*, Jonathan Cape, London, 1994.

Smakov, Gennady, *The Great Russian Dancers*, Alfred A. Knopf, New York, 1984.

Solway, Diane, *Nureyev: His Life*, William Morrow, 1998.

Sorley Walker, Kathrine, *Ninette de Valois, Idealist without Illusions*, Hamish Hamilton, London, 1987.

Spender, Stephen, *Journals 1939–1983*, Faber and Faber, London, 1985.

Stassinopoulos, Arianna, *Maria Callas – the Woman behind the Legend*, Simon & Schuster, New York, 1981.

Stuart, Otis, *Perpetual Motion – The Public and Private Lives of Rudolf Nureyev*, Simon & Schuster, New York, 1995.

Tallchief, Maria, with Kaplan, Larry, *Maria Tallchief – America's Prima Ballerina*, Henry Holt, New York, 1997.

Tomkinson, Constance, *Dancing Attendance*, Michael Joseph, London, 1965.

Tooley, John, *In House: Covent Garden: 50 Years of Opera and Ballet*, Faber and Faber, London, 1999.

Tynan, Kenneth, *Curtains*, Longmans, Green, London, 1961.

Tynan, Kenneth, *He That Plays the King*, Longmans, Green, London, 1950.

Tynan, Kenneth, *Tynan Right and Left*, Longmans, Green, London, 1967.

Van Praagh, Peggy, and Brinson, Peter, *The Choreographic Art*, with a foreword by Cyril Beaumont, A. & C. Black, London, 1963.

Vaughan, David, *Frederick Ashton and his Ballets*, A. & C. Black, London, 1977.

Vaughan, David, *The Royal Ballet at Covent Garden*, photographs by Leslie E. Spatt and Jennie Walton, with Edward Griffiths, Mike Humphrey and Rosemary Winckley, Dance Books, 1975.

Vickers, Hugo, *Cecil Beaton*, Weidenfeld & Nicolson, London, 1993.

Watson, Peter, *Nureyev – A Biography*, Hodder & Stoughton, London, 1994.

Wilson, G. B. L., *A Dictionary of Ballet*, 3rd edition, A. & C. Black, London, 1974.

Index